NETWORKS OF INFLUENCE

The Political Power of the Communications Industry

THE CENTER FOR PUBLIC INTEGRITY

Investigative Journalism in the Public Interest   www.publicintegrity.org

Table of Contents

About the Project

Well Connected is an ongoing investigation by the The Center for Public Integrity of the businesses that control the information pipelines in the United States as well as their government overseers. Well Connected is made possible by a start-up grant from the Ford Foundation. To learn more about Well Connected, please visit: **www.publicintegrity.org/telecom/** or **www.openairwaves.org**.

The Investigative Team

Project Manager: **John Dunbar**

Editors: **Teo Furtado** and **Alan Green**

Writers: **John Dunbar, Daniel Lathrop, Robert Morlino**

Database Developer and Web Programmer: **Scott Singleton**

Web Developer: **Han Nguyen**

Database Editors: **Aron Pilhofer, Daniel Lathrop**

Research Editors: **Neil Gordon, Alexander Cohen, Peter Newbatt Smith**

Researchers: **Michael Baxter, Katie Mills, Angela White**

IT Manager: **Javed Khan**

The Center for Public Integrity

Executive Director: **Roberta Baskin**

Managing Editor: **Bill Allison**

Director of Communications and Outreach: **Ann Pincus**

Director of Development: **Barbara Schecter**

Director of Finance and Administration: **Cathy Sweeney**

Methodology

This report is the result of an eight-month investigation into the ties between the companies that make up the bulk of the nation's electronic communications industry and the government regulators whose job it is to protect the public interest. The Center for Public Integrity examined three main sectors of that industry: cable television, broadcasting and telecommunications. The measures used to gauge influence are campaign contributions, lobby spending and industry-funded trips for certain members of Congress. Researchers also compiled an unprecedented database of government employees who have left public service to apply their expertise in the private sector in jobs at communications companies.

The Center focused on the 41 companies and their trade associations that dominate the communications industry in the United States.

Lobbying

The Center looked at lobbying activities by the industry and others on their behalf as reported to the Senate Office of Public Records under the Lobbying Disclosure Act of 1995. Those filings provide the amounts that companies, associations and unions spend on lobbying Congress and federal agencies as well as the amounts paid to consultants hired to affect policy. The Center tracked filings since 1998—the most recent year for which the Senate makes filings electronically available—through June 30, 2004.

Campaign Contributions

Campaign finance totals for this report are from 1998 through September 2004. To determine totals of campaign contributions, the Center identified employees and political action committees of companies regulated by the FCC. We also examined contributions from industry trade associations and unions to federally registered political campaigns and political parties. These contributions were combined with the unlimited "soft money" contributions those companies, associations and unions were allowed to make to federally registered political parties before the passage of the Bipartisan Campaign Reform Act of 2002.

Industry-funded trips

The Center examined trips taken by members of the House and Senate commerce committees and their staffs between January of 2000 and March of 2004. Paper filings were obtained from the House Legislative Resource Center and Senate Office of Public Records. Those records were scanned into electronic files and sent to an outside data entry contractor, where the information from thousands of pages of documents was typed into a database that could be analyzed and trips sponsored by the communications industry identified. The House and Senate commerce committees, which oversee the FCC, are the primary forum for legislative action related to the communications industry.

Revolvers

Center researchers spent hundreds of hours over several months tracking the careers of senior government officials who have left public service. The review focused on those who left the FCC and the House and Senate commerce committees since 1996, along with all those who have registered to lobby for the industry since 1998. Because there is no centralized tracking of former government employees who lobby and required self-reporting in public filings is often incomplete or ambiguous, the Center reviewed hundreds of separate documents filed with the Senate Office of Public Records, documents issued by the FCC and press accounts going back more than a decade to create the most comprehensive outline to date of the back-and-forth movement of people from government to industry. To search for government employees who have taken a trip through the revolving door, please visit the Well Connected Web site: **www.publicintegrity.org/telecom/** or **www.openairwaves.org.**

Introduction

The Center for Public Integrity created the Well Connected project to monitor the corporations that control the flow of information to the public and the government overseers whose job it is to regulate them. The communications industry is in a unique position. It spends hundreds of millions of dollars to affect government policy but at the same time asks for the public's trust in delivering information on those activities.

Our research focuses on the "pipeline" companies: those that control telephone lines, cable television systems and valuable, publicly owned slices of the airwaves—in short, all the modes of electronic communication that exist in the economy. For the first time ever, we have been able to determine exactly how much telecommunications companies spend to sway powerful decision-makers in Washington, D.C.

The project is an ambitious one. Our analysis includes traditional telephone companies like Verizon Communications Inc., cable providers like Comcast Corp. and giant broadcasters like News Corp. You would normally expect these conglomerates to have little in common. But as communications technologies converge, companies that were once in segregated lines of business are becoming direct competitors.

For example, cable television companies now provide telephone service; traditional telephone companies are spending billions on fiber optic lines to deliver video programming to homes. And although only a small percentage of Americans receive their television signals over the air, giant broadcast companies still control most of the programming we see every day.

Our report attempts to take a snapshot of the industry as a whole. And the numbers are staggering.

The communications industry spent $957 million to lobby the federal government and spent another $145 million in contributions to members of Congress from 1998 through mid-2004. Another $704,000 was spent to fly lawmakers and their staff all over the country in an attempt to influence key regulatory issues.

As part of our investigation, Center researchers and writers looked at broadcasters, who have increased spending on lobbying by 74 percent from 1998 through 2003 and are working furiously behind the scenes to defeat rules that block giant media mergers. We tracked the en masse movement of the authors of the landmark Telecommunications Act of 1996 from government to industry. We examined what is one of the most sophisticated and multi-layered lobbying machines in Washington, D.C., the cable television industry and its occasionally strange bedfellows. Finally, we showed how much members of the House and Senate commerce committees—the powerful men and women in Congress who write communications laws and oversee the Federal Communications Commission—received in political contributions and how many industry-sponsored trips they took.

The result is a comprehensive guide to the nation's largest communications companies, their holdings and how much they spend on lobbying and contributions.

For more information about the Well Connected project, or to search for media ownership information, government employees who have stepped through the revolving door and much more, please visit the project Web site at: **www.publicintegrity.org/telecom/** or **www.openairwaves.org**.

Networks of Influence
The political power of the communications industry

A new Center for Public Integrity investigation of campaign contributions, lobbying expenditures and other spending shows that the communications industry has spent $1.1 billion from 1998 to mid-2004 to affect election outcomes and influence legislation before Congress and the White House.

The report focuses on the three primary communications industry sectors that control the information pipelines in the United States – broadcasting, cable television and telecommunications. Researchers also examined lobbying and contribution activity of other companies regulated by the Federal Communications Commission, including satellite television and radio companies.

In addition to corporate spending on lobbying and campaign contributions, the total includes industry-funded trips for members of the House and Senate committees that oversee the FCC. Center researchers also undertook an unprecedented study of former key FCC and congressional officials who left their government jobs for positions in the communications field.

A breakdown shows:

- Total lobbying expenditures from 1998 through mid-2004 by the industry were more than $957 million. In comparison, the oil and gas industry spent $396 million over the same period, the Center has found.
- Campaign contributions from 1998 through September 2004 were $145.6 million. The total includes both hard and soft money donations from industry employees, labor unions representing employees in the communications industry and political action committees.
- The Center identified 450 industry-funded trips valued at $704,229 from 2000 through March of 2004.

The study is part of the Center's ongoing examination of the companies that control the nation's airwaves, telephone and cable lines and the hundreds of millions of dollars they spend to influence policies that affect how electronic communications are regulated in the United States. The survey took roughly eight months and involved the work of as many as a dozen researchers.

The influence of these industries is particularly important given that they control the information that helps all Americans formulate their views on everything from who to elect for president to what movie they want to see this weekend.

In addition to studying political spending, researchers were able to identify 311 former top congressional aides and FCC officials who have left government service and gone to work in the communications industry.

In an effort to help both journalists and citizens better understand the staggering influence the industry has on government, the Center has created "Influence Tracker," a searchable database that includes information on contributions, lobbying, frequent flyers and

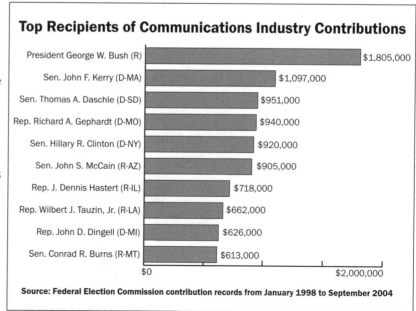

Top Recipients of Communications Industry Contributions

President George W. Bush (R)	$1,805,000
Sen. John F. Kerry (D-MA)	$1,097,000
Sen. Thomas A. Daschle (D-SD)	$951,000
Rep. Richard A. Gephardt (D-MO)	$940,000
Sen. Hillary R. Clinton (D-NY)	$920,000
Sen. John S. McCain (R-AZ)	$905,000
Rep. J. Dennis Hastert (R-IL)	$718,000
Rep. Wilbert J. Tauzin, Jr. (R-LA)	$662,000
Rep. John D. Dingell (D-MI)	$626,000
Sen. Conrad R. Burns (R-MT)	$613,000

Source: Federal Election Commission contribution records from January 1998 to September 2004

employees who have stepped through the revolving door between government and industry. To search the database, go to www.publicintegrity.org/telecom/ or www.openairwaves.org.

The database used for this report contains 105,991 records, including 74,302 contribution records and information from roughly 9,000 lobbyist disclosure reports.

Of the three sectors, traditional telecommunications companies spend far more on contributions and lobbying than broadcasters or cable companies. A sector breakdown shows:

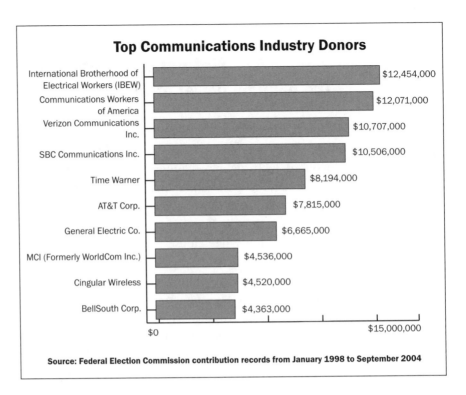

Top Communications Industry Donors

International Brotherhood of Electrical Workers (IBEW)	$12,454,000
Communications Workers of America	$12,071,000
Verizon Communications Inc.	$10,707,000
SBC Communications Inc.	$10,506,000
Time Warner	$8,194,000
AT&T Corp.	$7,815,000
General Electric Co.	$6,665,000
MCI (Formerly WorldCom Inc.)	$4,536,000
Cingular Wireless	$4,520,000
BellSouth Corp.	$4,363,000

Source: Federal Election Commission contribution records from January 1998 to September 2004

- Telephone companies like Verizon Communications Inc. and AT&T Corp. spent $498 million on lobbying, $60.5 million on campaign contributions and $276,000 on trips for an overall total of $559 million.
- Broadcasters spent $222.3 million on lobbying and $26.5 million on campaign contributions and $165,000 on trips for a total of $248.9 million.
- Cable television providers spent $119.9 million lobbying, $20.5 million on contributions and $226,000 on trips for a total of $140.6 million.

Lobbying

While contributions to politicians are a major expense for communications companies, it pales in comparison to the amount that is spent on making sure the legal and regulatory climate remains favorable.

The $957 million spent by the industry affected legislation ranging from local telephone competition to media consolidation to the deregulation of the cable television industry. The survey shows that spending on lobbying by communications companies rose from $145.3 million in 1998 to $169.2 million in 2003, an increase of 16 percent.

Among the top spenders on lobbying:

- General Electric Co., which owns 80 percent of NBC Universal in addition to a number of cable networks, topped the lobby spending list at $105.2 million. (The total includes all lobbying by the giant conglomerate, even though it draws only a portion of its revenue from broadcast operations. Federal disclosure rules do not require companies to separate lobbying expenditures by subject.)
- Second by a small margin was Verizon Communications Inc., the nation's largest phone company. The former regional Bell operating company spent $102.5 million from 1998 through mid 2004. Verizon has key financial interests in local and long-distance phone regulation, spectrum

Contribution Party Breakdown for the Communications Industry

Party	Total	Percentage
Democratic Party	$82,632,000	56.19%
Republican Party	$63,473,000	43.17%
Other/Independent	$942,000	0.64%
Total	**$147,047,000**	

Source: Federal Election Commission contribution records from January 1998 to September 2004

allocation for its wireless division and a multitude of other issues.
- Third on the list of top lobby spenders was AT&T Corp. at $75 million.

AT&T is followed by competitors SBC Communications Inc., at $72.8 million and Sprint Corp. with $46.8 million.

The Center also looked at the top communications industry lobbying shops in Washington.

Number one on the list in billings was Patton Boggs at $10.9 million; second was Akin Gump Strauss Hauer & Feld at $9.6 million; third was PodestaMattoon at $9.3 million. Fourth was Piper Rudnick at $8.8 million and rounding out the top five was Hill & Knowlton at $8.4 million.

Contributions

The partisan preference of the communications industry as a whole has leaned toward the Democratic Party. Total contributions were split 56.2 percent for Democratic candidates and party organizations and 43.2 percent for Republicans through September 2004. That did not extend to the two most recent candidates for the White House: President Bush led Sen. John Kerry by a wide margin, $1.8 million to $1.1 million.

The two largest contributors over the study period were both labor unions.

- The International Brotherhood of Electrical Workers spent $12.5 million since 1998.
- Second was the Communication Workers of America at $12.1 million.
- Third on the list of top contributors was Verizon Communications at $10.7 million.

Verizon is followed by another former Bell, SBC Communications Inc., at $10.5 million. Media conglomerate Time Warner Inc., with holdings in publishing, film production, the Internet and cable television, was fifth at $8.2 million.

A significant portion of the union total (24 percent from the IBEW, 43 percent from the CWA) came from unregulated "soft money" contributions. Such contributions are now banned by the McCain-Feingold Bipartisan Campaign Reform Act which went into effect late in 2002.

Bush's top communications patron is SBC Communications Inc., the San Antonio-based former Bell operating company that has waged a long battle with the government over the Telecommunications

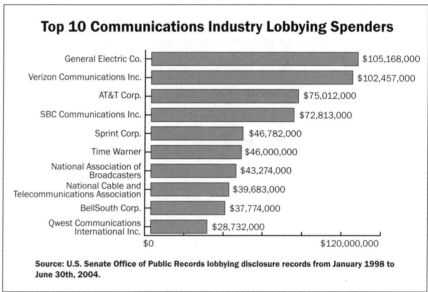

Top 10 Communications Industry Lobbying Spenders

General Electric Co.	$105,168,000
Verizon Communications Inc.	$102,457,000
AT&T Corp.	$75,012,000
SBC Communications Inc.	$72,813,000
Sprint Corp.	$46,782,000
Time Warner	$46,000,000
National Association of Broadcasters	$43,274,000
National Cable and Telecommunications Association	$39,683,000
BellSouth Corp.	$37,774,000
Qwest Communications International Inc.	$28,732,000

Source: U.S. Senate Office of Public Records lobbying disclosure records from January 1998 to June 30th, 2004.

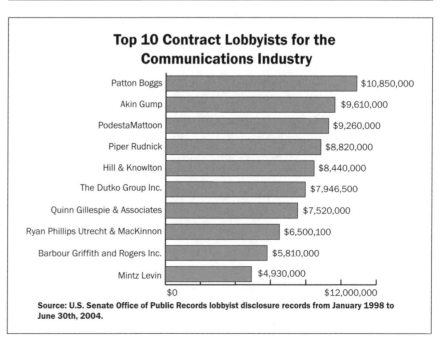

Top 10 Contract Lobbyists for the Communications Industry

Patton Boggs	$10,850,000
Akin Gump	$9,610,000
PodestaMattoon	$9,260,000
Piper Rudnick	$8,820,000
Hill & Knowlton	$8,440,000
The Dutko Group Inc.	$7,946,500
Quinn Gillespie & Associates	$7,520,000
Ryan Phillips Utrecht & MacKinnon	$6,500,100
Barbour Griffith and Rogers Inc.	$5,810,000
Mintz Levin	$4,930,000

Source: U.S. Senate Office of Public Records lobbyist disclosure records from January 1998 to June 30th, 2004.

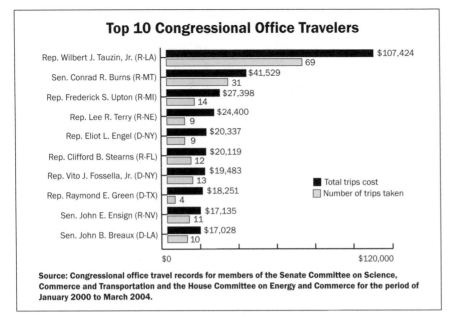

Top 10 Congressional Office Travelers

- Rep. Wilbert J. Tauzin, Jr. (R-LA): $107,424 / 69
- Sen. Conrad R. Burns (R-MT): $41,529 / 31
- Rep. Frederick S. Upton (R-MI): $27,398 / 14
- Rep. Lee R. Terry (R-NE): $24,400 / 9
- Rep. Eliot L. Engel (D-NY): $20,337 / 9
- Rep. Clifford B. Stearns (R-FL): $20,119 / 12
- Rep. Vito J. Fossella, Jr. (D-NY): $19,483 / 13
- Rep. Raymond E. Green (D-TX): $18,251 / 4
- Sen. John E. Ensign (R-NV): $17,135 / 11
- Sen. John B. Breaux (D-LA): $17,028 / 10

■ Total trips cost
□ Number of trips taken

$0 — $120,000

Source: Congressional office travel records for members of the Senate Committee on Science, Commerce and Transportation and the House Committee on Energy and Commerce for the period of January 2000 to March 2004.

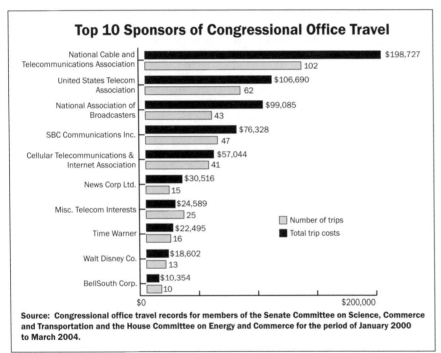

Top 10 Sponsors of Congressional Office Travel

- National Cable and Telecommunications Association: $198,727 / 102
- United States Telecom Association: $106,690 / 62
- National Association of Broadcasters: $99,085 / 43
- SBC Communications Inc.: $76,328 / 47
- Cellular Telecommunications & Internet Association: $57,044 / 41
- News Corp Ltd.: $30,516 / 15
- Misc. Telecom Interests: $24,589 / 25
- Time Warner: $22,495 / 16
- Walt Disney Co.: $18,602 / 13
- BellSouth Corp.: $10,354 / 10

□ Number of trips
■ Total trip costs

$0 — $200,000

Source: Congressional office travel records for members of the Senate Committee on Science, Commerce and Transportation and the House Committee on Energy and Commerce for the period of January 2000 to March 2004.

$951,000. He is followed by Rep. Dick Gephardt (D-Mo.) at $940,000. New York Democratic Sen. Hillary Rodham Clinton, despite her status as a freshman legislator, was next on the list, having collected an impressive $920,000. Sen. John McCain (R-Ariz.), chairman of the Senate Committee on Commerce, Science and Transportation, came in fifth at $905,000.

Then there were the bundlers. At least 10 figures in the communications industry raised $100,000 or more for President Bush's reelection, including the top executives at the largest and second largest telephone companies in the nation.

On the list of "Pioneers" were Salem Communications CEO Edward Atsinger; IDT Corp. CEO James Courter; lobbyist Ronald Kauffman, senior managing partner of the Dutko Group; Liggett Communications CEO Robert Liggett; lobbyist and former member of Congress Bill Paxon of Akin Gump Strauss Hauer & Feld; Univision Communications CEO Jerry Perenchio; Edge Wireless CEO Wayne Perry and Verizon CEO Ivan Seidenberg. SBC Communications CEO Edward Whitacre was named a "Ranger" for hitting the $200,000 mark.

Act of 1996, which was supposed to create competition in local phone service. SBC has donated $178,000 since 1998. Bush's second biggest booster from the communications business is Time Warner ($167,000) and third is General Electric ($151,000).

Kerry's top communications patron is Time Warner, which has donated $242,000 over the same period. Second is broadcast giant and owner of CBS, Viacom Inc., at $118,000. Verizon is third at $116,000.

Behind Bush and Kerry on the list of recipients of the most communications dollars is former Senate Minority Leader Tom Daschle (D-S.D.), who received

Trips

Closely related to lobbying was the much criticized Washington practice of "fact-finding trips" by lawmakers and staff, which are also referred to more derisively as "junkets."

Since 2000, the communications industry has sponsored 450 trips for members, family and staff of the Senate Committee on Science, Commerce and Transportation and the House Committee on Energy and Commerce. The top sponsor marks the first entry

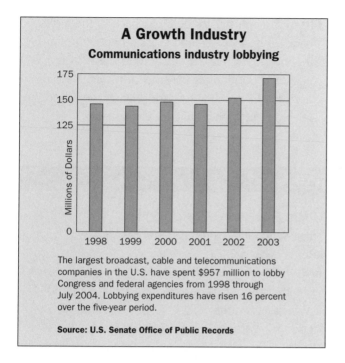

A Growth Industry
Communications industry lobbying

The largest broadcast, cable and telecommunications companies in the U.S. have spent $957 million to lobby Congress and federal agencies from 1998 through July 2004. Lobbying expenditures have risen 16 percent over the five-year period.

Source: U.S. Senate Office of Public Records

of the cable industry into a top five category of influence in the Center survey of communications companies.

The National Cable and Telecommunications Association funded 102 trips since 2000 worth $198,727. Second was another lobbying group, the United States Telecom Association, with 62 trips at $106,689. Third was SBC Communications Inc. with 47 trips valued at $76,327. Fourth was the National Association of Broadcasters with 43 trips at $99,084 and fifth was the Cellular Telecommunications & Internet Association with 41 trips valued at $57,044.

In May 2003, the Center did a survey on members of the FCC and staff who accepted free travel from industry. Over the eight-year period covered in the survey, businesses paid for $2.8 million in free travel for FCC staff. Since the publication of that report, the practice has largely ceased.

The frequent flyer award among members of Congress was no contest. The top recipient was retiring Louisiana Rep. Billy Tauzin, former chairman of the House Committee on Energy and Commerce. Tauzin and members of his office staff went on 69 trips valued at $107,424. Tauzin's office was top traveler in every communications sector examined by the Center.

A distant second is Sen. Conrad Burns (R-Mont.) at 31 trips valued at $41,529 and in third place is Rep.

Fred Upton (R-Mich.) with 14 trips worth $27,398.

Revolvers

The Center also examined the practice of government officials leaving their jobs to work for the industries they used to regulate. It is a common practice in Washington and has been the subject of recent reports on the U.S. Department of Agriculture and the Department of Defense.

The practice raises concern for a number of reasons, the most serious being that a federal employee may be tempted to show a regulated company favorable treatment in hopes of getting a job at the end of his government service.

The U.S. Office of Government Ethics has rules on post-employment activity by former federal workers, but they are narrowly drawn and easily sidestepped.

While the Center study did not find any former FCC or congressional employee who appeared to violate those rules, researchers found that an extraordinary number of them—398, in fact—have gone to work for companies they used to regulate.

For example, all eight previous chairmen of the FCC have either worked for or represented corporations that are regulated by the agency. Two are registered lobbyists.

Among some of the others:

- Republican Commissioner Kathleen Abernathy, once worked for Baby Bell USWEST (now part of Qwest). She is on at least her second time through the revolving door between the FCC and the phone companies. In the 1990s, she was a lobbyist for private companies with business before the FCC after having served in senior staff roles to the FCC and two FCC commissioners.
- Lyndon K. Boozer, BellSouth's vice president of federal relations, is an FCC alumnus who worked as a special assistant in the agency's Office of Legislation and Intergovernmental Affairs before leaving for his lucrative job at BellSouth.
- Peter Davidson, Verizon's senior vice president of federal government relations, has passed twice through the revolving door between government and industry. After serving as policy director to

then-House Majority Leader Dick Armey (R-Texas), he worked for Qwest, then worked under the U.S. Trade Representative in the Bush administration until taking his position with Verizon.

- Marsha MacBride, currently the executive vice president for legal and regulatory affairs with the National Association of Broadcasters, has gone

from the industry to the FCC, back to the industry, back to the FCC again and then once more into the industry. Over the course of 13 years, she has occupied positions at the uppermost echelons of both media corporations and organizations and the government agency that regulates them.

Former FCC Chairs Cash In

All eight previous chairmen of the Federal Communications Commission have either worked for or represented corporations that are regulated by the agency. Two are registered lobbyists.

William E. Kennard (1997–2001)
Firm: The Carlyle Group, investment banking
Role: Managing director in global telecommunications and Media
Other positions: Boards of directors of Nextel Communications, Inc., The New York Times Company, Dex Media Inc. and eAccess Ltd. Prior to FCC, partner at Verner, Liipfert, Bernhard, McPherson and Hand.

Reed E. Hundt (1993–1997)
Firm: McKinsey and Company, worldwide management consulting business
Role: Senior advisor on information industries
Other positions: Boards of directors of Allegiance Telecom Inc., Expedia, Polyserve and Intel Corp. Special advisor to private equity firm Blackstone Group; venture partner at Benchmark Capital, firm specializing in investments in high-tech companies.

James H. Quello (1993)
Firm: Wiley Rein & Fielding
Role: Government affairs consultant
Former position: Vice president and general manager, WJR, Detroit.

Alfred C. Sikes (1989–1993)
Firm: Hearst Corp.
Role: Consultant on technology-enabled investment
Other positions: Board member Hughes Electronics, iVillage and Cymfony, in addition to several nonprofit and educational organizations.

Source: Reporting by The Center for Public Integrity

Dennis Patrick (1987–1989)
Firm: National Geographic Ventures
Role: President
Former Positions: CEO of Time Warner Communications; co-founder, Milliwave, acquired by Winstar; president/CEO, Doeg Hill Ventures (funded start-up telecom ventures); Patrick Communications, a telecommunications consulting firm; AOL Wireless.

Mark Fowler (1981–1987)
Firm: Talk America; Beasley Broadcast Group
Role: Director
Former positions: Senior communications counsel, Lathman & Watkins; founder and chairman/CEO of PowerFone Holdings, acquired by Nextel; founder and chairman of UniSite, antenna site developer; founder of AssureSat; director of Pao-West Telecomm.

Charles Ferris (1977–1981)
Firm: Mintz, Levin, Cohn, Ferris, Glovsky and Popeo
Role: Lobbyist, chairman of federal law section, practice focuses on communications and federal relations law.
Other positions: Prior to FCC, chief counsel to then-Senate Majority Leader Mike Mansfield, Served as general counsel to former House Speaker Thomas P. O'Neill.

Richard Wiley (1974–1977)
Firm: Wiley Rein & Fielding LLP
Role: Lobbyist, head of 70-attorney communications law practice.
Clients: Viacom Inc. (CBS), Gannett Company Inc., Belo Corp., Emmis Communications Corp., Gray Television, Verizon Communications Inc., SBC Communications Inc., BellSouth Corp., Motorola, and the Newspaper Association of America.

Broadcast Lobbying Tops $222 Million
One story you won't hear on the news

The broadcast industry spent more than $222 million lobbying the federal government from 1998 through June 2004—a period of increasingly intense battles over ownership rules.

In addition, television and radio companies contributed more than $26.5 million to federal candidates and lawmakers during the same period. The companies and their principal representative organization—the National Association of Broadcasters—also sponsored 84 trips for lawmakers and regulators at a cost of $165,474, bringing total spending to affect policy and elections by the industry to $248.9 million.

The volatile political climate also saw 24 individuals with close ties to both the industry and its regulatory overseers make lucrative moves back and forth between the two.

From 1998 through June 30, 2004, lobbying expenditures by the broadcast industry rose 74 percent, from nearly $26 million to a high of more than $45 million during 2003. It was during that last year of record lobbying that the FCC proposed significant relaxation of the ownership rules, which would have allowed corporations to own more media outlets than ever before and reach a greater percentage of the national audience.

The top spenders:

- General Electric Co., which owns 80 percent of NBC Universal in addition to a number of cable networks, topped the lobby spending list for broadcasters at $105 million. The total includes all lobbying. The giant conglomerate draws only a portion of its revenue from broadcast operations, but broadcast-related lobbying numbers are not reported separately.

- Second in broadcast lobbying is the National Association of Broadcasters, an influential trade group that represents the interests of free, over-the-

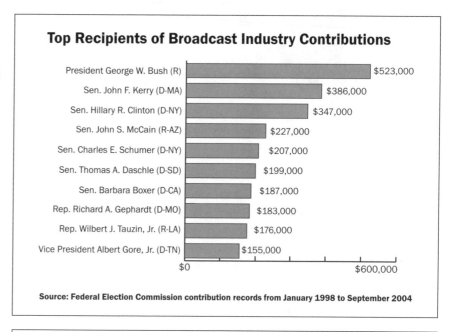

Top Recipients of Broadcast Industry Contributions

President George W. Bush (R)	$523,000
Sen. John F. Kerry (D-MA)	$386,000
Sen. Hillary R. Clinton (D-NY)	$347,000
Sen. John S. McCain (R-AZ)	$227,000
Sen. Charles E. Schumer (D-NY)	$207,000
Sen. Thomas A. Daschle (D-SD)	$199,000
Sen. Barbara Boxer (D-CA)	$187,000
Rep. Richard A. Gephardt (D-MO)	$183,000
Rep. Wilbert J. Tauzin, Jr. (R-LA)	$176,000
Vice President Albert Gore, Jr. (D-TN)	$155,000

Source: Federal Election Commission contribution records from January 1998 to September 2004

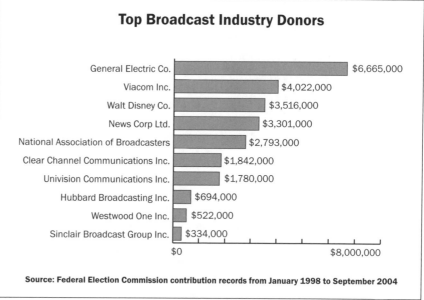

Top Broadcast Industry Donors

General Electric Co.	$6,665,000
Viacom Inc.	$4,022,000
Walt Disney Co.	$3,516,000
News Corp Ltd.	$3,301,000
National Association of Broadcasters	$2,793,000
Clear Channel Communications Inc.	$1,842,000
Univision Communications Inc.	$1,780,000
Hubbard Broadcasting Inc.	$694,000
Westwood One Inc.	$522,000
Sinclair Broadcast Group Inc.	$334,000

Source: Federal Election Commission contribution records from January 1998 to September 2004

Contribution Party Breakdown (Broadcasters)

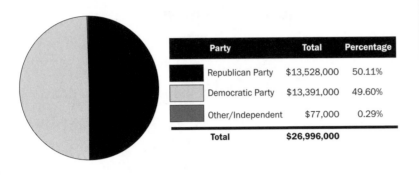

Party	Total	Percentage
Republican Party	$13,528,000	50.11%
Democratic Party	$13,391,000	49.60%
Other/Independent	$77,000	0.29%
Total	**$26,996,000**	

Source: Federal Election Commission contribution records from January 1998 to September 2004

Top 10 Broadcast Industry Lobbying Spenders

General Electric Co.	$105,168,000
National Association of Broadcasters	$43,274,000
Walt Disney Co.	$24,227,000
Viacom Inc.	$16,112,000
News Corp Ltd.	$15,782,000
Gannett Company	$3,192,000
Clear Channel Communications Inc.	$2,821,000
Belo Corp.	$1,620,000
Washington Post Co.	$1,320,000
Hubbard Broadcasting Inc.	$1,050,000

Source: U.S. Senate Office of Public Records lobbying disclosure records from January 1998 to June 30th, 2004.

Top 10 Broadcast Industry Contract Lobbyists

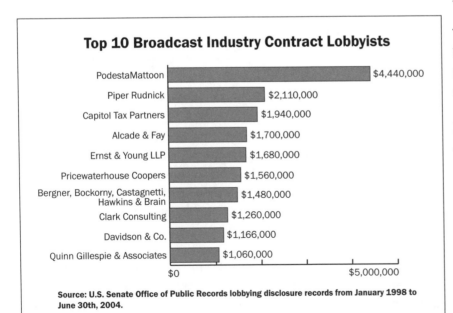

PodestaMattoon	$4,440,000
Piper Rudnick	$2,110,000
Capitol Tax Partners	$1,940,000
Alcade & Fay	$1,700,000
Ernst & Young LLP	$1,680,000
Pricewaterhouse Coopers	$1,560,000
Bergner, Bockorny, Castagnetti, Hawkins & Brain	$1,480,000
Clark Consulting	$1,260,000
Davidson & Co.	$1,166,000
Quinn Gillespie & Associates	$1,060,000

Source: U.S. Senate Office of Public Records lobbying disclosure records from January 1998 to June 30th, 2004.

air radio and television broadcasters. The NAB spent $43.2 million lobbying, according to records.

- Walt Disney Co., owner of the ABC television network, is a distant third at $24.2 million.

The steady rise in lobbying dollars followed the passage of the Telecommunications Act of 1996, which stipulated that both caps on station ownership and the percentage of the national audience a broadcast company may reach directly be reviewed every two years. Since 1998, the industry has responded by steadily increasing spending on lobbying.

As for contributions, in the three election cycles between 1998 and 2004, broadcasters contributed more than $26.5 million to federal candidates and sitting officials. President George W. Bush and his Democratic challenger, Sen. John F. Kerry, ranked first and second through September 2004, with donations of $523,000 and $386,000, respectively. Sen. Hillary Rodham Clinton, the freshman from New York and former first lady, ranked third with $347,000.

The last election cycled was a boon to both Bush and Kerry, who raked in unprecedented amounts of contributions.

Broadcasters gave nearly identical amounts to Republicans and Democrats during the period analyzed. Of all contributions, 50.1 percent went to Republicans and 49.6 percent went to Democrats.

Almost half of the contributions went to the national party committees—$6.4 million to Democrats and $5.7 million to Republicans—

which then redistributed the money to affect local elections. Contributions made directly to individual candidates, such as Kerry and Clinton, made up the roughly $2 million difference between the two parties.

Once again, the industry's top donors of federal campaign dollars were major broadcast owners, with General Electric leading the way ($6.7 million), followed by Viacom Inc. ($4.0 million) and Disney ($3.5 million).

Broadcasters have also sponsored $165,474 in trips and junkets for members, family and staff of the Senate Committee on Science, Commerce and Transportation and the House Committee on Energy and Commerce.

First on the list by a large margin is former Rep. Billy Tauzin and his staff, who accepted 18 trips valued at $25,006, according to records. The Louisiana Republican was chairman of the House Committee on Energy and Commerce.

The NAB has been by far the greatest sponsor of such outings, having paid for 43 of the 84 industry-sponsored trips over the past six years. During that time, the trade association accounted for two-thirds of all broadcast-industry junket and trip spending. News Corp. and Disney followed the NAB with 15 and 13 trips, respectively.

As lobbying has increased and campaign contributions and industry trips have continued at a steady clip, some two dozen individuals have moved through the lucrative "revolving door"—that is, between the broadcast industry and the government offices and agencies that regulate it.

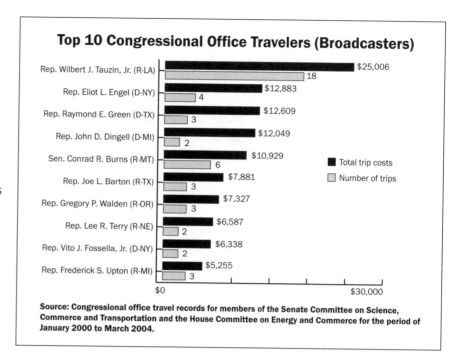

Top 10 Congressional Office Travelers (Broadcasters)

Rep. Wilbert J. Tauzin, Jr. (R-LA) — $25,006 / 18
Rep. Eliot L. Engel (D-NY) — $12,883 / 4
Rep. Raymond E. Green (D-TX) — $12,609 / 3
Rep. John D. Dingell (D-MI) — $12,049 / 2
Sen. Conrad R. Burns (R-MT) — $10,929 / 6
Rep. Joe L. Barton (R-TX) — $7,881 / 3
Rep. Gregory P. Walden (R-OR) — $7,327 / 3
Rep. Lee R. Terry (R-NE) — $6,587 / 2
Rep. Vito J. Fossella, Jr. (D-NY) — $6,338 / 2
Rep. Frederick S. Upton (R-MI) — $5,255 / 3

■ Total trip costs
☐ Number of trips

$0 — $30,000

Source: Congressional office travel records for members of the Senate Committee on Science, Commerce and Transportation and the House Committee on Energy and Commerce for the period of January 2000 to March 2004.

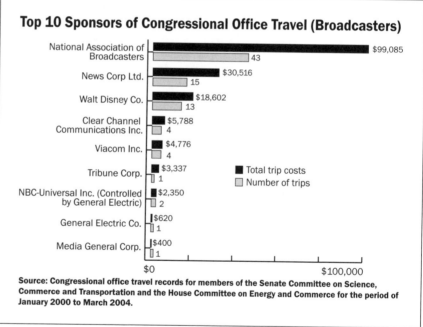

Top 10 Sponsors of Congressional Office Travel (Broadcasters)

National Association of Broadcasters — $99,085 / 43
News Corp Ltd. — $30,516 / 15
Walt Disney Co. — $18,602 / 13
Clear Channel Communications Inc. — $5,788 / 4
Viacom Inc. — $4,776 / 4
Tribune Corp. — $3,337 / 1
NBC-Universal Inc. (Controlled by General Electric) — $2,350 / 2
General Electric Co. — $620 / 1
Media General Corp. — $400 / 1

■ Total trip costs
☐ Number of trips

$0 — $100,000

Source: Congressional office travel records for members of the Senate Committee on Science, Commerce and Transportation and the House Committee on Energy and Commerce for the period of January 2000 to March 2004.

■ Marsha MacBride, currently the NAB's executive vice president for legal and regulatory affairs, has ping-ponged at a dizzying clip over the last 13 years: she went from the industry to the FCC, back to the industry, and then back to the FCC before landing—at least for now—at the NAB.

■ Clear Channel Communications Inc., which had virtually no Washington lobbying presence for years, got into the influence business in a big way when it hired Andrew Levin. Levin was Minority Counsel for the House Committee on Energy and

Commerce, where virtually all broadcast legislation is heard, before moving on to become senior vice president of government relations for the radio giant.

- Finally, David Goodfriend, interim executive vice president and general counsel for liberal radio network Air America, was at one time deputy staff secretary at the White House under President Bill Clinton, director of legal and business affairs at satellite television broadcaster EchoStar, legal advisor to Commissioner Susan Ness and a telecommunications lawyer with Willkie Farr & Gallagher.

Sinclair Flap Proves Exception to the Rule
Broadcasters split the ticket when it comes to contributions

An examination of contributions by broadcasters and their chief lobbying organization, the National Association of Broadcasters, reveals that when it comes to politics, the industry does not play favorites: between 1998 and September 2004, records show, broadcasters have donated $13,528,000 to Democratic candidates and party organizations and $13,391,000 to Republicans.

A glaring exception to this evenhanded approach can be found at Sinclair Broadcasting Group, which recently endured a firestorm of negative publicity for ordering its 62 television stations to air a documentary—just days before the election—critical of Democratic presidential nominee John Kerry.

A little more than 95 percent of Sinclair's $334,000 in contributions have gone to Republicans—a lopsided record of giving unmatched by any other major television broadcaster, the Center found. News Corp., for example, whose Fox cable-news operation is often criticized for its perceived right wing bias, has actually given 64 percent of its contributions to Democrats since 1998 and 36 percent to Republicans. (Contributions by longtime Democratic fundraiser Haim Saban, who owned half of Fox Family Worldwide, are excluded from that ratio; when included, News Corp. contributions skew in favor of

Democrats by 81 percent to 19 percent.) And Clear Channel Communications Inc., whose board of directors includes the businessman who bought the Texas Rangers baseball team from President George W. Bush, only favors Republicans by about 63 percent to 37 percent.

Reporters, editors and news executives insist that their employers' campaign contributions have no bearing on how the news is reported. But recent events involving Sinclair and other large broadcasters, such as Viacom Inc., coupled with an escalating lobbying effort to remove government controls, raise questions about whether the broadcast industry's corporate goals may be affecting news coverage.

Bad business

The controversy involving Sinclair was kindled when management ordered the company's television stations, several of which are in so-called swing states, to pre-empt regular primetime programming for an unflattering documentary about Kerry's Vietnam service, *Stolen Honor: Wounds That Never Heal.*

But if Sinclair's goal was to help itself by helping President Bush, whose administration has consistently supported deregulation of major media corporations,

Broadcaster	Republican	Democratic	Total Contribtions
News Corporation Limited.* (Fox Entertainment Group Inc.)	35.57%	63.88%	$840,106
CBS Television Network (Viacom Inc.)	31.19%	68.56%	$4,022,089
NBC Universal Inc. (General Electric Co.)	57.50%	42.10%	$6,664,859
Tribune Co.	54.43%	45.04%	$188,395
ABC Inc. (Walt Disney Co.)	48.87%	50.78%	$3,516,037
Gannett Company, Inc.	46.79%	50.66%	$40,075
Hearst-Argyle Television, Inc. (Hearst Corp.)	49.68%	47.18%	$159,304
Sinclair Broadcast Group Inc.	95.56%	4.44%	$334,425
Belo Corp.	49.90%	50.10%	$24,150
Cox Enterprises Inc.	32.00%	68.00%	$651,01

*Totals for News Corp. exclude contributions by Haim Saban, once half-owner of Fox Family Worldwide.
Saban and News Corp. sold that property to the Walt Disney Co. in 2001.

the move clearly backfired. By ordering the airing of an overtly political broadcast so close to the election, the company managed to cast a negative light on the media ownership issue in general, and a harsh spotlight on itself in particular.

"This is an abuse of the public trust," FCC Commissioner Michael Copps said of the Sinclair flap in a prepared statement. "And it is proof positive of media consolidation run amok when one owner can use the public airwaves to blanket the country with its political ideology—whether liberal or conservative."

It wasn't the first time Sinclair became the subject of a newscast, as opposed to the producer of one. Six months earlier, for example, the company earned an unwelcome spotlight for instructing its ABC affiliates to pre-empt a "Nightline" program devoted entirely to the reading of a list of American soldiers who had died in the Iraq war. In explaining its decision, Sinclair claimed that "Despite the denials by a spokeswoman for the show, ABC appears to be motivated by a political agenda designed to undermine the efforts of the United States in Iraq." Two months earlier, Sinclair had dispatched news crews to Iraq to cover the "good news" that it believed the rest of the media had missed.

Sinclair was founded by Julian Sinclair Smith in 1971 with a single Baltimore television station that is now the company flagship. Led by Smith's son, David, Sinclair grew into the nation's largest owner of television stations—a collection of mostly small-market broadcasters that reach nearly 25 percent of all households.

The company has made no secret of its conservative leanings. In 2002, it created its "News Central" production to centrally manage news operations for all of its stations. Daily broadcasts include commentaries by Mark Hyman, the company's vice president for corporate relations, whose minute-long segments have often included questionable claims. In one segment, for instance, Hyman said that Kerry enlisted in the Navy to avoid being drafted into the Army.

Overall, however, Sinclair has shown its partisan colors with impunity—at least until now.

When news surfaced of the company's plans to air *Stolen Honor*, advertisers threatened to boycott, Wall Street analysts criticized the company and the stock dropped to a 52-week low. Shareholders threatened lawsuits over the broadcast of the anti-Kerry documentary, prompting Sinclair to issue a statement saying it would not air the film in its entirety, but rather broadcast segments from it as part of a news program.

But as bad as it was for Sinclair, the controversy is worse for the broadcast industry as a whole by raising concerns about one company controlling too large a portion of the airwaves.

"Sinclair has replaced Clear Channel as the new poster child for the ills of media consolidation," Jeffrey Chester, executive director of the Center for Digital Democracy in Washington, told the Center for Public Integrity.

Top priority

Since 1998, lobbying expenditures by the broadcast industry have risen 74 percent, from nearly $26 million to a high of more than $45 million in 2003. It was during that last year of record lobbying that the FCC proposed significant relaxation of the ownership rules, which would have allowed corporations to own more media outlets than ever before and reach a greater percentage of the national audience.

Media deregulation is a top priority for broadcasters. And former FCC Chairman Michael Powell, who was appointed by Bush, shares their views.

That was made clear during Powell's first public appearance as chairman-designate. At a meeting of the Association of Local Television Stations on January 22, 2001, the commissioner agreed with fellow Republican FCC Commissioner Harold Furchtgott-Roth that the agency had in effect become a needless third federal antitrust regulator, given its restrictions over media ownership.

Gradually, the impending deregulation found its way into the national discourse. By June 2003, the FCC had received more than 700,000 public comments about the issue, with 99 percent opposed to any further deregulation. They constituted the largest public response in the agency's history.

"There's a gut reaction," said Chester, noting that these complaints came despite the fact that "you've never gotten a single report from any of the major news broadcasts or newspapers about what the owners are lobbying about." Despite not being well-informed by major news organizations about the agendas of their parent companies, "the public," he said, "understands that things are out of whack."

Nevertheless, on June 2, 2003, Powell led the other Republican commissioners in voting to increase the national broadcast television audience cap to 45 percent (up from 35 percent) and eliminate the so-called duopoly rule (a prohibition against owning two TV stations in the same market) and the media cross-ownership rules.

Perhaps convinced by the public outcry, though, the Senate commerce committee quickly called on the FCC to defend the new rules and, at the same time, crafted a bill that would override the attempt to set the national audience cap at 45 percent. Ultimately, the White House stepped in and the 45 percent cap was reduced to 39 percent. Some of the nation's largest broadcasters, including Fox and Viacom, are all bumping against or exceeding that limit.

Since then, a federal appeals court sent the new rules, other than the audience cap, back to the FCC for re-justification, forcing the agency to re-submit the proposed changes with new supporting research. Eventually, the agency will do just that, and the ultimate decision as to whether the rules will be loosened further will rest with the federal government.

Battle not over

It is disturbing to many to think of media companies as politically active. But it would be naïve not to. Big broadcasters are required to consider both the public interest and the interest of their shareholders, but too often the shareholders' interest wins at the expense of the public's.

"The standards and practices are determined within the corporate environment," said Danny Schechter, executive editor of Mediachannel.org, a Web site that tracks media issues.

Schechter was at one time news director and principal newscaster at WBCN-FM in Boston. He said that news staffers would take "ascertainment" trips into the community to determine issues of importance, then run documentaries on them. Over a number of years, however, WBCN went from being owned by a small company with a few radio stations to one of 183 owned by Viacom, and that same period saw significant decline in the quality of news production.

"The bottom line is much more important than the public interest," he told the Center. "Yes, government policy has favored [deregulation], but corporations have run with it beyond what they've envisioned."

All good journalists follow the money. And in the media consolidation debate, the money has been flying out of the bank for lobbying.

Major broadcasters sharply increased the amount of money they spent lobbying during 2003, the peak of the consolidation debate. In addition to the impact on national audience caps, the decisions also affected so-called cross-ownership—how many different kinds of media outlets, such as newspapers and television stations—a company may own in one market.

Belo Corp., owner of television stations and newspapers, had consistently spent $200,000 a year from 1998 through 2002. In 2003, however, the company more than doubled that amount to $420,000. Clear Channel Communications Inc., the largest radio station owner in the country, went from an average yearly lobbying total of $76,000 for 1998-2002 to a whopping $2.3 million in 2003. Both the National Association of Broadcasters and the Washington Post Co., which also owns television stations, saw significant increases.

The most obvious sign of this shift comes not from hard-core Republicans like David Smith and his three brothers, who control Sinclair, but from the 81-year-old self-described "liberal Democrat" who controls Viacom Inc., owner of CBS, and one of the largest media conglomerates in the world.

Sumner Redstone tacitly endorsed George Bush for re-election in late September, at a meeting of CEOs in Hong Kong. The election of a Republican administration, Redstone told his audience, "is a better deal" in Viacom's view, "because the Republican administration has stood for many things we believe in, deregulation and so on."

Newsweek reported that Redstone's remarks were viewed by many as a breach of an understood code of silence regarding political endorsements that most media conglomerates respect. Several other executives from the top broadcasters were asked to comment, and most repudiated any notion of political favor, while a public interest lobbyist pointed to the remarks as evidence of "what we have known all along"—a comfortable relationship between the industry and its government regulators.

When asked to comment on Redstone's endorsement of Bush, a News Corp. spokesman told Newsweek, "We run these businesses not to promote an ideology or political agenda, but to make them successful."

Broadcast Company Rankings

The world of television and radio broadcasting has been in turmoil as the Federal Communications Commission, Congress, the White House and the courts have wrestled with limits on how many stations one company may own. After years of rulemaking, court cases, legislation and more court cases, the issue is still unresolved.

A federal appeals court in Philadelphia stayed a series of rules approved by the FCC that would greatly relax the restrictions on how many broadcast outlets a single company may own. One change will stand, however. Congress mandated that a single television broadcast company may reach no more than 39 percent of Americans.

Top 10 Television Broadcast Companies

Australian-born billionaire Rupert Murdoch moved the corporate headquarters of News Corp. to the United States, where he is closer to his television holdings and his new stake in the DirecTV satellite broadcasting company. His television broadcast empire is tops in the nation.

Rank	Company	Stations	Revenue (in thousands)
1.	News Corporation Limited. (Fox Entertainment Group Inc.)	37	$2,435,850
2.	CBS Television Network (Viacom Inc.)	41	$2,000,550
3.	NBC Universal Inc. (General Electric Co.)	44	$1,944,450
4.	Tribune Co.	30	$1,328,900
5.	ABC (Walt Disney Co.)	10	$1,247,925
6.	Gannett Company, Inc.	21	$918,800
7.	Hearst-Argyle Television, Inc. (Hearst Corp.)	36	$827,225
8.	Belo Corp.	20	$731,950
9.	Univision Communications Inc.	62	$644,350
10.	Cox Enterprises Inc.	16	$649,400

Source: BIA Financial Network Inc., 2004 Estimated Revenues, 4/2005

Top 10 Radio Broadcast Companies

Clear Channel Communications Inc. is still No. 1 in the U.S. by a large margin, both in number of stations and in revenue.

Rank	Company	Stations	Revenue (in thousands)
1.	Clear Channel Communications, Inc.	1,195	$3,570,650
2.	Infinity Broadcasting Corp. (Viacom Inc.)	179	$2,223,700
3.	Entercom Communications Corp.	106	$487,775
4.	Cox Radio Inc. (Cox Enterprises Inc.)	78	$485,800
5.	ABC Radio Networks (Walt Disney Co.)	73	$454,850
6.	Citadel Broadcasting Corp.	224	$412,782
7.	Radio One Inc.	68	$377,200
8.	Univision Communications Inc.	70	$338,875
9.	Cumulus Media Inc.	303	$325,700
10.	Emmis Communications Corp.	25	$311,175

Source: BIA Financial Network Inc. 2004 Estimated Revenues, 4/2005

Satellite Radio Broadcast Companies (through June 30, 2004)

This category has only two entrants, and the future looks bright for both. An increasing number of vehicle manufacturers are offering the satellite radio service in new cars, and the FCC's crackdown on indecent broadcasting is expected to drive raunchy disc jockeys and their loyal listeners to pay radio.

Rank	Company	Subscribers*
1.	XM Satellite Radio Holdings Inc.	2,100,352
2.	Sirius Satellite Radio Inc.	480,341

* Through second quarter, 2004.

Source: Securities and Exchange Commission filings.

Bells vs. AT&T
Telephone lobbying surpasses half-billion

The four former "Baby Bell" local phone companies and their rivals have spent nearly a half-billion dollars lobbying Congress and the executive branch from 1998 through mid-2004 in an effort to influence federal telecommunications policy.

Led by Verizon Communications Inc. at $102 million, the former Bells collectively have far outspent chief rival AT&T in an attempt to win favor with Congress, the Federal Communications Commission and other government agencies.

All telecommunications companies combined have spent $498 million lobbying from 1998 through June 30, 2004, making the industry among the most prolific spenders in Washington, D.C. By comparison, the powerful oil and gas industry spent $396 million.

In addition, phone companies have contributed some $60.5 million to federal campaigns and political parties from 1998 through September 2004 and paid for $276,072 worth of travel for members and staff of Congress, bringing total spending to affect policy and politics to over $559 million.

"They make huge contributions and they pay for both sides," Mark Cooper, research director of Consumer Federation of America, said in response to the Center's findings. "They hire these lobbyists and they [the lobbyists] live in the halls of the FCC."

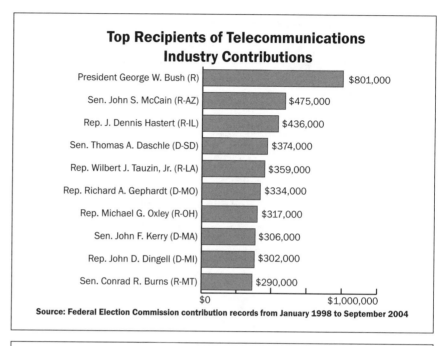

Top Recipients of Telecommunications Industry Contributions

President George W. Bush (R)	$801,000
Sen. John S. McCain (R-AZ)	$475,000
Rep. J. Dennis Hastert (R-IL)	$436,000
Sen. Thomas A. Daschle (D-SD)	$374,000
Rep. Wilbert J. Tauzin, Jr. (R-LA)	$359,000
Rep. Richard A. Gephardt (D-MO)	$334,000
Rep. Michael G. Oxley (R-OH)	$317,000
Sen. John F. Kerry (D-MA)	$306,000
Rep. John D. Dingell (D-MI)	$302,000
Sen. Conrad R. Burns (R-MT)	$290,000

Source: Federal Election Commission contribution records from January 1998 to September 2004

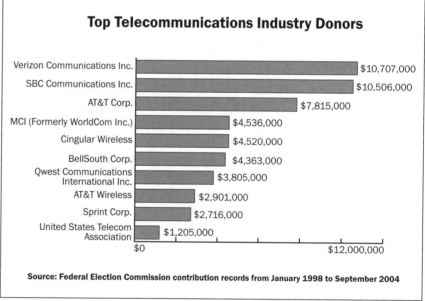

Top Telecommunications Industry Donors

Verizon Communications Inc.	$10,707,000
SBC Communications Inc.	$10,506,000
AT&T Corp.	$7,815,000
MCI (Formerly WorldCom Inc.)	$4,536,000
Cingular Wireless	$4,520,000
BellSouth Corp.	$4,363,000
Qwest Communications International Inc.	$3,805,000
AT&T Wireless	$2,901,000
Sprint Corp.	$2,716,000
United States Telecom Association	$1,205,000

Source: Federal Election Commission contribution records from January 1998 to September 2004

Second behind Verizon in lobby spending is AT&T. Despite experiencing tough economic times over the period, the phone giant nevertheless spent $75 million on lobbying from January 1998 through June 2004. SBC Communications Inc. was third spending $73 million.

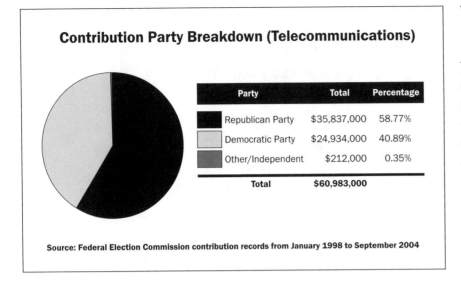

Contribution Party Breakdown (Telecommunications)

Party	Total	Percentage
Republican Party	$35,837,000	58.77%
Democratic Party	$24,934,000	40.89%
Other/Independent	$212,000	0.35%
Total	**$60,983,000**	

Source: Federal Election Commission contribution records from January 1998 to September 2004

Top 10 Telecommunications Industry Lobbying Spenders

Verizon Communications Inc.	$102,457,000
AT&T Corp.	$75,012,000
SBC Communications Inc.	$72,813,000
Sprint Corp.	$46,782,000
BellSouth Corp.	$37,744,000
Qwest Communications International Inc.	$28,732,000
Cellular Telecommunications & Internet Association	$26,032,000
MCI (Formerly WorldCom Inc.)	$21,361,000
United States Telecom Association	$21,309,000
Deutsche Telekom AG (T-Mobile)	$9,530,000

Source: U.S. Senate Office of Public Records lobbying disclosure records from January 1998 to June 30th, 2004.

White House counsel from late 1995 to early 1997.

Third place went to the Dutko Group, whose roster of high-profile lobbyists includes former officials from the administrations of George H.W. Bush, Clinton and President George W. Bush.

As for contributions, telephone companies prefer Republicans to Democrats. Since 1998, telecommunications companies gave 58.8 percent of contributions to Republican parties and candidates and 40.9 percent to Democrats.

The three companies that led the pack in lobbying also topped the list of campaign contributors: Verizon shelled out $10.7 million, while SBC spent $10.5 million and AT&T spent $7.8 million.

The top recipient of telecommunications industry campaign contributions is President Bush with $801,000; Sen. John McCain (R-Ariz.), former chairman of the Committee on Commerce, Science & Transportation, is second at $475,000; and Rep. Dennis Hastert (R-Ill.), the speaker of the House, is third at $436,000.

The lobbyists hired to represent these and other telecommunications heavyweights were some of the most politically well-connected in D.C.

The top hired gun for the telephone industry, with $7.1 million in fees, was Akin Gump Strauss Hauer & Feld. (Akin Gump was also the number two lobbyist for the overall communications industry, with $9.6 million in fees.) The firm is home to such Capitol Hill veterans as former Sen. Lauch Faircloth (R-N.C.) and former Rep. Bill Paxon (R-N.Y.).

Second-place honors went to Quinn Gillespie & Associates, whose principals include current Republican National Committee Chairman Ed Gillespie and Jack Quinn, President Bill Clinton's

Former Democratic presidential candidate John Kerry was eighth overall with $306,000.

From 1998 through September 2004, Bush outraised Kerry in phone contributions 5 to 2. Bush's top four phone supporters were the four Bell companies: SBC ($178,000), Verizon ($129,000), BellSouth ($122,000) and Qwest ($64,000). Together the Bells gave Bush 62 percent of the money he received from telephone interests and favored him over Kerry almost 3 to 1.

Kerry's top four phone contributors are: Verizon ($116,000), AT&T ($31,000), SBC ($29,000) and MCI ($23,000). Together the Bells gave Kerry a bit more than half of the money he has received from phone interests.

The telephone industry is also a frequent sponsor of trips for members, family and staff of the two congressional committees that regulate the industry – the Senate Committee on Science, Commerce and Transportation and the House Committee on Energy and Commerce.

The telephone industry as a whole paid for 195 trips by congressmen, senators and congressional staffers from the House and Senate commerce committees between 2000 and early 2004, valued at $276,071, according to documents.

The congressional office of former Rep. Billy Tauzin (R-La.), former chairman of the House Committee on Energy and Commerce, racked up the most miles at industry expense by a large margin. Tauzin or members of his staff went on 23 trips at a cost of $36,568.

Tauzin personally took trips home to New Orleans and to a number of California locales, including San Diego and Palm Springs, at a cost of $6,894 to the industry. Tauzin's wife Cecile accompanied him on the California outings, while son Michael went along on one of the trips to New Orleans.

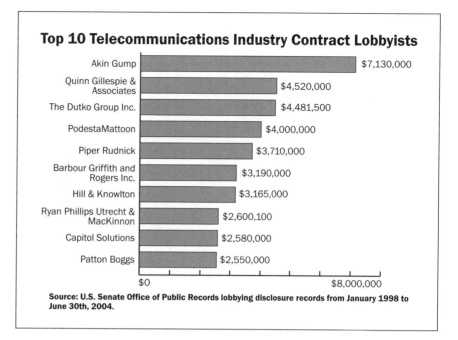

Top 10 Telecommunications Industry Contract Lobbyists

Akin Gump	$7,130,000
Quinn Gillespie & Associates	$4,520,000
The Dutko Group Inc.	$4,481,500
PodestaMattoon	$4,000,000
Piper Rudnick	$3,710,000
Barbour Griffith and Rogers Inc.	$3,190,000
Hill & Knowlton	$3,165,000
Ryan Phillips Utrecht & MacKinnon	$2,600,100
Capitol Solutions	$2,580,000
Patton Boggs	$2,550,000

Source: U.S. Senate Office of Public Records lobbying disclosure records from January 1998 to June 30th, 2004.

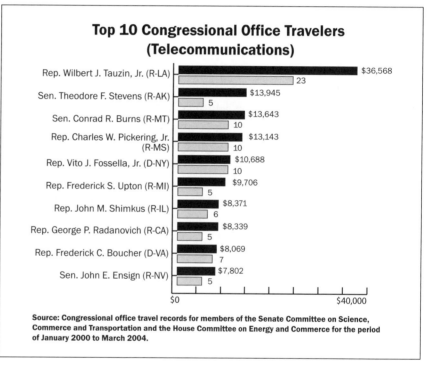

Top 10 Congressional Office Travelers (Telecommunications)

Member	Cost	Trips
Rep. Wilbert J. Tauzin, Jr. (R-LA)	$36,568	23
Sen. Theodore F. Stevens (R-AK)	$13,945	5
Sen. Conrad R. Burns (R-MT)	$13,643	10
Rep. Charles W. Pickering, Jr. (R-MS)	$13,143	10
Rep. Vito J. Fossella, Jr. (D-NY)	$10,688	10
Rep. Frederick S. Upton (R-MI)	$9,706	5
Rep. John M. Shimkus (R-IL)	$8,371	6
Rep. George P. Radanovich (R-CA)	$8,339	5
Rep. Frederick C. Boucher (D-VA)	$8,069	7
Sen. John E. Ensign (R-NV)	$7,802	5

Source: Congressional office travel records for members of the Senate Committee on Science, Commerce and Transportation and the House Committee on Energy and Commerce for the period of January 2000 to March 2004.

Another indication of the coziness between the industry and federal regulators is the large number of former government workers who become lobbyists. Indeed, at least 58 current and former FCC, congressional and executive branch officials have worked for the phone industry. At least 23 have worked for the Bells or their trade association, the United States Telecom Association. Many others have been hired as outside consultants and contract lobbyists on the industry's behalf.

For example, FCC Commissioner Kathleen Abernathy, who once worked for Baby Bell U S West, Inc. (since acquired by Qwest), is on her second pass through the revolving door between the FCC and the phone companies. In the 1990s, she was a lobbyist for private companies with business before the FCC after having served in senior staff roles at the FCC.

Lyndon K. Boozer, BellSouth's vice president of federal relations, previously worked as a special assistant in the FCC's Office of Legislative and Intergovernmental Affairs.

Peter Davidson, Verizon's senior vice president for federal government relations, has also passed twice through the revolving door. After serving as general counsel and policy director to then-House Majority Leader Dick Armey (R-Texas), Davidson worked for Qwest, then with the U.S. Trade Representative in the Bush administration. He joined Verizon in April 2003.

The companies that enlisted the help of these commission veterans have reaped a substantial return on investment. In particular, the Bell companies have scored a series of victories at the FCC since former FCC Chairmen Reed Hundt, who openly favored new competitors at their expense, left the commission. His successor, William Kennard, another Clinton appointee, hewed closer to the Bells while former Chairman Michael Powell, a Bush appointee, went even further by favoring the Bells on most key decisions.

The industry's political largesse means that the Bells

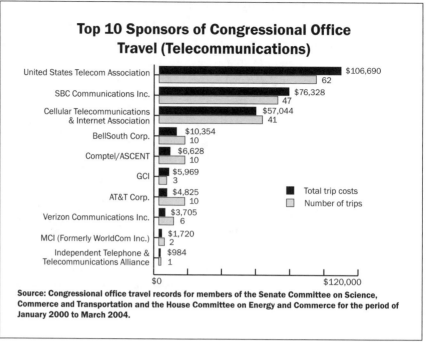

Top 10 Sponsors of Congressional Office Travel (Telecommunications)

Sponsor	Total trip costs	Number of trips
United States Telecom Association	$106,690	62
SBC Communications Inc.	$76,328	47
Cellular Telecommunications & Internet Association	$57,044	41
BellSouth Corp.	$10,354	10
Comptel/ASCENT	$6,628	10
GCI	$5,969	3
AT&T Corp.	$4,825	10
Verizon Communications Inc.	$3,705	6
MCI (Formerly WorldCom Inc.)	$1,720	2
Independent Telephone & Telecommunications Alliance	$984	1

Source: Congressional office travel records for members of the Senate Committee on Science, Commerce and Transportation and the House Committee on Energy and Commerce for the period of January 2000 to March 2004.

will have allies among Republicans as well as Democrats on the powerful House and Senate panels poised to undertake a wholesale realignment of the telecommunications laws in the coming year.

Last summer, when a federal judge threw out rules opposed by the Bells, the administration chose not to appeal—a decision that left Bell competitors to face price hikes until new rules are written.

From Government Service to Private Practice
Writers of telecom law move to K Street

What do nearly all of the tight-knit group of congressional aides who crafted the pro-business Telecommunications Act of 1996 now have in common? Salaries as industry lobbyists.

Some call it cashing in. Some call it an opportunity they can't pass up. Others call it an offer they can't refuse.

"Some people had no choice but to go through the revolving door because you have to make a living on what you do and what you know," said Christopher McLean, who went on to senior roles in the Clinton administration and then left government for a Washington, D.C.-based lobbying firm following President George W. Bush's 2000 election victory.

Whatever their motives, the aides have taken the common route from political staff member to champion of private interests.

Through press accounts, primary sources and detailed interviews, The Center for Public Integrity has identified a short list of the 15 staffers most involved in the years-long process of drafting the 1996 act. Thirteen of them, it turns out, became lobbyists, and another is a lawmaker who gets generous financial support for his campaigns from telephone companies. Another worked for a telecom lobbyist before helping to draft the law.

Those staffers have defended the integrity of their work on the 1996 act, but some telecom observers have their doubts. Adam Thierer, for example, an analyst at the libertarian Cato Institute, has called it a fundamentally flawed law loaded with contradictory giveaways and payoffs to various industry players.

The Center identified at least 199 current or former Federal Communications Commission officials and congressional staff who have worked as registered lobbyists, many leaving the FCC to work for the communications industry and later returning to government. Most notable among them is FCC

Commissioner Kathleen Abernathy. Abernathy was appointed by President George W. Bush after executive jobs in government affairs for US West (since acquired by Qwest Communications International) and AirTouch Communications Inc.

Abernathy declined a request for an interview.

"I think there's no doubt that there's what some people call an almost incestuous relationship," said Thierer of Cato "The real question at the end of the day for someone like me is, What are they fighting over? They're fighting over control of the government's ability to influence private decision making."

Rep. Chip Pickering (R-Miss.), who worked on the act as a staffer to Sen. Trent Lott (R-Miss.), now holds the most prominent position of the group, having run for office immediately after leaving Lott's payroll. Pickering may not have gone to work for the industry, but the phone companies nevertheless found a way to boost his career: along with their employees, they've donated $264,000 to his campaigns from 1998 through September 2004. That's just a small slice of the more than 35,000 contributions—totaling more than $60 million—the industry has made to House, Senate and presidential candidates.

Records show that between 2000 and March 2004, telephone interests have paid for 10 trips for Pickering or members of his staff, at a cost of more than $11,000. Among the trips: a two-day outing to New Orleans during Mardi Gras that Pickering took at the expense of the trade group representing cell phone providers.

Pickering's office did not respond to the Center's request for an interview.

John Windhausen Jr., a former Senate Committee on Commerce, Science and Transportation staffer reporting to Sen. Ernest "Fritz" Hollings (D-S.C.), went on to head the Association for Local Telecommunication Services, a trade group for local phone-service providers that compete against the major phone companies.

"It wasn't going to get any better than that. After the '96 act I'd accomplished everything a staffer could accomplish," Windhausen told the Center.

Of course, congressional and FCC staffers aren't alone in moving from public servants to telephone industry lobbyists. They are joined by FCC commissioners, administration officials and even members of Congress.

Indeed, at least two congressmen and one senator who played key roles on the 1996 bill became lobbyists whose clients have included one of the "Baby Bell" companies that now appear to be the ultimate winners from the law: former Reps. Jack Fields (R-Texas) and Thomas Bliley (R-Va.) and former Sen. Larry Pressler (R-S.D.). At the time the 1996 act passed, Pressler was chairman of the Senate Committee on Commerce, Science and Transportation, but lost a tough re-election fight later that year. Bliley was chairman of the House Committee on Energy and Commerce.

The only other lawmaker centrally involved in crafting the 1996 law who has left office is Sen. James Exon (D-Neb.), the veteran politician who retired after his final term ended in January 1997.

Indeed, the Center has found that in 2003 nearly 1,000 lobbyists plied the halls of Congress and the FCC on behalf of the phone companies. The cost to the industry for this swarm has been more than $498 million from 1998 through June 30, 2004. In 2003 alone, phone companies spent nearly $83 million on lobbying.

Besides Pickering and Windhausen, the Center identified the following staffers who had major involvement in the '96 bill:

Earl Comstock: Then a staffer for Sen. Ted Stevens (R-Alaska), he has gone on to be a partner and head of the telecommunications practice group at the Washington, D.C., law firm Sher & Blackwell. His clients have included Nextel Communications, AT&T and Winstar.

Donald McClellan: Then a Senate commerce committee staffer reporting to Sen. Pressler, he is now chief lobbyist for computer maker Gateway Inc.

Gerard Waldron: Then a committee staffer reporting to Rep. Edward Markey (D-Mass.), he is now a lobbyist at the Washington, D.C., law firm Covington & Burling. His clients there have included satellite powerhouse COMSAT and the Network Affiliated Stations Alliance.

James "J.D." Derderian: Then a committee staffer for Rep. Bliley (R-Va.), Derderian became a partner in the Cormac Group, where his clients included AT&T, AT&T Wireless, XO Communications and DSL provider Covad Communications. In 2003 he co-founded another lobbying and consulting firm, the Stanton Park Group.

Katie King: Then majority communications counsel for the Senate commerce committee, King is now special counsel in the FCC's Telecommunications Access Policy Division. While she didn't leave government to become a lobbyist, she does have a tie to the lobbying industry: Before working on Capitol Hill, King was a lawyer at Wiley Rein & Fielding, one of the biggest telecommunications lobbying firms in D.C.

Kevin Joseph: Then a senior minority counsel for the Senate commerce committee, Joseph went on to jobs with AT&T and Allegiance Telecom Inc. before opening his own lobbying firm.

Catherine M. Reid: Then the majority counsel for the House commerce committee, she later worked at cable TV giant Time Warner and at the law and lobbying firm Williams & Jensen, where her clients included the National Cable & Telecommunications Association and phone company LCI International (now Qwest Communications).

David Leach: Then a staffer for Rep. Anna Eshoo (D-Calif.), Leach became a lobbyist at Dewey Ballantine LLP. He started his own lobbying firm with clients including Verizon, SBC Communications and wireless phone provider NextWave Telecom Inc.

Harold Furchtgott-Roth: Then the chief economist for the House commerce committee, he went on to serve as an FCC commissioner and later as a visiting fellow at the American Enterprise Institute. He also started his own company, Furchtgott-Roth Economic Enterprises. While not a registered lobbyist, his Web site advertises services including "development of regulatory strategies."

Michael Regan: Then a senior staffer on the House commerce committee, Regan went on to be senior vice president of external affairs for NextWave Telecom and now serves as senior vice president of government affairs at News Corp., owner of the Fox broadcasting and cable networks.

Christopher McLean: Then a staffer for Sen. Exon, he helped draft provisions of the act related to rural telephone service and the "universal service" tax fund. He later worked as administrator of the Rural Utilities Service in the Clinton administration. Now he is a lobbyist with the government affairs firm e-Copernicus, where he helps companies and organizations get money from the federal government's rural service and universal service funds.

Gregory Rohde: Then a staffer for Sen. Byron Dorgan (D-N.D.), Rohde worked with McLean on the rural and universal service aspects of the 1996 bill. He went on to serve as administrator of the Commerce Department's National Telecommunications and Information Administration for President Clinton, then resumed his partnership with McLean as president of e-Copernicus. In addition, he serves as head of the E9-1-1 Institute, the nonprofit arm of the Congressional E9-1-1 Caucus. Their clients include BellSouth Corp and Motorola.

Paddy Link: Served as staff director of the Senate commerce committee during the drafting of the 1996 act and went on to other senior congressional staff roles before becoming a lobbyist. Link is now a lobbyist at Wexler & Walker Public Policy Associates (part of Hill & Knowlton), where her client list includes MCI Inc.

Kevin Curtin: A staffer on the Senate commerce committee during the drafting of the 1996 act, he is now a lobbyist whose clients include Verizon.

Telephone Company Rankings

With the advent of cellular and Internet-based phone service, it's never been easier to reach out and touch someone.

The old telephone lines controlled by the former Baby Bells still carry most of our calls, but cellular services have been gaining ground at an astonishing pace. By the end of 2003, there were more than 160 million subscribers. A mere decade ago, the total number of subscribers was 16 million. And cable companies are chipping away further at local and long-distance companies as they offer telephone service over the Internet.

What does this mean for the near future? First and foremost, the entire Telecommunications Act of 1996 – a hugely important rewrite of communications law that was supposed to create competition in local phone service – is in danger of becoming obsolete. Second, the Federal Communications Commission will have to decide exactly how to regulate phone service that's really computer data in disguise. But the good news is that the consumer has more choices as wireline, cellular and wireless companies compete with one another. The bad news is, some of those services are actually owned by the same company.

Local Telephone Service Providers (by access lines)

The top local telephone service providers are ranked according to the number of access lines each company controls. So long as customers want to pick up their phones and hear a good-old-fashioned dial tone, chances are they will use one of these four carriers.

While competition in the local telephone industry has picked up in recent years, most of the business is still dominated by the four former Bell operating companies that are what's left of the old AT&T telephone monopoly. The largest provider is Verizon Communications Inc., with SBC Communications Inc. a very close second.

Rank	Company	Lines*
1.	Verizon Communications Inc.	55.5 million
2.	SBC Communications Inc.	54.7 million
3.	BellSouth Corp.	23.7 million
4.	Qwest Communications International Inc.	16.2 million

* Totals through year-end 2003. An access line connects a telephone company's central office to a point usually on the customer's premises.
Source: Securities and Exchange Commission filings.

Long-distance Phone Service Providers (by revenue)

Long distance companies are ranked by amount of money they take in each year on toll-calls. The former Baby Bells continue to chip away at the traditional long-distance market. Many cell phone plans now offer free long distance. The share of the three largest providers is down to 62 percent, according to the most recent revenue figures from the FCC. These numbers will most likely continue to drop as more customers turn to cellular service and the Internet to make the calls that have been considered "long distance" up until now.

Rank	Company	Revenue*	Market Share
1.	AT&T Corp.	$27,094	32%
2.	MCI Inc.	$17,659	21%
3.	Sprint Corp.	$7,077	9%
Top 3		$51,829	62%
	Other		38%

* Totals through year-end 2002, in thousands.
Source: FCC Statistics of Communications Common Carriers

Wireless Service Providers

In 2003, wireless telephone service crossed a major milestone, as the nationwide subscriber rate rose from 48 percent to 54 percent; for the first time, a majority of Americans are cellular subscribers—more than 160 million in all. Customers are also talking on the cell phones for more minutes per month than ever before—more than 500 on average—and sending an increasing number of text messages through their cell phones. As usage continues to skyrocket, however, the number of providers remains relatively static. The top 10 service providers account for 88.7 percent of all subscribers.

Rank	Carrier	Subscribers	Market Share
1.	Verizon Wireless Inc. (Verizon Communications Inc.)	37,522,000	23.3%
2.	Cingular Wireless LLC	24,027,000	14.9%
3.	AT&T Wireless Services Inc.	21,980,000	13.6%
4.	Sprint PCS (Sprint Corp.)	15,900,000	9.9%
5.	T-Mobile USA (Deutsche Telekom AG)	13,128,000	8.1%
6.	Nextel Communications, Inc.	12,882,000	8.0%
7.	ALLTEL Corp.	8,023,000	4.9%
8.	United States Cellular Corp. (Telephone and Data Systems Inc.)	4,409,000	2.7%
9.	Dobson Communications, Inc.	1,552,000	1.0%
10.	Leap Wireless International Inc.	1,473,000	0.9%
	Other		12.7%

Source: 2004 FCC Annual Report and Analysis of Competitive Market Conditions With Respect to Commercial Mobile Services.

Industry Battles Re-regulation
Cable lobbying climbs by 50 percent

The cable television industry has steadily increased the amount it spends to sway opinion in Congress and at the Federal Communications Commission since 1998.

The industry spent $16.2 million on lobbying in 1998 compared with $24.3 million in 2003, a jump of 50 percent, according to records. All told, the industry spent $120 million on lobbying from 1998 through mid-2004.

The cable television industry also spent $20.5 million on political campaigns from 1998 through September 2004 and sponsored 127 trips for members, family and staff of the two congressional committees that oversee the industry from 2000 through the first quarter of 2004 at a cost of $225,670.

In addition to contributions, lobbying and junkets, the Center also analyzed employment patterns of former FCC staff and senior employees of the House and Senate commerce committees. Researchers identified 16 former senior government officials who went to work for the cable industry since 1996.

The top spenders on lobbying among cable systems are:

- Time Warner Inc. leads the list at $46 million. The total includes spending from non-cable divisions of the media conglomerate. Time Warner is the nation's second largest cable systems operator, with nearly 11 million subscribers. Its holdings also include several cable television networks, including news channel CNN.

- Second on the lobbying list is the National Cable & Telecommunications Association, the cable industry's Washington representative, at $39.7 million.

- Third is Comcast, the nation's largest cable television company with 21.5 million subscribers, at $15.6 million.

The most important issues facing the cable industry deal mostly with staving off federal regulation. The industry is fighting to keep broadband Internet service free from similar "common carrier" rules that affect telephone companies. The industry is also fighting a proposal that would require them to carry multiple

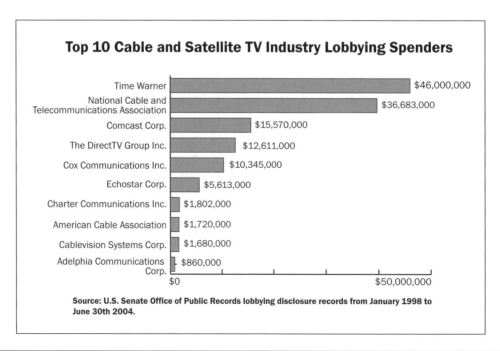

Top 10 Cable and Satellite TV Industry Lobbying Spenders

Time Warner	$46,000,000
National Cable and Telecommunications Association	$36,683,000
Comcast Corp.	$15,570,000
The DirectTV Group Inc.	$12,611,000
Cox Communications Inc.	$10,345,000
Echostar Corp.	$5,613,000
Charter Communications Inc.	$1,802,000
American Cable Association	$1,720,000
Cablevision Systems Corp.	$1,680,000
Adelphia Communications Corp.	$860,000

$0 $50,000,000

Source: U.S. Senate Office of Public Records lobbying disclosure records from January 1998 to June 30th 2004.

digital broadcast signals on their systems from a single broadcaster and is in the midst of a massive lobbying effort to snuff out attempts to require that channels be made available on an "a la carte" basis rather than in tiers.

While cable television is still by far the most popular means of receiving video programming, direct broadcast satellite has become a legitimate competitor. The DirecTV group is now the second largest provider of pay-television service with 11.6 million subscribers. EchoStar Communication Corp. ranks fourth behind Time Warner with 8.8 million customers.

These two companies have also become big Washington influence players. DirecTV and Echostar collectively spent $18.2 million on lobbying and $2.2 million on campaign contributions between 1998 and September 2004. DirecTV, controlled by News Corp., spent $12.6 million on lobbying while EchoStar spent $5.6 million.

The partisan preference of the cable television industry skews Democratic. Contributions were split 52.5 percent for Democratic candidates and party organizations and 47.2 percent for Republicans.

Time Warner is the top contributor in the sector at $8.2 million. Comcast is a distant second with $3.2 million and the National Cable & Telecommunications Association is third with $3.1 million.

The top recipient of cable contributions is President George W. Bush at $375,000. Sen. John Kerry, Bush's 2004 Democratic opponent, is second at $323,000, while Senate Minority Leader Tom Daschle, Democrat of South Dakota, was third at $224,000.

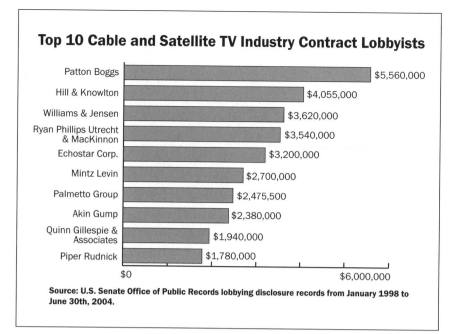

Top 10 Cable and Satellite TV Industry Contract Lobbyists

Patton Boggs	$5,560,000
Hill & Knowlton	$4,055,000
Williams & Jensen	$3,620,000
Ryan Phillips Utrecht & MacKinnon	$3,540,000
Echostar Corp.	$3,200,000
Mintz Levin	$2,700,000
Palmetto Group	$2,475,500
Akin Gump	$2,380,000
Quinn Gillespie & Associates	$1,940,000
Piper Rudnick	$1,780,000

Source: U.S. Senate Office of Public Records lobbying disclosure records from January 1998 to June 30th, 2004.

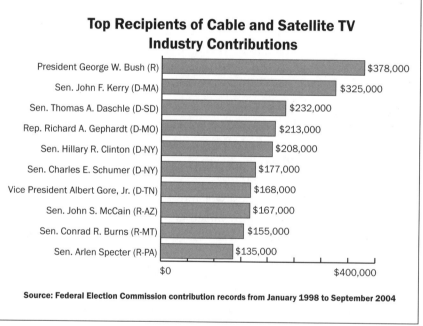

Top Recipients of Cable and Satellite TV Industry Contributions

President George W. Bush (R)	$378,000
Sen. John F. Kerry (D-MA)	$325,000
Sen. Thomas A. Daschle (D-SD)	$232,000
Rep. Richard A. Gephardt (D-MO)	$213,000
Sen. Hillary R. Clinton (D-NY)	$208,000
Sen. Charles E. Schumer (D-NY)	$177,000
Vice President Albert Gore, Jr. (D-TN)	$168,000
Sen. John S. McCain (R-AZ)	$167,000
Sen. Conrad R. Burns (R-MT)	$155,000
Sen. Arlen Specter (R-PA)	$135,000

Source: Federal Election Commission contribution records from January 1998 to September 2004

The cable industry is also a frequent sponsor of trips for members, family and staff of the two congressional committees that regulate the industry – the Senate Committee on Science, Commerce and Transportation and the House Committee on Energy and Commerce.

The NCTA, which puts particular emphasis on its annual trade show, is far and away the cable industry's largest underwriter of travel for members of those committees; in fact, it is No. 1 in the communications industry as a whole.

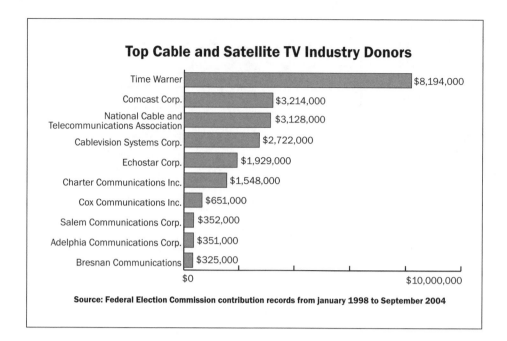

Top Cable and Satellite TV Industry Donors

Time Warner	$8,194,000
Comcast Corp.	$3,214,000
National Cable and Telecommunications Association	$3,128,000
Cablevision Systems Corp.	$2,722,000
Echostar Corp.	$1,929,000
Charter Communications Inc.	$1,548,000
Cox Communications Inc.	$651,000
Salem Communications Corp.	$352,000
Adelphia Communications Corp.	$351,000
Bresnan Communications	$325,000

Source: Federal Election Commission contribution records from January 1998 to September 2004

(The NCTA also spent $192,609 on 102 trips over an eight-year period flying FCC commissioners and staff to various events, according to a 2003 Center study. The practice all but stopped due to congressional pressure following the Center's report.)

Second for spending on congressional travel was Time Warner with 16 trips worth $22,495. Comcast was a distant third with $2,810 worth of trips.

According to the survey, the most-well-traveled congressional office—with 21 trips valued at $38,037—was that of former Rep. Billy Tauzin (R-La.), who was chairman of the House commerce committee. Second, with 12 trips valued at $15,514 was the office of Sen. Conrad Burns (R-Mont.), a member of the Subcommittee on Communications of the Senate commerce committee.

Among former government officials now working for the cable industry, perhaps the most well known is Victoria "Torie" Clarke. Clarke was the Pentagon spokeswoman during the most recent Iraq war and is widely credited with creating the "embedding" system

of attaching reporters to troops in the field. Clarke, who had previously served as chief spokeswoman for the NCTA, took a job with Comcast as senior adviser for communications and government affairs.

One of the top cable lobbyists in Washington is Daniel Brenner, senior vice president for law and regulatory policy with the NCTA. Brenner was senior legal adviser to former FCC Chairman Mark Fowler from 1981 to 1986.

Among Time Warner's heavy-hitting lobbyists is Susan Brophy, who was director of congressional relations for the Clinton-Gore transition team, and then deputy director of legislative affairs at the White House. She joined Time Warner as senior vice president of domestic policy in 2001 and now serves as vice president for global public policy.

As for satellite broadcasters, DirecTV hired Susan Eid as vice president of government relations. Eid was senior legal adviser to FCC Chairman Michael Powell before joining DirecTV.

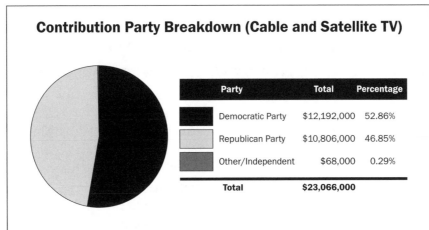

Contribution Party Breakdown (Cable and Satellite TV)

Party	Total	Percentage
Democratic Party	$12,192,000	52.86%
Republican Party	$10,806,000	46.85%
Other/Independent	$68,000	0.29%
Total	**$23,066,000**	

Source: Federal Election Commission contribution records from January 1998 to September 2004

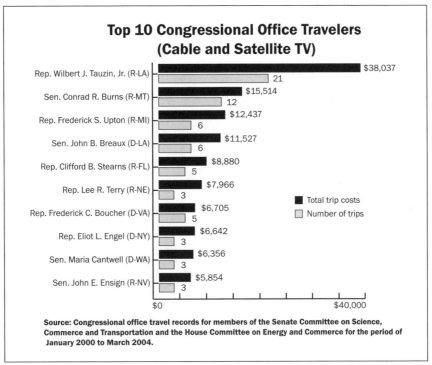

Top 10 Congressional Office Travelers (Cable and Satellite TV)

Rep. Wilbert J. Tauzin, Jr. (R-LA) — $38,037 / 21
Sen. Conrad R. Burns (R-MT) — $15,514 / 12
Rep. Frederick S. Upton (R-MI) — $12,437 / 6
Sen. John B. Breaux (D-LA) — $11,527 / 6
Rep. Clifford B. Stearns (R-FL) — $8,880 / 5
Rep. Lee R. Terry (R-NE) — $7,966 / 3
Rep. Frederick C. Boucher (D-VA) — $6,705 / 5
Rep. Eliot L. Engel (D-NY) — $6,642 / 3
Sen. Maria Cantwell (D-WA) — $6,356 / 3
Sen. John E. Ensign (R-NV) — $5,854 / 3

■ Total trip costs
□ Number of trips

$0 — $40,000

Source: Congressional office travel records for members of the Senate Committee on Science, Commerce and Transportation and the House Committee on Energy and Commerce for the period of January 2000 to March 2004.

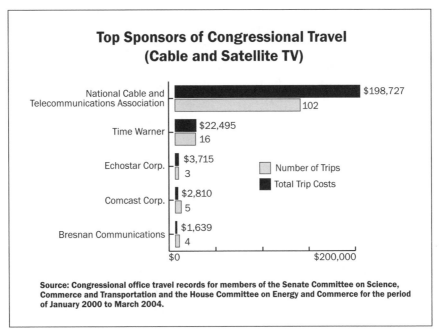

Top Sponsors of Congressional Travel (Cable and Satellite TV)

National Cable and Telecommunications Association — $198,727 / 102
Time Warner — $22,495 / 16
Echostar Corp. — $3,715 / 3
Comcast Corp. — $2,810 / 5
Bresnan Communications — $1,639 / 4

□ Number of Trips
■ Total Trip Costs

$0 — $200,000

Source: Congressional office travel records for members of the Senate Committee on Science, Commerce and Transportation and the House Committee on Energy and Commerce for the period of January 2000 to March 2004.

Anatomy of a Lobbying Blitz
Cable industry enlists diverse crowd in high-level influence campaign

When a conservative member of Congress floated the idea of allowing consumers to pick which channels they want to pay for rather than having to buy a "bundle" of channels they may never watch, it seemed like a pretty good idea.

Rather than pay a flat fee for dozens of channels, consumers could choose a handful of channels "a la carte," or from a menu—and possibly pay far less for their service.

Among the hundreds of initiatives tracked by the cable television industry and its army of lobbyists, a la carte is among the most feared. A re-regulation of the industry could cost cable companies control over programming and jeopardize an economic model that has helped the industry maintain huge profits over the years. The industry has argued that a la carte service would increase costs to consumers rather than lower their cable bills.

In addition to warning of higher prices, the industry's chief argument for bundling channels is that cable networks that cater to minorities will wither and die if people are allowed to choose their own programming.

The cable industry, largely unregulated since 1999, has had a problematic track record with consumers. Cable prices have risen 40 percent from 1997 to 2002 and subscribers in 98 percent of markets have only one cable provider, according to a study by the Government Accountability Office.

Surveys by J.D. Power show a low level of public satisfaction with cable service providers.

But rather than spark an uprising of consumer support, the proposal to offer channels on an a la carte basis was blasted by elected officials at every level of government. Joining the chorus were nationally known and respected civil rights organizations and a large collection of women's groups, all of whom appeared to be singing from the same page.

A Center for Public Integrity investigation of hundreds of filings with the Federal Communications Commission, lobbying reports and other documents reveals that the "grass roots" opposition to a la carte is actually a highly sophisticated lobbying campaign where seemingly disinterested third parties—like non-profits and legislators—are spreading the anti-a la carte message using minority programming as the key issue.

In fact, rather than being disinterested, these third parties have much to gain. The Center has identified hundreds of thousands of dollars in donations and other benefits showered by cable companies on some of these nonprofits. The Center also found one instance in which free airtime was made available to a mayors group and identified nearly $60,000 in contributions to one key pro-cable congressman.

One measure of the campaign's effectiveness is an August 13, 2004, comment filed by the National Cable and Telecommunications Association, the key lobbying arm of the cable television industry, with the Federal Communications Commission, pointing out the overwhelming number of letters that had been filed in opposition to a la carte. Among those letters pointed out by the NCTA, some 64 were from nonprofits and politicians whose comments were derived from one of five basic form letters, one of which was written by four cable executives, another circulated by an industry lobbyist.

It is not unusual for a special interest group to orchestrate mass-mailing campaigns, on either side of the political spectrum. But what's not so common is for nationally recognized civil rights leaders, members of Congress, city council members and state legislators to sign their names to an industry-generated letter.

Among the signers of one of the five letters were two members of Congress, six mayors, seven members of the New York City Council, six members of the New York state legislature, one Florida state legislator, one Arizona state legislator, one Illinois state legislator and the comptroller of the state of Connecticut.

"The difference with this campaign, the ethnic community is at the vanguard," said Brian Woolfolk, who is working pro bono for small cable networks that are in favor of a la carte pricing. "Strategically, it completely disarms the Democratic caucus. The Democratic caucus is going to be sensitive to civil rights organizations and civil rights issues."

Among the minority nonprofits who signed form letters in opposition to a la carte pricing were the National Urban League, the Rainbow/PUSH Coalition and the National Congress of Black Women Inc.

Strange bedfellows

The cable a la carte issue actually dates back to the 1980s, when cable companies offered it as a pricing option. Though a la carte service never caught on, demand for the option resurfaces periodically depending on the level of public dissatisfaction with service and cost. By March 31, 1999, provisions of the Telecommunications Act of 1996 had phased out cable price regulation and prices began to spiral upward. But the a la carte issue got red hot exposure when conservative groups started pushing the issue.

The Janet Jackson Super Bowl stunt emboldened social conservatives like Rep. Nathan Deal, a Republican from Georgia, to push for a la carte as a means to keep risqué programming out of households that don't want it. Joining the cable a la carte debate was Consumers Union and its senior director of policy Gene Kimmelman, albeit grudgingly.

"A la carte emerged in the consumer agenda only after efforts to prevent concentration of ownership and price gouging all failed," he said. "It was kind of a fall-back position. It was never viewed as the totally optimal approach."

Consumers Union is the respected nonprofit publisher of *Consumer Reports* magazine. The organization accepts no corporate contributions.

Kimmelman and others expected resistance from the industry. But they were certainly caught off guard by the allies that cable mustered to its side.

The Congressional Black Caucus, which was founded in 1969, is a group of 39 lawmakers who list among

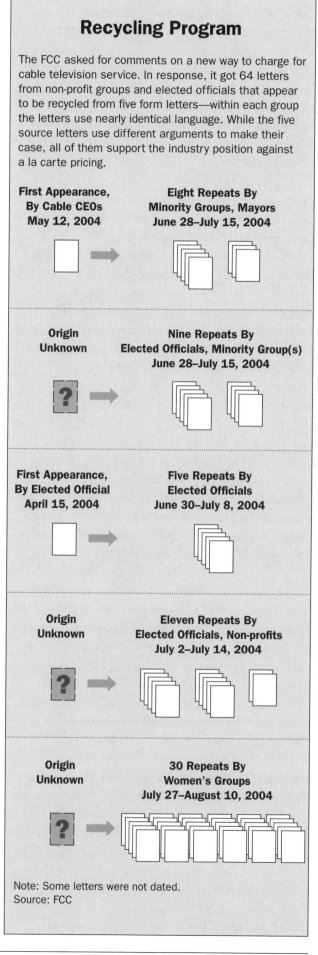

Recycling Program

The FCC asked for comments on a new way to charge for cable television service. In response, it got 64 letters from non-profit groups and elected officials that appear to be recycled from five form letters—within each group the letters use nearly identical language. While the five source letters use different arguments to make their case, all of them support the industry position against a la carte pricing.

First Appearance, By Cable CEOs May 12, 2004

Eight Repeats By Minority Groups, Mayors June 28–July 15, 2004

Origin Unknown

Nine Repeats By Elected Officials, Minority Group(s) June 28–July 15, 2004

First Appearance, By Elected Official April 15, 2004

Five Repeats By Elected Officials June 30–July 8, 2004

Origin Unknown

Eleven Repeats By Elected Officials, Non-profits July 2–July 14, 2004

Origin Unknown

30 Repeats By Women's Groups July 27–August 10, 2004

Note: Some letters were not dated.
Source: FCC

their legislative priorities the creation of a living wage, guaranteed health insurance for all Americans, and strengthening and better enforcing civil rights laws. The caucus has long been concerned with the lack of diversity in cable programming, ownership and in the senior ranks of system operators. In early 2003, the caucus, led by Rep. Bobby Scott, D-Va., wrote a letter to the cable industry threatening severe regulatory consequences if cable's prospects for minorities did not improve.

"Since we have not seen ample progress in the diversification of content and ownership to assuage our apprehensions, we may no longer be able to justify our current hands-off approach to regulating the cable industry," the letter reads in part.

A portion of the letter was published in a trade magazine, but it was never actually mailed, according to Woolfolk, its author. A series of meetings between cable television representatives and the caucus followed, and the diversity issue appeared to fade away.

Not long after the meetings, the a la carte movement began to get some traction thanks to the Janet Jackson scandal and general public outrage regarding indecent broadcasting. Deal authored an amendment to a bill that would require cable and satellite companies to give customers the option of buying channels one at a time, rather than as a package.

Alfred Liggins, chairman of TV One, a new African-American-themed cable television network co-owned by broadcaster Radio One and cable giant Comcast Corp., wrote an April 12, 2004 op-ed piece in the *Washington Times* arguing against the idea. Liggins, whose network benefits from being bundled with other channels, argued that minority networks would be squeezed out if consumers were allowed to choose their own channels.

On May 12, 2004, the Congressional Black Caucus went from being a key cable industry threat to an ally.

The caucus sent a letter to Reps. Joe Barton and John Dingell, the chairman and ranking member of the House Committee on Energy and Commerce respectively, arguing against the a la carte idea. The letter, which quotes the Liggins piece in the *Washington Times*, shifted the focus of the a la carte

debate from lowering consumer costs to preserving minority programming.

Over the past few years, the nonprofit Congressional Black Caucus Foundation—a separate and distinct entity from the caucus that nevertheless boasts 11 caucus members on its board of directors and two caucus members among its top officers—has drawn considerable support from the cable industry.

In its 2002 annual report, the foundation, which ranks donors within ranges, lists Time Warner (then AOL Time Warner) as contributing between $50,000 and $99,999. In the 2003 report, the company jumped a tier, contributing between $100,000 and $249,999. Comcast also upped its contribution, from between $30,000 and $49,999 in 2002 to between $50,000 and $99,999 in 2003.

Viacom companies are listed as contributing between $20,000 and $44,998 in 2002, but in 2003 only Viacom was listed as contributing between $5,000 and $14,999. The NCTA donated between $5,000 and $14,999 in 2002 and 2003.

In addition, Comcast, the NCTA, Time Warner and Viacom are all regular sponsors of the caucus's annual legislative conference. In all, over the two years, those companies contributed as much as $589,991.

Calls to the director of communications for the Congressional Black Caucus were not returned.

Touching off the deluge

The same day the caucus sent its letter—May 12— another missive was directed at the Commerce Committee. Four cable executives—Debra Lee (BET Holdings Inc.); Jeff Valdez (Sí TV, a Hispanic-themed network whose investors include Time Warner and EchoStar); Johnathan Rodgers (TV One) and Kent Rice (International Channel, which was acquired by Comcast in July)—wrote the committee a letter objecting to the a la carte concept.

The executives' letter was posted on NCTA's Web site; the trade group has cited it in its filings with the FCC.

Portions of the letter were identical to the op-ed Liggins penned for the *Washington Times*.

It opens: "We understand that some Members of Congress have suggested requiring cable and satellite companies to sell basic cable networks on a channel-by-channel, or 'a la carte,' basis. On the surface, this idea sounds appealing, but a deeper look can only lead to the conclusion that a la carte packaging and pricing of programming would have a chilling effect on programming diversity in America."

A week later, Congress opted to bail out of the a la carte debate and let the FCC deal with it. Leadership of the House committee that regulates cable wrote a letter to FCC Chairman Michael Powell asking the FCC to study the issue. Sen. John McCain, chairman of the Senate Committee on Commerce, Science and Transportation, also wrote a letter, arguing forcefully for an la carte option. On May 25, 2004, the FCC officially opened the issue for comment, in anticipation of filing a report in the fall.

And the floodgates were opened.

On July 15, 2004, the NCTA released a study funded by the association that said a la carte would hike rates. The study, conducted by Booz Allen Hamilton Inc., determined that if cable operators had to offer all channels a la carte while still offering tiered programming, costs would rise between 7 percent and 15 percent just to outfit cable systems with the a la carte technology. Booz Allen argued that consumers would end up paying more for fewer channels, and an a la carte system would make it difficult for new networks (like minority themed channels) to get into the business.

Civil rights groups join debate

On the same day, the nation's "oldest, largest and most diverse civil and human rights coalition," the Leadership Conference on Civil Rights, also filed comments with the FCC opposing a la carte on grounds that it would hurt diversity in cable programming. The organization quoted Liggins in its filing.

The Leadership Conference counts among its victories passage of the Civil Rights Act of 1964, the Voting Rights Act of 1965, and the Fair Housing Act of 1968. More recently, the group has worked to eliminate the so-called "digital divide" in America and worked to provide the advantages of Internet access and other technology to disadvantaged schoolchildren.

In the a la carte issue, the civil rights organization sided with the cable companies.

On June 23, 2004, the LCCR in conjunction with TV One and others sponsored a lunch briefing opposing the a la carte effort. Titled "Cable A La Carte: The Beginning of the End for Media Diversity on Cable TV?" the event was organized by its lobbyist, Leslie Harris of Leslie Harris and Associates. Among Harris's other clients is Time Warner Inc.

Leading the charge for LCCR against a la carte was the group's deputy director, Nancy Zirkin, who targeted Kimmelman and Consumers Union specifically because he was supporting an issue that was also backed by conservative groups like the Parents Television Council and Concerned Women of America.

"Every one of these groups that Consumers Union is allied with has fought us on the increase of diversity," Zirkin said.

Zirkin could not be reached for comment for this report.

The AOL Time Warner Foundation reported in its calendar 2001 tax filing with the IRS that it pledged $100,000 to the Leadership Conference on Civil Rights and another $200,000 to the Leadership Conference Education Fund. For 2002, the foundation reported a payment of $100,000 to the Leadership Conference on Civil Rights.

Among contributions to other nonprofits who signed letters opposing cable a la carte, the AOL Foundation has given $300,000 to City Year, $100,000 in 2000, 2001 and 2002; and the Comcast Foundation has contributed $50,000 to the National Urban League, $78,600 to the Women in Cable & Telecommunications, $70,000 to City Year Philadelphia and $50,000 to City Year Detroit.

Each organization signed form letters supporting the cable industry.

Then the letter campaign began. First to be heard from were the civil rights groups. The first was from the National Congress of Black Women Inc., signed by national chairwoman C. DeLores Tucker on June 28, 2004.

"We would like to voice our concerns about the potential affects of requiring cable and satellite companies to sell basic cable networks on a channel-by-channel, or 'a la carte' basis," she writes. "On the surface, this idea sounds appealing, but a deeper look can only lead to the conclusion that a la carte packaging would have a chilling effect on programming diversity in America."

Tucker's letter is nearly a word for word copy of the one written by the cable executives. She also penned an op-ed piece published in the *Boston Globe* and *Chicago Sun-Times* arguing that "If these would-be regulators succeed, the diversity in cable programming—a fruit of the civil rights movement—will die with it."

Tucker led a high profile crusade against misogynist lyrics in rap music. Ironically, Tucker's chief target was Time Warner's music division. A call to Tucker's office was not returned.

Other groups who signed the same letter to the FCC as Tucker include the National Urban League, the Rainbow/PUSH Coalition and the Brotherhood Crusade.

Also submitting the same basic letter were three members of the board of directors of the National Conference of Black Mayors—Harvey Johnson Jr., mayor of Jackson, Miss., and president of the conference; Irene Brodie, mayor of the village of Robbins, Ill. and assistant secretary for the group; and Roosevelt F. Dorn, mayor of Inglewood, Calif. who is 2nd vice president of the mayoral conference. The letters were dated July 12, 2004.

On April 27 of that year, the group hosted its annual conference in Philadelphia, the hometown of Comcast. The conference's "premium" sponsors were Comcast and TV One, employer of Alfred Liggins. TV One president and CEO Johnathan Rodgers spoke at the event, which also included an "hour-long TV interview program that will include a panel of mayors discussing issues facing major urban cities and mayors today."

Another mayoral organization chimed in on the debate—the National Conference of Democratic Mayors. The NCDM lists the NCTA as a sponsor.

Cable goes to Towns

Among cable television's best friends is Rep. Edolphus Towns, a member of the Congressional Black Caucus who signed the May 12 anti-a la carte letter.

Towns also submitted another letter, this one to the FCC, on July 8. The letter was nearly identical to five others—one by Florida state Rep. Bob Henriquez, three by members of the New York state legislature and one by a New York City Council member.

But unlike those elected representatives, Towns is in a position to do more than comment on the issue. The one portion of his letter that does appear to be original reads: "As a senior member of the House Committee on Energy and Commerce, I implore you to reject the 'a la carte' system and urge you to keep diverse programming on the air," he wrote.

Any legislation that would re-regulate the cable industry would originate from that committee. Towns submitted his comment despite the fact that Chairman Barton, ranking member Dingell and three other representatives had asked the FCC to prepare the report on the feasibility of a la carte.

From 1988 through September of 2004, Towns accepted $58,897 from the employees, their immediate family members, and the political action committees of the nation's largest cable television companies, sixth-highest among House Democrats over that period.

Towns spokesman Andrew Delia submitted a statement to the Center in response to a set of detailed questions.

"Congressman Towns believed and continues to believe that on the whole, an a la carte system would hurt niche and diversity programming. While there are legitimate concerns about diversity in the media, a la carte is not the solution to such a problem," the statement reads.

Towns contends that some channels would disappear if they were located on fewer systems because they would be unable to generate advertising revenue. Programmers would have to raise rates to make up the difference and niche channels would suffer. The result would be higher costs for consumers for fewer channels.

The response from the congressman's office did not answer the question of who wrote the letter he submitted to the FCC or whether the cable industry's support of his campaigns or the Congressional Black Caucus Foundation—Towns is a member of its board of directors—played a role in his position.

Bundling support

The cable industry found support in other quarters. Rep. Raul M. Grijalva of Arizona was one of 12 elected officials to sign another version of one of the industry's form letters. Grijalva is a member of the Congressional Hispanic Caucus. Among others who submitted the same letter were Hispanic officeholders in the New York state legislature and New York City Council in addition to a number of nonprofits.

In case the FCC was still unconvinced, the cable lobby had one more "grass roots" coalition join the battle—and this would be the largest outpouring yet. In late July and early August, a truly impressive cross-section of women's groups began sending letters to the FCC, asking it not to support cable a la carte pricing.

Once again, the letters sounded familiar. In fact, 30 of them were virtually identical. Among the signers were the Sexuality Information and Education Council of the United States, the Global Fund for Women, the Feminist Majority, American Women in Radio and Television Inc. and the National Council of Women's Organizations.

In this case, it wasn't hard to find the source. The firm of Leslie Harris, the Time Warner lobbyist who also represents the Leadership Conference on Civil Rights orchestrated the campaign. Her firm advertised its role on its Web site.

After being retained by a "major media company" Leslie Harris and Associates "organized a well-attended briefing where minority and women's programmers laid out the case against the proposal and then worked with dozens of organizations to file comments at the FCC. One measure of our success: working closely with Oxygen Media, we were able to organize over 30 prominent women's organizations against the proposal."

Harris filed a lobbyist registration statement listing

Time Warner as a client on July 23. Harris, through a spokeswoman, declined to comment for the record.

Oxygen Media is a 24-hour cable television network aimed at women. Founded in 1998, the network is independently owned and now available in over 52 million cable households, according to its Web site. Its chairwoman and CEO, Geraldine Laybourne, is also on the board of directors of NCTA. Time Warner is an investor in the network.

The letters argue that the a la carte proposal could have a "significant negative impact on the so-called niche networks, such as Oxygen, that cater to particular interests or demographics such as women, minorities, gays and lesbians and non-English language speakers."

In a detailed email to NCTA senior director of communications Brian Dietz, the Center asked whether it was disingenuous to point to a groundswell of opposition to a la carte when so many of the letters were industry generated.

Dietz replied that "As a matter of policy, NCTA does not comment on our lobbying or PAC activity." But the association included a generic statement.

"Many of the individuals and organizations that have voiced opposition to a la carte are concerned that such regulation would further reduce diversity in media, which directly affects the constituents they represent. NCTA welcomes this support and will continue to work with organizations that are concerned about these issues," it reads in part.

So the question is, are the commissioners aware that the anti-a la carte comments they are being inundated with are not as spontaneous as they seem? And does it really matter?

The Center sent a list of detailed questions to former FCC Chairman Michael Powell through a spokesman. Powell did not respond, but the Center was provided with a written statement from then-FCC Media Bureau Chief Kenneth Ferree.

"In the A La Carte proceeding, as with all FCC proceedings, we value, and read, comments from any and all persons and parties on all sides of the issue. Our job is to then evaluate the pros and cons, and strengths and weaknesses, of all the arguments, positions, and studies presented to us, and then make our best public policy judgments based on the entire record," it reads.

"It is interesting to note that the practice of a party on one side of an issue soliciting letters of support is not uncommon. For example, most recently, a very high percentage of letters in the media ownership rule proceeding were form letters generated by self-interested organizations. As to the A La Carte proceeding, we are in the process of evaluating the record at the present time and do not comment on any individual filings."

Currently, the anti-a la carte comments outnumber pro a la carte comments by about six to one. Among the pro camp are Consumers Union, the Consumer Federation of America, the New Jersey Ratepayer Advocate, the Urban Broadcasting Company and the city of Seattle. There is no indication of coordination among the comments filed supporting a la carte.

Wired for influence

From 1988 through September 2004, the nation's cable television companies spent $22.7 million in campaign contributions to national party organizations, members of Congress and presidential races. Leading the pack is Time Warner with $8.2 million. Second is Comcast at $3.2 million and third is the NCTA with $3.1 million.

The money came from PACs, soft money donations (before they were banned by the Bipartisan Campaign Reform Act of 2002) and individual contributions from company executives, employees and their families.

In addition to the donations, cable television companies can provide something worth more than greenbacks—airtime. No politician, no matter how skilled or principled, can turn his or her back on reaching large blocs of the voting public through public affairs programming.

Corporations can also play the sponsorship game. With millions to give away, the Time Warner Foundation funds good works all over the country, including the activities of civil rights groups.

The industry's trade group, the NCTA, is among the most deep-pocketed and influential lobbying organizations in Washington. The association sponsored 102 trips worth $198,727 from 2000 through March 2004, flying members of Congress and their staff to various events around the country.

The NCTA is also a major sponsor of travel for FCC commissioners and staff, having spent $192,609 flying over an eight-year period, according to a previous Center study.

In addition to its campaign contributions and its all-expenses-paid junkets, the trade group spent $39.7 million on lobbying from 1988 through June 30, 2004. The NCTA's top lobbyist, Daniel Brenner, was senior legal adviser to former FCC Chairman Mark Fowler in the 1980s.

While campaign contributions get the most coverage in Washington politics, the real money is being spent on lobbying.

The cable television industry has been steadily increasing the amount it spends to sway opinion in Congress and the FCC. The industry spent $16.2 million on lobbying in 1998 compared with $24.3 million in 2003, a jump of 50 percent, according to lobbying records. The industry spent $120 million total on lobbying from 1998 through mid-2004.

Time Warner is No. 1 at $46 million, while the NCTA is a close second.

While the dollar amount is impressive, it is the people who are doing the lobbying that are the real key.

The cable, broadcasting and telecommunications lobby in Washington is stacked with former FCC commissioners, bureau chiefs, top-level aides and former congressional staffers who have helped write communications laws.

For the cable industry alone, Center researchers were able to identify 17 former key government officials who now lobby Congress and the FCC. The "revolving door" situation at the FCC is so prevalent, it is at times difficult to keep straight whether someone is still in government or representing one communications firm or another.

Among former government officials who now work for the cable industry, the best known is Victoria Clarke, who had nothing to do with the FCC. Clark was the Pentagon spokeswoman during the Iraq war and is widely credited with creating the "embedding" system of attaching reporters to troops in the field. Clarke took a job with Comcast as senior adviser, communications and government affairs.

As to the a la carte issue specifically, the NCTA is using Brenner as well as Jill Luckett, vice president of program network policy, formerly a special adviser to former FCC Commissioner Rachelle Chong, and before that, legislative director for former Sen. Bob Packwood of Oregon.

Leslie Harris and Associates, whose clients include Time Warner and the Leadership Conference on Civil Rights, employs Jon Bernstein, who before becoming a lobbyist was an attorney adviser with the FCC. Prior to that, he was a lobbyist for the National Education Association.

Working for Viacom on the issue is Wiley Rein & Fielding. Richard E. Wiley heads the firm's 70-attorney communications practice, which it bills as the largest in the nation. Wiley was chairman of the FCC from 1970 to 1977 and was a chief advocate of deregulation of the communications industry. Lawrence W. Secrest III, a partner with the firm overseeing the media practice and Wiley's former assistant at the FCC, is also on the a la carte beat.

That's a lot of high-priced talent to be spending on what seems like a relatively small issue that is barely on the regulatory radar screen. The FCC is merely collecting comment for a report. There is no realistic expectation that the issue will make it into any legislation.

Kimmelman believes the lobbying campaign has more to do with the issue's potential than what it means right now. He believes that "there was a potential out-of-control grass-roots uprising against the way large cable and broadcast companies control programming and how it's distributed to the public," he said.

"I think they recognized this was so attractive to people from all political perspectives and so volatile in terms of spiraling cable rates and concerns about smarmy programming – they needed to deep six and absolutely wipe the debate off the ledgers before policy makers got into it."

Cable and Satellite TV Company Rankings

The cable television industry's stranglehold on America's pay television market is slipping. Only a decade ago, the idea that television signals broadcast directly from satellites would create real competition for cable seemed laughable. But no one is laughing now, especially cable television executives.

The Federal Communications Commission reports that as of June 2003, there were 106,641,910 television households in America, and only 11.7 percent of them received their signal over the air. Of those who pay for programming, the cable industry is the service of choice for about 74.9 percent, while subscribers to

direct broadcast satellite providers like The DirecTV Group Inc. and EchoStar Communications Corp. make up roughly 21.6 percent.

Overall, a small number of pay television companies control most of the market. The top 10 providers, for example, are responsible for 82.3 percent of "multichannel video programming" households, according to the FCC and industry figures. But just as satellite companies are taking customers from cable providers, cable companies are hoping to persuade customers of traditional telephone companies to sign up for phone service through their cable service.

Rank	Company	Subscribers*	Market Share
1.	Comcast Corp.	21,364,100	22.7%
2.	The DirecTV Group	11,600,000	12.3%
3.	Time Warner Cable (Time Warner Inc.)	10,938,000	11.6%
4.	EchoStar Communications Corp.	8,800,000	9.3%
5.	Charter Communications Inc.	6,486,900	6.9%
6.	Cox Communications Inc. (Cox Enterprises Inc.)	6,278,500	6.7%
7.	Adelphia Communications Corp.	5,400,000	5.7%
8.	Cablevision Systems Corp.	3,000,000	3.2%
9.	Advance/Newhouse Communications Inc.	2,062,900	2.2%
10.	Mediacom Communications Corp.	1,560,000	1.7%
	Other		17.7%

* Totals are through June, 2003.

Sources: FCC, National Cable & Telecommunications Association, Securities and Exchange Commission filings.

Appendix A - Communications Companies

The Well Connected project staff has compiled detailed information on the largest communications companies in America. In determining what companies to include, we considered three basic categories – broadcasting, telecommunications and cable/satellite television.

We chose to examine the largest players in each of the three categories. That amounts to a total of 41 separate companies. Several are active in more than one category.

Each company profile includes:
- a brief company history
- basic financial information including profits, revenue, stock holdings by board members and executive salaries

- a detailed list of media holdings, including a regional grouping of radio and television stations
- campaign contribution breakdowns, including partisan preference
- lobbying expenditures by year
- details of company-sponsored trips for members of Congress and their staff.

The information was gleaned from dozens of sources, including Securities and Exchange Commission filings, Federal Election Commission records, published reports and interviews by Center researchers. Newspaper circulation information was provided by VNU eMedia Inc.

Communications Companies - Index

Adelphia Communications Corp.

Address:	1 N. Main St.	Stock Symbol:	ADELQ
	Coudersport, PA 16915-1141	Telephone:	814-274-9830
		Fax:	814-274-8631
Total Employees:	Not Reported	Website:	www.adelphia.net

In 1952, John Rigas spent $300 on a license that allowed him to string coaxial cable from house to house in the small Pennsylvania town of Coudersport. Five decades later, he would be chief executive of a cable television powerhouse with millions of subscribers in prime markets.

Adelphia Communications Corp. made so much money that Rigas would mail checks to down-on-their-luck citizens he read about in the newspaper.

That wonderful rags-to-riches story was blown away when Rigas and his son were convicted of pilfering millions from the company to support an extravagant lifestyle. The 79-year-old entrepreneur was found guilty of multiple counts of fraud and could spend the rest of his natural life in jail. (One of Rigas's sons was also convicted. The jury could not reach a verdict for another, Adelphia Vice President Michael Rigas, on charges of fraud, resulting in a mistrial. Prosecutors say they will refile.)

The verdict signaled the end of one of the handful of corporate fraud trials that have made crooked CEOs the bane of the American public. Only a few years ago, Adelphia was the envy of the cable industry. It had more than 5 million subscribers, nearly all of them clustered in prime markets such as Los Angeles and South Florida. The company enjoyed one of the highest profit margins in the industry.

At the time, Rigas flew around the country in a Gulfstream jet Adelphia had purchased from King Hussein of Jordan. Problem was, he used the jet for personal use, as he and other family members did with billions of dollars of the company's money. Their financial abuse was enough to bring down the Rigas empire in the summer of 2002. Rigas was hauled off in handcuffs, the whole nasty affair beamed nationwide by television crews alerted by investigators. He and three of his sons were forced to surrender control of the company and resign from the board of directors, accused of looting the company's coffers. By some estimates, the wrongdoing has cost shareholders as much as $60 billion.

In addition, the Securities and Exchange Commission began a massive investigation, even setting up an office in Coudersport. Adelphia's stock was de-listed and its operating units were forced into Chapter 11 bankruptcy. The company itself filed a racketeering lawsuit against the Rigases.

Through it all, and despite technically being run by a New York bankruptcy court as of April 2003, Adelphia has continued to operate as the nation's fifth largest cable company, still claiming more than 5.3 million subscribers in 30 states.

Like many other cable companies, Adelphia is trying to become a one-stop-shop for telecom services. In addition to its cable operations, Adelphia offers digital cable, high-speed internet access, long distance telephone service and home security.

In March 2003, the company brought in two former executives of the defunct AT&T Broadband cable venture to lift Adelphia out of bankruptcy. Both stood to profit handsomely if they could pull it off. New Chairman and CEO William T. Schleyer was promised as much as $24.6 million over three years under his incentive-laden contract. New President and COO Ronald Cooper could make $16.2 million.

Schleyer was chief executive officer of AT&T Broadband and Cooper was chief operating officer there before the company was acquired by cable industry leader Comcast Corp. in November 2002.

Their efforts provided a windfall for Adelphia stakeholders in April of 2005 when Time Warner Inc. and Comcast Corp. announced a joint acquisition of the company. Adelphia investors will reap $12.7 billion in cash and hold 16 percent of the new company, which will be publicly traded under Time Warner.

—Bob Williams, Robert Morlino

April 28, 2005

Sources: Company Web site, Securities and Exchange Commission filings, Yahoo! Finance Online, Dow Jones News Service, Hoover's Online, Fortune magazine, Rhode Island Providence Journal, The Times UK.

Adelphia Communications Corp. Recent Financial Information		
Year	Revenue	Net Income (Net Loss)
1998	$630,999,000	($133,267,000)
1999	$1,287,968,000	($240,719,000)
2000	$2,909,351,000	($547,568,000)

Adelphia Communications Corp. Board of Directors				
Name	Position	Relevant Stock		Qty
Kailbourne, Erland	Director		N/A	N/A
Cornelius, Rod	Director		N/A	N/A
Coyle, Dennis	Director		N/A	N/A
Gelber, Leslie	Director		N/A	N/A
Kronman, Anthony	Director		N/A	N/A
Metros, Pete	Director		N/A	N/A
Schleyer, William	Chairman		N/A	N/A

Adelphia Communications Corp. Corporate Officers			
Name	Position	Salary	Bonuses
Schleyer, William	Chairman and CEO	N/A	N/A
Whitman, Vanessa	CFO	N/A	N/A
Cooper, Ronald	President and COO	N/A	N/A

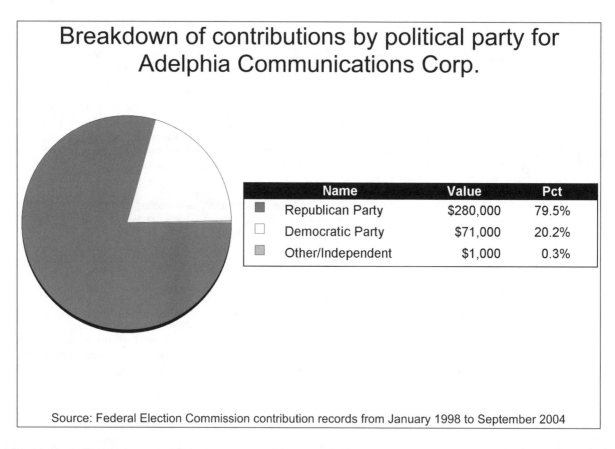

Breakdown of contributions by political party for Adelphia Communications Corp.

Name	Value	Pct
Republican Party	$280,000	79.5%
Democratic Party	$71,000	20.2%
Other/Independent	$1,000	0.3%

Source: Federal Election Commission contribution records from January 1998 to September 2004

Top 10 Recipients of Contributions Sourced to Adelphia Communications Corp.	
Recipient	Amount
National Republican Party Committees	$166,000
National Democratic Party Committees	$28,000
Rep John E Peterson (R-PA)	$17,000
Republican Federal Committee Of Pennsylvania	$16,000
Sen Arlen Specter (R-PA)	$14,000
Sen Richard J Santorum (R-PA)	$12,000
Rep Ronald P Klink (D-PA)	$9,000
President George W Bush (R)	$9,000
Sen John E Sununu (R-NH)	$6,000
Rep Jack Quinn, Jr (R-NY)	$4,000
Total:	$281,000
Source: Federal Election Commission contribution records from January 1998 to September 2004	

Adelphia Communications Corp. Lobbying Expenditures by Year	
Year	Amount
1998	$100,000
1999	$100,000
2000	$80,000
2002	$100,000
2003	$260,000
2004	$220,000
Total:	$860,000
Source: U.S. Senate Office of Public Records lobbying disclosure records from January 1998 to June 30th, 2004.	

Advance/Newhouse Communications Inc.

Address:	950 Fingerboard Rd.	Stock Symbol:	N/A
	Staten Island, NY 10305	Telephone:	718-891-1234
		Fax:	718-981-1456
Total Employees:	27,585	Website:	www.advance.net

Earlier this year, when media giant Advance/Newhouse Communications Inc. christened the new headquarters of its cable television operation in Bradenton, Fla., the unmistakable theme was optimism. A black-tie gala celebration called "Night under the Stars" attracted 300 guests, including community and civic leaders, who ate gourmet food and watched classic films projected onto the walls of the new facility.

Bright House Networks, as the cable division of Advance/Newhouse was officially named about a year earlier, is looking to the future. That's because behind it lies the unpleasant memory of a seven-year partnership with Time Warner Inc. that didn't work out so well.

Back in 1995, Advance/Newhouse, a media conglomerate that includes newspapers, television production companies and several major magazines through publisher Conde Nast, entered into an agreement with Time Warner to combine the cable television operations of both companies.

At the time, Advance/Newhouse served 1.5 million customers, which were added to Time Warner's 3 million. The union created the second-largest cable company at that time. The honeymoon ended when AOL came to town.

The disastrous merger between the new and old media giants left Advance/Newhouse stuck with a partnership that was quickly souring. As AOL Time Warner's stock continued to plummet amid Justice Department and SEC investigations, the company decided it was time for a divorce.

In the end, Advance/Newhouse walked away with 2.1 million subscribers to call its own, as part of an agreement wherein Time Warner will still oversee some aspects of programming, marketing and engineering.

But Bright House Networks clearly intends to form a successful operation independent of the ill-fated Time Warner deal. In 2003, along with the renaming, the company launched an aggressive marketing campaign to build brand awareness. The company has invested in several of the newer technologies available to cable subscribers, including high-speed Internet, on-demand and high definition programming.

Bright House has maintained its subscriber base of more than 2 million customers, making it the ninth-largest pay television provider. Its markets are concentrated in six major markets—Central Florida, Tampa Bay, Alabama, Indiana, Michigan and Bakersfield, Calif.

Financials are not available because the company remains under the control of the privately-owned Advance/Newhouse. The company's president, Steve Miron, is the son of Advance/Newhouse chairman and CEO Robert Miron. Robert's mother was the sister of Advance/Newhouse founder Samuel I. Newhouse Sr. The parent is still controlled by S. I. Newhouse Jr.and his younger brother Donald. Forbes magazine has estimated the brothers' fortune at more than $15 billion.

—Robert Morlino, Bob Williams

August 4, 2004

Sources: Company Web site, Hoover's Online, The Bradenton Herald, Securities and Exchange Commission filings, Yahoo! Finance Online, St. Petersburg Times, Fortune magazine.

Breakdown of contributions by political party for Advance/Newhouse Communications Inc.

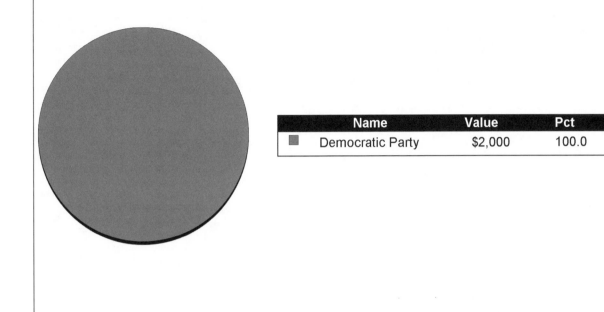

	Name	Value	Pct
▪	Democratic Party	$2,000	100.0

Source: Federal Election Commission contribution records from January 1998 to September 2004

Top 10 Recipients of Contributions Sourced to Advance/Newhouse Communications Inc.	
Recipient	Amount
Sen Hillary Rodham Clinton (D-NY)	$2,000
Total:	$2,000
Source: Federal Election Commission contribution records from January 1998 to September 2004	

Advance/Newhouse Communications Inc. Lobbying Expenditures by Year	
Year	Amount
2003	$120,000
2004	$120,000
Total:	$240,000
Source: U.S. Senate Office of Public Records lobbying disclosure records from January 1998 to June 30th, 2004.	

Print Media Subsidiaries for Advance/Newhouse Communications Inc.			
Company Name	Market City	Weekday Circulation	Sunday Circulation
Bridgeton News	Bridgeton, NJ	7,647	0
Jackson Citizen Patriot	Jackson, MI	34,313	39,300
Kalamazoo Gazette	Kalamazoo, MI	56,299	74,144
Mobile Register	Mobile, AL	100,244	118,391
Staten Island Advance	Staten Island, NY	65,607	81,830
The Ann Arbor News	Ann Arbor, MI	52,432	65,708
The Bay City Times	Bay City, MI	31,126	44,368
The Birmingham News	Birmingham, AL	153,195	189,087
The Express-Times	Easton, PA	50,439	49,596
The Flint Journal	Flint, MI	84,313	102,154
The Gloucester County Times	Woodbury, NJ	23,827	26,929
The Grand Rapids Press	Grand Rapids, MI	139,216	187,174
The Huntsville Times	Huntsville, AL	55,951	76,401
The Jersey Journal	Jersey City, NJ	28,375	0
The Mississippi Press	Pascagoula, MS	19,539	20,189
The Muskegon Chronicle	Muskegon, MI	44,738	49,945
The Oregonian	Portland, OR	342,040	412,113
The Patriot-News	Harrisburg, PA	101,524	152,153
The Plain Dealer	Cleveland, OH	367,528	480,540

Print Media Subsidiaries for Advance/Newhouse Communications Inc.			
Company Name	Market City	Weekday Circulation	Sunday Circulation
The Post-Standard	Syracuse, NY	119,158	174,581
The Republican	Springfield, MA	84,694	127,024
The Saginaw News	Saginaw, MI	45,918	56,307
The Star-Ledger	Newark, NJ	407,945	610,542
The Times	Trenton, NJ	73,235	76,718
The Times-Picayune	New Orleans, LA	262,008	286,802
Today's Sunbeam	Salem, NJ	9,867	9,627

ALLTEL Corp.

Address:	1 Allied Dr. Little Rock, AR 72202	Stock Symbol:	AT
		Telephone:	501-905-8000
		Fax:	501-905-5444
Total Employees:	19,986	Website:	www.alltel.com

Though it doesn't sit atop any lists of telecommunications companies, ALLTEL Corp. nevertheless is a major player in the industry. The company has maintained a solid performance relative to the competition by targeting customer bases in local sectors and offering a diverse package of services.

It is a national leader in bundled services, providing local telephone, wireless, long-distance, paging and Internet service to more than 12 million customers in 26 states. And it is a leading provider of competitive local phone service in 25 markets where it isn't the local phone company. In addition, the Little Rock, Ark.-based company publishes phone directories and sells telecommunications equipment.

Following a trend, ALLTEL has entered into partnerships with other providers to utilize emerging technologies such as Voice-over Internet Protocol, or VoIP. Recently the company chose Lucent Technologies to deliver ALLTEL combined voice and data service to the University of Kentucky. This strategy, which some analysts describe as "hollowing out," will allow ALLTEL to deliver its packages without the cost of owning and operating an actual delivery infrastructure.

The company that would become ALLTEL was founded as Allied Telephone in Little Rock, Ark. in 1943. In 1983, Allied merged with a group of Midwestern phone companies called Mid-Continent to form ALLTEL.

Weldon Case, who had been head of Mid-Continent, was CEO of ALLTEL from the 1983 merger until 1991. He was succeeded by Allied Telephone veteran Joe T. Ford, who was chairman and CEO of ALLTEL until 2002, when he turned over the CEO reins to his son, Scott T. Ford.

Although it launched its first wireless system in 1983, ALLTEL became the large and diversified company it is today primarily under the senior Ford's leadership.

In 1993, the company purchased GTE Corp.'s telephone operations in Georgia, as well as its telephone directory publishing contracts. In 1996, the company began offering long-distance service.

In 1997, ALLTEL bought PCS wireless licenses for 73 markets in 12 states. That same year it combined its wireline and wireless businesses into a single unit, which began to offer a full suite of telecommunications services to customers.

In 1998 ALLTEL merged with troubled wireless company 360° Communications in a deal valued at more than $6 billion.

In 1999, ALLTEL and Aliant Communications completed a $1.8 billion merger, adding Nebraska to ALLTEL's service area. It also completed a $600 million merger with Liberty Cellular, a privately held communications company that offered wireless, paging, long-distance and Internet services in Kansas.

In 2000, ALLTEL completed a wireless exchange with Bell Atlantic and GTE, which set up a roaming agreement covering 95 percent of the country. Later that year the company introduced "Total Freedom," a nationwide wireless calling plan that eliminated roaming and long-distance charges nationwide.

In 2002, ALLTEL completed an acquisition of Verizon local access lines in Kentucky and bought CenturyTel's wireless operations for $1.59 billion in cash.

In early 2003, ALLTEL sold the financial services arm of its ALLTEL Information Services subsidiary to Fidelity National Financial in a cash and stock deal valued at $1.05 billion.

-Bob Williams, Robert Morlino

August 20, 2004

Sources: Company Web site, Securities and Exchange Commission filings, Yahoo! Finance Online, Hoover's Online, Fortune magazine.

ALLTEL Corp. Recent Financial Information		
Year	Revenue	Net Income (Net Loss)
2001	$6,615,800,000	$1,067,000,000
2002	$7,112,400,000	$924,300,000
2003	$7,979,900,000	$1,330,100,000

ALLTEL Corp. Board of Directors				
Name	Position	Relevant Stock		Qty
Ford, Joe	Chairman		AT	2,275,594
Ford, Scott	Director, President and CEO		AT	1,349,032
Belk, John	Director		AT	56,497
Foster, Dennis	Director		AT	400,699
Gellerstedt, Lawrence	Director		AT	55,826
Mahony, Emon	Director		AT	102,162
McConnell, John	Director		AT	57,797
Natori, Josie	Director		AT	55,171
Penske, Gregory	Director		AT	33,500
Reed, Frank	Director		AT	62,203
Stephens, Warren	Director		AT	10,842,837
Townsend, Ronald	Director		AT	32,803

ALLTEL Corp. Corporate Officers			
Name	Position	Salary	Bonuses
Ford, Scott	President, CEO, and Director	$850,000	$1,889,550
Beebe, Kevin	Group President, Communications	$550,000	$893,475
Flynn, Michael	Assistant CEO	$425,000	$645,075
Frantz, Francis	EVP	$450,000	$692,550

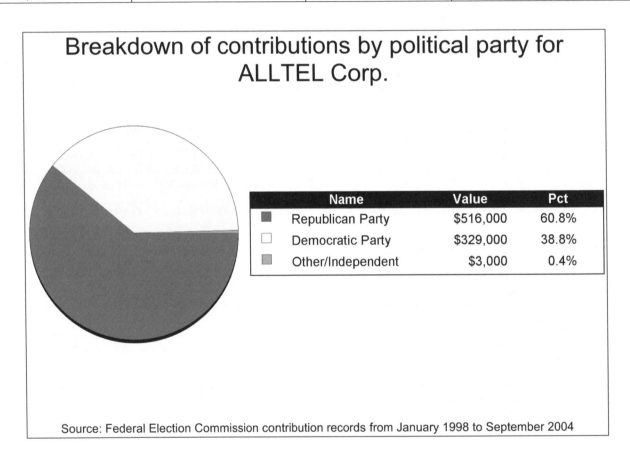

Breakdown of contributions by political party for ALLTEL Corp.

Name	Value	Pct
Republican Party	$516,000	60.8%
Democratic Party	$329,000	38.8%
Other/Independent	$3,000	0.4%

Source: Federal Election Commission contribution records from January 1998 to September 2004

Top 10 Recipients of Contributions Sourced to ALLTEL Corp.	
Recipient	Amount
President George W Bush (R)	$38,000
Sen Blanche Lambert Lincoln (D-AR)	$32,000
Rep Jay Woodson Dickey, Jr (R-AR)	$26,000
Sen Tim Hutchison (R-AR)	$22,000
Rep Victor Frederick Snyder (D-AR)	$15,000
Rep Robert Marion Berry (D-AR)	$15,000
Rep Michael G Oxley (R-OH)	$13,000
Sen Mark Lunsford Pryor (D-AR)	$13,000
National Democratic Party Committees	$12,000
Rep Michael Avery Ross (D-AR)	$12,000
Total:	$198,000
Source: Federal Election Commission contribution records from January 1998 to September 2004	

ALLTEL Corp. Lobbying Expenditures by Year	
Year	Amount
1998	$130,000
1999	$220,000
2000	$230,000
2001	$280,000
2002	$280,000
2003	$220,000
2004	$50,000
Total:	$1,410,000
Source: U.S. Senate Office of Public Records lobbying disclosure records from January 1998 to June 30th, 2004.	

AT&T Corp.

Address:	One AT&T Way	Stock Symbol:	T
	Bedminster, NJ 07921	Telephone:	908-221-2000
		Fax:	908-221-2528
Total Employees:	61,600	Website:	www.att.com

Alexander Graham Bell's phone company ain't what it used to be. In fact, AT&T Corp. has reinvented itself so many times, it's hard to say exactly what sort of company it is. After a very public and very embarrassing foray into the cable television business, the nation's oldest phone company has shifted gears once again, and is now looking to one of the newest types of communications technology. The latest shift attracted the attention of SBC Communications Inc. – itself one of the traditional phone carriers created by the breakup of AT&T in 1984 – which will pay $16 billion to acquire AT&T by the end of 2006.

Under new chief executive officer David W. Dorman, AT&T is hollowing out its operations and shifting toward a model based on the emerging Voice over Internet Protocol, or VoIP—the Internet-based telephone service. The company has announced that it expects to have more than 1 million VoIP customers by the end of 2005.

Dorman told analysts during a conference call back in January, "If current interest is any indication of future adoption, we're on the verge of a Voice over IP revolution which AT&T intends to lead at both a consumer and business level."

In fact, the company has already planned its first marketing blitz to make it so, and Dorman told the Boston Globe, "I think it's going to be huge. I think it's going to be pervasive. We are going to be leaders here. If you watch the Olympics this summer, I promise you will become completely sick of ads for AT&T VoIP services."

AT&T is also focusing more on packages of services to customers, negotiated with other providers, than simply being a service provider itself.

The strategy marks yet another turning point in the history of a company that has endured despite numerous, and significant, setbacks. After a century of domination, AT&T's nationwide telephone monopoly was broken up in 1984. Local service monopolies were passed on to seven so-called "Baby Bells." AT&T got to keep the long distance business along with the equipment manufacturing unit of the monopoly.

AT&T is still the country's largest long-distance company, although it controlled only about 32 percent of long distance revenues by 2003, according to the Federal Communications Commission. The company is also making a lot less on each long distance call as keen competition from companies such as MCI (formerly WorldCom) and Sprint Corp. has driven down rates. The company's long-distance revenue is expected to continue to decline in years to come, in no small part due to new competition from wireless carriers.

AT&T tried to recoup from the cable business what it had lost in the long-distance race. The company began pushing into cable in the late 1990s at the peak of the dot.com technology boom. It hoped to bypass its old sister companies, the Baby Bells, to reach the homes of millions of potential new customers.

AT&T jumped into the cable business in earnest in early 1999 with its purchase of cable giant TCI. A year later, AT&T became the country's largest cable company when it outbid then-industry leader Comcast for Media One.

AT&T's plan to offer phone service, Internet access and a whole host of new services over its cable systems fell flat, however, as most of those markets turned out to be much slower to develop than the company had hoped. As a result, AT&T's domination of the cable business was short-lived. Awash in debt, it decided in late 2001 to sell its cable business to Comcast Corp. for $47 billion in stock and $25 billion in assumed debt.

AT&T was also a major player in the wireless business, but the company decided to spin off its AT&T Wireless subsidiary in 2001. AT&T Wireless was at one point the third-largest cellular provider, behind Verizon Wireless and Cingular Wireless. However, last year, Cingular moved to acquire the company and the merger created what is now the No. 1 wireless provider, with about 30 percent of the market and more than 46 million combined subscribers.

Although it is a mere shadow of its former self—AT&T was the world's largest company before it was broken up in 1984—it is still huge by any measure. With revenues of more than $34 billion and more than 61,000 employees, AT&T held the number 40 spot on the 2004 Fortune 500 list. That was down sharply from its number 22 position one year earlier, which itself was down sharply from 15th the year before.

—Bob Williams, Robert Morlino

April 28, 2005

Sources: Company Web site, Securities and Exchange Commission filings, Yahoo! Finance Online, Hoover's Online, Fortune magazine, Werbach.com, Boston Globe, Bergen Record.

AT&T Corp. Recent Financial Information		
Year	Revenue	Net Income (Net Loss)
2000	$46,850,000,000	$4,669,000,000
2001	$42,197,000,000	($7,715,000,000)
2002	$37,827,000,000	($13,082,000,000)
2003	$34,529,000,000	$1,865,000,000

AT&T Corp. Board of Directors				
Name	Position	Relevant Stock		Qty
Dorman, David	Chairman and CEO		T	1,252,927
Derr, Kenneth	Director		T	2,773
Eickhoff, M.	Director		T	3,183
Henkel, Herbert	Director		T	N/A
McHenry, Donald	Director		T	2,664
Jackson, Shirley	Director		T	1,450
Herringer, Frank	Director		T	16,885
Madonna, Jon	Director		T	3,151
White, Tony	Director		T	2,851
Aldinger, William	Director		T	3,000

AT&T Corp. Corporate Officers			
Name	Position	Salary	Bonuses
Dorman, David	Chairman and CEO	$1,268,750	$2,648,000
Horton, Thomas	SEVP	$625,000	$940,000
Cicconi, James	General Counsel and EVP	$605,000	$840,300

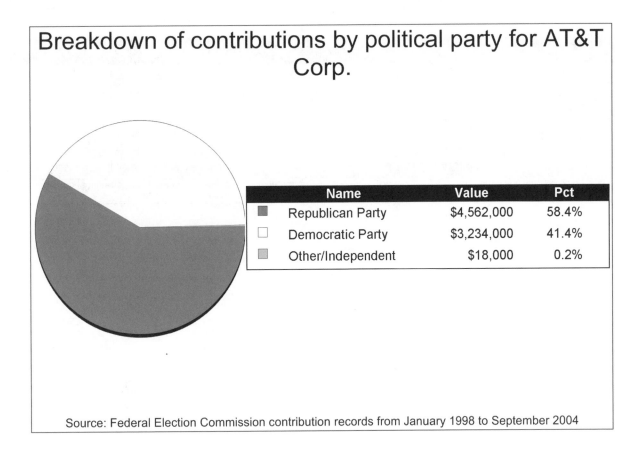

Breakdown of contributions by political party for AT&T Corp.

Name	Value	Pct
Republican Party	$4,562,000	58.4%
Democratic Party	$3,234,000	41.4%
Other/Independent	$18,000	0.2%

Source: Federal Election Commission contribution records from January 1998 to September 2004

Top 10 Recipients of Contributions Sourced to AT&T Corp.	
Recipient	Amount
National Republican Party Committees	$4,176,000
National Democratic Party Committees	$2,798,000
President George W Bush (R)	$49,000
Sen John F Kerry (D-MA)	$31,000
Sen John S McCain (R-AZ)	$29,000
Vice President Albert Gore, Jr (D-TN)	$28,000
Rep Richard A Gephardt (D-MO)	$22,000
Rep Edward John Markey (D-MA)	$22,000
Sen Tim Johnson (D-SD)	$20,000
Rep Charles W Pickering, Jr (R-MS)	$15,000
Total:	$7,190,000
Source: Federal Election Commission contribution records from January 1998 to September 2004	

AT&T Corp. Lobbying Expenditures by Year	
Year	Amount
1998	$9,964,000
1999	$11,826,000
2000	$8,661,000
2001	$14,285,000
2002	$12,145,000
2003	$12,480,000
2004	$5,650,610
Total:	$75,011,610
Source: U.S. Senate Office of Public Records lobbying disclosure records from January 1998 to June 30th, 2004.	

AT&T Corp. Sponsored Trips for Congressional Staff		
Congressional Office	Number of Trips	$ Amount
Sen Conrad R Burns (R-MT)	2	$1,180
Sen Theodore F Stevens (R-AK)	2	$1,180
Rep Barbara Lynn Cubin (R-WY)	1	$590
Rep Stephen Michael Largent (R-OK)	1	$590
Rep Charles W Pickering, Jr (R-MS)	2	$555
Sen Trent Lott (R-MS)	1	$520
Rep Carolyn McCarthy (D-NY)	1	$210
Total:	10	$4,825
Source: Congressional office travel records for members of the Senate Committee on Commerce, Science & Transportation and the House Committee on Energy and Commerce for the period of January 2000 to March 2004.		

BellSouth Corp.

Address:	1155 Peachtree St. NE	**Stock Symbol:**	BLS
	Room 15G03	**Telephone:**	404-249-2000
	Atlanta, GA 30309-3610	**Fax:**	404-249-2071
Total Employees:	76,000	**Website:**	www.bellsouth.com

Florida state Rep. Julio Robaina was on the statehouse floor considering whether to vote in favor of a bill that would freeze local phone rates when he got a telephone call that couldn't wait. On the other end was BellSouth lobbyist and vice president Eliseo Gomez.

The Miami Republican paid particular attention given that he is a long-time employee of the company. As the votes were cast one by one by other members of the Florida House, Gomez kept Robaina talking. Neither party disclosed the substance of the conversation afterward, but lawmakers told the Miami Herald that, as the call went on, Robaina became increasingly distressed, appearing "flustered and teary-eyed" by the end of the call.

For his part, Gomez admitted that he had lobbied Robaina hard to vote against the rate freeze, but denied having ever threatened the lawmaker's employment status. In the end, Robaina was able to cast a late vote with the House clerk—one that he subsequently changed twice before settling on a vote in favor of the freeze. Nevertheless, the measure lost in the House by a wide margin.

BellSouth has 26 lobbyists working in the Florida Legislature alone. The company is third among the four remaining Bell telephone service providers, with more than 44 million customers, behind Verizon and SBC. It continues its intense lobbying against rate freezes in many of the nine southern states where it provides local service: Alabama, Florida, Georgia, Kentucky, Louisiana, Mississippi, North Carolina, South Carolina and Tennessee.

Of the seven "Baby Bells" that were created when AT&T was broken apart in 1984, only BellSouth Corp. has kept its name. And despite a push by all the former Bells to diversify services, BellSouth still relies heavily on the revenue it derives from its local phone service, which is regulated at the state level.

In addition to protecting its local phone base, BellSouth has also aggressively pursued the long distance customers, with mixed success. The company reported 4.6 million long distance subscribers through the first quarter of 2004. In 1998 the FCC turned down BellSouth's request to begin offering long distance service in Louisiana and South Carolina, saying the company had not done enough to open its local markets to competition.

BellSouth is also active in the wireless business through its Cingular Wireless partnership with SBC in which BellSouth holds a 40 percent stake. Cingular serves more than 22 million wireless customers in 38 states and the District of Columbia, and is poised to double its subscriber base as it moves to complete its purchase of AT&T Wireless.

One of the company's fastest growing businesses is high speed DSL (digital subscriber line) Internet service. BellSouth has more than one million DSL customers in 74 markets. In 2002, the company teamed up with Dell Corp. to sell DSL-equipped computers. The company also has telecommunications interests in 11 Latin American countries, serving nearly 12 million local service and wireless customers.

BellSouth has also moved away from certain businesses. It quit the pay-telephone business in 2001, citing diminishing revenues and returns. In 2002 it swapped its minority ownership in the German wireless company E-Plus for a nine percent stake in the Dutch telecom company Royal KPN. BellSouth later sold its Royal KPN stake, however, and said it plans to divest itself of its other European holdings.

Despite BellSouth's best efforts, it may be facing a much tougher opponent than telephone technicians in the Florida statehouse: the emerging Voice-over Internet Protocol, a technology that will allow other telecom companies such as AT&T, and the cable giants such as Comcast Corp., to offer phone service over cable and data lines.

—Robert Morlino, Bob Williams

August 18, 2004

Sources: Company Web site, Securities and Exchange Commission filings, Yahoo! Finance Online, Hoover's Online, Fortune magazine, Miami Herald.

BellSouth Corp. Recent Financial Information		
Year	Revenue	Net Income (Net Loss)
2000	$26,151,000,000	$4,220,000,000
2001	$24,130,000,000	$2,570,000,000
2002	$22,440,000,000	$1,423,000,000
2003	$22,635,000,000	$3,904,000,000

BellSouth Corp. Board of Directors				
Name	Position	Relevant Stock		Qty
Ackerman, F.	Chairman		BLS	4,002,470
Anderson, Reuben	Director		BLS	41,421
Blanchard, James	Director		BLS	73,487
Brown, J.	Director		BLS	120,774
Codina, Armando	Director		BLS	98,814
Feldstein, Kathleen	Director		BLS	20,292
Kelly, James	Director		BLS	15,047
Mullin, Leo	Director		BLS	46,520
Murphy, Eugene	Director		BLS	33,519
Smith, Robin	Director		BLS	39,345
Stavropoulos, William	Director		BLS	32,041

BellSouth Corp. Corporate Officers			
Name	Position	Salary	Bonuses
Ackerman, F.	Chairman, President, and CEO	$1,365,000	$2,939,000
Dykes, Ronald	CFO	$658,200	$1,278,200
Morgan, Charles	EVP and General Counsel	$507,500	$702,900

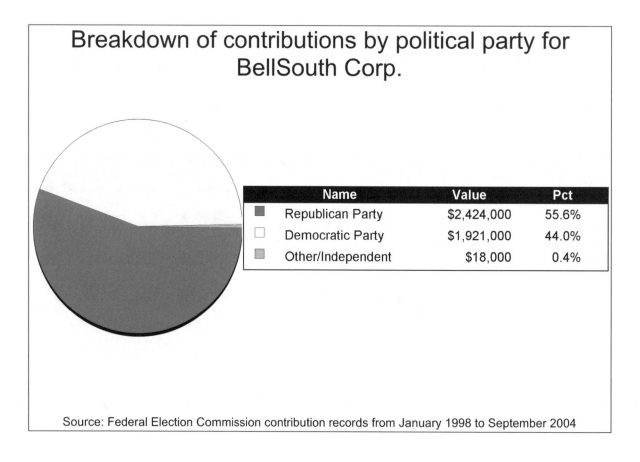

Breakdown of contributions by political party for BellSouth Corp.

Name	Value	Pct
Republican Party	$2,424,000	55.6%
Democratic Party	$1,921,000	44.0%
Other/Independent	$18,000	0.4%

Source: Federal Election Commission contribution records from January 1998 to September 2004

Top 10 Recipients of Contributions Sourced to BellSouth Corp.	
Recipient	Amount
National Republican Party Committees	$1,416,000
National Democratic Party Committees	$1,150,000
President George W Bush (R)	$122,000
Rep John D Dingell (D-MI)	$70,000
Vice President Albert Gore, Jr (D-TN)	$68,000
Rep Wilbert J Tauzin, Jr (R-LA)	$63,000
Sen Max Cleland (D-GA)	$59,000
Sen Mitch McConnell (R-KY)	$44,000
Sen John S McCain (R-AZ)	$40,000
Sen Zell Bryan Miller (D-GA)	$34,000
Total:	$3,066,000
Source: Federal Election Commission contribution records from January 1998 to September 2004	

BellSouth Corp. Lobbying Expenditures by Year	
Year	Amount
1998	$6,309,000
1999	$5,717,000
2000	$3,801,112
2001	$3,928,428
2002	$7,458,828
2003	$5,894,991
2004	$4,634,468
Total:	$37,743,827
Source: U.S. Senate Office of Public Records lobbying disclosure records from January 1998 to June 30th, 2004.	

BellSouth Corp. Sponsored Trips for Congressional Staff		
Congressional Office	Number of Trips	$ Amount
Rep Wilbert J Tauzin, Jr (R-LA)	1	$1,890
Rep Michael Bilirakis (R-FL)	1	$1,503
Rep George P Radanovich (R-CA)	1	$1,298
Rep John Mondy Shimkus (R-IL)	1	$1,215
Rep Vito J Fossella, Jr (D-NY)	2	$1,151
Rep Joe Linus Barton (R-TX)	1	$921
Rep Christopher Charles John (D-LA)	1	$921
Rep Mary Bono (R-CA)	1	$841
Sen George Allen (R-VA)	1	$612
Total:	10	$10,354
Source: Congressional office travel records for members of the Senate Committee on Commerce, Science & Transportation and the House Committee on Energy and Commerce for the period of January 2000 to March 2004.		

Belo Corp.

Address:	400 S. Record St.	**Stock Symbol:**	BLC
	Dallas, TX 75202-4841	**Telephone:**	214-977-6606
		Fax:	214-977-6603
Total Employees:	7,900	**Website:**	www.belo.com

In the age of media consolidation, among the first casualties to suffer from the relentless focus on the bottom line is political news coverage. Dallas-based Belo Corp. is an exception.

At a time when the major broadcast networks are opting to reduce coverage of the two national conventions in favor of "Trading Spouses" and repeats of "CSI," Belo's television stations are expanding coverage. For the fifth consecutive election cycle, the company will run the "It's Your Time" program, which gives each congressional and gubernatorial candidate five free minutes of air time to make his or her pitch directly to voters.

And in the lead-up to November's general election, Belo stations will air at least an hour's worth of political coverage every week, including debates and interviews with candidates of all levels, plus features on local issues.

It's all part of a strategy Belo conceived in 1996, and since that time more than 400 candidates have participated. Robert W. Decherd, the president, chairman and chief executive officer of Belo, told The Dallas Morning News, "Belo took this groundbreaking step eight years ago to ensure that we were doing all we could to create an informed electorate in the communities we serve."

Incidentally, The Dallas Morning News is the flagship property of Belo, which got its start way back in 1876, when Alfred Horatio Belo purchased the Galveston Daily News. Nine years later, he sent an associate to find a proper location to establish a sister publication. In 1885, that paper—The Dallas Morning News—began printing.

The Belo associate who took a chance on Dallas—George Dealey—eventually became owner of the company, naming it A. H. Belo Corporation after its founder. (The initials were dropped in 2001.) The company opened its first radio station in 1922.

The Dallas Morning News was key to Belo's success. Its good performance led to the purchase of the company's first television station, also in Dallas, in the early 1950s. In 1991, Belo purchased The Dallas Morning News' competing daily, the Times-Herald, and shut the paper down. Dallas officially became a one-daily city, and Belo went on to expand significantly.

The company bought the Providence Journal newspaper in 1997, along with several television stations, for $1.5 billion from the Providence Journal Company.

Today Belo is the eighth largest broadcast television company by revenue, with 20 stations in all. In addition to the Morning News, it publishes three major dailies (including the Providence Journal and the Press-Enterprise of Riverside, Calif.) as well as a handful of community papers.

There have been setbacks along the way, most notably the failed 19-month partnership with Time Warner that was News 24 TV, a 24-hour cable news network launched in 2002 in the Houston market. Sagging ratings led both companies to pull the plug in July, with Belo taking an $18.7 million loss on the deal, which had included cable news stations in San Antonio and Charlotte, N.C.

And there was the 12 percent stake in the Dallas Mavericks that Belo paid $24 million for in 1999; the team's majority owner, Mark Cuban, had agreed to buy Belo's share back for $34 million, but after a public battle they settled on a price tag of $27 million.

The setbacks were the exception, though, and the company continues to prosper financially, as operating revenues and net income have increased at a healthy rate. The company had a profit $128.5 million in 2003.

Belo's philanthropic arm, The Belo Foundation, has awarded grants over the past half-century totaling $20 million.

—Robert Morlino

August 20, 2004

Sources: Company Web site, Hoover's Online, The Dallas Morning News, The Houston Chronicle, Dow Jones Business News

Belo Corp. Recent Financial Information		
Year	Revenue	Net Income (Net Loss)
1999	$1,434,086,000	$178,306,000
2000	$1,589,392,000	$150,825,000
2001	$1,364,703,000	($2,686,000)
2002	$1,427,907,000	$131,126,000
2003	$1,436,011,000	$128,525,000

Belo Corp. Board of Directors				
Name	Position	Relevant Stock		Qty
Decherd, Robert	Chairman, President, CEO		BLC	8,971,519
Becton, Henry	Director		BLC	91,907
Caldera, Louis	Director		BLC	23,985
Cordova, France	Director		BLC	9,080
Craven, Judith	Director		BLC	75,982
Enrico, Roger	Director		BLC	138,099
Hamblett, Stephen	Director		BLC	592,239
Herndon, Dealey	Director		BLC	3,835,139
Hirsch, Laurence	Director		BLC	93,035
Sanders, Wayne	Director		BLC	12,080
Solomon, William	Director		BLC	116,432
Ward, Lloyd	Director		BLC	38,895
Williams, J.	Director		BLC	82,404

Belo Corp. Corporate Officers			
Name	Position	Salary	Bonuses
Decherd, Robert	Chairman, President, CEO	$855,000	$45,800
Sander, John	President, Media Operations	$600,000	$23,600
Kerr, Guy	SVP, Law and Government	$405,000	$10,900

Breakdown of contributions by political party for Belo Corp.

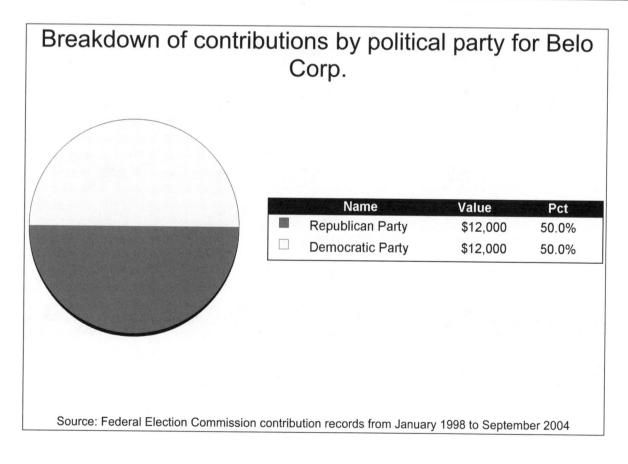

Name	Value	Pct
Republican Party	$12,000	50.0%
Democratic Party	$12,000	50.0%

Source: Federal Election Commission contribution records from January 1998 to September 2004

Top 10 Recipients of Contributions Sourced to Belo Corp.	
Recipient	Amount
Rep Martin Frost (D-TX)	$4,000
Sen John S McCain (R-AZ)	$4,000
Rep Ralph Moody Hall (D-TX)	$2,000
Rep Raymond E Green (D-TX)	$2,000
Sen Theodore F Stevens (R-AK)	$2,000
Sen Lincoln D Chafee (R-RI)	$2,000
Rep Bart T Stupak (D-MI)	$1,000
Sen Donald Lee Nickles (R-OK)	$1,000
Rep Edward John Markey (D-MA)	$1,000
Rep Ronald Kirk (D-TX)	$1,000
Total:	$20,000

Source: Federal Election Commission contribution records from January 1998 to September 2004

Belo Corp. Lobbying Expenditures by Year	
Year	Amount
1998	$200,000
1999	$200,000
2000	$200,000
2001	$210,000
2002	$200,000
2003	$420,000
2004	$190,000
Total:	$1,620,000

Source: U.S. Senate Office of Public Records lobbying disclosure records from January 1998 to June 30th, 2004.

TV Station Subsidiaries for Belo Corp.			
Call Sign	Channel and Type	Subsidiary Name	Area of Service
WHAS-TV	11 TV Commercial	BELO KENTUCKY, INC.	LOUISVILLE, KY
KASW	61 TV Commercial	KASW-TV, INC.	PHOENIX, AZ
KENS-TV	5 TV Commercial	KENS-TV, INC.	SAN ANTONIO, TX
KHOU-TV	11 TV Commercial	KHOU-TV, L.P.	HOUSTON, TX
KTFT-LP	38 TV Low Power (UHF)	KING BROADCASTING COMPANY	TWIN FALLS, ID
KING-TV	5 TV Commercial	KING BROADCASTING COMPANY	SEATTLE, WA
KTVB	7 TV Commercial	KING BROADCASTING COMPANY	BOISE, ID
KREM-TV	2 TV Commercial	KING BROADCASTING COMPANY	SPOKANE, WA
KGW	8 TV Commercial	KING BROADCASTING COMPANY	PORTLAND, OR
KMOV	4 TV Commercial	KMOV-TV, INC.	ST. LOUIS, MO
KMSB-TV	11 TV Commercial	KMSB-TV, INC.	TUCSON, AZ
KONG-TV	16 TV Commercial	KONG-TV, INC.	EVERETT, WA
KSKN	22 TV Commercial	KSKN TELEVISION, INC.	SPOKANE, WA
KTTU-TV	18 TV Commercial	KTTU-TV, INC.	TUCSON, AZ
KTVK	3 TV Commercial	KTVK, INC.	PHOENIX, AZ
KVUE	24 TV Commercial	KVUE TELEVISION, INC.	AUSTIN, TX
WCNC-TV	36 TV Commercial	WCNC-TV, INC.	CHARLOTTE, NC
WFAA-TV	8 TV Commercial	WFAA-TV, L.P.	DALLAS, TX
WVEC-TV	13 TV Commercial	WVEC TELEVISION, INC.	HAMPTON, VA
WWL-TV	4 TV Commercial	WWL-TV, INC.	NEW ORLEANS, LA

Print Media Subsidiaries for Belo Corp.			
Company Name	Market City	Weekday Circulation	Sunday Circulation
Denton Record-Chronicle	Denton, TX	17,435	17,435
The Dallas Morning News	Dallas, TX	519,014	755,912
The Press-Enterprise	Riverside, CA	191,802	191,290
The Providence Journal	Providence, RI	166,460	234,147

Cablevision Systems Corp.

Address: 1111 Stewart Ave.
          Bethpage, NY 11714

Total Employees: 18,820

Stock Symbol: CVC
Telephone: 516-803-2300
Fax: 516-803-2273
Website: www.cablevision.com

Cablevision is about as New York as it gets.

It starts with the company's more than 3 million cable subscribers in the New York City metropolitan area.

Next add in the Big Apple's sports temple, Madison Square Garden, which Cablevision controls and operates. Toss in the city's beloved New York Knicks basketball team and New York Rangers hockey team, which Cablevision controls.

Still not enough? Add Radio City Music Hall to the list, including its high-kicking icons, the Rockettes.

Cablevision's ties to New York should come as no surprise.

It was born in the city when founder Charles Dolan, one of the pioneers in the cable business, helped form a company called Sterling Manhattan Cable in 1954. The company got its big break in 1965, when it won the cable franchise for lower Manhattan. Just two years later, Sterling started televising Knicks and Ranger games.

In 1970, Dolan founded Home Box Office, the country's first nationwide pay television station. Three years later he changed the company's name to Sterling Communications and took it public. Time Inc. quickly swooped in and bought an 80 percent interest in the company.

Time soured on Sterling quickly, however, and liquidated the company just a few months later. The only piece Time retained was HBO.

Dolan bought back Sterling's New York franchises and formed a new company called Long Island Cable Communications Development, which would eventually become Cablevision. He also formed a new subsidiary called Rainbow Programming, which started boutique cable networks such as American Movie Classics and the Bravo Channel.

Dolan took Cablevision public in 1986, using part of the proceeds to buy three New England cable systems over the following year.

He continued to dabble in new businesses as well. He partnered with NBC to start its cable network CNBC, eventually selling his interest in the venture to the television network.

The company started offering phone service over its cable network in Long Island in 1995, well ahead of most other cable companies, when it teamed up with Baby Bell NYNEX to offer local phone service in the New York area. Cablevision and ITT got together in 1995 to buy Madison Square Garden, a deal that included the Knicks and the Rangers. MSG bought control of Radio City Music Hall in 1997.

During the early 1990s, Cablevision was also buying up cable systems throughout the country. By 1997 it had systems in 19 states.

At that point, Dolan again decided to shift the focus of the company's cable business back to New York. Through a series of deals the company swapped its subscribers in other parts of the country for New York customers.

Cablevision even took a flyer in the electronics business, buying the New York-based "The Wiz" retail chain in a bankruptcy proceeding in 1998. The company then sold its interests in the colorful electronics chain, a New York fixture for many years, as part of an effort to focus on its cable operations.

The company then fired the first shot in the looming war between the regional Bell local phone companies and the cable industry when it began offering what amounted to free local phone service. Cablevision utilized VoIP technology, or Voice-over Internet Protocol, in a bundled package of Internet and cable services. Verizon Communications Inc., now Cablevision's competitor for local phone service in New York, dismissed the offer as a promotional gimmick. But VoIP threatens the Bells' dominance like no other technology because cable doesn't have to rely on the local phone companies to deliver the "last mile" of wire to customers' homes.

Charles Dolan's son James took over as chief executive officer of Cablevision in 1996, although the elder Dolan retained his title as chairman.

With more than 18,000 employees and overall revenues of just over $4.1 billion in 2003, Cablevision checked in at number 409 on the latest Fortune 500 list.

—Bob Williams

August 19, 2004

Sources: Company Web site, Securities and Exchange Commission filings, Yahoo! Finance Online, Hoover's Online, Fortune magazine.

Cablevision Systems Corp. Recent Financial Information		
Year	Revenue	Net Income (Net Loss)
2000	$4,411,000,000	$229,300,000
2001	$4,404,500,000	$1,007,700,000
2002	$4,003,400,000	$90,200,000
2003	$4,177,100,000	($297,200,000)

Cablevision Systems Corp. Board of Directors				
Name	Position	Relevant Stock		Qty
Dolan, Charles	Chairman		CNYG	37,920,966
Dolan, James	Director		CNYG	3,069,248
Mahony, Sheila	Director		CNYG	168,464
Ferris, Charles	Director		CNYG	101,755
Hochman, Richard	Director		CNYG	108,737
Oristano, Victor	Director		CNYG	47,512
Tatta, John	Director		CNYG	142,497
Tese, Vincent	Director		CNYG	60,275
Reifenheiser, Thomas	Director		CNYG	35,843
Ryan, John	Director		CNYG	35,843
Dolan, Thomas	Director		CNYG	2,121,197
Dolan, Patrick	Director		CNYG	2,044,625
Rattner, Steven	Director		CNYG	48,843
Ratner, Hank	Vice Chairman		CNYG	550,181
Bell, William	Vice Chairman		CNYG	400,312

Cablevision Systems Corp. Corporate Officers			
Name	Position	Salary	Bonuses
Dolan, Charles	Chairman	$1,600,000	$4,800,000
Bell, William	Vice Chairman	$1,000,000	$1,345,000
Dolan, James	President, CEO, Director	$1,600,000	$2,800,000
Ratner, Hank	Vice Chairman	$1,087,019	$2,000,000
Hildenbrand, Wilton	EVP, Engineering and Technology	$750,000	$675,000

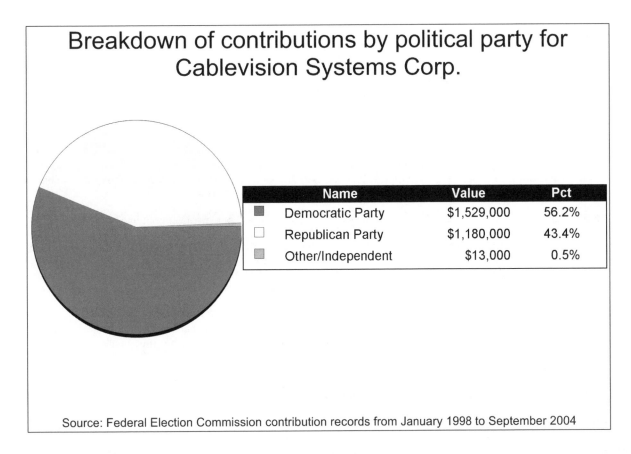

Breakdown of contributions by political party for Cablevision Systems Corp.

Name	Value	Pct
Democratic Party	$1,529,000	56.2%
Republican Party	$1,180,000	43.4%
Other/Independent	$13,000	0.5%

Source: Federal Election Commission contribution records from January 1998 to September 2004

Top 10 Recipients of Contributions Sourced to Cablevision Systems Corp.	
Recipient	Amount
National Republican Party Committees	$990,000
National Democratic Party Committees	$981,000
Sen Hillary Rodham Clinton (D-NY)	$72,000
Sen Charles E Schumer (D-NY)	$51,000
Vice President Albert Gore, Jr (D-TN)	$44,000
President George W Bush (R)	$40,000
Sen Robert G Torricelli (D-NJ)	$38,000
Sen John F Kerry (D-MA)	$23,000
Sen Christopher J Dodd (D-CT)	$23,000
Rep Charles B Rangel (D-NY)	$22,000
Total:	$2,284,000

Source: Federal Election Commission contribution records from January 1998 to September 2004

Cablevision Systems Corp. Lobbying Expenditures by Year	
Year	Amount
1998	$100,000
1999	$60,000
2000	$140,000
2001	$180,000
2002	$560,000
2003	$580,000
2004	$60,000
Total:	$1,680,000

Source: U.S. Senate Office of Public Records lobbying disclosure records from January 1998 to June 30th, 2004.

Charter Communications Inc.

Address:	12405 Powerscourt Dr. Ste. 100 St. Louis, MO 63131-3660	Stock Symbol: Telephone: Fax:	CHTR 314-965-0555 314-965-9745
Total Employees:	15,500	Website:	www.chartercom.com

The arrival of the world's largest privately owned yacht at the annual cable-industry convention in New Orleans this past May was perhaps more remarkable for its owner than for itself. On board was billionaire Paul Allen, Microsoft co-founder and chairman of the third-largest cable television company in the United States, Charter Communications Inc.

"His presence was notable...It means that Paul is not a seller as much as a buyer," one media analyst told the Los Angeles Times.

Just one year ago, Charter Communications, the company in which Allen bought a controlling interest in 1998, appeared to be in dire straits beyond the ministrations even of the third-richest man in America. The mogul's initial investment in the company had spurred a buying binge that put the company more than $21 billion in debt after the dot.com bubble burst, and the Securities and Exchange Commission opened an investigation that led to the indictment of four former executives for improper financial reporting (neither Allen nor CEO Carl Vogel have been implicated).

Fast forward one year later to New Orleans, and Allen is in the process of re-positioning himself in the industry by introducing a new set-top digital box that integrates multiple data and home entertainment functions, and potentially buying more cable markets that come up for sale as bankrupt Adelphia Communications Corp. disintegrates.

The odds for Allen and Charter improved with the help of an $8 billion refinancing deal completed earlier in the year with several major banks. Part of the deal included the largest institutional loan ever taken.

Meanwhile Vogel has been cleaning house, appointing a new chief financial officer and executive vice president. The company has held steady as the third-largest cable provider, with more than 6 million subscribers and 1.7 million high-speed Internet customers.

Charter was intended to be the cornerstone of Allen's concept of a "wired world," where customers would receive everything from entertainment to basic phone service through fat data transmission lines provided by the company.

Allen called it "a vision of a wired world where everyone would be interconnected in a global network, providing immediate availability to information and resources anywhere in the world." It was an idea Allen had been kicking around for more than 25 years, but it only began in earnest with his takeover of Charter—a first step that would drop his net worth by more than $7 billion.

The company was started by three executives of a local cable franchise in St. Louis in 1992. Crown Media, a unit of the Hallmark greeting card empire, had just bought their company when the three decided to start their own cable acquisition and management company. Two years later, the new company paid about $900 million for a controlling interest in Crown. Charter went on to spend more than $3 billion to acquire more than a dozen cable companies over the next four years.

The deals only got bigger when Allen arrived on the scene. In 1998 Charter paid $2.8 billion to acquire Dallas cable company Marcus Communications. Next came Falcon Communications, which added more than a million cable subscribers to the mix.

Other acquisitions and cable system swaps had grown Charter's subscriber base to more than 6.8 million by the end of 2002. Nearly 2.3 million of those customers had digital cable service and nearly 750,000 had broadband Internet service.

—Bob Williams, Robert Morlino

August 17, 2004

Sources: Company Web site, Securities and Exchange Commission filings, Yahoo! Finance Online, New York Post, Associated Press, Hoover's Online, Fortune magazine, Los Angeles Times, Multichannel News, Seattle Times

Charter Communications Inc. Recent Financial Information		
Year	Revenue	Net Income (Net Loss)
1999	$1,428,000,000	($66,000,000)
2000	$3,141,000,000	($858,000,000)
2001	$3,807,000,000	($1,167,000,000)
2002	$4,566,000,000	($2,514,000,000)
2003	$4,819,000,000	($238,000,000)

Charter Communications Inc. Board of Directors			
Name	Position	Relevant Stock	Qty
Allen, Paul	Chairman	CHTR	29,160,640
Nathanson, Marc	Director	CHTR	370,000
Vogel, Carl	Director	CHTR	80,208
Peretsman, Nancy	Director	CHTR	60,000
Tory, John	Director	CHTR	4,300
Wangberg, Larry	Director	CHTR	3,000
Lilis, Charles	Director	N/A	N/A
Merritt, David	Director	N/A	N/A
Patton, Jo	Director	N/A	N/A

Charter Communications Inc. Corporate Officers			
Name	Position	Salary	Bonuses
Vogel, Carl	President, CEO, and Director	$1,000,000	$150,000
Shaw, Curtis	SVP, General Counsel, and Secretary	$275,782	$37,500
Bellville, Margaret	EVP, COO	$581,730	$203,125
Schumm, Steven	EVP, CAO	$448,077	$45,000
Silva, Stephen	Former EVP	$213,005	N/A

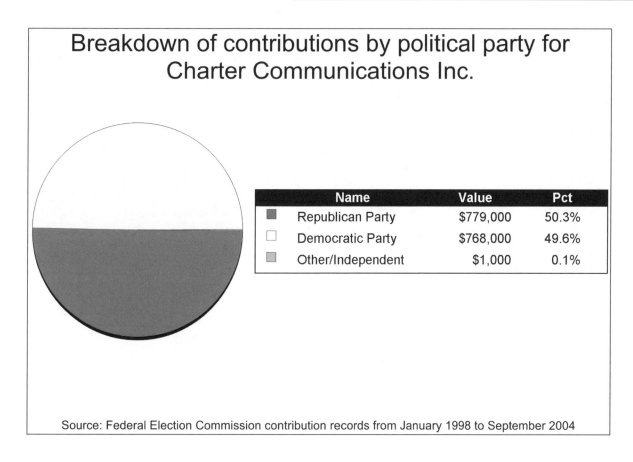

Breakdown of contributions by political party for Charter Communications Inc.

Name	Value	Pct
Republican Party	$779,000	50.3%
Democratic Party	$768,000	49.6%
Other/Independent	$1,000	0.1%

Source: Federal Election Commission contribution records from January 1998 to September 2004

Top 10 Recipients of Contributions Sourced to Charter Communications Inc.	
Recipient	Amount
National Republican Party Committees	$637,000
National Democratic Party Committees	$543,000
Rep Richard A Gephardt (D-MO)	$65,000
Sen Jean A Carnahan (D-MO)	$17,000
Sen Mel Carnahan (D-MO)	$16,000
Rep Robert R Simmons (R-CT)	$10,000
President George W Bush (R)	$9,000
Vice President Albert Gore, Jr (D-TN)	$8,000
Rep Roy Blunt (R-MO)	$8,000
Sen John David Ashcroft (R-MO)	$7,000
Total:	$1,320,000
Source: Federal Election Commission contribution records from January 1998 to September 2004	

Charter Communications Inc. Lobbying Expenditures by Year	
Year	Amount
1998	$232,500
1999	$189,500
2000	$220,000
2001	$440,000
2002	$600,000
2003	$120,000
Total:	$1,802,000
Source: U.S. Senate Office of Public Records lobbying disclosure records from January 1998 to June 30th, 2004.	

Cingular Wireless LLC

Address: 5565 Glenridge Connector
Ste. 1401
Atlanta, GA 30342
Total Employees: 39,400

Stock Symbol: N/A
Telephone: 404-236-7895
Fax: 404-236-6005
Website: www.cingular.com

The product of a union between the wireless divisions of two former Baby Bells—SBC Communications Inc. and BellSouth Corp.—Cingular is poised to become the nation's number one wireless carrier. Currently second, behind Verizon Communications Inc., the company is in the process of buying AT&T's wireless division, adding more than 22 million subscribers to its own base of more than 22 million.

SBC owns 60 percent of the company and BellSouth owns 40 percent, based on the value of the assets both contributed to the venture when it began in April 2000.

Cingular was the first U.S. wireless carrier to offer Rollover, the wireless plan that lets customers keep their unused monthly minutes. The company provides cellular/PCS (personal communications system) service in 43 of the top 50 markets nationwide. It also provides corporate e-mail and other types of advanced data services.

Cingular's revenue was more than $15 billion in 2003.

—Bob Williams

August 20, 2004

*See also BellSouth Corp. and SBC Communications Inc.

Sources: Company Web site, Securities and Exchange Commission filings, Yahoo! Finance Online, Hoover's Online, Reuters

Cingular Wireless Recent Financial Information		
Year	Revenue	Net Income (Net Loss)
2001	$14,268,000,000	$1,692,000,000
2002	$14,903,000,000	$1,207,000,000
2003	$15,483,000,000	$1,022,000,000

Cingular Wireless Board of Directors			
Name	Position	Relevant Stock	Qty
Dykes, Ronald	Director	N/A	N/A
Anderson, Richard	Director	N/A	N/A
Stephenson, Randall	Chairman	N/A	N/A
Wilkins, Rayford	Director	SBC	431,692

Cingular Wireless Corporate Officers			
Name	Position	Salary	Bonuses
Sigman, Stanley	President and CEO	$900,000	$1,876,000
Feidler, Mark	Former COO	$555,654	$730,600
Lindner, Richard	CFO	$383,635	$407,550
Carbonell, Joaquin	EVP and General Counsel	$314,277	$286,000
Vega, Ralph	COO	$410,319	$716,000
Arroyo, F.	CIO	$346,500	$332,250

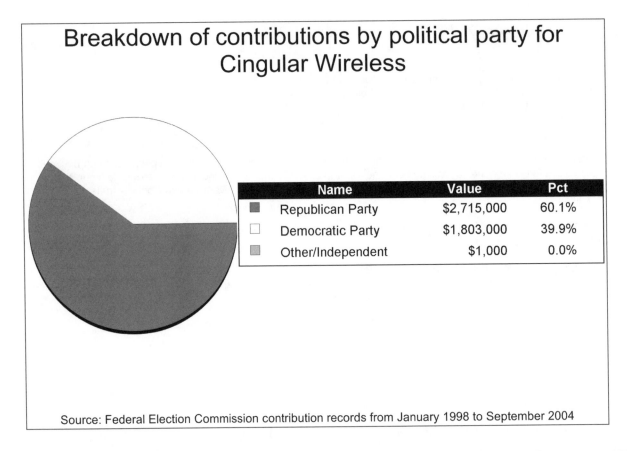

Breakdown of contributions by political party for Cingular Wireless

	Name	Value	Pct
■	Republican Party	$2,715,000	60.1%
☐	Democratic Party	$1,803,000	39.9%
■	Other/Independent	$1,000	0.0%

Source: Federal Election Commission contribution records from January 1998 to September 2004

Top 10 Recipients of Contributions Sourced to Cingular Wireless	
Recipient	Amount
National Republican Party Committees	$539,000
National Democratic Party Committees	$412,000
Rep J Dennis Hastert (R-IL)	$61,000
Rep Roy Blunt (R-MO)	$52,000
Rep Thomas Dale Delay (R-TX)	$49,000
Sen Thomas Andrew Daschle (D-SD)	$39,000
Rep John D Dingell (D-MI)	$37,000
Rep Martin Frost (D-TX)	$36,000
Rep Wilbert J Tauzin, Jr (R-LA)	$35,000
President George W Bush (R)	$35,000
Total:	$1,295,000

Source: Federal Election Commission contribution records from January 1998 to September 2004

Cingular Wireless Lobbying Expenditures by Year	
Year	Amount
2001	$3,200,000
2002	$2,220,000
2003	$3,760,000
2004	$340,000
Total:	$9,520,000

Source: U.S. Senate Office of Public Records lobbying disclosure records from January 1998 to June 30th, 2004.

Citadel Broadcasting Corp.

Address: 7201 W. Lake Mead Blvd.
Ste. 400
Las Vegas, NV 89128
Total Employees: 2,400

Stock Symbol: CDL
Telephone: 702-804-5200
Fax: 702-804-5936
Website: www.citadelbroadcasting.com

The next big radio conglomerate to challenge the likes of Clear Channel Communications Inc. and Viacom's Infinity division will be ... Citadel Communications Corp. Well, maybe.

Citadel stands out as the only major radio broadcast company owned by a powerful Wall Street leveraged buyout firm. Forstmann Little & Co. bought Citadel from its public shareholders in June 2001 for $2 billion.

In January, Forstmann took the company public again, but Citadel stock soon hit a one-year low. In June, the company announced that it would be buying back outstanding shares, with a combined value of as much as $100 million.

Despite Citadel's questionable financial future, the company's history reads like a business school finance class.

Leveraged buyouts, or LBOs, were a phenomenon rampant in the 1980s, but are rarely seen these days. Generally, a firm raises a huge sum of money to buy out shareholders of an undervalued company, be it its own or another, thus taking it private. (The largest of these was in 1988 when Kohlberg Kravis Roberts & Co. paid shareholders $25 billion to take RJR Nabisco private.)

Citadel itself was founded in 1984. The company grew steadily through the 1990s, but really took off after passage of the 1996 Telecommunications Act when Congress eliminated or loosened restrictions on how many radio stations could be owned by a single company. In 1997, the company raised money with a preferred stock offering and shortly after purchased 61 radio stations for $230 million.

In 1998 it completed an initial public offering, selling 6.2 million shares of stock for $106.9 million, and continued its acquisition spree. Forstmann took the company private in January 2001, and continued buying stations. Citadel owns 220 stations in 44 markets and is the sixth-largest radio broadcaster in the nation.

Citadel focuses on buying stations in "mid-sized markets" because they are "less competitive, have fewer signals, derive a significant portion of their revenue from local advertisers and offer substantial opportunities for further consolidation." (It's difficult to find any mention of responsible stewardship of the public airwaves in the company's corporate strategy.)

The company's Web site includes the slogan, "Reaching Across America One Station at a Time," but dominating mid-sized markets is the company's actual practice. Citadel owns 11 stations in Wilkes Barre/Scranton, Pa., and 11 in and around Little Rock, Ark., for example.

Citadel has its work cut out if it wants to compete with Clear Channel. Last year, the FCC voted to tighten rules on how many stations a company may own in a single market by using maps created by the Arbitron ratings firm rather than the FCC's flawed "contour method" that has allowed the creation of behemoths like Clear Channel. A federal appeals court stayed that decision, but earlier this month, the commission asked the court to lift the stay as it applies to the radio rules.

—John Dunbar, Robert Morlino

August 19, 2004

Sources: Citadel Communications Corp. Web site, New York Post, Broadcasting & Cable.

Citadel Broadcasting Corp. Recent Financial Information		
Year	Revenue	Net Income (Net Loss)
1999	$178,495,000	($8,928,000)
2000	$284,824,000	($39,224,000)
2001	$323,484,000	($202,973,000)
2002	$348,869,000	($89,160,000)
2003	$371,509,000	($89,570,000)

Citadel Broadcasting Corp. Board of Directors				
Name	Position	Relevant Stock		Qty
Suleman, Farid	Chairman		CDL	3,704,574
Forstmann, J.	Director		CDL	12,500
Forstmann, Theodore	Director		CDL	76,277,703
Holmes, Gordon	Director		CDL	N/A
Horbach, Sandra	Director		CDL	76,277,703
Miles, Michael	Director		CDL	12,500
Checketts, David	Director		CDL	51,500
Rose, Charles	Director		CDL	32,500
Siegel, Herbert	Director		CDL	N/A

Citadel Broadcasting Corp. Corporate Officers			
Name	Position	Salary	Bonuses
Suleman, Farid	Chairman and CEO	$1,000,000	N/A
Proffitt, D.	President	$179,642	N/A
Ellis, Judith	COO	$320,883	$229,167
Taylor, Randy	VP, Finance	$225,000	$25,000

Radio Station Subsidiaries for Citadel Broadcasting Corp.				
State	City	Call Sign	Frequency	Subsidiary Name
AL	BIRMINGHAM	WJOX	690 AM Station	CITADEL BROADCASTING COMPANY
AL	BIRMINGHAM	WZRR	99.5 FM Commercial	CITADEL BROADCASTING COMPANY
AL	BIRMINGHAM	WAPI	1070 AM Station	CITADEL BROADCASTING COMPANY
AL	BIRMINGHAM	WYSF	94.5 FM Commercial	CITADEL BROADCASTING COMPANY
AL	BIRMINGHAM	WRAX	107.7 FM Commercial	CITADEL BROADCASTING COMPANY
AR	CABOT	KARN-FM	102.5 FM Commercial	CITADEL BROADCASTING COMPANY
AR	HUMNOKE	KKRN	101.7 FM Commercial	CITADEL BROADCASTING COMPANY
AR	LITTLE ROCK	KURB	98.5 FM Commercial	CITADEL BROADCASTING COMPANY
AR	LITTLE ROCK	KLIH	1250 AM Station	CITADEL BROADCASTING COMPANY
AR	LITTLE ROCK	KAAY	1090 AM Station	CITADEL BROADCASTING COMPANY
AR	LITTLE ROCK	KARN	920 AM Station	CITADEL BROADCASTING COMPANY
AR	PINE BLUFF	KIPR	92.3 FM Commercial	CITADEL BROADCASTING COMPANY
AR	SHERIDAN	KVLO	102.9 FM Commercial	CITADEL BROADCASTING COMPANY
AR	SHERWOOD	KOKY	102.1 FM Commercial	CITADEL BROADCASTING COMPANY
AR	WRIGHTSVILLE	KLAL	107.7 FM Commercial	CITADEL BROADCASTING COMPANY
AZ	ORO VALLEY	KSZR	97.5 FM Commercial	CITADEL BROADCASTING COMPANY
AZ	TUCSON	KCUB	1290 AM Station	CITADEL BROADCASTING COMPANY
AZ	TUCSON	KIIM-FM	99.5 FM Commercial	CITADEL BROADCASTING COMPANY
AZ	TUCSON	KHYT	107.5 FM Commercial	CITADEL BROADCASTING COMPANY
AZ	TUCSON	KTUC	1400 AM Station	CITADEL BROADCASTING COMPANY
CA	LODI	KWIN	97.7 FM Commercial	CITADEL BROADCASTING COMPANY
CA	MARIPOSA	KDJK	103.9 FM Commercial	CITADEL BROADCASTING COMPANY
CA	MODESTO	KATM	103.3 FM Commercial	CITADEL BROADCASTING COMPANY
CA	MODESTO	KHKK	104.1 FM Commercial	CITADEL BROADCASTING COMPANY
CA	MODESTO	KESP	970 AM Station	CITADEL BROADCASTING COMPANY
CA	OAKDALE	KHOP	95.1 FM Commercial	CITADEL BROADCASTING COMPANY
CA	SOUTH LAKE TAHOE	KWYL	102.9 FM Commercial	CITADEL BROADCASTING COMPANY
CA	STOCKTON	KJOY	99.3 FM Commercial	CITADEL BROADCASTING COMPANY
CA	TURLOCK	KWNN	98.3 FM Commercial	CITADEL BROADCASTING COMPANY
CO	COLORADO SPRINGS	KKFM	98.1 FM Commercial	CITADEL BROADCASTING COMPANY
CO	COLORADO SPRINGS	KSPZ	92.9 FM Commercial	CITADEL BROADCASTING COMPANY
CO	COLORADO SPRINGS	KBZC	1300 AM Station	CITADEL BROADCASTING COMPANY
CO	COLORADO SPRINGS	KVOR	740 AM Station	CITADEL BROADCASTING COMPANY
CO	PUEBLO	KKMG	98.9 FM Commercial	CITADEL BROADCASTING COMPANY
CT	GROTON	WSUB	980 AM Station	CITADEL BROADCASTING COMPANY
CT	GROTON	WQGN-FM	105.5 FM Commercial	CITADEL BROADCASTING COMPANY
CT	STONINGTON	WXLM	102.3 FM Commercial	CITADEL BROADCASTING COMPANY
IA	BOONE	KBGG-FM	98.3 FM Commercial	CITADEL BROADCASTING COMPANY
IA	DES MOINES	KGGO	94.9 FM Commercial	CITADEL BROADCASTING COMPANY
IA	DES MOINES	KHKI	97.3 FM Commercial	CITADEL BROADCASTING COMPANY
IA	DES MOINES	KBGG	1700 AM Station	CITADEL BROADCASTING COMPANY
IA	WEST DES MOINES	KJJY	92.5 FM Commercial	CITADEL BROADCASTING COMPANY
ID	BOISE	KIZN	92.3 FM Commercial	CITADEL BROADCASTING COMPANY

State	City	Call Sign	Frequency	Subsidiary Name
ID	BOISE	KBOI	670 AM Station	CITADEL BROADCASTING COMPANY
ID	BOISE	KQFC	97.9 FM Commercial	CITADEL BROADCASTING COMPANY
ID	NAMPA	KKGL	96.9 FM Commercial	CITADEL BROADCASTING COMPANY
ID	NAMPA	KTIK	1350 AM Station	CITADEL BROADCASTING COMPANY
ID	NEW PLYMOUTH	KZMG	93.1 FM Commercial	CITADEL BROADCASTING COMPANY
IL	BLOOMINGTON	WJBC	1230 AM Station	CITADEL BROADCASTING COMPANY
IL	BLOOMINGTON	WBNQ	101.5 FM Commercial	CITADEL BROADCASTING COMPANY
IL	DWIGHT	WJEZ	98.9 FM Commercial	LIVINGSTON COUNTY BROADCASTERS, INC.
IL	LE ROY	WBWN	104.1 FM Commercial	CITADEL BROADCASTING COMPANY
IL	PONTIAC	WTRX-FM	93.7 FM Commercial	LIVINGSTON COUNTY BROADCASTERS, INC.
IN	KOKOMO	WWKI	100.5 FM Commercial	CITADEL BROADCASTING COMPANY
IN	NEW CASTLE	WMDH	1550 AM Station	CITADEL BROADCASTING COMPANY
IN	NEW CASTLE	WMDH-FM	102.5 FM Commercial	CITADEL BROADCASTING COMPANY
LA	BATON ROUGE	WIBR	1300 AM Station	CITADEL BROADCASTING COMPANY
LA	BATON ROUGE	WXOK	1460 AM Station	CITADEL BROADCASTING COMPANY
LA	BELLE CHASSE	KMEZ	102.9 FM Commercial	CITADEL BROADCASTING COMPANY
LA	HAMMOND	WBBE	103.3 FM Commercial	CITADEL BROADCASTING COMPANY
LA	KENTWOOD	WEMX	94.1 FM Commercial	CITADEL BROADCASTING COMPANY
LA	LACOMBE	WOPR	94.7 FM Commercial	CITADEL BROADCASTING COMPANY
LA	LAFAYETTE	KRRQ	95.5 FM Commercial	CITADEL BROADCASTING COMPANY
LA	LAFAYETTE	KDYS	1520 AM Station	CITADEL BROADCASTING COMPANY
LA	LAFAYETTE	KSMB	94.5 FM Commercial	CITADEL BROADCASTING COMPANY
LA	LAFAYETTE	KVOL	1330 AM Station	CITADEL BROADCASTING COMPANY
LA	LAPLACE	WCKW-FM	92.3 FM Commercial	CITADEL BROADCASTING COMPANY
LA	MAURICE	KFXZ	106.3 FM Commercial	CITADEL BROADCASTING COMPANY
LA	NEW IBERIA	KXKC	99.1 FM Commercial	CITADEL BROADCASTING COMPANY
LA	NEW IBERIA	KOOJ	93.7 FM Commercial	CITADEL BROADCASTING COMPANY
LA	NEW ROADS	KQXL-FM	106.5 FM Commercial	CITADEL BROADCASTING COMPANY
LA	PORT SULPHUR	KKND	106.7 FM Commercial	CITADEL BROADCASTING COMPANY
LA	RESERVE	WPRF	94.9 FM Commercial	CITADEL BROADCASTING COMPANY
LA	WASHINGTON	KNEK-FM	104.7 FM Commercial	CITADEL BROADCASTING COMPANY
LA	WASHINGTON	KNEK	1190 AM Station	CITADEL BROADCASTING COMPANY
MA	FAIRHAVEN	WFHN	107.1 FM Commercial	CITADEL BROADCASTING COMPANY
MA	FITCHBURG	WXLO	104.5 FM Commercial	CITADEL BROADCASTING COMPANY
MA	NEW BEDFORD	WBSM	1420 AM Station	CITADEL BROADCASTING COMPANY
MA	SOUTHBRIDGE	WWFX	100.1 FM Commercial	CITADEL BROADCASTING COMPANY
MA	SPRINGFIELD	WMAS-FM	94.7 FM Commercial	CITADEL BROADCASTING COMPANY
MA	SPRINGFIELD	WMAS	1450 AM Station	CITADEL BROADCASTING COMPANY
MA	WEBSTER	WORC-FM	98.9 FM Commercial	CITADEL BROADCASTING COMPANY
ME	AUGUSTA	WEZW	1400 AM Station	CITADEL BROADCASTING COMPANY
ME	AUGUSTA	WMME-FM	92.3 FM Commercial	CITADEL BROADCASTING COMPANY
ME	BIDDEFORD	WCYY	94.3 FM Commercial	CITADEL BROADCASTING COMPANY
ME	BRUNSWICK	WCLZ	98.9 FM Commercial	CITADEL BROADCASTING COMPANY
ME	KITTERY	WSHK	105.3 FM Commercial	CITADEL BROADCASTING COMPANY
ME	LEWISTON	WCYI	93.9 FM Commercial	CITADEL BROADCASTING COMPANY
ME	PORTLAND	WBLM	102.9 FM Commercial	CITADEL BROADCASTING COMPANY
ME	PORTLAND	WJBQ	97.9 FM Commercial	CITADEL BROADCASTING COMPANY
ME	PRESQUE ISLE	WBPW	96.9 FM Commercial	CITADEL BROADCASTING COMPANY
ME	PRESQUE ISLE	WQHR	96.1 FM Commercial	CITADEL BROADCASTING COMPANY
ME	PRESQUE ISLE	WOZI	101.9 FM Commercial	CITADEL BROADCASTING COMPANY
ME	WATERVILLE	WEBB	98.5 FM Commercial	CITADEL BROADCASTING COMPANY
ME	WATERVILLE	WTVL	1490 AM Station	CITADEL BROADCASTING COMPANY
MI	BAY CITY	WHNN	96.1 FM Commercial	CITADEL BROADCASTING COMPANY
MI	BAY CITY	WIOG	102.5 FM Commercial	CITADEL BROADCASTING COMPANY
MI	EAST LANSING	WVFN	730 AM Station	CITADEL BROADCASTING COMPANY
MI	EAST LANSING	WMMQ	94.9 FM Commercial	CITADEL BROADCASTING COMPANY
MI	EAST LANSING	WFMK	99.1 FM Commercial	CITADEL BROADCASTING COMPANY
MI	FLINT	WFBE	95.1 FM Commercial	CITADEL BROADCASTING COMPANY
MI	FLINT	WTRX	1330 AM Station	CITADEL BROADCASTING COMPANY
MI	GRAND RAPIDS	WBBL	1340 AM Station	CITADEL BROADCASTING COMPANY
MI	GRAND RAPIDS	WLAV-FM	96.9 FM Commercial	CITADEL BROADCASTING COMPANY
MI	GREENVILLE	WODJ	107.3 FM Commercial	CITADEL BROADCASTING COMPANY
MI	HOLLAND	WKLQ	94.5 FM Commercial	CITADEL BROADCASTING COMPANY
MI	LANSING	WITL-FM	100.7 FM Commercial	CITADEL BROADCASTING COMPANY

Radio Station Subsidiaries for Citadel Broadcasting Corp.				
State	City	Call Sign	Frequency	Subsidiary Name
MI	LANSING	WJIM	1240 AM Station	CITADEL BROADCASTING COMPANY
MI	LANSING	WJIM-FM	97.5 FM Commercial	CITADEL BROADCASTING COMPANY
MI	MIDLAND	WKQZ	93.3 FM Commercial	CITADEL BROADCASTING COMPANY
MI	PINCONNING	WYLZ	100.9 FM Commercial	CITADEL BROADCASTING COMPANY
MI	SAGINAW	WILZ	104.5 FM Commercial	CITADEL BROADCASTING COMPANY
MN	MORRIS	KKOK-FM	95.7 FM Commercial	IOWA CITY BROADCASTING COMPANY
NH	DOVER	WOKQ	97.5 FM Commercial	CITADEL BROADCASTING COMPANY
NH	HAMPTON	WSAK	102.1 FM Commercial	CITADEL BROADCASTING COMPANY
NH	MT. WASHINGTON	WHOM	94.9 FM Commercial	CITADEL BROADCASTING COMPANY
NH	NORTH CONWAY	WPKQ	103.7 FM Commercial	CITADEL BROADCASTING COMPANY
NM	ALBUQUERQUE	KRST	92.3 FM Commercial	CITADEL BROADCASTING COMPANY
NM	ALBUQUERQUE	KKOB-FM	93.3 FM Commercial	CITADEL BROADCASTING COMPANY
NM	ALBUQUERQUE	KKOB	770 AM Station	CITADEL BROADCASTING COMPANY
NM	ALBUQUERQUE	KMGA	99.5 FM Commercial	CITADEL BROADCASTING COMPANY
NM	ALBUQUERQUE	KNML	610 AM Station	CITADEL BROADCASTING COMPANY
NM	ALBUQUERQUE	KBZU	96.3 FM Commercial	CITADEL BROADCASTING COMPANY
NM	ALBUQUERQUE	KTZO	103.3 FM Commercial	CITADEL BROADCASTING COMPANY
NM	LOS RANCHOS	KTBL	1050 AM Station	CITADEL BROADCASTING COMPANY
NV	CARSON CITY	KBUL-FM	98.1 FM Commercial	CITADEL BROADCASTING COMPANY
NV	RENO	KKOH	780 AM Station	CITADEL BROADCASTING COMPANY
NV	RENO	KNEV	95.5 FM Commercial	CITADEL BROADCASTING COMPANY
NY	BINGHAMTON	WNBF	1290 AM Station	CITADEL BROADCASTING COMPANY
NY	BINGHAMTON	WHWK	98.1 FM Commercial	CITADEL BROADCASTING COMPANY
NY	BINGHAMTON	WAAL	99.1 FM Commercial	CITADEL BROADCASTING COMPANY
NY	BINGHAMTON	WYOS	1360 AM Station	CITADEL BROADCASTING COMPANY
NY	BUFFALO	WMNY	1120 AM Station	CITADEL BROADCASTING COMPANY
NY	BUFFALO	WHTT-FM	104.1 FM Commercial	CITADEL BROADCASTING COMPANY
NY	BUFFALO	WGRF	96.9 FM Commercial	CITADEL BROADCASTING COMPANY
NY	BUFFALO	WEDG	103.3 FM Commercial	CITADEL BROADCASTING COMPANY
NY	CHENANGO BRIDGE	WWYL	104.1 FM Commercial	CITADEL BROADCASTING COMPANY
NY	CORTLAND	WIII	99.9 FM Commercial	CITADEL BROADCASTING COMPANY
NY	CORTLAND	WKRT	920 AM Station	CITADEL BROADCASTING COMPANY
NY	MANLIUS	WAQX-FM	95.7 FM Commercial	CITADEL BROADCASTING COMPANY
NY	MONTAUK	WMOS	104.7 FM Commercial	CITADEL BROADCASTING COMPANY
NY	NIAGARA FALLS	WHLD	1270 AM Station	CITADEL BROADCASTING COMPANY
NY	SYRACUSE	WLTI	105.9 FM Commercial	CITADEL BROADCASTING COMPANY
NY	SYRACUSE	WNTQ	93.1 FM Commercial	CITADEL BROADCASTING COMPANY
NY	SYRACUSE	WNSS	1260 AM Station	CITADEL BROADCASTING COMPANY
OK	BETHANY	WWLS-FM	104.9 FM Commercial	CITADEL BROADCASTING COMPANY
OK	EDMOND	KKWD	97.9 FM Commercial	CITADEL BROADCASTING COMPANY
OK	KINGFISHER	KSYY	105.3 FM Commercial	CITADEL BROADCASTING COMPANY
OK	MOORE	WWLS	640 AM Station	CITADEL BROADCASTING COMPANY
OK	OKLAHOMA CITY	WKY	930 AM Station	CITADEL BROADCASTING COMPANY
OK	OKLAHOMA CITY	KATT-FM	100.5 FM Commercial	CITADEL BROADCASTING COMPANY
OK	OKLAHOMA CITY	KYIS	98.9 FM Commercial	CITADEL BROADCASTING COMPANY
PA	ALLENTOWN	WLEV	100.7 FM Commercial	CITADEL BROADCASTING COMPANY
PA	CARLISLE	WCAT-FM	102.3 FM Commercial	CITADEL BROADCASTING COMPANY
PA	EASTON	WCTO	96.1 FM Commercial	CITADEL BROADCASTING COMPANY
PA	HAZLETON	WBSX	97.9 FM Commercial	CITADEL BROADCASTING COMPANY
PA	MOUNTAIN TOP	WBHT	97.1 FM Commercial	CITADEL BROADCASTING COMPANY
PA	OLYPHANT	WBHD	95.7 FM Commercial	CITADEL BROADCASTING COMPANY
PA	SCRANTON	WARM	590 AM Station	CITADEL BROADCASTING COMPANY
PA	WILKES-BARRE	WMGS	92.9 FM Commercial	CITADEL BROADCASTING COMPANY
PA	YORK	WQXA-FM	105.7 FM Commercial	CITADEL BROADCASTING COMPANY
PA	YORK	WQXA	1250 AM Station	CITADEL BROADCASTING COMPANY
RI	MIDDLETOWN	WKKB	100.3 FM Commercial	CITADEL BROADCASTING COMPANY
RI	PROVIDENCE	WWLI	105.1 FM Commercial	CITADEL BROADCASTING COMPANY
RI	PROVIDENCE	WSKO	790 AM Station	CITADEL BROADCASTING COMPANY
RI	PROVIDENCE	WPRO-FM	92.3 FM Commercial	CITADEL BROADCASTING COMPANY
RI	PROVIDENCE	WPRO	630 AM Station	CITADEL BROADCASTING COMPANY
RI	WAKEFIELD-PEACEDALE	WSKO-FM	99.7 FM Commercial	CITADEL BROADCASTING COMPANY
SC	CHARLESTON	WXTC	1390 AM Station	CITADEL BROADCASTING COMPANY
SC	CHARLESTON	WSUY	96.9 FM Commercial	CITADEL BROADCASTING COMPANY
SC	CHARLESTON	WTMA	1250 AM Station	CITADEL BROADCASTING COMPANY

\multicolumn{5}{c}{Radio Station Subsidiaries for Citadel Broadcasting Corp.}				

State	City	Call Sign	Frequency	Subsidiary Name
SC	CHARLESTON	WSSX-FM	95.1 FM Commercial	CITADEL BROADCASTING COMPANY
SC	COLUMBIA	WISW	1320 AM Station	CITADEL BROADCASTING COMPANY
SC	COLUMBIA	WOMG	103.1 FM Commercial	CITADEL BROADCASTING COMPANY
SC	DORCHESTER TERR.-BRE	WTMZ	910 AM Station	CITADEL BROADCASTING COMPANY
SC	LEXINGTON	WLXC	98.5 FM Commercial	CITADEL BROADCASTING COMPANY
SC	ORANGEBURG	WTCB	106.7 FM Commercial	CITADEL BROADCASTING COMPANY
SC	RAVENEL	WMGL	101.7 FM Commercial	CITADEL BROADCASTING COMPANY
SC	ST. GEORGE	WNKT	107.5 FM Commercial	CITADEL BROADCASTING COMPANY
SC	SUMMERVILLE	WWWZ	93.3 FM Commercial	CITADEL BROADCASTING COMPANY
TN	BLOUNTVILLE	WGOC	640 AM Station	CITADEL BROADCASTING COMPANY
TN	CHATTANOOGA	WSKZ	106.5 FM Commercial	CITADEL BROADCASTING COMPANY
TN	CHATTANOOGA	WGOW	1150 AM Station	CITADEL BROADCASTING COMPANY
TN	EAST RIDGE	WOGT	107.9 FM Commercial	CITADEL BROADCASTING COMPANY
TN	GALLATIN	WGFX	104.5 FM Commercial	CITADEL BROADCASTING COMPANY
TN	JOHNSON CITY	WJCW	910 AM Station	CITADEL BROADCASTING COMPANY
TN	JOHNSON CITY	WQUT	101.5 FM Commercial	CITADEL BROADCASTING COMPANY
TN	KINGSPORT	WKOS	104.9 FM Commercial	CITADEL BROADCASTING COMPANY
TN	KINGSPORT	WKIN	1320 AM Station	CITADEL BROADCASTING COMPANY
TN	KNOXVILLE	WNOX	990 AM Station	CITADEL BROADCASTING COMPANY
TN	KNOXVILLE	WIVK-FM	107.7 FM Commercial	CITADEL BROADCASTING COMPANY
TN	LOUDON	WNOX-FM	99.1 FM Commercial	CITADEL BROADCASTING COMPANY
TN	MEMPHIS	WGKX	105.9 FM Commercial	CITADEL BROADCASTING COMPANY
TN	MILLINGTON	WSRR-FM	98.1 FM Commercial	CITADEL BROADCASTING COMPANY
TN	MUNFORD	WJZN	98.9 FM Commercial	CITADEL BROADCASTING COMPANY
TN	NASHVILLE	WKDF	103.3 FM Commercial	CITADEL BROADCASTING COMPANY
TN	OLIVER SPRINGS	WYIL-FM	98.7 FM Commercial	CITADEL BROADCASTING COMPANY
TN	SODDY-DAISY	WGOW-FM	102.3 FM Commercial	CITADEL BROADCASTING COMPANY
UT	MURRAY	KJQS	1230 AM Station	CITADEL BROADCASTING COMPANY
UT	OGDEN	KBER	101.1 FM Commercial	CITADEL BROADCASTING COMPANY
UT	OREM	KENZ	107.5 FM Commercial	CITADEL BROADCASTING COMPANY
UT	SALT LAKE CITY	KBEE-FM	98.7 FM Commercial	CITADEL BROADCASTING COMPANY
UT	SALT LAKE CITY	KFNZ	1320 AM Station	CITADEL BROADCASTING COMPANY
UT	SALT LAKE CITY	KUBL-FM	93.3 FM Commercial	CITADEL BROADCASTING COMPANY
UT	SALT LAKE CITY	KBEE	860 AM Station	CITADEL BROADCASTING COMPANY
WA	CHENEY	KEYF-FM	101.1 FM Commercial	CITADEL BROADCASTING COMPANY
WA	DISHMAN	KEYF	1050 AM Station	CITADEL BROADCASTING COMPANY
WA	SPOKANE	KGA	1510 AM Station	CITADEL BROADCASTING COMPANY
WA	SPOKANE	KJRB	790 AM Station	CITADEL BROADCASTING COMPANY
WA	SPOKANE	KDRK-FM	93.7 FM Commercial	CITADEL BROADCASTING COMPANY
WA	SPOKANE	KZBD	105.7 FM Commercial	CITADEL BROADCASTING COMPANY
WA	SPOKANE	KYWL	103.9 FM Commercial	CITADEL BROADCASTING COMPANY

\multicolumn{4}{c}{TV Station Subsidiaries for Citadel Broadcasting Corp.}			

Call Sign	Channel and Type	Subsidiary Name	Area of Service
WOI-TV	5 TV Commercial	CAPITAL COMMUNICATIONS COMPANY, INC.	AMES, IA
KCAU-TV	9 TV Commercial	CITADEL COMMUNICATIONS CO.LTD.	SIOUX CITY, IA
KLKE	24 TV Commercial	CITADEL COMMUNICATIONS, L.L.C.	ALBION, NE
KLKN	8 TV Commercial	CITADEL COMMUNICATIONS, L.L.C.	LINCOLN, NE

Clear Channel Communications Inc.

Address:	200 E. Basse Rd. San Antonio, TX 78209	Stock Symbol: Telephone: Fax:	CCU 210-822-2828 210-822-2299
Total Employees:	36,500	Website:	www.clearchannel.com

Huge fines, more bad publicity and illness have rocked radio giant Clear Channel Communications Inc. over the past year, but despite all the bad news, the company's bankers are still smiling.

Clear Channel founder and chief executive officer Lowry Mays, 68, checked into a hospital in May to remove a blood clot from his brain and has yet to fully recover. In June, the company agreed to pay a record $1.75 million to settle broadcast indecency complaints. And most recently, the company was sued for refusing to place an anti-war advertisement on one of its Times Square billboards in New York City.

Despite all that, the company posted a slight increase it in its second-quarter 2004 Net Income (Net Loss). Clear Channel's second quarter profit was $254 million. And it continues to be a cash machine, bringing in nearly $4.5 billion in revenue in the first half of the year.

Those profits can be traced directly to Lowry Mays's hardnosed approach to the radio business.

"If anyone said we were in the radio business, it wouldn't be someone from our company," Mays told Fortune magazine in a now-notorious interview. "We're not in the business of providing news and information. We're not in the business of providing well-researched music. We're simply in the business of selling our customers' products."

Mays' matter-of-fact business philosophy makes clear what many critics of the company allege: that the radio giant is interested in the bottom line, not its responsibility to the public in its stewardship of publicly owned airwaves. Even pro-deregulation FCC Chairman Michael Powell has expressed concern about consolidation in the radio industry.

Clear Channel is a regulatory phenomenon—or more accurately, a deregulatory phenomenon. It was born in 1972 when Mays and Red McCombs formed San Antonio Broadcasting Company to acquire an FM radio station in Texas. Three years later, they acquired their first "clear channel" station, meaning it was on a frequency reserved exclusively for its own use and broadcast nationwide. The company grew steadily through the 1980s and 1990s, but the expansion was nothing compared to what happened after the Telecommunications Act of 1996. The act eliminated national ownership limits on radio stations, and drastically reduced them in individual markets. Clear Channel acquired the bulk of its empire in two huge transactions. In 1998, it paid $4.4 billion for Jacor Communications and two years later, its $15.9 billion acquisition of AMFM Inc. made it the No. 1 radio broadcaster. As of 2005, the company reported 1194 radio stations and $3.5 billion in revenue from radio operations. It broadcasts in all 50 states and claims 110 million listeners every week.

The company is also one of the nation's largest outdoor advertising company and has been expanding overseas.

Some critics have called Clear Channel the poster child for why consolidation of media is a bad idea, mostly from a diversity standpoint. Critics also allege that Clear Channel cuts cost at every opportunity, often hurting news divisions in the process. The company received a black eye in Minot, North Dakota, where it owns six of seven local radio stations. Clear Channel often centralizes programming, far from where it is being broadcast. None of the stations picked up the phone when authorities sought to warn residents of a dangerous ammonia spill, according to police. The company disputes the allegations.

Clear Channel has also been criticized for its music promotion practices where independent music promoters pay to receive airplay for songs. (The company has said it would halt the practice.) Finally, Clear Channel has raised concerns for using its radio stations as bullhorns promoting the war in Iraq.

—John Dunbar

August 19, 2004

Sources: Fortune Magazine, Clear Channel Communications Inc. Web site, Form 10-K.

Clear Channel Communications Inc. Recent Financial Information		
Year	Revenue	Net Income (Net Loss)
2000	$5,345,306,000	$248,808,000
2001	$7,970,003,000	($1,144,026,000)
2002	$8,421,055,000	($16,053,703,000)
2003	$8,930,899,000	$1,145,591,000

Clear Channel Communications Inc. Board of Directors				
Name	Position	Relevant Stock		Qty
Mays, L	Chairman		CCU	31,840,668
Mays, Mark	Director		CCU	10,647,471
Mays, Randall	Director		CCU	6,032,777
Feld, Alan	Director		CCU	47,329
Hicks, Thomas	Director		CCU	37,733,292
Lewis, Perry	Director		CCU	179,332
McCombs, Billy	Director		CCU	11,182,481
Riggins, Phyllis	Director		CCU	3,850
Strauss, Theodore	Director		CCU	237,975
Watts, Julius	Director		CCU	1,500
Williams, John	Director		CCU	36,089

Clear Channel Communications Inc. Corporate Officers			
Name	Position	Salary	Bonuses
Mays, L.	Chairman (on leave from CEO position)	$1,012,838	$1,000,000
Mays, Mark	Interim CEO, President, COO and Director	$697,093	$1,000,000
Mays, Randall	EVP, CFO, and Director	$692,617	$1,000,000
Wilson, David	SVP and CIO	N/A	N/A
Wyker, Kenneth	SVP, General Counsel, and Secretary	N/A	N/A
Becker, Brian	CEO, Entertainment	$495,983	$325,000

Breakdown of contributions by political party for Clear Channel Communications Inc.

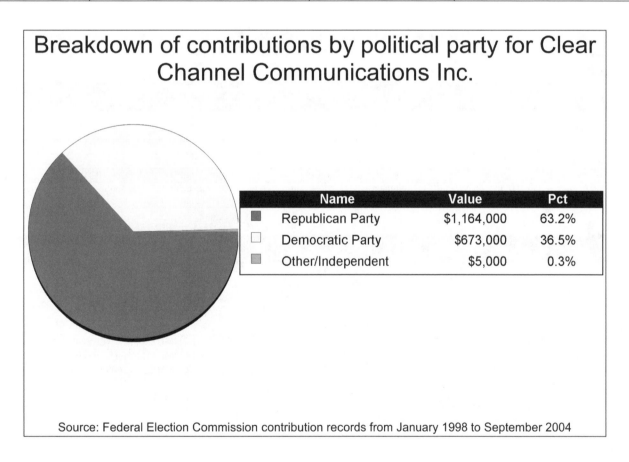

Name	Value	Pct
Republican Party	$1,164,000	63.2%
Democratic Party	$673,000	36.5%
Other/Independent	$5,000	0.3%

Source: Federal Election Commission contribution records from January 1998 to September 2004

Top 10 Recipients of Contributions Sourced to Clear Channel Communications Inc.

Recipient	Amount
National Republican Party Committees	$593,000
National Democratic Party Committees	$355,000
President George W Bush (R)	$114,000
Michael McCaul (R-TX)	$38,000
Sen Hillary Rodham Clinton (D-NY)	$29,000
Sen Charles E Schumer (D-NY)	$19,000
Rep J Dennis Hastert (R-IL)	$16,000
Sen John F Kerry (D-MA)	$16,000
Rep Martin Frost (D-TX)	$15,000
Rep Thomas Dale Delay (R-TX)	$15,000
Total:	$1,210,000

Source: Federal Election Commission contribution records from January 1998 to September 2004

Clear Channel Communications Inc. Lobbying Expenditures by Year

Year	Amount
1998	$60,000
1999	$120,000
2000	$120,000
2001	$12,000
2002	$68,675
2003	$2,280,000
2004	$160,000
Total:	$2,820,675

Source: U.S. Senate Office of Public Records lobbying disclosure records from January 1998 to June 30th, 2004.

Clear Channel Communications Inc. Sponsored Trips for Congressional Staff

Congressional Office	Number of Trips	$ Amount
Rep Eliot L Engel (D-NY)	1	$1,601
Rep John Mondy Shimkus (R-IL)	1	$1,547
Rep Karen McCarthy (D-MO)	1	$1,344
Rep Clement Leroy Otter (R-ID)	1	$1,296
Total:	4	$5,788

Source: Congressional office travel records for members of the Senate Committee on Commerce, Science & Transportation and the House Committee on Energy and Commerce for the period of January 2000 to March 2004.

Radio Station Subsidiaries for Clear Channel Communications Inc.

State	City	Call Sign	Frequency	Subsidiary Name
AK	ANCHORAGE	KASH-FM	107.5 FM Commercial	CAPSTAR TX LIMITED PARTNERSHIP
AK	ANCHORAGE	KBFX	100.5 FM Commercial	CAPSTAR TX LIMITED PARTNERSHIP
AK	ANCHORAGE	KYMG	98.9 FM Commercial	CAPSTAR TX LIMITED PARTNERSHIP
AK	ANCHORAGE	KGOT	101.3 FM Commercial	CAPSTAR TX LIMITED PARTNERSHIP
AK	ANCHORAGE	KENI	650 AM Station	CAPSTAR TX LIMITED PARTNERSHIP
AK	ANCHORAGE	KTZN	550 AM Station	CAPSTAR TX LIMITED PARTNERSHIP
AK	FAIRBANKS	KKED	104.7 FM Commercial	CAPSTAR TX LIMITED PARTNERSHIP
AK	FAIRBANKS	KIAK-FM	102.5 FM Commercial	CAPSTAR TX LIMITED PARTNERSHIP
AK	FAIRBANKS	KIAK	970 AM Station	CAPSTAR TX LIMITED PARTNERSHIP
AK	FAIRBANKS	KAKQ-FM	101.1 FM Commercial	CAPSTAR TX LIMITED PARTNERSHIP
AL	ALEXANDER CITY	WSTH-FM	106.1 FM Commercial	CLEAR CHANNEL BROADCASTING LICENSES, INC.
AL	BIRMINGHAM	WMJJ	96.5 FM Commercial	CAPSTAR TX LIMITED PARTNERSHIP
AL	BIRMINGHAM	WERC	960 AM Station	CAPSTAR TX LIMITED PARTNERSHIP
AL	CARROLLTON	WZBQ	94.1 FM Commercial	CAPSTAR TX LIMITED PARTNERSHIP
AL	DECATUR	WHOS	800 AM Station	CAPSTAR TX LIMITED PARTNERSHIP
AL	DECATUR	WDRM	102.1 FM Commercial	CAPSTAR TX LIMITED PARTNERSHIP
AL	FAYETTE	WTXT	98.1 FM Commercial	CAPSTAR TX LIMITED PARTNERSHIP
AL	FORT MITCHELL	WAGH	98.3 FM Commercial	CLEAR CHANNEL BROADCASTING LICENSES, INC.
AL	GADSDEN	WAAX	570 AM Station	CAPSTAR TX LIMITED PARTNERSHIP
AL	GADSDEN	WQEN	103.7 FM Commercial	CAPSTAR TX LIMITED PARTNERSHIP
AL	GLENCOE	WGMZ	93.1 FM Commercial	CAPSTAR TX LIMITED PARTNERSHIP
AL	HARTSELLE	WTAK-FM	106.1 FM Commercial	CAPSTAR TX LIMITED PARTNERSHIP
AL	HUNTSVILLE	WBHP	1230 AM Station	CAPSTAR TX LIMITED PARTNERSHIP
AL	JASPER	WDXB	102.5 FM Commercial	CAPSTAR TX LIMITED PARTNERSHIP

		Radio Station Subsidiaries for Clear Channel Communications Inc.		
State	City	Call Sign	Frequency	Subsidiary Name
AL	LUVERNE	WQLD	104.3 FM Commercial	CAPSTAR TX LIMITED PARTNERSHIP
AL	MERIDIANVILLE	WXQW	94.1 FM Commercial	CAPSTAR TX LIMITED PARTNERSHIP
AL	MILLBROOK	WMCZ	97.1 FM Commercial	CAPSTAR TX LIMITED PARTNERSHIP
AL	MOBILE	WNTM	710 AM Station	CLEAR CHANNEL BROADCASTING LICENSES, INC.
AL	MOBILE	WMXC	99.9 FM Commercial	CLEAR CHANNEL BROADCASTING LICENSES, INC.
AL	MOBILE	WRKH	96.1 FM Commercial	CLEAR CHANNEL BROADCASTING LICENSES, INC.
AL	MOBILE	WKSJ-FM	94.9 FM Commercial	CLEAR CHANNEL BROADCASTING LICENSES, INC.
AL	MUSCLE SHOALS	WVNA-FM	105.5 FM Commercial	CLEAR CHANNEL BROADCASTING LICENSES, INC.
AL	MUSCLE SHOALS	WLAY	1450 AM Station	CLEAR CHANNEL BROADCASTING LICENSES, INC.
AL	PHENIX CITY	WGSY	100.1 FM Commercial	CLEAR CHANNEL BROADCASTING LICENSES, INC.
AL	PHENIX CITY/COLUMBUS	WHAL	1460 AM Station	CLEAR CHANNEL BROADCASTING LICENSES, INC.
AL	RUSSELLVILLE	WMXV	103.5 FM Commercial	CLEAR CHANNEL BROADCASTING LICENSES, INC.
AL	SMITHS	WBFA	101.3 FM Commercial	CLEAR CHANNEL BROADCASTING LICENSES, INC.
AL	TRINITY	WWXQ	92.5 FM Commercial	CAPSTAR TX LIMITED PARTNERSHIP
AL	TROY	WZHT	105.7 FM Commercial	CAPSTAR TX LIMITED PARTNERSHIP
AL	TRUSSVILLE	WENN	105.9 FM Commercial	CAPSTAR TX LIMITED PARTNERSHIP
AL	TUSCALOOSA	WACT	1420 AM Station	CAPSTAR TX LIMITED PARTNERSHIP
AL	TUSCALOOSA	WRTR	105.5 FM Commercial	CAPSTAR TX LIMITED PARTNERSHIP
AL	TUSCUMBIA	WLAY-FM	100.3 FM Commercial	CLEAR CHANNEL BROADCASTING LICENSES, INC.
AL	TUSCUMBIA	WVNA	1590 AM Station	CLEAR CHANNEL BROADCASTING LICENSES, INC.
AR	ASHDOWN	KMJI	93.3 FM Commercial	CLEAR CHANNEL BROADCASTING LICENSES, INC.
AR	BENTON	KHKN	106.7 FM Commercial	CLEAR CHANNEL BROADCASTING LICENSES, INC.
AR	CONWAY	KMJX	105.1 FM Commercial	CLEAR CHANNEL BROADCASTING LICENSES, INC.
AR	FAYETTEVILLE	KKIX	103.9 FM Commercial	CAPSTAR TX LIMITED PARTNERSHIP
AR	FAYETTEVILLE	KEZA	107.9 FM Commercial	CAPSTAR TX LIMITED PARTNERSHIP
AR	FORT SMITH	KMAG	99.1 FM Commercial	CAPSTAR TX LIMITED PARTNERSHIP
AR	FORT SMITH	KYHN	1320 AM Station	CAPSTAR TX LIMITED PARTNERSHIP
AR	FT. SMITH	KWHN	1650 AM Station	CAPSTAR TX LIMITED PARTNERSHIP
AR	HARRISBURG	KBZR	95.9 FM Commercial	CLEAR CHANNEL BROADCASTING LICENSES, INC.
AR	JACKSONVILLE	KDJE	100.3 FM Commercial	CLEAR CHANNEL BROADCASTING LICENSES, INC.
AR	JONESBORO	KNEA	970 AM Station	CLEAR CHANNEL BROADCASTING LICENSES, INC.
AR	JONESBORO	KFIN	107.9 FM Commercial	CAPSTAR TX LIMITED PARTNERSHIP
AR	JONESBORO	KBTM	1230 AM Station	CAPSTAR TX LIMITED PARTNERSHIP
AR	JONESBORO	KIYS	101.9 FM Commercial	CAPSTAR TX LIMITED PARTNERSHIP
AR	LITTLE ROCK	KSSN	95.7 FM Commercial	CLEAR CHANNEL BROADCASTING LICENSES, INC.
AR	LOWELL	KMXF	101.9 FM Commercial	CAPSTAR TX LIMITED PARTNERSHIP
AR	MAUMELLE	KMSX	94.9 FM Commercial	CLEAR CHANNEL BROADCASTING LICENSES, INC.
AR	TEXARKANA	KYGL	106.3 FM Commercial	CAPSTAR TX LIMITED PARTNERSHIP
AR	TEXARKANA	KOSY	790 AM Station	CAPSTAR TX LIMITED PARTNERSHIP
AZ	CHINLE	KFXR-FM	107.3 FM Commercial	CLEAR CHANNEL BROADCASTING LICENSES, INC.
AZ	GREEN VALLEY	KTZR-FM	97.1 FM Commercial	CAPSTAR TX LIMITED PARTNERSHIP
AZ	MARANA	KOHT	98.3 FM Commercial	CLEAR CHANNEL BROADCASTING LICENSES, INC.
AZ	MESA	KZZP	104.7 FM Commercial	CITICASTERS LICENSES, L.P.
AZ	PHOENIX	KGME	910 AM Station	AMFM RADIO LICENSES, L.L.C.
AZ	PHOENIX	KFYI	550 AM Station	AMFM RADIO LICENSES, L.L.C.
AZ	PHOENIX	KNIX-FM	102.5 FM Commercial	CLEAR CHANNEL BROADCASTING LICENSES, INC.
AZ	PHOENIX	KMXP	96.9 FM Commercial	CITICASTERS LICENSES, L.P.
AZ	PHOENIX	KYOT-FM	95.5 FM Commercial	AMFM RADIO LICENSES, L.L.C.
AZ	PHOENIX	KOY	1230 AM Station	AMFM RADIO LICENSES, L.L.C.
AZ	PHOENIX	KESZ	99.9 FM Commercial	CLEAR CHANNEL BROADCASTING LICENSES, INC.
AZ	SOUTH TUCSON	KXEW	1600 AM Station	CLEAR CHANNEL BROADCASTING LICENSES, INC.
AZ	TUCSON	KWFM	1450 AM Station	CLEAR CHANNEL BROADCASTING LICENSES, INC.
AZ	TUCSON	KNST	790 AM Station	CAPSTAR TX LIMITED PARTNERSHIP
AZ	TUCSON	KRQQ	93.7 FM Commercial	CAPSTAR TX LIMITED PARTNERSHIP
AZ	TUCSON	KWMT-FM	92.9 FM Commercial	CAPSTAR TX LIMITED PARTNERSHIP
AZ	WILLCOX	KWCX-FM	104.9 FM Commercial	LAKESHORE MEDIA, LLC
AZ	YUMA	KBLU	560 AM Station	CAPSTAR TX LIMITED PARTNERSHIP
AZ	YUMA	KTTI	95.1 FM Commercial	CAPSTAR TX LIMITED PARTNERSHIP
AZ	YUMA	KYJT	100.9 FM Commercial	CAPSTAR TX LIMITED PARTNERSHIP
CA	APPLE VALLEY	KIXW	960 AM Station	CAPSTAR TX LIMITED PARTNERSHIP
CA	APPLE VALLEY	KZXY-FM	102.3 FM Commercial	CAPSTAR TX LIMITED PARTNERSHIP
CA	AUBURN	KHYL	101.1 FM Commercial	AMFM RADIO LICENSES, L.L.C.
CA	BAKERSFIELD	KDFO	800 AM Station	CLEAR CHANNEL BROADCASTING LICENSES, INC.
CA	BAKERSFIELD	KKXX-FM	96.5 FM Commercial	CLEAR CHANNEL BROADCASTING LICENSES, INC.

State	City	Call Sign	Frequency	Subsidiary Name
\multicolumn{5}{c}{Radio Station Subsidiaries for Clear Channel Communications Inc.}

State	City	Call Sign	Frequency	Subsidiary Name
CA	BAKERSFIELD	KGET	970 AM Station	CLEVELAND RADIO LICENSES, LLC
CA	CARLSBAD	KUSS	95.7 FM Commercial	CITICASTERS LICENSES, L.P.
CA	CARPINTERIA	KSBL	101.7 FM Commercial	CITICASTERS LICENSES, L.P.
CA	CHICO	KMXI	95.1 FM Commercial	CAPSTAR TX LIMITED PARTNERSHIP
CA	CHICO	KPAY	1290 AM Station	CAPSTAR TX LIMITED PARTNERSHIP
CA	DELANO	KKDJ	105.3 FM Commercial	CLEAR CHANNEL BROADCASTING LICENSES, INC.
CA	DELANO	KDFO-FM	98.5 FM Commercial	CLEAR CHANNEL BROADCASTING LICENSES, INC.
CA	DINUBA	KRDU	1130 AM Station	CAPSTAR TX LIMITED PARTNERSHIP
CA	DINUBA	KSOF	98.9 FM Commercial	CAPSTAR TX LIMITED PARTNERSHIP
CA	EL CAJON	KHTS-FM	93.3 FM Commercial	CITICASTERS LICENSES, L.P.
CA	ELLWOOD	KSPE-FM	94.5 FM Commercial	CITICASTERS LICENSES, L.P.
CA	FOWLER	KEZL	96.7 FM Commercial	CAPSTAR TX LIMITED PARTNERSHIP
CA	FRESNO	KALZ	102.7 FM Commercial	CAPSTAR TX LIMITED PARTNERSHIP
CA	FRESNO	KCBL	1340 AM Station	CAPSTAR TX LIMITED PARTNERSHIP
CA	GEORGE	KATJ-FM	100.7 FM Commercial	CAPSTAR TX LIMITED PARTNERSHIP
CA	GREENACRES	KRAB	106.1 FM Commercial	CLEAR CHANNEL BROADCASTING LICENSES, INC.
CA	GROVER BEACH	KURQ	107.3 FM Commercial	CLEAR CHANNEL BROADCASTING LICENSES, INC.
CA	HANFORD	KRZR	103.7 FM Commercial	CAPSTAR TX LIMITED PARTNERSHIP
CA	LANCASTER	KAVL	610 AM Station	CITICASTERS LICENSES, L.P.
CA	LOMPOC	KSMY	106.7 FM Commercial	CLEAR CHANNEL BROADCASTING LICENSES, INC.
CA	LOS ANGELES	KLAC	570 AM Station	AMFM RADIO LICENSES, L.L.C.
CA	LOS ANGELES	KHHT	92.3 FM Commercial	AMFM RADIO LICENSES, L.L.C.
CA	LOS ANGELES	KYSR	98.7 FM Commercial	AMFM RADIO LICENSES, L.L.C.
CA	LOS ANGELES	KBIG-FM	104.3 FM Commercial	AMFM RADIO LICENSES, L.L.C.
CA	LOS ANGELES	KIIS-FM	102.7 FM Commercial	CITICASTERS LICENSES, L.P.
CA	LOS ANGELES	KXTA	1150 AM Station	CITICASTERS LICENSES, L.P.
CA	LOS ANGELES	KOST	103.5 FM Commercial	CAPSTAR TX LIMITED PARTNERSHIP
CA	LOS ANGELES	KFI	640 AM Station	CAPSTAR TX LIMITED PARTNERSHIP
CA	LOS OSOS-BAYWOOD PAR	KSTT-FM	101.3 FM Commercial	CLEAR CHANNEL BROADCASTING LICENSES, INC.
CA	LUCERNE VALLEY	KIXA	106.5 FM Commercial	CAPSTAR TX LIMITED PARTNERSHIP
CA	MANTECA	KMRQ	96.7 FM Commercial	CAPSTAR TX LIMITED PARTNERSHIP
CA	MARINA	KTOM-FM	92.7 FM Commercial	CLEAR CHANNEL BROADCASTING LICENSES, INC.
CA	MODESTO	KFIV	1360 AM Station	CAPSTAR TX LIMITED PARTNERSHIP
CA	MODESTO	KJSN	102.3 FM Commercial	CAPSTAR TX LIMITED PARTNERSHIP
CA	MOJAVE	KVVS	97.7 FM Commercial	CITICASTERS LICENSES, L.P.
CA	MOJAVE	KTPI	1340 AM Station	CLEAR CHANNEL BROADCASTING LICENSES, INC.
CA	OAKLAND	KABL	960 AM Station	AMFM RADIO LICENSES, L.L.C.
CA	OAKLAND	KNEW	910 AM Station	AMFM RADIO LICENSES, L.L.C.
CA	OROVILLE	KHHZ	97.7 FM Commercial	CLEAR CHANNEL BROADCASTING LICENSES, INC.
CA	OROVILLE	KEWE	1340 AM Station	CLEAR CHANNEL BROADCASTING LICENSES, INC.
CA	PACIFIC GROVE	KOCN	105.1 FM Commercial	CLEAR CHANNEL BROADCASTING LICENSES, INC.
CA	PARADISE	KHSL-FM	103.5 FM Commercial	CAPSTAR TX LIMITED PARTNERSHIP
CA	PATTERSON	KOSO	93.1 FM Commercial	CAPSTAR TX LIMITED PARTNERSHIP
CA	RANCHO CORDOVA	KSTE	650 AM Station	AMFM RADIO LICENSES, L.L.C.
CA	RIVERSIDE	KDIF	1440 AM Station	CITICASTERS LICENSES, L.P.
CA	RIVERSIDE	KGGI	99.1 FM Commercial	AMFM RADIO LICENSES, L.L.C.
CA	ROSAMOND	KOSS	105.5 FM Commercial	CLEAR CHANNEL BROADCASTING LICENSES, INC.
CA	SACRAMENTO	KFBK	1530 AM Station	AMFM RADIO LICENSES, L.L.C.
CA	SACRAMENTO	KGBY	92.5 FM Commercial	AMFM RADIO LICENSES, L.L.C.
CA	SALINAS	KZFX	1380 AM Station	CLEAR CHANNEL BROADCASTING LICENSES, INC.
CA	SALINAS	KPRC-FM	100.7 FM Commercial	CLEAR CHANNEL BROADCASTING LICENSES, INC.
CA	SALINAS	KDON-FM	102.5 FM Commercial	CLEAR CHANNEL BROADCASTING LICENSES, INC.
CA	SALINAS	KION	1460 AM Station	CLEAR CHANNEL BROADCASTING LICENSES, INC.
CA	SAN BERNARDINO	KKDD	1290 AM Station	AMFM RADIO LICENSES, L.L.C.
CA	SAN BERNARDINO	KTDD	1350 AM Station	CITICASTERS LICENSES, L.P.
CA	SAN DIEGO	KMYI	94.1 FM Commercial	CITICASTERS LICENSES, L.P.
CA	SAN DIEGO	KOGO	600 AM Station	CITICASTERS LICENSES, L.P.
CA	SAN DIEGO	KIOZ	105.3 FM Commercial	CITICASTERS LICENSES, L.P.
CA	SAN DIEGO	KPOP	1360 AM Station	CITICASTERS LICENSES, L.P.
CA	SAN DIEGO	KGB-FM	101.5 FM Commercial	CITICASTERS LICENSES, L.P.
CA	SAN FRANCISCO	KIOI	101.3 FM Commercial	AMFM RADIO LICENSES, L.L.C.
CA	SAN FRANCISCO	KYLD	94.9 FM Commercial	AMFM RADIO LICENSES, L.L.C.
CA	SAN FRANCISCO	KISQ	98.1 FM Commercial	AMFM RADIO LICENSES, L.L.C.

		Radio Station Subsidiaries for Clear Channel Communications Inc.		
State	City	Call Sign	Frequency	Subsidiary Name
CA	SAN FRANCISCO	KMEL	106.1 FM Commercial	AMFM RADIO LICENSES, L.L.C.
CA	SAN FRANCISCO	KKSF	103.7 FM Commercial	AMFM RADIO LICENSES, L.L.C.
CA	SAN JOSE	KUFX	98.5 FM Commercial	CITICASTERS LICENSES, L.P.
CA	SAN JOSE	KSJO	92.3 FM Commercial	CITICASTERS LICENSES, L.P.
CA	SAN LUIS OBISPO	KVEC	920 AM Station	CLEVELAND RADIO LICENSES, LLC
CA	SAN LUIS OBISPO	KSLY-FM	96.1 FM Commercial	CLEAR CHANNEL BROADCASTING LICENSES, INC.
CA	SANTA BARBARA	KBKO	1490 AM Station	CITICASTERS LICENSES, L.P.
CA	SANTA BARBARA	KTLK	1340 AM Station	CITICASTERS LICENSES, L.P.
CA	SANTA BARBARA	KTYD	99.9 FM Commercial	CITICASTERS LICENSES, L.P.
CA	SANTA BARBARA	KTMS	990 AM Station	CITICASTERS LICENSES, L.P.
CA	SANTA BARBARA	KIST-FM	107.7 FM Commercial	CITICASTERS LICENSES, L.P.
CA	SANTA MARIA	KSNI-FM	102.5 FM Commercial	CLEAR CHANNEL BROADCASTING LICENSES, INC.
CA	SANTA MARIA	KSMA	1240 AM Station	CLEAR CHANNEL BROADCASTING LICENSES, INC.
CA	SANTA MARIA	KXFM	99.1 FM Commercial	CLEAR CHANNEL BROADCASTING LICENSES, INC.
CA	STOCKTON	KUYL	1280 AM Station	CAPSTAR TX LIMITED PARTNERSHIP
CA	STOCKTON	KQOD	100.1 FM Commercial	CAPSTAR TX LIMITED PARTNERSHIP
CA	SUNNYVALE	KCNL	104.9 FM Commercial	CLEAR CHANNEL BROADCASTING LICENSES, INC.
CA	TEHACHAPI	KTPI-FM	103.1 FM Commercial	CLEAR CHANNEL BROADCASTING LICENSES, INC.
CA	TEMECULA	KMYT	94.5 FM Commercial	CLEAR CHANNEL BROADCASTING LICENSES, INC.
CA	TEMECULA	KGBB	103.3 FM Commercial	CLEAR CHANNEL BROADCASTING LICENSES, INC.
CA	THOUSAND OAKS	KIIS	850 AM Station	CITICASTERS LICENSES, L.P.
CA	VISALIA	KVBL	1400 AM Station	CAPSTAR TX LIMITED PARTNERSHIP
CA	VISALIA	KFSO-FM	92.9 FM Commercial	CAPSTAR TX LIMITED PARTNERSHIP
CA	YERMO	KRSX-FM	105.3 FM Commercial	CITICASTERS LICENSES, L.P.
CO	BOULDER	KBCO-FM	97.3 FM Commercial	CITICASTERS LICENSES, L.P.
CO	DENVER	KFMD	95.7 FM Commercial	CITICASTERS LICENSES, L.P.
CO	DENVER	KHOW	630 AM Station	CITICASTERS LICENSES, L.P.
CO	DENVER	KOA	850 AM Station	JACOR BROADCASTING OF COLORADO, INC.
CO	DENVER	KBPI	106.7 FM Commercial	JACOR BROADCASTING OF COLORADO, INC.
CO	DENVER	KRFX	103.5 FM Commercial	JACOR BROADCASTING OF COLORADO, INC.
CO	FORT COLLINS	KPAW	107.9 FM Commercial	JACOR BROADCASTING OF COLORADO, INC.
CO	FORT COLLINS	KIIX	1410 AM Station	JACOR BROADCASTING OF COLORADO, INC.
CO	FORT COLLINS	KTCL	93.3 FM Commercial	JACOR BROADCASTING OF COLORADO, INC.
CO	FOUNTAIN	KMOM	96.1 FM Commercial	AMFM RADIO LICENSES, LLC
CO	GREELEY	KSME	96.1 FM Commercial	JACOR BROADCASTING OF COLORADO, INC.
CO	PUEBLO	KCSJ	590 AM Station	CLEAR CHANNEL BROADCASTING LICENSES, INC.
CO	PUEBLO	KGHF	1350 AM Station	CLEAR CHANNEL BROADCASTING LICENSES, INC.
CO	PUEBLO	KVUU	99.9 FM Commercial	CAPSTAR TX LIMITED PARTNERSHIP
CO	PUEBLO	KCCY	96.9 FM Commercial	CAPSTAR TX LIMITED PARTNERSHIP
CO	PUEBLO	KDZA-FM	107.9 FM Commercial	CAPSTAR TX LIMITED PARTNERSHIP
CO	ROCKY FORD	KJQY	95.5 FM Commercial	CAPSTAR TX LIMITED PARTNERSHIP
CO	THORNTON	KKZN	760 AM Station	JACOR BROADCASTING OF COLORADO, INC.
CO	WELLINGTON	KCOL	600 AM Station	JACOR BROADCASTING OF COLORADO, INC.
CO	WIDEFIELD	KKLI	106.3 FM Commercial	CAPSTAR TX LIMITED PARTNERSHIP
CT	ENFIELD	WPKX	97.9 FM Commercial	CAPSTAR TX LIMITED PARTNERSHIP
CT	HAMDEN	WKCI-FM	101.3 FM Commercial	CLEAR CHANNEL BROADCASTING LICENSES, INC.
CT	HARTFORD	WHCN	105.9 FM Commercial	CAPSTAR TX LIMITED PARTNERSHIP
CT	HARTFORD	WPOP	1410 AM Station	CAPSTAR TX LIMITED PARTNERSHIP
CT	HARTFORD-MERIDEN	WKSS	95.7 FM Commercial	CAPSTAR TX LIMITED PARTNERSHIP
CT	NEW HAVEN	WELI	960 AM Station	CLEAR CHANNEL BROADCASTING LICENSES, INC.
CT	NEW HAVEN	WAVZ	1300 AM Station	CLEAR CHANNEL BROADCASTING LICENSES, INC.
CT	WATERBURY	WPHH	104.1 FM Commercial	CAPSTAR TX LIMITED PARTNERSHIP
CT	WATERBURY	WWYZ	92.5 FM Commercial	CAPSTAR TX LIMITED PARTNERSHIP
DC	WASHINGTON	WASH	97.1 FM Commercial	AMFM RADIO LICENSES, L.L.C.
DC	WASHINGTON	WMZQ-FM	98.7 FM Commercial	AMFM RADIO LICENSES, L.L.C.
DC	WASHINGTON	WIHT	99.5 FM Commercial	AMFM RADIO LICENSES, L.L.C.
DC	WASHINGTON	WBIG-FM	100.3 FM Commercial	AMFM RADIO LICENSES, L.L.C.
DC	WASHINGTON	WWRC	1260 AM Station	AMFM RADIO LICENSES, L.L.C.
DC	WASHINGTON	WWDC-FM	101.1 FM Commercial	AMFM RADIO LICENSES, L.L.C.
DC	WASHINGTON	WTEM	980 AM Station	AMFM RADIO LICENSES, L.L.C.
DE	BETHANY BEACH	WOSC	95.9 FM Commercial	CAPSTAR TX LIMITED PARTNERSHIP
DE	DOVER	WRDX	94.7 FM Commercial	CAPSTAR TX LIMITED PARTNERSHIP
DE	DOVER	WDOV	1410 AM Station	CAPSTAR TX LIMITED PARTNERSHIP
DE	FENWICK ISLAND	WLBW	92.1 FM Commercial	CAPSTAR TX LIMITED PARTNERSHIP

State	City	Call Sign	Frequency	Subsidiary Name
			Radio Station Subsidiaries for Clear Channel Communications Inc.	
DE	SMYRNA	WDSD	92.9 FM Commercial	CAPSTAR TX LIMITED PARTNERSHIP
DE	WILMINGTON	WWTX	1290 AM Station	CAPSTAR TX LIMITED PARTNERSHIP
FL	BRADENTON	WTBT	103.5 FM Commercial	CITICASTERS LICENSES, L.P.
FL	CALLAHAN	WPLA	93.3 FM Commercial	CLEAR CHANNEL BROADCASTING LICENSES, INC.
FL	CHARLOTTE HARBOR	WIKX	92.9 FM Commercial	CITICASTERS LICENSES, L.P.
FL	CLEARWATER	WBTP	95.7 FM Commercial	CLEAR CHANNEL BROADCASTING LICENSES, INC.
FL	CLEARWATER	WXTB	97.9 FM Commercial	CITICASTERS LICENSES, L.P.
FL	COCOA	WMMV	1350 AM Station	CAPSTAR TX LIMITED PARTNERSHIP
FL	COCOA	WLRQ-FM	99.3 FM Commercial	CAPSTAR TX LIMITED PARTNERSHIP
FL	COCOA BEACH	WTKS-FM	104.1 FM Commercial	CLEAR CHANNEL BROADCASTING LICENSES, INC.
FL	COCOA BEACH	WJRR	101.1 FM Commercial	CLEAR CHANNEL BROADCASTING LICENSES, INC.
FL	CORAL COVE	WSRZ-FM	107.9 FM Commercial	CITICASTERS LICENSES, L.P.
FL	ENGLEWOOD	WTZB	105.9 FM Commercial	CITICASTERS LICENSES, L.P.
FL	FORT LAUDERDALE	WMIB	103.5 FM Commercial	CLEAR CHANNEL BROADCASTING LICENSES, INC.
FL	FORT LAUDERDALE	WHYI-FM	100.7 FM Commercial	CLEAR CHANNEL BROADCASTING LICENSES, INC.
FL	FORT LAUDERDALE	WBGG-FM	105.9 FM Commercial	CLEAR CHANNEL BROADCASTING LICENSES, INC.
FL	FORT MYERS	WOLZ	95.3 FM Commercial	CLEAR CHANNEL BROADCASTING LICENSES, INC.
FL	FORT PIERCE	WKGR	98.7 FM Commercial	CLEAR CHANNEL BROADCASTING LICENSES, INC.
FL	FORT PIERCE	WLDI	95.5 FM Commercial	CLEAR CHANNEL BROADCASTING LICENSES, INC.
FL	GIFFORD	WSYR-FM	94.7 FM Commercial	CAPSTAR TX LIMITED PARTNERSHIP
FL	GREEN COVE SPRINGS	WJBT	92.7 FM Commercial	CITICASTERS LICENSES, L.P.
FL	HOBE SOUND	WOLL	105.5 FM Commercial	CLEAR CHANNEL BROADCASTING LICENSES, INC.
FL	JACKSONVILLE	WQIK-FM	99.1 FM Commercial	CITICASTERS LICENSES, L.P.
FL	JACKSONVILLE	WFXJ	930 AM Station	CLEAR CHANNEL BROADCASTING LICENSES, INC.
FL	JACKSONVILLE	WROO	107.3 FM Commercial	CLEAR CHANNEL BROADCASTING LICENSES, INC.
FL	KEY WEST	WKEY-FM	93.5 FM Commercial	CLEAR CHANNEL BROADCASTING LICENSES, INC.
FL	KEY WEST	WAIL	99.5 FM Commercial	CLEAR CHANNEL BROADCASTING LICENSES, INC.
FL	KEY WEST	WEOW	92.7 FM Commercial	CLEAR CHANNEL BROADCASTING LICENSES, INC.
FL	LEHIGH ACRES	WDRR	107.1 FM Commercial	CLEAR CHANNEL BROADCASTING LICENSES, INC.
FL	MELBOURNE	WMMB	1240 AM Station	CAPSTAR TX LIMITED PARTNERSHIP
FL	MELBOURNE	WBVD	95.1 FM Commercial	CAPSTAR TX LIMITED PARTNERSHIP
FL	MEXICO BEACH	WPBH	99.3 FM Commercial	CLEAR CHANNEL BROADCASTING LICENSES, INC.
FL	MIAMI	WRFX	940 AM Station	CLEAR CHANNEL BROADCASTING LICENSES, INC.
FL	MIAMI	WIOD	610 AM Station	CLEAR CHANNEL BROADCASTING LICENSES, INC.
FL	MIAMI BEACH	WLVE	93.9 FM Commercial	CLEAR CHANNEL BROADCASTING LICENSES, INC.
FL	MIAMI BEACH	WZTA	94.9 FM Commercial	CLEAR CHANNEL BROADCASTING LICENSES, INC.
FL	MIDWAY	WBWT	100.7 FM Commercial	CLEAR CHANNEL BROADCASTING LICENSES, INC.
FL	MOUNT DORA	WMGF	107.7 FM Commercial	CLEAR CHANNEL BROADCASTING LICENSES, INC.
FL	NAPLES PARK	WBTT	105.5 FM Commercial	CLEAR CHANNEL BROADCASTING LICENSES, INC.
FL	NEPTUNE BEACH	WFKS	97.9 FM Commercial	CLEAR CHANNEL BROADCASTING LICENSES, INC.
FL	ORLANDO	WQTM	740 AM Station	CLEAR CHANNEL BROADCASTING LICENSES, INC.
FL	ORLANDO	WEBG	100.3 FM Commercial	CLEAR CHANNEL BROADCASTING LICENSES, INC.
FL	PANAMA CITY	WDIZ	590 AM Station	CLEAR CHANNEL BROADCASTING LICENSES, INC.
FL	PANAMA CITY	WFSY	98.5 FM Commercial	CLEAR CHANNEL BROADCASTING LICENSES, INC.
FL	PANAMA CITY	WPAP-FM	92.5 FM Commercial	CLEAR CHANNEL BROADCASTING LICENSES, INC.
FL	PARKER	WFBX	94.5 FM Commercial	CLEAR CHANNEL BROADCASTING LICENSES, INC.
FL	PENSACOLA	WTKX-FM	101.5 FM Commercial	CLEAR CHANNEL BROADCASTING LICENSES, INC.
FL	PENSACOLA	WYCL	107.3 FM Commercial	CLEAR CHANNEL BROADCASTING LICENSES, INC.
FL	PINE HILLS	WFLF	540 AM Station	CLEAR CHANNEL BROADCASTING LICENSES, INC.
FL	PLANTATION KEY	WCTH	100.3 FM Commercial	CLEAR CHANNEL BROADCASTING LICENSES, INC.
FL	PLANTATION KEY	WFKZ	103.1 FM Commercial	CLEAR CHANNEL BROADCASTING LICENSES, INC.
FL	PORT CHARLOTTE	WCKT	100.1 FM Commercial	CLEAR CHANNEL BROADCASTING LICENSES, INC.
FL	PORT ST. JOE	WEBZ	93.5 FM Commercial	CITICASTERS LICENSES, L.P.
FL	PUNTA GORDA	WCCF	1580 AM Station	CITICASTERS LICENSES, L.P.
FL	QUINCY	WXSR	101.5 FM Commercial	CLEAR CHANNEL BROADCASTING LICENSES, INC.
FL	RIVIERA BEACH	WZZR	94.3 FM Commercial	CLEAR CHANNEL BROADCASTING LICENSES, INC.
FL	SARASOTA	WSRQ	1450 AM Station	CITICASTERS LICENSES, L.P.
FL	SARASOTA	WCTQ	106.5 FM Commercial	CITICASTERS LICENSES, L.P.
FL	SOLANA	WKII	1070 AM Station	CLEAR CHANNEL BROADCASTING LICENSES, INC.
FL	SOLANA	WCVU	104.9 FM Commercial	CITICASTERS LICENSES, L.P.
FL	ST. PETERSBURG	WDAE	620 AM Station	CLEAR CHANNEL BROADCASTING LICENSES, INC.
FL	STUART	WAVW	92.7 FM Commercial	CAPSTAR TX LIMITED PARTNERSHIP
FL	TALLAHASSEE	WTNT-FM	94.9 FM Commercial	CLEAR CHANNEL BROADCASTING LICENSES, INC.
FL	TALLAHASSEE	WNLS	1270 AM Station	CLEAR CHANNEL BROADCASTING LICENSES, INC.

State	City	Call Sign	Frequency	Subsidiary Name
		Radio Station Subsidiaries for Clear Channel Communications Inc.		
FL	TAMPA	WHNZ	1250 AM Station	CITICASTERS LICENSES, L.P.
FL	TAMPA	WMTX	100.7 FM Commercial	CITICASTERS LICENSES, L.P.
FL	TAMPA	WFLA	970 AM Station	CITICASTERS LICENSES, L.P.
FL	TAMPA	WFLZ-FM	93.3 FM Commercial	CITICASTERS LICENSES, L.P.
FL	TAVARES	WXXL	106.7 FM Commercial	AMFM RADIO LICENSES, L.L.C.
FL	TAVERNIER	WKEZ-FM	96.9 FM Commercial	CLEAR CHANNEL BROADCASTING LICENSES, INC.
FL	VENICE	WDDV	92.1 FM Commercial	CITICASTERS LICENSES, L.P.
FL	VENICE	WAMR	1320 AM Station	CITICASTERS LICENSES, L.P.
FL	VERO BEACH	WCZR	101.7 FM Commercial	CAPSTAR TX LIMITED PARTNERSHIP
FL	VERO BEACH	WAXE	1370 AM Station	CAPSTAR TX LIMITED PARTNERSHIP
FL	VERO BEACH	WQOL	103.7 FM Commercial	CAPSTAR TX LIMITED PARTNERSHIP
FL	WEST PALM BEACH	WRLX	92.1 FM Commercial	CAPSTAR TX LIMITED PARTNERSHIP
FL	WEST PALM BEACH	WBZT	1230 AM Station	CAPSTAR TX LIMITED PARTNERSHIP
FL	WEST PALM BEACH	WJNO	1290 AM Station	CLEAR CHANNEL BROADCASTING LICENSES, INC.
GA	ALBANY	WJIZ-FM	96.3 FM Commercial	CLEAR CHANNEL BROADCASTING LICENSES, INC.
GA	ALBANY	WJYZ	960 AM Station	CLEAR CHANNEL BROADCASTING LICENSES, INC.
GA	ATLANTA	WKLS	96.1 FM Commercial	CITICASTERS LICENSES, L.P.
GA	ATLANTA	WGST	640 AM Station	CITICASTERS LICENSES, L.P.
GA	ATLANTA	WLTM	94.9 FM Commercial	CITICASTERS LICENSES, L.P.
GA	AUGUSTA	WEKL	102.3 FM Commercial	CAPSTAR TX LIMITED PARTNERSHIP
GA	AUGUSTA	WINZ	1340 AM Station	CAPSTAR TX LIMITED PARTNERSHIP
GA	AUGUSTA	WBBQ-FM	104.3 FM Commercial	CAPSTAR TX LIMITED PARTNERSHIP
GA	AUGUSTA	WZNY	105.7 FM Commercial	CAPSTAR TX LIMITED PARTNERSHIP
GA	BAINBRIDGE	WRAK-FM	97.3 FM Commercial	CLEAR CHANNEL BROADCASTING LICENSES, INC.
GA	BOWDON	WMAX-FM	105.3 FM Commercial	CLEAR CHANNEL BROADCASTING LICENSES, INC.
GA	BRUNSWICK	WSOL-FM	101.5 FM Commercial	CITICASTERS LICENSES, L.P.
GA	CANTON	WLCL	105.7 FM Commercial	CLEAR CHANNEL BROADCASTING LICENSES, INC.
GA	CHATSWORTH	WQMT	98.9 FM Commercial	CLEAR CHANNEL BROADCASTING LICENSES, INC.
GA	COLUMBUS	WVRK	102.9 FM Commercial	CLEAR CHANNEL BROADCASTING LICENSES, INC.
GA	COLUMBUS	WDAK	540 AM Station	CLEAR CHANNEL BROADCASTING LICENSES, INC.
GA	DALTON	WYYU	104.5 FM Commercial	CLEAR CHANNEL BROADCASTING LICENSES, INC.
GA	DALTON	WDAL	1430 AM Station	CLEAR CHANNEL BROADCASTING LICENSES, INC.
GA	DALTON	WBLJ	1230 AM Station	CLEAR CHANNEL BROADCASTING LICENSES, INC.
GA	DRY BRANCH	WMWR	1670 AM Station	CLEVELAND RADIO LICENSES, LLC
GA	FORT VALLEY	WQBZ	106.3 FM Commercial	CLEVELAND RADIO LICENSES, LLC
GA	FORT VALLEY	WIBB-FM	97.9 FM Commercial	CLEVELAND RADIO LICENSES, LLC
GA	GRAY	WYNF	96.5 FM Commercial	CLEVELAND RADIO LICENSES, LLC
GA	HELEN	WHEL	105.1 FM Commercial	CITICASTERS LICENSES, L.P.
GA	HOGANSVILLE	WMGP	98.1 FM Commercial	CITICASTERS LICENSES, L.P.
GA	HOGANSVILLE	WVCC	720 AM Station	CITICASTERS LICENSES, L.P.
GA	MACON	WLCG	1280 AM Station	CLEVELAND RADIO LICENSES, LLC
GA	MARTINEZ	WPRW-FM	107.7 FM Commercial	CAPSTAR TX LIMITED PARTNERSHIP
GA	NEWNAN	WCOH	1400 AM Station	CITICASTERS CO
GA	PEACHTREE CITY	WBZY-FM	96.7 FM Commercial	CITICASTERS LICENSES, L.P.
GA	RINGGOLD	WTUN	101.9 FM Commercial	CLEAR CHANNEL BROADCASTING LICENSES, INC.
GA	ROSSVILLE	WUUS	980 AM Station	CAPSTAR TX LIMITED PARTNERSHIP
GA	ROSSVILLE	WRXR-FM	105.5 FM Commercial	CAPSTAR TX LIMITED PARTNERSHIP
GA	SAVANNAH	WAEV	97.3 FM Commercial	CAPSTAR TX LIMITED PARTNERSHIP
GA	SAVANNAH	WSOK	1230 AM Station	CAPSTAR TX LIMITED PARTNERSHIP
GA	SAVANNAH	WQBT	94.1 FM Commercial	CAPSTAR TX LIMITED PARTNERSHIP
GA	SAVANNAH	WTKS	1290 AM Station	CAPSTAR TX LIMITED PARTNERSHIP
GA	THOMASVILLE	WTLY	107.1 FM Commercial	CLEAR CHANNEL BROADCASTING LICENSES, INC.
GA	TIFTON	WOBB	100.3 FM Commercial	CLEAR CHANNEL BROADCASTING LICENSES, INC.
GA	WARNER ROBINS	WRBV	101.7 FM Commercial	CLEVELAND RADIO LICENSES, LLC
GA	WARNER ROBINS	WEBL	102.5 FM Commercial	CLEVELAND RADIO LICENSES, LLC
HI	HONOLULU	KSSK	590 AM Station	CAPSTAR TX LIMITED PARTNERSHIP
HI	HONOLULU	KHBZ	990 AM Station	CAPSTAR TX LIMITED PARTNERSHIP
HI	HONOLULU	KDNN	98.5 FM Commercial	CAPSTAR TX LIMITED PARTNERSHIP
HI	HONOLULU	KHVH	830 AM Station	CAPSTAR TX LIMITED PARTNERSHIP
HI	HONOLULU	KIKI-FM	93.9 FM Commercial	CAPSTAR TX LIMITED PARTNERSHIP
HI	PEARL CITY	KUCD	101.9 FM Commercial	CAPSTAR TX LIMITED PARTNERSHIP
HI	WAIPAHU	KSSK-FM	92.3 FM Commercial	CAPSTAR TX LIMITED PARTNERSHIP
IA	AMES	KCCQ	105.1 FM Commercial	CITICASTERS LICENSES, L.P.
IA	AMES	KASI	1430 AM Station	CITICASTERS LICENSES, L.P.

State	City	Call Sign	Frequency	Subsidiary Name
\multicolumn{5}{c}{**Radio Station Subsidiaries for Clear Channel Communications Inc.**}

State	City	Call Sign	Frequency	Subsidiary Name
IA	ANKENY	KDRB	106.3 FM Commercial	CITICASTERS LICENSES, L.P.
IA	BURLINGTON	KGRS	107.3 FM Commercial	CITICASTERS LICENSES, L.P.
IA	BURLINGTON	KBUR	1490 AM Station	CITICASTERS LICENSES, L.P.
IA	CEDAR RAPIDS	WMT	600 AM Station	CITICASTERS LICENSES, L.P.
IA	CEDAR RAPIDS	WMT-FM	96.5 FM Commercial	CITICASTERS LICENSES, L.P.
IA	CEDAR RAPIDS	KMJM	1360 AM Station	CAPSTAR TX LIMITED PARTNERSHIP
IA	CHARLES CITY	KCHA-FM	95.9 FM Commercial	CLEAR CHANNEL BROADCASTING LICENSES, INC.
IA	CHARLES CITY	KCHA	1580 AM Station	CLEAR CHANNEL BROADCASTING LICENSES, INC.
IA	CLEAR LAKE	KLKK	103.7 FM Commercial	CLEAR CHANNEL BROADCASTING LICENSES, INC.
IA	CLINTON	KMXG	96.1 FM Commercial	CITICASTERS LICENSES, L.P.
IA	DAVENPORT	WOC	1420 AM Station	CITICASTERS LICENSES, L.P.
IA	DAVENPORT	WLLR-FM	103.7 FM Commercial	CITICASTERS LICENSES, L.P.
IA	DAVENPORT	KCQQ	106.5 FM Commercial	CITICASTERS LICENSES, L.P.
IA	DES MOINES	KKDM	107.5 FM Commercial	CLEAR CHANNEL BROADCASTING LICENSES, INC.
IA	DES MOINES	WHO	1040 AM Station	CITICASTERS LICENSES, L.P.
IA	DES MOINES	KMXD	100.3 FM Commercial	CITICASTERS LICENSES, L.P.
IA	DES MOINES	KXNO	1460 AM Station	CAPSTAR TX LIMITED PARTNERSHIP
IA	FORT DODGE	KWMT	540 AM Station	CLEAR CHANNEL BROADCASTING LICENSES, INC.
IA	FORT DODGE	KKEZ	94.5 FM Commercial	CLEAR CHANNEL BROADCASTING LICENSES, INC.
IA	FORT MADISON	KBKB	1360 AM Station	CITICASTERS LICENSES, L.P.
IA	FORT MADISON	KBKB-FM	101.7 FM Commercial	CITICASTERS LICENSES, L.P.
IA	GLENWOOD	KXKT	103.7 FM Commercial	CAPSTAR TX LIMITED PARTNERSHIP
IA	IOWA CITY	KXIC	800 AM Station	CITICASTERS LICENSES, L.P.
IA	IOWA CITY	KKRQ	100.7 FM Commercial	CITICASTERS LICENSES, L.P.
IA	MASON CITY	KGLO	1300 AM Station	CLEAR CHANNEL BROADCASTING LICENSES, INC.
IA	MASON CITY	KIAI	93.9 FM Commercial	CLEAR CHANNEL BROADCASTING LICENSES, INC.
IA	NEW HAMPTON	KCZE	95.1 FM Commercial	CLEAR CHANNEL BROADCASTING LICENSES, INC.
IA	OSAGE	KSMA-FM	98.7 FM Commercial	CLEAR CHANNEL BROADCASTING LICENSES, INC.
IA	SIOUX CITY	KSEZ	97.9 FM Commercial	CLEVELAND RADIO LICENSES, LLC
IA	SIOUX CITY	KMNS	620 AM Station	CLEVELAND RADIO LICENSES, LLC
IA	SIOUX CITY	KGLI	95.5 FM Commercial	CLEVELAND RADIO LICENSES, LLC
IA	SIOUX CITY	KWSL	1470 AM Station	CLEVELAND RADIO LICENSES, LLC
ID	BOISE	KFXD	630 AM Station	CITICASTERS LICENSES, L.P.
ID	BOISE	KLTB	104.3 FM Commercial	CITICASTERS LICENSES, L.P.
ID	CALDWELL	KSAS-FM	103.3 FM Commercial	CITICASTERS LICENSES, L.P.
ID	CHUBBUCK	KLLP	98.5 FM Commercial	CITICASTERS LICENSES, L.P.
ID	EAGLE	KXLT-FM	107.9 FM Commercial	CITICASTERS LICENSES, L.P.
ID	GARDEN CITY	KCIX	105.9 FM Commercial	CITICASTERS LICENSES, L.P.
ID	IDAHO FALLS	KID	590 AM Station	CITICASTERS LICENSES, L.P.
ID	IDAHO FALLS	KID-FM	96.1 FM Commercial	CITICASTERS LICENSES, L.P.
ID	NAMPA	KIDO	580 AM Station	CITICASTERS LICENSES, L.P.
ID	POCATELLO	KPKY	94.9 FM Commercial	CITICASTERS LICENSES, L.P.
ID	POCATELLO	KWIK	1240 AM Station	CITICASTERS LICENSES, L.P.
ID	POST FALLS	KCDA	103.1 FM Commercial	CAPSTAR TX LIMITED PARTNERSHIP
ID	TWIN FALLS	KEZJ-FM	95.7 FM Commercial	CITICASTERS LICENSES, L.P.
ID	TWIN FALLS	KLIX	1310 AM Station	CITICASTERS LICENSES, L.P.
ID	TWIN FALLS	KLIX-FM	96.5 FM Commercial	CITICASTERS LICENSES, L.P.
IL	ALTON	KATZ-FM	100.3 FM Commercial	CITICASTERS LICENSES, L.P.
IL	CHICAGO	WNUA	95.5 FM Commercial	AMFM RADIO LICENSES, L.L.C.
IL	CHICAGO	WGRB	1390 AM Station	AMFM RADIO LICENSES, L.L.C.
IL	CHICAGO	WGCI-FM	107.5 FM Commercial	AMFM RADIO LICENSES, L.L.C.
IL	CHICAGO	WKSC-FM	103.5 FM Commercial	AMFM RADIO LICENSES, L.L.C.
IL	CHICAGO	WLIT-FM	93.9 FM Commercial	AMFM RADIO LICENSES, L.L.C.
IL	COLUMBIA	KMJM-FM	104.9 FM Commercial	CITICASTERS LICENSES, L.P.
IL	EAST MOLINE	KUUL	101.3 FM Commercial	CITICASTERS LICENSES, L.P.
IL	HERRIN	WVZA	92.7 FM Commercial	CLEAR CHANNEL BROADCASTING LICENSES, INC.
IL	HILLSBORO	WXAJ	99.7 FM Commercial	CLEAR CHANNEL BROADCASTING LICENSES, INC.
IL	JOHNSTON CITY	WDDD	810 AM Station	CLEAR CHANNEL BROADCASTING LICENSES, INC.
IL	MARION	WDDD-FM	107.3 FM Commercial	CLEAR CHANNEL BROADCASTING LICENSES, INC.
IL	MOLINE	WFXN	1230 AM Station	CITICASTERS LICENSES, L.P.
IL	MURPHYSBORO	WTAO-FM	105.1 FM Commercial	CLEAR CHANNEL BROADCASTING LICENSES, INC.
IL	OAK PARK	WVAZ	102.7 FM Commercial	AMFM RADIO LICENSES, L.L.C.
IL	SPRINGFIELD	WFMB-FM	104.5 FM Commercial	CAPSTAR TX LIMITED PARTNERSHIP
IL	SPRINGFIELD	WFMB	1450 AM Station	CAPSTAR TX LIMITED PARTNERSHIP

State	City	Call Sign	Frequency	Subsidiary Name
			Radio Station Subsidiaries for Clear Channel Communications Inc.	
IL	VIRDEN	WCVS-FM	96.7 FM Commercial	CAPSTAR TX LIMITED PARTNERSHIP
IL	WEST FRANKFORT	WQUL	97.7 FM Commercial	CLEAR CHANNEL BROADCASTING LICENSES, INC.
IL	WEST FRANKFORT	WFRX	1300 AM Station	CLEAR CHANNEL BROADCASTING LICENSES, INC.
IN	CLARKSVILLE	WJZL	93.1 FM Commercial	CLEAR CHANNEL BROADCASTING LICENSES, INC.
IN	INDIANAPOLIS	WRZX	103.3 FM Commercial	CAPSTAR TX LIMITED PARTNERSHIP
IN	INDIANAPOLIS	WFBQ	94.7 FM Commercial	CAPSTAR TX LIMITED PARTNERSHIP
IN	INDIANAPOLIS	WNDE	1260 AM Station	CAPSTAR TX LIMITED PARTNERSHIP
IN	JEFFERSONVILLE	WQMF	95.7 FM Commercial	CLEAR CHANNEL BROADCASTING LICENSES, INC.
IN	SALEM	WZKF	98.9 FM Commercial	CLEAR CHANNEL BROADCASTING LICENSES, INC.
KS	HUTCHINSON	KZSN	102.1 FM Commercial	CAPSTAR TX LIMITED PARTNERSHIP
KS	WICHITA	KRBB	97.9 FM Commercial	CAPSTAR TX LIMITED PARTNERSHIP
KY	BURNSIDE	WKEQ	910 AM Station	CAPSTAR TX LIMITED PARTNERSHIP
KY	BURNSIDE	WLLK	93.9 FM Commercial	CAPSTAR TX LIMITED PARTNERSHIP
KY	DANVILLE	WHIR-FM	107.1 FM Commercial	CLEAR CHANNEL BROADCASTING LICENSES, INC.
KY	FRANKFORT	WKED-FM	103.7 FM Commercial	CLEAR CHANNEL BROADCASTING LICENSES, INC.
KY	FRANKFORT	WFKY	1490 AM Station	CLEAR CHANNEL BROADCASTING LICENSES, INC.
KY	FRANKFORT	WKYW	104.9 FM Commercial	CLEAR CHANNEL BROADCASTING LICENSES, INC.
KY	GEORGETOWN	WXRA	1580 AM Station	CITICASTERS LICENSES, L.P.
KY	LEXINGTON	WBUL-FM	98.1 FM Commercial	CITICASTERS LICENSES, L.P.
KY	LEXINGTON	WMXL	94.5 FM Commercial	CITICASTERS LICENSES, L.P.
KY	LEXINGTON	WLAP	630 AM Station	CITICASTERS LICENSES, L.P.
KY	LEXINGTON-FAYETTE	WLKT	104.5 FM Commercial	CITICASTERS LICENSES, L.P.
KY	LOUISVILLE	WXXA	790 AM Station	CLEAR CHANNEL BROADCASTING LICENSES, INC.
KY	LOUISVILLE	WKJK	1080 AM Station	CLEAR CHANNEL BROADCASTING LICENSES, INC.
KY	LOUISVILLE	WTFX-FM	100.5 FM Commercial	CLEAR CHANNEL BROADCASTING LICENSES, INC.
KY	LOUISVILLE	WAMZ	97.5 FM Commercial	CLEAR CHANNEL BROADCASTING LICENSES, INC.
KY	LOUISVILLE	WHAS	840 AM Station	CLEAR CHANNEL BROADCASTING LICENSES, INC.
KY	MOUNT STERLING	WMKJ	105.5 FM Commercial	CAPSTAR TX LIMITED PARTNERSHIP
KY	RUSSELLVILLE	WUBT	101.1 FM Commercial	CAPSTAR TX LIMITED PARTNERSHIP
KY	SHELBYVILLE	WJZO	101.7 FM Commercial	CLEAR CHANNEL BROADCASTING LICENSES, INC.
KY	SHELBYVILLE	WCND	940 AM Station	CLEAR CHANNEL BROADCASTING LICENSES, INC.
KY	SOMERSET	WSEK	97.1 FM Commercial	CAPSTAR TX LIMITED PARTNERSHIP
KY	SOMERSET	WSFC	1240 AM Station	CAPSTAR TX LIMITED PARTNERSHIP
KY	WINCHESTER	WKQQ	100.1 FM Commercial	CITICASTERS LICENSES, L.P.
LA	ALEXANDRIA	KZMZ	96.9 FM Commercial	CAPSTAR TX LIMITED PARTNERSHIP
LA	ALEXANDRIA	KDBS	1410 AM Station	CAPSTAR TX LIMITED PARTNERSHIP
LA	ALEXANDRIA	KRRV-FM	100.3 FM Commercial	CAPSTAR TX LIMITED PARTNERSHIP
LA	BATON ROUGE	WFMF	102.5 FM Commercial	CAPSTAR TX LIMITED PARTNERSHIP
LA	BATON ROUGE	WJBO	1150 AM Station	CAPSTAR TX LIMITED PARTNERSHIP
LA	BATON ROUGE	WYNK-FM	101.5 FM Commercial	CAPSTAR TX LIMITED PARTNERSHIP
LA	BATON ROUGE	WYNK	1380 AM Station	CAPSTAR TX LIMITED PARTNERSHIP
LA	BRUSLY	KRVE	96.1 FM Commercial	CAPSTAR TX LIMITED PARTNERSHIP
LA	DENHAM SPRINGS	WSKR	1210 AM Station	CAPSTAR TX LIMITED PARTNERSHIP
LA	HOUMA	KSTE-FM	104.1 FM Commercial	CLEAR CHANNEL BROADCASTING LICENSES, INC.
LA	NEW ORLEANS	WYLD-FM	98.5 FM Commercial	CLEAR CHANNEL BROADCASTING LICENSES, INC.
LA	NEW ORLEANS	WQUE-FM	93.3 FM Commercial	CLEAR CHANNEL BROADCASTING LICENSES, INC.
LA	NEW ORLEANS	WRNO-FM	99.5 FM Commercial	CLEAR CHANNEL BROADCASTING LICENSES, INC.
LA	NEW ORLEANS	WODT	1280 AM Station	CLEAR CHANNEL BROADCASTING LICENSES, INC.
LA	NEW ORLEANS	WYLD	940 AM Station	CLEAR CHANNEL BROADCASTING LICENSES, INC.
LA	NEW ORLEANS	WNOE-FM	101.1 FM Commercial	CLEAR CHANNEL BROADCASTING LICENSES, INC.
LA	OAKDALE	KKST	98.7 FM Commercial	CAPSTAR TX LIMITED PARTNERSHIP
LA	SHREVEPORT	KVKI-FM	96.5 FM Commercial	CITICASTERS LICENSES, L.P.
LA	SHREVEPORT	KRUF	94.5 FM Commercial	CITICASTERS LICENSES, L.P.
LA	SHREVEPORT	KWKH	1130 AM Station	CITICASTERS LICENSES, L.P.
LA	SHREVEPORT	KXKS-FM	93.7 FM Commercial	CITICASTERS LICENSES, L.P.
LA	SHREVEPORT	KEEL	710 AM Station	CITICASTERS LICENSES, L.P.
MA	BOSTON	WJMN	94.5 FM Commercial	AMFM RADIO LICENSES, L.L.C.
MA	EVERETT	WXKS	1430 AM Station	AMFM RADIO LICENSES, L.L.C.
MA	FRAMINGHAM	WKOX	1200 AM Station	CAPSTAR TX LIMITED PARTNERSHIP
MA	MEDFORD	WXKS-FM	107.9 FM Commercial	AMFM RADIO LICENSES, L.L.C.
MA	SPRINGFIELD	WHYN-FM	93.1 FM Commercial	CLEAR CHANNEL BROADCASTING LICENSES, INC.
MA	SPRINGFIELD	WHYN	560 AM Station	CLEAR CHANNEL BROADCASTING LICENSES, INC.
MA	TAUNTON	WSNE-FM	93.3 FM Commercial	CAPSTAR TX LIMITED PARTNERSHIP
MA	WESTFIELD	WNNZ	640 AM Station	CLEAR CHANNEL BROADCASTING LICENSES, INC.

State	City	Call Sign	Frequency	Subsidiary Name
			Radio Station Subsidiaries for Clear Channel Communications Inc.	
MA	WORCESTER	WSRS	96.1 FM Commercial	CAPSTAR TX LIMITED PARTNERSHIP
MA	WORCESTER	WTAG	580 AM Station	CAPSTAR TX LIMITED PARTNERSHIP
MD	BALTIMORE	WPOC	93.1 FM Commercial	CITICASTERS LICENSES, L.P.
MD	BALTIMORE	WCAO	600 AM Station	CITICASTERS LICENSES, L.P.
MD	BALTIMORE	WSMJ	104.3 FM Commercial	CITICASTERS LICENSES, L.P.
MD	BETHESDA	WTNT	570 AM Station	AMFM RADIO LICENSES, L.L.C.
MD	FREDERICK	WFMD	930 AM Station	CAPSTAR TX LIMITED PARTNERSHIP
MD	FREDERICK	WFRE	99.9 FM Commercial	CAPSTAR TX LIMITED PARTNERSHIP
MD	OCEAN CITY	WWFG	99.9 FM Commercial	CAPSTAR TX LIMITED PARTNERSHIP
MD	OCEAN CITY-SALISBURY	WQHQ	104.7 FM Commercial	CAPSTAR TX LIMITED PARTNERSHIP
MD	SALISBURY	WLVW-FM	105.5 FM Commercial	CAPSTAR TX LIMITED PARTNERSHIP
MD	SALISBURY	WTGM	960 AM Station	CAPSTAR TX LIMITED PARTNERSHIP
MD	SALISBURY	WJDY	1470 AM Station	CAPSTAR TX LIMITED PARTNERSHIP
MD	SALISBURY	WSBY-FM	98.9 FM Commercial	CAPSTAR TX LIMITED PARTNERSHIP
ME	AUGUSTA	WKCG	101.3 FM Commercial	CAPSTAR TX LIMITED PARTNERSHIP
ME	BANGOR	WABI	910 AM Station	CLEAR CHANNEL BROADCASTING LICENSES, INC.
ME	BANGOR	WWBX	97.1 FM Commercial	CLEAR CHANNEL BROADCASTING LICENSES, INC.
ME	BAR HARBOR	WLKE	99.1 FM Commercial	CLEAR CHANNEL BROADCASTING LICENSES, INC.
ME	BELFAST	WBFB	104.7 FM Commercial	CLEAR CHANNEL BROADCASTING LICENSES, INC.
ME	BOOTHBAY HARBOR	WCME	96.7 FM Commercial	CAPSTAR TX LIMITED PARTNERSHIP
ME	CAMDEN	WQSS	102.5 FM Commercial	CLEAR CHANNEL BROADCASTING LICENSES, INC.
ME	DEXTER	WGUY	102.1 FM Commercial	CLEAR CHANNEL BROADCASTING LICENSES, INC.
ME	ELLSWORTH	WKSQ	94.5 FM Commercial	CLEAR CHANNEL BROADCASTING LICENSES, INC.
ME	GARDINER	WFAU	1280 AM Station	CAPSTAR TX LIMITED PARTNERSHIP
ME	GARDINER	WABK-FM	104.3 FM Commercial	CAPSTAR TX LIMITED PARTNERSHIP
ME	HOWLAND	WVOM	103.9 FM Commercial	CLEAR CHANNEL BROADCASTING LICENSES, INC.
ME	MADISON	WIGY	97.5 FM Commercial	CAPSTAR TX LIMITED PARTNERSHIP
ME	ROCKLAND	WRKD	1450 AM Station	CAPSTAR TX LIMITED PARTNERSHIP
ME	ROCKLAND	WMCM	103.3 FM Commercial	CAPSTAR TX LIMITED PARTNERSHIP
ME	SEARSPORT	WFZX	101.7 FM Commercial	CLEAR CHANNEL BROADCASTING LICENSES, INC.
ME	SKOWHEGAN	WTOS-FM	105.1 FM Commercial	CAPSTAR TX LIMITED PARTNERSHIP
ME	WINTER HARBOR	WNSX	97.7 FM Commercial	CLEAR CHANNEL BROADCASTING LICENSES, INC.
ME	YORK CENTER	WUBB	95.3 FM Commercial	CAPSTAR TX LIMITED PARTNERSHIP
MI	ANN ARBOR	WWWW	102.9 FM Commercial	CAPSTAR TX LIMITED PARTNERSHIP
MI	ANN ARBOR	WTKA	1050 AM Station	CAPSTAR TX LIMITED PARTNERSHIP
MI	ANN ARBOR	WQKL	107.1 FM Commercial	CAPSTAR TX LIMITED PARTNERSHIP
MI	BATTLE CREEK	WBCK	930 AM Station	CAPSTAR TX LIMITED PARTNERSHIP
MI	BATTLE CREEK	WBXX	95.3 FM Commercial	CAPSTAR TX LIMITED PARTNERSHIP
MI	BATTLE CREEK	WRCC	1400 AM Station	CAPSTAR TX LIMITED PARTNERSHIP
MI	DEARBORN	WXDX	1310 AM Station	AMFM RADIO LICENSES, L.L.C.
MI	DEARBORN	WNIC	100.3 FM Commercial	AMFM RADIO LICENSES, L.L.C.
MI	DETROIT	WKQI	95.5 FM Commercial	AMFM RADIO LICENSES, L.L.C.
MI	DETROIT	WJLB	97.9 FM Commercial	AMFM RADIO LICENSES, L.L.C.
MI	DETROIT	WMXD	92.3 FM Commercial	AMFM RADIO LICENSES, L.L.C.
MI	DETROIT	WDTW	106.7 FM Commercial	AMFM RADIO LICENSES, L.L.C.
MI	DETROIT	WDFN	1130 AM Station	AMFM RADIO LICENSES, L.L.C.
MI	GRAND RAPIDS	WOOD	1300 AM Station	CLEAR CHANNEL BROADCASTING LICENSES, INC.
MI	GRAND RAPIDS	WOOD-FM	105.7 FM Commercial	CLEAR CHANNEL BROADCASTING LICENSES, INC.
MI	GRAND RAPIDS	WBCT	93.7 FM Commercial	CLEAR CHANNEL BROADCASTING LICENSES, INC.
MI	GRAND RAPIDS	WBFX	101.3 FM Commercial	CLEAR CHANNEL BROADCASTING LICENSES, INC.
MI	GRAND RAPIDS	WTKG	1230 AM Station	CLEAR CHANNEL BROADCASTING LICENSES, INC.
MI	HOLLAND	WVTI	96.1 FM Commercial	CLEAR CHANNEL BROADCASTING LICENSES, INC.
MI	MARSHALL	WWKN	104.9 FM Commercial	CAPSTAR TX LIMITED PARTNERSHIP
MI	MUSKEGON	WMHG	1600 AM Station	CUMULUS LICENSING LLC
MI	MUSKEGON	WSNX-FM	104.5 FM Commercial	CLEAR CHANNEL BROADCASTING LICENSES, INC.
MI	MUSKEGON	WMUS-FM	106.9 FM Commercial	CLEAR CHANNEL BROADCASTING LICENSES, INC.
MI	MUSKEGON	WMUS	1090 AM Station	CLEAR CHANNEL BROADCASTING LICENSES, INC.
MI	MUSKEGON	WSHZ	107.9 FM Commercial	CLEAR CHANNEL BROADCASTING LICENSES, INC.
MI	MUSKEGON HEIGHTS	WMRR	101.7 FM Commercial	CLEAR CHANNEL BROADCASTING LICENSES, INC.
MI	SALINE	WHNE	1290 AM Station	CAPSTAR TX LIMITED PARTNERSHIP
MN	ANOKA	KQQL	107.9 FM Commercial	AMFM RADIO LICENSES, L.L.C.
MN	AUSTIN	KNFX	970 AM Station	CLEAR CHANNEL BROADCASTING LICENSES, INC.
MN	CROOKSTON	KQHT	96.1 FM Commercial	CITICASTERS LICENSES, L.P.
MN	DETROIT LAKES	KRVI	95.1 FM Commercial	CAPSTAR TX LIMITED PARTNERSHIP

State	City	Call Sign	Frequency	Subsidiary Name
		Radio Station Subsidiaries for Clear Channel Communications Inc.		
MN	DULUTH	KKCB	105.1 FM Commercial	CLEAR CHANNEL BROADCASTING LICENSES, INC.
MN	DULUTH	WEBC	560 AM Station	CLEAR CHANNEL BROADCASTING LICENSES, INC.
MN	DULUTH	KLDJ	101.7 FM Commercial	CLEAR CHANNEL BROADCASTING LICENSES, INC.
MN	LAKE CITY	KMFX-FM	102.5 FM Commercial	CLEAR CHANNEL BROADCASTING LICENSES, INC.
MN	MANKATO	KYSM	1230 AM Station	CLEAR CHANNEL BROADCASTING LICENSES, INC.
MN	MANKATO	KYSM-FM	103.5 FM Commercial	CLEAR CHANNEL BROADCASTING LICENSES, INC.
MN	MINNEAPOLIS	KFXN	690 AM Station	AMFM RADIO LICENSES, L.L.C.
MN	MINNEAPOLIS	KTCZ-FM	97.1 FM Commercial	AMFM RADIO LICENSES, L.L.C.
MN	MINNEAPOLIS	KJZI	100.3 FM Commercial	AMFM RADIO LICENSES, L.L.C.
MN	MINNEAPOLIS	KFAN	1130 AM Station	AMFM RADIO LICENSES, LLC
MN	MOORHEAD	KVOX	1280 AM Station	CAPSTAR TX LIMITED PARTNERSHIP
MN	NEW ULM	KXLP	93.1 FM Commercial	CLEAR CHANNEL BROADCASTING LICENSES, INC.
MN	PROCTOR	KBMX	107.7 FM Commercial	CLEAR CHANNEL BROADCASTING LICENSES, INC.
MN	RICHFIELD	KDWB-FM	101.3 FM Commercial	AMFM RADIO LICENSES, L.L.C.
MN	ROCHESTER	KWEB	1270 AM Station	CLEAR CHANNEL BROADCASTING LICENSES, INC.
MN	ROCHESTER	KRCH	101.7 FM Commercial	CLEAR CHANNEL BROADCASTING LICENSES, INC.
MN	ST. PAUL	KEEY-FM	102.1 FM Commercial	AMFM RADIO LICENSES, L.L.C.
MN	THIEF RIVER FALLS	KSNR	100.3 FM Commercial	CITICASTERS LICENSES, L.P.
MN	WABASHA	KMFX	1190 AM Station	CLEAR CHANNEL BROADCASTING LICENSES, INC.
MO	AURORA	KGMY-FM	100.5 FM Commercial	CLEAR CHANNEL BROADCASTING LICENSES, INC.
MO	NIXA	KGBX-FM	105.9 FM Commercial	CLEAR CHANNEL BROADCASTING LICENSES, INC.
MO	PLEASANT HOPE	KTOZ-FM	95.5 FM Commercial	CLEAR CHANNEL BROADCASTING LICENSES, INC.
MO	SELIGMAN	KIGL	93.3 FM Commercial	CAPSTAR TX LIMITED PARTNERSHIP
MO	SPRINGFIELD	KGMY	1400 AM Station	CLEAR CHANNEL BROADCASTING LICENSES, INC.
MO	SPRINGFIELD	KXUS	97.3 FM Commercial	CLEAR CHANNEL BROADCASTING LICENSES, INC.
MO	ST. LOUIS	KSD	93.7 FM Commercial	CITICASTERS LICENSES, L.P.
MO	ST. LOUIS	KLOU	103.3 FM Commercial	CITICASTERS LICENSES, L.P.
MO	ST. LOUIS	KSLZ	107.7 FM Commercial	CITICASTERS LICENSES, L.P.
MO	ST. LOUIS	KATZ	1600 AM Station	CITICASTERS LICENSES, L.P.
MS	ABERDEEN	WWKZ	105.3 FM Commercial	CAPSTAR TX LIMITED PARTNERSHIP
MS	BALDWYN	WESE	92.5 FM Commercial	CAPSTAR TX LIMITED PARTNERSHIP
MS	BILOXI	WMJY	93.7 FM Commercial	CLEAR CHANNEL BROADCASTING LICENSES, INC.
MS	BOONEVILLE	WBIP-FM	99.3 FM Commercial	CLEAR CHANNEL BROADCASTING LICENSES, INC.
MS	ELLISVILLE	WJKX	102.5 FM Commercial	CLEAR CHANNEL BROADCASTING LICENSES, INC.
MS	HATTIESBURG	WUSW	103.7 FM Commercial	CLEAR CHANNEL BROADCASTING LICENSES, INC.
MS	HATTIESBURG	WFOR	1400 AM Station	CLEAR CHANNEL BROADCASTING LICENSES, INC.
MS	HEIDELBERG	WHER	99.3 FM Commercial	CLEAR CHANNEL BROADCASTING LICENSES, INC.
MS	JACKSON	WZRX	1590 AM Station	CAPSTAR TX LIMITED PARTNERSHIP
MS	JACKSON	WJDX	620 AM Station	CAPSTAR TX LIMITED PARTNERSHIP
MS	JACKSON	WMSI-FM	102.9 FM Commercial	CAPSTAR TX LIMITED PARTNERSHIP
MS	JACKSON	WHLH	95.5 FM Commercial	CAPSTAR TX LIMITED PARTNERSHIP
MS	KOSCIUSKO	WQJQ	105.1 FM Commercial	CAPSTAR TX LIMITED PARTNERSHIP
MS	LAUREL	WNSL	100.3 FM Commercial	CLEAR CHANNEL BROADCASTING LICENSES, INC.
MS	LAUREL	WEEZ	890 AM Station	CLEAR CHANNEL BROADCASTING LICENSES, INC.
MS	MARION	WYYW	95.1 FM Commercial	CLEAR CHANNEL BROADCASTING LICENSES, INC.
MS	MERIDIAN	WFFX	1450 AM Station	CLEAR CHANNEL BROADCASTING LICENSES, INC.
MS	MERIDIAN	WJDQ	101.3 FM Commercial	CLEAR CHANNEL BROADCASTING LICENSES, INC.
MS	MOSS POINT	WBUV	104.9 FM Commercial	CLEAR CHANNEL BROADCASTING LICENSES, INC.
MS	NEW ALBANY	WWZD-FM	106.7 FM Commercial	CAPSTAR TX LIMITED PARTNERSHIP
MS	NEWTON	WMSO	97.9 FM Commercial	CLEAR CHANNEL BROADCASTING LICENSES, INC.
MS	OCEAN SPRINGS	WQYZ	92.5 FM Commercial	GOLDEN GULF COAST BROADCASTING, INC.
MS	OLIVE BRANCH	WHAL-FM	95.7 FM Commercial	CLEAR CHANNEL BROADCASTING LICENSES, INC.
MS	PASCAGOULA	WKNN-FM	99.1 FM Commercial	CLEAR CHANNEL BROADCASTING LICENSES, INC.
MS	PETAL	WZLD	106.3 FM Commercial	CLEAR CHANNEL BROADCASTING LICENSES, INC.
MS	TUPELO	WTUP	1490 AM Station	CAPSTAR TX LIMITED PARTNERSHIP
MS	TUPELO	WKMQ	1060 AM Station	CAPSTAR TX LIMITED PARTNERSHIP
MS	UNION	WZKS	104.1 FM Commercial	CLEAR CHANNEL BROADCASTING LICENSES, INC.
MS	VICKSBURG	WSTZ-FM	106.7 FM Commercial	CAPSTAR TX LIMITED PARTNERSHIP
MT	BELGRADE	KISN	96.7 FM Commercial	CAPSTAR TX LIMITED PARTNERSHIP
MT	BILLINGS	KBUL	970 AM Station	CLEAR CHANNEL BROADCASTING LICENSES, INC.
MT	BILLINGS	KCTR-FM	102.9 FM Commercial	CLEAR CHANNEL BROADCASTING LICENSES, INC.
MT	BILLINGS	KKBR	97.1 FM Commercial	CLEAR CHANNEL BROADCASTING LICENSES, INC.
MT	BILLINGS	KBBB	103.7 FM Commercial	CLEAR CHANNEL BROADCASTING LICENSES, INC.
MT	BOZEMAN	KMMS	1450 AM Station	CAPSTAR TX LIMITED PARTNERSHIP

State	City	Call Sign	Frequency	Subsidiary Name
		Radio Station Subsidiaries for Clear Channel Communications Inc.		
MT	BOZEMAN	KMMS-FM	95.1 FM Commercial	CAPSTAR TX LIMITED PARTNERSHIP
MT	BOZEMAN	KZMY	103.5 FM Commercial	CAPSTAR TX LIMITED PARTNERSHIP
MT	EAST MISSOULA	KLCY	930 AM Station	CAPSTAR TX LIMITED PARTNERSHIP
MT	HAMILTON	KLYQ	1240 AM Station	CAPSTAR TX LIMITED PARTNERSHIP
MT	HAMILTON	KBAZ	96.3 FM Commercial	CAPSTAR TX LIMITED PARTNERSHIP
MT	HARDIN	KMHK	95.5 FM Commercial	CLEAR CHANNEL BROADCASTING LICENSES, INC.
MT	LIVINGSTON	KXLB	100.7 FM Commercial	CAPSTAR TX LIMITED PARTNERSHIP
MT	LIVINGSTON	KPRK	1340 AM Station	CAPSTAR TX LIMITED PARTNERSHIP
MT	MISSOULA	KYSS-FM	94.9 FM Commercial	CAPSTAR TX LIMITED PARTNERSHIP
MT	MISSOULA	KGVO	1290 AM Station	CAPSTAR TX LIMITED PARTNERSHIP
MT	SHELBY	KSEN	1150 AM Station	CAPSTAR TX LIMITED PARTNERSHIP
MT	SHELBY	KZIN-FM	96.7 FM Commercial	CAPSTAR TX LIMITED PARTNERSHIP
MT	SUPERIOR	KLTC-FM	107.5 FM Commercial	CLEAR CHANNEL BROADCASTING LICENSES, INC.
NC	ASHEVILLE	WWNC	570 AM Station	CAPSTAR TX LIMITED PARTNERSHIP
NC	BURLINGTON	WRSN	93.9 FM Commercial	CAPSTAR TX LIMITED PARTNERSHIP
NC	DURHAM	WDCG	105.1 FM Commercial	CAPSTAR TX LIMITED PARTNERSHIP
NC	DURHAM	WDUR	1490 AM Station	CLEAR CHANNEL BROADCASTING LICENSES, INC.
NC	EDEN	WGBT	94.5 FM Commercial	CLEAR CHANNEL BROADCASTING LICENSES, INC.
NC	FAIRVIEW	WPEK	880 AM Station	CLEAR CHANNEL BROADCASTING LICENSES, INC.
NC	HENDERSONVILLE	WMYI	102.5 FM Commercial	CAPSTAR TX LIMITED PARTNERSHIP
NC	HICKORY	WLYT	102.9 FM Commercial	CAPSTAR TX LIMITED PARTNERSHIP
NC	HIGH POINT	WMAG	99.5 FM Commercial	CAPSTAR TX LIMITED PARTNERSHIP
NC	HIGH POINT	WVBZ	100.3 FM Commercial	CAPSTAR TX LIMITED PARTNERSHIP
NC	KANNAPOLIS	WRFX-FM	99.7 FM Commercial	CAPSTAR TX LIMITED PARTNERSHIP
NC	OLD FORT	WQNQ	104.3 FM Commercial	CLEAR CHANNEL BROADCASTING LICENSES, INC.
NC	OLD FORT	WKSF	99.9 FM Commercial	CAPSTAR TX LIMITED PARTNERSHIP
NC	ROCKY MOUNT	WTRG	100.7 FM Commercial	CAPSTAR TX LIMITED PARTNERSHIP
NC	SALISBURY	WEND	106.5 FM Commercial	CAPSTAR TX LIMITED PARTNERSHIP
NC	SHELBY	WWMG	96.1 FM Commercial	CLEAR CHANNEL BROADCASTING LICENSES, INC.
NC	STATESVILLE	WKKT	96.9 FM Commercial	CAPSTAR TX LIMITED PARTNERSHIP
NC	STATESVILLE	WSIC	1400 AM Station	CAPSTAR TX LIMITED PARTNERSHIP
NC	WAYNESVILLE	WQNS	104.9 FM Commercial	CLEAR CHANNEL BROADCASTING LICENSES, INC.
NC	WAYNESVILLE	WMXF	1400 AM Station	CLEAR CHANNEL BROADCASTING LICENSES, INC.
NC	WILSON	WRDU	106.1 FM Commercial	CAPSTAR TX LIMITED PARTNERSHIP
NC	WINSTON-SALEM	WTQR	104.1 FM Commercial	CLEAR CHANNEL BROADCASTING LICENSES, INC.
ND	BISMARCK	KYYY	92.9 FM Commercial	CITICASTERS LICENSES, L.P.
ND	BISMARCK	KFYR	550 AM Station	CITICASTERS LICENSES, L.P.
ND	BISMARCK	KSSS	101.5 FM Commercial	CLEAR CHANNEL BROADCASTING LICENSES, INC.
ND	BISMARCK	KXMR	710 AM Station	CLEAR CHANNEL BROADCASTING LICENSES, INC.
ND	BISMARCK	KQDY	94.5 FM Commercial	CLEAR CHANNEL BROADCASTING LICENSES, INC.
ND	BISMARCK	KBMR	1130 AM Station	CLEAR CHANNEL BROADCASTING LICENSES, INC.
ND	DICKINSON	KCAD	99.1 FM Commercial	CLEAR CHANNEL BROADCASTING LICENSES, INC.
ND	DICKINSON	KZRX	92.1 FM Commercial	CLEAR CHANNEL BROADCASTING LICENSES, INC.
ND	DICKINSON	KLTC	1460 AM Station	CLEAR CHANNEL BROADCASTING LICENSES, INC.
ND	FARGO	KFGO	790 AM Station	CAPSTAR TX LIMITED PARTNERSHIP
ND	FARGO	KKBX	101.9 FM Commercial	CAPSTAR TX LIMITED PARTNERSHIP
ND	FARGO	WDAY-FM	93.7 FM Commercial	CAPSTAR TX LIMITED PARTNERSHIP
ND	GRAND FORKS	KKXL	1440 AM Station	CITICASTERS LICENSES, L.P.
ND	GRAND FORKS	KKXL-FM	92.9 FM Commercial	CITICASTERS LICENSES, L.P.
ND	GRAND FORKS	KJKJ	107.5 FM Commercial	CITICASTERS LICENSES, L.P.
ND	HOPE	KDAM	104.7 FM Commercial	CLEAR CHANNEL BROADCASTING LICENSES, INC.
ND	KINDRED	KFAB-FM	92.7 FM Commercial	CAPSTAR TX LIMITED PARTNERSHIP
ND	MINOT	KZPR	105.3 FM Commercial	CLEAR CHANNEL BROADCASTING LICENSES, INC.
ND	MINOT	KRRZ	1390 AM Station	CLEAR CHANNEL BROADCASTING LICENSES, INC.
ND	MINOT	KIZZ	93.7 FM Commercial	CLEAR CHANNEL BROADCASTING LICENSES, INC.
ND	MINOT	KYYX	97.1 FM Commercial	CLEAR CHANNEL BROADCASTING LICENSES, INC.
ND	MINOT	KCJB	910 AM Station	CLEAR CHANNEL BROADCASTING LICENSES, INC.
ND	MINOT	KMXA-FM	99.9 FM Commercial	CLEAR CHANNEL BROADCASTING LICENSES, INC.
NE	BEATRICE	KTGL	92.9 FM Commercial	CAPSTAR TX LIMITED PARTNERSHIP
NE	BENNINGTON	KHUS	93.3 FM Commercial	CAPSTAR TX LIMITED PARTNERSHIP
NE	CRETE	KIBZ	104.1 FM Commercial	CAPSTAR TX LIMITED PARTNERSHIP
NE	OGALLALA	KOGA	930 AM Station	CAPSTAR TX LIMITED PARTNERSHIP
NE	OGALLALA	KOGA-FM	99.7 FM Commercial	CAPSTAR TX LIMITED PARTNERSHIP
NE	OGALLALA	KMCX-FM	106.5 FM Commercial	CAPSTAR TX LIMITED PARTNERSHIP

State	City	Call Sign	Frequency	Subsidiary Name
			Radio Station Subsidiaries for Clear Channel Communications Inc.	
NE	OMAHA	KEFM	96.1 FM Commercial	CLEAR CHANNEL BROADCASTING LICENSES, INC.
NE	OMAHA	KGOR	99.9 FM Commercial	CAPSTAR TX LIMITED PARTNERSHIP
NE	OMAHA	KFAB	1110 AM Station	CAPSTAR TX LIMITED PARTNERSHIP
NE	SEWARD	KZKX	96.9 FM Commercial	CAPSTAR TX LIMITED PARTNERSHIP
NE	SOUTH SIOUX CITY	KSFT-FM	107.1 FM Commercial	CLEVELAND RADIO LICENSES, LLC
NH	EXETER	WERZ	107.1 FM Commercial	CAPSTAR TX LIMITED PARTNERSHIP
NH	EXETER	WGIP	1540 AM Station	CAPSTAR TX LIMITED PARTNERSHIP
NH	HANOVER	WGXL	92.3 FM Commercial	CAPSTAR TX LIMITED PARTNERSHIP
NH	HANOVER	WTSL	1400 AM Station	CAPSTAR TX LIMITED PARTNERSHIP
NH	LEBANON	WXXK	100.5 FM Commercial	CAPSTAR TX LIMITED PARTNERSHIP
NH	MANCHESTER	WGIR	610 AM Station	CAPSTAR TX LIMITED PARTNERSHIP
NH	MANCHESTER	WGIR-FM	101.1 FM Commercial	CAPSTAR TX LIMITED PARTNERSHIP
NH	NEWPORT	WVRR	101.7 FM Commercial	CAPSTAR TX LIMITED PARTNERSHIP
NH	PORTSMOUTH	WHEB	100.3 FM Commercial	CAPSTAR TX LIMITED PARTNERSHIP
NH	PORTSMOUTH	WMYF	1380 AM Station	CAPSTAR TX LIMITED PARTNERSHIP
NH	ROCHESTER	WGIN	930 AM Station	CAPSTAR TX LIMITED PARTNERSHIP
NH	ROCHESTER	WQSO	96.7 FM Commercial	CAPSTAR TX LIMITED PARTNERSHIP
NJ	BLAIRSTOWN	WHCY	106.3 FM Commercial	CLEAR CHANNEL BROADCASTING LICENSES, INC.
NJ	FRANKLIN	WSUS	102.3 FM Commercial	CLEAR CHANNEL BROADCASTING LICENSES, INC.
NJ	NEWARK	WHTZ	100.3 FM Commercial	AMFM RADIO LICENSES, L.L.C.
NJ	NEWTON	WNNJ-FM	103.7 FM Commercial	CLEAR CHANNEL BROADCASTING LICENSES, INC.
NJ	NEWTON	WNNJ	1360 AM Station	CLEAR CHANNEL BROADCASTING LICENSES, INC.
NM	ALBUQUERQUE	KPEK	100.3 FM Commercial	CITICASTERS LICENSES, L.P.
NM	ALBUQUERQUE	KBQI	107.9 FM Commercial	CITICASTERS LICENSES, L.P.
NM	ALBUQUERQUE	KXKS	1190 AM Station	CLEAR CHANNEL BROADCASTING LICENSES, INC.
NM	ALBUQUERQUE	KABQ	1350 AM Station	CLEAR CHANNEL BROADCASTING LICENSES, INC.
NM	ALBUQUERQUE	KZRR	94.1 FM Commercial	CLEAR CHANNEL BROADCASTING LICENSES, INC.
NM	AZTEC	KCQL	1340 AM Station	CAPSTAR TX LIMITED PARTNERSHIP
NM	BLOOMFIELD	KKFG	104.5 FM Commercial	CAPSTAR TX LIMITED PARTNERSHIP
NM	BOSQUE FARMS	KTEG	104.7 FM Commercial	CLEAR CHANNEL BROADCASTING LICENSES, INC.
NM	CORRALES	KSYU	95.1 FM Commercial	CLEAR CHANNEL BROADCASTING LICENSES, INC.
NM	FARMINGTON	KDAG	96.9 FM Commercial	CAPSTAR TX LIMITED PARTNERSHIP
NM	FARMINGTON	KTRA-FM	102.1 FM Commercial	CAPSTAR TX LIMITED PARTNERSHIP
NM	GALLUP	KGLX	99.1 FM Commercial	CLEAR CHANNEL BROADCASTING LICENSES, INC.
NM	GALLUP	KFMQ	106.1 FM Commercial	CLEAR CHANNEL BROADCASTING LICENSES, INC.
NM	KIRTLAND	KAZX	102.9 FM Commercial	CAPSTAR TX LIMITED PARTNERSHIP
NM	LAS VEGAS	KBAC	98.1 FM Commercial	CLEAR CHANNEL BROADCASTING LICENSES, INC.
NM	SANTA FE	KABQ-FM	104.1 FM Commercial	CITICASTERS LICENSES, L.P.
NM	THOREAU	KXTC	99.9 FM Commercial	CLEAR CHANNEL BROADCASTING LICENSES, INC.
NM	WHITE ROCK	KSFQ	101.1 FM Commercial	CLEAR CHANNEL BROADCASTING LICENSES, INC.
NV	HENDERSON	KWNR	95.5 FM Commercial	CITICASTERS LICENSES, L.P.
NV	LAS VEGAS	KSNE-FM	106.5 FM Commercial	CITICASTERS LICENSES, L.P.
NV	LAS VEGAS	KWID	101.9 FM Commercial	CITICASTERS LICENSES, L.P.
NV	LAS VEGAS	KQOL-FM	93.1 FM Commercial	CITICASTERS LICENSES, L.P.
NY	ALBANY	WHRL	103.1 FM Commercial	CLEAR CHANNEL BROADCASTING LICENSES, INC.
NY	ALBANY	WPYX	106.5 FM Commercial	CAPSTAR TX LIMITED PARTNERSHIP
NY	AUBURN	WPHR	106.9 FM Commercial	CLEAR CHANNEL BROADCASTING LICENSES, INC.
NY	BALLSTON SPA	WKKF	102.3 FM Commercial	CLEAR CHANNEL BROADCASTING LICENSES, INC.
NY	BINGHAMTON	WINR	680 AM Station	CLEVELAND RADIO LICENSES, LLC
NY	CANANDAIGUA	WISY	102.3 FM Commercial	CITICASTERS LICENSES, L.P.
NY	CATSKILL	WCTW	98.5 FM Commercial	CLEAR CHANNEL BROADCASTING LICENSES, INC.
NY	CONKLIN	WKGB-FM	92.5 FM Commercial	CLEAR CHANNEL BROADCASTING LICENSES, INC.
NY	DERUYTER	WWDG	105.1 FM Commercial	CLEAR CHANNEL BROADCASTING LICENSES, INC.
NY	EAST PATCHOGUE	WALK	1370 AM Station	AMFM RADIO LICENSES, L.L.C.
NY	ELLENVILLE	WELV	1370 AM Station	CLEAR CHANNEL BROADCASTING LICENSES, INC.
NY	ELLENVILLE	WFKP	99.3 FM Commercial	CLEAR CHANNEL BROADCASTING LICENSES, INC.
NY	ENDICOTT	WENE	1430 AM Station	CLEAR CHANNEL BROADCASTING LICENSES, INC.
NY	ENDICOTT	WMRV-FM	105.7 FM Commercial	CLEAR CHANNEL BROADCASTING LICENSES, INC.
NY	ENDWELL	WBBI	107.5 FM Commercial	CLEAR CHANNEL BROADCASTING LICENSES, INC.
NY	ESSEX	WCPV	101.3 FM Commercial	CAPSTAR TX LIMITED PARTNERSHIP
NY	FULTON	WBBS	104.7 FM Commercial	CITICASTERS LICENSES, L.P.
NY	HIGHLAND	WRWD-FM	107.3 FM Commercial	CLEVELAND RADIO LICENSES, LLC
NY	HONEOYE FALLS	WNVE	95.1 FM Commercial	CITICASTERS LICENSES, L.P.
NY	HUDSON	WHUC	1230 AM Station	CLEAR CHANNEL BROADCASTING LICENSES, INC.

State	City	Call Sign	Frequency	Subsidiary Name
	Radio Station Subsidiaries for Clear Channel Communications Inc.			
NY	HUDSON	WZCR	93.5 FM Commercial	CLEAR CHANNEL BROADCASTING LICENSES, INC.
NY	IRONDEQUOIT	WKGS	106.7 FM Commercial	CITICASTERS LICENSES, L.P.
NY	KINGSTON	WGHQ	920 AM Station	CLEVELAND RADIO LICENSES, LLC
NY	LAKE SUCCESS	WKTU	103.5 FM Commercial	AMFM RADIO LICENSES, L.L.C.
NY	LITTLE FALLS	WSKU	105.5 FM Commercial	CAPSTAR TX LIMITED PARTNERSHIP
NY	LITTLE FALLS	WLFH	1230 AM Station	CAPSTAR TX LIMITED PARTNERSHIP
NY	NEW PALTZ	WBWZ	93.3 FM Commercial	CLEVELAND RADIO LICENSES, LLC
NY	NEW YORK	WLTW	106.7 FM Commercial	AMFM NEW YORK LICENSES, LLC
NY	NEW YORK	WAXQ	104.3 FM Commercial	AMFM NEW YORK LICENSES, LLC
NY	NEW YORK	WWPR-FM	105.1 FM Commercial	AMFM RADIO LICENSES, L.L.C.
NY	PATCHOGUE	WALK-FM	97.5 FM Commercial	AMFM RADIO LICENSES, L.L.C.
NY	PLATTSBURGH	WEAV	960 AM Station	CLEAR CHANNEL BROADCASTING LICENSES, INC.
NY	PORT HENRY	WVTK	92.1 FM Commercial	CAPSTAR TX LIMITED PARTNERSHIP
NY	PORT JERVIS	WDLC	1490 AM Station	PORT JERVIS BROADCASTING CO., INC.
NY	PORT JERVIS	WTSX	96.7 FM Commercial	PORT JERVIS BROADCASTING CO., INC.
NY	POUGHKEEPSIE	WRNQ	92.1 FM Commercial	CLEAR CHANNEL BROADCASTING LICENSES, INC.
NY	POUGHKEEPSIE	WPKF	96.1 FM Commercial	CLEAR CHANNEL BROADCASTING LICENSES, INC.
NY	POUGHKEEPSIE	WKIP	1450 AM Station	CLEAR CHANNEL BROADCASTING LICENSES, INC.
NY	REMSEN	WUCL	93.5 FM Commercial	CLEAR CHANNEL BROADCASTING LICENSES, INC.
NY	REMSEN	WADR	1480 AM Station	CLEAR CHANNEL BROADCASTING LICENSES, INC.
NY	ROCHESTER	WHAM	1180 AM Station	CITICASTERS LICENSES, L.P.
NY	ROCHESTER	WVOR-FM	100.5 FM Commercial	CITICASTERS LICENSES, L.P.
NY	ROCHESTER	WHTK	1280 AM Station	CITICASTERS LICENSES, L.P.
NY	ROME	WUMX	102.5 FM Commercial	CLEAR CHANNEL BROADCASTING LICENSES, INC.
NY	ROME	WRNY	1350 AM Station	CLEAR CHANNEL BROADCASTING LICENSES, INC.
NY	ROTTERDAM	WTRY-FM	98.3 FM Commercial	CAPSTAR TX LIMITED PARTNERSHIP
NY	SCHENECTADY	WGY	810 AM Station	CLEAR CHANNEL BROADCASTING LICENSES, INC.
NY	SCHENECTADY	WRVE	99.5 FM Commercial	CLEAR CHANNEL BROADCASTING LICENSES, INC.
NY	SOUTH BRISTOL TOWNSH	WFXF	107.3 FM Commercial	CITICASTERS LICENSES, L.P.
NY	SYRACUSE	WHEN	620 AM Station	CLEAR CHANNEL BROADCASTING LICENSES, INC.
NY	SYRACUSE	WWHT	107.9 FM Commercial	CLEAR CHANNEL BROADCASTING LICENSES, INC.
NY	SYRACUSE	WYYY	94.5 FM Commercial	CLEAR CHANNEL BROADCASTING LICENSES, INC.
NY	SYRACUSE	WSYR	570 AM Station	CLEAR CHANNEL BROADCASTING LICENSES, INC.
NY	TROY	WOFX	980 AM Station	CAPSTAR TX LIMITED PARTNERSHIP
NY	UTICA	WUTQ	1550 AM Station	CLEAR CHANNEL BROADCASTING LICENSES, INC.
NY	UTICA	WOUR	96.9 FM Commercial	CLEAR CHANNEL BROADCASTING LICENSES, INC.
NY	VESTAL	WMXW	103.3 FM Commercial	CLEAR CHANNEL BROADCASTING LICENSES, INC.
NY	WHITESBORO	WSKS	97.9 FM Commercial	CAPSTAR TX LIMITED PARTNERSHIP
NY	WILLSBORO	WXZO	96.7 FM Commercial	CAPSTAR TX LIMITED PARTNERSHIP
OH	AKRON	WTOU	1350 AM Station	CAPSTAR TX LIMITED PARTNERSHIP
OH	AKRON	WAKS	96.5 FM Commercial	CAPSTAR TX LIMITED PARTNERSHIP
OH	AKRON	WHLO	640 AM Station	CLEAR CHANNEL BROADCASTING LICENSES, INC.
OH	ASHLAND	WNCO-FM	101.3 FM Commercial	CAPSTAR TX LIMITED PARTNERSHIP
OH	ASHLAND	WNCO	1340 AM Station	CAPSTAR TX LIMITED PARTNERSHIP
OH	ASHTABULA	WFUN	970 AM Station	CLEAR CHANNEL BROADCASTING LICENSES, INC.
OH	ASHTABULA	WREO-FM	97.1 FM Commercial	CLEAR CHANNEL BROADCASTING LICENSES, INC.
OH	BEAVERCREEK	WXEG	103.9 FM Commercial	CITICASTERS LICENSES, L.P.
OH	BELPRE	WNUS	107.1 FM Commercial	CLEAR CHANNEL BROADCASTING LICENSES, INC.
OH	CANTON	WKDD	98.1 FM Commercial	CITICASTERS LICENSES, L.P.
OH	CHILLICOTHE	WBEX	1490 AM Station	CITICASTERS LICENSES, L.P.
OH	CHILLICOTHE	WLZT	93.3 FM Commercial	CLEAR CHANNEL BROADCASTING LICENSES, INC.
OH	CHILLICOTHE	WKKJ	94.3 FM Commercial	CLEAR CHANNEL BROADCASTING LICENSES, INC.
OH	CHILLICOTHE	WCHI	1350 AM Station	CLEAR CHANNEL BROADCASTING LICENSES, INC.
OH	CINCINNATI	WSAI	1530 AM Station	JACOR BROADCASTING CORPORATION
OH	CINCINNATI	WOFX-FM	92.5 FM Commercial	JACOR BROADCASTING CORPORATION
OH	CINCINNATI	WCKY	1360 AM Station	JACOR BROADCASTING CORPORATION
OH	CINCINNATI	WVMX	94.1 FM Commercial	CITICASTERS LICENSES, L.P.
OH	CINCINNATI	WKRC	550 AM Station	JACOR BROADCASTING CORPORATION
OH	CINCINNATI	WLW	700 AM Station	JACOR BROADCASTING CORPORATION
OH	CINCINNATI	WEBN	102.7 FM Commercial	JACOR BROADCASTING CORPORATION
OH	CLEVELAND	WMVX	106.5 FM Commercial	JACOR BROADCASTING CORPORATION
OH	CLEVELAND	WTAM	1100 AM Station	JACOR BROADCASTING CORPORATION
OH	CLEVELAND	WGAR-FM	99.5 FM Commercial	CITICASTERS LICENSES, L.P.

		Radio Station Subsidiaries for Clear Channel Communications Inc.		
State	City	Call Sign	Frequency	Subsidiary Name
OH	CLEVELAND	WMMS	100.7 FM Commercial	CITICASTERS LICENSES, L.P.
OH	CLEVELAND	WMJI	105.7 FM Commercial	CITICASTERS LICENSES, L.P.
OH	CLYDE	WMJK	100.9 FM Commercial	CITICASTERS LICENSES, L.P.
OH	COAL GROVE	WBVB	97.1 FM Commercial	CAPSTAR TX LIMITED PARTNERSHIP
OH	COLUMBUS	WCOL-FM	92.3 FM Commercial	CITICASTERS LICENSES, L.P.
OH	COLUMBUS	WCOL	1230 AM Station	CITICASTERS LICENSES, L.P.
OH	COLUMBUS	WTVN	610 AM Station	CITICASTERS LICENSES, L.P.
OH	COLUMBUS	WNCI	97.9 FM Commercial	CITICASTERS LICENSES, L.P.
OH	COLUMBUS GROVE	WLWD	93.9 FM Commercial	CLEAR CHANNEL BROADCASTING LICENSES, INC.
OH	DAYTON	WTUE	104.7 FM Commercial	CITICASTERS LICENSES, L.P.
OH	DAYTON	WONE	980 AM Station	CITICASTERS LICENSES, L.P.
OH	DAYTON	WMMX	107.7 FM Commercial	CITICASTERS LICENSES, L.P.
OH	DEFIANCE	WONW	1280 AM Station	CLEAR CHANNEL BROADCASTING LICENSES, INC.
OH	DEFIANCE	WZOM	105.7 FM Commercial	CLEAR CHANNEL BROADCASTING LICENSES, INC.
OH	DEFIANCE	WDFM	98.1 FM Commercial	CITICASTERS LICENSES, L.P.
OH	DOVER	WJER-FM	101.7 FM Commercial	CLEAR CHANNEL BROADCASTING LICENSES, INC.
OH	DOVER-NEW PHILADELPH	WJER	1450 AM Station	CLEAR CHANNEL BROADCASTING LICENSES, INC.
OH	EDGEWOOD	WZOO-FM	102.5 FM Commercial	CLEAR CHANNEL BROADCASTING LICENSES, INC.
OH	ENGLEWOOD	WDKF	94.5 FM Commercial	CITICASTERS LICENSES, L.P.
OH	FORT SHAWNEE	WZRX-FM	107.5 FM Commercial	JACOR BROADCASTING CORPORATION
OH	FREDERICKTOWN	WWBK	98.3 FM Commercial	CAPSTAR TX LIMITED PARTNERSHIP
OH	GALION	WFXN-FM	102.3 FM Commercial	CAPSTAR TX LIMITED PARTNERSHIP
OH	GREENVILLE	WDSJ	106.5 FM Commercial	CITICASTERS LICENSES, L.P.
OH	HILLIARD	WFJX	105.7 FM Commercial	CITICASTERS LICENSES, L.P.
OH	HILLSBORO	WSRW	1590 AM Station	CLEAR CHANNEL BROADCASTING LICENSES, INC.
OH	HILLSBORO	WSRW-FM	106.7 FM Commercial	CLEAR CHANNEL BROADCASTING LICENSES, INC.
OH	IRONTON	WIRO	1230 AM Station	CAPSTAR TX LIMITED PARTNERSHIP
OH	IRONTON	WBKS	107.1 FM Commercial	CAPSTAR TX LIMITED PARTNERSHIP
OH	KETTERING	WLQT	99.9 FM Commercial	CITICASTERS LICENSES, L.P.
OH	LIMA	WIMT	102.1 FM Commercial	JACOR BROADCASTING CORPORATION
OH	LIMA	WIMA	1150 AM Station	JACOR BROADCASTING CORPORATION
OH	LOUDONVILLE	WBZW	107.7 FM Commercial	CAPSTAR TX LIMITED PARTNERSHIP
OH	MANSFIELD	WMAN	1400 AM Station	CAPSTAR TX LIMITED PARTNERSHIP
OH	MANSFIELD	WYHT	105.3 FM Commercial	CAPSTAR TX LIMITED PARTNERSHIP
OH	MARIETTA	WRVB	102.1 FM Commercial	CLEAR CHANNEL BROADCASTING LICENSES, INC.
OH	MARIETTA	WLTP	910 AM Station	CLEAR CHANNEL BROADCASTING LICENSES, INC.
OH	MARION	WDIF	94.3 FM Commercial	CITICASTERS LICENSES, L.P.
OH	MARION	WMRN	1490 AM Station	CITICASTERS LICENSES, L.P.
OH	MARION	WMRN-FM	106.9 FM Commercial	CITICASTERS LICENSES, L.P.
OH	MILFORD	WKFS	107.1 FM Commercial	JACOR BROADCASTING CORPORATION
OH	MOUNT VERNON	WMVO	1300 AM Station	CAPSTAR TX LIMITED PARTNERSHIP
OH	MOUNT VERNON	WQIO	93.7 FM Commercial	CAPSTAR TX LIMITED PARTNERSHIP
OH	NAPOLEON	WNDH	103.1 FM Commercial	CLEAR CHANNEL BROADCASTING LICENSES, INC.
OH	NILES	WBBG	106.1 FM Commercial	CITICASTERS LICENSES, L.P.
OH	NORTH BALTIMORE	WPFX-FM	107.7 FM Commercial	CITICASTERS LICENSES, L.P.
OH	NORTH KINGSVILLE	WFXJ-FM	107.5 FM Commercial	CLEAR CHANNEL BROADCASTING LICENSES, INC.
OH	OTTAWA	WBUK	106.3 FM Commercial	CITICASTERS LICENSES, L.P.
OH	SANDUSKY	WLEC	1450 AM Station	CITICASTERS LICENSES, L.P.
OH	SANDUSKY	WCPZ	102.7 FM Commercial	CITICASTERS LICENSES, L.P.
OH	SHADYSIDE	WVKF	95.7 FM Commercial	CAPSTAR TX LIMITED PARTNERSHIP
OH	SHELBY	WSWR	100.1 FM Commercial	CAPSTAR TX LIMITED PARTNERSHIP
OH	SPRINGFIELD	WIZE	1340 AM Station	CITICASTERS LICENSES, L.P.
OH	ST. MARYS	WMLX	103.3 FM Commercial	JACOR BROADCASTING CORPORATION
OH	TIFFIN	WCKY-FM	103.7 FM Commercial	CITICASTERS LICENSES, L.P.
OH	TIFFIN	WTTF	1600 AM Station	CITICASTERS LICENSES, L.P.
OH	TOLEDO	WSPD	1370 AM Station	CITICASTERS LICENSES, L.P.
OH	TOLEDO	WRVF	101.5 FM Commercial	CITICASTERS LICENSES, L.P.
OH	TOLEDO	WCWA	1230 AM Station	JACOR BROADCASTING CORPORATION
OH	TOLEDO	WIOT	104.7 FM Commercial	JACOR BROADCASTING CORPORATION
OH	TOLEDO	WVKS	92.5 FM Commercial	CITICASTERS LICENSES, L.P.
OH	UPPER SANDUSKY	WYNT	95.9 FM Commercial	CLEAR CHANNEL BROADCASTING LICENSES, INC.
OH	WASHINGTON COURT HOU	WCHO-FM	105.5 FM Commercial	CITICASTERS LICENSES, L.P.

State	City	Call Sign	Frequency	Subsidiary Name
OH	WASHINGTON CT HOUSE	WCHO	1250 AM Station	CITICASTERS LICENSES, L.P.
OH	YOUNGSTOWN	WKBN	570 AM Station	CITICASTERS LICENSES, L.P.
OH	YOUNGSTOWN	WMXY	98.9 FM Commercial	CITICASTERS LICENSES, L.P.
OH	YOUNGSTOWN	WNCD	93.3 FM Commercial	CITICASTERS LICENSES, L.P.
OH	YOUNGSTOWN	WNIO	1390 AM Station	CITICASTERS LICENSES, L.P.
OK	BROKEN ARROW	KIZS	92.1 FM Commercial	CLEAR CHANNEL BROADCASTING LICENSES, INC.
OK	COLLINSVILLE	KTBT	101.5 FM Commercial	CLEAR CHANNEL BROADCASTING LICENSES, INC.
OK	LAWTON	KLAW	101.3 FM Commercial	CAPSTAR TX LIMITED PARTNERSHIP
OK	LAWTON	KZCD	94.1 FM Commercial	CAPSTAR TX LIMITED PARTNERSHIP
OK	MIDWEST CITY	KTLV	1220 AM Station	FIRST CHOICE BROADCASTING, INC.
OK	OKLAHOMA CITY	KJYO	102.7 FM Commercial	CLEAR CHANNEL BROADCASTING LICENSES, INC.
OK	OKLAHOMA CITY	KTOK	1000 AM Station	CLEAR CHANNEL BROADCASTING LICENSES, INC.
OK	OKLAHOMA CITY	KXXY-FM	96.1 FM Commercial	CLEAR CHANNEL BROADCASTING LICENSES, INC.
OK	OKLAHOMA CITY	KTST	101.9 FM Commercial	CLEAR CHANNEL BROADCASTING LICENSES, INC.
OK	OKLAHOMA CITY	KHBZ-FM	94.7 FM Commercial	CLEAR CHANNEL BROADCASTING LICENSES, INC.
OK	OWASSO	KQLL-FM	106.1 FM Commercial	CLEAR CHANNEL BROADCASTING LICENSES, INC.
OK	POTEAU	KZBB	97.9 FM Commercial	CAPSTAR TX LIMITED PARTNERSHIP
OK	SALLISAW	KKBD	95.9 FM Commercial	CAPSTAR TX LIMITED PARTNERSHIP
OK	TULSA	KAKC	1300 AM Station	CLEAR CHANNEL BROADCASTING LICENSES, INC.
OK	TULSA	KMOD-FM	97.5 FM Commercial	CLEAR CHANNEL BROADCASTING LICENSES, INC.
OK	TULSA	KTBZ	1430 AM Station	CLEAR CHANNEL BROADCASTING LICENSES, INC.
OR	ALBANY	KRKT-FM	99.9 FM Commercial	CITICASTERS LICENSES, L.P.
OR	ALBANY	KRKT	990 AM Station	CITICASTERS LICENSES, L.P.
OR	ASHLAND	KIFS	107.5 FM Commercial	CITICASTERS LICENSES, L.P.
OR	BEAVERTON	KKCW	103.3 FM Commercial	CITICASTERS LICENSES, L.P.
OR	CORVALLIS	KLOO	1340 AM Station	CITICASTERS LICENSES, L.P.
OR	CORVALLIS	KEJO	1240 AM Station	CITICASTERS LICENSES, L.P.
OR	CORVALLIS	KFLY	101.5 FM Commercial	CITICASTERS LICENSES, L.P.
OR	CORVALLIS	KLOO-FM	106.3 FM Commercial	CITICASTERS LICENSES, L.P.
OR	EAGLE POINT	KZZE	106.3 FM Commercial	CITICASTERS LICENSES, L.P.
OR	EUGENE	KODZ	99.1 FM Commercial	CAPSTAR TX LIMITED PARTNERSHIP
OR	EUGENE	KPNW	1120 AM Station	CAPSTAR TX LIMITED PARTNERSHIP
OR	FLORENCE	KDUK-FM	104.7 FM Commercial	CAPSTAR TX LIMITED PARTNERSHIP
OR	GOLD HILL	KRWQ	100.3 FM Commercial	CITICASTERS LICENSES, L.P.
OR	MEDFORD	KMED	1440 AM Station	CITICASTERS LICENSES, L.P.
OR	MEDFORD	KLDZ	103.5 FM Commercial	CITICASTERS LICENSES, L.P.
OR	MILTON-FREEWATER	KOLW	97.9 FM Commercial	CAPSTAR TX LIMITED PARTNERSHIP
OR	PORTLAND	KEX	1190 AM Station	CITICASTERS LICENSES, L.P.
OR	PORTLAND	KKRZ	100.3 FM Commercial	CITICASTERS LICENSES, L.P.
OR	PORTLAND	KPOJ	620 AM Station	CITICASTERS LICENSES, L.P.
PA	ALLENTOWN	WKAP	1470 AM Station	CAPSTAR TX LIMITED PARTNERSHIP
PA	ALLENTOWN	WAEB	790 AM Station	CAPSTAR TX LIMITED PARTNERSHIP
PA	ALLENTOWN	WAEB-FM	104.1 FM Commercial	CAPSTAR TX LIMITED PARTNERSHIP
PA	BETHLEHEM	WZZO	95.1 FM Commercial	CAPSTAR TX LIMITED PARTNERSHIP
PA	ELLWOOD CITY	WJST	92.1 FM Commercial	CITICASTERS LICENSES, L.P.
PA	HARRISBURG	WHP	580 AM Station	CLEAR CHANNEL BROADCASTING LICENSES, INC.
PA	HARRISBURG	WKBO	1230 AM Station	CLEAR CHANNEL BROADCASTING LICENSES, INC.
PA	HARRISBURG	WRVV	97.3 FM Commercial	CLEAR CHANNEL BROADCASTING LICENSES, INC.
PA	HARRISBURG	WTKT	1460 AM Station	CLEAR CHANNEL BROADCASTING LICENSES, INC.
PA	HARRISBURG	WHKF	99.3 FM Commercial	CLEAR CHANNEL BROADCASTING LICENSES, INC.
PA	HARRISBURG	WRBT	94.9 FM Commercial	CLEAR CHANNEL BROADCASTING LICENSES, INC.
PA	HUGHESVILLE	WRKK	1200 AM Station	CLEAR CHANNEL BROADCASTING LICENSES, INC.
PA	LANCASTER	WLAN-FM	96.9 FM Commercial	CLEAR CHANNEL BROADCASTING LICENSES, INC.
PA	LANCASTER	WLAN	1390 AM Station	CLEAR CHANNEL BROADCASTING LICENSES, INC.
PA	MILL HALL	WVRT	97.7 FM Commercial	CAPSTAR TX LIMITED PARTNERSHIP
PA	NEW CASTLE	WBZY	1280 AM Station	CITICASTERS LICENSES, L.P.
PA	NEW CASTLE	WKST	1200 AM Station	CITICASTERS LICENSES, L.P.
PA	PHILADELPHIA	WDAS	1480 AM Station	AMFM RADIO LICENSES, L.L.C.
PA	PHILADELPHIA	WDAS-FM	105.3 FM Commercial	AMFM RADIO LICENSES, L.L.C.
PA	PHILADELPHIA	WIOQ	102.1 FM Commercial	AMFM RADIO LICENSES, L.L.C.
PA	PHILADELPHIA	WUSL	98.9 FM Commercial	AMFM RADIO LICENSES, L.L.C.
PA	PHILADELPHIA	WJJZ	106.1 FM Commercial	AMFM RADIO LICENSES, L.L.C.
PA	PHILADELPHIA	WSNI-FM	104.5 FM Commercial	AMFM RADIO LICENSES, L.L.C.
PA	PITTSBURGH	WDVE	102.5 FM Commercial	CAPSTAR TX LIMITED PARTNERSHIP

State	City	Call Sign	Frequency	Subsidiary Name
		Radio Station Subsidiaries for Clear Channel Communications Inc.		
PA	PITTSBURGH	WWSW-FM	94.5 FM Commercial	AMFM RADIO LICENSES, L.L.C.
PA	PITTSBURGH	WXDX-FM	105.9 FM Commercial	CAPSTAR TX LIMITED PARTNERSHIP
PA	PITTSBURGH	WPGB	104.7 FM Commercial	CAPSTAR TX LIMITED PARTNERSHIP
PA	PITTSBURGH	WKST-FM	96.1 FM Commercial	CAPSTAR TX LIMITED PARTNERSHIP
PA	PITTSBURGH	WBGG	970 AM Station	AMFM RADIO LICENSES, L.L.C.
PA	READING	WRAW	1340 AM Station	CLEAR CHANNEL BROADCASTING LICENSES, INC.
PA	READING	WRFY-FM	102.5 FM Commercial	CLEAR CHANNEL BROADCASTING LICENSES, INC.
PA	SALLADASBURG	WBYL	95.5 FM Commercial	CLEAR CHANNEL BROADCASTING LICENSES, INC.
PA	SHAMOKIN	WBLJ-FM	95.3 FM Commercial	CLEAR CHANNEL BROADCASTING LICENSES, INC.
PA	SHARPSVILLE	WAKZ	95.9 FM Commercial	CITICASTERS LICENSES, L.P.
PA	WILLIAMSPORT	WRAK	1400 AM Station	CLEAR CHANNEL BROADCASTING LICENSES, INC.
PA	WILLIAMSPORT	WKSB	102.7 FM Commercial	CLEAR CHANNEL BROADCASTING LICENSES, INC.
RI	PROVIDENCE	WWBB	101.5 FM Commercial	CLEAR CHANNEL BROADCASTING LICENSES, INC.
RI	PROVIDENCE	WHJY	94.1 FM Commercial	CAPSTAR TX LIMITED PARTNERSHIP
RI	PROVIDENCE	WHJJ	920 AM Station	CAPSTAR TX LIMITED PARTNERSHIP
SC	AIKEN	WKSP	96.3 FM Commercial	CAPSTAR TX LIMITED PARTNERSHIP
SC	BEAUFORT	WYKZ	98.7 FM Commercial	CAPSTAR TX LIMITED PARTNERSHIP
SC	CAYCE	WLTY	96.7 FM Commercial	CAPSTAR TX LIMITED PARTNERSHIP
SC	CHARLESTON	WEZL	103.5 FM Commercial	CITICASTERS LICENSES, L.P.
SC	CHARLESTON	WALC	100.5 FM Commercial	CITICASTERS LICENSES, L.P.
SC	CHARLESTON	WSCC	730 AM Station	CITICASTERS LICENSES, L.P.
SC	COLUMBIA	WNOK	104.7 FM Commercial	CAPSTAR TX LIMITED PARTNERSHIP
SC	COLUMBIA	WCOS-FM	97.5 FM Commercial	CAPSTAR TX LIMITED PARTNERSHIP
SC	COLUMBIA	WCOS	1400 AM Station	CAPSTAR TX LIMITED PARTNERSHIP
SC	COLUMBIA	WVOC	560 AM Station	CAPSTAR TX LIMITED PARTNERSHIP
SC	GOOSE CREEK	WSSP	94.3 FM Commercial	CLEAR CHANNEL BROADCASTING LICENSES, INC.
SC	GRAY COURT	WSSL-FM	100.5 FM Commercial	CAPSTAR TX LIMITED PARTNERSHIP
SC	GREENVILLE	WGVL	1440 AM Station	CAPSTAR TX LIMITED PARTNERSHIP
SC	GREENVILLE	WESC-FM	92.5 FM Commercial	CLEAR CHANNEL BROADCASTING LICENSES, INC.
SC	GREENVILLE	WLFJ	660 AM Station	CLEAR CHANNEL BROADCASTING LICENSES, INC.
SC	HARDEEVILLE	WLVH	101.1 FM Commercial	CAPSTAR TX LIMITED PARTNERSHIP
SC	MAULDIN	WBZT-FM	96.7 FM Commercial	CLEAR CHANNEL BROADCASTING LICENSES, INC.
SC	MOUNT PLEASANT	WRFQ	104.5 FM Commercial	CITICASTERS LICENSES, L.P.
SC	NORTH AUGUSTA	WPCH	1380 AM Station	CAPSTAR TX LIMITED PARTNERSHIP
SC	NORTH CHARLESTON	WXLY	102.5 FM Commercial	CITICASTERS LICENSES, L.P.
SC	WEST COLUMBIA	WXBT	100.1 FM Commercial	CAPSTAR TX LIMITED PARTNERSHIP
SD	ABERDEEN	KBFO	106.7 FM Commercial	CLEAR CHANNEL BROADCASTING LICENSES, INC.
SD	ABERDEEN	KKAA	1560 AM Station	CLEAR CHANNEL BROADCASTING LICENSES, INC.
SD	ABERDEEN	KQAA	94.9 FM Commercial	CLEAR CHANNEL BROADCASTING LICENSES, INC.
SD	ABERDEEN	KSDN-FM	94.1 FM Commercial	CLEAR CHANNEL BROADCASTING LICENSES, INC.
SD	ABERDEEN	KSDN	930 AM Station	CLEAR CHANNEL BROADCASTING LICENSES, INC.
TN	CLEVELAND	WUSY	100.7 FM Commercial	CAPSTAR TX LIMITED PARTNERSHIP
TN	COOKEVILLE	WHUB	1400 AM Station	CLEAR CHANNEL BROADCASTING LICENSES, INC.
TN	COOKEVILLE	WGIC	98.5 FM Commercial	CLEAR CHANNEL BROADCASTING LICENSES, INC.
TN	COOKEVILLE	WGSQ	94.7 FM Commercial	CLEAR CHANNEL BROADCASTING LICENSES, INC.
TN	COOKEVILLE	WPTN	780 AM Station	CLEAR CHANNEL BROADCASTING LICENSES, INC.
TN	JACKSON	WTJS	1390 AM Station	CAPSTAR TX LIMITED PARTNERSHIP
TN	JACKSON	WTNV	104.1 FM Commercial	CAPSTAR TX LIMITED PARTNERSHIP
TN	LEBANON	WRVW	107.5 FM Commercial	CAPSTAR TX LIMITED PARTNERSHIP
TN	MCMINNVILLE	WBMC	960 AM Station	CITICASTERS LICENSES, L.P.
TN	MCMINNVILLE	WTRZ-FM	103.9 FM Commercial	CITICASTERS LICENSES, L.P.
TN	MCMINNVILLE	WAKI	1230 AM Station	CITICASTERS LICENSES, L.P.
TN	MEMPHIS	WREC	600 AM Station	CLEAR CHANNEL BROADCASTING LICENSES, INC.
TN	MEMPHIS	WEGR	102.7 FM Commercial	CLEAR CHANNEL BROADCASTING LICENSES, INC.
TN	MEMPHIS	KWAM	990 AM Station	CONCORD MEDIA GROUP, INC.
TN	MEMPHIS	KJMS	101.1 FM Commercial	CLEAR CHANNEL BROADCASTING LICENSES, INC.
TN	MEMPHIS	WDIA	1070 AM Station	CLEAR CHANNEL BROADCASTING LICENSES, INC.
TN	MEMPHIS	WHRK	97.1 FM Commercial	CLEAR CHANNEL BROADCASTING LICENSES, INC.
TN	MILAN	WYNU	92.3 FM Commercial	CAPSTAR TX LIMITED PARTNERSHIP
TN	NASHVILLE	WLAC	1510 AM Station	CAPSTAR TX LIMITED PARTNERSHIP
TN	NASHVILLE	WNRQ	105.9 FM Commercial	CAPSTAR TX LIMITED PARTNERSHIP
TN	NASHVILLE	WSIX-FM	97.9 FM Commercial	CAPSTAR TX LIMITED PARTNERSHIP
TN	SIGNAL MOUNTAIN	WKXJ	98.1 FM Commercial	CAPSTAR TX LIMITED PARTNERSHIP
TN	SOUTH PITTSBURG	WMXF-FM	97.3 FM Commercial	CAPSTAR TX LIMITED PARTNERSHIP

State	City	Call Sign	Frequency	Subsidiary Name
		Radio Station Subsidiaries for Clear Channel Communications Inc.		
TN	SPARTA	WSMT	1050 AM Station	CLEAR CHANNEL BROADCASTING LICENSES, INC.
TN	SPARTA	WRKK-FM	105.5 FM Commercial	CLEAR CHANNEL BROADCASTING LICENSES, INC.
TN	SPARTA	WTZX	860 AM Station	CLEAR CHANNEL BROADCASTING LICENSES, INC.
TN	SPENCER	WKZP	107.3 FM Commercial	CITICASTERS LICENSES, L.P.
TN	ST. JOSEPH	WJOR-FM	101.5 FM Commercial	CLEAR CHANNEL BROADCASTING LICENSES, INC.
TX	ABILENE	KEAN-FM	105.1 FM Commercial	CCB TEXAS LICENSES, L.P.
TX	ABILENE	KSLI	1280 AM Station	CCB TEXAS LICENSES, L.P.
TX	ABILENE	KULL	92.5 FM Commercial	CCB TEXAS LICENSES, L.P.
TX	ABILENE	KEYJ-FM	107.9 FM Commercial	CCB TEXAS LICENSES, L.P.
TX	ABILENE	KYYW	1470 AM Station	CCB TEXAS LICENSES, L.P.
TX	ABILENE	KHYS	100.7 FM Commercial	CCB TEXAS LICENSES, L.P.
TX	AMARILLO	KATP	101.9 FM Commercial	AMFM RADIO LICENSES, L.L.C.
TX	AMARILLO	KMXJ-FM	94.1 FM Commercial	CAPSTAR TX LIMITED PARTNERSHIP
TX	AMARILLO	KMML-FM	96.9 FM Commercial	CAPSTAR TX LIMITED PARTNERSHIP
TX	AMARILLO	KPRF	98.7 FM Commercial	CAPSTAR TX LIMITED PARTNERSHIP
TX	AMARILLO	KIXZ	940 AM Station	CAPSTAR TX LIMITED PARTNERSHIP
TX	AUSTIN	KPEZ	102.3 FM Commercial	CCB TEXAS LICENSES, L.P.
TX	AUSTIN	KASE-FM	100.7 FM Commercial	CAPSTAR TX LIMITED PARTNERSHIP
TX	AUSTIN	KVET	1300 AM Station	CAPSTAR TX LIMITED PARTNERSHIP
TX	AUSTIN	KVET-FM	98.1 FM Commercial	CAPSTAR TX LIMITED PARTNERSHIP
TX	BEAUMONT	KLVI	560 AM Station	CAPSTAR TX LIMITED PARTNERSHIP
TX	BEAUMONT	KYKR	95.1 FM Commercial	CAPSTAR TX LIMITED PARTNERSHIP
TX	BLOOMINGTON	KLUB	106.9 FM Commercial	CAPSTAR TX LIMITED PARTNERSHIP
TX	BROWNSVILLE	KTEX	100.3 FM Commercial	CAPSTAR TX LIMITED PARTNERSHIP
TX	BROWNSVILLE	KQXX	1600 AM Station	CLEAR CHANNEL BROADCASTING LICENSES, INC.
TX	BROWNSVILLE	KVNS	1700 AM Station	CLEAR CHANNEL BROADCASTING LICENSES, INC.
TX	BRYAN	KKYS	104.7 FM Commercial	CCB TEXAS LICENSES, L.P.
TX	BRYAN	KNFX-FM	99.5 FM Commercial	CCB TEXAS LICENSES, L.P.
TX	CARTHAGE	KTUX	98.9 FM Commercial	CITICASTERS LICENSES, L.P.
TX	CORPUS CHRISTI	KKTX	1360 AM Station	CAPSTAR TX LIMITED PARTNERSHIP
TX	CORPUS CHRISTI	KRYS-FM	99.1 FM Commercial	CAPSTAR TX LIMITED PARTNERSHIP
TX	CORPUS CHRISTI	KMXR	93.9 FM Commercial	CAPSTAR TX LIMITED PARTNERSHIP
TX	CORPUS CHRISTI	KUNO	1400 AM Station	CAPSTAR TX LIMITED PARTNERSHIP
TX	DALLAS	KZPS	92.5 FM Commercial	AMFM TEXAS LICENSES LIMITED PARTNERSHIP
TX	DALLAS	KFXR	1190 AM Station	CAPSTAR TX LIMITED PARTNERSHIP
TX	DALLAS	KDMX	102.9 FM Commercial	CITICASTERS LICENSES, L.P.
TX	DENTON	KHKS	106.1 FM Commercial	AMFM TEXAS LICENSES LIMITED PARTNERSHIP
TX	DIBOLL	KAFX-FM	95.5 FM Commercial	CAPSTAR TX LIMITED PARTNERSHIP
TX	EDINBURG	KBFM	104.1 FM Commercial	CAPSTAR TX LIMITED PARTNERSHIP
TX	EL PASO	KTSM	690 AM Station	CCB TEXAS LICENSES, L.P.
TX	EL PASO	KHEY-FM	96.3 FM Commercial	CCB TEXAS LICENSES, L.P.
TX	EL PASO	KPRR	102.1 FM Commercial	CCB TEXAS LICENSES, L.P.
TX	EL PASO	KTSM-FM	99.9 FM Commercial	CCB TEXAS LICENSES, L.P.
TX	EL PASO	KHEY	1380 AM Station	CCB TEXAS LICENSES, L.P.
TX	FORT WORTH	KEGL	97.1 FM Commercial	CITICASTERS LICENSES, L.P.
TX	FORT WORTH-DALLAS	KDGE	102.1 FM Commercial	CAPSTAR TX LIMITED PARTNERSHIP
TX	GARDENDALE	KFZX	102.1 FM Commercial	CAPSTAR TX LIMITED PARTNERSHIP
TX	GEORGETOWN	KHFI-FM	96.7 FM Commercial	CCB TEXAS LICENSES, L.P.
TX	GROVES	KCOL-FM	92.5 FM Commercial	CLEAR CHANNEL BROADCASTING LICENSES, INC.
TX	HILLSBORO	KBRQ	102.5 FM Commercial	CLEAR CHANNEL BROADCASTING LICENSES, INC.
TX	HOOKS	KPWW	95.9 FM Commercial	CAPSTAR TX LIMITED PARTNERSHIP
TX	HOUSTON	KODA	99.1 FM Commercial	AMFM TEXAS LICENSES LIMITED PARTNERSHIP
TX	HOUSTON	KLOL	101.1 FM Commercial	AMFM TEXAS LICENSES LIMITED PARTNERSHIP
TX	HOUSTON	KTRH	740 AM Station	AMFM TEXAS LICENSES LIMITED PARTNERSHIP
TX	HOUSTON	KHMX	96.5 FM Commercial	CITICASTERS LICENSES, L.P.
TX	HOUSTON	KTBZ-FM	94.5 FM Commercial	AMFM TEXAS LICENSES LIMITED PARTNERSHIP
TX	HOUSTON	KBME	790 AM Station	AMFM TEXAS LICENSES LIMITED PARTNERSHIP
TX	HOUSTON	KKRW	93.7 FM Commercial	CAPSTAR TX LIMITED PARTNERSHIP
TX	HOUSTON	KPRC	950 AM Station	CCB TEXAS LICENSES, L.P.
TX	KILGORE	KBGE	1240 AM Station	CAPSTAR TX LIMITED PARTNERSHIP
TX	KILGORE	KKTX-FM	96.1 FM Commercial	CAPSTAR TX LIMITED PARTNERSHIP
TX	KILLEEN	KIIZ-FM	92.3 FM Commercial	CAPSTAR TX LIMITED PARTNERSHIP
TX	LORENZO	KKCL	98.1 FM Commercial	CAPSTAR TX LIMITED PARTNERSHIP
TX	LUBBOCK	KZII-FM	102.5 FM Commercial	CAPSTAR TX LIMITED PARTNERSHIP

State	City	Call Sign	Frequency	Subsidiary Name
			Radio Station Subsidiaries for Clear Channel Communications Inc.	
TX	LUBBOCK	KFYO	790 AM Station	CAPSTAR TX LIMITED PARTNERSHIP
TX	LUBBOCK	KKAM	1340 AM Station	CAPSTAR TX LIMITED PARTNERSHIP
TX	LUBBOCK	KFMX-FM	94.5 FM Commercial	CAPSTAR TX LIMITED PARTNERSHIP
TX	LUBBOCK	KQBR	99.5 FM Commercial	CAPSTAR TX LIMITED PARTNERSHIP
TX	LUFKIN	KYKS	105.1 FM Commercial	CAPSTAR TX LIMITED PARTNERSHIP
TX	MADISONVILLE	KAGG	96.1 FM Commercial	CCB TEXAS LICENSES, L.P.
TX	MERCEDES	KHKZ	106.3 FM Commercial	CLEAR CHANNEL BROADCASTING LICENSES, INC.
TX	MIDLAND	KCRS	550 AM Station	CCB TEXAS LICENSES, L.P.
TX	MIDLAND	KCHX	106.7 FM Commercial	CAPSTAR TX LIMITED PARTNERSHIP
TX	MIDLAND	KCRS-FM	103.3 FM Commercial	CCB TEXAS LICENSES, L.P.
TX	MISSION	KQXX-FM	105.5 FM Commercial	CLEAR CHANNEL BROADCASTING LICENSES, INC.
TX	NACOGDOCHES	KTBQ	107.7 FM Commercial	CAPSTAR TX LIMITED PARTNERSHIP
TX	NACOGDOCHES	KSFA	860 AM Station	CAPSTAR TX LIMITED PARTNERSHIP
TX	NOLANVILLE	KLFX	107.3 FM Commercial	CLEAR CHANNEL BROADCASTING LICENSES, INC.
TX	ODESSA	KMRK-FM	96.1 FM Commercial	CAPSTAR TX LIMITED PARTNERSHIP
TX	ORANGE	KKMY	104.5 FM Commercial	CAPSTAR TX LIMITED PARTNERSHIP
TX	ORANGE	KIOC	106.1 FM Commercial	CAPSTAR TX LIMITED PARTNERSHIP
TX	ROBSTOWN	KSAB	99.9 FM Commercial	CAPSTAR TX LIMITED PARTNERSHIP
TX	ROUND ROCK	KFMK	105.9 FM Commercial	CAPSTAR TX LIMITED PARTNERSHIP
TX	SAN ANTONIO	KXXM	96.1 FM Commercial	CCB TEXAS LICENSES, L.P.
TX	SAN ANTONIO	KAJA	97.3 FM Commercial	CCB TEXAS LICENSES, L.P.
TX	SAN ANTONIO	KTKR	760 AM Station	CCB TEXAS LICENSES, L.P.
TX	SAN ANTONIO	WOAI	1200 AM Station	CCB TEXAS LICENSES, L.P.
TX	SAN ANTONIO	KQXT-FM	101.9 FM Commercial	CCB TEXAS LICENSES, L.P.
TX	SINTON	KNCN	101.3 FM Commercial	CAPSTAR TX LIMITED PARTNERSHIP
TX	SOMERSET	KSJL	810 AM Station	MARANATHA BROADCASTING, INC.
TX	TEXARKANA	KKYR-FM	102.5 FM Commercial	CAPSTAR TX LIMITED PARTNERSHIP
TX	TYLER	KNUE	101.5 FM Commercial	CAPSTAR TX LIMITED PARTNERSHIP
TX	TYLER	KTYL-FM	93.1 FM Commercial	CAPSTAR TX LIMITED PARTNERSHIP
TX	VICTORIA	KQVT	92.3 FM Commercial	CAPSTAR TX LIMITED PARTNERSHIP
TX	VICTORIA	KIXS	107.9 FM Commercial	CAPSTAR TX LIMITED PARTNERSHIP
TX	WACO	KBGO	95.7 FM Commercial	CAPSTAR TX LIMITED PARTNERSHIP
TX	WACO	KWTX	1230 AM Station	CAPSTAR TX LIMITED PARTNERSHIP
TX	WACO	KWTX-FM	97.5 FM Commercial	CAPSTAR TX LIMITED PARTNERSHIP
TX	WACO	WACO-FM	99.9 FM Commercial	CAPSTAR TX LIMITED PARTNERSHIP
TX	WHITEHOUSE	KISX	107.3 FM Commercial	CAPSTAR TX LIMITED PARTNERSHIP
TX	WICHITA FALLS	KNIN-FM	92.9 FM Commercial	CCB TEXAS LICENSES, L.P.
TX	WICHITA FALLS	KBZS	106.3 FM Commercial	CCB TEXAS LICENSES, L.P.
TX	WICHITA FALLS	KWFS	1290 AM Station	CCB TEXAS LICENSES, L.P.
TX	WICHITA FALLS	KWFS-FM	102.3 FM Commercial	CCB TEXAS LICENSES, L.P.
UT	BOUNTIFUL	KURR	99.5 FM Commercial	CITICASTERS LICENSES, L.P.
UT	CENTERVILLE	KCPX	105.7 FM Commercial	CITICASTERS LICENSES, L.P.
UT	NORTH SALT LAKE CITY	KALL	700 AM Station	CITICASTERS LICENSES, L.P.
UT	SALT LAKE CITY	KNRS	570 AM Station	CITICASTERS LICENSES, L.P.
UT	SALT LAKE CITY	KZHT	97.1 FM Commercial	CLEAR CHANNEL BROADCASTING LICENSES, INC.
UT	SALT LAKE CITY	KODJ	94.1 FM Commercial	CITICASTERS LICENSES, L.P.
UT	SPANISH FORK	KOSY-FM	106.5 FM Commercial	CITICASTERS LICENSES, L.P.
VA	AMHERST	WYYD	107.9 FM Commercial	CAPSTAR TX LIMITED PARTNERSHIP
VA	APPOMATTOX	WMJA	102.7 FM Commercial	CAPSTAR TX LIMITED PARTNERSHIP
VA	CHARLOTTESVILLE	WCHV	1260 AM Station	CLEAR CHANNEL BROADCASTING LICENSES, INC.
VA	CHARLOTTESVILLE	WKAV	1400 AM Station	CLEAR CHANNEL BROADCASTING LICENSES, INC.
VA	CROZET	WSUH	102.3 FM Commercial	CLEAR CHANNEL BROADCASTING LICENSES, INC.
VA	ELKTON	WACL	98.5 FM Commercial	CAPSTAR TX LIMITED PARTNERSHIP
VA	FRONT ROYAL	WFQX	99.3 FM Commercial	CAPSTAR TX LIMITED PARTNERSHIP
VA	HARRISONBURG	WKCY-FM	104.3 FM Commercial	CAPSTAR TX LIMITED PARTNERSHIP
VA	HARRISONBURG	WKCY	1300 AM Station	CAPSTAR TX LIMITED PARTNERSHIP
VA	LYNCHBURG	WVGM	1320 AM Station	CAPSTAR TX LIMITED PARTNERSHIP
VA	LYNCHBURG	WJJX	101.7 FM Commercial	CAPSTAR TX LIMITED PARTNERSHIP
VA	MARTINSVILLE	WROV-FM	96.3 FM Commercial	CAPSTAR TX LIMITED PARTNERSHIP
VA	NORFOLK	WOWI	102.9 FM Commercial	CLEAR CHANNEL BROADCASTING LICENSES, INC.
VA	RICHMOND	WBTJ	106.5 FM Commercial	CAPSTAR TX LIMITED PARTNERSHIP
VA	RICHMOND	WTVR-FM	98.1 FM Commercial	CLEAR CHANNEL BROADCASTING LICENSES, INC.
VA	RICHMOND	WRVA	1140 AM Station	CLEAR CHANNEL BROADCASTING LICENSES, INC.
VA	RICHMOND	WRVQ	94.5 FM Commercial	CLEAR CHANNEL BROADCASTING LICENSES, INC.

State	City	Call Sign	Frequency	Subsidiary Name
			Radio Station Subsidiaries for Clear Channel Communications Inc.	
VA	RICHMOND	WRNL	910 AM Station	CLEAR CHANNEL BROADCASTING LICENSES, INC.
VA	RICHMOND	WRXL	102.1 FM Commercial	CLEAR CHANNEL BROADCASTING LICENSES, INC.
VA	ROANOKE	WMGR-FM	104.9 FM Commercial	CAPSTAR TX LIMITED PARTNERSHIP
VA	ROANOKE	WGMN	1240 AM Station	CAPSTAR TX LIMITED PARTNERSHIP
VA	RUCKERSVILLE	WHTE-FM	101.9 FM Commercial	CLEAR CHANNEL BROADCASTING LICENSES, INC.
VA	SALEM	WSNV	93.5 FM Commercial	CAPSTAR TX LIMITED PARTNERSHIP
VA	STAUNTON	WCYK-FM	99.7 FM Commercial	CLEAR CHANNEL BROADCASTING LICENSES, INC.
VA	STAUNTON	WSVO	93.1 FM Commercial	CLEAR CHANNEL BROADCASTING LICENSES, INC.
VA	STAUNTON	WKDW	900 AM Station	CLEAR CHANNEL BROADCASTING LICENSES, INC.
VA	VINTON	WJJS-FM	106.1 FM Commercial	CAPSTAR TX LIMITED PARTNERSHIP
VA	WAYNESBORO	WKCI	970 AM Station	CLEAR CHANNEL BROADCASTING LICENSES, INC.
VA	WINCHESTER	WUSQ-FM	102.5 FM Commercial	CAPSTAR TX LIMITED PARTNERSHIP
VA	WINCHESTER	WTFX	610 AM Station	CAPSTAR TX LIMITED PARTNERSHIP
VA	WINDSOR	WJCD	107.7 FM Commercial	CLEAR CHANNEL BROADCASTING LICENSES, INC.
VA	WOODSTOCK	WAZR	93.7 FM Commercial	CLEAR CHANNEL BROADCASTING LICENSES, INC.
VT	BURLINGTON	WEZF	92.9 FM Commercial	CAPSTAR TX LIMITED PARTNERSHIP
VT	RANDOLPH	WWWT	1320 AM Station	CAPSTAR TX LIMITED PARTNERSHIP
VT	RANDOLPH	WCVR-FM	102.1 FM Commercial	CAPSTAR TX LIMITED PARTNERSHIP
VT	RUTLAND	WSYB	1380 AM Station	CAPSTAR TX LIMITED PARTNERSHIP
VT	RUTLAND	WZRT	97.1 FM Commercial	CAPSTAR TX LIMITED PARTNERSHIP
VT	SPRINGFIELD	WXKK	93.5 FM Commercial	CLEAR CHANNEL BROADCASTING LICENSES, INC.
VT	WOODSTOCK	WMXR	93.9 FM Commercial	CLEAR CHANNEL BROADCASTING LICENSES, INC.
WA	CENTRALIA	KMNT	102.9 FM Commercial	CITICASTERS LICENSES, L.P.
WA	CENTRALIA-CHEHALIS	KELA	1470 AM Station	CITICASTERS LICENSES, L.P.
WA	EATONVILLE	KFNK	104.9 FM Commercial	ACKERLEY MEDIA GROUP, INC.
WA	NACHES	KQSN	99.3 FM Commercial	CAPSTAR TX LIMITED PARTNERSHIP
WA	OPPORTUNITY	KIXZ-FM	96.1 FM Commercial	CAPSTAR TX LIMITED PARTNERSHIP
WA	PASCO	KEYW	98.3 FM Commercial	CAPSTAR TX LIMITED PARTNERSHIP
WA	PASCO	KFLD	870 AM Station	CAPSTAR TX LIMITED PARTNERSHIP
WA	RICHLAND	KORD-FM	102.7 FM Commercial	CAPSTAR TX LIMITED PARTNERSHIP
WA	SEATTLE	KJR-FM	95.7 FM Commercial	ACKERLEY MEDIA GROUP, INC.
WA	SEATTLE	KJR	950 AM Station	ACKERLEY MEDIA GROUP, INC.
WA	SEATTLE	KUBE	93.3 FM Commercial	ACKERLEY MEDIA GROUP, INC.
WA	SPOKANE	KKZX	98.9 FM Commercial	CAPSTAR TX LIMITED PARTNERSHIP
WA	SPOKANE	KAQQ	1280 AM Station	CAPSTAR TX LIMITED PARTNERSHIP
WA	SPOKANE	KQNT	590 AM Station	CAPSTAR TX LIMITED PARTNERSHIP
WA	SPOKANE	KISC	98.1 FM Commercial	CAPSTAR TX LIMITED PARTNERSHIP
WA	TACOMA	KHHO	850 AM Station	ACKERLEY MEDIA GROUP, INC.
WA	TOPPENISH	KDBL	92.9 FM Commercial	CITICASTERS LICENSES, L.P.
WA	VANCOUVER	KRVO	105.9 FM Commercial	CITICASTERS LICENSES, L.P.
WA	WALLA WALLA	KXRX	97.1 FM Commercial	CAPSTAR TX LIMITED PARTNERSHIP
WA	YAKIMA	KATS	94.5 FM Commercial	CITICASTERS LICENSES, L.P.
WA	YAKIMA	KIT	1280 AM Station	CITICASTERS LICENSES, L.P.
WA	YAKIMA	KUTI	1460 AM Station	CITICASTERS LICENSES, L.P.
WA	YAKIMA	KFFM	107.3 FM Commercial	CITICASTERS LICENSES, L.P.
WI	ALTOONA	WISM-FM	98.1 FM Commercial	CLEAR CHANNEL BROADCASTING LICENSES, INC.
WI	BLOOMER	WQRB	95.1 FM Commercial	CAPSTAR TX LIMITED PARTNERSHIP
WI	CHETEK	WATQ	106.7 FM Commercial	CAPSTAR TX LIMITED PARTNERSHIP
WI	EAU CLAIRE	WBIZ	1400 AM Station	CAPSTAR TX LIMITED PARTNERSHIP
WI	EAU CLAIRE	WBIZ-FM	100.7 FM Commercial	CAPSTAR TX LIMITED PARTNERSHIP
WI	MADISON	WIBA	1310 AM Station	CAPSTAR TX LIMITED PARTNERSHIP
WI	MADISON	WIBA-FM	101.5 FM Commercial	CAPSTAR TX LIMITED PARTNERSHIP
WI	MADISON	WTSO	1070 AM Station	CAPSTAR TX LIMITED PARTNERSHIP
WI	MADISON	WZEE	104.1 FM Commercial	CAPSTAR TX LIMITED PARTNERSHIP
WI	MENOMONIE	WMEQ-FM	92.1 FM Commercial	CAPSTAR TX LIMITED PARTNERSHIP
WI	MENOMONIE	WMEQ	880 AM Station	CAPSTAR TX LIMITED PARTNERSHIP
WI	MILWAUKEE	WLTQ	97.3 FM Commercial	CAPSTAR TX LIMITED PARTNERSHIP
WI	MILWAUKEE	WISN	1130 AM Station	CAPSTAR TX LIMITED PARTNERSHIP
WI	MILWAUKEE	WRIT-FM	95.7 FM Commercial	CLEAR CHANNEL BROADCASTING LICENSES, INC.
WI	MILWAUKEE	WOKY	920 AM Station	CLEAR CHANNEL BROADCASTING LICENSES, INC.
WI	RACINE	WKKV-FM	100.7 FM Commercial	CLEAR CHANNEL BROADCASTING LICENSES, INC.
WI	SAUK CITY	WMAD	96.3 FM Commercial	CAPSTAR TX LIMITED PARTNERSHIP
WI	SUN PRAIRIE	WXXM	92.1 FM Commercial	CAPSTAR TX LIMITED PARTNERSHIP
WI	WAUKESHA	WMIL-FM	106.1 FM Commercial	CLEAR CHANNEL BROADCASTING LICENSES, INC.

Radio Station Subsidiaries for Clear Channel Communications Inc.

State	City	Call Sign	Frequency	Subsidiary Name
WV	CHARLES TOWN	WKSI-FM	98.3 FM Commercial	CLEVELAND RADIO LICENSES, LLC
WV	CHARLESTOWN	WMRE	1550 AM Station	CLEVELAND RADIO LICENSES, LLC
WV	ELIZABETH	WRZZ	106.1 FM Commercial	CLEAR CHANNEL BROADCASTING LICENSES, INC.
WV	HUNTINGTON	WKEE-FM	100.5 FM Commercial	CAPSTAR TX LIMITED PARTNERSHIP
WV	HUNTINGTON	WTCR-FM	103.3 FM Commercial	CAPSTAR TX LIMITED PARTNERSHIP
WV	HUNTINGTON	WVHU	800 AM Station	CAPSTAR TX LIMITED PARTNERSHIP
WV	KENOVA	WTCR	1420 AM Station	CAPSTAR TX LIMITED PARTNERSHIP
WV	MILTON	WZZW	1600 AM Station	CAPSTAR TX LIMITED PARTNERSHIP
WV	MILTON	WAMX	106.3 FM Commercial	CAPSTAR TX LIMITED PARTNERSHIP
WV	VIENNA	WDMX	100.1 FM Commercial	CLEAR CHANNEL BROADCASTING LICENSES, INC.
WV	WHEELING	WWVA	1170 AM Station	CAPSTAR TX LIMITED PARTNERSHIP
WV	WHEELING	WOVK	98.7 FM Commercial	CAPSTAR TX LIMITED PARTNERSHIP
WV	WHEELING	WBBD	1400 AM Station	CAPSTAR TX LIMITED PARTNERSHIP
WV	WHEELING	WKWK-FM	97.3 FM Commercial	CAPSTAR TX LIMITED PARTNERSHIP
WV	WHEELING	WEGW	107.5 FM Commercial	CAPSTAR TX LIMITED PARTNERSHIP
WY	BURNS	KIGN	101.9 FM Commercial	CITICASTERS LICENSES, L.P.
WY	CASPER	KKTL	1400 AM Station	CITICASTERS LICENSES, L.P.
WY	CASPER	KTWO	1030 AM Station	CITICASTERS LICENSES, L.P.
WY	CASPER	KWYY	95.5 FM Commercial	CLEAR CHANNEL BROADCASTING LICENSES, INC.
WY	CASPER	KTRS-FM	104.7 FM Commercial	CLEAR CHANNEL BROADCASTING LICENSES, INC.
WY	CASPER	KMGW	96.7 FM Commercial	CLEAR CHANNEL BROADCASTING LICENSES, INC.
WY	CHEYENNE	KLEN	106.3 FM Commercial	CITICASTERS LICENSES, L.P.
WY	CHEYENNE	KOLZ	100.7 FM Commercial	CITICASTERS LICENSES, L.P.
WY	CHEYENNE	KQLF	97.9 FM Commercial	CITICASTERS LICENSES, L.P.
WY	LARAMIE	KCGY	95.1 FM Commercial	CLEAR CHANNEL BROADCASTING LICENSES, INC.
WY	LARAMIE	KOWB	1290 AM Station	CLEAR CHANNEL BROADCASTING LICENSES, INC.
WY	MIDWEST	KRVK	107.9 FM Commercial	CLEAR CHANNEL BROADCASTING LICENSES, INC.
WY	ORCHARD VALLEY	KGAB	650 AM Station	CITICASTERS LICENSES, L.P.

TV Station Subsidiaries for Clear Channel Communications Inc.

Call Sign	Channel and Type	Subsidiary Name	Area of Service
KGPE	47 TV Commercial	ACKERLEY BROADCASTING - FRESNO, LLC	FRESNO, CA
KTVF	11 TV Commercial	ACKERLEY MEDIA GROUP, INC.	FAIRBANKS, AK
KMTZ	23 TV Commercial	ACKERLEY MEDIA GROUP, INC.	COOS BAY, OR
KMTX-TV	46 TV Commercial	ACKERLEY MEDIA GROUP, INC.	ROSEBURG, OR
KMTR	16 TV Commercial	ACKERLEY MEDIA GROUP, INC.	EUGENE, OR
KVIQ	6 TV Commercial	ACKERLEY MEDIA GROUP, INC.	EUREKA, CA
KCOY-TV	12 TV Commercial	ACKERLEY MEDIA GROUP, INC.	SANTA MARIA, CA
KVOS-TV	12 TV Commercial	ACKERLEY MEDIA GROUP, INC.	BELLINGHAM, WA
KION-TV	46 TV Commercial	ACKERLEY MEDIA GROUP, INC.	MONTEREY, CA
KKFX-CA	24 Class A TV (UHF)	ACKERLEY MEDIA GROUP, INC.	SAN LUIS OBISPO, CA
KFTY	50 TV Commercial	ACKERLEY MEDIA GROUP, INC.	SANTA ROSA, CA
KGET-TV	17 TV Commercial	ACKERLEY MEDIA GROUP, INC.	BAKERSFIELD, CA
WOAI-TV	4 TV Commercial	CCB TEXAS LICENSES, L.P.	SAN ANTONIO, TX
WIVT	34 TV Commercial	CENTRAL NY NEWS, INC.	BINGHAMTON, NY
WOKR	13 TV Commercial	CENTRAL NY NEWS, INC.	ROCHESTER, NY
WIXT-TV	9 TV Commercial	CENTRAL NY NEWS, INC.	SYRACUSE, NY
WBGH-CA	20 Class A TV (UHF)	CENTRAL NY NEWS, INC.	BINGHAMTON, NY
WWTI	50 TV Commercial	CENTRAL NY NEWS, INC.	WATERTOWN, NY
WKRC-TV	12 TV Commercial	CITICASTERS CO.	CINCINNATI, OH
WDFM-LP	26 TV Low Power (UHF)	CITICASTERS LICENSES, L.P.	DEFIANCE, OH
KBDK	14 TV Commercial	CLEAR CHANNEL BROADCASTING LICENSES, INC.	HOISINGTON, KS
WPTY-TV	24 TV Commercial	CLEAR CHANNEL BROADCASTING LICENSES, INC.	MEMPHIS, TN
WPMI	15 TV Commercial	CLEAR CHANNEL BROADCASTING LICENSES, INC.	MOBILE, AL
WHP-TV	21 TV Commercial	CLEAR CHANNEL BROADCASTING LICENSES, INC.	HARRISBURG, PA
WJTC	44 TV Commercial	CLEAR CHANNEL BROADCASTING LICENSES, INC.	PENSACOLA, FL
KASN	38 TV Commercial	CLEAR CHANNEL BROADCASTING LICENSES, INC.	PINE BLUFF, AR
KTFO	41 TV Commercial	CLEAR CHANNEL BROADCASTING LICENSES, INC.	TULSA, OK
WLMT	30 TV Commercial	CLEAR CHANNEL BROADCASTING LICENSES, INC.	MEMPHIS, TN
WJKT	16 TV Commercial	CLEAR CHANNEL BROADCASTING LICENSES, INC.	JACKSON, TN
KTVX	4 TV Commercial	CLEAR CHANNEL BROADCASTING LICENSES, INC.	SALT LAKE CITY, UT
WTEV-TV	47 TV Commercial	CLEAR CHANNEL BROADCASTING LICENSES, INC.	JACKSONVILLE, FL
WAWS	30 TV Commercial	CLEAR CHANNEL BROADCASTING LICENSES, INC.	JACKSONVILLE, FL

TV Station Subsidiaries for Clear Channel Communications Inc.			
Call Sign	Channel and Type	Subsidiary Name	Area of Service
KOKI-TV	23 TV Commercial	CLEAR CHANNEL BROADCASTING LICENSES, INC.	TULSA, OK
KSAS-TV	24 TV Commercial	CLEAR CHANNEL BROADCASTING LICENSES, INC.	WICHITA, KS
KAAS-TV	18 TV Commercial	CLEAR CHANNEL BROADCASTING LICENSES, INC.	SALINA, KS
KSCC-LP	14 TV Low Power (UHF)	CLEAR CHANNEL BROADCASTING LICENSES, INC.	GREAT BEND, KS
K28AK	28 TV Low Power (UHF)	CLEAR CHANNEL BROADCASTING LICENSES, INC.	COLLEGE STATION, TX
KLRT-TV	16 TV Commercial	CLEAR CHANNEL BROADCASTING LICENSES, INC.	LITTLE ROCK, AR
KSAS-LP	29 TV Low Power (UHF)	CLEAR CHANNEL BROADCASTING LICENSES, INC.	DODGE CITY, KS
KAAS-LP	31 TV Low Power (UHF)	CLEAR CHANNEL BROADCASTING LICENSES, INC.	GARDEN CITY, KS
WXXA-TV	23 TV Commercial	CLEAR CHANNEL BROADCASTING LICENSES, INC.	ALBANY, NY

Comcast Corp.

Address:	1500 Market St.	Stock Symbol:	CMCSA
	Philadelphia, PA 19102-2148	Telephone:	215-665-1700
		Fax:	215-981-7790
Total Employees:	68,000	Website:	www.comcast.com

Having conquered the cable industry, Comcast Corp. revealed in 2004 its intention to extend its dominance beyond mere delivery of programming.

Comcast stunned the industry when it attempted (unsuccessfully) to buy the Walt Disney Co., including all of its film and television production facilities and theme parks. And weeks later, it sent shockwaves through the telecommunications sector when it announced plans to offer Internet-based telephone service to more than 40 million households by 2006.

The bid to buy Disney and the aggressive move into the telephone business signaled a clear change of direction for a company that until now has been content to merely provide the pipeline for television programming.

But despite its mammoth size and rapidly expanding power, Comcast is still very much a family business. It was founded in 1969 by Ralph J. Roberts, Daniel Aaron and Julian A. Brodsky, when the trio purchased a 1,200 subscriber cable system in Tupelo, Miss. The company went public in 1972, trading on NASDAQ.

Like most of today's largest cable companies, Comcast got big through acquisitions. In 1986 it purchased a stake in Group W Cable and made a founding investment in the QVC home shopping network. In 1988 Comcast bought a 50 percent stake in Storer Communications, boosting its number of cable subscribers to more than 2 million.

That same year Comcast got into the cellular telephone business with the purchase of AMCELL (American Cellular Network Corp.), whose New Jersey and Delaware service territory covered a population of 2 million. In 1992 Comcast combined AMCELL with Metrophone, tripling the population area served to 7 million, according to a company-prepared timeline. Comcast would eventually sell its cellular business to SBC Communications of San Antonio, Texas, for $1.7 billion in 1999.

In 1995 Comcast bought a majority stake in QVC and assumed management of the electronics retailer. Comcast later sold its interest to Liberty Media for $7.9 billion. The company also acquired E.W. Scripps cable systems, adding another 800,000 subscribers and bringing Comcast's customer total to 4.3 million.

Microsoft invested $1 billion in Comcast in 1997. The company continued to grow rapidly the next few years through acquisitions and subscriber swaps with other leading cable companies, including Adelphia and Jones Intercable.

In late 1999, Comcast and MediaOne announced a $60 billion merger agreement with great fanfare, but the deal would eventually fall apart. When the merger agreement was canceled, Comcast collected a $1.5 billion termination fee and announced an agreement to acquire 2 million AT&T subscribers.

In December 2001, AT&T Broadband agreed to sell its cable unit to Comcast for $47 billion in stock and $25 billion in assumed debt. That deal, by far the largest ever in the cable business, was completed in November 2002. The acquisition gave the company nearly 22 million cable subscribers in 41 states, nearly double the size of its nearest competitor, Time Warner Cable. Comcast also has 6.3 million digital video customers, 3.3 million high-speed data customers, and 1.3 million cable phone subscribers. It will see an additional 1.8 million cable subscribers with the recent deal with Time Warner Inc. to acquire Adelphia.

Despite Comcast's domination of the cable services business, the majority of the media giant's business comes from other sources. Nearly half of Comcast's revenues in 2001 came from its 57 percent stake in QVC Corp, which itself had sales of nearly $4 billion in 2001.

The company is also the majority owner of the Philadelphia Flyers hockey team and the Philadelphia 76ers basketball team. Another Comcast venture, regional cable network Sportsnet, broadcasts Flyers, 76ers, and Philadelphia Phillies games. Other cable programming ventures include regional sports network Comcast Sports Southeast (72 percent), E! entertainment channel (40 percent), the Golf Channel (91 percent), Outdoor Life Network (100 percent) , Style Network (40 percent), and sports and public affairs regional programmer The Sunshine Network (16 percent). In addition, Comcast holds an 11 percent stake of the In Demand pay-per-view network.

Following the withdrawal of the Disney bid, C. Michael Armstrong announced at the annual shareholders meeting that he was stepping down as chairman of the board of Comcast, a position he held since November 2002. Prior to that he was chairman and CEO of AT&T Corporation from 1997 to February 2002. He was chairman and CEO of Hughes Electronic Corporation from 1992 to 1997, and an officer of IBM Corp. from 1961 to 1992. He is currently a director of Parsons Corp. and Citigroup Inc.

The company's largest individual stockholders are Roberts, now 83 years old, and his son, Comcast President and CEO Brian Roberts, 43, who succeeded Armstrong as board chairman. Together they control about 33 percent of Comcast's voting stock

—Bob Williams, Robert Morlino

April 28, 2005

Sources: Company Web site, Securities and Exchange Commission filings, Yahoo! Finance Online, Hoover's Online, Fortune magazine, Bloomberg.com

Comcast Corp. Recent Financial Information		
Year	Revenue	Net Income (Net Loss)
1999	$3,465,000,000	$1,066,000,000
2000	$4,836,000,000	$2,021,000,000
2001	$5,937,000,000	$609,000,000
2002	$8,102,000,000	($274,000,000)
2003	$18,348,000,000	$3,240,000,000

Comcast Corp. Board of Directors			
Name	Position	Relevant Stock	Qty
Bacon, Kenneth	Director	CMCSA	15,300
Bonovitz, Sheldon	Director	CMCSA	20,925
Roberts, Brian	Chairman and CEO	CMCSK	3,017
Roberts, Ralph	Director	N/A	N/A
Rodin, Judith	Director	CMCSA	8,584
Anstrom, S.	Director	CMCSA	8,584
Brodsky, Julian	Director	CMCSK	124,457
Cook, J.	Director	CMCSA	14,359
Sovern, Michael	Director	CMCSA	14,989
Castle, Joseph	Director	CMCSA	6,000
Armstrong, C.	Non-executive chairman of the Board	CMCSA	2,633,050

Comcast Corp. Corporate Officers			
Name	Position	Salary	Bonuses
Roberts, Brian	President and CEO	$2,001,000	$6,000,000
Roberts, Ralph	Chairman of the Executive and Finance Committee of the Board of Directors	$1,601,000	$1,600,000
Burke, Stephen	EVP and President, Comcast Cable	$1,167,886	$5,166,886
Smith, Lawrence	Co-CFO and EVP	$1,040,500	$1,039,500
Alchin, John	Co-CFO, EVP, Treasurer	$883,000	$882,000
Armstrong, C.	Non-Executive Chairman of the Board	$1,801,000	$2,700,000

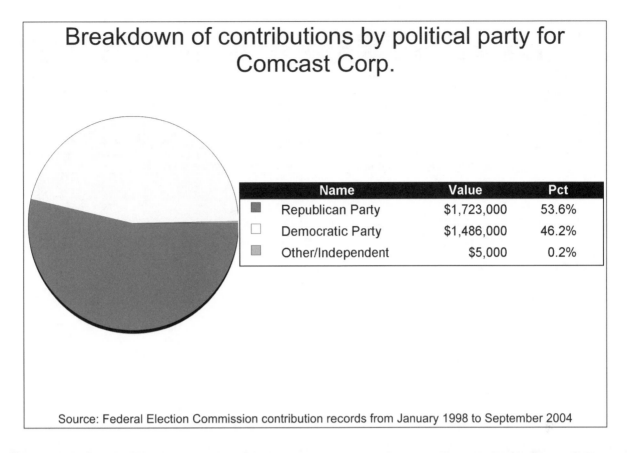

Breakdown of contributions by political party for Comcast Corp.

Name	Value	Pct
Republican Party	$1,723,000	53.6%
Democratic Party	$1,486,000	46.2%
Other/Independent	$5,000	0.2%

Source: Federal Election Commission contribution records from January 1998 to September 2004

Top 10 Recipients of Contributions Sourced to Comcast Corp.	
Recipient	Amount
National Republican Party Committees	$851,000
National Democratic Party Committees	$669,000
President George W Bush (R)	$109,000
Sen Arlen Specter (R-PA)	$77,000
Rep John D Dingell (D-MI)	$55,000
Sen Thomas Andrew Daschle (D-SD)	$50,000
Sen Conrad R Burns (R-MT)	$35,000
Rep Heather Ann Wilson (R-NM)	$34,000
Sen John F Kerry (D-MA)	$33,000
Rep Charles W Pickering, Jr (R-MS)	$29,000
Total:	$1,942,000

Source: Federal Election Commission contribution records from January 1998 to September 2004

Comcast Corp. Lobbying Expenditures by Year	
Year	Amount
1998	$2,220,000
1999	$1,540,000
2000	$960,000
2001	$1,720,000
2002	$4,850,000
2003	$3,780,000
2004	$500,000
Total:	$15,570,000

Source: U.S. Senate Office of Public Records lobbying disclosure records from January 1998 to June 30th, 2004.

Comcast Corp. Sponsored Trips for Congressional Staff		
Congressional Office	Number of Trips	$ Amount
Rep Peter Russell Deutsch (D-FL)	1	$1,021
Rep Frederick Carlyle Boucher (D-VA)	1	$518
Rep Charles F Bass (R-NH)	1	$517
Rep Michael J Rogers (R-MI)	1	$503
Sen John E Sununu (R-NH)	1	$251
Total:	5	$2,810
Source: Congressional office travel records for members of the Senate Committee on Commerce, Science & Transportation and the House Committee on Energy and Commerce for the period of January 2000 to March 2004.		

Cox Enterprises Inc.

Address: 6500 Peachtree Dunwoody Rd.
Atlanta, GA 30328

Stock Symbol: N/A
Telephone: 678-645-0000
Fax: 678-645-1079
Website: www.coxenterprises.com

Total Employees: 77,000

When Cox Enterprises Inc. announced its intention to take its cable subsidiary Cox Communications Inc. private in August, the news was enough to lift the bulk of the cable sector on Wall Street. Cox competitors saw a significant boost in their stock price. Cablevision Systems Corp., rumored to be a prime takeover target for Cox, saw its shares rise 11 percent after the announcement.

If the cable company is eventually taken private, it won't be without precedent. Cox Communications, 63 percent owned by Cox Enterprises, is but one part of one of the nation's leading media companies. And the cable company has gone private before, only to revert to public ownership when it suited the interests of the parent.

Through its major operating subsidiaries, Cox Enterprises has significant holdings in multiple sectors of the telecommunications and media industries. All told, Cox delivers cable television services to more than 6 million subscribers, owns 15 broadcast television stations, 78 radio stations, 17 daily newspapers including the Atlanta Journal-Constitution, and 23 weeklies. And to boot, the company is also a major player in the automobile auction business.

Cox Enterprises has traveled a long road to get where it is today, but it may never have even existed were it not for President Warren G. Harding. In 1920, Harding defeated Cox founder and three-term Ohio Governor James M. Cox to win the White House. (Cox's running mate was a young newcomer to the Democrat Party named Franklin D. Roosevelt.)

Harding went to Washington, where his legacy would be the Teapot Dome oil field scandal. Cox, who already owned the Dayton Daily News newspaper, stayed in Ohio and started to build a media empire.

Cox was an early investor in radio—he started Dayton's first radio station in 1934. James Cox Jr., who took over the company upon his father's death in 1957, was one of the first big investors in cable television.

James C. Kennedy, the grandson of company founder James M. Cox, has been chairman and chief executive officer of Cox Enterprises since 1987.

James Robbins has been president of Cox Communications since 1985 and CEO since 1995, when the company went public. Robbins came to Cox from Viacom Communications Inc., where he was senior vice president of operations.

The company has made it clear it believes the sale of bundled services—cable, Internet access, telephone and other telecommunications services—will be the key to future growth. Unlike some of its competitors, the company doesn't charge customers extra for the bundling service—a risky position given the cost.

In fact, confidence in that strategy led to the announcement that the parent company intends to take Cox Communications private once more, believing that it can make better progress without having to answer to investors.

Indeed, such concerns have contributed to the sagging stock prices across the cable industry, as investors have become spooked by the prospects of direct broadcast satellite television. Despite enjoying six consecutive quarters of growth, the company's stock was down 25 percent from the beginning of the year.

But with the announcement—seen by industry analysts as a sign of strength in the cable industry as a whole—Cox Communications stock jumped 20 percent.

—Bob Williams, Robert Morlino

August 3, 2004

Sources: Company Web site, Securities and Exchange Commission filings, Yahoo! Finance Online, Hoover's Online, Fortune magazine, Multichannel News

Cox Enterprises Inc. Recent Financial Information		
Year	Revenue	Net Income (Net Loss)
1991	$2,314,500,000	Not reported
1992	$2,486,300,000	Not reported
1993	$2,637,700,000	Not reported
1994	$2,844,400,000	Not reported
1995	$3,634,800,000	Not reported
1996	$4,289,000,000	Not reported
1997	$4,791,900,000	Not reported
1998	$5,223,500,000	Not reported

Cox Enterprises Inc. Recent Financial Information		
Year	Revenue	Net Income (Net Loss)
1999	$6,097,300,000	Not reported
2000	$7,823,600,000	Not reported
2001	$8,691,200,000	Not reported

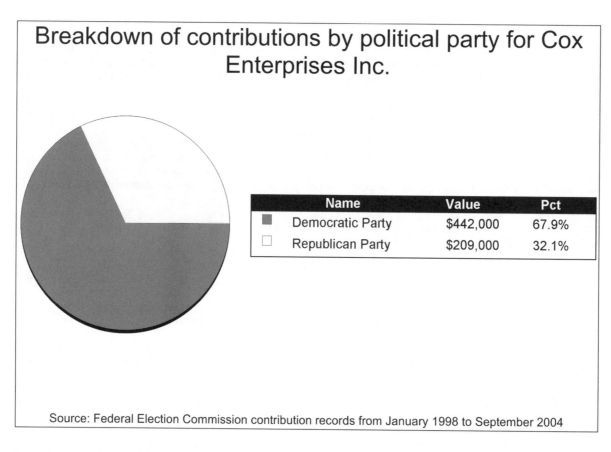

Breakdown of contributions by political party for Cox Enterprises Inc.

	Name	Value	Pct
	Democratic Party	$442,000	67.9%
	Republican Party	$209,000	32.1%

Source: Federal Election Commission contribution records from January 1998 to September 2004

Top 10 Recipients of Contributions Sourced to Cox Enterprises Inc.	
Recipient	Amount
National Democratic Party Committees	$295,000
National Republican Party Committees	$70,000
President George W Bush (R)	$24,000
Sen Saxby Chambliss (R-GA)	$12,000
Michael J Coles (D-GA)	$12,000
Sen Harry Reid (D-NV)	$11,000
Rep Wilbert J Tauzin, Jr (R-LA)	$11,000
Erskine B Bowles (D-NC)	$11,000
Sen Max Cleland (D-GA)	$10,000
Sen John S McCain (R-AZ)	$9,000
Total:	$465,000

Source: Federal Election Commission contribution records from January 1998 to September 2004

Cox Enterprises Inc. Lobbying Expenditures by Year	
Year	Amount
1998	$980,000
1999	$960,000
2000	$1,156,000
2001	$2,582,000
2002	$1,902,000
2003	$1,961,614
2004	$803,753
Total:	$10,345,367

Source: U.S. Senate Office of Public Records lobbying disclosure records from January 1998 to June 30th, 2004.

Radio Station Subsidiaries for Cox Enterprises Inc.

State	City	Call Sign	Frequency	Subsidiary Name
AL	BIRMINGHAM	WZZK-FM	104.7 FM Commercial	CXR HOLDINGS, INC.
AL	BIRMINGHAM	WBPT	106.9 FM Commercial	CXR HOLDINGS, INC.
AL	BIRMINGHAM	WZZK	1320 AM Station	CXR HOLDINGS, INC.
AL	HOMEWOOD	WODL	97.3 FM Commercial	CXR HOLDINGS, INC.
AL	TUSCALOOSA	WBHJ	95.7 FM Commercial	CXR HOLDINGS, INC.
AL	WARRIOR	WBHK	98.7 FM Commercial	CXR HOLDINGS, INC.
CT	BRIDGEPORT	WEZN-FM	99.9 FM Commercial	CXR HOLDINGS, INC.
CT	NEW HAVEN	WPLR	99.1 FM Commercial	COX RADIO, INC.
CT	NORWALK	WNLK	1350 AM Station	COX RADIO, INC.
CT	NORWALK	WEFX	95.9 FM Commercial	COX RADIO, INC.
CT	STAMFORD	WKHL	96.7 FM Commercial	COX RADIO, INC.
CT	STAMFORD	WSTC	1400 AM Station	COX RADIO, INC.
FL	ATLANTIC BEACH	WFYV-FM	104.5 FM Commercial	COX RADIO, INC.
FL	CORAL GABLES	WHQT	105.1 FM Commercial	COX RADIO, INC.
FL	DAYTONA BEACH	WCFB	94.5 FM Commercial	COX RADIO, INC.
FL	HOLIDAY	WSUN-FM	97.1 FM Commercial	COX RADIO, INC
FL	JACKSONVILLE	WAPE-FM	95.1 FM Commercial	COX RADIO, INC.
FL	JACKSONVILLE	WKQL	96.9 FM Commercial	COX RADIO, INC.
FL	JACKSONVILLE	WOKV	690 AM Station	COX RADIO, INC.
FL	JACKSONVILLE	WMXQ	102.9 FM Commercial	COX RADIO, INC.
FL	MAITLAND	WPYO	95.3 FM Commercial	CXR HOLDINGS, INC.
FL	MIAMI	WFLC	97.3 FM Commercial	COX RADIO, INC.
FL	MIAMI	WEDR	99.1 FM Commercial	COX RADIO, INC.
FL	MIAMI	WPYM	93.1 FM Commercial	COX RADIO-MIAMI, LLC
FL	NEW PORT RICHEY	WDUV	105.5 FM Commercial	CXR HOLDINGS, INC.
FL	ORLANDO	WWKA	92.3 FM Commercial	COX RADIO, INC.
FL	ORLANDO	WDBO	580 AM Station	COX RADIO, INC.
FL	ORLANDO	WHTQ	96.5 FM Commercial	COX RADIO, INC.
FL	ORLANDO	WMMO	98.9 FM Commercial	COX RADIO, INC.
FL	SARASOTA	WHPT	102.5 FM Commercial	CXR HOLDINGS, INC.
FL	ST. PETERSBURG	WPOI	101.5 FM Commercial	CXR HOLDINGS, INC.
FL	ST. PETERSBURG	WXGL	107.3 FM Commercial	COX RADIO, INC.
FL	TAMPA	WWRM	94.9 FM Commercial	COX RADIO, INC.
GA	ATHENS	WBTS	95.5 FM Commercial	CXR HOLDINGS, INC.
GA	ATLANTA	WSB	750 AM Station	CXR HOLDINGS, INC.
GA	ATLANTA	WSB-FM	98.5 FM Commercial	CXR HOLDINGS, INC.
GA	GAINESVILLE	WFOX	97.1 FM Commercial	COX RADIO, INC.
GA	LA GRANGE	WALR-FM	104.1 FM Commercial	CXR HOLDINGS, INC.
GA	WOODBINE	WCGA	1100 AM Station	COX BROADCAST GROUP, INC.
HI	AIEA	KGMZ-FM	107.9 FM Commercial	HONOLULU BROADCASTING, INC.
HI	HONOLULU	KCCN-FM	100.3 FM Commercial	CXR HOLDINGS, INC.
HI	HONOLULU	KINE-FM	105.1 FM Commercial	CXR HOLDINGS, INC.
HI	KAILUA	KRTR-FM	96.3 FM Commercial	CXR HOLDINGS, INC.
HI	KANEOHE	KXME	104.3 FM Commercial	CXR HOLDINGS, INC.
IN	CORYDON	WSFR	107.7 FM Commercial	CXR HOLDINGS, INC.
KY	LOUISVILLE	WVEZ	106.9 FM Commercial	CXR HOLDINGS, INC.
KY	LOUISVILLE	WPTI	103.9 FM Commercial	CXR HOLDINGS, INC.
KY	ST. MATTHEWS	WRKA	103.1 FM Commercial	CXR HOLDINGS, INC.
NY	BABYLON	WBAB	102.3 FM Commercial	CXR HOLDINGS, INC.
NY	PATCHOGUE	WBLI	106.1 FM Commercial	CXR HOLDINGS, INC.
NY	SOUTHAMPTON	WHFM	95.3 FM Commercial	CXR HOLDINGS, INC.
OH	DAYTON	WHIO	1290 AM Station	CXR HOLDINGS, INC.
OH	DAYTON	WHKO	99.1 FM Commercial	CXR HOLDINGS, INC.
OH	PIQUA	WDPT	95.7 FM Commercial	CXR HOLDINGS, INC.
OH	XENIA	WZLR	95.3 FM Commercial	CXR HOLDINGS, INC.
OK	SAND SPRINGS	KRTQ	102.3 FM Commercial	CXR HOLDINGS, INC.
OK	TULSA	KRMG	740 AM Station	CXR HOLDINGS, INC.
OK	TULSA	KJSR	103.3 FM Commercial	CXR HOLDINGS, INC.
OK	TULSA	KWEN	95.5 FM Commercial	CXR HOLDINGS, INC.
OK	TULSA	KRAV-FM	96.5 FM Commercial	CXR HOLDINGS, INC.
SC	ANDERSON	WJMZ-FM	107.3 FM Commercial	CXR HOLDINGS, INC.
SC	SENECA	WHZT	98.1 FM Commercial	CXR HOLDINGS, INC.
TX	CLEVELAND	KTHT	97.1 FM Commercial	CXR HOLDINGS, INC.
TX	CONROE	KHPT	106.9 FM Commercial	CXR HOLDINGS, INC.

State	City	Call Sign	Frequency	Subsidiary Name
\multicolumn{5}{c}{Radio Station Subsidiaries for Cox Enterprises Inc.}

State	City	Call Sign	Frequency	Subsidiary Name
TX	HELOTES	KONO-FM	101.1 FM Commercial	CXR HOLDINGS, INC.
TX	LAKE JACKSON	KLDE	107.5 FM Commercial	CXR HOLDINGS, INC.
TX	PASADENA	KKBQ-FM	92.9 FM Commercial	CXR HOLDINGS, INC.
TX	SAN ANTONIO	KONO	860 AM Station	CXR HOLDINGS, INC.
TX	SAN ANTONIO	KCYY	100.3 FM Commercial	CXR HOLDINGS, INC.
TX	SAN ANTONIO	KKYX	680 AM Station	CXR HOLDINGS, INC.
TX	SAN ANTONIO	KISS-FM	99.5 FM Commercial	CXR HOLDINGS, INC.
TX	SEGUIN	KSMG	105.3 FM Commercial	CXR HOLDINGS, INC.
TX	TERRELL HILLS	KELZ-FM	106.7 FM Commercial	CXR HOLDINGS, INC.
VA	CHESTER	WDYL	101.1 FM Commercial	CXR HOLDINGS, INC.
VA	COLONIAL HEIGHTS	WKHK	95.3 FM Commercial	COX RADIO, INC.
VA	FORT LEE	WKLR	96.5 FM Commercial	COX RADIO, INC.
VA	RICHMOND	WMXB	103.7 FM Commercial	COX RADIO, INC.

TV Station Subsidiaries for Cox Enterprises Inc.

Call Sign	Channel and Type	Subsidiary Name	Area of Service
KIRO-TV	7 TV Commercial	KIRO-TV HOLDINGS, INC.	SEATTLE, WA
KFOX-TV	14 TV Commercial	KTVU PARTNERSHIP	EL PASO, TX
KRXI-TV	11 TV Commercial	KTVU PARTNERSHIP	RENO, NV
KTVU	2 TV Commercial	KTVU PARTNERSHIP	OAKLAND, CA
KICU-TV	36 TV Commercial	KTVU PARTNERSHIP	SAN JOSE, CA
WRDQ	27 TV Commercial	WFTV-TV HOLDINGS, INC.	ORLANDO, FL
WFTV	9 TV Commercial	WFTV-TV HOLDINGS, INC.	ORLANDO, FL
WHIO-TV	7 TV Commercial	WHIO-TV HOLDINGS, INC.	DAYTON, OH
WJAC-TV	6 TV Commercial	WPXI-TV HOLDINGS, INC.	JOHNSTOWN, PA
WPXI	11 TV Commercial	WPXI-TV HOLDINGS, INC.	PITTSBURGH, PA
WSB-TV	2 TV Commercial	WSB-TV HOLDINGS, INC.	ATLANTA, GA
WAXN-TV	64 TV Commercial	WSOC-TV HOLDINGS, INC.	KANNAPOLIS, NC
WSOC-TV	9 TV Commercial	WSOC-TV HOLDINGS, INC.	CHARLOTTE, NC
WTOV-TV	9 TV Commercial	WTOV-TV HOLDINGS, INC.	STEUBENVILLE, OH

Print Media Subsidiaries for Cox Enterprises Inc.

Company Name	Market City	Weekday Circulation	Sunday Circulation
Austin American-Statesman	Austin, TX	184,907	234,409
Dayton Daily News	Dayton, OH	124,702	192,003
JournalNews	Hamilton, OH	22,208	24,568
Longview News-Journal	Longview, TX	29,509	36,457
Marshall News Messenger	Marshall, TX	6,994	7,519
Middletown Journal	Middletown, OH	20,556	22,432
Palm Beach Daily News	Palm Beach, FL	6,270	6,270
Rocky Mount Telegram	Rocky Mount, NC	14,518	16,902
Springfield News-Sun	Springfield, OH	28,525	35,726
The Atlanta Journal-Constitution	Atlanta, GA	389,580	629,505
The Daily Advance	Elizabeth City, NC	10,514	10,383
The Daily Reflector	Greenville, NC	20,265	22,863
The Daily Sentinel	Grand Junction, CO	29,975	33,842
The Daily Sentinel	Nacogdoches, TX	8,238	10,040
The Lufkin Daily News	Lufkin, TX	13,697	16,138
The Palm Beach Post	West Palm Beach, FL	168,147	208,286
Waco Tribune-Herald	Waco, TX	40,699	49,628

Cumulus Media Inc.

Address:	3535 Piedmont Rd. Building 14, Floor 14 Atlanta, GA 30305	Stock Symbol: Telephone: Fax:	CMLS 404-949-0700 404-949-0740
Total Employees:	2,800	Website:	www.cumulus.com

Virtually all of the major radio broadcast companies have taken advantage of the 1996 law that loosened limits on how many stations a single company can own to grow bigger. But Cumulus Media is the only major broadcaster that actually formed because of that controversial piece of legislation.

Now the second-largest radio station owner in the United States by number of stations (ninth by total revenue), Cumulus is following the same corporate strategy as radio kingpin Clear Channel Communications Inc.: buy as many stations in each market as possible, cut costs and raise revenue. The strategy seems to be working, as the company has continued to scoop up stations.

Cumulus focuses on building "clusters" of radio stations in mid-sized markets. The clustering approach allows Cumulus and other large broadcasting companies to save money through shared administrative, sales and production operations.

Cumulus was created in 1997 by radio consultant and Harvard-trained MBA Lew Dickey and Milwaukee investor Richard Weening. At the time, Dickey was working for some Caribbean radio stations owned by Weening. The two sought to capitalize on changes made in the Telecommunications Act of 1996. The legislation eliminated the national cap on how many radio stations a single company can own.

The pair raised money for the company's acquisitions from the State of Wisconsin Investment Board and NationsBank Capital, among others. Cumulus went public in 1998, greatly accelerating its expansion. In only six years, Cumulus has grown to 305 radio stations in nearly 60 U.S. cities.

Dickey spearheaded the company's acquisition efforts, which consisted of more than 130 separate transactions.

Dickey, now chairman, president and CEO of Cumulus, is a second generation broadcaster. Prior to Cumulus, he founded Stratford Research, a market research and consulting firm for the radio and television industry. Dickey and his family control a small percentage of total Cumulus stock, but Lewis Dickey owns all of the company's "class C" shares, which means he controls about a third of the voting stock.

Despite the favorable regulatory climate and a wealth of experience, Cumulus has had some problems financially.

While revenue has increased steadily (with the exception of 2001, a terrible year for radio), Cumulus wasn't profitable until 2003, posting a $5 million net gain, up from the $92.8 million net loss of the previous year.

Of more concern to investors and regulators, the company was forced to restate earnings for three quarters in 1999, and was the subject of a number of shareholder lawsuits.

In late 2003, Cumulus reached a settlement agreement with the Securities and Exchange Commission related to an investigation into whether, in 1999, its then-top managers violated securities law. In settling the matter, the company neither admitted nor denied the allegations. The charges concerned the way Weening had managed the company's finances, reportedly to meet investor expectations, in 1999. As part of the settlement, Weening personally agreed to pay $75,000. Part of the SEC's reasoning behind settling the case was the potential damage to shareholders that would be caused by litigation against Cumulus, and the fact that Weening and the other two executives involved in the case were no longer with the company.

The company's problems with the SEC didn't hinder its expansion plans. Just prior to the announcement of the settlement, Cumulus bought 15 stations in the Midwest for a cool $78 million. Earlier this year, it coughed up another $38.75 million for seven more stations in Missouri.

Cumulus continues to expand despite concerns that the company has used its stations to punish artists whose politics don't agree with those of its management. Cumulus briefly banned the Dixie Chicks from its play list for their criticism of President Bush and the war in Iraq in 2003. Dickey told a U.S. Senate panel the Chicks were pulled from the air because of a "groundswell of negative reaction by our listeners against the band and we had never seen anything like it before."

—John Dunbar, Robert Morlino

August 20, 2004

Sources: Cumulus Media Inc. Web site, Hoover's Online company profile, Cumulus Form 10-K, Los Angeles Times, The Daily Deal, Milwaukee Journal Sentinel

Cumulus Media Inc. Recent Financial Information		
Year	Revenue	Net Income (Net Loss)
1998	$98,787,000	($11,282,000)
1999	$180,230,000	($13,622,000)
2000	$226,640,000	($2,298,000)
2001	$202,087,000	($30,553,000)
2002	$252,597,000	($92,753,000)
2003	$281,971,000	$5,041,000

Cumulus Media Inc. Board of Directors				
Name	Position	Relevant Stock		Qty
Everett, Ralph	Director		CMLS	114,370
Green, Holcombe	Director		CMLS	50,310
Robison, Eric	Director		CMLS	106,778
Sheridan, Robert	Director		CMLS	34,999
Dickey, Lewis	Chairman		CMLS	4,708,005

Cumulus Media Inc. Corporate Officers			
Name	Position	Salary	Bonuses
Dickey, Lewis	Chairman, President, and CEO	$577,496	$288,750
Pinch, John	SVP and COO	$425,000	$85,000
Gausvik, Martin	EVP, CFO, and Treasurer	$423,329	$212,000
Dickey, John	EVP	$440,000	$220,000

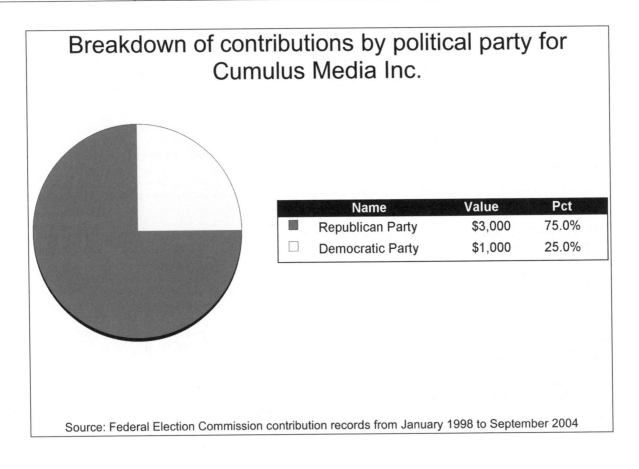

Breakdown of contributions by political party for Cumulus Media Inc.

	Name	Value	Pct
■	Republican Party	$3,000	75.0%
□	Democratic Party	$1,000	25.0%

Source: Federal Election Commission contribution records from January 1998 to September 2004

Top 10 Recipients of Contributions Sourced to Cumulus Media Inc.

Recipient	Amount
Rep Frederick Stephen Upton (R-MI)	$2,000
National Republican Party Committees	$1,000
Sen Debbie Stabenow (D-MI)	$1,000
Eshagpoor, Jane	-
Sen John F Kerry (D-MA)	-
Georgia Republican Party	-
Total:	$4,000

Source: Federal Election Commission contribution records from January 1998 to September 2004

Cumulus Media Inc. Lobbying Expenditures by Year

Year	Amount
1999	$100,000
2000	$80,000
Total:	$180,000

Source: U.S. Senate Office of Public Records lobbying disclosure records from January 1998 to June 30th, 2004.

Radio Station Subsidiaries for Cumulus Media Inc.

State	City	Call Sign	Frequency	Subsidiary Name
AL	ATHENS	WZYP	104.3 FM Commercial	CUMULUS LICENSING LLC
AL	ATHENS	WVNN	770 AM Station	CUMULUS LICENSING LLC
AL	ATMORE	WYOK	104.1 FM Commercial	CUMULUS LICENSING LLC
AL	CHICKASAW	WDLT-FM	98.3 FM Commercial	CUMULUS LICENSING LLC
AL	DAPHNE	WAVH	106.5 FM Commercial	BALDWIN BROADCASTING COMPANY, DEBTOR IN POSSESSION
AL	FAIRHOPE	WDLT	660 AM Station	CUMULUS LICENSING LLC
AL	MADISON	WUMP	730 AM Station	CUMULUS LICENSING LLC
AL	MOBILE	WGOK	900 AM Station	CUMULUS LICENSING LLC
AL	MOBILE	WBLX-FM	92.9 FM Commercial	CUMULUS LICENSING LLC
AL	MONTGOMERY	WMSP	740 AM Station	CUMULUS LICENSING LLC
AL	MONTGOMERY	WLWI-FM	92.3 FM Commercial	CUMULUS LICENSING LLC
AL	MONTGOMERY	WNZZ	950 AM Station	CUMULUS LICENSING LLC
AL	MONTGOMERY	WMXS	103.3 FM Commercial	CUMULUS LICENSING LLC
AL	MONTGOMERY	WLWI	1440 AM Station	CUMULUS LICENSING LLC
AL	MONTGOMERY	WHHY-FM	101.9 FM Commercial	CUMULUS LICENSING LLC
AL	PRATTVILLE	WXFX	95.1 FM Commercial	CUMULUS LICENSING LLC
AR	BENTONVILLE	KQSM-FM	98.3 FM Commercial	CUMULUS LICENSING LLC
AR	FARMINGTON	KFAY	1030 AM Station	CUMULUS LICENSING LLC
AR	FAYETTEVILLE	KKEG	92.1 FM Commercial	CUMULUS LICENSING LLC
AR	FORT SMITH	KBBQ-FM	100.7 FM Commercial	CUMULUS LICENSING LLC
AR	MAGNOLIA	KVMA-FM	107.9 FM Commercial	COLUMBIA BROADCASTING CO., INC.
AR	PRAIRIE GROVE	KYNF	94.9 FM Commercial	CUMULUS LICENSING LLC
AR	ROGERS	KAMO-FM	94.3 FM Commercial	CUMULUS LICENSING LLC
AR	SILOAM SPRINGS	KMCK-FM	105.7 FM Commercial	CUMULUS LICENSING LLC
AR	SPRINGDALE	KZRA	1590 AM Station	CUMULUS LICENSING LLC
AR	VAN BUREN	KLSZ-FM	102.7 FM Commercial	CUMULUS LICENSING LLC
AR	VAN BUREN	KAYR	1060 AM Station	CUMULUS LICENSING LLC
CA	GOLETA	KKSB	106.3 FM Commercial	CUMULUS LICENSING LLC
CA	SANTA BARBARA	KRUZ	103.3 FM Commercial	CUMULUS LICENSING LLC
CA	SANTA BARBARA	KMGQ	97.5 FM Commercial	CUMULUS LICENSING LLC
CA	VENTURA	KBBY-FM	95.1 FM Commercial	CUMULUS LICENSING LLC
CA	VENTURA	KVEN	1450 AM Station	CUMULUS LICENSING LLC
CA	VENTURA	KHAY	100.7 FM Commercial	CUMULUS LICENSING LLC
CO	DELTA	KKNN	95.1 FM Commercial	CUMULUS LICENSING LLC
CO	FRUITA	KEKB	99.9 FM Commercial	CUMULUS LICENSING LLC
CO	GRAND JUNCTION	KEXO	1230 AM Station	CUMULUS LICENSING LLC
CO	GRAND JUNCTION	KMXY	104.3 FM Commercial	CUMULUS LICENSING LLC
CO	GRAND JUNCTION	KBKL	107.9 FM Commercial	CUMULUS LICENSING LLC
CT	BRIDGEPORT	WICC	600 AM Station	CUMULUS LICENSING LLC
CT	BROOKFIELD	WINE	940 AM Station	CUMULUS LICENSING LLC
CT	BROOKFIELD	WRKI	95.1 FM Commercial	CUMULUS LICENSING LLC
CT	WESTPORT	WEBE	107.9 FM Commercial	CUMULUS LICENSING LLC
FL	FORT WALTON	WZNS	96.5 FM Commercial	CUMULUS LICENSING LLC

Radio Station Subsidiaries for Cumulus Media Inc.				
State	City	Call Sign	Frequency	Subsidiary Name
	BEACH			
FL	FORT WALTON BEACH	WFTW	1260 AM Station	CUMULUS LICENSING LLC
FL	FORT WALTON BEACH	WKSM	99.5 FM Commercial	CUMULUS LICENSING LLC
FL	GULF BREEZE	WRRX	106.1 FM Commercial	CUMULUS LICENSING LLC
FL	MARY ESTHER	WYZB	105.5 FM Commercial	CUMULUS LICENSING LLC
FL	MELBOURNE	WAOA-FM	107.1 FM Commercial	CUMULUS LICENSING LLC
FL	MELBOURNE	WINT	1560 AM Station	CUMULUS LICENSING LLC
FL	NICEVILLE	WNCV	100.3 FM Commercial	CUMULUS LICENSING LLC
FL	PENSACOLA	WCOA	1370 AM Station	CUMULUS LICENSING LLC
FL	PENSACOLA	WJLQ	100.7 FM Commercial	CUMULUS LICENSING LLC
FL	ROCKLEDGE	WHKR	102.7 FM Commercial	CUMULUS LICENSING LLC
FL	SEBASTIAN	WSJZ-FM	95.9 FM Commercial	SEBASTIAN BROADCASTING COMPANY
FL	TALLAHASSEE	WBZE	98.9 FM Commercial	CUMULUS LICENSING LLC
FL	TALLAHASSEE	WHBX	96.1 FM Commercial	CUMULUS LICENSING LLC
FL	TALLAHASSEE	WHBT	1410 AM Station	CUMULUS LICENSING LLC
FL	TALLAHASSEE	WGLF	104.1 FM Commercial	CUMULUS LICENSING LLC
GA	ALBANY	WGPC	1450 AM Station	CUMULUS LICENSING LLC
GA	ALBANY	WKAK	104.5 FM Commercial	CUMULUS LICENSING LLC
GA	ALBANY	WALG	1590 AM Station	CUMULUS LICENSING LLC
GA	ALBANY	WNUQ	101.7 FM Commercial	CUMULUS LICENSING LLC
GA	CAIRO	WWLD	102.3 FM Commercial	CUMULUS LICENSING LLC
GA	CAMILLA	WQVE	105.5 FM Commercial	CUMULUS LICENSING LLC
GA	JEFFERSONVILLE	WPEZ	93.7 FM Commercial	CUMULUS LICENSING LLC
GA	LEESBURG	WJAD	103.5 FM Commercial	CUMULUS LICENSING LLC
GA	MACON	WDEN	1500 AM Station	CUMULUS LICENSING LLC
GA	MACON	WAYS	105.5 FM Commercial	CUMULUS LICENSING LLC
GA	MACON	WMKS	92.3 FM Commercial	CUMULUS LICENSING LLC
GA	MACON	WDDO	1240 AM Station	CUMULUS LICENSING LLC
GA	MACON	WDEN-FM	99.1 FM Commercial	CUMULUS LICENSING LLC
GA	MACON	WMAC	940 AM Station	CUMULUS LICENSING LLC
GA	MONTEZUMA	WMGB	95.1 FM Commercial	CUMULUS LICENSING LLC
GA	SASSER	WEGC	107.7 FM Commercial	CUMULUS LICENSING LLC
GA	SAVANNAH	WZAT	102.1 FM Commercial	CUMULUS LICENSING LLC
GA	SAVANNAH	WJCL-FM	96.5 FM Commercial	CUMULUS LICENSING LLC
GA	SAVANNAH	WJLG	900 AM Station	CUMULUS LICENSING LLC
GA	SAVANNAH	WEAS-FM	93.1 FM Commercial	CUMULUS LICENSING LLC
GA	SAVANNAH	WIXV	95.5 FM Commercial	CUMULUS LICENSING LLC
GA	SAVANNAH	WBMQ	630 AM Station	CUMULUS LICENSING LLC
GA	SPRINGFIELD	WSIS	103.9 FM Commercial	CUMULUS LICENSING LLC
GA	SYLVESTER	WZBN	102.1 FM Commercial	CUMULUS LICENSING LLC
IA	ASBURY	WJOD	103.3 FM Commercial	CUMULUS LICENSING LLC
IA	CEDAR FALLS	KOEL-FM	98.5 FM Commercial	CUMULUS LICENSING LLC
IA	CEDAR RAPIDS	KHAK	98.1 FM Commercial	CUMULUS LICENSING LLC
IA	CEDAR RAPIDS	KDAT	104.5 FM Commercial	CUMULUS LICENSING LLC
IA	DAVENPORT	KJOC	1170 AM Station	CUMULUS LICENSING LLC
IA	DE WITT	KBOB-FM	104.9 FM Commercial	CUMULUS LICENSING LLC
IA	DUBUQUE	KLYV	105.3 FM Commercial	CUMULUS LICENSING LLC
IA	DUBUQUE	KXGE	102.3 FM Commercial	CUMULUS LICENSING LLC
IA	DUBUQUE	WDBQ	1490 AM Station	CUMULUS LICENSING LLC
IA	GRUNDY CENTER	KCRR	97.7 FM Commercial	CUMULUS LICENSING LLC
IA	IOWA CITY	KRNA	94.1 FM Commercial	CUMULUS LICENSING LLC
IA	MUSCATINE	KBEA-FM	99.7 FM Commercial	CUMULUS LICENSING LLC
IA	OELWEIN	KKHQ-FM	92.3 FM Commercial	CUMULUS LICENSING LLC
IA	OELWEIN	KOEL	950 AM Station	CUMULUS LICENSING LLC
IL	FREEPORT	WXXQ	98.5 FM Commercial	CUMULUS LICENSING LLC
IL	GALENA	WDBQ-FM	107.5 FM Commercial	CUMULUS LICENSING LLC
IL	LOVES PARK	WKGL-FM	96.7 FM Commercial	CUMULUS LICENSING LLC
IL	MOLINE	WXLP	96.9 FM Commercial	CUMULUS LICENSING LLC
IL	ROCKFORD	WZOK	97.5 FM Commercial	CUMULUS LICENSING LLC
IL	ROCKFORD	WROK	1440 AM Station	CUMULUS LICENSING LLC
KS	OTTAWA	KCHZ	95.7 FM Commercial	SYNCOM RADIO CORPORATION
KS	ST. MARYS	KQTP	102.9 FM Commercial	CUMULUS LICENSING LLC

		Radio Station Subsidiaries for Cumulus Media Inc.		
State	City	Call Sign	Frequency	Subsidiary Name
KS	TOPEKA	KTOP	1490 AM Station	CUMULUS LICENSING LLC
KS	TOPEKA	KDVV	100.3 FM Commercial	CUMULUS LICENSING LLC
KS	TOPEKA	KMAJ-FM	107.7 FM Commercial	CUMULUS LICENSING LLC
KS	TOPEKA	KMAJ	1440 AM Station	CUMULUS LICENSING LLC
KS	TOPEKA	KWIC	99.3 FM Commercial	CUMULUS LICENSING LLC
KY	CYNTHIANA	WCYN-FM	102.3 FM Commercial	CUMULUS LICENSING LLC
KY	GEORGETOWN	WXZZ	103.3 FM Commercial	CUMULUS LICENSING LLC
KY	HAROLD	WXLR	104.9 FM Commercial	ADAM D GEARHEART
KY	LEXINGTON	WLXX	92.9 FM Commercial	CUMULUS LICENSING LLC
KY	LEXINGTON	WVLK	590 AM Station	CUMULUS LICENSING LLC
KY	NICHOLASVILLE	WLTO	102.5 FM Commercial	CUMULUS LICENSING LLC
KY	RICHMOND	WLRO	101.5 FM Commercial	CUMULUS LICENSING LLC
LA	LAKE CHARLES	KYKZ	96.1 FM Commercial	CUMULUS LICENSING LLC
LA	LAKE CHARLES	KXZZ	1580 AM Station	CUMULUS LICENSING LLC
LA	LAKE CHARLES	KBIU	103.7 FM Commercial	CUMULUS LICENSING LLC
LA	SHREVEPORT	KRMD-FM	101.1 FM Commercial	CUMULUS LICENSING LLC
LA	SHREVEPORT	KRMD	1340 AM Station	CUMULUS LICENSING LLC
LA	SHREVEPORT	KBED	102.9 FM Commercial	CUMULUS LICENSING LLC
LA	SHREVEPORT	KMJJ-FM	99.7 FM Commercial	CUMULUS LICENSING LLC
LA	SULPHUR	KKGB	101.3 FM Commercial	CUMULUS LICENSING LLC
ME	BANGOR	WEZQ	92.9 FM Commercial	CUMULUS LICENSING LLC
ME	BREWER	WQCB	106.5 FM Commercial	CUMULUS LICENSING LLC
ME	ELLSWORTH	WDEA	1370 AM Station	CUMULUS LICENSING LLC
ME	ELLSWORTH	WWMJ	95.7 FM Commercial	CUMULUS LICENSING LLC
ME	OLD TOWN	WBZN	107.3 FM Commercial	CUMULUS LICENSING LLC
MI	BATTLE CREEK	WKFR-FM	103.3 FM Commercial	CUMULUS LICENSING LLC
MI	FLINT	WDZZ-FM	92.7 FM Commercial	CUMULUS LICENSING LLC
MI	FLINT	WWCK-FM	105.5 FM Commercial	CUMULUS LICENSING LLC
MI	FLINT	WWCK	1570 AM Station	CUMULUS LICENSING LLC
MI	KALAMAZOO	WKMI	1360 AM Station	CUMULUS LICENSING LLC
MI	LUNA PIER	WTWR-FM	98.3 FM Commercial	CUMULUS LICENSING LLC
MI	OWOSSO	WRSR	103.9 FM Commercial	CUMULUS LICENSING LLC
MI	PORTAGE	WRKR	107.7 FM Commercial	CUMULUS LICENSING LLC
MN	FARIBAULT	KQCL	95.9 FM Commercial	CUMULUS LICENSING LLC
MN	FARIBAULT	KDHL	920 AM Station	CUMULUS LICENSING LLC
MN	OWATONNA	KRFO	1390 AM Station	CUMULUS LICENSING LLC
MN	OWATONNA	KRFO-FM	104.9 FM Commercial	CUMULUS LICENSING LLC
MN	PRESTON	KFIL-FM	103.1 FM Commercial	KFIL, INC.
MN	PRESTON	KFIL	1060 AM Station	KFIL, INC.
MN	ROCHESTER	KROC	1340 AM Station	SOUTHERN MINNESOTA BROADCASTING CO.
MN	ROCHESTER	KROC-FM	106.9 FM Commercial	SOUTHERN MINNESOTA BROADCASTING CO.
MN	ROCHESTER	KOLM	1520 AM Station	CUMULUS LICENSING LLC
MN	ROCHESTER	KWWK	96.5 FM Commercial	CUMULUS LICENSING LLC
MN	SPRING VALLEY	KVGO	104.3 FM Commercial	KVGO, INC.
MN	ST. CHARLES	KLCX	107.7 FM Commercial	CUMULUS LICENSING LLC
MN	STEWARTVILLE	KYBA	105.3 FM Commercial	SOUTHERN MINNESOTA BROADCASTING CO
MO	ASHLAND	KOQL	106.1 FM Commercial	MID-MISSOURI BROADCASTING, INC.
MO	COLUMBIA	KPLA	101.5 FM Commercial	COLUMBIA FM, INC.
MO	COLUMBIA	KFRU	1400 AM Station	COLUMBIA AM, INC.
MO	COLUMBIA	KBXR	102.3 FM Commercial	FT. SMITH FM, INC.
MO	JEFFERSON CITY	KJMO	104.1 FM Commercial	PREMIER RADIO GROUP, L.L.C.
MO	JEFFERSON CITY	KLIK	1240 AM Station	PREMIER RADIO GROUP
MO	JEFFERSON CITY	KBBM	100.1 FM Commercial	PREMIER RADIO GROUP
MO	LEXINGTON	KMJK	107.3 FM Commercial	CUMULUS KC LICENSING CORP.
MO	STOCKTON	KRLK	107.7 FM Commercial	CUMULUS LICENSING LLC
MS	ARTESIA	WSMS	99.9 FM Commercial	CUMULUS LICENSING LLC
MS	COLUMBUS	WJWF	1400 AM Station	CUMULUS LICENSING LLC
MS	COLUMBUS	WMBC	103.1 FM Commercial	CUMULUS LICENSING LLC
MS	COLUMBUS	WKOR-FM	94.9 FM Commercial	CUMULUS LICENSING LLC
MS	STARKVILLE	WSSO	1230 AM Station	CUMULUS LICENSING LLC
MS	STARKVILLE	WMXU	106.1 FM Commercial	CUMULUS LICENSING LLC
MS	STARKVILLE	WKOR	980 AM Station	CUMULUS LICENSING LLC
NC	DUNN	WRCQ	103.5 FM Commercial	CUMULUS LICENSING LLC
NC	FAYETTEVILLE	WQSM	98.1 FM Commercial	CUMULUS LICENSING LLC

State	City	Call Sign	Frequency	Subsidiary Name
			Radio Station Subsidiaries for Cumulus Media Inc.	
NC	FAYETTEVILLE	WFNC	640 AM Station	CUMULUS LICENSING LLC
NC	LELAND	WKXS-FM	94.1 FM Commercial	CUMULUS LICENSING LLC
NC	LELAND	WAAV	980 AM Station	CUMULUS LICENSING LLC
NC	LUMBERTON	WFNC-FM	102.3 FM Commercial	CUMULUS LICENSING LLC
NC	SOUTHERN PINES	WKQB	106.9 FM Commercial	CUMULUS LICENSING CORP.
NC	WILMINGTON	WWQQ-FM	101.3 FM Commercial	CUMULUS LICENSING LLC
NC	WILMINGTON	WMNX	97.3 FM Commercial	CUMULUS LICENSING LLC
NC	WILMINGTON	WGNI	102.7 FM Commercial	CUMULUS LICENSING LLC
ND	BISMARCK	KBYZ	96.5 FM Commercial	CUMULUS LICENSING LLC
ND	BISMARCK	KACL	98.7 FM Commercial	CUMULUS LICENSING LLC
ND	BISMARCK	KKCT	97.5 FM Commercial	CUMULUS LICENSING LLC
ND	BISMARCK-MANDAN	KLXX	1270 AM Station	CUMULUS LICENSING LLC
NY	ARLINGTON	WRRB	96.9 FM Commercial	CUMULUS LICENSING LLC
NY	BREWSTER	WPUT	1510 AM Station	CUMULUS LICENSING LLC
NY	HYDE PARK	WCZX	97.7 FM Commercial	CUMULUS LICENSING LLC
NY	JEFFERSONVILLE	WPDA	106.1 FM Commercial	CUMULUS LICENSING LLC
NY	KINGSTON	WKXP	94.3 FM Commercial	CUMULUS LICENSING CORP.
NY	KINGSTON	WKNY	1490 AM Station	CUMULUS LICENSING LLC
NY	MIDDLETOWN	WRRV	92.7 FM Commercial	CUMULUS LICENSING LLC
NY	MIDDLETOWN	WALL	1340 AM Station	CUMULUS LICENSING LLC
NY	MOUNT KISCO	WFAF	106.3 FM Commercial	CUMULUS LICENSING LLC
NY	PATTERSON	WDBY	105.5 FM Commercial	CUMULUS LICENSING LLC
NY	POUGHKEEPSIE	WEOK	1390 AM Station	CUMULUS LICENSING LLC
NY	POUGHKEEPSIE	WPDH	101.5 FM Commercial	CUMULUS LICENSING LLC
NY	WHITE PLAINS	WFAS-FM	103.9 FM Commercial	CUMULUS LICENSING LLC
NY	WHITE PLAINS	WFAS	1230 AM Station	CUMULUS LICENSING LLC
NY	WURTSBORO	WZAD	97.3 FM Commercial	CUMULUS LICENSING LLC
OH	BOWLING GREEN	WRQN	93.5 FM Commercial	CUMULUS LICENSING LLC
OH	CANTON	WRQK-FM	106.9 FM Commercial	CUMULUS LICENSING LLC
OH	DELTA	WRWK	106.5 FM Commercial	CUMULUS LICENSING LLC
OH	PORT CLINTON	WXKR	94.5 FM Commercial	CUMULUS LICENSING LLC
OH	SALEM	WSOM	600 AM Station	CUMULUS LICENSING LLC
OH	SALEM	WQXK	105.1 FM Commercial	CUMULUS LICENSING LLC
OH	SYLVANIA	WWWM-FM	105.5 FM Commercial	CUMULUS LICENSING LLC
OH	TOLEDO	WTOD	1560 AM Station	CUMULUS LICENSING LLC
OH	TOLEDO	WKKO	99.9 FM Commercial	CUMULUS LICENSING CORP.
OH	TOLEDO	WLQR	1470 AM Station	CUMULUS LICENSING LLC
OH	YOUNGSTOWN	WHOT-FM	101.1 FM Commercial	CUMULUS LICENSING LLC
OH	YOUNGSTOWN	WBBW	1240 AM Station	CUMULUS LICENSING LLC
OK	POTEAU	KOMS	107.3 FM Commercial	CUMULUS LICENSING LLC
OR	BROWNSVILLE	KEHK	102.3 FM Commercial	CUMULUS LICENSING LLC
OR	CRESWELL	KUJZ	95.3 FM Commercial	CUMULUS LICENSING LLC
OR	EUGENE	KZEL-FM	96.1 FM Commercial	CUMULUS LICENSING LLC
OR	EUGENE	KUGN	590 AM Station	CUMULUS LICENSING LLC
OR	EUGENE	KSCR	1320 AM Station	CUMULUS LICENSING LLC
OR	EUGENE	KNRQ-FM	97.9 FM Commercial	CUMULUS LICENSING LLC
PA	HARRISBURG	WTCY	1400 AM Station	CUMULUS LICENSING LLC
PA	HARRISBURG	WNNK-FM	104.1 FM Commercial	CUMULUS LICENSING LLC
PA	MECHANICSBURG	WTPA	93.5 FM Commercial	CUMULUS LICENSING LLC
PA	MERCER	WWIZ	103.9 FM Commercial	CUMULUS LICENSING LLC
PA	MERCER	WLLF	96.7 FM Commercial	CUMULUS LICENSING LLC
PA	PALMYRA	WWKL	92.1 FM Commercial	CUMULUS LICENSING LLC
PA	SHARON	WPIC	790 AM Station	CUMULUS LICENSING LLC
PA	SHARON	WYFM	102.9 FM Commercial	CUMULUS LICENSING LLC
SC	ATLANTIC BEACH	WSEA	100.3 FM Commercial	CUMULUS LICENSING LLC
SC	CONWAY	WIQB	1050 AM Station	CUMULUS LICENSING LLC
SC	CONWAY	WJXY-FM	93.9 FM Commercial	CUMULUS LICENSING LLC
SC	FLORENCE	WYNN	540 AM Station	CUMULUS LICENSING LLC
SC	FLORENCE	WYNN-FM	106.3 FM Commercial	CUMULUS LICENSING LLC
SC	GEORGETOWN	WSYN	106.5 FM Commercial	CUMULUS LICENSING LLC
SC	GEORGETOWN	WXJY	93.7 FM Commercial	CUMULUS LICENSING LLC
SC	HARTSVILLE	WBZF	98.5 FM Commercial	CUMULUS LICENSING LLC
SC	HARTSVILLE	WHSC	1450 AM Station	CUMULUS LICENSING LLC
SC	LAKE CITY	WWFN	100.1 FM Commercial	CUMULUS LICENSING LLC

State	City	Call Sign	Frequency	Subsidiary Name
		Radio Station Subsidiaries for Cumulus Media Inc.		
SC	LATTA	WCMG	94.3 FM Commercial	CUMULUS LICENSING LLC
SC	MANNING	WYMB	920 AM Station	CUMULUS LICENSING LLC
SC	MARION	WHLZ	100.5 FM Commercial	CUMULUS LICENSING LLC
SC	PAMPLICO	WMXT	102.1 FM Commercial	CUMULUS LICENSING LLC
SC	PAWLEYS ISLAND	WDAI	98.5 FM Commercial	CUMULUS LICENSING LLC
SC	SURFSIDE BEACH	WYAK-FM	103.1 FM Commercial	CUMULUS LICENSING LLC
SD	CANTON	KYBB	102.7 FM Commercial	SOUTHERN MINNESOTA B/C COMPANY
SD	SALEM	KIKN-FM	100.5 FM Commercial	SOUTHERN MINNESOTA B/CNG. COMPANY
SD	SIOUX FALLS	KSOO	1140 AM Station	SOUTHERN MINNESOTA BROADCASTING CO.
SD	SIOUX FALLS	KMXC	97.3 FM Commercial	SOUTHERN MINNESOTA BROADCASTING CO.
SD	SIOUX FALLS	KKLS-FM	104.7 FM Commercial	SOUTHERN MINNESOTA BROADCASTING CO.
SD	SIOUX FALLS	KXRB	1000 AM Station	SOUTHERN MINNESOTA BROADCASTING CO.
TN	BELLE MEADE	WNPL	106.7 FM Commercial	CUMULUS LICENSING LLC
TN	GOODLETTSVILLE	WRQQ	97.1 FM Commercial	CUMULUS LICENSING LLC
TN	HENDERSONVILLE	WQQK	92.1 FM Commercial	CUMULUS LICENSING LLC
TN	MANCHESTER	WWTN	99.7 FM Commercial	CUMULUS LICENSING LLC
TN	NASHVILLE	WSM-FM	95.5 FM Commercial	CUMULUS LICENSING LLC
TN	TULLAHOMA	WHRP	93.3 FM Commercial	CUMULUS LICENSING LLC
TX	AMARILLO	KQIZ-FM	93.1 FM Commercial	CUMULUS LICENSING LLC
TX	AMARILLO	KPUR	1440 AM Station	CUMULUS LICENSING LLC
TX	ANSON	KFQX-FM	98.1 FM Commercial	CUMULUS LICENSING LLC
TX	BEAUMONT	KIKR	1450 AM Station	CUMULUS LICENSING LLC
TX	BEAUMONT	KRWP	97.5 FM Commercial	CUMULUS LICENSING LLC
TX	BEAUMONT	KQXY-FM	94.1 FM Commercial	CUMULUS LICENSING LLC
TX	BEAUMONT	KTCX	102.5 FM Commercial	CUMULUS LICENSING LLC
TX	BELTON	KOOC	106.3 FM Commercial	CUMULUS LICENSING LLC
TX	BURKBURNETT	KYYI	104.7 FM Commercial	CUMULUS LICENSING LLC
TX	CANYON	KZRK-FM	107.9 FM Commercial	CUMULUS LICENSING LLC
TX	CANYON	KZRK	1550 AM Station	CUMULUS LICENSING LLC
TX	CANYON	KPUR-FM	107.1 FM Commercial	CUMULUS LICENSING LLC
TX	CLAUDE	KARX	95.7 FM Commercial	CUMULUS LICENSING LLC
TX	COPPERAS COVE	KSSM	103.1 FM Commercial	CUMULUS LICENSING LLC
TX	CRYSTAL BEACH	KSTB	101.5 FM Commercial	CUMULUS LICENSING LLC
TX	ELECTRA	KOLI	94.9 FM Commercial	CUMULUS LICENSING LLC
TX	HAMLIN	KCDD	103.7 FM Commercial	CUMULUS LICENSING LLC
TX	HARKER HEIGHTS	KUSJ	105.5 FM Commercial	CUMULUS LICENSING LLC
TX	MERKEL	KHXS	102.7 FM Commercial	CUMULUS LICENSING LLC
TX	MIDLAND	KBAT	93.3 FM Commercial	CUMULUS LICENSING LLC
TX	MIDLAND	KMND	1510 AM Station	CUMULUS LICENSING LLC
TX	MIDLAND	KNFM	92.3 FM Commercial	CUMULUS LICENSING LLC
TX	MONAHANS	KGEE	99.9 FM Commercial	CUMULUS LICENSING LLC
TX	NEDERLAND	KQHN	1510 AM Station	CUMULUS LICENSING LLC
TX	ODESSA	KODM	97.9 FM Commercial	CUMULUS LICENSING LLC
TX	ODESSA	KRIL	1410 AM Station	CUMULUS LICENSING LLC
TX	PECOS	KKLY	97.3 FM Commercial	CUMULUS LICENSING LLC
TX	SILSBEE	KAYD-FM	101.7 FM Commercial	HILCO COMMUNICATIONS, INC.
TX	STANTON	KKJW	105.9 FM Commercial	UNIQUE BROADCASTING, L.L.C.
TX	TEMPLE	KLTD	101.7 FM Commercial	CUMULUS LICENSING LLC
TX	TEMPLE	KTEM	1400 AM Station	CUMULUS LICENSING LLC
TX	TYE	KBCY	99.7 FM Commercial	CUMULUS LICENSING LLC
TX	WICHITA FALLS	KQXC-FM	103.9 FM Commercial	CUMULUS LICENSING LLC
TX	WICHITA FALLS	KLUR	99.9 FM Commercial	CUMULUS LICENSING LLC
VA	BEDFORD	WBWR	106.9 FM Commercial	BEDFORD RADIO PARTNERS, LLC
VA	BLACKSBURG	WFNR	710 AM Station	NEW RIVER VALLEY RADIO PARTNERS, L.L.C.
VA	BLACKSBURG	WBRW	105.3 FM Commercial	NEW RIVER VALLEY RADIO PARTNERS, LLC
VA	CHRISTIANSBURG	WFNR-FM	100.7 FM Commercial	NEW RIVER VALLEY RADIO PARTNERS, LLC
VA	PULASKI	WPSK-FM	107.1 FM Commercial	NEW RIVER VALLEY RADIO PARTNERS, LLC
VA	RADFORD	WWBU	101.7 FM Commercial	NEW RIVER VALLEY RADIO PARTNERS, LLC
VA	RADFORD	WRAD	1460 AM Station	NEW RIVER VALLEY RADIO PARTNERS, LLC
WI	ALLOUEZ	WJLW	106.7 FM Commercial	CUMULUS LICENSING LLC
WI	BRILLION	WDUZ	107.5 FM Commercial	CUMULUS LICENSING LLC
WI	DENMARK	WPCK	104.9 FM Commercial	CUMULUS LICENSING LLC
WI	GREEN BAY	WNGB	1400 AM Station	CUMULUS LICENSING LLC
WI	GREEN BAY	WQLH	98.5 FM Commercial	CUMULUS LICENSING LLC

Radio Station Subsidiaries for Cumulus Media Inc.				
State	City	Call Sign	Frequency	Subsidiary Name
WI	KAUKAUNA	WOGB	103.1 FM Commercial	CUMULUS LICENSING LLC
WI	NEENAH-MENASHA	WNAM	1280 AM Station	CUMULUS LICENSING LLC
WI	OMRO	WPKR	99.5 FM Commercial	CUMULUS LICENSING LLC
WI	OSHKOSH	WWWX	96.9 FM Commercial	CUMULUS LICENSING LLC
WI	OSHKOSH	WOSH	1490 AM Station	CUMULUS LICENSING LLC
WI	WINNECONNE	WVBO	103.9 FM Commercial	CUMULUS LICENSING LLC

Deutsche Telekom AG

Address:	Friedrich-Ebert-Allee 140	Stock Symbol:	DT
	53113 Bonn, Germany,	Telephone:	49-228-181-0
		Fax:	49-228-181-8872
Total Employees:	248,519	Website:	www.telekom.de

You need a scorecard to keep up with the various names and owners of the firm now known as T-Mobile USA, the country's fifth-largest wireless company.

In 1994, two cellular startups called General Cellular and Pacific Northwest Cellular merged to form Western Wireless, based in Bellevue, Wash.

In 1995, the company won Federal Communications Commission auctions for wireless PCS licenses for Portland, Honolulu, Albuquerque, El Paso, Des Moines, Oklahoma City and Salt Lake City. In 1996 Western Wireless completed an initial public offering and two bond offerings, raising $600 million. Later that year the company launched service under the VoiceStream name in the six markets where it held PCS licenses.

In 1998, Western Wireless established an alliance with Hong Kong-based Hutchison Whampoa Ltd., which invested approximately $325 million in the company.

In May 1999, VoiceStream Wireless was spun off from its parent company, Western Wireless. The next year, VoiceStream completed merger transactions with two other wireless companies, Omnipoint Communications and Aerial Communications. With those mergers complete, VoiceStream went national, serving such major markets as New York, Philadelphia, Miami, Tampa and Detroit.

In June 2001, VoiceStream was bought by German telecom behemoth Deutsche Telekom AG in a deal valued at about $30 billion. The company was added to Deutsche Telekom's mobile telecommunications subsidiary, T-Mobile International.

Got all that?

Throughout its existence, there have been two constants at the company.

The first is beautiful spokeswomen. It was actress Jamie Lee Curtis when the company was VoiceStream. It changed to actress Catherine Zeta-Jones when the company officially switched to the T-Mobile brand name in the United States in 2002.

The second constant has been wireless industry veteran John Stanton. Stanton started both of the companies that merged to form Western Wireless. He was also a co-founder of McCaw Cellular Communications, one of the original pioneers in the wireless business.

Stanton is chairman of T-Mobile USA, although he gave up the CEO title in March 2003, saying he was toying with a run for political office. He is also chairman and CEO of Western Wireless.

T-Mobile USA has more than 13 million wireless customers and has more than 22,000 U.S. employees.

T-Mobile International operates in10 countries through its subsidiaries and holdings. Worldwide, Deutsche Telekom offers mobile services to more than 80 million customers.

Unlike most of its competitors, T-Mobile USA operates on the globally dominant GSM technology, which stands for Global System for Mobile Communications. GSM technology is the most used technology in virtually every other country besides the U.S.

Of the other top wireless providers, Cingular and AT&T also operate on GSM platforms, although the former is in negotiations to acquire the latter; a successful fusion of the two would create the nation's top wireless provider with more than 40 million subscribers.

T-Mobile has also begun to offer wireless broadband Internet service at more than 4,700 public locations nationwide, including Borders and Starbucks stores and American Airlines' Admirals Clubs, through its T-Mobile HotSpot division.

—Bob Williams, Robert Morlino

August 20, 2004

Sources: Company Web site, Securities and Exchange Commission filings, Yahoo! Finance Online, Seattle Times, Hoover's Online, Fortune magazine, USA Today.

Deutsche Telekom AG Recent Financial Information		
Year	Revenue	Net Income (Net Loss)
2000	$38,556,000,000	$5,581,000,000
2001	$43,058,000,000	($3,079,000,000)
2002	$56,390,000,000	($25,824,000,000)
2003	$70,200,000,000	$1,575,000,000

Deutsche Telekom AG Board of Directors			
Name	Position	Relevant Stock	Qty
Ricke, Kai-Uwe	Chairman	N/A	N/A
Eick, Karl-Gerhard	Deputy Chairman	N/A	N/A
Klinkhammer, Heinz	Director	N/A	N/A
Brauner, Josef	Director	N/A	N/A
Obermann, Rene	Director	N/A	N/A
Holtrop, Thomas	Director	N/A	N/A
Reiss, Konrad	Director	N/A	N/A

Deutsche Telekom AG Corporate Officers			
Name	Position	Salary	Bonuses
Ricke, Kai-Uwe	Chairman and CEO	N/A	N/A
Eick, Karl-Gerhard	Deputy Chair, CFO	N/A	N/A

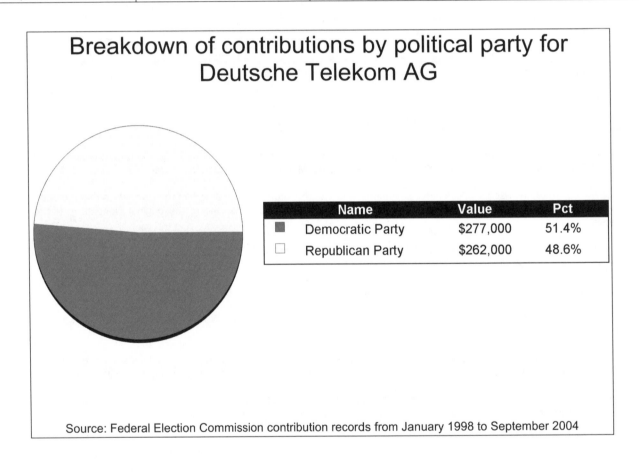

Breakdown of contributions by political party for Deutsche Telekom AG

Name	Value	Pct
Democratic Party	$277,000	51.4%
Republican Party	$262,000	48.6%

Source: Federal Election Commission contribution records from January 1998 to September 2004

Top 10 Recipients of Contributions Sourced to Deutsche Telekom AG	
Recipient	Amount
National Democratic Party Committees	$163,000
National Republican Party Committees	$149,000
Sen Thomas Andrew Daschle (D-SD)	$10,000
Sen Byron L Dorgan (D-ND)	$9,000
Rep J Dennis Hastert (R-IL)	$8,000
Sen Patty Murray (D-WA)	$7,000
Sen Conrad R Burns (R-MT)	$7,000
Rep David Adam Smith (D-WA)	$6,000
Rep Joe Linus Barton (R-TX)	$6,000
Rep Roy Blunt (R-MO)	$6,000
Total:	$371,000
Source: Federal Election Commission contribution records from January 1998 to September 2004	

Deutsche Telekom AG Lobbying Expenditures by Year	
Year	Amount
1998	$20,000
1999	$80,000
2000	$1,640,000
2001	$3,390,000
2002	$2,420,100
2003	$1,780,000
2004	$200,000
Total:	$9,530,100
Source: U.S. Senate Office of Public Records lobbying disclosure records from January 1998 to June 30th, 2004.	

EchoStar Communications Corp.

Address:	5701 S. Santa Fe Drive	Stock Symbol:	DISH
	Littleton, CO 80120	Telephone:	303- 723-1000
		Fax:	303-723-1399
Total Employees:	15,000	Website:	www.dishnetwork.com

Remember those giant satellite dishes people used to put up in their back yards in the 1980s? You know, those huge skyward-pointing metal daisies that drove neighbors crazy and the cable companies even crazier? Charles W. "Charlie" Ergen does.

The chairman and CEO of EchoStar Communications, Ergen got his start in 1980 selling satellite systems to people in rural Colorado who couldn't get cable, or just weren't satisfied with it. The business became obsolete as cable became more accessible, and cable companies started scrambling their signals. Seeing the writing on the wall, Ergen moved on to a new business—Direct Broadcast Satellite television.

Rather than grab feeds off other satellites, Ergen applied for a license to launch his own satellites and supply programming directly to subscribers. EchoStar I was put into orbit in December 1995. As of the close of 2003, EchoStar's DISH Network brand has 9.4 million subscribers who choose from up to 500 television channels.

There are only two competitors in the direct broadcast television business, EchoStar's DISH Network and DirecTV, which until recently was controlled by General Motors Corp. Hughes Electronics Corp., the unit that operated DirecTV, had been for sale since 2001, and at one point was to be merged with EchoStar. The Federal Communications Commission nixed the sale, and a controlling interest in Hughes was eventually sold to Rupert Murdoch's News Corp.

It would seem that allowing the only two competitors in an industry to merge would be anti-competitive and that consumer advocates would have supported the FCC's decision to kill the deal. That is not the case. Cable television is still the dominant provider of video entertainment in the U.S., and in most markets, the cable company has a monopoly. Consumers Union, for one, had hoped the merger of the two direct satellite providers would provide some real competition for companies like Comcast and Time Warner.

The collapse of the merger was more than an inconvenience for EchoStar—it also hurt financially. According to company filings with the SEC, the company lost $690 million in termination costs related to the merger.

For now, Ergen and EchoStar are focusing on high speed Internet service, one area where cable has a distinct advantage. EchoStar has reached a deal with SES Americom Inc., which would allow the company to offer broadband through a new satellite scheduled for launch this month. EchoStar also has an agreement with EarthLink Inc. to offer wired digital subscriber line service to Dish Network subscribers at a special rate.

EchoStar has also entered into agreements with phone companies such as SBC Communications, Sprint Corp. and Qwest Communications to deliver telecom services.

—John Dunbar, Robert Morlino

August 17, 2004

Sources: EchoStar Communications Web site and Form 10-K, Consumers Union, SES Americom, Hoover's Online.

EchoStar Communications Corp. Recent Financial Information		
Year	Revenue	Net Income (Net Loss)
1999	$1,602,841,000	($792,847,000)
2000	$2,715,220,000	($650,326,000)
2001	$4,001,138,000	($215,498,000)
2002	$4,820,825,000	($852,034,000)
2003	$5,739,296,000	$224,506,000

EchoStar Communications Corp. Board of Directors				
Name	Position	Relevant Stock		Qty
Dea, Peter	Director		DISH	15,000
DeFranco, James	Director		DISH	7,310,804
Ergen, Cantey	Director		DISH	240,513,780
Ergen, Charles	Chairman		DISH	240,857,780
Friedlob, Raymond	Director		DISH	43,000
Goodbarn, Steven	Director		DISH	15,000
Moskowitz, David	Director		DISH	910,515
Messier, Jean-Marie	Director		DISH	N/A

EchoStar Communications Corp. Board of Directors			
Name	Position	Relevant Stock	Qty
Schroeder, C.	Director	DISH	23,600
Dugan, Michael	Director	DISH	839,671
Daines, O.	Director	DISH	N/A

EchoStar Communications Corp. Corporate Officers			
Name	Position	Salary	Bonuses
Ergen, Charles	Chairman and CEO	$283,847	N/A
Moskowitz, David	SVP, General Counsel and Director	$235,393	N/A
Dugan, Michael	President and COO	$295,405	N/A
Hesabi-Cartwright, Soraya	EVP, DISH Network	$256,958	N/A

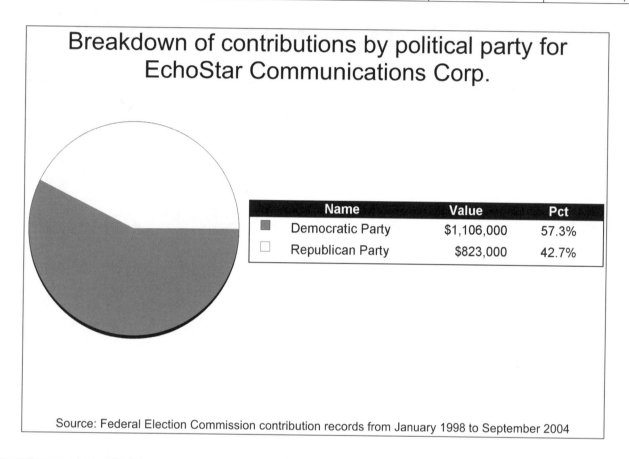

Breakdown of contributions by political party for EchoStar Communications Corp.

	Name	Value	Pct
■	Democratic Party	$1,106,000	57.3%
☐	Republican Party	$823,000	42.7%

Source: Federal Election Commission contribution records from January 1998 to September 2004

Top 10 Recipients of Contributions Sourced to EchoStar Communications Corp.	
Recipient	Amount
National Democratic Party Committees	$873,000
National Republican Party Committees	$583,000
Rep Edward John Markey (D-MA)	$23,000
Sen John S McCain (R-AZ)	$21,000
Sen Arlen Specter (R-PA)	$18,000
Sen Ronald Lee Wyden (D-OR)	$18,000
Sen A Wayne Allard (R-CO)	$16,000
Rep J Dennis Hastert (R-IL)	$12,000
Rep Mike Doyle (D-PA)	$11,000
Vermont Democratic Fed. Campaign Comm.	$10,000
Total:	$1,585,000

Source: Federal Election Commission contribution records from January 1998 to September 2004

EchoStar Communications Corp. Lobbying Expenditures by Year	
Year	Amount
1998	$33,000
1999	$1,440,000
2000	$60,000
2001	$720,000
2002	$2,200,000
2003	$960,000
2004	$200,000
Total:	$5,613,000

Source: U.S. Senate Office of Public Records lobbying disclosure records from January 1998 to June 30th, 2004.

EchoStar Communications Corp. Sponsored Trips for Congressional Staff		
Congressional Office	Number of Trips	$ Amount
Rep Frederick Stephen Upton (R-MI)	1	$2,048
	1	$842
Rep Mike Doyle (D-PA)	1	$825
Total:	3	$3,715

Source: Congressional office travel records for members of the Senate Committee on Commerce, Science & Transportation and the House Committee on Energy and Commerce for the period of January 2000 to March 2004.

Emmis Communications Corp.

Address:	One Emmis Plaza	Stock Symbol:	EMMS
	40 Monument Circle, Ste. 700	Telephone:	317-266-0100
	Indianapolis, IN 46204	Fax:	317-631-3750
Total Employees:	3,114	Website:	www.emmis.com

In an era of corporate media ownership, maximization of profits and concentration on the bottom line, Emmis Communications is a company that "takes its corporate citizenship seriously," according to its corporate profile.

Whether you believe that or not, making corporate citizenship a priority certainly is a departure from most other corporate media owners—especially in the radio business, where Emmis ranks No. 10. The fact that the company has a section on "public service" on its Web site in itself distinguishes it from many other media companies.

Emmis owns 25 radio stations, a tiny number compared to corporate giants like Clear Channel Communications Corp. But the stations are mostly in big-market cities like Los Angeles, New York and Chicago, garnering big ratings and bringing in lots of revenue. Emmis is also the 23rd largest television broadcaster by audience reach and boasts a publishing division.

Emmis is the creation of 56-year-old CEO, Jeffrey Smulyan, who founded the company in Indiana in 1979. Smulyan purchased WSVL, a small station in Shelbyville, Ind. In 1984 he bought stations in St. Louis and Los Angeles and continued to expand throughout the 1980s. In 1989, Smulyan and partners bought the Seattle Mariners baseball team. His ownership of the team was stormy, to say the least. He was accused of blackmailing the city for a better stadium deal by threatening to move the team to St. Petersburg, Fla. He eventually sold to a partnership that included the Nintendo computer game company in 1992.

In 1994, Emmis became a public company. According to the company's 2004 proxy statement, Smulyan controls 53 percent of the company thanks to his sole ownership of all 5.6 million Class B super-voting shares.

In March 1998, Emmis entered the television business by acquiring four Fox affiliates from SF Broadcasting and two other stations from Wabash Valley Broadcasting. Currently Emmis owns 16 network-affiliated television stations.

Smulyan created the nation's first 24-hour all-sports radio station (WFAN in New York City). Emmis (the Hebrew word for "truth") at one point owned the top-rated stations in Los Angeles and New York simultaneously.

Not satisfied to stay within the U.S. borders, Emmis opened a station in Hungary, which now reaches 4 million of the nation's 11 million citizens, according to the company. The company also owns a total of 9 stations in Belgium.

In addition to its radio and television holdings, Emmis also publishes books and several regional magazines, including Indianapolis Monthly, Los Angeles Magazine, Atlanta, Cincinnati Magazine and Texas Monthly.

—John Dunbar

August 19, 2004

Sources: Emmis Communications Corp. Web site and Form 10-K, Broadcasting & Cable, Hoover's Online.

Emmis Communications Corp. Recent Financial Information		
Year	Revenue	Net Income (Net Loss)
2000	$325,265,000	($33,000)
2001	$473,345,000	$13,736,000
2002	$539,822,000	($64,108,000)
2003	$562,363,000	($164,468,000)
2004	$591,868,000	$2,256,000

Emmis Communications Corp. Board of Directors				
Name	Position	Relevant Stock		Qty
Smulyan, Jeffrey	Chairman		EMMS	6,107,021
Berger, Walter	Director		EMMS	206,331
Kaseff, Gary	Director		EMMS	207,814
Bayh, Susan	Director		EMMS	38,481
Leventhal, Richard	Director		EMMS	61,934
Sica, Frank	Director		EMMS	33,334
Sorrel, Lawrence	Director		EMMS	43,674
Nathanson, Greg	Director		EMMS	217,063
Lund, Peter	Director		N/A	N/A

Emmis Communications Corp. Corporate Officers			
Name	Position	Salary	Bonuses
Smulyan, Jeffrey	Chairman, President, and CEO	$640,105	$822,246
Berger, Walter	EVP, CFO, Treasurer, and Director	$369,750	$403,988
Kaseff, Gary	EVP, General Counsel, and Director	$340,000	$227,844
Cummings, Richard	President, Radio Division	$391,500	$291,255
Bongarten, Randall	President, Television Division	$382,800	$315,558

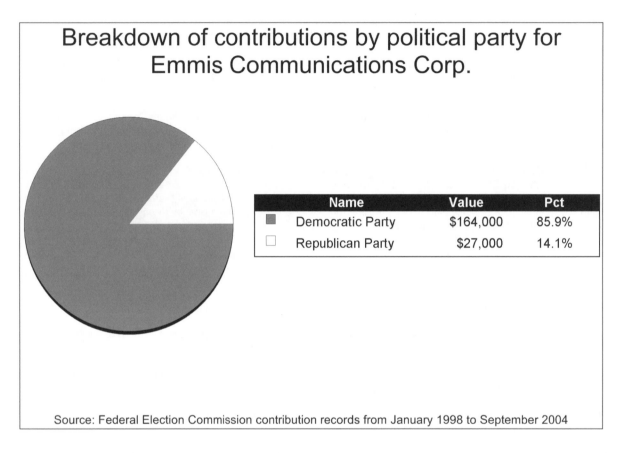

Breakdown of contributions by political party for Emmis Communications Corp.

Name	Value	Pct
Democratic Party	$164,000	85.9%
Republican Party	$27,000	14.1%

Source: Federal Election Commission contribution records from January 1998 to September 2004

Top 10 Recipients of Contributions Sourced to Emmis Communications Corp.	
Recipient	Amount
National Democratic Party Committees	$69,000
Sen Evan Bayh (D-IN)	$23,000
Indiana Democratic Congressional Victory Committee	$20,000
President George W Bush (R)	$9,000
Rep Baron Paul Hill (D-IN)	$8,000
Wesley K Clark (D)	$6,000
Vice President Albert Gore, Jr (D-TN)	$5,000
David Lawther Johnson (D-IN)	$4,000
Sen John F Kerry (D-MA)	$4,000
Sen Richard G Lugar (R-IN)	$4,000
Total:	$152,000

Source: Federal Election Commission contribution records from January 1998 to September 2004

Radio Station Subsidiaries for Emmis Communications Corp.				
State	City	Call Sign	Frequency	Subsidiary Name
AZ	GLENDALE	KKFR	92.3 FM Commercial	EMMIS RADIO LICENSE CORPORATION
AZ	PHOENIX	KMVP	860 AM Station	EMMIS RADIO LICENSE CORPORATION
AZ	PHOENIX	KKLT	98.7 FM Commercial	EMMIS RADIO LICENSE CORPORATION
AZ	PHOENIX	KTAR	620 AM Station	EMMIS RADIO LICENSE CORPORATION
CA	LOS ANGELES	KPWR	105.9 FM Commercial	EMMIS RADIO LICENSE CORPORATION
CA	LOS ANGELES	KZLA-FM	93.9 FM Commercial	EMMIS RADIO LICENSE CORPORATION
IL	CHICAGO	WKQX	101.1 FM Commercial	EMMIS RADIO LICENSE CORPORATION
IL	JERSEYVILLE	WRDA	104.1 FM Commercial	EMMIS RADIO LICENSE CORPORATION
IN	INDIANAPOLIS	WIBC	1070 AM Station	EMMIS RADIO LICENSE CORPORATION

Radio Station Subsidiaries for Emmis Communications Corp.

State	City	Call Sign	Frequency	Subsidiary Name
IN	INDIANAPOLIS	WNOU	93.1 FM Commercial	EMMIS RADIO LICENSE CORPORATION
IN	INDIANAPOLIS	WYXB	105.7 FM Commercial	EMMIS RADIO LICENSE CORPORATION
IN	SHELBYVILLE	WENS	97.1 FM Commercial	EMMIS RADIO LICENSE CORPORATION
IN	TERRE HAUTE	WTHI-FM	99.9 FM Commercial	EMMIS RADIO LICENSE CORPORATION
IN	WEST TERRE HAUTE	WWVR	105.5 FM Commercial	EMMIS RADIO LICENSE CORPORATION
MO	CRESTWOOD	KSHE	94.7 FM Commercial	EMMIS RADIO LICENSE CORPORATION
MO	FLORISSANT	KFTK	97.1 FM Commercial	EMMIS RADIO LICENSE CORPORATION
MO	ST. GENEVIEVE	KPNT	105.7 FM Commercial	EMMIS RADIO LICENSE CORPORATION
MO	ST. LOUIS	KIHT	96.3 FM Commercial	EMMIS RADIO LICENSE CORPORATION
NY	NEW YORK	WRKS	98.7 FM Commercial	EMMIS RADIO LICENSE CORPORATION OF NEW YORK
NY	NEW YORK	WQCD	101.9 FM Commercial	EMMIS RADIO LICENSE CORPORATION
NY	NEW YORK	WQHT	97.1 FM Commercial	EMMIS LICENSE CORPORATION OF NEW YORK
TX	AUSTIN	KLBJ	590 AM Station	EMMIS AUSTIN RADIO BROADCASTING COMPANY, L.P.
TX	AUSTIN	KLBJ-FM	93.7 FM Commercial	EMMIS AUSTIN RADIO BROADCASTING COMPANY, L.P.
TX	BASTROP	KGSR	107.1 FM Commercial	EMMIS AUSTIN RADIO BROADCASTING COMPANY, L.P.
TX	BUDA	KROX-FM	101.5 FM Commercial	EMMIS AUSTIN RADIO BROADCASTING COMPANY, L.P.
TX	CEDAR PARK	KDHT	93.3 FM Commercial	EMMIS AUSTIN RADIO BROADCASTING COMPANY, L.P.
TX	SAN MARCOS	KEYI-FM	103.5 FM Commercial	EMMIS AUSTIN RADIO BROADCASTING COMPANY, L.P.

TV Station Subsidiaries for Emmis Communications Corp.

Call Sign	Channel and Type	Subsidiary Name	Area of Service
WALA-TV	10 TV Commercial	EMMIS TELEVISION LICENSE CORPORATION	MOBILE, AL
KHON-TV	2 TV Commercial	EMMIS TELEVISION LICENSE CORPORATION	HONOLULU, HI
KAII-TV	7 TV Commercial	EMMIS TELEVISION LICENSE CORPORATION	WAILUKU, HI
KHAW-TV	11 TV Commercial	EMMIS TELEVISION LICENSE CORPORATION	HILO, HI
WVUE	8 TV Commercial	EMMIS TELEVISION LICENSE CORPORATION	NEW ORLEANS, LA
WLUK-TV	11 TV Commercial	EMMIS TELEVISION LICENSE CORPORATION	GREEN BAY, WI
WBPG	55 TV Commercial	EMMIS TELEVISION LICENSE CORPORATION	GULF SHORES, AL
W04CN	4 TV Low Power (VHF)	EMMIS TELEVISION LICENSE CORPORATION	COCOA, ETC., FL
WKCF	18 TV Commercial	EMMIS TELEVISION LICENSE CORPORATION	CLERMONT, FL
WFTX	36 TV Commercial	EMMIS TELEVISION LICENSE CORPORATION	CAPE CORAL, FL
WTHI-TV	10 TV Commercial	EMMIS TELEVISION LICENSE CORPORATION	TERRE HAUTE, IN
KMTV	3 TV Commercial	EMMIS TELEVISION LICENSE CORPORATION	OMAHA, NE
KOIN	6 TV Commercial	EMMIS TELEVISION LICENSE CORPORATION	PORTLAND, OR
K11SE	11 TV Low Power (VHF)	EMMIS TELEVISION LICENSE CORPORATION	BEND, OR
WSAZ-TV	3 TV Commercial	EMMIS TELEVISION LICENSE CORPORATION	HUNTINGTON, WV
KGMD-TV	9 TV Commercial	EMMIS TELEVISION LICENSE CORPORATION	HILO, HI
KGMB	9 TV Commercial	EMMIS TELEVISION LICENSE CORPORATION	HONOLULU, HI
KGUN	9 TV Commercial	EMMIS TELEVISION LICENSE CORPORATION	TUCSON, AZ
KGMV	3 TV Commercial	EMMIS TELEVISION LICENSE CORPORATION	WAILUKU, HI
W16CE	16 TV Low Power (UHF)	EMMIS TELEVISION LICENSE CORPORATION	CHARLESTON, WV
KBIM-TV	10 TV Commercial	EMMIS TELEVISION LICENSE CORPORATION	ROSWELL, NM
KRQE	13 TV Commercial	EMMIS TELEVISION LICENSE CORPORATION	ALBUQUERQUE, NM
KREZ-TV	6 TV Commercial	EMMIS TELEVISION LICENSE CORPORATION	DURANGO, CO
KSNT	27 TV Commercial	EMMIS TELEVISION LICENSE CORPORATION OF TOPEKA	TOPEKA, KS
KSNW	3 TV Commercial	EMMIS TELEVISION LICENSE CORPORATION OF WICHITA	WICHITA, KS
KSNC	2 TV Commercial	EMMIS TELEVISION LICENSE CORPORATION OF WICHITA	GREAT BEND, KS
KSNG	11 TV Commercial	EMMIS TELEVISION LICENSE CORPORATION OF WICHITA	GARDEN CITY, KS
KSNK	8 TV Commercial	EMMIS TELEVISION LICENSE CORPORATION OF WICHITA	McCOOK, NE

Entercom Communications Corp.

Address: 401 City Ave.
              Ste. 409
              Bala Cynwyd, PA   19004

Total Employees: 2,493

Stock Symbol: ETM
Telephone: 610-660-5610
Fax: 610-660-5620
Website: www.entercom.com

The founder of Entercom Communications Corp. based his company's strategy on a technological innovation in radio, and his son is hoping to further that legacy by focusing on another change.

Seventy-two-year old Joseph M. Field founded Entercom in 1968 with the idea that FM broadcasting was the future. He believed (rightly) that it would eventually overtake AM as the radio band of choice among listeners.

New Entercom CEO David Field, son of Joseph, is vice chairman of the radio board of the National Association of Broadcasters, the industry trade and lobbying group. He's been talking about the next great technological shift in the industry, the transition from analog to digital.

Joseph Field founded Entercom after 14 years as a lawyer, including a stint as an assistant U.S. Attorney. During his tenure as CEO, the company grew steadily. (Field is still chairman, but turned over CEO duties to his son David in May 2002.) Growth accelerated in the 1990s with changes in station ownership rules.

In 1992, when the FCC began allowing radio broadcasters to own two stations in a single market, Entercom began doubling up.

After the Telecommunications Act of 1996 was passed, the company expanded more quickly. In 1999, it acquired 45 stations from Sinclair Broadcast Group Inc., and bought 10 more stations from other companies. It has continued its acquisition strategy through the subsequent five years.

Earlier this year, Entercom submitted a $9 million bid to acquire a second sports station in the Buffalo market—WNSA, owned by bankrupt cable television company Adelphia Communications Corp.

Pending approval of its purchase by the Federal Communications Commission and bankruptcy court, Entercom will likely shift broadcasts of the Buffalo Sabres hockey games from WNSA to WGR, the other sports station already owned by the company. The sports format for WNSA would likely be dropped. The $9 million bid is nearly twice the $5 million Adelphia paid to acquire WNSA four years ago.

Today, Entercom, which is traded on the New York Stock Exchange, owns 103 stations in 19 markets and trails only Clear Channel Communications Corp., Infinity and Cox Radio Inc. in total revenue. The station owner's programming is varied, from oldies to rock, news/talk and country. It also broadcasts games of a number of professional and college sports teams.

Unlike the television industry's changeover to a digital signal, the transition from analog to digital for radio has not gotten a lot of press. The technology is very much in its infancy, and radio sets that can receive a digital signal have only just entered the market. Still, the switch is less expensive than television's; what's more, the FCC is not forcing the change on the industry. David Field insists that the expansion into digital technology is an opportunity.

"[Radio is] free, it's ubiquitous," he told the Las Vegas Review-Journal at an NAB annual convention. "Once a consumer pays for a new set, they'll get digital quality. And they'll continue to get current radio on their existing sets. It's a win-win."

—John Dunbar, Robert Morlino

August 19, 2004

Sources: Entercom Communications Corp. Form 10-K, Data Monitor Company Profiles, Los Angeles Times, Buffalo News, Las Vegas Review-Journal

Entercom Communications Corp. Recent Financial Information		
Year	Revenue	Net Income (Net Loss)
2000	$352,025,000	$47,254,000
2001	$332,897,000	$17,268,000
2002	$391,289,000	($83,052,000)
2003	$401,056,000	$71,780,000

Entercom Communications Corp. Board of Directors				
Name	Position	Relevant Stock		Qty
Berkman, David	Director		ETM	19,857
Donlevie, John	Director		ETM	186,612
Field, David	Director		ETM	2,738,392
Field, Joseph	Chairman		ETM	8,484,091
Kean, Herbert	Director		ETM	655,099
Gold, Daniel	Director		ETM	412
West, Edward	Director		ETM	1,662
Wiesenthal, Robert	Director		N/A	N/A

Entercom Communications Corp. Corporate Officers			
Name	Position	Salary	Bonuses
Field, Joseph	Chairman	$505,145	$250,000
Field, David	President, CEO, and Director	$656,688	$500,000
Fisher, Stephen	EVP and CFO	$353,601	$300,000
Donlevie, John	EVP, Secretary, General Counsel, and Director	$282,881	$100,000

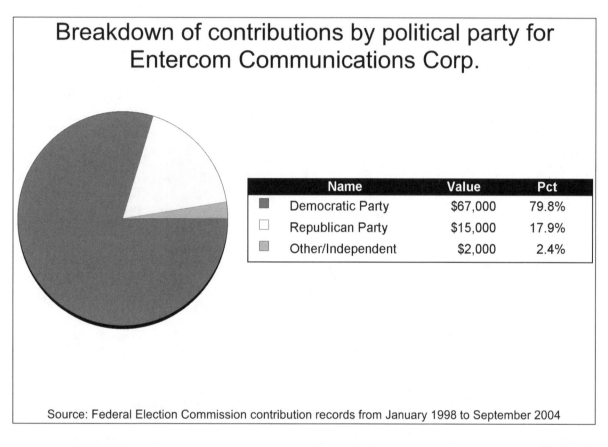

Breakdown of contributions by political party for Entercom Communications Corp.

	Name	Value	Pct
■	Democratic Party	$67,000	79.8%
□	Republican Party	$15,000	17.9%
▦	Other/Independent	$2,000	2.4%

Source: Federal Election Commission contribution records from January 1998 to September 2004

Top 10 Recipients of Contributions Sourced to Entercom Communications Corp.	
Recipient	Amount
National Democratic Party Committees	$50,000
Sen Arlen Specter (R-PA)	$11,000
Sen John F Kerry (D-MA)	$6,000
Wesley K Clark (D)	$4,000
Sen Richard Craig Shelby (R-AL)	$2,000
Sen Richard J Santorum (R-PA)	$2,000
Levin, Murray S	$2,000
Rep Chris John (D-LA)	$2,000
Rudolph W Giuliani (R-NY)	$1,000
Joseph M Torsella (D-PA)	$1,000
Total:	$81,000
Source: Federal Election Commission contribution records from January 1998 to September 2004	

State	City	Call Sign	Frequency	Subsidiary Name
			Radio Station Subsidiaries for Entercom Communications Corp.	
CA	FAIR OAKS	KSSJ	94.7 FM Commercial	ENTERCOM SACRAMENTO LICENSE, LLC
CA	SACRAMENTO	KRXQ	98.5 FM Commercial	ENTERCOM SACRAMENTO LICENSE, LLC
CA	SACRAMENTO	KSEG	96.9 FM Commercial	ENTERCOM SACRAMENTO LICENSE, LLC
CA	SACRAMENTO	KWOD	106.5 FM Commercial	ENTERCOM SACRAMENTO LICENSE, LLC
CA	SACRAMENTO	KCTC	1320 AM Station	ENTERCOM SACRAMENTO LICENSE, LLC
CA	SACRAMENTO	KDND	107.9 FM Commercial	ENTERCOM SACRAMENTO LICENSE, LLC
CO	AURORA	KEZW	1430 AM Station	ENTERCOM DENVER LICENSE, LLC
CO	DENVER	KOSI	101.1 FM Commercial	ENTERCOM DENVER LICENSE, LLC
CO	DENVER	KALC	105.9 FM Commercial	ENTERCOM DENVER LICENSE, LLC
CO	DENVER	KQMT	99.5 FM Commercial	ENTERCOM DENVER LICENSE, LLC
FL	CRYSTAL RIVER	WKTK	98.5 FM Commercial	ENTERCOM GAINESVILLE LICENSE, LLC
FL	MICANOPY	WSKY-FM	97.3 FM Commercial	ENTERCOM GAINESVILLE LICENSE, LLC
KS	ANDOVER	KDGS	93.9 FM Commercial	ENTERCOM WICHITA LICENSE, LLC
KS	CLEARWATER	KFH-FM	98.7 FM Commercial	ENTERCOM WICHITA LICENSE, LLC
KS	HAYSVILLE	KFBZ	105.3 FM Commercial	ENTERCOM WICHITA LICENSE, LLC
KS	KANSAS CITY	KKHK	1250 AM Station	ENTERCOM KANSAS CITY LICENSE, LLC
KS	KANSAS CITY	KXTR	1660 AM Station	ENTERCOM KANSAS CITY LICENSE, LLC
KS	KANSAS CITY	KUDL	98.1 FM Commercial	ENTERCOM KANSAS CITY LICENSE, LLC
KS	LEAVENWORTH	KQRC-FM	98.9 FM Commercial	ENTERCOM KANSAS CITY LICENSE, LLC
KS	WICHITA	KNSS	1240 AM Station	ENTERCOM WICHITA LICENSE, LLC
KS	WICHITA	KEYN-FM	103.7 FM Commercial	ENTERCOM WICHITA LICENSE, LLC
KS	WICHITA	KFH	1330 AM Station	ENTERCOM WICHITA LICENSE, LLC
LA	KENNER	WKZN	105.3 FM Commercial	ENTERCOM NEW ORLEANS LICENSE, LLC
LA	NEW ORLEANS	WSMB	1350 AM Station	ENTERCOM NEW ORLEANS LICENSE, LLC
LA	NEW ORLEANS	WTKL	95.7 FM Commercial	ENTERCOM NEW ORLEANS LICENSE, LLC
LA	NEW ORLEANS	WEZB	97.1 FM Commercial	ENTERCOM NEW ORLEANS LICENSE, LLC
LA	NEW ORLEANS	WLMG	101.9 FM Commercial	ENTERCOM NEW ORLEANS LICENSE, LLC
LA	NEW ORLEANS	WWL	870 AM Station	ENTERCOM NEW ORLEANS LICENSE, LLC
MA	BOSTON	WRKO	680 AM Station	ENTERCOM BOSTON LICENSE, LLC
MA	BOSTON	WEEI	850 AM Station	ENTERCOM BOSTON LICENSE, LLC
MA	LAWRENCE	WQSX	93.7 FM Commercial	ENTERCOM BOSTON LICENSE, LLC
MA	WESTBOROUGH	WAAF	107.3 FM Commercial	ENTERCOM BOSTON LICENSE, LLC
MA	WORCESTER	WVEI	1440 AM Station	ENTERCOM BOSTON LICENSE, LLC
MO	KANSAS CITY	KRBZ	96.5 FM Commercial	ENTERCOM KANSAS CITY LICENSE, LLC
MO	KANSAS CITY	KCSP	610 AM Station	ENTERCOM KANSAS CITY LICENSE, LLC
MO	KANSAS CITY	KYYS	99.7 FM Commercial	ENTERCOM KANSAS CITY LICENSE, LLC
MO	KANSAS CITY	KMBZ	980 AM Station	ENTERCOM KANSAS CITY LICENSE, LLC
MO	LIBERTY	WDAF-FM	106.5 FM Commercial	ENTERCOM KANSAS CITY LICENSE, LLC
NC	GREENSBORO	WPET	950 AM Station	ENTERCOM GREENSBORO LICENSE, LLC
NC	GREENSBORO	WOZN	98.7 FM Commercial	ENTERCOM GREENSBORO LICENSE, LLC
NC	GREENSBORO	WEAL	1510 AM Station	ENTERCOM GREENSBORO LICENSE, LLC
NC	GREENSBORO	WQMG-FM	97.1 FM Commercial	ENTERCOM GREENSBORO LICENSE, LLC
NC	REIDSVILLE	WJMH	102.1 FM Commercial	ENTERCOM GREENSBORO LICENSE, LLC
NC	WINSTON-SALEM	WMQX-FM	93.1 FM Commercial	ENTERCOM GREENSBORO LICENSE, LLC
NY	BUFFALO	WWKB	1520 AM Station	ENTERCOM BUFFALO LICENSE, LLC
NY	BUFFALO	WGR	550 AM Station	ENTERCOM BUFFALO LICENSE, LLC
NY	BUFFALO	WWWS	1400 AM Station	ENTERCOM BUFFALO LICENSE, LLC
NY	BUFFALO	WBEN	930 AM Station	ENTERCOM BUFFALO LICENSE, LLC
NY	BUFFALO	WTSS	102.5 FM Commercial	ENTERCOM BUFFALO LICENSE, LLC
NY	FAIRPORT	WBBF-FM	93.3 FM Commercial	ENTERCOM ROCHESTER LICENSE, LLC.
NY	NIAGARA FALLS	WKSE	98.5 FM Commercial	ENTERCOM BUFFALO LICENSE, LLC
NY	ROCHESTER	WBZA	98.9 FM Commercial	ENTERCOM ROCHESTER LICENSE, LLC.
NY	ROCHESTER	WROC	950 AM Station	ENTERCOM ROCHESTER LICENSE, LLC.
NY	ROCHESTER	WBEE-FM	92.5 FM Commercial	ENTERCOM ROCHESTER LICENSE, LLC.
OR	CANNON BEACH	KCBZ	94.9 FM Commercial	ALC COMMUNICATIONS
OR	MOLALLA	KRSK	105.1 FM Commercial	ENTERCOM PORTLAND LICENSE, LLC
OR	PORTLAND	KWJJ-FM	99.5 FM Commercial	ENTERCOM PORTLAND LICENSE, LLC
OR	PORTLAND	KGON	92.3 FM Commercial	ENTERCOM PORTLAND LICENSE, LLC (DE)
OR	PORTLAND	KKSN-FM	97.1 FM Commercial	ENTERCOM PORTLAND LICENSE, LLC (DE)
OR	PORTLAND	KFXX	1080 AM Station	ENTERCOM PORTLAND LICENSE, LLC
OR	SALEM	KSLM	1390 AM Station	ENTERCOM PORTLAND LICENSE, LLC (DE)
PA	BENTON	WGGI	95.9 FM Commercial	ENTERCOM WILKES-BARRE SCRANTON, LLC
PA	FREELAND	WKRZ	98.5 FM Commercial	ENTERCOM WILKES-BARRE SCRANTON, LLC

	Radio Station Subsidiaries for Entercom Communications Corp.			
State	City	Call Sign	Frequency	Subsidiary Name
PA	PITTSTON	WDMT	102.3 FM Commercial	ENTERCOM WILKES-BARRE SCRANTON, LLC
PA	SCRANTON	WGBI	910 AM Station	ENTERCOM WILKES-BARRE SCRANTON, LLC
PA	SCRANTON	WGGY	101.3 FM Commercial	ENTERCOM WILKES-BARRE SCRANTON, LLC
PA	TOBYHANNA	WKRF	107.9 FM Commercial	ENTERCOM WILKES-BARRE SCRANTON, LLC
PA	WEST HAZLETON	WOGY	1300 AM Station	ENTERCOM WILKES-BARRE SCRANTON, LLC
PA	WILKES-BARRE	WILK	980 AM Station	ENTERCOM WILKES-BARRE SCRANTON, LLC
SC	EASLEY	WOLI	103.9 FM Commercial	ENTERCOM GREENVILLE LICENSE, LLC
SC	GREENVILLE	WYRD	1330 AM Station	ENTERCOM GREENVILLE LICENSE, LLC
SC	GREENVILLE	WFBC-FM	93.7 FM Commercial	ENTERCOM GREENVILLE LICENSE, LLC
SC	GREER	WOLT	103.3 FM Commercial	ENTERCOM GREENVILLE LICENSE, LLC
SC	SPARTANBURG	WORD	950 AM Station	ENTERCOM GREENVILLE LICENSE, LLC
SC	SPARTANBURG	WSPA-FM	98.9 FM Commercial	ENTERCOM GREENVILLE LICENSE, LLC
SC	SPARTANBURG	WSPA	910 AM Station	ENTERCOM GREENVILLE LICENSE, LLC
TN	GERMANTOWN	WMBZ	94.1 FM Commercial	ENTERCOM MEMPHIS LICENSE, LLC
TN	MEMPHIS	WRVR-FM	104.5 FM Commercial	ENTERCOM MEMPHIS LICENSE, LLC
TN	MEMPHIS	WJCE	680 AM Station	ENTERCOM MEMPHIS LICENSE, LLC
VA	HAMPTON	WWDE-FM	101.3 FM Commercial	ENTERCOM NORFOLK LICENSE, LLC
VA	NORFOLK	WVKL	95.7 FM Commercial	ENTERCOM NORFOLK LICENSE, LLC
VA	NORFOLK	WNVZ	104.5 FM Commercial	ENTERCOM NORFOLK LICENSE, LLC
VA	VIRGINIA BEACH	WPTE	94.9 FM Commercial	ENTERCOM NORFOLK LICENSE, LLC
WA	AUBURN-FEDERAL WAY	KNWX	1210 AM Station	ENTERCOM SEATTLE LICENSE, LLC
WA	CAMAS	KNRK	94.7 FM Commercial	ENTERCOM PORTLAND LICENSE, LLC (DE)
WA	CASTLE ROCK	KRQT	107.1 FM Commercial	ENTERCOM LONGVIEW LICENSE, LLC
WA	KELSO	KLYK	94.5 FM Commercial	ENTERCOM LONGVIEW LICENSE, LLC
WA	LONGVIEW	KBAM	1270 AM Station	ENTERCOM LONGVIEW LICENSE, LLC
WA	LONGVIEW	KEDO	1400 AM Station	ENTERCOM LONGVIEW LICENSE, LLC
WA	SEATTLE	KISW	99.9 FM Commercial	ENTERCOM SEATTLE LICENSE, LLC
WA	SEATTLE	KNDD	107.7 FM Commercial	ENTERCOM SEATTLE LICENSE, LLC
WA	SEATTLE	KTTH	770 AM Station	ENTERCOM SEATTLE LICENSE, LLC
WA	SEATTLE	KIRO	710 AM Station	ENTERCOM SEATTLE LICENSE, LLC
WA	SEATTLE	KQBZ	100.7 FM Commercial	ENTERCOM SEATTLE LICENSE, LLC
WA	TACOMA	KMTT	103.7 FM Commercial	ENTERCOM SEATTLE LICENSE, LLC
WA	TACOMA	KBSG-FM	97.3 FM Commercial	ENTERCOM SEATTLE LICENSE, LLC
WA	VANCOUVER	KOTK	910 AM Station	ENTERCOM PORTLAND LICENSE, LLC (DE)
WI	BARABOO	WOLX-FM	94.9 FM Commercial	ENTERCOM MADISON LICENSE, LLC.
WI	MILWAUKEE	WMYX-FM	99.1 FM Commercial	ENTERCOM MILWAUKEE LICENSE, LLC
WI	MILWAUKEE	WEMP	1250 AM Station	ENTERCOM MILWAUKEE LICENSE, LLC
WI	VERONA	WMMM-FM	105.5 FM Commercial	ENTERCOM MADISON LICENSE, LLC.
WI	WAUNAKEE	WBZU	105.1 FM Commercial	ENTERCOM MADISON LICENSE, LLC.
WI	WAUWATOSA	WXSS	103.7 FM Commercial	ENTERCOM MILWAUKEE LICENSE, LLC

Gannett Co. Inc.

Address:	7950 Jones Branch Drive	Stock Symbol:	GCI
	McLean, VA 22107-0910	Telephone:	703-854-6000
		Fax:	703-854-2046
Total Employees:	53,000	Website:	www.gannett.com

The unparalleled giant of the American newspaper business just keeps getting bigger, and not even a journalistic scandal at its flagship paper—USA Today, the nation's biggest—was enough to slow down Gannett Co. Inc., Inc.

The Gannett empire was built through the accumulation of lots of smaller newspapers. The vast majority of the chain's papers—more than 100 in all—are in small towns like Chillicothe, Ohio and Muskogee, Okla. In July, Gannett announced it was accumulating a few more—23 newspapers and 11 specialty publications in all, purchased from a privately held publisher in Wisconsin.

The purchase put to rest a struggle between Gannett and publisher Frank Wood that has played out for nearly a quarter-century, with Wood accusing the company of unfair business practices. In the end, Wood's papers couldn't compete with those of Gannett, and he relented.

Fellow publisher Richard McCord, who also has gone head-to-head with Gannett, wrote a book about Wood's fight against the media giant. He told the Chicago Tribune, "Frank has put up an astonishing struggle to remain community based and independent in an age of media conglomerates."

Astonishing though it may have been, given Gannett's size and power in the industry, Wood's surrender was, in a word, inevitable. Gannett boasts a combined daily circulation of 7.6 million. USA Today has a circulation of 2.3 million, far more than No. 2 Wall Street Journal with 1.8 million. Some of the company's other larger market newspapers include the Detroit News, the Arizona Republic, the Cincinnati Enquirer, the Louisville Courier-Journal and the Indianapolis Star.

In addition to its newspaper holdings, Gannett is also the sixth-largest television broadcast company in the United States with 23 stations. With its 1995 purchase of Multimedia Inc., Gannett expanded the business into radio and cable television systems. Since then, it has concentrated on newspapers and television, in addition to InfiNet, its Internet access and service venture that it acquired sole ownership of in 2003.

The news chain was founded in 1906 when Frank E. Gannett and associates bought half interest in the Elmira Gazette in New York. Throughout the early years of the company, Gannett acquired more newspapers in upstate New York and by the late 1940s his company owned 21 newspapers and seven radio stations.

Gannett died in 1957, but his company was only getting started. By 1967, the chain had gone public. Allen H. Neuharth, who later wrote the best-selling autobiography Confessions of an S.O.B., became chief executive in 1973 and chairman in 1979, during the company's most aggressive period of growth. In 1982, Gannett launched USA Today, the first general circulation newspaper aimed at the entire nation.

Skeptics derisively dubbed the daily "McPaper" and criticized its extravagant use of color, short articles contained within single pages and graphics with titles like "What We Are Eating." But the public loved it, and USA Today became an unprecedented success.

In recent years, the newspaper has fought to be recognized for its serious journalism. But those efforts suffered a serious setback in early 2004, when one of the paper's star reporters, Jack Kelley, was accused of plagiarism and fabrication. Reported on the heels of the Jayson Blair meltdown, the Kelley scandal saw the resignation of not only the reporter himself but several top editors as well. Nevertheless, Gannett raised the cover price by a quarter just a few months later, the first hike since 1985.

With Gannett's considerable holdings in both newspapers and television stations, it has been an active participant in the debate before the FCC over media consolidation. Not surprisingly, Gannett supports the elimination of the rule that would prevent a company from owning a newspaper and broadcast station in the same market.

Last year, media ownership activist Andrew Schwartzman, president of Media Access Project, criticized Gannett for failing to cover a hearing in Phoenix about the FCC's then-ending decision on whether to loosen media ownership rules. Gannett, which supports deregulation, owns a local television station and the dominant newspaper, the Arizona Republic, in Phoenix. A corporate spokeswoman said coverage of the event was up to local management.

—John Dunbar, Robert Morlino

August 20, 2004

Sources: Gannett Co. Inc. Inc. Web site, Form 10-K, Broadcasting & Cable, Chicago Tribune

---

Gannett Co. Inc. Recent Financial Information		
Year	Revenue	Net Income (Net Loss)
2000	$6,184,086,000	$1,719,077,000
2001	$6,299,606,000	$831,197,000
2002	$6,422,249,000	$1,160,128,000
2003	$6,711,000,000	$1,211,000,000

Gannett Co. Inc. Board of Directors				
Name	Position	Relevant Stock		Qty
McCorkindale, Douglas	Chairman		GCI	1,768,174
Arnelle, H.	Director		GCI	4,881
Brokaw, Meredith	Director		GCI	14,659
Johnson, James	Director		GCI	4,155
Munn, Stephen	Director		GCI	3,625
Shalala, Donna	Director		GCI	5,466
Trujillo, Solomon	Director		GCI	2,297
Williams, Karen	Director		GCI	4,886
Boccardi, Louis	Director		GCI	2,537

Gannett Co. Inc. Corporate Officers			
Name	Position	Salary	Bonuses
McCorkindale, Douglas	Chairman, President, and CEO	$1,600,000	$2,250,000
Martore, Gracia	SVP and CFO	N/A	N/A
Chapple, Thomas	SVP, Secretary, and General Counsel	$391,667	$285,000
Watson, Gary	President, Newspaper Divison	$700,000	$710,000
Dubow, Craig	President, Broadcasting Division	$500,000	$325,000

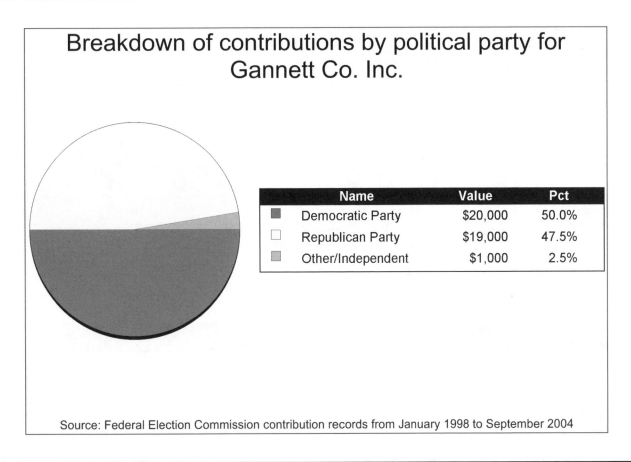

Breakdown of contributions by political party for Gannett Co. Inc.

Name	Value	Pct
Democratic Party	$20,000	50.0%
Republican Party	$19,000	47.5%
Other/Independent	$1,000	2.5%

Source: Federal Election Commission contribution records from January 1998 to September 2004

Top 10 Recipients of Contributions Sourced to Gannett Co. Inc.	
Recipient	Amount
National Democratic Party Committees	$10,000
Sen John S McCain (R-AZ)	$2,000
Rep Ralph Moody Hall (D-TX)	$2,000

Top 10 Recipients of Contributions Sourced to Gannett Co. Inc.	
Recipient	Amount
Rep Richard A Zimmer (R-NJ)	$2,000
Rep Brian Phillip Bilbray (R-CA)	$2,000
Rep Frederick Carlyle Boucher (D-VA)	$2,000
President George W Bush (R)	$2,000
Sen Thomas R Carper (D-DE)	$2,000
Sen Lincoln D Chafee (R-RI)	$2,000
Sen Thomas Andrew Daschle (D-SD)	$2,000
Total:	$28,000

Source: Federal Election Commission contribution records from January 1998 to September 2004

Gannett Co. Inc. Lobbying Expenditures by Year	
Year	Amount
1998	$452,000
1999	$480,000
2000	$480,000
2001	$460,000
2002	$520,000
2003	$560,000
2004	$240,000
Total:	$3,192,000

Source: U.S. Senate Office of Public Records lobbying disclosure records from January 1998 to June 30th, 2004.

TV Station Subsidiaries for Gannett Co. Inc.			
Call Sign	Channel and Type	Subsidiary Name	Area of Service
KTHV	11 TV Commercial	ARKANSAS TELEVISION COMPANY	LITTLE ROCK, AR
WZZM-TV	13 TV Commercial	COMBINED COMMUNICATIONS CORP. OF OKLAHOMA, INC.	GRAND RAPIDS, MI
WXIA-TV	11 TV Commercial	GANNETT GEORGIA, L.P.	ATLANTA, GA
WMAZ-TV	13 TV Commercial	GANNETT GEORGIA, L.P.	MACON, GA
WBIR-TV	10 TV Commercial	GANNETT PACIFIC CORPORATION	KNOXVILLE, TN
WJXX	25 TV Commercial	GANNETT RIVER STATES PUBLISHING CORPORATION	ORANGE PARK, FL
KXTV	10 TV Commercial	KXTV, INC.	SACRAMENTO, CA
WGRZ-TV	2 TV Commercial	MULTIMEDIA ENTERTAINMENT, INC.	BUFFALO, NY
KPNX	12 TV Commercial	MULTIMEDIA HOLDINGS CORPORATION	MESA, AZ
WTLV	12 TV Commercial	MULTIMEDIA HOLDINGS CORPORATION	JACKSONVILLE, FL
KUSA-TV	9 TV Commercial	MULTIMEDIA HOLDINGS CORPORATION	DENVER, CO
KARE	11 TV Commercial	MULTIMEDIA HOLDINGS CORPORATION	MINNEAPOLIS, MN
KNAZ-TV	2 TV Commercial	MULTIMEDIA HOLDINGS CORPORATION	FLAGSTAFF, AZ
KMOH-TV	6 TV Commercial	MULTIMEDIA HOLDINGS CORPORATION	KINGMAN, AZ
KSDK	5 TV Commercial	MULTIMEDIA KSDK, INC.	ST. LOUIS, MO
WTSP	10 TV Commercial	PACIFIC AND SOUTHERN COMPANY, INC.	ST. PETERSBURG, FL
WLTX	19 TV Commercial	PACIFIC AND SOUTHERN COMPANY, INC.	COLUMBIA, SC
WLBZ	2 TV Commercial	PACIFIC AND SOUTHERN COMPANY, INC.	BANGOR, ME
WCSH	6 TV Commercial	PACIFIC AND SOUTHERN COMPANY, INC.	PORTLAND, ME
WUSA	9 TV Commercial	THE DETROIT NEWS, INC.	WASHINGTON, DC
WFMY-TV	2 TV Commercial	WFMY TELEVISION CORPORATION	GREENSBORO, NC
WKYC-TV	3 TV Commercial	WKYC-TV, INC.	CLEVELAND, OH

Print Media Subsidiaries for Gannett Co. Inc.			
Company Name	Market City	Weekday Circulation	Sunday Circulation
Alamogordo Daily News	Alamogordo, NM	6,854	8,156
Argus Leader	Sioux Falls, SD	54,700	76,131
Asbury Park Press	Neptune, NJ	161,937	217,636
Battle Creek Enquirer	Battle Creek, MI	24,831	33,071
Carlsbad Current-Argus	Carlsbad, NM	8,030	8,189
Chillicothe Gazette	Chillicothe, OH	16,018	15,956
Chronicle-Tribune	Marion, IN	17,881	20,279
Coshocton Tribune	Coshocton, OH	7,060	7,286
Courier News	Bridgewater, NJ	42,148	41,601
Courier-Post	Cherry Hill, NJ	79,400	94,762
Daily Record	Parsippany, NJ	42,665	43,930
Daily Tribune	Wisconsin Rapids, WI	13,109	0
Deming Headlight	Deming, NM	3,541	0

Print Media Subsidiaries for Gannett Co. Inc.			
Company Name	Market City	Weekday Circulation	Sunday Circulation
El Paso Times	El Paso, TX	74,278	90,232
Florida Today	Melbourne, FL	88,244	106,590
Fort Collins Coloradoan	Fort Collins, CO	28,415	34,240
Great Falls Tribune	Great Falls, MT	33,436	36,757
Green Bay Press-Gazette	Green Bay, WI	56,858	82,691
Herald Times Reporter	Manitowoc, WI	15,746	16,460
Home News Tribune	East Brunswick, NJ	61,417	68,661
Iowa City Press-Citizen	Iowa City, IA	15,077	0
Journal and Courier	Lafayette, IN	36,784	43,615
Lancaster Eagle-Gazette	Lancaster, OH	15,055	14,856
Las Cruces Sun-News	Las Cruces, NM	22,168	24,664
Marshfield News-Herald	Marshfield, WI	13,519	0
Montgomery Advertiser	Montgomery, AL	51,524	61,208
Muskogee Daily Phoenix & Times-Democrat	Muskogee, OK	17,209	18,364
News Journal	Mansfield, OH	32,641	41,493
News-Herald	Port Clinton, OH	5,675	0
Norwich Bulletin	Norwich, CT	27,569	31,659
Observer-Dispatch	Utica, NY	43,653	51,068
Oshkosh Northwestern	Oshkosh, WI	21,748	25,193
Palladium-Item	Richmond, IN	18,241	22,283
Pensacola News Journal	Pensacola, FL	63,357	81,218
Poughkeepsie Journal	Poughkeepsie, NY	40,504	50,393
Press & Sun-Bulletin	Binghamton, NY	55,237	69,460
Public Opinion	Chambersburg, PA	17,414	0
Reno Gazette-Journal	Reno, NV	67,023	84,813
Rochester Democrat and Chronicle	Rochester, NY	169,697	228,567
Rockford Register Star	Rockford, IL	65,685	78,932
Springfield News-Leader	Springfield, MO	61,608	89,516
St. Cloud Times	Saint Cloud, MN	28,199	37,598
Star-Gazette	Elmira, NY	28,826	39,578
Statesman Journal	Salem, OR	56,298	62,374
Stevens Point Journal	Stevens Point, WI	12,726	0
Telegraph-Forum	Bucyrus, OH	7,190	0
The Advertiser	Lafayette, LA	46,361	56,361
The Advocate	Newark, OH	22,217	23,188
The Arizona Republic	Phoenix, AZ	466,926	587,159
The Asheville Citizen-Times	Asheville, NC	55,982	69,558
The Baxter Bulletin	Mountain Home, AR	11,217	0
The Bellingham Herald	Bellingham, WA	24,346	30,877
The Burlington Free Press	Burlington, VT	47,278	55,782
The Californian	Salinas, CA	18,464	0
The Cincinnati Enquirer	Cincinnati, OH	192,246	309,608
The Clarion-Ledger	Jackson, MS	100,731	110,981
The Courier-Journal	Louisville, KY	216,934	279,611
The Daily Journal	Vineland, NJ	17,941	0
The Daily News Journal	Murfreesboro, TN	15,938	18,730
The Daily News Leader	Staunton, VA	18,262	21,252
The Daily Times	Farmington, NM	18,144	19,965
The Daily Times	Salisbury, MD	27,512	31,293
The Daily World	Opelousas, LA	10,053	11,851
The Des Moines Register	Des Moines, IA	155,898	246,246
The Desert Sun	Palm Springs, CA	58,527	60,691
The Detroit News	Detroit, MI	225,174	705,148
The Greenville News	Greenville, SC	91,714	117,195
The Hattiesburg American	Hattiesburg, MS	22,419	25,889
The Herald-Dispatch	Huntington, WV	31,423	37,523
The Honolulu Advertiser	Honolulu, HI	145,943	166,585
The Idaho Statesman	Boise, ID	65,714	86,586
The Indianapolis Star	Indianapolis, IN	253,778	367,995
The Ithaca Journal	Ithaca, NY	17,861	0
The Jackson Sun	Jackson, TN	35,561	40,979
The Journal News	White Plains, NY	142,145	164,636
The Lansing State Journal	Lansing, MI	73,594	93,914
The Leaf-Chronicle	Clarksville, TN	21,452	25,374

Print Media Subsidiaries for Gannett Co. Inc.			
Company Name	Market City	Weekday Circulation	Sunday Circulation
The Marion Star	Marion, OH	14,213	13,994
The News Journal	Wilmington, DE	117,859	141,283
The News-Messenger	Fremont, OH	13,432	0
The News-Press	Fort Myers, FL	90,950	108,858
The News-Star	Monroe, LA	36,619	40,891
The Olympian	Olympia, WA	34,482	41,687
The Post-Crescent	Appleton, WI	54,193	69,484
The Reporter	Fond du Lac, WI	18,116	19,269
The Sheboygan Press	Sheboygan, WI	23,863	25,665
The Spectrum	Saint George, UT	23,069	24,865
The Star Press	Muncie, IN	33,068	35,905
The Tennessean	Nashville, TN	176,231	243,796
The Times	Shreveport, LA	66,614	80,312
The Town Talk	Alexandria, LA	35,248	40,479
The Wausau Daily Herald	Wausau, WI	22,757	47,890
Times Herald	Port Huron, MI	29,488	39,178
Times Recorder	Zanesville, OH	21,329	20,721
Tucson Citizen	Tucson, AZ	32,712	0
Tulare Advance-Register	Tulare, CA	7,802	0
USA TODAY	McLean, VA	2,154,539	0
Visalia Times-Delta	Visalia, CA	21,771	0

General Electric Co.

Address:	3135 Easton Tpke. Fairfield, CT 06828-0001	Stock Symbol: Telephone: Fax:	GE 203-373-2211 203-373-3131
Total Employees:	305,000	Website:	www.ge.com

Considered the quiet giant in the media business, General Electric made news in a big way in May of 2004 with the completion of the blockbuster purchase of Vivendi Universal Entertainment. The resulting combination added badly needed film and television production capability to NBC, something competing media giants have had for years.

The $14 billion deal resulted in the creation of a new company, NBC Universal. The venture is 80 percent owned by GE and run by longtime media industry heavyweight Bob Wright, who is chairman and CEO of the new company. Wright also maintains his position as vice chairman of GE's board of directors.

Vivendi Universal has 16,000 employees and is expecting 2005 revenues of $15 billion. But the company is still just a small cog in the huge corporate machine that is GE. Consider that GE's roughly $134 billion in revenue is more than Time Warner Inc., Walt Disney Co. and Viacom Inc. combined.

The network generated only 5.1 percent of the company's total 2003 revenues, according to its most recent 10K filing. But make no mistake; NBC has always been a major media player, with 14 owned and operated television stations plus more than 230 affiliates. NBC also owns 15 stations through its purchase of the Spanish language Telemundo network.

GE, through the NBC network, owns Telemundo, the Spanish language broadcasting network and partially owns cable news channel MSNBC, business network CNBC and cable channels A&E Television Networks, American Movie Classics and Bravo.

General Electric, created in part by Thomas Alva Edison, is a true broadcast pioneer, having founded NBC in 1926 in the early days of radio with RCA and Westinghouse. GE profited from producing shows and selling the radios people used to listen to them. RCA took over NBC in 1932, but GE got back in the business when it bought RCA in 1986. Today, GE's operating interests include aircraft engines, broadcasting, consumer finance, consumer products, insurance and power systems.

In addition to NBC's brand holdings, GE also has a non-voting interest in Paxson Communications Inc. (Ironically, GE has all but given up on radio, having sold most of its stations in the late 1980s.) It also has a strategic alliance with Dow Jones, publisher of the Wall Street Journal.

Wright, the new chief at NBC Universal, has considerable clout in Washington as well as on Wall Street. Wright was actively involved in efforts last year to get the FCC to overturn limits on the number of television stations that can be owned by a single company. While the FCC's decision to loosen limits was rejected by a federal court, Wright and other network honchos enjoyed a partial victory. The White House signed a bill raising the national audience cap for television station owners to 39 percent from 35 percent.

—John Dunbar, Robert Morlino

August 20, 2004

Sources: General Electric Form 10-K, NBC Web site, Broadcasting & Cable, New York Post.

General Electric Co. Recent Financial Information		
Year	Revenue	Net Income (Net Loss)
1999	$11,215,000,000	$10,717,000,000
2000	$130,385,000,000	$12,735,000,000
2001	$126,416,000,000	$13,684,000,000
2002	$132,210,000,000	$14,118,000,000
2003	$134,187,000,000	$15,002,000,000

General Electric Co. Board of Directors				
Name	Position	Relevant Stock		Qty
Immelt, Jeffrey	Chairman and CEO		GE	2,624,420
Dammerman, Dennis	Vice Chairman		GE	2,962,517
Wright, Robert	Vice Chairman		GE	3,596,318
Cash, James	Director		GE	92,936
Fudge, Ann	Director		GE	45,853
Gonzalez, Claudio	Director		GE	221,652
Jung, Andrea	Director		GE	64,500
Lafley, Alan	Director		GE	5,755
Langone, Kenneth	Director		GE	340,649
Larsen, Ralph	Director		GE	19,659
Lazarus, Rochelle	Director		GE	27,043
Nunn, Sam	Director		GE	97,500
Penske, Roger	Director		GE	154,500
Swieringa, Robert	Director		GE	2,685
Warner, Douglas	Director		GE	181,888

General Electric Co. Corporate Officers			
Name	Position	Salary	Bonuses
Immelt, Jeffrey	Chairman and CEO	$3,000,000	$4,325,000
Dammerman, Dennis	Vice Chairman and Executive Officer	$2,266,667	$4,325,000
Wright, Robert	Vice Chairman and Executive Officer	$2,354,167	$4,950,000
Heineman, Benjamin	SVP, General Counsel and Secretary	$1,475,000	$2,890,000
Rogers, Gary	Former Vice Chairman and Executive Officer	$1,700,000	$2,160,000

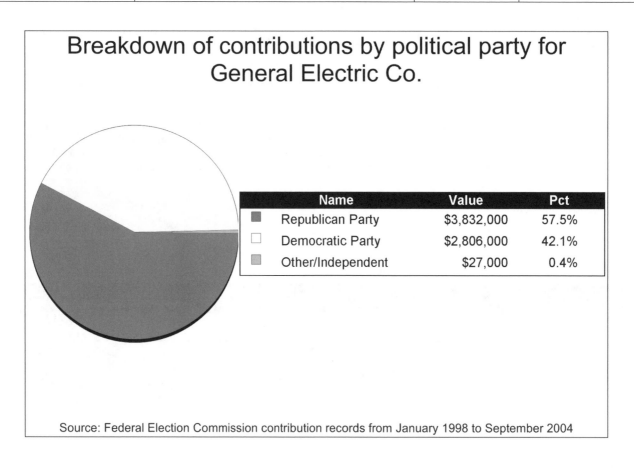

Breakdown of contributions by political party for General Electric Co.

Name	Value	Pct
Republican Party	$3,832,000	57.5%
Democratic Party	$2,806,000	42.1%
Other/Independent	$27,000	0.4%

Source: Federal Election Commission contribution records from January 1998 to September 2004

Top 10 Recipients of Contributions Sourced to General Electric Co.

Recipient	Amount
National Republican Party Committees	$901,000
National Democratic Party Committees	$757,000
President George W Bush (R)	$151,000
Sen Hillary Rodham Clinton (D-NY)	$66,000
Sen John F Kerry (D-MA)	$59,000
Rep Charles B Rangel (D-NY)	$58,000
Sen Charles E Schumer (D-NY)	$57,000
Rep Anne Meagher Northup (R-KY)	$47,000
Sen Mitch McConnell (R-KY)	$46,000
Rep Eric Ivan Cantor (R-VA)	$44,000
Total:	$2,186,000

Source: Federal Election Commission contribution records from January 1998 to September 2004

General Electric Co. Lobbying Expenditures by Year

Year	Amount
1998	$9,220,000
1999	$10,331,000
2000	$19,568,356
2001	$18,157,000
2002	$17,275,900
2003	$21,638,500
2004	$8,977,500
Total:	$105,168,256

Source: U.S. Senate Office of Public Records lobbying disclosure records from January 1998 to June 30th, 2004.

General Electric Co. Sponsored Trips for Congressional Staff

Congressional Office	Number of Trips	$ Amount
Sen Charles E Schumer (D-NY)	1	$1,540
Rep Steven Buyer (R-IN)	1	$810
Sen John F Kerry (D-MA)	1	$620
Total:	3	$2,970

Source: Congressional office travel records for members of the Senate Committee on Commerce, Science & Transportation and the House Committee on Energy and Commerce for the period of January 2000 to March 2004.

TV Station Subsidiaries for General Electric Co.

Call Sign	Channel and Type	Subsidiary Name	Area of Service
WNJU	47 TV Commercial	NBC TELEMUNDO LICENSE CO.	LINDEN, NJ
WVIT	30 TV Commercial	NBC TELEMUNDO LICENSE CO.	NEW BRITAIN, CT
WVTM-TV	13 TV Commercial	NBC TELEMUNDO LICENSE CO.	BIRMINGHAM, AL
KPHZ	11 TV Commercial	NBC TELEMUNDO LICENSE CO.	HOLBROOK, AZ
K34FB	34 TV Low Power (UHF)	NBC TELEMUNDO LICENSE CO.	PUEBLO, CO
KSBS-LP	67 Class A TV (UHF)	NBC TELEMUNDO LICENSE CO.	DENVER, CO
KMAS-LP	63 TV Low Power (VHF)	NBC TELEMUNDO LICENSE CO.	DENVER, CO
KNSO	51 TV Commercial	NBC TELEMUNDO LICENSE CO.	MERCED, CA
WSNS-TV	44 TV Commercial	NBC TELEMUNDO LICENSE CO.	CHICAGO, IL
KNTV	11 TV Commercial	NBC TELEMUNDO LICENSE CO.	SAN JOSE, CA
WNBC	4 TV Commercial	NBC TELEMUNDO LICENSE CO.	NEW YORK, NY
WJAR	10 TV Commercial	NBC TELEMUNDO LICENSE CO.	PROVIDENCE, RI
KVDA	60 TV Commercial	NBC TELEMUNDO LICENSE CO.	SAN ANTONIO, TX
WSCV	51 TV Commercial	NBC TELEMUNDO LICENSE CO.	FORT LAUDERDALE, FL
KEJT-LP	50 Class A TV (UHF)	NBC TELEMUNDO LICENSE CO.	SALT LAKE CITY, UT
K27EI	27 TV Low Power (UHF)	NBC TELEMUNDO LICENSE CO.	SANTA MARIA, CA
K15CU	15 Class A TV (UHF)	NBC TELEMUNDO LICENSE CO.	SALINAS, CA
K49CJ	49 TV Low Power (UHF)	NBC TELEMUNDO LICENSE CO.	COLORADO SPRINGS, CO
KTMD	48 TV Commercial	NBC TELEMUNDO LICENSE CO.	GALVESTON, TX
KSTS	48 TV Commercial	NBC TELEMUNDO LICENSE CO.	SAN JOSE, CA
K52FF	52 TV Low Power (UHF)	NBC TELEMUNDO LICENSE CO.	RENO, NV
WCMH-TV	4 TV Commercial	NBC TELEMUNDO LICENSE CO.	COLUMBUS, OH
WNCN	17 TV Commercial	NBC TELEMUNDO LICENSE CO.	GOLDSBORO, NC
WRC-TV	4 TV Commercial	NBC TELEMUNDO LICENSE CO.	WASHINGTON, DC
WMAQ-TV	5 TV Commercial	NBC TELEMUNDO LICENSE CO.	CHICAGO, IL

TV Station Subsidiaries for General Electric Co.			
Call Sign	Channel and Type	Subsidiary Name	Area of Service
KNBC	4 TV Commercial	NBC TELEMUNDO LICENSE CO.	LOS ANGELES, CA
WNEU	60 TV Commercial	NBC TELEMUNDO LICENSE CO.	MERRIMACK, NH
WCAU	10 TV Commercial	NBC TELEMUNDO LICENSE CO.	PHILADELPHIA, PA
WTVJ	6 TV Commercial	NBC TELEMUNDO LICENSE CO.	MIAMI, FL
KDRX-CA	48 Class A TV (UHF)	NBC TELEMUNDO LICENSE CO.	PHOENIX, AZ
KWHY-LP	22 TV Low Power (UHF)	NBC TELEMUNDO LICENSE CO.	SANTA BARBARA, CA
KWHY-TV	22 TV Commercial	NBC TELEMUNDO LICENSE CO.	LOS ANGELES, CA
K47GD	47 TV Low Power (UHF)	NBC TELEMUNDO LICENSE CO.	SAN LUIS OBISPO, CA
KVEA	52 TV Commercial	NBC TELEMUNDO LICENSE CO.	CORONA, CA
KMAS-TV	24 TV Commercial	NBC TELEMUNDO LICENSE CO.	STEAMBOAT SPRINGS, CO
KHRR	40 TV Commercial	NBC TELEMUNDO LICENSE CO.	TUCSON, AZ
KXTX-TV	39 TV Commercial	NBC TELEMUNDO LICENSE CO.	DALLAS, TX
KPHZ-LP	58 TV Low Power (UHF)	NBC TELEMUNDO LICENSE CO.	PHOENIX, AZ
KNSD	39 TV Commercial	STATION VENTURE OPERATIONS, LP	SAN DIEGO, CA
KXAS-TV	5 TV Commercial	STATION VENTURE OPERATIONS, LP	FORT WORTH, TX
WKAQ-TV	2 TV Commercial	TELEMUNDO OF PUERTO RICO	SAN JUAN, PR

Hearst Corp.

Address: 959 8th Ave
New York, NY 10019

Total Employees: 17,320

Stock Symbol: N/A
Telephone: 212-649-2000
Fax: 212-765-3528
Website: http://www.hearstcorp.com

Though publicly traded corporations dominate today's media landscape, family dynasties built the country's first media empires. A few family-owned companies have survived into the 21st century, and none has played a more prominent role in the development of mass media than Hearst Corp.

Hearst, No. 42 on Forbes magazine's list of the largest private companies in 2003, publishes 12 daily newspapers, including the San Francisco Chronicle and the Houston Chronicle. The company's 18 magazines are among the most well-known and widely read in the country. Hearst publishes Cosmopolitan, Esquire, Good Housekeeping, O, The Oprah Magazine, Redbook and Popular Mechanics, among others. It also controls King Features Syndicate, the largest distributor of comics in the United States, in addition to other entertainment. But it is the company's television broadcast holdings that probably hold the most influence.

Hearst-Argyle Television Inc. owns or manages 27 television stations in cities like Boston, Tampa, Pittsburgh, Sacramento and Baltimore. While Hearst Corp. is a private company, Hearst-Argyle is traded on the New York Stock Exchange. The company was created in August 1997 when Hearst joined with Argyle Television Inc. Hearst Corp. is majority shareholder.

Hearst Corp. traces its roots to 1887, when William Randolph Hearst became "proprietor" of the San Francisco Examiner. History has not been kind to the memory of Hearst, who, along with his competitor Joseph Pulitzer, was a progenitor of "yellow journalism," a type of sensational reporting whose primary function was to create scary headlines, sell newspapers and pump up circulation and advertising revenue. Both men were accused of goading America into a war with Spain in an effort to sell newspapers. Hearst's life was loosely chronicled in the movie classic Citizen Kane, starring Orson Welles as a Hearst-like media tycoon.

Whatever history's opinion of Hearst, his company has endured. Upon his death, he directed all the company stock be placed in a trust, to be controlled by family members and outside directors who act as trustees in accordance with his will.

His penchant for competition seems as antiquated as the Victorian age. For 21 years, Hearst's Seattle Post-Intelligencer has had a joint operating agreement—an exemption from antitrust law that allows the paper to cooperate with a rival—with The Seattle Times. The Blethen family, which controls 50.5 percent of the Times, informed Hearst that the paper had lost money three years in a row. This development activated a clause in the JOA that would lead either to the termination of the agreement or see the Post-Intelligencer shut down. Hearst has said it would close the paper if the operating agreement ends.

A civic action group called the Committee for a Two-Newspaper Town has asked the Justice Department to intervene and preserve the joint operating agreement; there have been reports of recent backdoor negotiations between the two sides as well. Whatever the outcome, the chapter doesn't quite jibe with Hearst mythology.

Though the company's origins were in broadsheets and linotype, Hearst has expanded into more modern means of media communications. Hearst holds stakes in cable television networks A&E, Lifetime and ESPN. It also owns a 30 percent stake in iVillage, a Web network aimed at women.

Not surprisingly, last year, when the FCC considered whether to eliminate a rule preventing newspaper owners from owning television stations in the same market, Hearst came out in favor of eliminating the ban.

—John Dunbar, Robert Morlino

August 20, 2004

Sources: Hearst Corp., Forbes magazine Web site, TNT Web site, Broadcasting & Cable, The Seattle Times

Hearst Corp. Corporate Officers			
Name	Position	Salary	Bonuses
Hearst, George	Chairman	N/A	N/A
Bennnack, Frank	Vice Chairman	N/A	N/A
Ganzi, Victor	President and CEO; Chairman, HTV	N/A	N/A
Barrett, David	President and CEO, HTV	N/A	N/A

Breakdown of contributions by political party for Hearst Corp.

	Name	Value	Pct
■	Republican Party	$79,000	49.7%
□	Democratic Party	$75,000	47.2%
■	Other/Independent	$5,000	3.1%

Source: Federal Election Commission contribution records from January 1998 to September 2004

Top 10 Recipients of Contributions Sourced to Hearst Corp.	
Recipient	Amount
National Republican Party Committees	$21,000
National Democratic Party Committees	$17,000
Sen Hillary Rodham Clinton (D-NY)	$14,000
Sen Evan Bayh (D-IN)	$9,000
President George W Bush (R)	$7,000
Rudolph W Giuliani (R-NY)	$6,000
Sen Elizabeth H Dole (R-NC)	$6,000
New York Republican County Committee	$5,000
Solutions America	$5,000
Sen John F Kerry (D-MA)	$5,000
Total:	$95,000

Source: Federal Election Commission contribution records from January 1998 to September 2004

Hearst Corp. Lobbying Expenditures by Year	
Year	Amount
1998	$160,000
1999	$192,000
2000	$164,000
2001	$34,000
2002	$12,000
2003	$80,000
Total:	$642,000

Source: U.S. Senate Office of Public Records lobbying disclosure records from January 1998 to June 30th, 2004.

Radio Station Subsidiaries for Hearst Corp.				
State	City	Call Sign	Frequency	Subsidiary Name
MD	BALTIMORE	WBAL	1090 AM Station	HEARST RADIO, INC.
MD	BALTIMORE	WIYY	97.9 FM Commercial	HEARST RADIO, INC.

| \multicolumn{5}{c}{TV Station Subsidiaries for Hearst Corp.} |
Call Sign	Channel and Type	Subsidiary Name	Area of Service
KCCI	8 TV Commercial	DES MOINES HEARST-ARGYLE TV, INC.	DES MOINES, IA
WPXL	49 TV Commercial	FLINN BROADCASTING CORPORATION	NEW ORLEANS, LA
W27BL	27 TV Low Power (UHF)	HEARST-ARGYLE PROPERTIES, INC.	BERLIN, NH
WMUR-TV	9 TV Commercial	HEARST-ARGYLE PROPERTIES, INC.	MANCHESTER, NH
W38CB	38 TV Low Power (UHF)	HEARST-ARGYLE PROPERTIES, INC.	LITTLETON, NH
WMUR-LP	29 TV Low Power (UHF)	HEARST-ARGYLE PROPERTIES, INC.	LITTLETON, NH
WNNE	31 TV Commercial	HEARST-ARGYLE STATIONS, INC.	HARTFORD, VT
KSBW	8 TV Commercial	HEARST-ARGYLE STATIONS, INC.	SALINAS, CA
WPTZ	5 TV Commercial	HEARST-ARGYLE STATIONS, INC.	NORTH POLE, NY
KCRA-TV	3 TV Commercial	KCRA HEARST-ARGYLE TELEVISION, INC.	SACRAMENTO, CA
KQCA	58 TV Commercial	KCRA HEARST-ARGYLE TELEVISION, INC.	STOCKTON, CA
KCWE	29 TV Commercial	KCWE-TV, INC.	KANSAS CITY, MO
KETV	7 TV Commercial	KETV HEARST-ARGYLE TELEVISION, INC.	OMAHA, NE
KHBS	40 TV Commercial	KHBS HEARST-ARGYLE TELEVISION, INC.	FORT SMITH, AR
KHOG-TV	29 TV Commercial	KHBS HEARST-ARGYLE TELEVISION, INC.	FAYETTEVILLE, AR
K55BB	55 TV Low Power (UHF)	KITV HEARST-ARGYLE TELEVISION, INC.	SOLDOTNA, AK
KHVO	13 TV Commercial	KITV HEARST-ARGYLE TV, INC. (CA CORP.)	HILO, HI
KITV	4 TV Commercial	KITV HEARST-ARGYLE TV, INC. (CA CORP.)	HONOLULU, HI
KMAU	12 TV Commercial	KITV HEARST-ARGYLE TV, INC. (CA CORP.)	WAILUKU, HI
KMBC-TV	9 TV Commercial	KMBC HEARST-ARGYLE TELEVISION, INC.	KANSAS CITY, MO
KOAT-TV	7 TV Commercial	KOAT HEARST-ARGYLE TELEVISION, INC.	ALBUQUERQUE, NM
KOCT	6 TV Commercial	KOAT HEARST-ARGYLE TELEVISION, INC.	CARLSBAD, NM
KOVT	10 TV Commercial	KOAT HEARST-ARGYLE TELEVISION, INC.	SILVER CITY, NM
WDSU	6 TV Commercial	NEW ORLEANS HEARST-ARGYLE TELEVISION, INC.	NEW ORLEANS, LA
KOCO-TV	5 TV Commercial	OHIO/OKLAHOMA HEARST- ARGYLE TELEVISION	OKLAHOMA CITY, OK
WLWT	5 TV Commercial	OHIO/OKLAHOMA HEARST-ARGYLE TV, INC	CINCINNATI, OH
WESH	2 TV Commercial	ORLANDO HEARST-ARGYLE TELEVISION, INC.	DAYTONA BEACH, FL
WAPT	16 TV Commercial	WAPT HEARST-ARGYLE TV, INC. (CA CORP.)	JACKSON, MS
WBAL-TV	11 TV Commercial	WBAL HEARST-ARGYLE TV, INC. (CA CORP.)	BALTIMORE, MD
WCVB-TV	5 TV Commercial	WCVB HEARST-ARGYLE TV, INC.	BOSTON, MA
WGAL	8 TV Commercial	WGAL HEARST-ARGYLE TELEVISION, INC.	LANCASTER, PA
WISN-TV	12 TV Commercial	WISN HEARST-ARGYLE TV, INC. (CA CORP.)	MILWAUKEE, WI
WLKY-TV	32 TV Commercial	WLKY HEARST-ARGYLE TELEVISION, INC.	LOUISVILLE, KY
WMOR-TV	32 TV Commercial	WMOR-TV COMPANY	LAKELAND, FL
WMTW-TV	8 TV Commercial	WMTW BROADCAST GROUP, LLC	POLAND SPRING, ME
WPBF	25 TV Commercial	WPBF-TV COMPANY	TEQUESTA, FL
WTAE-TV	4 TV Commercial	WTAE HEARST-ARGYLE TV, INC. (CA CORP.)	PITTSBURGH, PA
WXII-TV	12 TV Commercial	WXII HEARST-ARGYLE TELEVISION, INC.	WINSTON-SALEM, NC
WYFF	4 TV Commercial	WYFF HEARST-ARGYLE TELEVISION, INC.	GREENVILLE, SC

| \multicolumn{4}{c}{Print Media Subsidiaries for Hearst Corp.} |
Company Name	Market City	Weekday Circulation	Sunday Circulation
Edwardsville Intelligencer	Edwardsville, IL	5,092	0
Houston Chronicle	Houston, TX	549,300	740,002
Laredo Morning Times	Laredo, TX	21,396	23,895
Midland Daily News	Midland, MI	16,076	17,880
Midland Reporter-Telegram	Midland, TX	20,464	23,654
Plainview Daily Herald	Plainview, TX	6,481	6,481
San Antonio Express-News	San Antonio, TX	237,961	359,828
San Francisco Chronicle	San Francisco, CA	501,135	553,983
Seattle Post-Intelligencer	Seattle, WA	150,901	465,830
The Beaumont Enterprise	Beaumont, TX	53,718	61,825
The Huron Daily Tribune	Bad Axe, MI	7,339	7,603
Times Union	Albany, NY	99,957	144,368

Leap Wireless International Inc.

Address: 10307 Pacific Center Ct. Stock Symbol: LWINQ
San Diego, CA 92121 Telephone: 858-882-6000
Fax: 858-882-6010
Total Employees: 1,400 Website: www.leapwireless.com

Leap Wireless International was a high flyer in the cellular telephone business before taking a dive straight into bankruptcy. But Leap is on the verge of emerging and may yet see better days. A top executive from within the industry has just been named the new CEO, and the company's operating subsidiary continues to add subscribers.

After years of growth, Leap came crashing to Earth in April 2003. Staggering under more than $2.2 billion in debt and cutthroat competition from bigger wireless carriers such as Verizon, AT&T and Sprint, it filed for Chapter 11 bankruptcy.

The announcement of the bankruptcy dropped the value of Leap's shares to 9 cents a share—a far cry from its highs in early 2000, when Leap had traded for more than $100 a share. In December 2002 the company was de-listed by NASDAQ.

Leap was spun off by wireless equipment maker QUALCOMM Inc. in June 1998. Qualcomm co-founder and president Harvey P. White left to run Leap.

Despite having never shown a profit, Leap remains the nation's ninth-largest wireless company. Cricket Communications, a company subsidiary, continues to enjoy fast growth thanks to its flat-rate, no-limit local calling plan

Leap emerged from bankruptcy in August 2004. The FCC granted the company permission to sell some of its wireless spectrum licenses.

The company's new CEO, William Freeman, was previously at Verizon Communications. "I found a company whose business model still has some legs," he told the San Diego Union-Tribune.

At least one analyst disagrees, however, saying that the novelty of Cricket's flat-rate plan has been undercut by the dropping costs of standard, minute-based wireless plans. If Leap does emerge from bankruptcy, it could wind up being acquired by one of the larger wireless providers.

–Robert Morlino, Bob Williams

August 20, 2004

Sources: Company Web site, Securities and Exchange Commission filings, Yahoo! Finance Online, RCR Wireless News, the San Diego Union-Tribune, Hoover's Online, Fortune magazine

Leap Wireless International Inc. Recent Financial Information		
Year	Revenue	Net Income (Net Loss)
2000	$50,317,000	($168,000)
2001	$255,164,000	($483,297,000)
2002	Not Reported	($664,799,000)
2003	$751,296,000	($597,437,000)

Leap Wireless International Inc. Board of Directors			
Name	Position	Relevant Stock	Qty
White, Harvey	Chairman	LWINQ	976,678
Bernard, Thomas	Vice Chairman	LWINQ	257,204
Dynes, Robert	Director	LWINQ	39,000
Chase, Anthony	Director	LWINQ	130,049
Page, Thomas	Director	LWINQ	18,000
Targoff, Michael	Director	LWINQ	42,000

Leap Wireless International Inc. Corporate Officers			
Name	Position	Salary	Bonuses
White, Harvey	Chairman and CEO	$498,750	$348,536
Davis, David	SVP, Operations	N/A	N/A
Irving, Robert	SVP, General Counsel, Secretary	N/A	N/A
Swenson, Susan	Former President, COO, Director	$383,654	$256,567
Hutcheson, S.	EVP, CFO	$290,923	$159,841
Umetsu, Glenn	EVP, COO	$265,385	$100,248

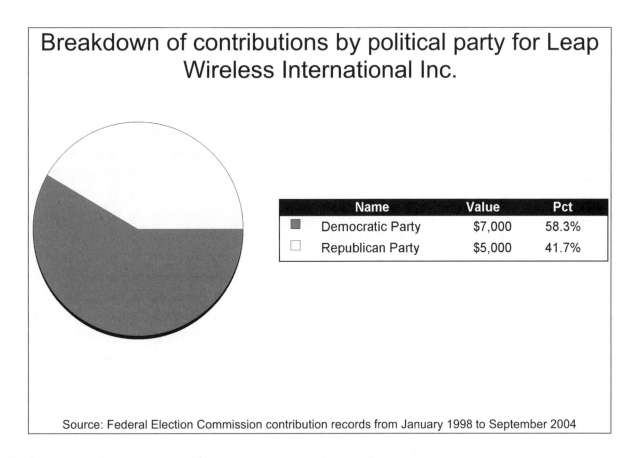

Breakdown of contributions by political party for Leap Wireless International Inc.

Name	Value	Pct
Democratic Party	$7,000	58.3%
Republican Party	$5,000	41.7%

Source: Federal Election Commission contribution records from January 1998 to September 2004

Top 10 Recipients of Contributions Sourced to Leap Wireless International Inc.	
Recipient	Amount
Davis, Susan A	$5,000
Sen Spencer Abraham (R-MI)	$2,000
Rep Thomas J Campbell (R-CA)	$1,000
Sen Bill Bradley (D-NJ)	$1,000
Sen George Allen (R-VA)	$1,000
Sen John S McCain (R-AZ)	$1,000
Rep Duncan Congressman Hunter (R-CA)	$1,000
Vice President Albert Gore, Jr (D-TN)	$1,000
Total:	$13,000

Source: Federal Election Commission contribution records from January 1998 to September 2004

Leap Wireless International Inc. Lobbying Expenditures by Year	
Year	Amount
1999	$320,000
2000	$160,000
2001	$220,000
2002	$40,000
2003	$60,000
Total:	$800,000

Source: U.S. Senate Office of Public Records lobbying disclosure records from January 1998 to June 30th, 2004.

MCI Inc.

Address:	22001 Loudoun County Parkway	Stock Symbol:	MCIAV
	Ashburn, VA 20147	Telephone:	703-886-5600
		Fax:	212-885-0570
Total Employees:	56,600	Website:	www.mci.com

The roller-coaster ride that is WorldCom—uh, make that MCI—showed no signs of stopping in 2005. After fielding a series of takeover bids, MCI announced that – at least as of this writing – it has deemed a bid from Qwest Communications International LLC superior to an offer from Verizon Communications Inc. Three times prior, MCI has signaled a preference for Verizon, even though those bids were significantly lower. The fight is far from over, however, as MCI is still concerned about the much smaller Qwest, and its $17 billion debt load. Regardless, the spirited bidding war may be the best indication yet that MCI has truly come back from the dead.

MCI, formerly known as WorldCom, formerly known as MCI, is in many ways a classic American success story. In 1983 a group of investors that included Mississippi hotel owner Bernard Ebbers reportedly sketched out on a napkin at a Hattiesburg, Miss., diner the original business plan for the company that would become WorldCom.

Originally called Long Distance Discount Services, the company took advantage of FCC rules that subsidized competitors to the newly disassembled AT&T.

By the early 1990s, Worldcom had begun a buying binge that would eventually include more than 60 separate deals. Nearly all of the deals were financed with WorldCom stock, which was driven ever upward by the hot market for telecom companies.

The culmination of the dealmaking would come in 1997 when WorldCom outbid GTE and British Telecom with a $37 billion offer to buy the nation's number two long-distance company, MCI Corp.

But things went bad quickly. The telecom powerhouse had to seek bankruptcy protection in July 2002. Ebbers and most of the company's other top executive resigned following the disclosure of accounting irregularities and a fraud suit filed by the Securities and Exchange Commission.

The scale of the company's financial problems was illustrated in stark terms in March 2003 when WorldCom announced plans to write off nearly $80 billion in the value of goodwill and other intangible assets and the value of networks and other property.

Former Compaq Computer Chairman and CEO Michael Capellas was brought in to try to rescue the company in November 2002. One of the first things he did was change the company's name to MCI Inc. and move the corporate headquarters from Mississippi to Virginia. He also began to aggressively promote flat fee packages for unlimited local and long-distance service for residential customers.

MCI emerged from the largest bankruptcy in U.S. history and officially resumed trading on the NASDAQ exchange in July. It also simultaneously announced a $125 million contract with Hewlett Packard to provide telecommunications services, part of a larger group of contracts totaling $1 billion.

Just two days prior, MCI announced that the investment group Leucadia National Corp. is seeking permission from the FTC to buy a controlling interest in the company. The result: a 16.8 percent bounce in the stock price. The company's new NASDAQ symbol is MCIP, with the IP half indicating the company's embrace of emerging data services. If the MCI phoenix hasn't quite yet risen from the ashes of Worldcom, it's at least begun to flap its wings.

As for former CEO Ebbers, the future doesn't look anywhere near as bright. Ebbers pleaded innocent to federal fraud and conspiracy charges accusing him of directing an accounting fraud estimated at about $11 billion. Trial is set for Nov. 9. Meanwhile, MCI has filed suit against Ebbers, alleging he owes the company more than $300 million in unpaid loans.

—Bob Williams, Robert Morlino, John Dunbar

April 28, 2005

Sources: Company Web site, Securities and Exchange Commission filings, Yahoo! Finance Online, Newark Star-Ledger, Hoover's Online, Fortune magazine.

MCI Inc. Recent Financial Information		
Year	Revenue	Net Income (Net Loss)
1999	$35,908,000,000	$3,941,000,000
2000	$39,090,000,000	$4,088,000,000
2000	$39,251,000,000	($48,909,000,000)
2001	$37,608,000,000	($15,616,000,000)
2001	$35,179,000,000	$1,384,000,000
2002	$32,189,000,000	($9,192,000,000)
2003	$27,315,000,000	$22,211,000,000

MCI Inc. Board of Directors				
Name	Position	Relevant Stock		Qty
Katzenbach, Nicholas	Director		N/A	N/A
Beresford, Dennis	Director		N/A	N/A
Rogers, C.B.	Director		N/A	N/A
Katzanbach, Nicholas	Chairman		N/A	N/A
Capellas, Michael	Director		MCIAV	841,515
Beresford, Dennis	Director		N/A	N/A
Gregory, W.	Director		N/A	N/A
Haberkorn, Judith	Director		N/A	N/A
Harris, Laurence	Director		N/A	N/A
Holder, Eric	Director		N/A	N/A
Neporent, Mark	Director		N/A	N/A
Rogers, C.B.	Director		N/A	N/A

MCI Inc. Corporate Officers			
Name	Position	Salary	Bonuses
Capellas, Michael	Chairman, President, and CEO	N/A	N/A
Blakely, Robert	CFO	N/A	N/A
Salsbury, Michael	EVP and General Counsel	N/A	N/A
Capellas, Michael	President, CEO, Director	$1,500,000	$1,500,000
Roscitt, Richard	President, COO	$380,800	$2,450,000
Biggs, Fred	President, Operations and Technology	$480,800	$795,000
Blakely, Robert	EVP, CFO	N/A	N/A
Kelly, Anastasia	EVP, General Counsel	N/A	N/A

Breakdown of contributions by political party for MCI, Inc.

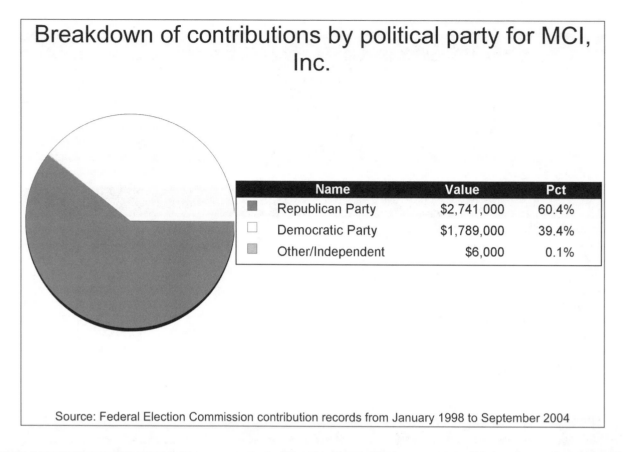

Name	Value	Pct
Republican Party	$2,741,000	60.4%
Democratic Party	$1,789,000	39.4%
Other/Independent	$6,000	0.1%

Source: Federal Election Commission contribution records from January 1998 to September 2004

Top 10 Recipients of Contributions Sourced to MCI Inc. Recipient	Amount
National Republican Party Committees	$1,444,000
National Democratic Party Committees	$741,000
President George W Bush (R)	$48,000
Sen Trent Lott (R-MS)	$47,000
Rep Charles W Pickering, Jr (R-MS)	$47,000
Sen Thomas Andrew Daschle (D-SD)	$39,000
Rep Heather Ann Wilson (R-NM)	$37,000
Rep Richard A Gephardt (D-MO)	$34,000
Sen Donald Lee Nickles (R-OK)	$34,000
Illinois Republican Party	$32,000
Total:	$2,503,000

Source: Federal Election Commission contribution records from January 1998 to September 2004

MCI Inc. Lobbying Expenditures by Year Year	Amount
1998	$3,542,863
1999	$670,000
2000	$3,683,553
2001	$4,037,981
2002	$3,185,984
2003	$5,885,086
2004	$356,000
Total:	$21,361,467

Source: U.S. Senate Office of Public Records lobbying disclosure records from January 1998 to June 30th, 2004.

MCI Inc. Sponsored Trips for Congressional Staff Congressional Office	Number of Trips	$ Amount
Sen Fritz Hollings (D-SC)	1	$865
Rep Ralph Moody Hall (D-TX)	1	$855
Total:	2	$1,720

Source: Congressional office travel records for members of the Senate Committee on Commerce, Science & Transportation and the House Committee on Energy and Commerce for the period of January 2000 to March 2004.

Mediacom Communications Corp.

Address:	100 Crystal Run Rd. Middletown, NY 10941	Stock Symbol:	MCCC
		Telephone:	845-695-2600
		Fax:	845-695-2699
Total Employees:	3,899	Website:	www.mediacomcc.com

Mediacom Communications likes to present itself as the cable company of rural and small town America, with some justification. The country's eighth-largest cable company and 10th-largest pay-television company if you include satellite broadcasters, provides service to such places as Moline, Ill., and Davenport, Iowa.

But don't get the idea that Mediacom is just another small-town, local cable franchiser. It has more than1.5 million basic cable subscribers in 23 states. More than 370,000 of those customers receive digital cable television service from Mediacom, while 302,000 customers tap into the Internet over the company's lines. The other customers receive standard cable service, not digital.

Those are pretty impressive numbers for such a young company. Mediacom was started in 1995 by cable industry veteran Rocco Commisso, who had served as executive vice president, chief financial officer and a director of Cablevision Industries Corp. from 1986 to 1995.

Immediately upon founding Mediacom, Commisso began buying up cable systems in non-metropolitan markets. The company's biggest deal came in 2001, when Mediacom bought several systems from AT&T Broadband serving more than 750,000 subscribers. AT&T Broadband was subsequently acquired by industry leader Comcast a year later.

That deal nearly doubled Mediacom's size and pushed up its revenue to almost $1 billion in 2002.

Mediacom has shown no sign it plans to change its strategy of concentrating on rural and small town systems scattered all over the country, even as most of the other major players in the cable business have been pushing hard to consolidate their holdings into clusters in and around metropolitan areas.

Instead, Mediacom has been spending money to upgrade its systems in order to offer digital cable television, high-speed Internet services and video-on-demand products.

Commisso, who has been an outspoken critic of rising cable programming costs, exercises complete control of Mediacom. He owns about 81 percent of the voting stock of the company.

Although Commisso calls all the shots, another media firm has a major stake in the company. Morris Communications, which also concentrates in non-metropolitan markets, owns 47 percent of the company.

Morris Communications, which is privately held, owns more than 50 newspapers, mostly in small towns or rural areas. It also owns more than 30 radio stations and dozens of specialty publications.

—Bob Williams

August 19, 2004

Sources: Company Web site, Securities and Exchange Commission filings, Yahoo! Finance Online, Hoover's Online.

Mediacom Communications Corp. Recent Financial Information		
Year	Revenue	Net Income (Net Loss)
1998	$129,297,000	($39,790,000)
1999	$174,961,000	($81,320,000)
2000	$328,258,000	($149,847,000)
2001	$585,175,000	($190,876,000)
2002	$923,033,000	($161,658,000)
2003	$1,004,889,000	($62,475,000)

Mediacom Communications Corp. Board of Directors				
Name	Position	Relevant Stock		Qty
Commisso, Rocco	Chairman		MCCC	28,861,939
Stephan, Mark	Director		MCCC	387,247
Mitchell, Craig	Director		MCCC	28,399,674
Morris, William	Director		MCCC	28,309,674
Reifenheiser, Thomas	Director		MCCC	10,000
Ricciardi, Natale	Director		MCCC	10,000
Winikoff, Robert	Director		MCCC	45,000

Mediacom Communications Corp. Corporate Officers			
Name	Position	Salary	Bonuses
Commisso, Rocco	Chairman and CEO	$800,000	$600,000
Stephan, Mark	EVP, CFO, Director	$230,000	$36,000
Carey, James	EVP, Operations	$202,500	$20,448

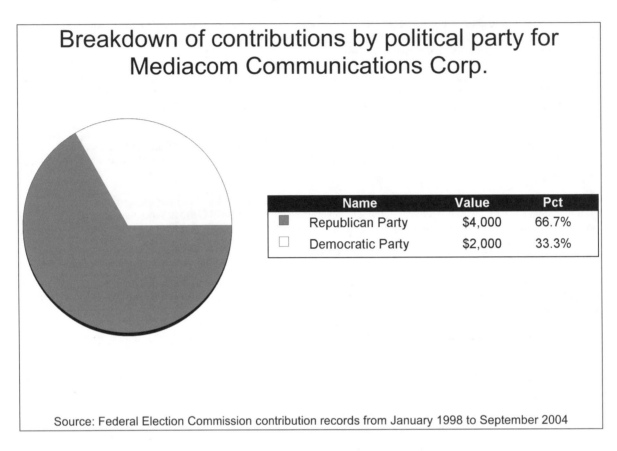

Breakdown of contributions by political party for Mediacom Communications Corp.

	Name	Value	Pct
	Republican Party	$4,000	66.7%
	Democratic Party	$2,000	33.3%

Source: Federal Election Commission contribution records from January 1998 to September 2004

Top 10 Recipients of Contributions Sourced to Mediacom Communications Corp.	
Recipient	Amount
Rep Rick A Lazio (R-NY)	$2,000
Sen Conrad R Burns (R-MT)	$1,000
Sen John S McCain (R-AZ)	$1,000
Rep William P Luther (D-MN)	$1,000
Sen John F Kerry (D-MA)	$1,000
Total:	$6,000

Source: Federal Election Commission contribution records from January 1998 to September 2004

Mediacom Communications Corp. Lobbying Expenditures by Year	
Year	Amount
2003	$60,000
Total:	$60,000

Source: U.S. Senate Office of Public Records lobbying disclosure records from January 1998 to June 30th, 2004.

News Corp. Limited

Address:	2 Holt St.	Stock Symbol:	NWS
	Sydney 2010, Australia,	Telephone:	61-2-9288-3000
		Fax:	61-2-9288-3292
Total Employees:	37,000	Website:	www.newscorp.com

In 1985, media mogul Rupert Murdoch became a United States citizen. In 2004, he revealed plans to bring his multi-billion-dollar media conglomerate with him. It only makes sense given that the company's U.S.-based business accounted for more than three-quarters of News Corp.'s roughly $20 billion in revenue last year.

The controversial Australian billionaire started small, inheriting his father's modest newspaper holdings in 1952. Murdoch showed a knack for the business, and began making a substantial profit. In the 1960s, he expanded his newspaper holdings to England with great success.

In 1973, he entered the U.S. market with the buyout of the San Antonio Express-News, now owned by Hearst Newspapers. He continued buying newspapers, but it was 1985 when he made his boldest move. That year, he bought Metromedia's seven independent television stations from John Kluge. That, combined with the purchase of Twentieth Century Fox Holdings, made it possible for Murdoch to create the first new television network since the mid-1950s.

Murdoch's decision to become a U.S. citizen was not necessarily related to any love of America—the Federal Communications Commission requires owners of television stations to be citizens. Even with the change in citizenship, the deal was still controversial.

Earlier this year, Murdoch announced he would move the headquarters of News Corp. as well as the company's stock listing to New York City. Analysts predict the move and reincorporation will produce numerous financial windfalls, including the improvement of trading liquidity and enhanced capital access. It will also help solidify the Murdoch family's control over the massive conglomerate.

The move comes on the heels of News Corp.'s 2003 acquisition of a controlling interest in satellite television broadcaster DirecTV. With the purchase, which Murdoch described at the company's annual meeting as "the missing link in a global satellite platform," Murdoch is able to deliver his product unimpeded to DirecTV's 12 million subscribers.

Today, News Corp.—roughly 30 percent controlled by Murdoch family members—owns a number of newspapers, including the Times of London and the New York Post. It also owns British Sky Broadcasting, a satellite television network, and HarperCollins book publishers.

The aggressive, conservative Australian magnate's most notable achievement of late has been the popularity of the Fox News Channel, the 24-hour news network. The news channel is consistently beating rival CNN in the ratings, but has also been blasted for its parade of right-wing commentators and accused of blatant bias in its reporting.

Regardless of politics, New Corp.'s broadcast empire includes 35 television stations and 200 affiliates for the Fox Network. And with the $6.6 billion purchase of DirecTV, those stations now have an independent means of continuing to broadcast the message.

—John Dunbar, Robert Morlino

August 20, 2004

Sources: News Corp. Web site and 2002 Annual Report, ketupa.net Media Profiles, Hoover's Online, The Hollywood Reporter, Contra Costa Times.

News Corp. Limited Recent Financial Information		
Year	Revenue	Net Income (Net Loss)
1999	$21,704,000,000	$963,000,000
2000	$2,237,000,000	($329,000,000)
2001	$25,387,000,000	($218,000,000)
2002	$28,776,000,000	($14,670,000,000)
2003	$29,752,000,000	$1,421,000,000

News Corp. Limited Board of Directors				
Name	Position	Relevant Stock		Qty
Murdoch, K.	Chairman		N/A	N/A
Bible, Geoffrey	Director		N/A	N/A
Chernin, Peter	Director		N/A	N/A
Cowley, Kenneth	Director		N/A	N/A

News Corp. Limited Board of Directors				
Name	Position	Relevant Stock		Qty
DeVoe, David	Director		N/A	N/A
Eddington, Rod	Director		N/A	N/A
Erkko, Juho	Director		N/A	N/A
Knight, Andrew	Director		N/A	N/A
Kraehe, Graham	Director		N/A	N/A
Murdoch, James	Director		N/A	N/A
Murdoch, Lachlan	Director		N/A	N/A
Perkins, Thomas	Director		N/A	N/A
Shuman, Stanley	Director		N/A	N/A
Siskind, Arthur	Director		N/A	N/A
Carey, Chase	Director		N/A	N/A

News Corp. Limited Corporate Officers			
Name	Position	Salary	Bonuses
Murdoch, K.	Chairman and CEO	$4,508,000	$7,500,000
Chernin, Peter	President and COO	$8,104,000	$8,000,000
Murdoch, Lachlan	Deputy COO	$1,403,000	$1,200,000
DeVoe, David	SEVP and CFO	$2,104,000	$7,150,000
Siskind, Arthur	SEVP and Group General Counsel	$1,965,000	$1,200,000
Murdoch, James	EVP; CEO, British Sky Broadcasting	$900,000	$1,200,000
Ailes, Roger	Chairman and CEO, Fox News Channel	$2,500,000	$5,956,000

Breakdown of contributions by political party for News Corp. Limited

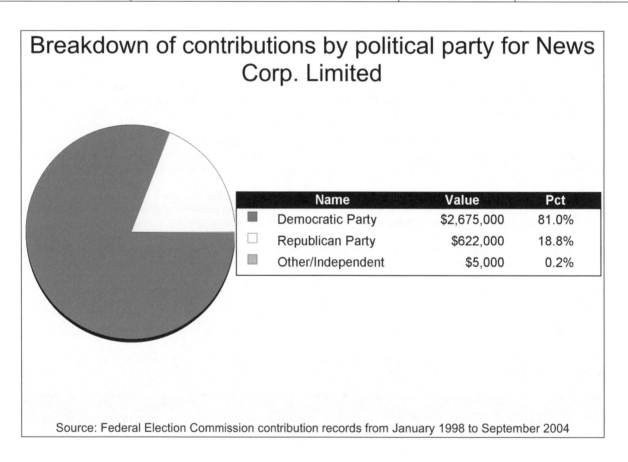

Name	Value	Pct
Democratic Party	$2,675,000	81.0%
Republican Party	$622,000	18.8%
Other/Independent	$5,000	0.2%

Source: Federal Election Commission contribution records from January 1998 to September 2004

Top 10 Recipients of Contributions Sourced to News Corp. Limited	
Recipient	Amount
National Democratic Party Committees	$2,080,000
National Republican Party Committees	$178,000
Sen John F Kerry (D-MA)	$90,000
Sen Hillary Rodham Clinton (D-NY)	$56,000
Sen Charles E Schumer (D-NY)	$41,000
Sen Barbara Boxer (D-CA)	$36,000
Sen John S McCain (R-AZ)	$30,000
Sen William H Frist (R-TN)	$28,000
President George W Bush (R)	$27,000
Rep Edward John Markey (D-MA)	$22,000
Total:	$2,588,000
Source: Federal Election Commission contribution records from January 1998 to September 2004	

News Corp. Limited Lobbying Expenditures by Year	
Year	Amount
1998	$1,950,000
1999	$1,715,000
2000	$2,335,000
2001	$1,860,000
2002	$3,718,000
2003	$3,884,000
2004	$320,000
Total:	$15,782,000
Source: U.S. Senate Office of Public Records lobbying disclosure records from January 1998 to June 30th, 2004.	

News Corp. Limited Sponsored Trips for Congressional Staff		
Congressional Office	Number of Trips	$ Amount
Rep Wilbert J Tauzin, Jr (R-LA)	2	$4,285
Rep Joe Linus Barton (R-TX)	2	$2,779
Rep Nathan Deal (R-GA)	1	$2,402
Rep Mary Bono (R-CA)	1	$2,358
Rep Vito J Fossella, Jr (D-NY)	1	$2,258
Rep Lee R Terry (R-NE)	1	$2,258
Rep Anna G Eshoo (D-CA)	1	$2,258
Rep Clifford Bundy Stearns (R-FL)	1	$2,258
Rep Frank Pallone, Jr (D-NJ)	1	$2,258
Sen John F Kerry (D-MA)	1	$1,957
Sen John B Breaux (D-LA)	1	$1,897
Sen John Eric Ensign (R-NV)	1	$1,897
Sen Trent Lott (R-MS)	1	$1,651
Total:	15	$30,516
Source: Congressional office travel records for members of the Senate Committee on Commerce, Science & Transportation and the House Committee on Energy and Commerce for the period of January 2000 to March 2004.		

TV Station Subsidiaries for News Corp. Limited			
Call Sign	Channel and Type	Subsidiary Name	Area of Service
WFXT	25 TV Commercial	FOX TELEVISION STATIONS INC.	BOSTON, MA
KSTU	13 TV Commercial	FOX TELEVISION STATIONS INC.	SALT LAKE CITY, UT
WWOR-TV	9 TV Commercial	FOX TELEVISION STATIONS, INC.	SECAUCUS, NJ
KFTC	26 TV Commercial	FOX TELEVISION STATIONS, INC.	BEMIDJI, MN
WJBK	2 TV Commercial	FOX TELEVISION STATIONS, INC.	DETROIT, MI
KMSP-TV	9 TV Commercial	FOX TELEVISION STATIONS, INC.	MINNEAPOLIS, MN
KUTP	45 TV Commercial	FOX TELEVISION STATIONS, INC.	PHOENIX, AZ
WOGX	51 TV Commercial	FOX TELEVISION STATIONS, INC.	OCALA, FL
WAGA	5 TV Commercial	FOX TELEVISION STATIONS, INC.	ATLANTA, GA
WOFL	35 TV Commercial	FOX TELEVISION STATIONS, INC.	ORLANDO, FL
WRBW	65 TV Commercial	FOX TELEVISION STATIONS, INC.	ORLANDO, FL
KCOP-TV	13 TV Commercial	FOX TELEVISION STATIONS, INC.	LOS ANGELES, CA
WDCA	20 TV Commercial	FOX TELEVISION STATIONS, INC.	WASHINGTON, DC
KTXH	20 TV Commercial	FOX TELEVISION STATIONS, INC.	HOUSTON, TX
WUTB	24 TV Commercial	FOX TELEVISION STATIONS, INC.	BALTIMORE, MD

TV Station Subsidiaries for News Corp. Limited			
Call Sign	Channel and Type	Subsidiary Name	Area of Service
WPWR-TV	50 TV Commercial	FOX TELEVISION STATIONS, INC.	GARY, IN
WFTC	29 TV Commercial	FOX TELEVISION STATIONS, INC.	MINNEAPOLIS, MN
WHBQ-TV	13 TV Commercial	FOX TELEVISION STATIONS, INC.	MEMPHIS, TN
KRIV	26 TV Commercial	FOX TELEVISION STATIONS, INC.	HOUSTON, TX
WNYW	5 TV Commercial	FOX TELEVISION STATIONS, INC.	NEW YORK, NY
WTTG	5 TV Commercial	FOX TELEVISION STATIONS, INC.	WASHINGTON, DC
KTTV	11 TV Commercial	FOX TELEVISION STATIONS, INC.	LOS ANGELES, CA
WFLD	32 TV Commercial	FOX TELEVISION STATIONS, INC.	CHICAGO, IL
KFCT	22 TV Commercial	FOX TELEVISION STATIONS, INC.	FORT COLLINS, CO
KDVR	31 TV Commercial	FOX TELEVISION STATIONS, INC.	DENVER, CO
WTXF-TV	29 TV Commercial	FOX TV STATIONS OF PHILADELPHIA	PHILADELPHIA, PA
KDFW	4 TV Commercial	KDFW LICENSE, INC.	DALLAS, TX
KSAZ-TV	10 TV Commercial	KSAZ LICENSE, INC.	PHOENIX, AZ
KTBC	7 TV Commercial	KTBC LICENSE, INC.	AUSTIN, TX
KTVI	2 TV Commercial	KTVI LICENSE, INC.	ST. LOUIS, MO
KDFI	27 TV Commercial	NEW DMIC, INC.	DALLAS, TX
WTVT	13 TV Commercial	TVT LICENSE, INC.	TAMPA, FL
WBRC	6 TV Commercial	WBRC LICENSE, INC.	BIRMINGHAM, AL
WDAF-TV	4 TV Commercial	WDAF LICENSE, INC.	KANSAS CITY, MO
WGHP	8 TV Commercial	WGHP LICENSE, INC.	HIGH POINT, NC
WITI	6 TV Commercial	WITI LICENSE, INC.	MILWAUKEE, WI
WJW	8 TV Commercial	WJW LICENSE, INC.	CLEVELAND, OH

Print Media Subsidiaries for News Corp. Limited			
Company Name	Market City	Weekday Circulation	Sunday Circulation
New York Post	New York, NY	678,012	445,094

Nextel Communications Inc.

Address:	2001 Edmund Halley Dr. Reston, VA 20191	Stock Symbol:	NXTL
		Telephone:	703-433-4000
		Fax:	703-433-4343
Total Employees:	17,000	Website:	www.nextel.com

Nextel Communications Inc. scored a major regulatory victory in 2004 when the FCC agreed to a request by the company to occupy a coveted new slice of the radio spectrum—a decision that was the subject of an intense battle between Nextel and rival Verizon Wireless, which objected vehemently. Competitor Sprint PCS, however, wasted no time in moving to acquire the company in a deal announced at the end of the year. Valued at $35 billion, the merger will create the No. 3 wireless carrier with a combined 35.4 million subscribers.

The FCC decision will keep Nextel from stepping on the toes of a number of public agencies, including police and firefighters, who occupy the 700 to 800 MHz range. Nextel will pay upward of $5 billion, between the value of the spectrum it will leave behind and a letter of credit to cover the relocation costs for the public agencies. Verizon called the decision a "multi-billion dollar windfall at taxpayer expense," and went so far as to call on members of Congress for help in blocking the plan.

And the Cellular Telecommunications & Internet Association was critical as well, arguing that the valuable section of the radio spectrum was being given away without a warranted public auction. Nevertheless, the FCC sided with Nextel, hardly surprising given the redoubtably well-connected members of the company's board.

Chairman William E. Conway is one of the founders and managing directors of the Carlyle Group, a huge, shadowy investment firm that employs former Secretary of State James Baker and until recently, former President George H.W. Bush. Then there is ex-Federal Communications Commission Chairman William Kennard, who also serves as a managing director of Carlyle with Conway.

The Nextel board is loaded with communications industry heavyweights—but wireless stalwart Craig McCaw is no longer among them. McCaw, who has invested more than $1 billion into the company, stepped down in December.

Also on hand at board meetings is a representative of telecom giant Motorola, which holds about 8 percent of Nextel's stock, is the company's partner on some ventures, and is its primary supplier of handsets and other equipment.

For most people, however, Nextel is known primarily for its cell phones that also work like walkie-talkies. Called Direct Connect, the digital service allows customers to reach other Nextel customers directly, without placing a phone call.

Nextel is the largest wireless company that doesn't trace its roots back to the old Bell System, the century-old phone monopoly broken up by the courts in 1984. Unlike larger wireless competitors Verizon, Cingular, AT&T and Sprint PCS, Nextel began in 1987 as a radio dispatch company under the name Fleet Call. It was founded by former FCC staffer Morgan O'Brien in 1987.

O'Brien had overseen the FCC's specialized mobile radio licensing division, the technology traditionally used to dispatch taxies and repairmen. He became convinced the old-line SMR technology could compete effectively with the newer cellular systems of the late 1980s.

He and some partners began buying up radio dispatch companies. The company went public in 1992, changing the name to Nextel.

In 1995, Motorola exchanged its SMR licenses in the 800 MHz spectrum band for a 20 percent ownership interest in Nextel.

In 1995 McCaw agreed to invest more than $1 billion in Nextel for an ownership stake. Daniel Akerson, was installed as chairman and CEO of Nextel until his departure in 2000. Founder O'Brien is vice chairman of the company.

Despite the Motorola deal, Nextel found itself seriously short of the wireless spectrum it needed to establish a nationwide network and grow into a viable national competitor. In 1999 Nextel made a bid to buy more than 190 wireless licenses from bankrupt telecom company Geotek, but was blocked from closing the deal by the Justice Department.

The government relented in 2000, however, allowing Nextel to buy the Geotek licenses. In the meantime, Nextel offered to buy hundreds of licenses owned by another bankrupt telecom startup, Nextwave, for $8.3 billion. Nextel eventually walked away from that deal after the government said it would try to reclaim the licenses from Nextwave.

Subsequently, the company concentrated on adding subscribers, using its two-way radio feature to build a dominant position in the wireless industry. With about 13 million subscribers currently, Nextel is the nation's sixth largest wireless company, and it's growing steadily.

Nextel enjoys one of the highest profit margins in the industry despite ranking sixth among major carriers in total subscribers. The company reported a second quarter profit of $1.3 billion, its ninth consecutive profitable quarter, and four times better than the previous year.

—Bob Williams, Robert Morlino

April 28, 2005

Sources: Company Web site, Securities and Exchange Commission filings, Yahoo! Finance Online, Hoover's Online, Fortune magazine, RCR Wireless News

Nextel Communications Inc. Recent Financial Information		
Year	Revenue	Net Income (Net Loss)
1998	$2,295,000,000	($1,652,000,000)
1999	$3,786,000,000	($1,338,000,000)
2000	$5,714,000,000	($815,000,000)
2001	$7,689,000,000	($2,625,000,000)
2002	$8,721,000,000	$1,386,000,000
2003	$10,820,000,000	$1,530,000,000

Nextel Communications Inc. Board of Directors				
Name	Position	Relevant Stock		Qty
Conway, William	Chairman		NXTL	1,323,930
O'Brien, Morgan	Vice Chairman		NXTL	1,117,324
Donahue, Timothy	Director		NXTL	4,270,016
Bane, Keith	Director		N/A	N/A
Drendel, Frank	Director		NXTL	191,247
Hill, V.	Director		NXTL	98,896
Kennard, William	Director		NXTL	65,302
Shem, Stephanie	Director		NXTL	10,000

Nextel Communications Inc. Corporate Officers			
Name	Position	Salary	Bonuses
O'Brien, Morgan	Vice Chairman	$444,769	$956,800
Donahue, Timothy	President, CEO, and Director	$938,461	$2,760,000
Kelly, Thomas	EVP and COO	$588,846	$1,204,000
Saleh, Paul	EVP and CFO	$516,769	$1,056,800
Kennedy, Leonard	SVP and General Counsel	$413,415	$574,080

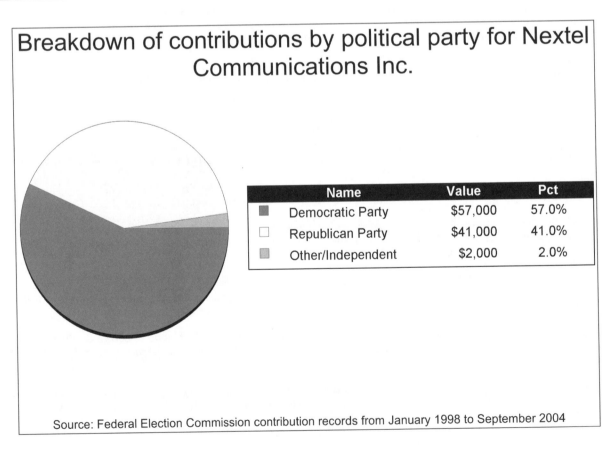

Breakdown of contributions by political party for Nextel Communications Inc.

Name	Value	Pct
Democratic Party	$57,000	57.0%
Republican Party	$41,000	41.0%
Other/Independent	$2,000	2.0%

Source: Federal Election Commission contribution records from January 1998 to September 2004

Top 10 Recipients of Contributions Sourced to Nextel Communications Inc.	
Recipient	Amount
National Republican Party Committees	$21,000
National Democratic Party Committees	$21,000
Sen John F Kerry (D-MA)	$9,000
President George W Bush (R)	$6,000
Sen John S McCain (R-AZ)	$4,000
Rep Constance A Morella (R-MD)	$4,000
Sen Patty Murray (D-WA)	$4,000
Sen Hillary Rodham Clinton (D-NY)	$4,000
Rep Jay Robert Inslee (D-WA)	$2,000
Rep Richard Ray Larsen (D-WA)	$2,000
Total:	$77,000
Source: Federal Election Commission contribution records from January 1998 to September 2004	

Nextel Communications Inc. Lobbying Expenditures by Year	
Year	Amount
1999	$960,000
2000	$150,000
2001	$20,000
2002	$280,000
2003	$2,283,000
2004	$520,000
Total:	$4,213,000
Source: U.S. Senate Office of Public Records lobbying disclosure records from January 1998 to June 30th, 2004.	

Qwest Communications International Inc.

Address:	1801 California St.	**Stock Symbol:**	Q
	Denver, CO 80202	**Telephone:**	303-992-1400
		Fax:	303-992-1724
Total Employees:	47,000	**Website:**	www.qwest.com

The hard-headed days for Qwest Communications appear to be over, giving way to a kinder, gentler telecommunications company. With the resignation of the company's pugnacious chief executive, and a propensity for settling disputes rather than fighting, the nation's fourth-largest local phone service provider appears to be sailing in smoother seas. Things are going so well, in fact, Qwest has decided to take on phone giant Verizon Communications Inc. in a bidding war for MCI. The transition hasn't been easy. The company has paid the two largest settlements in the history of the Federal Communications Commission, one for $9 million and one for $6.5 million, to settle FCC investigations for violating competition rules. The bad behavior took place under the reign of former CEO Joseph Nacchio.

It was also during Nacchio's tenure, in 2000 and 2001, that company revenues were inflated by $2.5 billion. The company is still recovering from that debacle—lawsuits and investigations continue—but recent business arrangements are helping put Qwest back on track...where it began, in a manner of speaking.

Qwest got its start hauling freight rather than voices and data. The company was the brainchild of Philip Anschutz, who bought the Southern Pacific Rail Corp. in 1988. That same year he formed Southern Pacific Telecommunications Co. and began laying fiber-optic cable along the railroad's right-of-way.

Within five years, the company was offering long distance telephone service throughout the southwestern region of the country. In 1995, SPT bought Qwest Communications, which operated a digital microwave communication system in the areas that the SPT fiber-optic network did not cover.

The combined company kept the Qwest name and struck out to build a high capacity, nationwide fiber-optic network capable of transmitting huge amounts of data and phone calls. Big customers such as MCI and GTE quickly lined up to purchase capacity on the network.

In 1996, Anschutz sold Southern Pacific Railroad to Union Pacific, but held on to the telecommunications business. A year later he brought in former AT&T executive Nacchio to run Qwest. The two took the company public in 1997, just in time to ride the crest of the dot.com boom of the late 1990s.

In 2000 Qwest jumped into the local phone business in a big way with a $43.5 billion acquisition of former Baby Bell U S West, a deal the company financed with its high-flying stock. The deal garnered Qwest about 25 million local phone customers.

The acquisition transformed Qwest into a huge force in the telecom industry, particularly in its 14-state home service area in the western and Midwestern United States, where it still dominates both the local and long distance market. The company also offers broadband and dial-up Internet access services, as well as wireless voice communications.

Qwest's rapid growth came with a share of legal and regulatory woes, including separate investigations of the company's accounting practices by the Securities and Exchange Commission and the Justice Department.

Four mid-level Qwest executives faced 11 charges including conspiracy and wire fraud in connection with helping the company improperly book $34 million in revenue, the Associated Press reported. In a trial in April, a jury failed to convict the four men. Grant Graham subsequently pleaded guilty to a charge of accessory after the fact to wire fraud. On June 9, a grand jury returned a new indictment against defendant Thomas Hall on four charges. That case is pending.

Nacchio was reportedly forced by the Qwest Board of Directors to resign as CEO in June 2002. His total compensation package of nearly $100 million in 2001 also left investors angry. Anschutz also bowed out of an active role with the company in June 2002.

The board brought in telecom veteran Richard Notebaert to replace Nacchio, naming him chairman and chief executive officer of the company. Prior to joining Qwest, Notebaert was president and CEO of equipment maker Tellabs Inc. Before that he was chairman of Baby Bell Ameritech, which was acquired by SBC in 1999.

Notebaert's stewardship of the company has earned praise from some of the previous management's harshest critics. W. Thomas Stephens, a board member whose criticisms of Nacchio came to light during congressional investigations into the corporate scandals that rocked the country in 2001 and 2002, resigned his post in July 2004. Stephens noted that Notebaert and his team had improved Qwest enough that he could focus on other business priorities.

Just a few weeks before Stephens resigned, Qwest announced an agreement to sell its wireless service infrastructure to Verizon, a deal that will add more than $400 million to the company's bottom line. The company has been shifting its customer base for several months, through a resale plan with Sprint PCS. Many of Qwest's 800,000-plus wireless subscribers already use Sprint's nationwide infrastructure for their service.

—Bob Williams, Robert Morlino

April 28, 2005

Sources: Company Web site, Securities and Exchange Commission filings, Yahoo! Finance Online, Hoover's Online, Fortune magazine.

Qwest Communications International Inc. Recent Financial Information		
Year	Revenue	Net Income (Net Loss)
2000	$14,148,000,000	($1,037,000,000)
2001	$16,530,000,000	($5,603,000,000)
2002	$15,371,000,000	($38,468,000,000)
2003	$14,288,000,000	$1,512,000,000

Qwest Communications International Inc. Board of Directors				
Name	Position	Relevant Stock		Qty
Khosla, Vinod	Director		Q	6,494
Popoff, Frank	Director		Q	106,665
Biggs, Charles	Director		Q	1,000
Notebaert, Richard	Chairman and CEO		Q	1,950,000
Anschutz, Philip	Director		Q	300,428,004
Alvarado, Linda	Director		Q	58,418
Brooksher, K.	Director		Q	5,000
Donohue, Thomas	Director		Q	16,274
Haines, Jordan	Director		Q	6,500
Harvey, Cannon	Director		Q	80,650
Hellman, Peter	Director		Q	60,146
Slater, Craig	Director		Q	124,650
Stephens, W.	Director		Q	20,059

Qwest Communications International Inc. Corporate Officers			
Name	Position	Salary	Bonuses
Baer, Richard	EVP and General Counsel	$500,000	$1,162,625
Shaffer, Oren	Vice Chairman and CFO	$800,000	$2,338,800
Notebaert, Richard	Chairman and CEO	$1,100,000	$2,925,000

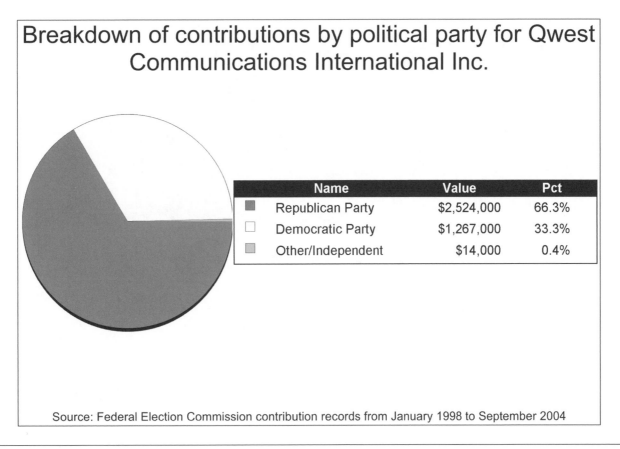

Breakdown of contributions by political party for Qwest Communications International Inc.

Name	Value	Pct
Republican Party	$2,524,000	66.3%
Democratic Party	$1,267,000	33.3%
Other/Independent	$14,000	0.4%

Source: Federal Election Commission contribution records from January 1998 to September 2004

Top 10 Recipients of Contributions Sourced to Qwest Communications International Inc.	
Recipient	Amount
National Republican Party Committees	$1,338,000
National Democratic Party Committees	$754,000
Sen John S McCain (R-AZ)	$117,000
President George W Bush (R)	$64,000
Sen Thomas Andrew Daschle (D-SD)	$45,000
Rep Michael G Oxley (R-OH)	$43,000
Rep J Dennis Hastert (R-IL)	$34,000
Rep Lee R Terry (R-NE)	$34,000
Sen Conrad R Burns (R-MT)	$33,000
Sen Larry E Craig (R-ID)	$27,000
Total:	$2,489,000
Source: Federal Election Commission contribution records from January 1998 to September 2004	

Qwest Communications International Inc. Lobbying Expenditures by Year	
Year	Amount
1998	$3,610,000
1999	$4,508,000
2000	$6,548,000
2001	$3,993,480
2002	$5,730,000
2003	$2,158,000
2004	$2,185,000
Total:	$28,732,480
Source: U.S. Senate Office of Public Records lobbying disclosure records from January 1998 to June 30th, 2004.	

Radio One Inc.

Address: 5900 Princess Garden Pkwy.
7th Floor
Lanham, MD 20706
Total Employees: 1,550

Stock Symbol: ROIA
Telephone: 301-306-1111
Fax: 301-306-9426
Website: www.radio-one.com

Under the stewardship of founder Catherine L. Hughes, Radio One has built itself into the largest radio broadcasting company in the U.S. targeting black Americans. That niche has helped the company become the seventh-largest radio broadcaster overall, with 65 stations in 22 markets.

With popular nationally syndicated personalities like Russ Parr, Radio One definitely knows its audience, and advertisers are aware. Thirty-six of Radio One's stations are in 14 of the top 20 African-American radio markets, including Atlanta, Baltimore, Cincinnati, Boston, Los Angeles, Philadelphia and Washington, D.C.

It has been a steady climb for Radio One, founded in 1980, and things are not slowing down a bit. In addition to its ownership of traditional broadcast outlets, the company also programs five channels for satellite radio company XM Satellite Radio Holdings. Most recently, it entered into an agreement with cable television giant Comcast Corp. to create a new cable television network targeting black Americans.

In a business that is being taken over by huge corporations, Radio One is very much a family affair. The president and CEO is Alfred C. Liggins III, son of the company's founder. Hughes, currently chairman of the board of the NASDAQ-traded company, got her start as general sales manager of WHUR-FM in Washington, D.C., the Howard University-owned urban contemporary station. Radio One got its start when Hughes purchased WOL-AM in 1980.

Hughes was CEO from 1980 to 1997 and has worked as president, general manager, general sales manager and even talk show host for the company.

Since its founding, Radio One has continued to expand. In August of 2000, Radio One bought 12 stations from Clear Channel Communications Corp. and AMFM (bought by Clear Channel) for approximately $1.3 billion. In February 2001, Radio One purchased all of the capital stock of Blue Chip Broadcasting, Inc. for approximately $190 million.

Radio One is well-known within the industry, but it made headlines when it inked a deal with Comcast. Under the agreement, Radio One will invest $70 million in the new cable television network, which will be targeted toward "25- to 54-year-old African-American viewers." The new network will feature entertainment, news, opinion and sports-related programming. The two companies hope it will offer a competitive alternative to BET, owned by media giant Viacom Inc.

The new venture is a clear departure for Radio One. Unlike radio, where it practically owns the franchise on marketing to black listeners, television will be a different story. BET has plenty of history and a loyal audience. However, BET has struggled a bit of late. The network was lambasted late last year when it cut most of its public affairs programming, despite scoring an interview with former Senate Majority Leader Trent Lott, who was in trouble for making racially insensitive remarks.

—John Dunbar

Sources: Radio One Inc. Web site, Form 10-K, Washington Post, Datamonitor Company Profiles.

Radio One Inc. Recent Financial Information		
Year	Revenue	Net Income (Net Loss)
1998	$46,109,000	$841,000
1999	$81,703,000	$133,000
2000	$155,666,000	($4,251,000)
2001	$243,804,000	($55,247,000)
2002	$295,851,000	$7,054,000
2003	$303,150,000	$53,783,000

Radio One Inc. Board of Directors			
Name	Position	Relevant Stock	Qty
Hughes, Catherine	Chairperson	ROIA	852,536
Liggins, Alfred	Director	ROIA	2,048,243
Armstrong, D.	Director	ROIA	10,000
Blaylock, Ronald	Director	N/A	N/A
Jones, Terry	Director	ROIA	313,888
Love, L.	Director	ROIA	250
McNeill, Brian	Director	ROIA	26,434

Radio One Inc. Corporate Officers			
Name	Position	Salary	Bonuses
Hughes, Catherine	Chairperson and Secretary	$399,000	$130,000
Liggins, Alfred	President, CEO, Treasurer, and Director	$500,000	$340,000
Royster, Scott	EVP and CFO	$375,000	$120,000
Sneed, Mary	COO	$375,000	$120,000
Vilardo, Linda	VP, General Counsel	$275,000	$140,000

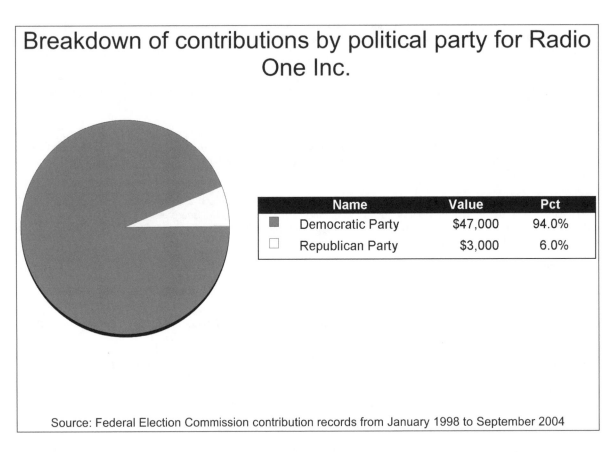

Breakdown of contributions by political party for Radio One Inc.

	Name	Value	Pct
	Democratic Party	$47,000	94.0%
	Republican Party	$3,000	6.0%

Source: Federal Election Commission contribution records from January 1998 to September 2004

Top 10 Recipients of Contributions Sourced to Radio One Inc.	
Recipient	Amount
Rev Alfred C Sharpton (D)	$16,000
Ronald Kirk (D-TX)	$4,000
Rep Martin T Meehan (D-MA)	$4,000
Sen Hillary Rodham Clinton (D-NY)	$4,000
Rep Elijah Eugene Cummings (D-MD)	$4,000
Glenn, Dylan C	$3,000
Kerry Victory 2004	$2,000
Sen Barack H Obama (D-IL)	$2,000
Rep Edolphus Towns (D-NY)	$2,000
Marlinga, Carl J	$1,000
Total:	$42,000
Source: Federal Election Commission contribution records from January 1998 to September 2004	

Radio Station Subsidiaries for Radio One Inc.				
State	City	Call Sign	Frequency	Subsidiary Name
CA	LOS ANGELES	KKBT	100.3 FM Commercial	RADIO ONE LICENSES, LLC
DC	WASHINGTON	WYCB	1340 AM Station	RADIO ONE LICENSES, LLC
DC	WASHINGTON	WKYS	93.9 FM Commercial	RADIO ONE LICENSES, LLC
DC	WASHINGTON	WOL	1450 AM Station	RADIO ONE LICENSES, LLC
FL	CORAL GABLES	WVCG	1080 AM Station	RADIO ONE LICENSES, LLC
GA	AUGUSTA	WFXA-FM	103.1 FM Commercial	RADIO ONE OF AUGUSTA, LLC
GA	AUGUSTA	WTHB	1550 AM Station	RADIO ONE OF AUGUSTA, LLC
GA	EVANS	WAEG	92.3 FM Commercial	RADIO ONE OF AUGUSTA, LLC

Radio Station Subsidiaries for Radio One Inc.				
State	City	Call Sign	Frequency	Subsidiary Name
GA	FAYETTEVILLE	WPZE	97.5 FM Commercial	ROA LICENSES, LLC
GA	HAMPTON	WHTA	107.9 FM Commercial	RADIO ONE LICENSES, LLC
GA	MABLETON	WAMJ	102.5 FM Commercial	NEW MABLETON BROADCASTING CORPORATION
GA	ROSWELL	WJZZ-FM	107.5 FM Commercial	ROA LICENSES, LLC
GA	WAYNESBORO	WTHB-FM	100.9 FM Commercial	RADIO ONE OF AUGUSTA, LLC
GA	WRENS	WAKB	96.9 FM Commercial	RADIO ONE OF AUGUSTA, LLC
IL	BETHALTO	WFUN-FM	95.5 FM Commercial	RADIO ONE LICENSES, LLC
IN	CHARLESTOWN	WEGK	104.3 FM Commercial	BLUE CHIP BROADCASTING LICENSES, LTD.
IN	CORYDON	WGZB-FM	96.5 FM Commercial	BLUE CHIP BROADCASTING LICENSES II, LTD.
IN	GREENWOOD	WTLC-FM	106.7 FM Commercial	RADIO ONE OF INDIANA, LLC
IN	INDIANAPOLIS	WTLC	1310 AM Station	RADIO ONE OF INDIANA, LLC
IN	INDIANAPOLIS	WHHH	96.3 FM Commercial	RADIO ONE OF INDIANA, LLC
IN	LEBANON	WYJZ	100.9 FM Commercial	RADIO ONE OF INDIANA, LLC
KY	ERLANGER	WIZF	100.9 FM Commercial	BLUE CHIP BROADCASTING LICENSES II, LTD.
KY	JEFFERSONTOWN	WMJM	101.3 FM Commercial	BLUE CHIP BROADCASTING LICENSES II, LTD.
KY	LOUISVILLE	WXMA	102.3 FM Commercial	BLUE CHIP BROADCASTING LICENSES II, LTD.
KY	LOUISVILLE	WDJX	99.7 FM Commercial	BLUE CHIP BROADCASTING LICENSES II, LTD.
KY	SHEPHERDSVILLE	WLRS	105.1 FM Commercial	BLUE CHIP BROADCASTING LICENSES II, LTD.
MA	BOSTON	WILD	1090 AM Station	RADIO ONE OF BOSTON LICENSES, LLC
MA	BROCKTON	WBOT	97.7 FM Commercial	RADIO ONE LICENSES, LLC
MD	BALTIMORE	WERQ-FM	92.3 FM Commercial	RADIO ONE LICENSES, LLC
MD	BALTIMORE	WWIN	1400 AM Station	RADIO ONE LICENSES, LLC
MD	BALTIMORE	WOLB	1010 AM Station	RADIO ONE LICENSES, LLC
MD	BETHESDA	WMMJ	102.3 FM Commercial	RADIO ONE LICENSES, LLC
MD	GLEN BURNIE	WWIN-FM	95.9 FM Commercial	RADIO ONE LICENSES, LLC
MI	DETROIT	WDTJ	105.9 FM Commercial	RADIO ONE OF DETROIT, LLC
MI	MOUNT CLEMENS	WDMK	102.7 FM Commercial	RADIO ONE OF DETROIT, LLC
MI	TAYLOR	WCHB	1200 AM Station	RADIO ONE OF DETROIT, LLC
MN	GLENCOE	KTTB	96.3 FM Commercial	BLUE CHIP BROADCASTING LICENSES II, LTD.
NC	DURHAM	WFXC	107.1 FM Commercial	RADIO ONE LICENSES, LLC
NC	FUQUAY-VARINA	WNNL	103.9 FM Commercial	RADIO ONE LICENSES, LLC
NC	HARRISBURG	WQNC	92.7 FM Commercial	RADIO ONE OF NORTH CAROLINA, LLC
NC	TARBORO	WFXK	104.3 FM Commercial	RADIO ONE LICENSES, LLC
NJ	PENNSAUKEN	WSNJ-FM	107.9 FM Commercial	RADIO ONE LICENSES, LLC
OH	CINCINNATI	WDBZ	1230 AM Station	BLUE CHIP COMMUNICATIONS, INC.
OH	CLEVELAND	WERE	1300 AM Station	BLUE CHIP BROADCASTING LICENSES, LTD
OH	CLEVELAND	WENZ	107.9 FM Commercial	BLUE CHIP BROADCASTING LICENSES, LTD
OH	CLEVELAND	WZAK	93.1 FM Commercial	BLUE CHIP BROADCASTING LICENSES, LTD
OH	CLEVELAND HEIGHTS	WJMO	1490 AM Station	BLUE CHIP BROADCASTING LICENSES, LTD
OH	COLUMBUS	WCKX	107.5 FM Commercial	BLUE CHIP BROADCASTING LICENSES, LTD
OH	DAYTON	WING	1410 AM Station	BLUE CHIP BROADCASTING LICENSES, LTD
OH	EATON	WGTZ	92.9 FM Commercial	BLUE CHIP BROADCASTING LICENSES, LTD
OH	LONDON	WJYD	106.3 FM Commercial	BLUE CHIP BROADCASTING LICENSES, LTD
OH	SPRINGFIELD	WDHT	102.9 FM Commercial	BLUE CHIP BROADCASTING LICENSES, LTD
OH	UPPER ARLINGTON	WXMG	98.9 FM Commercial	BLUE CHIP BROADCASTING LICENSES, LTD
OH	URBANA	WKSW	101.7 FM Commercial	BLUE CHIP BROADCASTING LICENSES, LTD
OH	WEST CARROLLTON	WRNB	92.1 FM Commercial	RADIO ONE OF DAYTON LICENSES, LLC
PA	JENKINTOWN	WPHI-FM	103.9 FM Commercial	RADIO ONE LICENSES, LLC
PA	MEDIA	WPLY	100.3 FM Commercial	RADIO ONE LICENSES, LLC
TX	DALLAS	KBFB	97.9 FM Commercial	RADIO ONE LICENSES, LLC
TX	GAINESVILLE	KSOC	94.5 FM Commercial	RADIO ONE LICENSES, LLC
TX	HOUSTON	KBXX	97.9 FM Commercial	RADIO ONE LICENSES, LLC
TX	HOUSTON	KMJQ	102.1 FM Commercial	RADIO ONE LICENSES, LLC
VA	CREWE	WKJS	104.7 FM Commercial	RADIO ONE LICENSES, LLC
VA	MECHANICSVILLE	WCDX	92.1 FM Commercial	RADIO ONE LICENSES, LLC
VA	PETERSBURG	WROU	1240 AM Station	RADIO ONE LICENSES, LLC
VA	PETERSBURG	WPZZ	99.3 FM Commercial	RADIO ONE LICENSES, LLC
VA	RICHMOND	WJMO-FM	105.7 FM Commercial	RADIO ONE LICENSES, LLC
VA	SOUTH BOSTON	WQOK	97.5 FM Commercial	RADIO ONE LICENSES, LLC

TV Station Subsidiaries for Radio One Inc.			
Call Sign	Channel and Type	Subsidiary Name	Area of Service
WDNI-LP	65 TV Low Power (UHF)	RADIO ONE OF INDIANA, LLC	INDIANAPOLIS, IN

SBC Communications Inc.

Address:	175 E. Houston		Stock Symbol:	SBC
	San Antonio, TX 78205-2233		Telephone:	210-821-4105
			Fax:	210-351-2071
Total Employees:	168,000		Website:	www.sbc.com

SBC Communications Inc. is the baby company that consumed its siblings and then its parent. It started out as one of the "Baby Bells" created by the 1984 government breakup of AT&T, and since that time has grown steadily through a marathon of acquisitions, culminating with a deal announced in 2005 to buy up what remains of AT&T for $16 billion.

Already the No. 2 provider of local telephone service, SBC also operates Cingular Wireless through a joint venture with BellSouth Corp. Cingular acquired AT&T's spun off wireless division last year, and that union created the largest cellular carrier in the nation.

SBC has been working on the all-out domination approach for nearly a decade. The original Southwestern Bell Corp.—from which SBC derives its name—remained primarily the local phone company for five southwestern states until passage of the Telecommunications Act of 1996.

Following passage of the landmark communications law rewrite, SBC went on an all-out acquisition binge, gobbling up two of its fellow Baby Bells and some other local phone companies in rapid succession.

In 1997 SBC acquired Pacific Telesis, the parent company of Pacific Bell and Nevada Bell. A year later it bought Southern New England Telecommunications, giving SBC a beachhead in the Northeast.

In 1999, SBC completed a $62 billion acquisition of Baby Bell Ameritech, giving it local dominance throughout the Midwest.

Those deals put SBC into a solid second place position behind Verizon in the domestic local telephone market with 54.7 million access lines in 13 states at year-end 2003, according to SEC documents filed by the company.

When Cingular acquired AT&T Wireless, SBC dethroned Verizon a second time. SBC owns a 60 percent stake in Cingular, which was created with BellSouth in 2000.

SBC also offers a variety of Internet services including dial-up access, high speed access, e-mail and Web hosting. In the fall of 2001, SBC acquired Prodigy Communications Corp., a residential and business Internet services company.

SBC has also teamed up with Web browser Yahoo! to offer joint DSL (digital subscriber line) Internet access in SBC's local markets and dial up service nationwide. As part of that deal SBC agreed to buy a three percent stake in Yahoo!

In 1999, SBC purchased a small stake in WilTel Communications, the long distance arm of Williams Communications Group, giving it a big jump on the long distance market, which was formerly off-limits. SBC now offers long distance in California, Connecticut, Kansas, Oklahoma, Texas, Arkansas, Illinois, Indiana, Michigan, Missouri, Nevada, Ohio and Wisconsin.

—Bob Williams, Robert Morlino

April 28, 2005

Sources: Company Web site, Securities and Exchange Commission filings, Yahoo! Finance Online, San Antonio Express-News, Hoover's Online, Fortune magazine.

SBC Communications Inc. Recent Financial Information		
Year	Revenue	Net Income (Net Loss)
1998	$46,241,000,000	$7,690,000,000
1999	$49,531,000,000	$8,159,000,000
2000	$51,374,000,000	$7,800,000,000
2001	$45,908,000,000	$7,008,000,000
2002	$43,138,000,000	$5,653,000,000
2003	$40,843,000,000	$8,505,000,000

SBC Communications Inc. Board of Directors				
Name	Position	Relevant Stock		Qty
Whitacre, Edward	Chairman and CEO		SBC	6,298,177
Amelio, Gilbert	Director		SBC	5,395
Barksdale, Clarence	Director		SBC	10,977
Barnes, James	Director		SBC	6,602
Busch, August	Director		SBC	46,354
Clark, William	Director		SBC	15,401

SBC Communications Inc. Board of Directors			
Name	Position	Relevant Stock	Qty
Tyson, Laura	Director	SBC	11,648
Eby, Martin	Director	SBC	26,856
Gallegos, Herman	Director	SBC	9,724
Hay, Jess	Director	SBC	12,010
Henderson, James	Director	SBC	23,476
Inman, Bobby	Director	SBC	7,363
Knight, Charles	Director	SBC	24,978
Martin, Lynn	Director	SBC	14,866
McCoy, John	Director	SBC	31,584
Metz, Mary	Director	SBC	12,883
Rembe, Toni	Director	SBC	24,790
Ritchey, S.	Director	SBC	17,249
Atterbury, James	Director	SBC	775,647
Wilkins, Rayford	Director	SBC	626,862
Ellis, James	Director	SBC	1,123,494
Daley, William	Director	SBC	180,970
Roche, Joyce	Director	SBC	2,041
Helu, Carlos	Director	SBC	5,002,002
Upton, Patricia	Director	SBC	12,060

SBC Communications Inc. Corporate Officers			
Name	Position	Salary	Bonuses
Whitacre, Edward	Chairman and CEO	$2,122,000	$5,700,000
Daley, William	President	$630,000	$890,000
Stephenson, Randall	SEVP and COO	N/A	N/A
Ellis, James	SEVP and General Counsel	$744,000	$925,000
Wilkins, Rayford	Group President	$777,000	$950,000
Sigman, Stanley	President and CEO, Cingular Wireless	$912,000	$921,000
Lindner, Richard	CFO	N/A	N/A

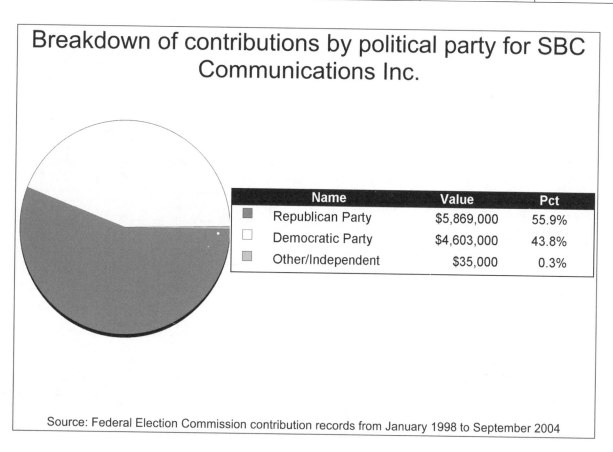

Breakdown of contributions by political party for SBC Communications Inc.

Name	Value	Pct
Republican Party	$5,869,000	55.9%
Democratic Party	$4,603,000	43.8%
Other/Independent	$35,000	0.3%

Source: Federal Election Commission contribution records from January 1998 to September 2004

Top 10 Recipients of Contributions Sourced to SBC Communications Inc.	
Recipient	**Amount**
National Democratic Party Committees	$1,913,000
National Republican Party Committees	$1,474,000
President George W Bush (R)	$178,000
Rep J Dennis Hastert (R-IL)	$132,000
Rep Richard A Gephardt (D-MO)	$129,000
Rep Michael G Oxley (R-OH)	$80,000
Rep Thomas Dale Delay (R-TX)	$69,000
Rep John Andrew Boehner (R-OH)	$67,000
Rep Martin Frost (D-TX)	$65,000
Rep Wilbert J Tauzin, Jr (R-LA)	$65,000
Total:	$4,172,000

Source: Federal Election Commission contribution records from January 1998 to September 2004

SBC Communications Inc. Lobbying Expenditures by Year	
Year	**Amount**
1998	$15,457,000
1999	$19,870,000
2000	$9,928,000
2001	$6,438,289
2002	$8,441,334
2003	$6,380,064
2004	$6,298,350
Total:	$72,813,037

Source: U.S. Senate Office of Public Records lobbying disclosure records from January 1998 to June 30th, 2004.

SBC Communications Inc. Sponsored Trips for Congressional Staff		
Congressional Office	**Number of Trips**	**$ Amount**
	4	$8,122
Rep Wilbert J Tauzin, Jr (R-LA)	5	$7,992
Rep George P Radanovich (R-CA)	3	$5,011
Rep Vito J Fossella, Jr (D-NY)	5	$4,944
Rep Mary Bono (R-CA)	3	$4,471
Rep John Mondy Shimkus (R-IL)	2	$3,667
Rep Nathan Deal (R-GA)	2	$3,326
Rep Frederick Stephen Upton (R-MI)	2	$3,141
Rep Steven Buyer (R-IN)	2	$2,793
Rep Bobby Lee Rush (D-IL)	1	$2,178
Sen Byron L Dorgan (D-ND)	1	$2,051
Rep Gregory Paul Walden (R-OR)	1	$1,965
Sen Donald Lee Nickles (R-OK)	1	$1,908
Rep Richard Mauze Burr (R-NC)	1	$1,838
Sen John Eric Ensign (R-NV)	1	$1,821
Rep Ralph Moody Hall (D-TX)	1	$1,813
Rep Edolphus Towns (D-NY)	1	$1,791
Rep Clifford Bundy Stearns (R-FL)	1	$1,771
Sen John B Breaux (D-LA)	1	$1,769
Rep Stephen Michael Largent (R-OK)	1	$1,711
Rep Paul Eugene Gillmor (R-OH)	1	$1,685
Rep Lee R Terry (R-NE)	1	$1,685
Sen George Allen (R-VA)	1	$1,685
Sen Conrad R Burns (R-MT)	1	$1,641
Sen Gordon Harold Smith (R-OR)	1	$1,630
Rep Edward Whitfield (R-KY)	1	$1,575
Rep Darrell E Issa (R-CA)	1	$1,266
Sen Tim Johnson (D-SD)	1	$1,077
Total:	47	$76,328

Source: Congressional office travel records for members of the Senate Committee on Commerce, Science & Transportation and the House Committee on Energy and Commerce for the period of January 2000 to March 2004.

Sinclair Broadcast Group Inc.

Address:	10706 Beaver Dam Road	Stock Symbol:	SBGI
	Hunt Valley, MD 21030	Telephone:	(410) 568-1500
		Fax:	
Total Employees:	3,266	Website:	www.sbgi.net

Throughout its 33-year history, Sinclair Broadcast Group has demonstrated a proclivity for buying up scads of television stations and attracting controversy. But two key decisions in 2004 on the part of the company's top management has transformed Sinclair into what one media analyst described as "the new poster child for the ills of media consolidation."

In April, when the ABC News program Nightline dedicated an entire show to reading the names of the more than 700 U.S. soldiers killed during the Iraq war to that point, Sinclair management issued an order to its seven ABC affiliates: do not air this program. That decision thrust Sinclair into the national and even international spotlight, with everyone from Nightline host Ted Koppel to Sen. John McCain coming out against the move.

McCain sent a public letter to Sinclair's CEO, David Smith, calling the decision not to air the Nightline tribute "unpatriotic." But despite that and overwhelming criticism from editorials to protests outside the company, Sinclair stuck to its guns, suggesting that the show was politics "disguised as news."

That was just a prelude, however, to what happened a few months later, just before the presidential election. Sinclair announced that it was ordering all of the television stations it programs—60 of the 62 in its overall group—to preempt regular primetime programming and air an unflattering documentary about Democratic presidential nominee John F. Kerry's Vietnam service.

An eruption of criticism—including from many of the company's own shareholders—followed. The Washington, D.C., bureau chief even spoke out against the decision, and was summarily dismissed. CNN contributor Howard Kurtz coined a slogan for the broadcaster: "Sinclair, we don't even pretend to be fair and balanced."

The company had never before received as much attention as it did in April and then in October, but anyone familiar with Sinclair's history wouldn't be surprised by the ability of its owners to withstand opposition.

Julian Sinclair Smith started out in 1971 with a single television station in Baltimore, Md., that is now the company's flagship; Smith's next acquisition was in Pittsburgh. After years of growth, by 1985, the company's board of directors tried to oust him. They failed when Smith and his son joined forces with one other board member, whose 10.2 percent stake combined with Smith's 40 percent to halt the move.

The Smith family then bought out the dissenting board members. In 1988 Smith's son David took over as chairman and CEO of the newly renamed Sinclair Broadcast Group. He became chairman of the board in 1990.

From there, the company embarked on a mission to get "as many TV stations as we can," in the words of Smith, and as of 2004 Sinclair owns more television stations than any other company in the United States, reaching nearly 25 percent of all households. The four sons of the company founder still control about 95 percent of Sinclair.

Despite its large collection of affiliates, the company has long had financial problems. The $75 million raised from Sinclair's IPO in 1995 was used to pay down debt. Three years later, still saddled with most of that debt, Sinclair paid out more than $1.3 billion for a total of 21 additional stations—14 from Sullivan Broadcast Holdings and seven from Guy Gannett Communications—and the company's debt grew.

During the same period of rapid expansion and escalating debt, Sinclair caught flack for violating the FCC rule against owning more than one UHF station in one market.

From 1999 to 2000, in an effort to recover financially, Sinclair sold all of its radio holdings, including 55 stations, to Entercom Communications for $920 million, thus making the company all-TV. Despite the sale, the company is still wrestling with significant debt. Sinclair is 11th among the top broadcast television companies, despite having 52 stations: revenues of about $756 million for 2002 are a fraction of the $2.3 billion that News Corp., with only 35 stations, pulled in.

As Sinclair has continually added stations, its role has become increasingly that of a content provider rather than a straight distributor. Most significantly, Sinclair reaches 25 percent of the national audience through its 62 stations, and owns more duopolies—two television stations in a single market—than any other broadcaster.

In 2002, Sinclair created News Central to manage news operations for all of its stations from a central location. The company prides itself on being an alternative to mainstream news media, broadcasting its own content under the name "News Central." The company's vice president for corporate relations, Mark Hyman, provides daily commentaries during broadcasts.

During the Iraq war, Sinclair dispatched its own reporters to Iraq in order to cover the positive stories coming out of the country that the company said were being spiked by the mainstream media.

But it was the Nightline flap that cast Sinclair as the unsung darling of conservative media. Robert Zelnick, chairman of Boston University's journalism department and former ABC News correspondent called the company "kind of a Triple-A Fox News," referring to News Corp.'s conservative cable news channel.

Sinclair has also given more money to Republicans in the form of campaign contributions, proportionately, than even Bush benefactor, Clear Channel Communications Inc. Between 1996 and mid-2004, Sinclair has contributed 89 percent of its $2.3 million in contributions to Republicans. Clear Channel, by comparison, has donated 65 percent of its $10 million in contributions to Republicans, according to a Center for Public Integrity analysis.

—Robert Morlino

October 20, 2004

Sources: Company Web site, Hoover's Online, The Hollywood Reporter, The Baltimore Sun, The Post and Courier, Television Week

Sinclair Broadcast Group Inc. Recent Financial Information		
Year	Revenue	Net Income (Net Loss)
2000	$758,511,000	$77,365,000
2001	$684,651,000	($127,722,000)
2002	$735,789,000	($564,494,000)
2003	$738,741,000	$24,392,000

Sinclair Broadcast Group Inc. Board of Directors				
Name	Position	Relevant Stock		Qty
Smith, David	Chairman, President, CEO		SBGI	34,249,033
Smith, Frederick	Vice President, Director		SBGI	17,219,697
Smith, J.	Secretary, Director		SBGI	22,001,972
Smith, Robert	Director		SBGI	15,731,791
Keith, Daniel	Director		SBGI	1,250
Leader, Martin	Director		SBGI	3,250
McCanna, Lawrence	Director		SBGI	1,850
Thomas, Basil	Director		SBGI	4,250

Sinclair Broadcast Group Inc. Corporate Officers			
Name	Position	Salary	Bonuses
Smith, David	Chairman, President and CEO	$1,000,000	N/A
Smith, Frederick	Vice President	$190,000	N/A
Smith, J.	Vice President and Secretary	$190,000	N/A
Amy, David	EVP and CFO	$300,000	$150,000
Faber, Barry	General Counsel	$250,000	$50,000

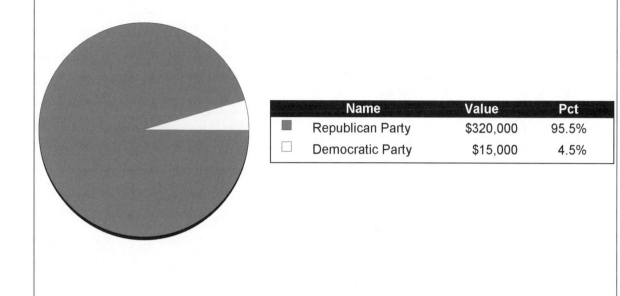

Breakdown of contributions by political party for Sinclair Broadcast Group Inc.

Name	Value	Pct
Republican Party	$320,000	95.5%
Democratic Party	$15,000	4.5%

Source: Federal Election Commission contribution records from January 1998 to September 2004

Top 10 Recipients of Contributions Sourced to Sinclair Broadcast Group Inc.	
Recipient	Amount
National Republican Party Committees	$217,000
President George W Bush (R)	$23,000
Rep Robert Leroy Ehrlich, Jr (R-MD)	$23,000
Sen John S McCain (R-AZ)	$19,000
Sen Conrad R Burns (R-MT)	$7,000
Republican State Central Committee Of Maryland	$5,000
Republican Party Of Florida Federal Campaign Account	$5,000
Vice President Albert Gore, Jr (D-TN)	$4,000
Rep Robert D Inglis (R-SC)	$4,000
Ruppersberger, C.a. Dutch	$4,000
Total:	$311,000

Source: Federal Election Commission contribution records from January 1998 to September 2004

Sinclair Broadcast Group Inc. Lobbying Expenditures by Year	
Year	Amount
2003	$60,000
Total:	$60,000

Source: U.S. Senate Office of Public Records lobbying disclosure records from January 1998 to June 30th, 2004.

TV Station Subsidiaries for Sinclair Broadcast Group Inc.			
Call Sign	Channel and Type	Subsidiary Name	Area of Service
WABM	68 TV Commercial	BIRMINGHAM (WABM-TV) LICENSEE, INC.	BIRMINGHAM, AL
KFBT	33 TV Commercial	CHANNEL 33, INC.	LAS VEGAS, NV
WBFF	45 TV Commercial	CHESAPEAKE TELEVISION LICENSEE, LLC	BALTIMORE, MD
KABB	29 TV Commercial	KABB LICENSEE, LLC	SAN ANTONIO, TX
KBSI	23 TV Commercial	KBSI LICENSEE L.P.	CAPE GIRARDEAU, MO
KDNL-TV	30 TV Commercial	KDNL LICENSEE, LLC	ST. LOUIS, MO
KDSM-TV	17 TV Commercial	KDSM LICENSEE, LLC	DES MOINES, IA
KGAN	2 TV Commercial	KGAN LICENSEE, LLC	CEDAR RAPIDS, IA
KMWB	23 TV Commercial	KLGT LICENSEE, LLC	MINNEAPOLIS, MN
KOCB	34 TV Commercial	KOCB LICENSEE, LLC	OKLAHOMA CITY, OK
KOKH-TV	25 TV Commercial	KOKH LICENSEE, LLC	OKLAHOMA CITY, OK

Call Sign	Channel and Type	TV Station Subsidiaries for Sinclair Broadcast Group Inc. Subsidiary Name	Area of Service
KSMO-TV	62 TV Commercial	KSMO LICENSEE, INC.	KANSAS CITY, MO
KVWB	21 TV Commercial	KUPN LICENSEE, LLC	LAS VEGAS, NV
WNYO-TV	49 TV Commercial	NEW YORK TELEVISION, INC.	BUFFALO, NY
WRDC	28 TV Commercial	RALEIGH (WRDC-TV) LICENSEE, INC.	DURHAM, NC
KRRT	35 TV Commercial	SAN ANTONIO (KRRT-TV) LICENSEE, INC.	KERRVILLE, TX
KOVR	13 TV Commercial	SCI - SACRAMENTO LICENSEE, LLC	STOCKTON, CA
WCGV-TV	24 TV Commercial	WCGV LICENSEE, LLC	MILWAUKEE, WI
WCHS-TV	8 TV Commercial	WCHS LICENSEE, LLC	CHARLESTON, WV
WCWB	22 TV Commercial	WCWB LICENSEE, LLC	PITTSBURGH, PA
WDKA	49 TV Commercial	WDKA ACQUISITION CORPORATION	PADUCAH, KY
WDKY-TV	56 TV Commercial	WDKY LICENSEE, LLC	DANVILLE, KY
WEAR-TV	3 TV Commercial	WEAR LICENSEE, LLC	PENSACOLA, FL
WEMT	39 TV Commercial	WEMT LICENSEE L.P.	GREENEVILLE, TN
WFGX	35 TV Commercial	WFGX LICENSEE, LLC	FORT WALTON BEACH, FL
WGGB-TV	40 TV Commercial	WGGB LICENSEE, LLC	SPRINGFIELD, MA
WGME-TV	13 TV Commercial	WGME LICENSEE, LLC	PORTLAND, ME
WICD	15 TV Commercial	WICD LICENSEE, LLC	CHAMPAIGN, IL
WICS	20 TV Commercial	WICS LICENSEE, LLC	SPRINGFIELD, IL
WKEF	22 TV Commercial	WKEF LICENSEE L.P.	DAYTON, OH
WLFL	22 TV Commercial	WLFL LICENSEE, LLC	RALEIGH, NC
WLOS	13 TV Commercial	WLOS LICENSEE, LLC	ASHEVILLE, NC
WMMP	36 TV Commercial	WMMP LICENSEE L.P.	CHARLESTON, SC
WMSN-TV	47 TV Commercial	WMSN LICENSEE, LLC	MADISON, WI
WPGH-TV	53 TV Commercial	WPGH LICENSEE, LLC	PITTSBURGH, PA
WRLH-TV	35 TV Commercial	WRLH LICENSEE, LLC	RICHMOND, VA
WSMH	66 TV Commercial	WSMH LICENSEE, LLC	FLINT, MI
WSTR-TV	64 TV Commercial	WSTR LICENSEE, INC.	CINCINNATI, OH
WSYT	68 TV Commercial	WSYT LICENSEE L.P.	SYRACUSE, NY
WSYX	6 TV Commercial	WSYX LICENSEE, INC.	COLUMBUS, OH
WTTO	21 TV Commercial	WTTO LICENSEE, LLC	HOMEWOOD, AL
WTVZ-TV	33 TV Commercial	WTVZ LICENSEE, LLC	NORFOLK, VA
WTWC-TV	40 TV Commercial	WTWC LICENSEE, LLC	TALLAHASSEE, FL
WUHF	31 TV Commercial	WUHF LICENSEE, LLC	ROCHESTER, NY
WUPN-TV	48 TV Commercial	WUPN LICENSEE, LLC	GREENSBORO, NC
WUTV	29 TV Commercial	WUTV LICENSEE, LLC	BUFFALO, NY
WUXP-TV	30 TV Commercial	WUXP LICENSEE, LLC	NASHVILLE, TN
WVTV	18 TV Commercial	WVTV LICENSEE, INC.	MILWAUKEE, WI
WXLV-TV	45 TV Commercial	WXLV LICENSEE, LLC	WINSTON-SALEM, NC
WYZZ-TV	43 TV Commercial	WYZZ LICENSEE, INC.	BLOOMINGTON, IL
WZTV	17 TV Commercial	WZTV LICENSEE, LLC	NASHVILLE, TN

Sirius Satellite Radio Inc.

Address:	1221 Avenue of the Americas	Stock Symbol:	SIRI
	Thirty-sixth Floor	Telephone:	212-584-5100
	New York, NY 10020	Fax:	212-584-5200
Total Employees:	375	Website:	www.siriusradio.com

Rap star Eminem once complained in a song, "...the FCC won't let me be, or let me be me." In July, taking a cue from radio talker Howard Stern's own struggles with the harsh, post-Janet Jackson-At-The-Super-Bowl world of increasing FCC indecency fines, he found what could be a solution for more and more broadcasters and artists. This fall, Eminem will have his own channel on the Sirius Satellite Radio network over which he can broadcast original, unedited versions of his music, as well as that of other artists.

"I can't wait to start dropping new material, exclusive tracks, and uncensored hip-hop featuring me and everyone else, freely saying whatever the hell we want," Eminem told an online music news site.

While artists like Eminem are clearly excited about the subscription-based, all-digital satellite radio concept, the radio-listening public is another issue. Sirius and competitor XM Satellite Radio Holdings have had lots to cheer about lately, but the big question is whether the market will support two providers. It looks increasingly like the battle between the two will depend on who can sign the biggest names with the most audience pull, with multi-million dollar contracts as the weapon of choice. And right now, Sirius is the underdog (no pun intended).But it's an underdog whose bark and bite are growing, as it proved later in 2004 when it bested XM by signing Howard Stern. Sirius enticed the disillusioned shock jock away from broadcast radio—the format he revolutionized—for $500 for the first five years.Sirius is betting that a large enough portion of Stern's 10 million-strong listener base will move to satellite along with him. The initial results seem promising. Even though Stern won't start broadcasting on Sirius until 2006, when his contract with Viacom expires, the company has already seen its subscriber base rise to 700,000.

Sirius broadcasts out of Rockefeller Center in the heart of Manhattan. Its service, similar to that of XM, has about 120 stations, with 65 devoted to commercial-free music and more than 50 devoted to sports, news and entertainment programming. Sirius costs a bit more. XM charges $9.99 per month, Sirius $12.95.

Neither includes the equipment required to receive the signal. Sirius lags far behind XM in the race for customers, although from 2003 to 2004 it expanded its subscription base dramatically to 480,341 as of June 30. XM leads the way with more than 2.5 million.

Despite launching its satellites first, Sirius has lagged behind XM from the beginning, since the latter was able to get to the marketplace first.

While both companies sell systems for existing vehicles and home use, marketing has shifted more and more toward negotiating deals with automakers to make the option available to new car buyers. Consequently, building relationships with automakers is critical to the success of the business. Sirius has agreements with DaimlerChrysler Corp., Mercedes Benz, and Freightliner LLC, the truck manufacturer. It also has agreements with the Ford Motor Company, BMW, Nissan and others. (Honda and GM are committed to XM.)

While things are looking up for satellite radio these days, there were some doubts about whether Sirius would survive without filing for bankruptcy. In the first quarter of 2003, it was saved when it renegotiated its debt and raised $200 million in new investment. The influx was critically important, but it remains to be seen whether Sirius can hold out long enough to become profitable.

Both Sirius and XM need more subscribers before they can break even. Sirius estimates it will start making a profit in 2005. In 2003, the company was more than $226 million in the red, and XM lost more than twice that amount.

—John Dunbar, Robert Morlino

October 20, 2004

Sources: Sirius Satellite Radio Web site, Multichannel News, New York Times, SoulShine.ca

Sirius Satellite Radio Inc. Recent Financial Information		
Year	Revenue	Net Income (Net Loss)
1998	Not reported	($48,396,000)
1999	Not reported	($62,822,000)
2000	Not reported	($134,744,000)
2001	Not reported	($235,763,000)
2002	$805,000	($422,481,000)
2003	$12,872,000	($226,215)

Sirius Satellite Radio Inc. Board of Directors				
Name	Position	Relevant Stock		Qty
Clayton, Joseph	Director		SIRI	5,418,869
Black, Leon	Director		N/A	N/A
Gilberti, Lawrence	Director		SIRI	67,000
Holden, James	Director		SIRI	40,000
McGuiness, Michael	Director		N/A	N/A
Lieberfarb, Warren	Director		N/A	N/A
Mooney, James	Director		SIRI	2,100

Sirius Satellite Radio Inc. Corporate Officers			
Name	Position	Salary	Bonuses
Clayton, Joseph	President, CEO, and Director	$600,000	$432,000
Donnelly, Patrick	EVP, General Counsel, and Secretary	$345,000	$235,700
Frear, David	EVP, CFO	$176,042	$98,583
Johnson, Guy	EVP, Sales	$400,000	$288,000

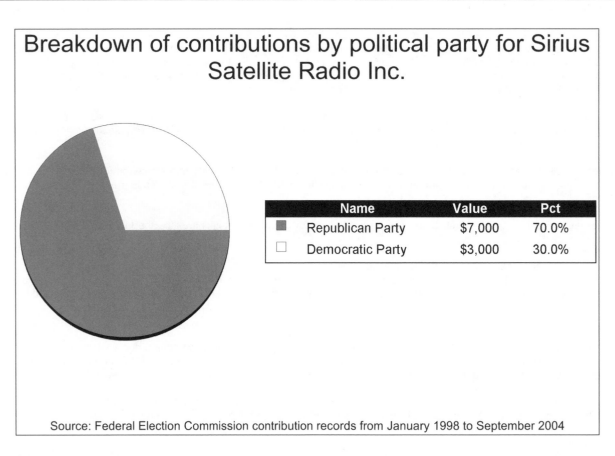

Breakdown of contributions by political party for Sirius Satellite Radio Inc.

	Name	Value	Pct
	Republican Party	$7,000	70.0%
	Democratic Party	$3,000	30.0%

Source: Federal Election Commission contribution records from January 1998 to September 2004

Top 10 Recipients of Contributions Sourced to Sirius Satellite Radio Inc.	
Recipient	Amount
Rep Thomas M Reynolds (R-NY)	$4,000
Sen John F Kerry (D-MA)	$3,000
Sen John Eric Ensign (R-NV)	$1,000
Sen Conrad R Burns (R-MT)	$1,000
Sen Spencer Abraham (R-MI)	$1,000
National Democratic Party Committees	$0
Total:	$10,000
Source: Federal Election Commission contribution records from January 1998 to September 2004	

Sirius Satellite Radio Inc. Lobbying Expenditures by Year	
Year	Amount
1998	$160,000
1999	$215,000
2000	$200,000
2001	$400,000
2002	$320,000
2003	$160,000
Total:	$1,455,000
Source: U.S. Senate Office of Public Records lobbying disclosure records from January 1998 to June 30th, 2004.	

Sprint Corp.

Address: 2330 Shawnee Mission Pkwy.
              Westwood, KS 66205

Stock Symbol: N/A
Telephone: 913-624-3000
Fax: 913-624-3281
Website: www.sprint.com

Total Employees: 66,900

It is a good time to be a shareholder of Sprint Corp., which is among the top five providers of local, long distance and cellular phone service in the nation. Under the tenure of Gary Forsee, who became CEO of the company in March 2003, shares have doubled in value.

It's not such a good time to be one of the company's 70,000 employees. During 2003 and 2004 alone, more than 22,000 Sprint workers have been laid off as part of a multi-year financial restructuring, and there doesn't seem to be any relief in sight. As late as June 2004, the company announced that up to 1,100 more workers would be dismissed.

Sprint is the largest local phone company that wasn't one of the seven original Baby Bells created by the breakup of AT&T in 1984. It is the third-largest long-distance company and will jump from fourth to third-largest cellular provider, as it completes its acquisition of former rival Nextel Communications. The $35 billion deal will add 15.3 million subscribers to Sprint's 20.1 million.

Sprint Corp. still comprises two business units—the FON Group and the PCS Group. The FON Group represents Sprint's core wireline telecommunications operations, which include long distance voice, data, and Internet; international voice and data; local telephone and product distribution businesses. The Sprint PCS Group consists of Sprint's wireless personal communications services.

Until 2004, the company traded under separate ticker symbols—one for wireline services (Sprint FON) and one for wireless (Sprint PCS)—but they were recombined in 2004 as Sprint continued efforts to stay competitive even as the telecom industry continued to evolve at a rapid pace.

The company provides local telephone service lines in 18 states. Nearly all of the company's local customers are served by digital switching technology, allowing Sprint to provide network-based voice, video and data services.

The company that would eventually become Sprint began in 1899 in Abilene, Kan., as one of the country's first non-Bell system phone service providers. A few years later it would combine with other Kansas phone companies to form United Telephone.

United continued to grow through the next several decades, mainly buying up other local telephone companies. In the 1960s it branched out into satellites and cable television, renaming itself United Telecommunications in 1971.

The Sprint name dates back to a microwave long-distance network put together by Southern Pacific along its railway lines in 1970s. Called Sprint, for Southern Pacific Railroad Internal Telecommunications, the network was bought by GTE Corp. in 1983.

Following the breakup of the Bell System in 1984, United Telecommunications bought GTE Sprint and began offering nationwide long distance service, competing with rivals such as MCI and AT&T. The company formally changed its name to Sprint in 1986.

France Telecom and Deutsche Telekom bought a 20 percent share of Sprint for $3.6 billion in 1996. That same year Sprint spun off its cellular business, renaming it 360 Communications. Sprint combined its Internet businesses with Internet service provider EarthLink in 1998.

Sprint itself became the target of a huge takeover battle between MCI Worldcom and BellSouth. Worldcom would eventually win out with a bid of $115 billion in stock and $14 billion in assumed debt, but the deal would be shot down by regulators a few months later. Sprint sold its R.H. Donnelley directory publishing subsidiary for $2.1 billion in early 2003.

Longtime Sprint CEO William Esrey stepped down in early 2003 amid allegations he and other top company officials accepted questionable tax shelter advice from Sprint auditor Ernst & Young.

Esrey was eventually replaced by Forsee, a former BellSouth executive, but not before his former employer took him to court. BellSouth charged that his acceptance of an offer from Sprint violated a non-compete clause in his contract. A federal arbitrator allowed Forsee to take the Sprint job, but imposed certain conditions during his first year on the job.

Nevertheless, Forsee has at least made investors happy, if not his new employees. As the layoffs continue, the company is aggressively seeking to solidify its wireless offerings and combat the "churning" that afflicts many of the top cellular providers; unhappy customers come and leave in droves. The pace has increased since the introduction of wireless number porting.

—Bob Williams, Robert Morlino

April 28, 2005

Sources: Company Web site, Securities and Exchange Commission filings, Yahoo! Finance Online, Hoover's Online, Fortune magazine.

Sprint Corp. Recent Financial Information		
Year	Revenue	Net Income (Net Loss)
1999	$19,856,000,000	($484,000,000)
2000	$23,166,000,000	$296,000,000
2001	$25,562,000,000	($901,000,000)
2002	$26,679,000,000	$2,100,000,000
2003	$26,197,000,000	$861,000,000

Sprint Corp. Board of Directors				
Name	Position	Relevant Stock		Qty
Bethune, Gordon	Director		N/A	N/A
Draper, E.	Director		N/A	N/A
Henretta, Deborah	Director		N/A	N/A
Storch, Gerald	Director		N/A	N/A
Forsee, Gary	Chairman and CEO		PCS	31,377
Rice, Charles	Director		FON	42,763
Rice, Charles	Director		PCS	33,357
Smith, Louis	Director		FON	11,074
Smith, Louis	Director		PCS	2,661
Lorimer, Linda	Director		FON	19,740
Lorimer, Linda	Director		PCS	39,900
Ausley, DuBose	Director		FON	16,917
Ausley, DuBose	Director		PCS	8,150
Hockaday, Irvine	Director		FON	11,589
Hockaday, Irvine	Director		PCS	49,777

Sprint Corp. Corporate Officers			
Name	Position	Salary	Bonuses
Esrey, William	Former Chairman and CEO	$2,572,796	$895,833
LeMay, Ronald	Former President and COO	$1,904,350	$322,500
Lauer, Len	COO and President of Sprint PCS Group	$652,318	$625,808
Forsee, Gary	Chairman and CEO	$813,410	$2,532,206
Fuller, Michael	President-Local Telecommunications Division	$641,705	$581,034
Dellinger, Robert	EVP and CFO	$511,343	$603,503

Breakdown of contributions by political party for Sprint Corp.

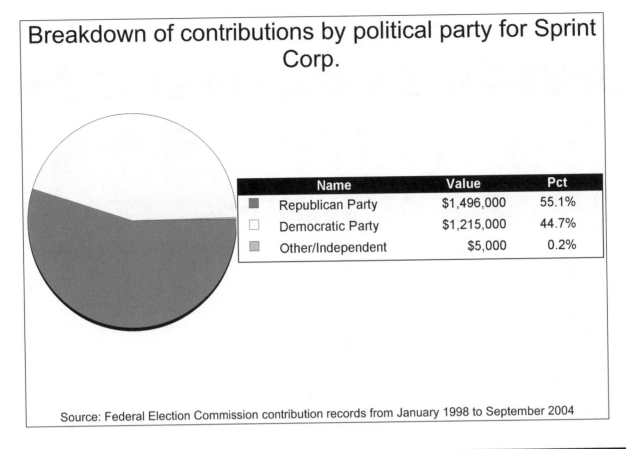

Name	Value	Pct
Republican Party	$1,496,000	55.1%
Democratic Party	$1,215,000	44.7%
Other/Independent	$5,000	0.2%

Source: Federal Election Commission contribution records from January 1998 to September 2004

Top 10 Recipients of Contributions Sourced to Sprint Corp.	
Recipient	Amount
National Republican Party Committees	$790,000
National Democratic Party Committees	$704,000
Rep Dennis Moore (D-KS)	$38,000
Sen Christopher S Bond (R-MO)	$38,000
Sen John David Ashcroft (R-MO)	$33,000
Rep John Conyers, Jr (D-MI)	$25,000
President George W Bush (R)	$22,000
Sen Jean A Carnahan (D-MO)	$19,000
Sen Byron L Dorgan (D-ND)	$18,000
Rep Edward John Markey (D-MA)	$16,000
Total:	$1,703,000

Source: Federal Election Commission contribution records from January 1998 to September 2004

Sprint Corp. Lobbying Expenditures by Year	
Year	Amount
1998	$7,508,665
1999	$8,145,000
2000	$7,145,000
2001	$8,355,920
2002	$7,717,000
2003	$7,910,000
Total:	$46,781,585

Source: U.S. Senate Office of Public Records lobbying disclosure records from January 1998 to June 30th, 2004.

Sprint Corp. Sponsored Trips for Congressional Staff		
Congressional Office	Number of Trips	$ Amount
Sen Trent Lott (R-MS)	1	$828
Total:	1	$828

Source: Congressional office travel records for members of the Senate Committee on Commerce, Science & Transportation and the House Committee on Energy and Commerce for the period of January 2000 to March 2004.

Telephone and Data Systems Inc.

Address:	30 North LaSalle St.	Stock Symbol:	TDS
	Ste. 4000	Telephone:	(312) 630-1900
	Chicago, IL 60602	Fax:	(312) 630-1908
Total Employees:	11,100	Website:	www.teldta.com

It's not unusual to see a cell phone company stage a public relations event when it enters a new market. But it is a little odd to have a governor show up for it.

That was the situation in downtown Oklahoma City in early July when United States Cellular Corp. officially began operating there. A celebratory event, attended by Oklahoma Gov. Brad Henry, saw confetti fired into the air as nearly 200 brand new US Cellular employees in red shirts cheered enthusiastically. Henry heralded the launch as a "great" and "exciting" day, lauding the company's multimillion dollar investment in the city.

Even as many of the top cellular companies are swapping customers at a high rate, especially since the advent of number portability, US Cellular has retained customers by focusing on satisfaction—a goal promised by the industry dominators but rarely delivered.

"We believe that the customer's experience is more important than the products we sell," US Cellular president and CEO Jack Rooney told the Daily Oklahoman.

Telephone and Data Systems Inc., parent company of US Cellular, is a Chicago-based corporation with a substantial presence both in the wireless and local telephone businesses. Chief subsidiary US Cellular is the nation's eighth-largest wireless company, providing service to more than 4 million customers in 28 states.

That business philosophy has allowed US Cellular, and indeed its parent company, TDS, to prosper by being the antidote to the industry giants. US Cellular, 82 percent controlled by TDS, generates about three-quarters of the parent company's revenue, with the rest coming from its local telephone operations.

The company that would evolve into TDS was started by LeRoy Carlson of Chicago in the 1950s. The Carlson family still holds about 53 percent of the company's voting shares.

Carlson bought several rural phone companies and brought them together under the name Telephones Inc. He sold Telephones Inc. to Contel in 1966, but continued to buy and consolidate rural phone companies. He would eventually bring his holdings together under the name Telephone and Data Systems in 1969.

Carlson soon began to dabble in new businesses. In 1981, TDS created a new subsidiary to offer paging services, American Paging. It also got into the cable television business in 1975, but sold all of its cable holdings in 1986.

In the early 1980s, Carlson also started pursuing cellular licenses, forming U.S. Cellular in 1983. U.S. Cellular went public in 1988, but TDS held onto about 80 percent of the company's voting stock.

It was a pattern TDS would repeat in 1993, when it created a new subsidiary named American Portable Telecom to pursue new PCS, or personal communications systems, wireless licenses being offered through lotteries by the Federal Communications Commission. American Portable Telecom, renamed Aerial Communications, went public in 1996, with TDS holding on to 82 percent of the voting shares.

Telecom Finland acquired a large minority stake in Aerial with a $200 million investment in the company in 1998. TDS toyed with the idea of spinning off Aerial, but eventually decided to sell its stake in the company to VoiceStream Wireless for $1.8 billion in 2000.

The deal left TDS with a 14 percent stake in VoiceStream, which it exchanged for cash and stock in Deutsche Telekom when the German telecom giant acquired VoiceStream in 2001.

LeRoy Carlson Jr., the son of TDS's founder, became CEO of TDS in 1986. Another son, Walter C.D. Carlson, is the company's chairman. The elder Carlson, now in his late 80s, is chairman emeritus of the company he founded.

This year, the board voted to declassify itself. The move will require the yearly election of every member of the board, a practice that corporate governance proponents support. The company went even further by webcasting its annual shareholders meeting in June.

—Bob Williams, Robert Morlino

August 19, 2004

Sources: Company Web site, Securities and Exchange Commission filings, Yahoo! Finance Online, Hoover's Online, Fortune magazine, Daily Oklahoman

Telephone and Data Systems Inc. Recent Financial Information		
Year	Revenue	Net Income (Net Loss)
1998	$1,803,639,000	$76,606,000
1999	$2,122,346,000	$178,687,000
2000	$2,326,856,000	$2,236,498,000
2001	$2,588,542,000	($198,513,000)
2002	$2,985,366,000	($984,798,000)
2003	$3,445,200,000	$61,500,000

Telephone and Data Systems Inc. Board of Directors				
Name	Position	Relevant Stock		Qty
Carlson, LeRoy	Chairman Emeritus		TDS	276,664
Carlson, Walter	Chairman		TDS	3,998
Carlson, LeRoy	Director		TDS	423,986
Helton, Sandra	Director		TDS	149,724
Barr, James	Director		TDS	48,560
Saranow, Mitchell	Director		TDS	1,000
Carlson, Letitia	Director		TDS	2,196
Mundt, Kevin	Director		TDS	1,970
Nebergall, Donald	Director		TDS	3,364
Off, George	Director		TDS	3,235
Solomon, Martin	Director		TDS	12,259
Wander, Herbert	Director		TDS	2,152

Telephone and Data Systems Inc. Corporate Officers			
Name	Position	Salary	Bonuses
Carlson, LeRoy	President and CEO	$910,000	$591,500
Carlson, LeRoy	Chairman Emeritus	$465,000	$233,000
Helton, Sandra	EVP and CFO	$550,000	$370,000
Barr, James	President and CEO of TDS Telecom	$539,000	$285,000
Rooney, John	President and CEO of US Cellular	$592,209	$360,000

Time Warner Inc.

Address:	One Time Warner Center New York, NY 10019	Stock Symbol: Telephone: Fax: Website:	TWX 212-484-8000 212-489-6183 www.timewarner.com
Total Employees:	80,000		

At the time, the idea of fusing old and new media seemed to make so much sense. But the subsequent 2000 marriage of AOL (new) and Time Warner (old) nearly drove the combined company into the ground, as AOL hemorrhaged subscribers and became a financial sink-hole.

Soon enough, "AOL" was removed from AOL Time Warner, a move that capped a more substantive re-positioning of online services within the giant media company and reflected an aggressive, successful turn-around engineered by Time Warner CEO Richard D. Parsons.

Although at the end of 2002, Time Warner posted a mind-boggling $98.2 billion loss—the largest in U.S. corporate history—under the stewardship of Parsons it posted a net profit of $2.6 billion just one year later.

Time Warner continues to rule over an expansive media empire, with businesses that include interactive services, cable systems, filmed entertainment, television networks, music and publishing. If it involves entertainment or communications, chances are Time Warner has a piece of the action.

Its cable division, Time Warner Cable, has maintained its second-place ranking in the cable industry, behind Comcast Corp, throughout the post-AOL recovery. For a time, though, Time Warner was shedding basic service subscribers. The company lost about 2 million cable subscribers when it unwound a complicated partnership with Advance/Newhouse Communications in 2002.

Time Warner still remains a potent force in the cable industry, however, leading the second tier of big companies that divide up the two-thirds of the business not controlled by Comcast. Following the Advance/Newhouse deal, Time Warner still had nearly 11 million subscribers, and it has retained that subscriber base.

In addition, Time Warner Cable has been aggressively upgrading its systems to high capacity digital technology, a move that allows it to offer expanded services such as broadband Internet, video-on-demand, and telephone service. Recently, the company entered into agreements with MCI and Sprint Corp. to offer telephone service to customers through its cable system, and expects to begin doing so within the year.

The company is currently a 79 percent-owned subsidiary of the parent, with 50-50 partnerships with rival Comcast in some of its cable systems. The company is exploring a deal to acquire the cable systems of bankrupt Adelphia Communications.

Time Warner Cable saw revenue growth during 2003 and 2004 thanks to gains across all its business units, except AOL. The Internet division was hemorrhaging subscribers to other low-cost providers. Analysts expected AOL to be expunged completely from Time Warner, but instead the company invested heavily in internet-based advertising deals, most recently forking over $435 million to purchase Advertising.com.

Parsons told Business Week, "Our emphasis is on building up the AOL business." To regain lost ground, AOL has diversified its offerings to customers, creating a range of services from low-cost, basic dial-up to on-demand, high-speed delivery programming.

The AOL turnaround and the shoring up of cable services were both smaller parts of a larger effort to turn things around financially for the parent company, where the bulk of revenue comes from the various entertainment properties, in the wake of the AOL merger.

In April of 2005, Time Warner Cable entered into an agreement with Comcast to jointly own and operate Adelphia Communications' cable properties. As part of the $17.6 billion cash and stock deal, Time Warner and Comcast will swap some of their customers in addition to acquiring those of Adelphia, an arrangement that will allow both companies to increase the concentration of their subscriber bases in some markets. All told, Time Warner Cable will see a net increase of 3.5 million basic cable subscribers.

—Bob Williams, Robert Morlino

April 28, 2005

Sources: Company Web site, Securities and Exchange Commission filings, Yahoo! Finance Online, CableFax magazine, Hoover's Online, Fortune magazine, Business Week

Time Warner Inc. Recent Financial Information		
Year	Revenue	Net Income (Net Loss)
2000	$7,605,000,000	$1,121,000,000
2001	$37,166,000,000	($4,934,000,000)
2002	$40,961,000,000	($98,696,000,000)
2003	$38,076,000,000	$2,639,000,000

Time Warner Inc. Board of Directors				
Name	Position	Relevant Stock		Qty
Case, Stephen	Director		TWX	16,567,584
Turner, R.E.	Director		TWX	39,644,676
Novack, Kenneth	Director		TWX	29,942
Parsons, Richard	Chairman		TWX	238,742
Barksdale, James	Director		TWX	3,491,231
Bollenbach, Stephen	Director		TWX	9,836
Caufield, Frank	Director		TWX	318,119
Gilburne, Miles	Director		TWX	255,149
Hills, Carla	Director		TWX	21,188
Mark, Reuben	Director		TWX	1,043,388
Miles, Michael	Director		TWX	48,929
Vincent, Francis	Director		TWX	75,039
Clark, Robert	Director		TWX	3,000

Time Warner Inc. Corporate Officers			
Name	Position	Salary	Bonuses
Parsons, Richard	Chairman and CEO	$1,000,000	$8,000,000
Pace, Wayne	EVP and CFO	$1,000,000	$2,700,000
Bewkes, Jeffrey	Chairman, Enterainment & Network Groups	$1,000,000	$6,500,000
Logan, Don	Chairman, Media & Communications Group	$1,000,000	$6,500,000
Kimmitt, Robert	EVP, Global Public Policy	$1,000,000	$2,175,000

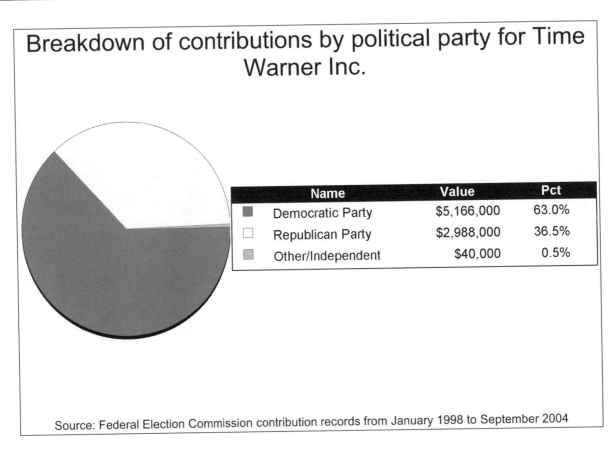

Breakdown of contributions by political party for Time Warner Inc.

Name	Value	Pct
Democratic Party	$5,166,000	63.0%
Republican Party	$2,988,000	36.5%
Other/Independent	$40,000	0.5%

Source: Federal Election Commission contribution records from January 1998 to September 2004

Top 10 Recipients of Contributions Sourced to Time Warner Inc.	
Recipient	Amount
National Democratic Party Committees	$2,114,000
National Republican Party Committees	$1,420,000
Sen John F Kerry (D-MA)	$242,000
President George W Bush (R)	$167,000
Sen Hillary Rodham Clinton (D-NY)	$128,000
Sen Thomas Andrew Daschle (D-SD)	$126,000
Sen Charles E Schumer (D-NY)	$116,000
Sen Barbara Boxer (D-CA)	$115,000
Vice President Albert Gore, Jr (D-TN)	$99,000
Rep Richard A Gephardt (D-MO)	$88,000
Total:	$4,615,000
Source: Federal Election Commission contribution records from January 1998 to September 2004	

Time Warner Inc. Lobbying Expenditures by Year	
Year	Amount
1998	$6,540,000
1999	$6,900,000
2000	$7,795,000
2001	$6,890,000
2002	$6,145,000
2003	$8,202,500
2004	$3,527,500
Total:	$46,000,000
Source: U.S. Senate Office of Public Records lobbying disclosure records from January 1998 to June 30th, 2004.	

Time Warner Inc. Sponsored Trips for Congressional Staff		
Congressional Office	Number of Trips	$ Amount
Rep Clifford Bundy Stearns (R-FL)	3	$4,806
Rep Wilbert J Tauzin, Jr (R-LA)	3	$4,545
Sen George Allen (R-VA)	3	$3,843
Rep Frederick Carlyle Boucher (D-VA)	2	$2,644
Rep Jim Davis (D-FL)	2	$1,840
Sen Donald Lee Nickles (R-OK)	1	$1,688
Rep Jane Harman (D-CA)	1	$1,627
Rep Barton Jennings Gordon (D-TN)	1	$1,502
Total:	16	$22,495
Source: Congressional office travel records for members of the Senate Committee on Commerce, Science & Transportation and the House Committee on Energy and Commerce for the period of January 2000 to March 2004.		

TV Station Subsidiaries for Time Warner Inc.			
Call Sign	Channel and Type	Subsidiary Name	Area of Service
WTBS	17 TV Commercial	SUPERSTATION, INC.	ATLANTA, GA
W34AX	34 TV Low Power (UHF)	TIME WARNER ENTERTAINMENT	HENDERSON, NC

Tribune Co.

Address:	435 N. Michigan Ave.
	Chicago, IL 60611
Total Employees:	23,800

Stock Symbol:	TRB
Telephone:	312-222-9100
Fax:	312-222-1573
Website:	www.tribune.com

What do five Pulitzers buy you these days in the corporate media marketplace? If you are the Los Angeles Times, the answer is layoffs.

The largest newspaper in the Tribune Co. chain announced it was laying off about 200 people. The announcement came only months after staffers there learned that the newspaper had won more Pulitzers than any other news organization. The layoffs combined with a scandal over inflated circulation figures and a disappointing appeals court decision regarding media consolidation rules have added up to a tough year for the conglomerate.

Despite the negative headlines, no one would dare predict that the long-term outlook for the Tribune Co. is anything but bright. It's simply too well-positioned in too many markets to stay down for long.

Known for more than a century as a family-owned, Chicago-centric publisher and broadcaster, Tribune went public in 1983 and has been expanding ever since. Its biggest acquisition by far was the Times Mirror Co., owner of the Times and Newsday, completed in June 2000 for $8.3 billion.

The company flagship, the Chicago Tribune, was founded in 1847, pre-dating even the Great Chicago Fire. Joseph Medill, editor and part owner, was elected mayor and led the city's reconstruction. In 1924, at the dawn of the radio age, WGN went on the air in Chicago. The call letters stand for "World's Greatest Newspaper." It was again a pioneer when television was created, establishing WGN-TV in 1948 and WPIX-TV in New York City. In the 1960s, Tribune bought the Fort Lauderdale Sun-Sentinel and the Orlando Sentinel. Later acquisitions included the Chicago Cubs baseball team.

Tribune Co. continued expanding when it bought KTLA-TV in Los Angeles for $510 million. But by far, the most far-reaching acquisition was Times Mirror. The merger doubled the size of the Tribune, making it the nation's No. 3 newspaper publisher. In addition to the Times and Newsday, the company added the Baltimore Sun, the Hartford Courant and four other newspapers to its stable. The merger made Tribune the only media company with newspapers and television stations in the top three markets in the U.S.—New York, Los Angeles and Chicago as well as a dominant position in Connecticut.

Normally, owning a dominant newspaper and television station in the same market is against FCC rules that are supposed to ensure "diversity, competition and localism" in the marketplace. Tribune Co.'s domination in Chicago is permissible because the media combinations were in place before the rule was created. But Los Angeles and New York are another story.

The Tribune Co. bought Times Mirror with the expectation that the commission would reject the newspaper-television cross-ownership rule, and lobbied hard to make sure that would happen. In fact, the FCC did loosen the rule, but a federal appeals court stayed the FCC's decision and kicked it back to Washington along with a slate of other measures that would allow large media companies to get larger. But there's no reason for Tribune Co. shareholders to get nervous—not yet anyway. In New York and Los Angeles, where the company is technically out of compliance, nothing can happen until the broadcast licenses come up for renewal, which is not until 2007 for New York and 2006 for Los Angeles.

A more pressing issue is the accusation that the company inflated circulation figures at Long Island newspaper Newsday and Spanish language publication Hoy. Advertising rates are based on circulation figures, and advertisers don't appreciate it when those numbers are lower than promised. Tribune Co. has agreed to pay advertisers $35 million to settle the dispute.

—John Dunbar, Robert Morlino

August 20, 2004

Sources: Tribune Co. Web site, Tribune Co. Form 10-K, Hoovers Online, ABCNews.com.

Tribune Co. Recent Financial Information		
Year	Revenue	Net Income (Net Loss)
1992	$1,833,031,000	$119,825,000
1993	$1,908,232,000	$188,606,000
1994	$2,034,633,000	$242,047,000
1995	$2,179,010,000	$278,165,000
1996	$2,248,520,000	$372,067,000
1997	$2,530,352,000	$393,625,000
1998	$2,689,690,000	$414,272,000
1999	$2,923,405,000	$1,468,709,000
2000	$4,950,830,000	$224,386,000
2001	$5,253,366,000	$111,136,000

Tribune Co. Recent Financial Information		
Year	Revenue	Net Income (Net Loss)
2002	$5,384,428,000	$442,922,000
2003	$5,595,000,000	$891,000,000

Tribune Co. Board of Directors				
Name	Position	Relevant Stock		Qty
FitzSimons, Dennis	Director		TRB	483,054
Fuller, Jack	Director		TRB	130,197
Chandler, Jeffrey	Director		TRB	4,913
Goodan, Roger	Director		TRB	11,255
Hernandez, Enrique	Director		TRB	5,128
Holden, Betsy	Director		TRB	2,597
Morrison, Robert	Director		TRB	6,992
Osborn, William	Director		TRB	6,207
Ryan, Patrick	Director		TRB	19,439
Stinehart, William	Director		TRB	6,571
Taft, Dudley	Director		TRB	84,908
Turner, Kathryn	Director		TRB	1,497

Tribune Co. Corporate Officers			
Name	Position	Salary	Bonuses
Madigan, John	Chairman	$865,385	$2,000,000
FitzSimons, Dennis	President, CEO and Director	$850,000	$1,200,000
Fuller, Jack	Director, President, Tribune Publishing	$591,723	$460,000
Grenesko, Donald	SVP, Finance and Administration	$462,877	$305,000
Kenney, Crane	SVP, General Counsel and Secretary	N/A	N/A
Mullen, Patrick	President, Tribune Broadcasting	$460,385	$330,000

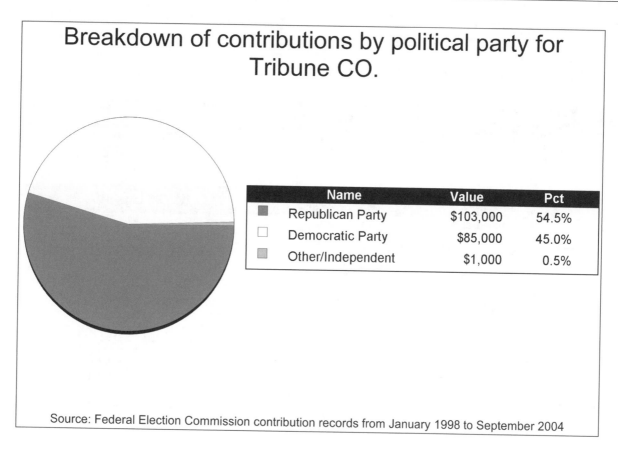

Breakdown of contributions by political party for Tribune CO.

Name	Value	Pct
Republican Party	$103,000	54.5%
Democratic Party	$85,000	45.0%
Other/Independent	$1,000	0.5%

Source: Federal Election Commission contribution records from January 1998 to September 2004

Top 10 Recipients of Contributions Sourced to Tribune Co.

Recipient	Amount
National Republican Party Committees	$53,000
National Democratic Party Committees	$53,000
Sen John F Kerry (D-MA)	$9,000
Andrew J McKenna (R-IL)	$9,000
Rep Edward John Markey (D-MA)	$8,000
Sen John S McCain (R-AZ)	$5,000
Rep Wilbert J Tauzin, Jr (R-LA)	$5,000
Rep Frederick Stephen Upton (R-MI)	$5,000
Sen Richard J Durbin (D-IL)	$4,000
Sen Conrad R Burns (R-MT)	$3,000
Total:	$154,000

Source: Federal Election Commission contribution records from January 1998 to September 2004

Tribune Co. Lobbying Expenditures by Year

Year	Amount
1998	$98,000
1999	$108,951
2000	$130,000
2001	$121,442
2002	$166,603
2003	$152,866
2004	$99,865
Total:	$877,727

Source: U.S. Senate Office of Public Records lobbying disclosure records from January 1998 to June 30th, 2004.

Tribune Co. Sponsored Trips for Congressional Staff

Congressional Office	Number of Trips	$ Amount
Rep Frederick Stephen Upton (R-MI)	1	$3,337
Total:	1	$3,337

Source: Congressional office travel records for members of the Senate Committee on Commerce, Science & Transportation and the House Committee on Energy and Commerce for the period of January 2000 to March 2004.

Radio Station Subsidiaries for Tribune Co.

State	City	Call Sign	Frequency	Subsidiary Name
IL	CHICAGO	WGN	720 AM Station	WGN CONTINENTAL BROADCASTING CO.

TV Station Subsidiaries for Tribune Co.

Call Sign	Channel and Type	Subsidiary Name	Area of Service
WBZL	39 TV Commercial	CHANNEL 39, INC.	MIAMI, FL
KTXL	40 TV Commercial	CHANNEL 40, INC.	SACRAMENTO, CA
KHWB	39 TV Commercial	KHWB, INC.	HOUSTON, TX
KPLR-TV	11 TV Commercial	KPLR, INC.	ST. LOUIS, MO
KSWB-TV	69 TV Commercial	KSWB INC.	SAN DIEGO, CA
KTLA-TV	5 TV Commercial	KTLA INC.	LOS ANGELES, CA
KWGN-TV	2 TV Commercial	KWGN INC.	DENVER, CO
KWBP	32 TV Commercial	TRIBUNE BROADCAST HOLDINGS, INC.	SALEM, OR
K24DX	24 TV Low Power (UHF)	TRIBUNE BROADCAST HOLDINGS, INC.	PENDLETON, ETC, OR
WTTV	4 TV Commercial	TRIBUNE BROADCAST HOLDINGS, INC.	BLOOMINGTON, IN
WTTK	29 TV Commercial	TRIBUNE BROADCAST HOLDINGS, INC.	KOKOMO, IN
K20ES	20 TV Low Power (UHF)	TRIBUNE BROADCASTING HOLDINGS, INC.	PENDLETON, ETC., OR
KWBP-LP	4 TV Low Power (VHF)	TRIBUNE BROADCASTING HOLDINGS, INC.	PORTLAND, OR
WXIN	59 TV Commercial	TRIBUNE TELEVISION COMPANY	INDIANAPOLIS, IN
WTIC-TV	61 TV Commercial	TRIBUNE TELEVISION COMPANY	HARTFORD, CT
KDAF	33 TV Commercial	TRIBUNE TELEVISION COMPANY	DALLAS, TX
WPHL-TV	17 TV Commercial	TRIBUNE TELEVISION COMPANY	PHILADELPHIA, PA
WPMT	43 TV Commercial	TRIBUNE TELEVISION COMPANY	YORK, PA
KTWB-TV	22 TV Commercial	TRIBUNE TELEVISION HOLDINGS, INC.	SEATTLE, WA
WXMI	17 TV Commercial	TRIBUNE TELEVISION HOLDINGS, INC.	GRAND RAPIDS, MI
WNOL-TV	38 TV Commercial	TRIBUNE TELEVISION NEW ORLEANS, INC.	NEW ORLEANS, LA

TV Station Subsidiaries for Tribune Co.			
Call Sign	Channel and Type	Subsidiary Name	Area of Service
WGNO	26 TV Commercial	TRIBUNE TELEVISION NEW ORLEANS, INC.	NEW ORLEANS, LA
KCPQ	13 TV Commercial	TRIBUNE TELEVISION NORTHWEST, INC.	TACOMA, WA
K54DX	54 TV Low Power (UHF)	TRIBUNE TELEVISION NORTHWEST, INC.	ELLENSBURG-KITTITAS, WA
K64ES	64 TV Low Power (UHF)	TRIBUNE TELEVISION NORTHWEST, INC.	CHELAN, WA
WATL	36 TV Commercial	WATL, LLC	ATLANTA, GA
WBDC-TV	50 TV Commercial	WBDC BROADCASTING, INC.	WASHINGTON, DC
WEWB-TV	45 TV Commercial	WEWB, L.L.C.	SCHENECTADY, NY
WGN-TV	9 TV Commercial	WGN CONTINENTAL BROADCASTING COMPANY	CHICAGO, IL
WLVI-TV	56 TV Commercial	WLVI, INC.	CAMBRIDGE, MA
WPIX	11 TV Commercial	WPIX, INC.	NEW YORK, NY
WTXX	20 TV Commercial	WTXX INC.	WATERBURY, CT

Print Media Subsidiaries for Tribune Co.			
Company Name	Market City	Weekday Circulation	Sunday Circulation
Chicago Tribune	Chicago, IL	693,978	1,002,398
Daily Pilot	Costa Mesa, CA	22,184	0
Daily Press	Newport News, VA	95,228	117,689
Greenwich Time	Greenwich, CT	12,047	13,107
Hoy (Spanish)	New York, NY	109,598	34,403
Los Angeles Times	Los Angeles, CA	983,727	1,392,672
News-Press	Glendale, CA	22,052	0
Newsday	Melville, NY	580,346	662,317
Orlando Sentinel	Orlando, FL	257,222	378,587
South Florida Sun-Sentinel	Fort Lauderdale, FL	233,634	357,133
The Hartford Courant	Hartford, CT	187,394	283,410
The Morning Call	Allentown, PA	112,392	167,335
The Stamford Advocate	Stamford, CT	27,350	31,798
The Sun	Baltimore, MD	301,186	465,807

Univision Communications Inc.

Address:	1999 Avenue of the Stars	**Stock Symbol:**	UVN
	Ste. 3050	**Telephone:**	310-556-7676
	Los Angeles, CA 90067	**Fax:**	310-556-7615
Total Employees:	4,300	**Website:**	www.univision.com

The 2000 Census tells us there are 35 million Hispanics in America, making up 12 percent of the population. That's 3 percentage points higher than the 1990 Census, making Hispanics the fastest-growing minority in America.

The Hispanic community constitutes a large and lucrative market for advertisers. And the best way to reach a Spanish speaking market is with a Spanish speaking network. Enter Univision.

Univision Communications Inc. is the largest Spanish-language television broadcast company in the United States, and owns the most stations overall, but is the ninth largest by revenue. The company is in an excellent position to take advantage of this exploding demographic. Univision owns 65 television stations and has more than 1,180 cable affiliates. It reaches 97 percent of Hispanic households in America.

Univision has become increasingly protective of its highly concentrated audience demographic. The company filed suit to block the distribution of the Nielsen rating system's new "local people meters" hardware in Los Angeles, the largest Spanish speaking market in the United States. Univision claimed that the new devices will under-represent the Hispanic community because they do not account for the language spoken in the homes they monitor.

A Los Angeles County Superior Court judge denied Univision's request for an injunction, allowing Nielsen to deploy the new meters, but did agree to set a trial date.

Lawsuits aside, business has been good for Univision. The network has grown and prospered by catering to people who speak a language other than English. Though the language is foreign, the ownership isn't—and federal restrictions on foreign ownership of broadcast stations had a great deal to do with how Univision came to be.

Televisa's Spanish International Network established the first Spanish language television stations in the United States in 1961. In 1986, the FCC ordered divestiture of the group, citing foreign ownership problems. The network was acquired by Hallmark, which later sold it back to Emilio Azcárraga, the original backer of the Spanish International Network, and Jerrold Perenchio, who became chairman and CEO.

Since then, the company has expanded its television empire, created a Spanish language Internet site and a Spanish language home shopping channel, gotten into the music business and watched its Miami station go to No. 1 in the market.

Perenchio, who is actually Italian-American, has also made a name for himself as a major supporter of President Bush and the Republican Party. During the past year, he became one of the top individual contributors to so-called 527 organizations, or political non-profits. Perenchio gave $1 million to Progress for America Voter Fund, a pro-Republican non-profit group that conducts get-out-the-vote operations.

Last year, Univision acquired Hispanic Broadcasting Corp. for $2.4 billion in stock, making it the 10th largest radio owner in the U.S. The broadcaster operates more than 60 radio stations in top Hispanic markets around the country. When that deal was completed, radio giant Clear Channel Communications ended up with a small stake in Univision because it owned stock in Hispanic Broadcasting. But earlier this year Univision announced it was buying back that stock, thus eliminating Clear Channel's investment in the company.

To win Justice Department approval of its acquisition of Hispanic Broadcasting Corp., Univision had to divest itself of two-thirds of its 31 percent ownership stake in Entravision Communications. Entravision is a diversified broadcast company that caters to the Hispanic market.

—John Dunbar, Robert Morlino

August 20, 2004

Sources: Hoover's Online, Ketupa.net media profiles, HispanicBusiness.com, Los Angeles Times

Univision Communications Inc. Recent Financial Information		
Year	Revenue	Net Income (Net Loss)
2000	$863,459,000	$116,923,000
2001	$887,870,000	$52,411,000
2002	$1,091,293,000	$86,528,000
2003	$1,311,015,000	$155,427,000

Univision Communications Inc. Board of Directors			
Name	Position	Relevant Stock	Qty
Perenchio, A.	Chairman	UVN	37,187,384
Cahill, Robert	Vice Chairman	UVN	1,274,250
Rodriguez, Ray	Director	UVN	1,025,700
Jean, Emilio	Director	UVN	30,193,784
Gaba, Harold	Director	UVN	324,750
Horn, Alan	Director	UVN	358,750
Perenchio, John	Director	UVN	569,485
Rivera, Alejandro	Director	UVN	2,008,750
Aguirre, Fernando	Director	UVN	2,000
Tichenor, McHenry	Director	UVN	2,862,564
Angoitia, Alfonso	Director	UVN	30,187,534
Cisneros, Gustavo	Director	UVN	17,837,164

Univision Communications Inc. Corporate Officers			
Name	Position	Salary	Bonuses
Perenchio, A.	Chairman and CEO	N/A	N/A
Rodriguez, Ray	President and COO	$800,000	$800,000
Cahill, Robert	Vice Chairman and Corporate Secretary	$600,000	$600,000
Blank, George	EVP and CFO	$600,000	$600,000
Kranwinkle, C.	EVP and General Counsel	$600,000	$600,000
Hobson, Andrew	EVP	$600,000	$600,000

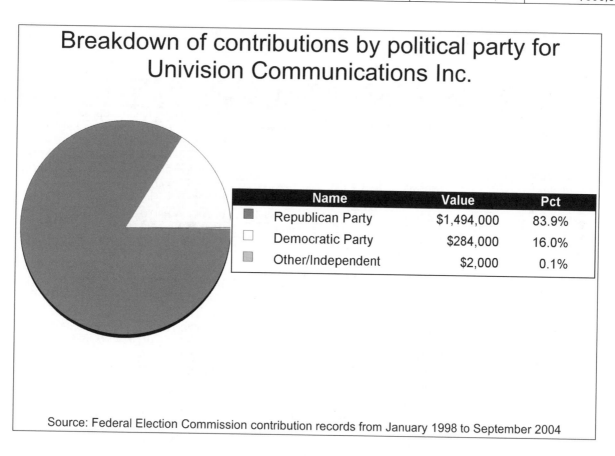

Breakdown of contributions by political party for Univision Communications Inc.

Name	Value	Pct
Republican Party	$1,494,000	83.9%
Democratic Party	$284,000	16.0%
Other/Independent	$2,000	0.1%

Source: Federal Election Commission contribution records from January 1998 to September 2004

Top 10 Recipients of Contributions Sourced to Univision Communications Inc.

Recipient	Amount
National Republican Party Committees	$1,299,000
National Democratic Party Committees	$85,000
President George W Bush (R)	$58,000
Hentschel, Noel Irwin	$33,000
Sen John S McCain (R-AZ)	$25,000
Sen Evan Bayh (D-IN)	$15,000
Sen Hillary Rodham Clinton (D-NY)	$15,000
Alex Penelas (D-FL)	$13,000
Rep Loretta Sanchez (D-CA)	$13,000
Rep Martin Frost (D-TX)	$11,000
Total:	$1,567,000

Source: Federal Election Commission contribution records from January 1998 to September 2004

Univision Communications Inc. Lobbying Expenditures by Year

Year	Amount
1998	$60,000
1999	$100,000
2000	$40,000
2001	$20,000
2002	$120,000
2003	$440,000
2004	$120,000
Total:	$900,000

Source: U.S. Senate Office of Public Records lobbying disclosure records from January 1998 to June 30th, 2004.

Radio Station Subsidiaries for Univision Communications Inc.

State	City	Call Sign	Frequency	Subsidiary Name
AZ	ARIZONA CITY	KKMR	106.5 FM Commercial	UNIVISION RADIO LICENSE CORPORATION
AZ	GLOBE	KMRR	100.3 FM Commercial	UNIVISION RADIO LICENSE CORPORATION
AZ	PARADISE VALLEY	KHOT-FM	105.9 FM Commercial	UNIVISION RADIO LICENSE CORPORATION
AZ	SUN CITY	KOMR	106.3 FM Commercial	UNIVISION RADIO LICENSE CORPORATION
AZ	WICKENBURG	KHOV-FM	105.3 FM Commercial	UNIVISION RADIO LICENSE CORPORATION
CA	CLOVIS	KOND	92.1 FM Commercial	UNIVISION RADIO LICENSE CORPORATION
CA	GLENDALE	KSCA	101.9 FM Commercial	UNIVISION RADIO LICENSE CORPORATION
CA	INGLEWOOD	KRCD	103.9 FM Commercial	UNIVISION RADIO LICENSE CORPORATION
CA	JACKSON	KOSL	94.3 FM Commercial	UNIVISION RADIO LICENSE CORPORATION
CA	LOS ANGELES	KTNQ	1020 AM Station	KTNQ-AM LICENSE CORP.
CA	LOS ANGELES	KLVE	107.5 FM Commercial	KLVE-FM LICENSE CORP.
CA	NORTH FORK	KZOL	107.9 FM Commercial	UNIVISION RADIO LICENSE CORPORATION
CA	SAN DIEGO	KLQV	102.9 FM Commercial	UNIVISION RADIO LICENSE CORPORATION
CA	SAN DIEGO	KLNV	106.5 FM Commercial	UNIVISION RADIO LICENSE CORPORATION
CA	SAN FRANCISCO	KSOL	98.9 FM Commercial	TMS LICENSE CALIFORNIA, INC
CA	SANTA CLARA	KEMR	105.7 FM Commercial	UNIVISION RADIO LICENSE CORPORATION
CA	SANTA CRUZ	KSQL	99.1 FM Commercial	TMS LICENSE CALIFORNIA, INC
CA	WEST COVINA	KRCV	98.3 FM Commercial	UNIVISION RADIO LICENSE CORPORATION
FL	GOULDS	WRTO-FM	98.3 FM Commercial	LICENSE CORPORATION #2
FL	MIAMI	WAQI	710 AM Station	LICENSE CORPORATION #1
FL	MIAMI	WAMR-FM	107.5 FM Commercial	WQBA-FM LICENSE CORP.
FL	MIAMI	WQBA	1140 AM Station	WQBA-AM LICENSE CORP.
IL	CHICAGO	WRTO	1200 AM Station	WLXX-AM LICENSE CORP.
IL	CHICAGO	WIND	560 AM Station	TICHENOR LICENSE CORPORATION
IL	EVANSTON	WOJO	105.1 FM Commercial	TICHENOR LICENSE CORPORATION
IL	HIGHLAND PARK	WVIV-FM	103.1 FM Commercial	UNIVISION RADIO LICENSE CORPORATION
IL	JOLIET	WVIX	93.5 FM Commercial	UNIVISION RADIO LICENSE CORPORATION
MN	NEW PRAGUE	KCHK	1350 AM Station	INGSTAD BROTHERS BROADCASTING, LLC
NJ	NEWARK	WCAA	105.9 FM Commercial	WADO-AM LICENSE CORP. ("WADO")
NM	ALBUQUERQUE	KJFA	101.3 FM Commercial	UNIVISION RADIO LICENSE CORPORATION
NM	LOS LUNAS	KIOT	102.5 FM Commercial	UNIVISION RADIO LICENSE CORPORATION
NM	RIO RANCHO	KAJZ	101.7 FM Commercial	UNIVISION RADIO LICENSE CORPORATION
NM	SANTA FE	KKSS	97.3 FM Commercial	UNIVISION RADIO LICENSE CORPORATION
NV	INDIAN SPRINGS	KQMR	99.3 FM Commercial	UNIVISION RADIO LICENSE CORPORATION
NV	LAS VEGAS	KISF	103.5 FM Commercial	UNIVISION RADIO LICENSE CORPORATION

Radio Station Subsidiaries for Univision Communications Inc.				
State	City	Call Sign	Frequency	Subsidiary Name
NV	WHITNEY	KLSQ	870 AM Station	KLSQ-AM LICENSE CORPORATION
NY	GARDEN CITY	WZAA	92.7 FM Commercial	UNIVISION RADIO LICENSE CORPORATION
NY	NEW YORK	WADO	1280 AM Station	WADO-AM LICENSE CORP.
PR	MAYAGUEZ	WUKQ-FM	99.1 FM Commercial	UNIVISION RADIO PUERTO RICO INC
PR	PONCE	WUKQ	1420 AM Station	UNIVISION RADIO PUERTO RICO INC
PR	SAN JUAN	WKAQ-FM	104.7 FM Commercial	UNIVISION RADIO PUERTO RICO INC
PR	SAN JUAN	WKAQ	580 AM Station	UNIVISION RADIO PUERTO RICO INC
TX	BENBROOK	KDXX	107.1 FM Commercial	KCYT-FM LICENSE CORP.
TX	COMFORT	KCOR-FM	95.1 FM Commercial	UNIVISION RADIO LICENSE CORPORATION
TX	CRYSTAL BEACH	KLTO	105.3 FM Commercial	TICHENOR LICENSE CORPORATION ("TLC")
TX	EL PASO	KBNA	920 AM Station	TICHENOR LICENSE CORPORATION
TX	EL PASO	KBNA-FM	97.5 FM Commercial	TICHENOR LICENSE CORPORATION
TX	EL PASO	KAMA	750 AM Station	TICHENOR LICENSE CORPORATION
TX	FORT WORTH	KLNO	94.1 FM Commercial	UNIVISION RADIO LICENSE CORPORATION
TX	GALVESTON	KOVE-FM	106.5 FM Commercial	UNIVISION RADIO LICENSE CORPORATION
TX	GEORGETOWN	KINV	107.7 FM Commercial	SIMMONS LONE STAR MEDIA, LTD
TX	HARLINGEN	KGBT	1530 AM Station	TICHENOR LICENSE CORPORATION
TX	HARLINGEN	KBTQ	96.1 FM Commercial	TICHENOR LICENSE CORPORATION
TX	HOUSTON	KLTN	102.9 FM Commercial	UNIVISION RADIO LICENSE CORPORATION
TX	HOUSTON	KLAT	1010 AM Station	TICHENOR LICENSE CORPORATION
TX	LEWISVILLE	KESS-FM	107.9 FM Commercial	KECS-FM LICENSE CORPORATION
TX	LLANO	KBAE	96.3 FM Commercial	RAWHIDE RADIO, LLC
TX	MCALLEN	KGBT-FM	98.5 FM Commercial	TICHENOR LICENSE CORPORATION
TX	MCQUEENEY	KNGT	97.7 FM Commercial	RAWHIDE RADIO, LLC
TX	MISSOURI CITY	KPTY	104.9 FM Commercial	TICHENOR LICENSE CORPORATION
TX	PORT ARTHUR	KQBU-FM	93.3 FM Commercial	TICHENOR LICENSE CORPORATION
TX	ROBINSON	KDOS	107.9 FM Commercial	KICI-FM LICENSE CORP.
TX	ROSENBURG/RICHMOND	KRTX	980 AM Station	TICHENOR LICENSE CORPORATION
TX	SAN ANTONIO	KCOR	1350 AM Station	TICHENOR LICENSE CORPORATION
TX	SAN ANTONIO	KXTN	1310 AM Station	TICHENOR LICENSE CORPORATION
TX	SAN ANTONIO	KROM	92.9 FM Commercial	TICHENOR LICENSE CORPORATION
TX	SAN ANTONIO	KXTN-FM	107.5 FM Commercial	TICHENOR LICENSE CORPORATION
TX	SCHERTZ	KBBT	98.5 FM Commercial	UNIVISION RADIO LICENSE CORPORATION
TX	WINNIE	KOBT	100.7 FM Commercial	TICHENOR LICENSE CORPORATION

TV Station Subsidiaries for Univision Communications Inc.			
Call Sign	Channel and Type	Subsidiary Name	Area of Service
KAKW-TV	62 TV Commercial	KAKW LICENSE PARTNERSHIP, L.P.	KILLEEN, TX
KDAS-CA	31 Class A TV (UHF)	KAKW LICENSE PARTNERSHIP, L.P.	AUSTIN, TX
KDTV-CA	28 Class A TV (UHF)	KDTV LICENSE PARTNERSHIP, G.P.	SANTA ROSA, CA
KDTV	14 TV Commercial	KDTV LICENSE PARTNERSHIP, G.P.	SAN FRANCISCO, CA
KABE-CA	39 Class A TV (UHF)	KFTV LICENSE PARTNERSHIP, G.P.	BAKERSFIELD, CA
KFTV	21 TV Commercial	KFTV LICENSE PARTNERSHIP, G.P.	HANFORD, CA
KMEX-TV	34 TV Commercial	KMEX LICENSE PARTNERSHIP, G.P.	LOS ANGELES, CA
KUVE-CA	38 Class A TV (UHF)	KTVW LICENSE PARTNERSHIP, G.P.	TUCSON, AZ
KTVW-CA	6 Class A TV (VHF)	KTVW LICENSE PARTNERSHIP, G.P.	FLAGSTAFF/DONEY PARK, AZ
KTVW-TV	33 TV Commercial	KTVW LICENSE PARTNERSHIP, G.P.	PHOENIX, AZ
KUVI-TV	45 TV Commercial	KUVI LICENSE PARTNERSHIP, G.P.	BAKERSFIELD, CA
KEAT-LP	22 TV Low Power (UHF)	KUVN LICENSE PARTNERSHIP, L.P.	AMARILLO, TX
KUVN-TV	23 TV Commercial	KUVN LICENSE PARTNERSHIP, L.P.	GARLAND, TX
KUVN-CA	31 Class A TV (UHF)	KUVN LICENSE PARTNERSHIP, L.P.	FORT WORTH, TX
KUVS-TV	19 TV Commercial	KUVS LICENSE PARTNERSHIP, G.P.	MODESTO, CA
KWEX-TV	41 TV Commercial	KWEX LICENSE PARTNERSHIP, L.P.	SAN ANTONIO, TX
KXLN-TV	45 TV Commercial	KXLN LICENSE PARTNERSHIP, L.P.	ROSENBERG, TX
KTFQ-TV	14 TV Commercial	TELEFUTURA ALBUQUERQUE LLC	ALBUQUERQUE, NM
KTFB-CA	4 Class A TV (VHF)	TELEFUTURA BAKERSFIELD LLC	BAKERSFIELD, CA
WUTF-TV	66 TV Commercial	TELEFUTURA BOSTON LLC	MARLBOROUGH, MA
WXFT-TV	60 TV Commercial	TELEFUTURA CHICAGO LLC	AURORA, IL
KSTR-TV	49 TV Commercial	TELEFUTURA DALLAS LLC	IRVING, TX
KTFF-TV	61 TV Commercial	TELEFUTURA FRESNO LLC	PORTERVILLE, CA
KFTH-TV	67 TV Commercial	TELEFUTURA HOUSTON LLC	ALVIN, TX
KFTR-TV	46 TV Commercial	TELEFUTURA LOS ANGELES LLC	ONTARIO, CA
WAMI-TV	69 TV Commercial	TELEFUTURA MIAMI LLC	HOLLYWOOD, FL

	TV Station Subsidiaries for Univision Communications Inc.		
Call Sign	Channel and Type	Subsidiary Name	Area of Service
WOTF-TV	43 TV Commercial	TELEFUTURA ORLANDO, INC.	MELBOURNE, FL
KFTU-TV	3 TV Commercial	TELEFUTURA PARTNERSHIP OF DOUGLAS	DOUGLAS, AZ
KFPH-TV	13 TV Commercial	TELEFUTURA PARTNERSHIP OF FLAGSTAFF	FLAGSTAFF, AZ
K45DX	45 TV Low Power (UHF)	TELEFUTURA PARTNERSHIP OF FLORESVILLE	FLORESVILLE, TX
KFPH-CA	39 Class A TV (UHF)	TELEFUTURA PARTNERSHIP OF PHOENIX	PHOENIX, AZ
KNIC-CA	17 Class A TV (UHF)	TELEFUTURA PARTNERSHIP OF SAN ANTONIO	SAN ANTONIO, TX
KFTO-CA	67 Class A TV (UHF)	TELEFUTURA PARTNERSHIP OF SAN ANTONIO	SAN ANTONIO, TX
KTAZ-CA	25 Class A TV (UHF)	TELEFUTURA PARTNERSHIP OF TUCSON	TUCSON, AZ
KTFK-TV	64 TV Commercial	TELEFUTURA SACRAMENTO LLC	STOCKTON, CA
KEZT-CA	23 Class A TV (UHF)	TELEFUTURA SACRAMENTO LLC	SACRAMENTO, CA
KEXT-CA	27 Class A TV (UHF)	TELEFUTURA SACRAMENTO LLC	MODESTO, CA
KFSF-TV	66 TV Commercial	TELEFUTURA SAN FRANCISCO LLC	VALLEJO, CA
WFTT-TV	50 TV Commercial	TELEFUTURA TAMPA LLC	TAMPA, FL
WUVG-TV	34 TV Commercial	UNIVISION ATLANTA LLC	ATHENS, GA
WQHS-TV	61 TV Commercial	UNIVISION CLEVELAND LLC	CLEVELAND, OH
WFTY-TV	67 TV Commercial	UNIVISION NEW YORK LLC	SMITHTOWN, NY
WFUT-TV	68 TV Commercial	UNIVISION NEW YORK LLC	NEWARK, NJ
WUVP-TV	65 TV Commercial	UNIVISION PHILADELPHIA LLC	VINELAND, NJ
KUVE-TV	46 TV Commercial	UNIVISION TELEVISION GROUP, INC.	GREEN VALLEY, AZ
WGBO-TV	66 TV Commercial	WGBO LICENSE PARTNERSHIP, G.P.	JOLIET, IL
WSUR-TV	9 TV Commercial	WLII/WSUR, INC.	PONCE, PR
WLII	11 TV Commercial	WLII/WSUR, INC.	CAGUAS, PR
WLTV	23 TV Commercial	WLTV LICENSE PARTNERSHIP, G.P.	MIAMI, FL
WUVC-TV	40 TV Commercial	WUVC LICENSE PARTNERSHIP G.P.	FAYETTEVILLE, NC
WTNC-LP	26 TV Low Power (UHF)	WUVC LICENSE PARTNERSHIP, G.P.	DURHAM, NC
WXTV	41 TV Commercial	WXTV LICENSE PARTNERSHIP, G.P.	PATERSON, NJ
WFPA-CA	28 Class A TV (UHF)	WXTV LICENSE PARTNERSHIP, G.P.	PHILADELPHIA, PA

Verizon Communications Inc.

Address: 1095 Avenue of the Americas
New York, NY 10036

Total Employees: 203,100

Stock Symbol: VZ
Telephone: 212-395-2121
Fax: 212-869-3265
Website: www.verizon.com

Verizon Communications has done the best job of reassembling the pieces of Ma Bell's nationwide telephone monopoly broken up by a federal judge in 1984. And as of this writing, the company is hoping to expand its empire further by winning a bidding war with Qwest Communications International LLC in an attempt to buy MCI Inc.

Once called Bell Atlantic, Verizon was one of the seven Regional Bell Operating Companies (RBOCs), or Baby Bells, carved out from the old Bell System monopoly under the landmark antitrust settlement. The settlement forced the Bell system to break up its local and long-distance businesses, which had successfully squashed competition for more than a century. Verizon didn't stay a Baby Bell long, however.

Through a series of huge mergers and acquisitions, Verizon became for a time the largest local telephone company in the country, claiming more than 140 million access lines in 29 states and the District of Columbia.

In 1997 Bell Atlantic nearly doubled its size with its acquisition of fellow Baby Bell NYNEX Corp. for $25.6 billion, at the time one of the biggest takeovers in corporate history.

But that deal was nothing compared to Bell Atlantic's $53 billion merger with GTE Corp. just two years later. The resulting company, Verizon, clocked in at number 12 on the Fortune 500 list last year, with revenues of nearly $68 billion and over 220,000 employees worldwide.

While local phone service remains at its heart, Verizon is also an aggressive player in other sectors of the telecommunications business. Although it was only allowed to get into the long-distance telephone business in 1999, Verizon has already claimed more than 10 million customers in that market. In addition, Verizon is the largest telephone directory publisher in the world and the largest wireless communications company in the U.S., claiming 40 million customers nationwide; the company's affiliates service 33 million customers around the world.

Verizon rose to the top of the wireless business in 2000, when Bell Atlantic combined its wireless operations with those of Newbury, England-based Vodafone Group Plc. The new company was the first with a nationwide wireless footprint and common digital technology.

Verizon Wireless is now a separate company, but a two-year-old plan for an initial public offering of its stock was dropped in early 2003. In the meantime, the company is partnering with Microsoft to develop and market wireless data services.

In the next two years, Verizon Wireless plans to spend $1 billion on the rollout of its broadband wireless services. The technology being used will allow Verizon Wireless to deliver the service over an expanded wireless infrastructure.

When Verizon Communications began operations in mid-2000, the leaders of Bell Atlantic and GTE shared management responsibility for the company. Former GTE Chairman and CEO Charles R. "Chuck" Lee became Verizon's founding chairman of the board and co-CEO, while former Bell Atlantic CEO Ivan Seidenberg became Verizon's founding president and co-CEO. In accordance with a leadership transition plan announced at the time of the merger, Lee retired from Verizon in 2002. He is currently serving as non-executive chairman of the board; Seidenberg is the sole CEO.

—Bob Williams

April 28, 2005

Sources: Company Web site, Securities and Exchange Commission filings, Yahoo! Finance Online, Hoover's Online, Fortune magazine.

Verizon Communications Inc. Recent Financial Information		
Year	Revenue	Net Income (Net Loss)
1998	$57,075,000,000	$4,980,000,000
1999	$58,194,000,000	$8,260,000,000
2000	$64,707,000,000	$11,797,000,000
2001	$67,190,000,000	$389,000,000
2002	$67,625,000,000	$4,079,000,000
2003	$67,752,000,000	$3,077,000,000

Verizon Communications Inc. Board of Directors				
Name	Position	Relevant Stock		Qty
Seidenberg, Ivan	Chairman and President		VZ	156,086
Barker, James	Director		VZ	5,124
Carrion, Richard	Director		VZ	2,730
Moose, Sandra	Director		VZ	696
Neubauer, Joseph	Director		VZ	587
O'Brien, Thomas	Director		VZ	3,163
Palmer, Russell	Director		VZ	2,684
Price, Hugh	Director		VZ	1,436
Shipley, Walter	Director		VZ	13,860
Stafford, John	Director		VZ	13,968
Storey, Robert	Director		VZ	366
Lane, Robert	Director		N/A	N/A

Verizon Communications Inc. Corporate Officers			
Name	Position	Salary	Bonuses
Seidenberg, Ivan	President and CEO	$1,500,000	$2,775,000
Babbio, Lawrence	Vice Chairman and President	$1,035,000	$1,418,000
Strigl, Dennis	EVP, President and CEO, Verizon Wireless	$875,000	$1,540,000
Toben, Doreen	EVP and CFO	$765,400	$777,000
Barr, William	EVP and General Counsel	$750,000	$834,000

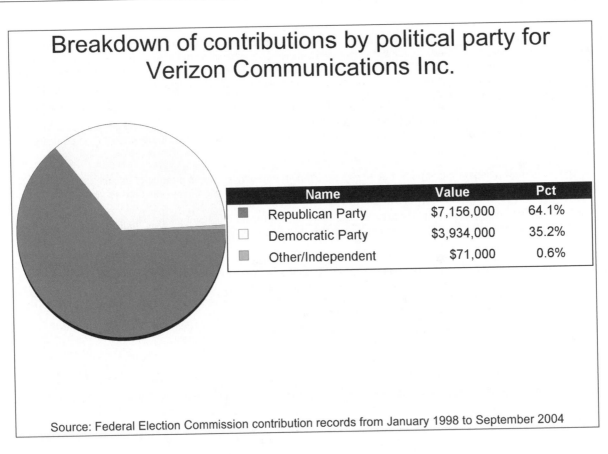

Breakdown of contributions by political party for Verizon Communications Inc.

Name	Value	Pct
Republican Party	$7,156,000	64.1%
Democratic Party	$3,934,000	35.2%
Other/Independent	$71,000	0.6%

Source: Federal Election Commission contribution records from January 1998 to September 2004

The Center for Public Integrity

Top 10 Recipients of Contributions Sourced to Verizon Communications Inc.

Recipient	Amount
National Republican Party Committees	$3,065,000
National Democratic Party Committees	$1,549,000
President George W Bush (R)	$138,000
Sen John F Kerry (D-MA)	$116,000
Sen John S McCain (R-AZ)	$84,000
Rep Wilbert J Tauzin, Jr (R-LA)	$72,000
Rep Roy Blunt (R-MO)	$64,000
Rep John D Dingell (D-MI)	$61,000
Rep J Dennis Hastert (R-IL)	$57,000
Rep Eliot L Engel (D-NY)	$57,000
Total:	$5,263,000

Source: Federal Election Commission contribution records from January 1998 to September 2004

Verizon Communications Inc. Lobbying Expenditures by Year

Year	Amount
1998	$28,382,684
1999	$15,016,588
2000	$14,580,412
2001	$12,794,353
2002	$12,302,387
2003	$15,471,000
2004	$4,910,000
Total:	$103,457,424

Source: U.S. Senate Office of Public Records lobbying disclosure records from January 1998 to June 30th, 2004.

Verizon Communications Inc. Sponsored Trips for Congressional Staff

Congressional Office	Number of Trips	$ Amount
Rep Wilbert J Tauzin, Jr (R-LA)	3	$1,825
Rep Frederick Carlyle Boucher (D-VA)	1	$750
Rep Eliot L Engel (D-NY)	1	$625
	1	$505
Total:	6	$3,705

Source: Congressional office travel records for members of the Senate Committee on Commerce, Science & Transportation and the House Committee on Energy and Commerce for the period of January 2000 to March 2004.

Viacom Inc.

Address: 1515 Broadway
New York, NY 10036
Total Employees: 117,750

Stock Symbol: VIA
Telephone: 212-258-6000
Fax: 212-258-6464
Website: www.viacom.com

Viacom Inc. didn't ask to be at the center of an election-year debate over broadcast indecency. But when a company is in a position to control the hearts and minds of Americans through a vast empire that includes television and radio stations, movie studios, cable networks and book publishing, attention is hard to avoid, unwanted or otherwise.

The now-infamous Janet Jackson Super Bowl stunt put the wheels in motion on indecency when angry viewers deluged the FCC with calls and e-mails. The breast seen around the world was first seen on Viacom's CBS. Thanks to the stunt, Viacom's 20 owned-and-operated stations are reportedly in line for fines of $27,500 each, for a total of $550,000, from the FCC.

But it didn't end there. Following the Jackson incident, the FCC targeted its indecency poster-boy, radio talker Howard Stern, whose show is syndicated through Viacom's Infinity Broadcasting. Clear Channel Communications Inc. dumped the program from all six of its radio stations that carry the program, and later reached a settlement with the FCC for $1.75 million to settle several indecency complaints against the broadcaster. It was the largest settlement for broadcast indecency in FCC history.

On top of the Stern/Jackson quagmire, the past year also saw Viacom announcing a separation from video rental giant Blockbuster, a money loser for the company, which held 81.5 percent of the chain's shares.

To top it off, Viacom's president, Mel Karmazin, suddenly resigned in June, the end-result of years of feuding with Viacom's Chairman and CEO Sumner Redstone over the best way to manage the company. Karmazin won accolades on Wall Street for having overseen CBS during the period when it became the most-watched broadcast network in primetime. He was also the shepherd for Viacom's vast network of radio stations, which have been a cash cow for the parent.

Immediately following Karmazin's departure, Redstone, who turned 81 in May, appointed chief CBS executive Leslie Moonves and MTV networks head Tom Freston as co- presidents and chief operating officers. In addition, he announced that he would step down as CEO within three years but remain as chairman.

The resignation seemed to further imperil Stern, who had always relied on staunch support from Karmazin throughout two decades of battles with the FCC, and some analysts saw his departure as a prelude to Stern's possible shift to satellite radio.

Instead, Stern announced in a press conference at the end of June that not only was he sticking to broadcast radio, but that Infinity was putting him back on the air on its own stations in several of the markets lost by the Clear Channel expulsion. Infinity is expected to fight the next wave of fines from the FCC, reportedly in the neighborhood of $1.5 million, which could land any day stemming from the Stern program that spurred the Clear Channel settlement.

When weathering a highly contentious political debate, it helps to be sitting on top of a media empire.

Redstone built his empire after amassing a fortune in the movie theater business. Redstone is chairman of closely held National Amusements Inc., and its 1,400 theaters, and National Amusements controls over two-thirds of Viacom. Redstone bought Viacom in 1987. At the time, Viacom owned a number of radio and television stations and pay television network Showtime. What followed was a series of acquisitions. In 1994, it bought Paramount Communications for $10 billion and Blockbuster for $8.4 billion. But the crescendo was in 2000 when Viacom bought CBS for $39.8 billion, one of the largest media mergers in history. Today, Viacom ranks No. 64 on the Fortune 500 list.

There's a good chance your favorite radio station is owned by Viacom's Infinity subsidiary (No. 2 in the industry by revenue). Viacom also owns the CBS and UPN television networks, as well as television stations that reach a larger audience than any company in the nation. It owns a number of major cable channels, including Showtime, perennial favorite Nickelodeon, MTV and BET. Beyond broadcast and cable, Viacom owns five major theme parks. Movie buffs are apt to see a Viacom-produced film through its Paramount Pictures subsidiary. Even bookworms are not immune—Viacom owns publisher Simon & Schuster and a number of other imprints.

The only thing missing from the company's impressive portfolio is a cable television system, but there's a reason for that—until recently, the FCC wouldn't allow a company to own both a national network and a cable television system, for fear it would give preferential treatment to its own programming. A court invalidated the rule, and it was repealed by the FCC last year. The first action in the wake of that decision was the failed bid by Comcast Corp. to acquire the Walt Disney Co.

Viacom is one of the world's largest media companies, reporting $26.6 billion in revenue in 2003 and a $1.4 billion profit.

In mid-2003, Viacom was reportedly looking into acquiring the entertainment properties of Vivendi Universal, but they were instead picked up by General Electric Co.

—Robert Morlino, John Dunbar

August 20, 2004

Sources: Viacom Inc. Form 10-K, Broadcasting & Cable, Hoover's Online, Fortune magazine, Knight-Ridder, Daily Variety

Viacom Inc. Recent Financial Information		
Year	Revenue	Net Income (Net Loss)
2000	$20,043,700,000	($816,100,000)
2001	$23,222,800,000	($223,500,000)
2002	$24,605,700,000	$725,700,000
2003	$26,585,300,000	$1,416,900,000

Viacom Inc. Board of Directors				
Name	Position	Relevant Stock		Qty
Redstone, Sumner	Chairman		VIA	93,658,908
Redstone, Sumner	Chairman		BBI	147,491,816
Karmazin, Mel	Director		N/A	N/A
Abrams, George	Director		VIA	18,295
Andelman, David	Director		VIA	2,466
Dauman, Philippe	Director		VIA	2,121
Dauman, Philippe	Director		BBI	2,994
Leschly, Jan	Director		VIA	3,172
McLaughlin, David	Director		VIA	N/A
Salerno, Frederic	Director		VIA	11,001
Schwartz, William	Director		VIA	18,477
Stonesifer, Patty	Director		VIA	3,619
Walter, Robert	Director		VIA	3,098
Califano, Joseph	Director		N/A	720
Cohen, Willam	Director		VIA	420
Greenberg, Alan	Director		N/A	N/A
Redstone, Shari	Director		N/A	N/A

Viacom Inc. Corporate Officers			
Name	Position	Salary	Bonuses
Redstone, Sumner	Chairman and CEO	$3,993,000	$15,000,000
Karmazin, Mel	President, COO, and Director	$3,993,000	$15,000,000
Bressler, Richard	SEVP and CFO	$1,155,625	$5,500,000
Fricklas, Michael	EVP and General Counsel	$1,004,327	$1,200,000

Breakdown of contributions by political party for Viacom Inc.

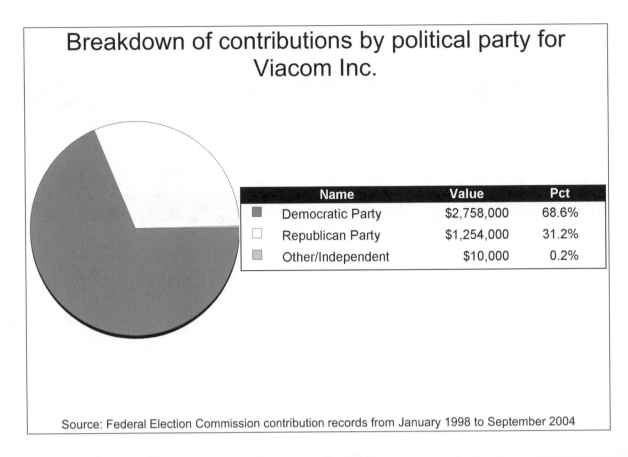

	Name	Value	Pct
■	Democratic Party	$2,758,000	68.6%
□	Republican Party	$1,254,000	31.2%
▨	Other/Independent	$10,000	0.2%

Source: Federal Election Commission contribution records from January 1998 to September 2004

Top 10 Recipients of Contributions Sourced to Viacom Inc.	
Recipient	Amount
National Democratic Party Committees	$1,291,000
National Republican Party Committees	$422,000
Sen John F Kerry (D-MA)	$118,000
Sen Hillary Rodham Clinton (D-NY)	$105,000
Vice President Albert Gore, Jr (D-TN)	$85,000
Sen Barbara Boxer (D-CA)	$81,000
Sen Charles E Schumer (D-NY)	$79,000
Sen John S McCain (R-AZ)	$70,000
Rep Richard A Gephardt (D-MO)	$60,000
Sen Thomas Andrew Daschle (D-SD)	$50,000
Total:	$2,361,000

Source: Federal Election Commission contribution records from January 1998 to September 2004

Viacom Inc. Lobbying Expenditures by Year	
Year	Amount
1998	$4,260,000
1999	$3,380,000
2000	$2,422,000
2001	$1,800,000
2002	$1,420,000
2003	$1,750,000
2004	$1,080,000
Total:	$16,112,000

Source: U.S. Senate Office of Public Records lobbying disclosure records from January 1998 to June 30th, 2004.

Viacom Inc. Sponsored Trips for Congressional Staff		
Congressional Office	Number of Trips	$ Amount
Rep Wilbert J Tauzin, Jr (R-LA)	4	$4,776
Total:	4	$4,776

Source: Congressional office travel records for members of the Senate Committee on Commerce, Science & Transportation and the House Committee on Energy and Commerce for the period of January 2000 to March 2004.

State	City	Call Sign	Frequency	Subsidiary Name
			Radio Station Subsidiaries for Viacom Inc.	
AZ	CHANDLER	KMLE	107.9 FM Commercial	INFINITY RADIO INC.
AZ	PHOENIX	KZON	101.5 FM Commercial	INFINITY RADIO INC.
AZ	PHOENIX	KOOL-FM	94.5 FM Commercial	INFINITY RADIO INC.
CA	CLOVIS	KOOR	790 AM Station	INFINITY RADIO INC.
CA	FRESNO	KOQO-FM	101.9 FM Commercial	INFINITY RADIO INC.
CA	FRESNO	KRNC	105.9 FM Commercial	INFINITY RADIO INC.
CA	FRESNO	KMJ	580 AM Station	INFINITY RADIO INC.
CA	FRESNO	KSKS	93.7 FM Commercial	INFINITY RADIO INC.
CA	FRESNO	KWYE	101.1 FM Commercial	INFINITY RADIO INC.
CA	FRESNO	KMGV	97.9 FM Commercial	INFINITY RADIO INC.
CA	GILROY	KBAA	94.5 FM Commercial	INFINITY RADIO INC.
CA	HESPERIA	KRAK	910 AM Station	INFINITY RADIO INC.
CA	LOS ANGELES	KCBS-FM	93.1 FM Commercial	INFINITY BROADCASTING EAST INC.
CA	LOS ANGELES	KNX	1070 AM Station	INFINITY BROADCASTING EAST INC.
CA	LOS ANGELES	KRTH-FM	101.1 FM Commercial	INFINITY BROADCASTING EAST INC.
CA	LOS ANGELES	KTWV	94.7 FM Commercial	INFINITY BROADCASTING EAST INC.
CA	LOS ANGELES	KLSX	97.1 FM Commercial	INFINITY BROADCASTING EAST INC.
CA	LOS ANGELES	KFWB	980 AM Station	INFINITY BROADCASTING EAST INC.
CA	PALM DESERT	KEZN	103.1 FM Commercial	INFINITY RADIO HOLDINGS, INC.
CA	PASADENA	KROQ-FM	106.7 FM Commercial	INFINITY BROADCASTING CORP. OF LOS ANGELES
CA	ROSEVILLE	KHWD	93.7 FM Commercial	INFINITY RADIO HOLDINGS, INC.
CA	SACRAMENTO	KYMX	96.1 FM Commercial	INFINITY RADIO INC.
CA	SACRAMENTO	KZZO	100.5 FM Commercial	INFINITY RADIO INC.
CA	SACRAMENTO	KHTK	1140 AM Station	INFINITY RADIO HOLDINGS, INC.
CA	SACRAMENTO	KNCI	105.1 FM Commercial	INFINITY RADIO HOLDINGS, INC.
CA	SAN BERNARDINO	KFRG	95.1 FM Commercial	INFINITY RADIO INC.
CA	SAN DIEGO	KPLN	103.7 FM Commercial	INFINITY RADIO INC.
CA	SAN DIEGO	KYXY	96.5 FM Commercial	INFINITY RADIO INC.
CA	SAN FRANCISCO	KLLC	97.3 FM Commercial	INFINITY BROADCASTING EAST INC.
CA	SAN FRANCISCO	KCBS	740 AM Station	INFINITY BROADCASTING EAST INC.
CA	SAN FRANCISCO	KBAY	93.3 FM Commercial	INFINITY BROADCASTING CORP. OF SAN FRANCISCO
CA	SAN FRANCISCO	KFRC	610 AM Station	INFINITY BROADCASTING CORPORATION OF LOS ANGELES
CA	SAN FRANCISCO	KFRC-FM	99.7 FM Commercial	INFINITY KFRC-FM, INC.
CA	SAN FRANCISCO	KITS	105.3 FM Commercial	INFINITY BROADCASTING EAST INC.
CA	SAN FRANCISCO	KYCY	1550 AM Station	INFINITY BROADCASTING EAST INC.
CA	SAN JOSE	KEZR	106.5 FM Commercial	INFINITY RADIO OF SAN JOSE, INC.
CA	SUN CITY	KXFG	92.9 FM Commercial	INFINITY RADIO INC.
CA	VICTORVILLE	KVFG	103.1 FM Commercial	INFINITY RADIO INC.
CA	WOODLAND	KSFM	102.5 FM Commercial	INFINITY RADIO OF SACRAMENTO, INC.
CO	BROOMFIELD	KDJM	92.5 FM Commercial	INFINITY RADIO INC.
CO	DENVER	KIMN	100.3 FM Commercial	INFINITY RADIO INC.
CO	DENVER	KXKL-FM	105.1 FM Commercial	INFINITY RADIO INC.
CT	HARTFORD	WZMX	93.7 FM Commercial	INFINITY RADIO INC.
CT	HARTFORD	WTIC	1080 AM Station	INFINITY RADIO INC.
CT	HARTFORD	WTIC-FM	96.5 FM Commercial	INFINITY RADIO INC.
CT	NEW BRITAIN	WRCH	100.5 FM Commercial	INFINITY RADIO INC.
FL	DAYTONA BEACH	WJHM	101.9 FM Commercial	INFINITY RADIO INC.
FL	DELAND	WOCL	105.9 FM Commercial	INFINITY RADIO INC.
FL	HOLMES BEACH	WLLD	98.7 FM Commercial	INFINITY RADIO INC.
FL	INDIANTOWN	WPBZ	103.1 FM Commercial	INFINITY RADIO INC.
FL	JENSEN BEACH	WMBX	102.3 FM Commercial	INFINITY RADIO INC.
FL	JUPITER	WJBW-FM	106.3 FM Commercial	INFINITY RADIO INC.
FL	LAKELAND	WSJT	94.1 FM Commercial	INFINITY RADIO INC.
FL	ORLANDO	WOMX-FM	105.1 FM Commercial	INFINITY RADIO INC.
FL	SAFETY HARBOR	WYUU	92.5 FM Commercial	INFINITY RADIO INC.
FL	SEFFNER	WQYK	1010 AM Station	INFINITY BROADCASTING CORPORATION OF TAMPA
FL	ST. PETERSBURG	WQYK-FM	99.5 FM Commercial	INFINITY BROADCASTING CORPORATION OF FLORIDA
FL	TAMPA	WRBQ-FM	104.7 FM Commercial	INFINITY RADIO INC.
FL	WEST PALM BEACH	WEAT-FM	104.3 FM Commercial	INFINITY RADIO INC.

State	City	Call Sign	Frequency	Subsidiary Name
			Radio Station Subsidiaries for Viacom Inc.	
FL	WEST PALM BEACH	WIRK-FM	107.9 FM Commercial	INFINITY RADIO INC.
GA	ATLANTA	WZGC	92.9 FM Commercial	INFINITY BROADCASTING CORP. OF ATLANTA
GA	ATLANTA	WAOK	1380 AM Station	INFINITY BROADCASTING EAST INC.
GA	ATLANTA	WVEE	103.3 FM Commercial	INFINITY BROADCASTING EAST INC.
IL	CHICAGO	WXRT-FM	93.1 FM Commercial	INFINITY BROADCASTING EAST INC.
IL	CHICAGO	WBBM	780 AM Station	INFINITY BROADCASTING EAST INC.
IL	CHICAGO	WBBM-FM	96.3 FM Commercial	INFINITY BROADCASTING EAST INC.
IL	CHICAGO	WSCR	670 AM Station	INFINITY BROADCASTING EAST INC.
IL	CHICAGO	WUSN	99.5 FM Commercial	INFINITY BROADCASTING CORPORATION OF CHICAGO
IL	CHICAGO	WJMK	104.3 FM Commercial	INFINITY BROADCASTING CORP. OF ILLINOIS
IL	ELMWOOD PARK	WCKG	105.9 FM Commercial	INFINITY HOLDINGS CORPORATION OF ORLANDO
KS	KANSAS CITY	KFKF-FM	94.1 FM Commercial	INFINITY RADIO HOLDINGS, INC.
KY	FORT THOMAS	WAQZ	97.3 FM Commercial	INFINITY RADIO INC.
MA	BOSTON	WODS	103.3 FM Commercial	INFINITY BROADCASTING EAST INC.
MA	BOSTON	WZLX	100.7 FM Commercial	INFINITY BROADCASTING CORPORATION OF BOSTON
MA	BOSTON	WBMX	98.5 FM Commercial	INFINITY RADIO INC.
MA	BOSTON	WBZ	1030 AM Station	INFINITY BROADCASTING EAST INC.
MA	BOSTON	WBCN	104.1 FM Commercial	HEMISPHERE BROADCASTING CORPORATION
MD	ANNAPOLIS	WHFS	99.1 FM Commercial	INFINITY BROADCASTING EAST INC.
MD	BALTIMORE	WWMX	106.5 FM Commercial	INFINITY RADIO INC.
MD	BALTIMORE	WBGR	860 AM Station	INFINITY RADIO INC.
MD	BALTIMORE	WQSR	102.7 FM Commercial	INFINITY BROADCASTING CORPORATION OF CHESAPEAKE
MD	BALTIMORE	WBMD	750 AM Station	INFINITY RADIO INC.
MD	BALTIMORE	WJFK	1300 AM Station	INFINITY WLIF-AM, INC.
MD	BALTIMORE	WLIF	101.9 FM Commercial	INFINITY WLIF, INC.
MD	BETHESDA	WARW	94.7 FM Commercial	INFINITY BROADCASTING EAST INC.
MD	CATONSVILLE	WXYV	105.7 FM Commercial	INFINITY RADIO INC.
MD	MORNINGSIDE	WPGC	1580 AM Station	INFINITY WPGC(AM), INC.
MD	MORNINGSIDE	WPGC-FM	95.5 FM Commercial	INFINITY BROADCASTING CORPORATION OF MARYLAND
MI	DETROIT	WYCD	99.5 FM Commercial	INFINITY BROADCASTING CORPORATION OF MICHIGAN
MI	DETROIT	WKRK-FM	97.1 FM Commercial	INFINITY BROADCASTING EAST INC.
MI	DETROIT	WWJ	950 AM Station	INFINITY BROADCASTING EAST INC.
MI	DETROIT	WVMV	98.7 FM Commercial	INFINITY BROADCASTING EAST INC.
MI	DETROIT	WXYT	1270 AM Station	INFINITY BROADCASTING CORP. OF DETROIT
MI	DETROIT	WOMC	104.3 FM Commercial	INFINITY BROADCASTING CORPORATION OF MICHIGAN
MN	MINNEAPOLIS	WLTE	102.9 FM Commercial	INFINITY MEDIA CORPORATION
MN	MINNEAPOLIS	WCCO	830 AM Station	INFINITY MEDIA CORPORATION
MN	ST. LOUIS PARK	WXPT	104.1 FM Commercial	THE AUDIO HOUSE, INC.
MN	ST. LOUIS PARK	KSNB	950 AM Station	THE AUDIO HOUSE, INC.
MO	KANSAS CITY	KSRC	102.1 FM Commercial	INFINITY RADIO INC.
MO	KANSAS CITY	KMXV	93.3 FM Commercial	INFINITY RADIO INC.
MO	KANSAS CITY	KBEQ-FM	104.3 FM Commercial	INFINITY RADIO HOLDINGS, INC.
MO	ST. LOUIS	KYKY	98.1 FM Commercial	INFINITY RADIO HOLDINGS, INC.
MO	ST. LOUIS	KEZK-FM	102.5 FM Commercial	INFINITY RADIO HOLDINGS, INC.
MO	ST. LOUIS	KMOX	1120 AM Station	INFINITY BROADCASTING EAST INC.
NC	CHARLOTTE	WKQC	104.7 FM Commercial	INFINITY RADIO HOLDINGS, INC.
NC	CHARLOTTE	WSOC-FM	103.7 FM Commercial	INFINITY RADIO HOLDINGS, INC.
NC	CHARLOTTE	WFNA	1660 AM Station	INFINITY RADIO HOLDINGS, INC.
NC	CHARLOTTE	WFNZ	610 AM Station	INFINITY RADIO HOLDINGS, INC.
NC	CHARLOTTE	WNKS	95.1 FM Commercial	INFINITY RADIO HOLDINGS, INC.
NC	CONCORD	WPEG	97.9 FM Commercial	INFINITY RADIO HOLDINGS, INC.
NC	GASTONIA	WBAV-FM	101.9 FM Commercial	INFINITY RADIO HOLDINGS, INC.
NC	GRAHAM	WSML	1200 AM Station	INFINITY RADIO INC.
NC	HIGH POINT	WMFR	1230 AM Station	INFINITY RADIO INC.
NC	WINSTON-SALEM	WSJS	600 AM Station	INFINITY RADIO INC.
NV	HENDERSON	KMXB	94.1 FM Commercial	INFINITY RADIO INC.
NV	HENDERSON	KMZQ-FM	100.5 FM Commercial	INFINITY RADIO INC.
NV	LAS VEGAS	KLUC-FM	98.5 FM Commercial	INFINITY RADIO INC.

State	City	Call Sign	Frequency	Subsidiary Name
			Radio Station Subsidiaries for Viacom Inc.	
NV	NORTH LAS VEGAS	KSFN	1140 AM Station	INFINITY RADIO INC.
NV	NORTH LAS VEGAS	KXNT	840 AM Station	INFINITY RADIO INC.
NV	PAHRUMP	KXTE	107.5 FM Commercial	INFINITY RADIO INC.
NY	BRIGHTON	WZNE	94.1 FM Commercial	INFINITY RADIO INC.
NY	BUFFALO	WYRK	106.5 FM Commercial	INFINITY RADIO INC.
NY	BUFFALO	WJYE	96.1 FM Commercial	INFINITY RADIO INC.
NY	BUFFALO	WBUF	92.9 FM Commercial	INFINITY RADIO INC.
NY	CHEEKTOWAGA	WECK	1230 AM Station	INFINITY RADIO INC.
NY	DEPEW	WBLK	93.7 FM Commercial	INFINITY RADIO INC.
NY	NEW YORK	WXRK	92.3 FM Commercial	INFINITY BROADCASTING EAST INC.
NY	NEW YORK	WCBS	880 AM Station	INFINITY BROADCASTING EAST INC.
NY	NEW YORK	WCBS-FM	101.1 FM Commercial	INFINITY BROADCASTING EAST INC.
NY	NEW YORK	WFAN	660 AM Station	INFINITY BROADCASTING EAST INC.
NY	NEW YORK	WINS	1010 AM Station	INFINITY BROADCASTING EAST INC.
NY	NEW YORK	WNEW	102.7 FM Commercial	INFINITY BROADCASTING EAST INC.
NY	ROCHESTER	WCMF-FM	96.5 FM Commercial	INFINITY RADIO INC.
NY	ROCHESTER	WRMM-FM	101.3 FM Commercial	INFINITY RADIO INC.
NY	ROCHESTER	WPXY-FM	97.9 FM Commercial	INFINITY RADIO INC.
OH	CINCINNATI	WUBE-FM	105.1 FM Commercial	INFINITY RADIO INC.
OH	CINCINNATI	WKRQ	101.9 FM Commercial	INFINITY RADIO INC.
OH	CIRCLEVILLE	WAZU	107.1 FM Commercial	INFINITY RADIO INC.
OH	CLEVELAND	WNCX	98.5 FM Commercial	INFINITY RADIO OF CLEVELAND INC.
OH	CLEVELAND	WDOK	102.1 FM Commercial	INFINITY RADIO INC.
OH	CLEVELAND	WQAL	104.1 FM Commercial	INFINITY RADIO INC.
OH	CLEVELAND HEIGHTS	WXTM	92.3 FM Commercial	INFINITY RADIO INC.
OH	COLUMBUS	WLVQ	96.3 FM Commercial	INFINITY RADIO INC.
OH	HAMILTON	WGRR	103.5 FM Commercial	INFINITY RADIO INC.
OH	LANCASTER	WHOK-FM	95.5 FM Commercial	INFINITY RADIO HOLDINGS, INC.
OR	BANKS	KVMX	107.5 FM Commercial	INFINITY RADIO INC.
OR	LAKE OSWEGO	KLTH	106.7 FM Commercial	INIFINITY RADIO OF PORTLAND INC.
OR	PORTLAND	KUPL-FM	98.7 FM Commercial	INFINITY RADIO OF PORTLAND INC.
OR	PORTLAND	KUPL	970 AM Station	INFINITY RADIO INC.
OR	PORTLAND	KUFO-FM	101.1 FM Commercial	INFINITY RADIO INC.
OR	PORTLAND	KINK	101.9 FM Commercial	INFINITY RADIO INC.
PA	NEW KENSINGTON	WZPT	100.7 FM Commercial	INFINITY RADIO HOLDINGS, INC.
PA	PHILADELPHIA	KYW	1060 AM Station	INFINITY BROADCASTING EAST INC.
PA	PHILADELPHIA	WOGL	98.1 FM Commercial	INFINITY BROADCASTING EAST INC.
PA	PHILADELPHIA	WPHT	1210 AM Station	INFINITY BROADCASTING EAST INC.
PA	PHILADELPHIA	WYSP	94.1 FM Commercial	INFINITY BROADCASTING EAST INC.
PA	PHILADELPHIA	WIP	610 AM Station	INFINITY BROADCASTING CORPORATION OF PHILADELPHIA
PA	PITTSBURGH	KDKA	1020 AM Station	INFINITY BROADCASTING EAST INC.
PA	PITTSBURGH	WDSY-FM	107.9 FM Commercial	INFINITY RADIO HOLDINGS, INC.
PA	PITTSBURGH	WBZZ	93.7 FM Commercial	INFINITY RADIO HOLDINGS, INC.
TN	BARTLETT	WMFS	92.9 FM Commercial	INFINITY BROADCASTING CORP. OF ILLINOIS
TN	MEMPHIS	WMC	790 AM Station	INFINITY RADIO INC.
TN	MEMPHIS	WMC-FM	99.7 FM Commercial	INFINITY RADIO INC.
TX	AUSTIN	KKMJ-FM	95.5 FM Commercial	TEXAS INFINITY RADIO L.P.
TX	DALLAS	KJKK	100.3 FM Commercial	INFINITY BROADCASTING CORP. OF FORT WORTH
TX	DALLAS	KLUV-FM	98.7 FM Commercial	INFINITY BROADCASTING CORPORATION OF DALLAS
TX	DALLAS	KRLD	1080 AM Station	TEXAS INFINITY BROADCASTING L.P.
TX	DALLAS	KLLI	105.3 FM Commercial	INFINITY BROADCASTING CORPORATION OF DALLAS
TX	FORT WORTH	KOAI	107.5 FM Commercial	INFINITY KOAI-FM, INC.
TX	HIGHLAND PARK-DALLAS	KVIL-FM	103.7 FM Commercial	INFINITY BROADCASTING CORPORATION OF TEXAS
TX	HOUSTON	KHJZ-FM	95.7 FM Commercial	TEXAS INFINITY BROADCASTING L.P.
TX	HOUSTON	KILT-FM	100.3 FM Commercial	TEXAS INFINITY BROADCASTING L.P.
TX	HOUSTON	KILT	610 AM Station	TEXAS INFINITY BROADCASTING L.P.
TX	LULING	KAMX	94.7 FM Commercial	TEXAS INFINITY RADIO L.P.
TX	PASADENA	KIKK	650 AM Station	TEXAS INFINITY BROADCASTING L.P.
TX	ROLLINGWOOD	KJCE	1370 AM Station	TEXAS INFINITY RADIO L.P.
TX	SAN ANTONIO	KSRX	102.7 FM Commercial	INFINITY BROADCASTING CORPORATION OF

Radio Station Subsidiaries for Viacom Inc.				
State	City	Call Sign	Frequency	Subsidiary Name
TX	SAN ANTONIO	KTSA	550 AM Station	SAN ANTONIO INFINITY BROADCASTING CORPORATION OF SAN ANTONIO
TX	TAYLOR	KQBT	104.3 FM Commercial	INFINITY RADIO INC.
VA	MANASSAS	WJFK-FM	106.7 FM Commercial	INFINITY BROADCASTING CORP. OF WASHINGTON, DC
WA	SEATTLE	KRQI-FM	96.5 FM Commercial	INFINITY RADIO HOLDINGS, INC.
WA	SEATTLE	KYCW	1090 AM Station	INFINITY RADIO HOLDINGS, INC.
WA	SEATTLE	KMPS-FM	94.1 FM Commercial	INFINITY RADIO HOLDINGS, INC.
WA	SEATTLE	KZOK-FM	102.5 FM Commercial	INFINITY RADIO HOLDINGS, INC.
WA	TACOMA	KBKS-FM	106.1 FM Commercial	INFINITY RADIO HOLDINGS, INC.

TV Station Subsidiaries for Viacom Inc.			
Call Sign	Channel and Type	Subsidiary Name	Area of Service
WLWC	28 TV Commercial	C-28 FCC LICENSEE SUBSIDIARY, LLC	NEW BEDFORD, MA
WTVX	34 TV Commercial	C-34 FCC LICENSEE SUBSIDIARY, LLC	FORT PIERCE, FL
KPIX-TV	5 TV Commercial	CBS BROADCASTING INC.	SAN FRANCISCO, CA
KYW-TV	3 TV Commercial	CBS BROADCASTING INC.	PHILADELPHIA, PA
KDKA-TV	2 TV Commercial	CBS BROADCASTING INC.	PITTSBURGH, PA
WCBS-TV	2 TV Commercial	CBS BROADCASTING INC.	NEW YORK, NY
WBBM-TV	2 TV Commercial	CBS BROADCASTING INC.	CHICAGO, IL
KCBS-TV	2 TV Commercial	CBS BROADCASTING INC.	LOS ANGELES, CA
WCCO-TV	4 TV Commercial	CBS BROADCASTING INC.	MINNEAPOLIS, MN
WJMN-TV	3 TV Commercial	CBS BROADCASTING INC.	ESCANABA, MI
KCCO-TV	7 TV Commercial	CBS BROADCASTING INC.	ALEXANDRIA, MN
WFRV-TV	5 TV Commercial	CBS BROADCASTING INC.	GREEN BAY, WI
KCCW-TV	12 TV Commercial	CBS BROADCASTING INC.	WALKER, MN
WWJ-TV	62 TV Commercial	CBS BROADCASTING INC.	DETROIT, MI
KEYE-TV	42 TV Commercial	CBS STATIONS GROUP OF TEXAS L.P.	AUSTIN, TX
KTVT	11 TV Commercial	CBS STATIONS GROUP OF TEXAS L.P.	FORT WORTH, TX
KCNC-TV	4 TV Commercial	CBS TELEVISION STATIONS INC.	DENVER, CO
WFOR-TV	4 TV Commercial	CBS TELEVISION STATIONS INC.	MIAMI, FL
KUSG	12 TV Commercial	KUTV HOLDINGS, INC.	ST. GEORGE, UT
KUTV	2 TV Commercial	KUTV HOLDINGS, INC.	SALT LAKE CITY, UT
KMAX-TV	31 TV Commercial	UPN STATIONS GROUP INC.	SACRAMENTO, CA
WNDY-TV	23 TV Commercial	UPN STATIONS GROUP INC.	MARION, IN
WWHO	53 TV Commercial	UPN STATIONS GROUP INC.	CHILLICOTHE, OH
WGNT	27 TV Commercial	UPN TELEVISION STATIONS INC.	PORTSMOUTH, VA
KSTW	11 TV Commercial	UPN TELEVISION STATIONS INC.	TACOMA, WA
WUPL	54 TV Commercial	UPN TELEVISION STATIONS INC.	SLIDELL, LA
WHDF	15 TV Commercial	VALLEY TELEVISION, LLC	FLORENCE, AL
WSBK-TV	38 TV Commercial	VIACOM INC.	BOSTON, MA
WJZ-TV	13 TV Commercial	VIACOM INC.	BALTIMORE, MD
WBZ-TV	4 TV Commercial	VIACOM INC.	BOSTON, MA
WTOG	44 TV Commercial	VIACOM INTERNATIONAL INC.	ST. PETERSBURG, FL
WUPA	69 TV Commercial	VIACOM STATIONS GROUP OF ATLANTA INC.	ATLANTA, GA
WKBD	50 TV Commercial	VIACOM STATIONS GROUP OF DETROIT INC.	DETROIT, MI
WBFS-TV	33 TV Commercial	VIACOM STATIONS GROUP OF MIAMI INC.	MIAMI, FL
KAUT-TV	43 TV Commercial	VIACOM STATIONS GROUP OF OKC LLC	OKLAHOMA CITY, OK
WPSG	57 TV Commercial	VIACOM STATIONS GROUP OF PHILADELPHIA INC.	PHILADELPHIA, PA
WNPA	19 TV Commercial	VIACOM STATIONS GROUP OF PITTSBURGH INC.	JEANNETTE, PA
KTXA	21 TV Commercial	VIACOM TELEVISION STATIONS GROUP OF DALLAS/FORT WORTH L.P.	FORT WORTH, TX
KCAL-TV	9 TV Commercial	VIACOM TELEVISION STATIONS GROUP OF LOS ANGELES LLC	LOS ANGELES, CA
KBHK-TV	44 TV Commercial	VIACOM TELEVISION STATIONS GROUP OF SAN FRANCISCO INC.	SAN FRANCISCO, CA

Walt Disney Co.

Address:	500 S. Buena Vista St.	Stock Symbol:	DIS
	Burbank, CA 91521-9722	Telephone:	818-560-1000
		Fax:	818-560-1930
Total Employees:	112,000	Website:	www.disney.go.com

The Mouse has had a rough year. The Walt Disney Co., a much-beloved producer of memorable movies and purveyor of theme park fun, weathered an unwelcome takeover bid from Comcast, a no-confidence vote for board chairman Michael Eisner and some unwelcome publicity from filmmaker and provocateur Michael Moore—all before Memorial Day. The rest of the year saw Eisner announce his intention to resign in 2006, and a court battle between shareholders and executives over the 1997 severance package given to talent agent Michael Ovitz.

In February, Disney's impressive inventory of content attracted unwanted attention from the nation's biggest information pipeline owner, cable television titan Comcast Corp. Comcast made a bid for the company, which was roundly rejected by the Disney board and it shareholders. Had it been successful it would have created the largest media company in the world.

The Comcast bid, once considered unthinkable, was taken more seriously thanks to the troubles of Disney CEO and golden boy Michael Eisner. Eisner survived an uprising led by board member Roy Disney and suffered a humiliating no-confidence vote by shareholders, but lost the chairmanship of the company.

Just when things seemed to be settling down a bit, filmmaker Michael Moore accused Eisner of blocking the distribution of Moore's newest film in an effort to avoid running afoul of Gov. Jeb Bush and jeopardizing tax breaks for Florida theme parks. The smash-hit documentary—Fahrenheit 9/11—was produced by Disney-owned Miramax studios and is a relentless attack on the Bush administration. Eisner denied that any tax breaks were a factor, but Moore had already used the controversy to vault the dispute over distribution into the national spotlight.

The dispute also reportedly strained contract negotiations between Miramax and Disney, spurring speculation that the studio may back out of its partnership with the Mouse, as the animation studio Pixar did earlier this year.

With his contract set to expire in 2006, Eisner concluded the months of turmoil by announcing that he would leave the company at that time. But the move didn't end the trouble. In October, Delaware courts heard arguments in a lawsuit between Disney shareholders and top executives over the $140 million severance agreement given to Michael Ovitz, who was courted by Eisner and then later let go when the two failed to achieve a working relationship.The case was described as a "test [of] whether directors can be held responsible for the outlandish pay of close colleagues" by the U.K. Telegraph, and with good reason. With $27 billion in 2003 revenue and 112,000 employees, Disney is the No. 2 media conglomerate in the world. It owns television stations, movie production companies and cable networks, in addition to Disneyland, Disneyworld, and other theme parks. In 1995, it became a mainstream media company with the $19 billion purchase of Capital Cities/ABC Inc. Since then, Disney has become one of the nation's biggest broadcast powers with 225 television affiliates across the country.

Unlike its current parent corporation, ABC began as an unwanted stepchild of sorts. It was established in the 1920s as the "Blue Network" part of General Electric's NBC radio. In 1941, the FCC ordered it to divest one of its networks, and the underperforming Blue was spun off and sold to Lifesavers candy king Edward Noble.

The new American Broadcasting Company struggled until its purchase by Paramount Studios (now part of Viacom) in 1951. In 1986 Capital Cities Communication, a major media conglomerate, bought the network. Nine years later, Disney took over. At the time, it was one of the largest media mergers in history.

ABC's relationship with Disney actually predates the purchase by decades. When Walt Disney was planning construction for his "Disneylandia" theme park in Anaheim, Calif., one of the investors who made his dream possible was ABC. The network invested $500,000 in 1954 and guaranteed Disney bank loans, in return receiving an ownership interest. Six years later, Disney easily bought out ABC's ownership interest and repaid the loans.

In addition to its affiliated stations, Disney owns 10 television stations and 74 radio stations. It also has considerable cable network holdings, including the Disney Channel, 80 percent of ESPN Inc., 38 percent of the A&E Television networks, and about 40 percent of E! Entertainment Television. Today, Disney ranks No. 60 on the Fortune magazine list of the 500 largest companies in America.

—John Dunbar, Robert Morlino

October 20, 2004

Sources: Hoover's Online, Fortune Magazine, ketupa.net media profiles, The Museum of Broadcast Communications, Walt Disney Co. Form 10-K, Philadelphia Inquirer, Salon.com, The Telegraph.

Walt Disney Co. Recent Financial Information		
Year	Revenue	Net Income (Net Loss)
2000	$25,325,000,000	$920,000,000
2001	$25,172,000,000	($158,000,000)
2002	$25,329,000,000	$1,236,000,000
2003	$27,061,000,000	$1,267,000,000

Walt Disney Co. Board of Directors				
Name	Position	Relevant Stock		Qty
Iger, Robert	Director		DIS	44,905
Bryson, John	Director		DIS	1,500
Estrin, Judith	Director		DIS	24,616
Lozano, Monica	Director		DIS	1,057
Matschullat, Robert	Director		DIS	8,000
Mitchell, George	Director		DIS	5,100
Watson, Raymond	Director		DIS	29,520
O'Donovan, Leo	Director		N/A	N/A
Eisner, Michael	Chairman and CEO		DIS	13,933,808
Chen, John	Director		DIS	5,793
Lewis, Aylwin	Director		DIS	1,100

Walt Disney Co. Corporate Officers			
Name	Position	Salary	Bonuses
Eisner, Michael	Chairman and CEO	$1,000,000	N/A
Iger, Robert	President, COO, and Director	$1,394,231	$4,000,000
Staggs, Thomas	SEVP and CFO	$841,827	$1,000,000
Murphy, Peter	SEVP and CSO	$841,827	$1,000,000
Braverman, Alan	SEVP and General Counsel	$685,291	$700,000

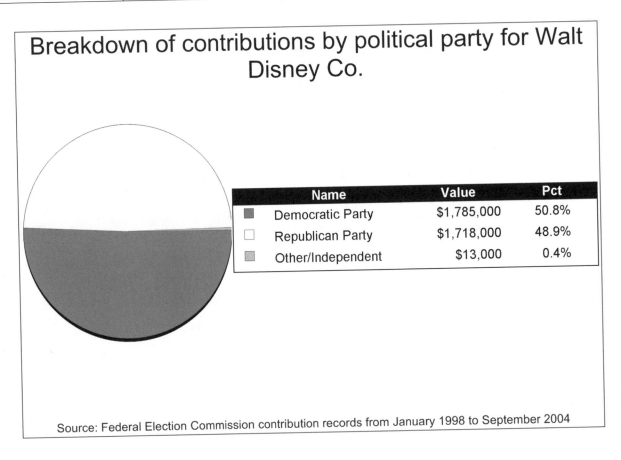

Breakdown of contributions by political party for Walt Disney Co.

Name	Value	Pct
Democratic Party	$1,785,000	50.8%
Republican Party	$1,718,000	48.9%
Other/Independent	$13,000	0.4%

Source: Federal Election Commission contribution records from January 1998 to September 2004

Top 10 Recipients of Contributions Sourced to Walt Disney Co.	
Recipient	Amount
National Republican Party Committees	$995,000
National Democratic Party Committees	$744,000
Sen John F Kerry (D-MA)	$60,000
Sen Hillary Rodham Clinton (D-NY)	$50,000
Sen Thomas Andrew Daschle (D-SD)	$50,000
Rep Howard L Berman (D-CA)	$47,000
Sen Bill Nelson (D-FL)	$43,000
Rep John D Dingell (D-MI)	$39,000
President George W Bush (R)	$38,000
Sen Patrick Joseph Leahy (D-VT)	$35,000
Total:	$2,101,000
Source: Federal Election Commission contribution records from January 1998 to September 2004	

Walt Disney Co. Lobbying Expenditures by Year	
Year	Amount
1998	$2,826,800
1999	$3,700,000
2000	$4,320,000
2001	$3,100,000
2002	$4,060,000
2003	$4,120,000
2004	$2,100,000
Total:	$24,226,800
Source: U.S. Senate Office of Public Records lobbying disclosure records from January 1998 to June 30th, 2004.	

Walt Disney Co. Sponsored Trips for Congressional Staff		
Congressional Office	Number of Trips	$ Amount
Rep John D Dingell (D-MI)	1	$6,295
Rep Wilbert J Tauzin, Jr (R-LA)	5	$5,032
Sen Tim Johnson (D-SD)	1	$2,483
Sen John F Kerry (D-MA)	1	$1,828
Sen Theodore F Stevens (R-AK)	1	$895
Sen Gordon Harold Smith (R-OR)	1	$571
Sen Byron L Dorgan (D-ND)	1	$571
Sen Donald Lee Nickles (R-OK)	1	$571
	1	$357
Total:	13	$18,602
Source: Congressional office travel records for members of the Senate Committee on Commerce, Science & Transportation and the House Committee on Energy and Commerce for the period of January 2000 to March 2004.		

Radio Station Subsidiaries for Walt Disney Co.				
State	City	Call Sign	Frequency	Subsidiary Name
AL	CITRONELLE	WQUA	102.1 FM Commercial	RADIO DISNEY GROUP, LLC
AR	LITTLE ROCK	KDIS-FM	99.5 FM Commercial	RADIO DISNEY GROUP, LLC
AZ	TEMPE	KMIK	1580 AM Station	RADIO DISNEY GROUP, LLC
CA	LOS ANGELES	KLOS	95.5 FM Commercial	KLOS-FM RADIO, INC.
CA	LOS ANGELES	KABC	790 AM Station	KABC-AM RADIO, INC.
CA	LOS ANGELES	KSPN	710 AM Station	KABC-AM RADIO, INC.
CA	OAKLAND	KMKY	1310 AM Station	KGO-AM RADIO, INC.
CA	PASADENA	KDIS	1110 AM Station	KABC-AM RADIO, INC.
CA	SACRAMENTO	KIID	1470 AM Station	RADIO DISNEY GROUP, LLC
CA	SAN FRANCISCO	KGO	810 AM Station	KGO-AM RADIO, INC.
CA	SAN FRANCISCO	KSFO	560 AM Station	KGO-AM RADIO, INC.
CO	ARVADA	KDDZ	1690 AM Station	RADIO DISNEY GROUP, LLC
CT	BLOOMFIELD	WDZK	1550 AM Station	RADIO DISNEY GROUP, LLC
DC	WASHINGTON	WMAL	630 AM Station	WMAL, INC.
DC	WASHINGTON	WRQX	107.3 FM Commercial	WMAL, INC.
FL	JACKSONVILLE	WBWL	600 AM Station	RADIO DISNEY GROUP, LLC
FL	MIAMI	WMYM	990 AM Station	RADIO DISNEY GROUP, LLC
FL	ORLANDO	WDYZ	990 AM Station	RADIO DISNEY GROUP, LLC
FL	RIVIERA BEACH	WMNE	1600 AM Station	RADIO DISNEY GROUP, LLC

\multicolumn{5}{c}{Radio Station Subsidiaries for Walt Disney Co.}
State	City	Call Sign	Frequency	Subsidiary Name
FL	ST. PETERSBURG	WWMI	1380 AM Station	RADIO DISNEY GROUP, LLC
GA	ATLANTA	WDWD	590 AM Station	RADIO DISNEY ATLANTA, LLC
GA	GAINSEVILLE	WYAY	106.7 FM Commercial	ABC RADIO ATLANTA, LLC
GA	MARIETTA	WKHX-FM	101.5 FM Commercial	ABC RADIO ATLANTA, LLC
IA	STORM LAKE	KAYL	990 AM Station	WMMP, LLC
IL	BELLEVILLE	WSDZ	1260 AM Station	RADIO DISNEY GROUP, LLC
IL	CHICAGO	WMVP	1000 AM Station	SPORTS RADIO CHICAGO, LLC
IL	CHICAGO	WLS	890 AM Station	WLS, INC.
IL	CHICAGO	WZZN	94.7 FM Commercial	ABC CHICAGO FM RADIO,INC.
IL	LA GRANGE	WRDZ	1300 AM Station	RADIO DISNEY CHICAGO, LLC
IN	PLAINFIELD	WRDZ-FM	98.3 FM Commercial	RADIO DISNEY GROUP, LLC
KS	WICHITA	KQAM	1480 AM Station	RADIO DISNEY GROUP, LLC
KY	NEWBURG	WDRD	680 AM Station	RADIO DISNEY GROUP, LLC
LA	NEW ORLEANS	WBYU	1450 AM Station	RADIO DISNEY GROUP, LLC
MA	BOSTON	WMKI	1260 AM Station	RADIO DISNEY GROUP, LLC
MI	DETROIT	WDRQ	93.1 FM Commercial	ABC RADIO DETROIT, LLC
MI	DETROIT	WJR	760 AM Station	ABC RADIO DETROIT, LLC
MI	DETROIT	WDVD	96.3 FM Commercial	ABC RADIO DETROIT, LLC
MI	FLINT	WFDF	910 AM Station	RADIO DISNEY GROUP, LLC
MN	CAMBRIDGE	WGVY	105.3 FM Commercial	KQRS, INC.
MN	EDEN PRAIRIE	WGVZ	105.7 FM Commercial	KQRS, INC.
MN	GOLDEN VALLEY	KDIZ	1440 AM Station	KQRS, INC.
MN	GOLDEN VALLEY	KQRS-FM	92.5 FM Commercial	KQRS, INC.
MN	LAKEVILLE	WGVX	105.1 FM Commercial	KQRS, INC.
MN	MINNEAPOLIS	KXXR	93.7 FM Commercial	KQRS, INC.
MO	KANSAS CITY	KPHN	1190 AM Station	RADIO DISNEY GROUP, LLC
NC	CHARLOTTE	WGFY	1480 AM Station	RADIO DISNEY GROUP, LLC
NJ	MOUNT HOLLY	WWJZ	640 AM Station	RADIO DISNEY GROUP, LLC
NM	LOS RANCHOS DE ALBUQ	KALY	1240 AM Station	RADIO DISNEY GROUP, LLC
NY	ALBANY	WDDY	1460 AM Station	RADIO DISNEY GROUP, LLC
NY	NEW YORK	WABC	770 AM Station	WABC-AM RADIO, INC.
NY	NEW YORK	WEPN	1050 AM Station	NEW YORK AM RADIO, LLC
NY	NEW YORK	WPLJ	95.5 FM Commercial	WPLJ-FM RADIO, INC.
OH	CLEVELAND	WWMK	1260 AM Station	RADIO DISNEY GROUP, LLC
OK	MUSKOGEE	KMUS	1380 AM Station	RADIO DISNEY GROUP, LLC
OR	LAKE OSWEGO	KDZR	1640 AM Station	RADIO DISNEY GROUP, LLC
OR	LAKE OSWEGO	KKSL	1290 AM Station	RADIO DISNEY GROUP, LLC
PA	PITTSBURGH	WEAE	1250 AM Station	SPORTS RADIO GROUP, LLC
RI	PAWTUCKET	WDDZ	550 AM Station	RADIO DISNEY GROUP, LLC
TX	ALLEN	KESN	103.3 FM Commercial	WBAP-KSCS OPERATING, LTD.
TX	FORT WORTH	WBAP	820 AM Station	WBAP-KSCS OPERATING, LTD.
TX	FORT WORTH	KSCS	96.3 FM Commercial	WBAP-KSCS OPERATING, LTD.
TX	HOUSTON	KMIC	1590 AM Station	RADIO DISNEY GROUP, LLC
TX	PLANO	KMKI	620 AM Station	RADIO DISNEY DALLAS, LLC
TX	SAN ANTONIO	KRDY	1160 AM Station	RADIO DISNEY GROUP, LLC
UT	SALT LAKE CITY	KWDZ	910 AM Station	RADIO DISNEY GROUP, LLC
VA	CLAREMONT	WPMH	670 AM Station	CHESAPEAKE-PORTSMOUTH BROADCASTING CORPORATION
VA	COLONIAL HEIGHTS	WDZY	1290 AM Station	RADIO DISNEY GROUP, LLC
VA	PORTSMOUTH	WHKT	1650 AM Station	RADIO DISNEY GROUP, LLC
VA	WOODBRIDGE	WJZW	105.9 FM Commercial	WMAL, INC.
WA	SEATTLE	KKDZ	1250 AM Station	WMAL, INC.
WI	SUSSEX	WKSH	1640 AM Station	RADIO DISNEY GROUP, LLC

\multicolumn{4}{c}{TV Station Subsidiaries for Walt Disney Co.}
Call Sign	Channel and Type	Subsidiary Name	Area of Service
KABC-TV	7 TV Commercial	ABC HOLDING COMPANY, INC.	LOS ANGELES, CA
WPVI-TV	6 TV Commercial	ABC, INC.	PHILADELPHIA, PA
WTVD	11 TV Commercial	ABC, INC.	DURHAM, NC
KFSN-TV	30 TV Commercial	ABC, INC.	FRESNO, CA
WABC-TV	7 TV Commercial	AMERICAN BROADCASTING COMPANIES, INC	NEW YORK, NY
WJRT-TV	12 TV Commercial	FLINT LICENSE SUBSIDIARY CORP.	FLINT, MI
KGO-TV	7 TV Commercial	KGO TELEVISION, INC.	SAN FRANCISCO, CA

TV Station Subsidiaries for Walt Disney Co.			
Call Sign	Channel and Type	Subsidiary Name	Area of Service
KTRK-TV	13 TV Commercial	KTRK TELEVISION, INC.	HOUSTON, TX
WLS-TV	7 TV Commercial	WLS TELEVISION, INC.	CHICAGO, IL
WTVG	13 TV Commercial	WTVG, INC.	TOLEDO, OH

Western Wireless Corp.

Address:	3650 131st Ave. SE	Stock Symbol:	WWCA
	Ste. 400	Telephone:	425-586-8700
	Bellevue, WA 98006	Fax:	425-586-8666
Total Employees:	2,357	Website:	www.wwireless.com

Western Wireless Corp. is the cellular provider that covers the widest geographical area of any company—a full 25 percent of the country is serviced under its Western Wireless and CellularONE brands. Yet for most of the company's 10-year history, it has failed to turn a profit. Part of the problem: the company targets an area of the country where the average population density is 11 people per square mile. (By comparison, New York City has 23,700 people per square mile.)

That equates to a large number of cell phone towers for a small number of customers.

But the company that cellular pioneer John Stanton formed to deliver wireless technology to the American West has held steady during the past decade and is showing increasing viability as it expands into the international market.

Stanton, who has spent the past 20 years wheeling and dealing in the cellular phone industry, formed Western Wireless Corp. in 1994 out of two startups he founded—General Cellular and Pacific Northwest Cellular.

In 1995, Western Wireless won Federal Communications Commission auctions for wireless personal communications service (PCS) licenses for Portland, Honolulu, Albuquerque, El Paso, Des Moines, Oklahoma City and Salt Lake City. In 1996, the company completed an initial public offering and two bond offerings, raising $600 million. Later that year, Western Wireless launched service under the VoiceStream name in the seven markets where it held PCS licenses.

In 1998, Western Wireless established an alliance with Hong Kong-based Hutchison Whampoa Ltd., which invested $248.4 million in the company through a subsidiary.

In May 1999, VoiceStream Wireless was spun off from Western Wireless. Stanton kept his hand in the business, however. When VoiceStream was acquired by German telecom giant Deutsche Telekom in 2001, Stanton was named to head its U.S. wireless operations, now called T-Mobile.

Stanton also remained chairman and CEO of Western Wireless. Stanton and Theresa Gillespie, his wife and company vice chairman, own about 43 percent of Western Wireless's voting shares.

Although smaller than it had once been, Western Wireless remains the country's 10th largest wireless company, serving more than 1.2 million customers located primarily in rural areas of 19 western states. The company briefly went into the black with a $65 million profit in 2000, but lost $155 million and $186 million over the subsequent two years.

During the past year, Western Wireless began to significantly build up its international markets, helping bring the company to the brink of profit by the end of 2003, when its loss amounted to $338,000 on revenues of $1.5 billion. Currently operating in seven countries, the company has invested heavily in Austria. Revenues from international operations nearly doubled in the first quarter of 2004.

In its second-largest international market—Ireland—the company has been adding subscribers at a fast clip.

—Bob Williams, Robert Morlino

August 19, 2004

Sources: Company Web site, Securities and Exchange Commission filings, Yahoo! Finance Online, Seattle Times, Hoover's Online, Fortune magazine, Investor's Business Daily

Western Wireless Corp. Recent Financial Information		
Year	Revenue	Net Income (Net Loss)
2000	$834,954,000	$65,406,000
2001	$1,037,959,000	($155,077,000)
2002	$1,186,610,000	($185,681,000)
2003	$1,501,324,000	($338,000)

Western Wireless Corp. Board of Directors				
Name	Position	Relevant Stock		Qty
Stanton, John	Chairman		WWCA	12,076,881
Thomsen, Mikal	Director		WWCA	906,783
Gillespie, Theresa	Vice Chair		WWCA	12,076,881
Bunce, John	Director		WWCA	290,089
Cohen, Mitchell	Director		WWCA	44,567
Evans, Daniel	Director		V	29,119
Nelson, Jonathan	Director		WWCA	685,582
van Oppen, Peter	Director		WWCA	285,425
Phillips, Peggy	Director		N/A	N/A

Western Wireless Corp. Corporate Officers			
Name	Position	Salary	Bonuses
Stanton, John	Chairman, CEO, and Director	$300,000	N/A
Thomsen, Mikal	President, COO, and Director	$325,000	N/A
Gillespie, Theresa	Vice Chair	N/A	N/A
Hertz, Eric	COO	$325,000	N/A
Wisehart, Wayne	EVP and CFO	$221,667	$54,000

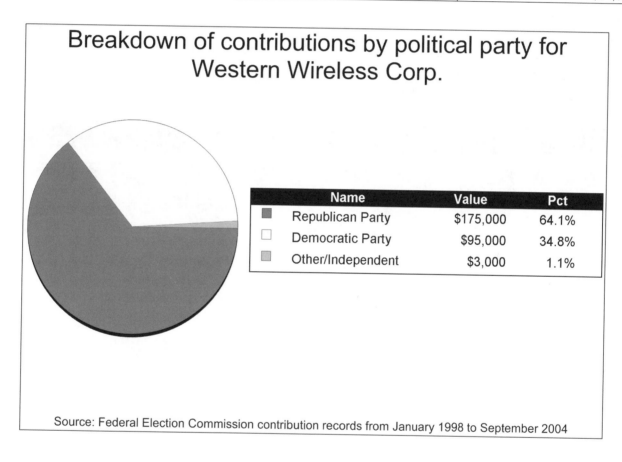

Breakdown of contributions by political party for Western Wireless Corp.

Name	Value	Pct
Republican Party	$175,000	64.1%
Democratic Party	$95,000	34.8%
Other/Independent	$3,000	1.1%

Source: Federal Election Commission contribution records from January 1998 to September 2004

Top 10 Recipients of Contributions Sourced to Western Wireless Corp.	
Recipient	Amount
National Republican Party Committees	$31,000
National Democratic Party Committees	$26,000
Rep J Dennis Hastert (R-IL)	$20,000
Sen Byron L Dorgan (D-ND)	$18,000
President George W Bush (R)	$14,000
Sen Slade Gorton (R-WA)	$11,000
Cathy McMorris (R-WA)	$10,000
Rep Jennifer B Dunn (R-WA)	$9,000
Sen John F Kerry (D-MA)	$8,000
Reichert, Dave	$8,000
Total:	$155,000
Source: Federal Election Commission contribution records from January 1998 to September 2004	

Western Wireless Corp. Lobbying Expenditures by Year	
Year	Amount
1998	$80,000
1999	$158,056
2000	$180,000
2001	$160,000
2002	$161,250
2003	$192,500
2004	$35,000
Total:	$966,806
Source: U.S. Senate Office of Public Records lobbying disclosure records from January 1998 to June 30th, 2004.	

Western Wireless Corp. Sponsored Trips for Congressional Staff		
Congressional Office	Number of Trips	$ Amount
Sen Conrad R Burns (R-MT)	1	$92
Total:	1	$92
Source: Congressional office travel records for members of the Senate Committee on Commerce, Science & Transportation and the House Committee on Energy and Commerce for the period of January 2000 to March 2004.		

XM Satellite Radio Holdings Inc.

Address:	1500 Eckington Place NE	Stock Symbol:	XMSR
	Washington, DC 20002	Telephone:	202-380-4000
		Fax:	202-380-4500
Total Employees:	425	Website:	www.xmradio.com

When radio giant Clear Channel Communications Inc. dropped the Howard Stern Show from six of its stations in the face of pending indecency fines from the FCC, the shock jock made the announcement that was music to XM Satellite Radio Holdings Inc.'s ears: In light of the increasingly hostile climate on broadcast radio, he would be exploring a future at one of the two major satellite radio providers.

Unfortunately for XM, he chose Sirius. Nevertheless, the publicity leading up to the choice was good for the company. In the second quarter of 2004, XM signed up 418,449 new subscribers, adding to its overall customer base, which now stand at more than 2.5 million. That's well ahead of the 700,000 subscribers of its only competitor, Sirius Satellite Radio Inc.Then in October, XM responded to the Stern loss by entering into an agreement with Major League Baseball to broadcast all regular season and play-off games, beginning in 2005. XM paid $650 million for the 11-year deal, a potentially better bargain than the $500 million Sirius for just five years of Howard Stern—if it translates into subscribers.

Washington, D.C.-based XM and its two satellites (one named Rock, one named Roll) offer more than 120 digital channels - including 68 commercial-free music stations - to homes and automobiles all over America for $9.99 a month.

XM began as American Mobile Radio Corp. in 1992. In 1997, it was granted a license by the FCC for a digital audio radio service. A year later, it entered into a contract with then-GM subsidiary Hughes Space and Communications International to build two satellites. In 1998 the company hired CEO Hugh Panero, who has guided the company through its considerable growing pains.

In July 1999, the company got a big financial boost of $250 million, including $50 million from GM and $75 million from broadcast radio giant Clear Channel Communications Inc. Shortly after, the company held a public offering and it was off to the races. The service was officially launched in September 2001 in Dallas and San Diego.

Some analysts were unconvinced that the company would convince people to pay for something they have been getting for free most of their lives. But XM offers some real advantages over commercial radio. First, the sound is digital and crisp. Unlike regular radio, you can't drive out of a station's coverage area. The program offerings are diverse, ranging from every imaginable music genre to news and sports offerings.

In addition, because the service is subscriber-based and not broadcast on public airwaves, content that would never see the light of day on free radio is available for customers. Thus the decades-worth of content that earned Howard Stern the title of preeminent shock-jock would pale in comparison to what he could do in such an environment.

The company's target audience is the "200 million-plus" automobile and truck drivers on the highways as well as home radio users. Along the way, XM has managed to attract a continuing flow of investment, and has made some important partnerships. Early in 2003, the company was able to defer payment of $250 million in debt and raise $225 million in new investment from GM and others.

Its two biggest investors are GM and American Honda Motor Company. Both firms are offering satellite radio as an option in new cars.

Despite its lagging numbers, Sirius isn't backing down, unveiling aggressive marketing plans in 2004, including exclusive agreements with Ford, BMW and Daimler-Chrysler.

XM's soaring subscriber rates notwithstanding, the company has a long way to go before making a profit. In 2003, it brought in nearly $92 million but netted a loss of more than $584 million.

—John Dunbar, Robert Morlino

October 20, 2004

Sources: XM Satellite Radio Web site, New York Times, Barron's.

XM Satellite Radio Holdings Inc. Recent Financial Information		
Year	Revenue	Net Income (Net Loss)
2001	$533,000	($284,379,000)
2002	$20,181,000	($495,012,000)
2003	$91,781,000	($585,535,000)

XM Satellite Radio Holdings Inc. Board of Directors				
Name	Position	Relevant Stock		Qty
Parsons, Gary	Chairman		XMSR	848,168
Panero, Hugh	Director		XMSR	978,796
Davis, Nathaniel	Director		XMSR	80,257
Donohue, Thomas	Director		XMSR	66,757
Huber, Chester	Director		N/A	N/A
Roberts, Pierce	Director		XMSR	120,312
Shaw, Jack	Director		XMSR	36,757
Elliott, Thomas	Director		N/A	N/A
Mohn, Jarl	Director		XMSR	500
Haywood, George	Director		XMSR	6,012,500

XM Satellite Radio Holdings Inc. Corporate Officers			
Name	Position	Salary	Bonuses
Parsons, Gary	Chairman	$250,000	$500,000
Panero, Hugh	President, CEO, Director	$412,000	$412,000
Cook, Stephen	EVP Sales, Marketing, and Customer Operations	$246,846	$125,150
Euteneuer, Joseph	EVP, CFO	$342,207	$134,108
Patsiokas, Stelios	EVP, Engineering and Technology	$271,920	$122,799

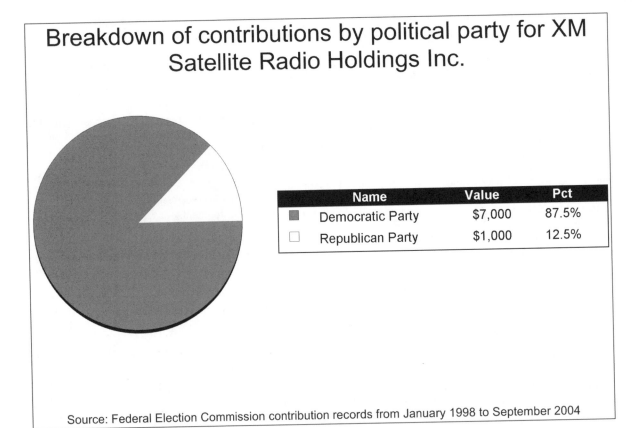

Breakdown of contributions by political party for XM Satellite Radio Holdings Inc.

Name	Value	Pct
Democratic Party	$7,000	87.5%
Republican Party	$1,000	12.5%

Source: Federal Election Commission contribution records from January 1998 to September 2004

Top 10 Recipients of Contributions Sourced to XM Satellite Radio Holdings Inc.	
Recipient	Amount
	$2,000
Rep Peter Russell Deutsch (D-FL)	$2,000
Howard Dean (D)	$1,000
Rep Thomas M Davis (R-VA)	$1,000
Sen Barack H Obama (D-IL)	$1,000
Sen John F Kerry (D-MA)	$1,000
Sen Tim Johnson (D-SD)	$1,000
Total:	$8,000

Source: Federal Election Commission contribution records from January 1998 to September 2004

| XM Satellite Radio Holdings Inc. Lobbying Expenditures by Year ||
Year	Amount
1998	$40,000
2002	$200,000
2003	$120,000
2004	$80,000
Total:	$440,000
Source: U.S. Senate Office of Public Records lobbying disclosure records from January 1998 to June 30th, 2004.	

Appendix B
Commerce Committee Members – 108th Congress (2003-2004)

Two committees in Congress oversee virtually all issues regarding broadcasting and telecommunications in the United States: the House Committee on Energy and Commerce and the Senate Committee on Commerce, Science & Transportation.

In an effort to gauge how much influence industry has over these committees, the Center has collected and categorized information about contributions from broadcasting, cable and telecommunications companies dating back to 1998.

We have also collected data on industry-sponsored trips taken by members of these committees.

To learn more, and to find an online searchable database of industry influence on Congress, please go to: www.publicintegrity.org/telecom/ or www.openairwaves.org.

House Committee on Energy and Commerce (2003-2004)

Allen, Tom

Representative (D-ME)

House Committee on Energy and Commerce

1717 Longworth House Office Building
Washington, DC 20515
Phone: (202) 225-6116
Fax: (202) 225-5590

Web Page: http://tomallen.house.gov/
Email: http://tomallen.house.gov/smartemail.asp

Contribution Summary By Telecommunications Sector	
Union	$38,000
Phones	$16,575
PayTV - Cable	$8,000
Broadcast	$4,500
Total:	$67,075
Source: Federal Election Commission contribution records from January 1998 to September 2004	

Contributions by Telecommunications Sector Organizations				
Company	Sector	#	Total	Avg.
International Brotherhood of Electrical Workers (IBEW)	Union	9	$36,000	$4,000
Verizon Communications Inc.	Phones	12	$9,326	$777
National Cable and Telecommunications Association	PayTV - Cable	1	$5,000	$5,000
Time Warner	PayTV - Cable	3	$3,000	$1,000
SBC Communications Inc.	Phones	2	$2,500	$1,250
National Association of Broadcasters	Broadcast	3	$2,000	$667
AT&T Wireless	Phones	3	$1,500	$500
General Electric Co.	Broadcast	3	$1,500	$500
Communications Workers of America	Union	1	$1,000	$1,000
Transportation Communications International Union	Union	2	$1,000	$500
Cingular Wireless	Phones	1	$1,000	$1,000
United States Cellular Corp.	Phones	2	$1,000	$500
Viacom Inc.	Broadcast	1	$1,000	$1,000
United States Telecom Association	Phones	2	$999	$500
AT&T Corp.	Phones	1	$250	$250
		Total:	$67,075	
Source: Federal Election Commission contribution records from January 1998 to September 2004				

Barton, Joe

Representative (R-TX)

House Committee on Energy and Commerce

Chairman; ex officio member of Subcommittee

2109 Rayburn House Office Building
Washington, DC 20515
Phone: (202) 225-2002
Fax: (202) 225-3052

Web Page: http://joebarton.house.gov/
Email: http://joebarton.house.gov/contact.asp

Contribution Summary By Telecommunications Sector	
Phones	$172,634
PayTV - Cable	$72,155
Broadcast	$70,212
Other	$6,500
PayTV - Satellite	$2,000
Satellite	$1,000
Total:	$324,501

Source: Federal Election Commission contribution records from January 1998 to September 2004

Contributions by Telecommunications Sector Organizations				
Company	Sector	#	Total	Avg.
SBC Communications Inc.	Phones	19	$37,034	$1,949
National Cable and Telecommunications Association	PayTV - Cable	10	$35,305	$3,531
Verizon Communications Inc.	Phones	25	$27,550	$1,102
General Electric Co.	Broadcast	20	$27,500	$1,375
Cingular Wireless	Phones	21	$26,750	$1,274
Comcast Corp.	PayTV - Cable	13	$15,300	$1,177
Viacom Inc.	Broadcast	12	$13,500	$1,125
AT&T Wireless	Phones	13	$11,000	$846
Qwest Communications International Inc.	Phones	8	$11,000	$1,375
Time Warner	PayTV - Cable	6	$9,500	$1,583
MCI (formerly WorldCom Inc.)	Phones	4	$8,000	$2,000
Sprint Corp.	Phones	7	$7,800	$1,114
News Corp Ltd.	Broadcast	6	$6,562	$1,094
National Association of Broadcasters	Broadcast	5	$6,500	$1,300
Charter Communications Inc.	PayTV - Cable	4	$6,500	$1,625
United States Telecom Association	Phones	5	$6,500	$1,300
Clear Channel Communications Inc.	Broadcast	3	$6,000	$2,000
Deutsche Telekom AG (T-Mobile)	Phones	2	$6,000	$3,000
ALLTEL Corp.	Phones	8	$6,000	$750
Walt Disney Co.	Broadcast	2	$5,000	$2,500
Western Wireless Corp.	Phones	2	$5,000	$2,500
Telephone Electronics Corp.	Phones	6	$4,750	$792
Cellular Telecommunications & Internet Association	Phones	4	$4,000	$1,000
VALOR Telecommunications	Phones	5	$3,750	$750
Level 3 Communications Inc.	Other	3	$3,500	$1,167
IDT Corp.	Other	3	$3,000	$1,000
AirTouch Communications Inc.	Phones	3	$3,000	$1,000
LIN TV Corp.	Broadcast	9	$2,750	$306
American Cable Association	PayTV - Cable	2	$2,500	$1,250
Cox Communications Inc.	PayTV - Cable	3	$2,000	$667
Echostar Corp.	PayTV - Satellite	2	$2,000	$1,000
National Telephone Cooperative Association	Phones	2	$2,000	$1,000
AT&T Corp.	Phones	1	$1,000	$1,000
Adelphia Communications Corp.	PayTV - Cable	1	$1,000	$1,000
Gannett Co. Inc.	Broadcast	1	$1,000	$1,000
Liberty Media Corp.	Broadcast	1	$1,000	$1,000
Loral Space & Communications Ltd.	Satellite	1	$1,000	$1,000
Association for Local Telecommunications Services	Phones	1	$500	$500
Focal Communications Corp.	Phones	1	$500	$500
Covad Communications Co.	Phones	1	$500	$500
Belo Corp.	Broadcast	1	$400	$400
SAVVIS Communications Corp.	PayTV - Cable	1	$50	$50
	Total:		$324,501	

Source: Federal Election Commission contribution records from January 1998 to September 2004

Telecommunications Company Provided Trips to Committee Member's Staff			
Company	Sector	#	Total $
National Association of Broadcasters	Broadcast	1	$5,102
National Cable and Telecommunications Association	PayTV - Cable	2	$3,105
News Corp Ltd.	Broadcast	2	$2,779
United States Telecom Association	Phones	1	$1,974
BellSouth Corp.	Phones	1	$921
Total:		7	$13,882

Source: Congressional office travel records for members of the Senate Committee on Commerce, Science & Transportation and the House Committee on Energy and Commerce for the period of January 2000 to March 2004.

Trips by Committee Member's Staff Sponsored by the Telecommunications Industry		
Individual	#	Total $
Barton, Joe	3	$8,482
Stansell, Heather	1	$1,699
Zerzan, Kelly	1	$1,504
Fried, Neil	1	$1,275
Couri, Heather	1	$921
Total:	7	$13,882

Source: Congressional office travel records for members of the Senate Committee on Commerce, Science & Transportation and the House Committee on Energy and Commerce for the period of January 2000 to March 2004.

Bass, Charles F.

Representative (R-NH)

House Committee on Energy and Commerce

2421 Rayburn House Office Building
Washington, DC 20515
Phone: (202) 225-5206
Fax: (202) 225-2946

Web Page: http://www.house.gov/bass/
Email: http://www.house.gov/bass/guestbook.html

Contribution Summary By Telecommunications Sector	
Phones	$57,729
PayTV - Cable	$16,720
Broadcast	$10,300
PayTV - Satellite	$3,000
Satellite	$500
Total:	$88,249

Source: Federal Election Commission contribution records from January 1998 to September 2004

Contributions by Telecommunications Sector Organizations				
Company	Sector	#	Total	Avg.
Verizon Communications Inc.	Phones	26	$24,500	$942
SBC Communications Inc.	Phones	11	$14,000	$1,273
National Cable and Telecommunications Association	PayTV - Cable	6	$13,720	$2,287
Cingular Wireless	Phones	8	$8,000	$1,000
General Electric Co.	Broadcast	12	$6,300	$525
United States Telecom Association	Phones	6	$5,229	$872
Qwest Communications International Inc.	Phones	4	$4,000	$1,000
Echostar Corp.	PayTV - Satellite	2	$3,000	$1,500
AT&T Corp.	Phones	5	$2,500	$500
Time Warner	PayTV - Cable	2	$2,000	$1,000
Clear Channel Communications Inc.	Broadcast	2	$2,000	$1,000
National Association of Broadcasters	Broadcast	1	$1,000	$1,000
Viacom Inc.	Broadcast	1	$1,000	$1,000
Charter Communications Inc.	PayTV - Cable	1	$500	$500
Comcast Corp.	PayTV - Cable	1	$500	$500
Motorola Inc.	Satellite	1	$500	$500
Cellular Telecommunications & Internet Association	Phones	1	($500)	($500)
		Total:	$88,249	

Source: Federal Election Commission contribution records from January 1998 to September 2004

Telecommunications Company Provided Trips to Committee Member's Staff			
Company	Sector	#	Total $
National Cable and Telecommunications Association	PayTV - Cable	1	$2,456
Comcast Corp.	PayTV - Cable	1	$517
	Total:	2	$2,974

Source: Congressional office travel records for members of the Senate Committee on Commerce, Science & Transportation and the House Committee on Energy and Commerce for the period of January 2000 to March 2004.

Trips by Committee Member's Staff Sponsored by the Telecommunications Industry		
Individual	#	Total $
Bass, Charles	1	$2,456
Furtado, Tad	1	$517
Total:	2	$2,974

Source: Congressional office travel records for members of the Senate Committee on Commerce, Science & Transportation and the House Committee on Energy and Commerce for the period of January 2000 to March 2004.

Bilirakis, Michael

Representative (R-FL)

House Committee on Energy and Commerce

2269 Rayburn House Office Building
Washington, DC 20515
Phone: (202) 225-5755
Fax:

Web Page: http://www.house.gov/bilirakis/
Email: http://www.house.gov/writerep

Contribution Summary By Telecommunications Sector	
Phones	$48,050
PayTV - Cable	$23,499
Broadcast	$16,500
PayTV - Satellite	$2,000
Total:	$90,049

Source: Federal Election Commission contribution records from January 1998 to September 2004

Contributions by Telecommunications Sector Organizations				
Company	Sector	#	Total	Avg.
National Cable and Telecommunications Association	PayTV - Cable	5	$17,499	$3,500
Verizon Communications Inc.	Phones	18	$16,000	$889
Cingular Wireless	Phones	14	$13,000	$929
BellSouth Corp.	Phones	4	$6,500	$1,625
Pappas Telecasting Cos.	Broadcast	5	$5,000	$1,000
SBC Communications Inc.	Phones	5	$5,000	$1,000
General Electric Co.	Broadcast	4	$4,000	$1,000
Time Warner	PayTV - Cable	4	$4,000	$1,000
Viacom Inc.	Broadcast	3	$3,000	$1,000
ALLTEL Corp.	Phones	3	$3,000	$1,000
National Association of Broadcasters	Broadcast	3	$3,000	$1,000
Adelphia Communications Corp.	PayTV - Cable	2	$2,000	$1,000
Echostar Corp.	PayTV - Satellite	2	$2,000	$1,000
Paxson Communications Corp.	Broadcast	1	$1,000	$1,000
AT&T Wireless	Phones	1	$1,000	$1,000
Cellular Telecommunications & Internet Association	Phones	2	$1,000	$500
MCI (formerly WorldCom Inc.)	Phones	1	$1,000	$1,000
AT&T Corp.	Phones	2	$550	$275
Meredith Corp.	Broadcast	1	$500	$500
Sprint Corp.	Phones	1	$500	$500
United States Telecom Association	Phones	1	$500	$500
	Total:		$90,049	

Source: Federal Election Commission contribution records from January 1998 to September 2004

Telecommunications Company Provided Trips to Committee Member's Staff			
Company	Sector	#	Total $
National Cable and Telecommunications Association	PayTV - Cable	1	$4,810
BellSouth Corp.	Phones	1	$1,503
	Total:	2	$6,313

Source: Congressional office travel records for members of the Senate Committee on Commerce, Science & Transportation and the House Committee on Energy and Commerce for the period of January 2000 to March 2004.

Trips by Committee Member's Staff Sponsored by the Telecommunications Industry		
Individual	#	Total $
Bilirakis, Michael	1	$4,810
Hyder, Rebecca	1	$1,503
Total:	2	$6,313

Source: Congressional office travel records for members of the Senate Committee on Commerce, Science & Transportation and the House Committee on Energy and Commerce for the period of January 2000 to March 2004.

Bono, Mary

Representative (R-CA)

House Committee on Energy and Commerce

404 Cannon House Office Building
Washington, DC 20515
Phone: (202) 225-5330
Fax: (202) 225-2961

Web Page: http://www.house.gov/bono/
Email: http://www.house.gov/bono/contact.html

Contribution Summary By Telecommunications Sector	
Phones	$71,604
Broadcast	$32,000
PayTV - Cable	$15,250
Total:	$118,854
Source: Federal Election Commission contribution records from January 1998 to September 2004	

Contributions by Telecommunications Sector Organizations				
Company	Sector	#	Total	Avg.
SBC Communications Inc.	Phones	15	$24,750	$1,650
Cingular Wireless	Phones	12	$14,500	$1,208
General Electric Co.	Broadcast	10	$11,000	$1,100
Verizon Communications Inc.	Phones	8	$10,500	$1,313
National Cable and Telecommunications Association	PayTV - Cable	2	$8,500	$4,250
United States Telecom Association	Phones	8	$7,354	$919
AT&T Wireless	Phones	9	$6,000	$667
Time Warner	PayTV - Cable	5	$5,750	$1,150
Clear Channel Communications Inc.	Broadcast	2	$5,000	$2,500
Walt Disney Co.	Broadcast	6	$5,000	$833
Viacom Inc.	Broadcast	4	$3,500	$875
News Corp Ltd.	Broadcast	5	$3,500	$700
Qwest Communications International Inc.	Phones	2	$3,000	$1,500
National Association of Broadcasters	Broadcast	4	$2,500	$625
Deutsche Telekom AG (T-Mobile)	Phones	2	$2,000	$1,000
MCI (formerly WorldCom Inc.)	Phones	2	$1,500	$750
Univision Communications Inc.	Broadcast	2	$1,500	$750
Comcast Corp.	PayTV - Cable	1	$1,000	$1,000
ALLTEL Corp.	Phones	1	$1,000	$1,000
Cellular Telecommunications & Internet Association	Phones	1	$500	$500
CenturyTel Inc.	Phones	1	$500	$500
		Total:	$118,854	
Source: Federal Election Commission contribution records from January 1998 to September 2004				

Telecommunications Company Provided Trips to Committee Member's Staff			
Company	Sector	#	Total $
SBC Communications Inc.	Phones	3	$4,471
News Corp Ltd.	Broadcast	1	$2,358
United States Telecom Association	Phones	1	$1,528
BellSouth Corp.	Phones	1	$841
	Total:	6	$9,198
Source: Congressional office travel records for members of the Senate Committee on Commerce, Science & Transportation and the House Committee on Energy and Commerce for the period of January 2000 to March 2004.			

Trips by Committee Member's Staff Sponsored by the Telecommunications Industry		
Individual	#	Total $
Sullivan, Michael	3	$5,820
Hall, James	1	$1,546
Cullen, Frank	1	$990
Baird, Jennifer	1	$841
Total:	6	$9,198
Source: Congressional office travel records for members of the Senate Committee on Commerce, Science & Transportation and the House Committee on Energy and Commerce for the period of January 2000 to March 2004.		

Boucher, Rick

Representative (D-VA)

House Committee on Energy and Commerce

2187 Rayburn House Office Building
Washington, DC 20515
Phone: (202) 225-3861
Fax: (202) 225-0442

Web Page: http://www.house.gov/boucher/
Email: Ninthnet@mail.house.gov

Contribution Summary By Telecommunications Sector	
Phones	$195,960
Broadcast	$38,800
Union	$27,000
PayTV - Satellite	$19,000
PayTV - Cable	$17,719
Satellite	$7,000
Other	$3,750
Total:	$309,229
Source: Federal Election Commission contribution records from January 1998 to September 2004	

Contributions by Telecommunications Sector Organizations				
Company	Sector	#	Total	Avg.
Verizon Communications Inc.	Phones	38	$48,312	$1,271
SBC Communications Inc.	Phones	29	$44,000	$1,517
Cingular Wireless	Phones	23	$31,500	$1,370
United States Telecom Association	Phones	17	$15,142	$891
National Association of Broadcasters	Broadcast	12	$14,500	$1,208
Communications Workers of America	Union	6	$13,500	$2,250
International Brotherhood of Electrical Workers (IBEW)	Union	7	$13,000	$1,857
ALLTEL Corp.	Phones	12	$11,250	$938
Qwest Communications International Inc.	Phones	11	$10,500	$955
Walt Disney Co.	Broadcast	8	$10,000	$1,250
Echostar Corp.	PayTV - Satellite	10	$10,000	$1,000
Cellular Telecommunications & Internet Association	Phones	13	$9,256	$712
The DirecTV Group Inc.	PayTV - Satellite	11	$9,000	$818
Time Warner	PayTV - Cable	9	$8,720	$969
National Cable and Telecommunications Association	PayTV - Cable	3	$8,499	$2,833
General Electric Co.	Broadcast	8	$6,000	$750
AT&T Wireless	Phones	6	$5,000	$833
Satellite Broadcasting & Communication Association	Satellite	5	$4,000	$800
MCI (formerly WorldCom Inc.)	Phones	6	$3,500	$583
Clear Channel Communications Inc.	Broadcast	3	$3,500	$1,167
Teligent	Phones	5	$3,000	$600
Western Wireless Corp.	Phones	3	$3,000	$1,000
Motorola Inc.	Satellite	3	$2,500	$833
AirTouch Communications Inc.	Phones	3	$2,500	$833
News Corp Ltd.	Broadcast	3	$2,000	$667
Deutsche Telekom AG (T-Mobile)	Phones	2	$2,000	$1,000
Gannett Co. Inc.	Broadcast	3	$1,800	$600
IDT Corp.	Other	2	$1,500	$750
United States Cellular Corp.	Phones	2	$1,500	$750
National Telephone Cooperative Association	Phones	3	$1,500	$500
Sprint Corp.	Phones	1	$1,000	$1,000
Cincinnati Bell Inc.	Phones	2	$1,000	$500
BellSouth Corp.	Phones	1	$1,000	$1,000
Level 3 Communications Inc.	Other	1	$1,000	$1,000
Misc. telecom interests	Other	2	$750	$375
Adelphia Communications Corp.	PayTV - Cable	1	$500	$500
Computer & Communications Industry Association	Other	1	$500	$500
Paxson Communications Corp.	Broadcast	1	$500	$500
Sinclair Broadcast Group Inc.	Broadcast	1	$500	$500
CenturyTel Inc.	Phones	1	$500	$500
ICG Communications Inc.	Phones	1	$500	$500

Contributions by Telecommunications Sector Organizations				
Company	Sector	#	Total	Avg.
Loral Space & Communications Ltd.	Satellite	1	$500	$500
Transportation Communications International Union	Union	1	$500	$500
		Total:	$309,229	
Source: Federal Election Commission contribution records from January 1998 to September 2004				

Telecommunications Company Provided Trips to Committee Member's Staff			
Company	Sector	#	Total $
United States Telecom Association	Phones	4	$4,606
National Cable and Telecommunications Association	PayTV - Cable	2	$3,543
Cellular Telecommunications & Internet Association	Phones	2	$2,713
Time Warner	PayTV - Cable	2	$2,644
National Association of Broadcasters	Broadcast	1	$1,761
Verizon Communications Inc.	Phones	1	$750
Comcast Corp.	PayTV - Cable	1	$518
Media General Corp.	Broadcast	1	$400
	Total:	14	$16,935
Source: Congressional office travel records for members of the Senate Committee on Commerce, Science & Transportation and the House Committee on Energy and Commerce for the period of January 2000 to March 2004.			

Trips by Committee Member's Staff Sponsored by the Telecommunications Industry		
Individual	#	Total $
Mikes, Johanna	6	$8,474
Boucher, Rick	6	$6,362
Brill, Hillary	2	$2,099
Total:	14	$16,935
Source: Congressional office travel records for members of the Senate Committee on Commerce, Science & Transportation and the House Committee on Energy and Commerce for the period of January 2000 to March 2004.		

Brown, Sherrod

Representative (D-OH)

House Committee on Energy and Commerce

2332 Rayburn House Office Building
Washington, DC 20515
Phone: (202) 225-3401
Fax: (202) 225-2266

Web Page: http://www.house.gov/sherrodbrown/
Email: sherrod@mail.house.gov

Contribution Summary By Telecommunications Sector	
Union	$80,000
Phones	$53,999
PayTV - Cable	$29,354
Broadcast	$9,000
PayTV - Satellite	-
Total:	$172,353
Source: Federal Election Commission contribution records from January 1998 to September 2004	

Contributions by Telecommunications Sector Organizations				
Company	Sector	#	Total	Avg.
International Brotherhood of Electrical Workers (IBEW)	Union	8	$40,000	$5,000
Communications Workers of America	Union	11	$37,000	$3,364
National Cable and Telecommunications Association	PayTV - Cable	8	$19,354	$2,419
AT&T Wireless	Phones	15	$9,999	$667
MCI (formerly WorldCom Inc.)	Phones	10	$9,500	$950
Sprint Corp.	Phones	13	$9,500	$731
SBC Communications Inc.	Phones	8	$7,500	$938
National Association of Broadcasters	Broadcast	6	$5,000	$833
Time Warner	PayTV - Cable	3	$4,000	$1,333
ALLTEL Corp.	Phones	4	$4,000	$1,000
General Electric Co.	Broadcast	6	$3,500	$583
Adelphia Communications Corp.	PayTV - Cable	2	$3,000	$1,500
Transportation Communications International Union	Union	6	$3,000	$500
Qwest Communications International Inc.	Phones	3	$2,500	$833
AT&T Corp.	Phones	3	$2,250	$750
Cincinnati Bell Inc.	Phones	1	$2,000	$2,000
Verizon Communications Inc.	Phones	2	$1,500	$750
Cingular Wireless	Phones	1	$1,000	$1,000
Covad Communications Co.	Phones	1	$1,000	$1,000
AirTouch Communications Inc.	Phones	2	$1,000	$500
CenturyTel Inc.	Phones	1	$1,000	$1,000
Cox Communications Inc.	PayTV - Cable	1	$1,000	$1,000
SAVVIS Communications Corp.	PayTV - Cable	1	$1,000	$1,000
American Cable Association	PayTV - Cable	1	$500	$500
Comcast Corp.	PayTV - Cable	1	$500	$500
News Corp Ltd.	Broadcast	1	$500	$500
Association for Local Telecommunications Services	Phones	1	$500	$500
National Telephone Cooperative Association	Phones	1	$500	$500
XO Communications Inc.	Phones	1	$250	$250
The DirecTV Group Inc.	PayTV - Satellite	2	-	-
Total:			$172,353	
Source: Federal Election Commission contribution records from January 1998 to September 2004				

Burr, Richard

Representative (R-NC)

House Committee on Energy and Commerce

Vice Chairman

1526 Longworth House Office Building
Washington, DC 20515
Phone: (202) 225-2071
Fax: (202) 225-2995

Web Page: http://www.house.gov/burr/
Email: Richard.BurrNC05@mail.house.gov

Contribution Summary By Telecommunications Sector	
Phones	$152,295
Broadcast	$78,919
PayTV - Cable	$24,930
Other	$5,500
PayTV - Satellite	$4,900
Satellite	$500
Total:	$267,044

Source: Federal Election Commission contribution records from January 1998 to September 2004

Contributions by Telecommunications Sector Organizations				
Company	Sector	#	Total	Avg.
BellSouth Corp.	Phones	32	$33,700	$1,053
National Association of Broadcasters	Broadcast	14	$33,100	$2,364
SBC Communications Inc.	Phones	15	$22,850	$1,523
General Electric Co.	Broadcast	24	$21,450	$894
Cingular Wireless	Phones	15	$21,250	$1,417
Verizon Communications Inc.	Phones	13	$20,500	$1,577
Salem Communications Corp.	PayTV - Cable	8	$13,000	$1,625
Qwest Communications International Inc.	Phones	10	$12,000	$1,200
ALLTEL Corp.	Phones	10	$11,445	$1,145
Clear Channel Communications Inc.	Broadcast	7	$9,419	$1,346
AT&T Wireless	Phones	11	$9,000	$818
United States Telecom Association	Phones	11	$7,750	$705
Sprint Corp.	Phones	7	$7,000	$1,000
Walt Disney Co.	Broadcast	4	$7,000	$1,750
National Cable and Telecommunications Association	PayTV - Cable	4	$6,430	$1,608
IDT Corp.	Other	1	$5,000	$5,000
Echostar Corp.	PayTV - Satellite	3	$4,900	$1,633
Time Warner	PayTV - Cable	5	$4,500	$900
Cellular Telecommunications & Internet Association	Phones	4	$3,200	$800
News Corp Ltd.	Broadcast	1	$2,000	$2,000
Sinclair Broadcast Group Inc.	Broadcast	2	$2,000	$1,000
Tribune Co.	Broadcast	6	$1,750	$292
Deutsche Telekom AG (T-Mobile)	Phones	2	$1,500	$750
Hearst Corp.	Broadcast	2	$1,200	$600
AT&T Corp.	Phones	2	$1,000	$500
Viacom Inc.	Broadcast	1	$1,000	$1,000
MCI (formerly WorldCom Inc.)	Phones	1	$1,000	$1,000
Motorola Inc.	Satellite	1	$500	$500
Telecommunications Industry Association	Other	1	$500	$500
American Cable Association	PayTV - Cable	1	$500	$500
Charter Communications Inc.	PayTV - Cable	1	$500	$500
United States Cellular Corp.	Phones	1	$100	$100
	Total:		$267,044	

Source: Federal Election Commission contribution records from January 1998 to September 2004

Telecommunications Company Provided Trips to Committee Member's Staff			
Company	Sector	#	Total $
National Association of Broadcasters	Broadcast	1	$3,415
National Cable and Telecommunications Association	PayTV - Cable	2	$2,946
United States Telecom Association	Phones	2	$2,503
SBC Communications Inc.	Phones	1	$1,838
	Total:	6	$10,703

Source: Congressional office travel records for members of the Senate Committee on Commerce, Science & Transportation and the House Committee on Energy and Commerce for the period of January 2000 to March 2004.

Trips by Committee Member's Staff Sponsored by the Telecommunications Industry		
Individual	#	Total $
Rhinehardt, Kimrey	4	$5,815
Burr, Richard	1	$3,415
Meli, Amelia	1	$1,473
Total:	6	$10,703
Source: Congressional office travel records for members of the Senate Committee on Commerce, Science & Transportation and the House Committee on Energy and Commerce for the period of January 2000 to March 2004.		

Buyer, Steve

Representative (R-IN)

House Committee on Energy and Commerce

2230 Rayburn House Office Building
Washington, DC 20515
Phone: (202) 225-5037
Fax:

Web Page: http://stevebuyer.house.gov/
Email: http://www.house.gov/writerep/

Contribution Summary By Telecommunications Sector

Phones	$89,925
Broadcast	$33,000
PayTV - Cable	$16,499
PayTV - Satellite	$1,000
Total:	$140,424

Source: Federal Election Commission contribution records from January 1998 to September 2004

Contributions by Telecommunications Sector Organizations

Company	Sector	#	Total	Avg.
SBC Communications Inc.	Phones	29	$32,000	$1,103
National Association of Broadcasters	Broadcast	11	$20,000	$1,818
Verizon Communications Inc.	Phones	13	$19,000	$1,462
Cingular Wireless	Phones	9	$14,500	$1,611
General Electric Co.	Broadcast	14	$12,000	$857
National Cable and Telecommunications Association	PayTV - Cable	5	$11,999	$2,400
United States Telecom Association	Phones	8	$7,925	$991
Deutsche Telekom AG (T-Mobile)	Phones	4	$5,500	$1,375
AT&T Wireless	Phones	4	$3,500	$875
Comcast Corp.	PayTV - Cable	3	$3,250	$1,083
Cellular Telecommunications & Internet Association	Phones	6	$3,000	$500
Sprint Corp.	Phones	4	$1,500	$375
News Corp Ltd.	Broadcast	1	$1,000	$1,000
Charter Communications Inc.	PayTV - Cable	1	$1,000	$1,000
The DirecTV Group Inc.	PayTV - Satellite	1	$1,000	$1,000
ALLTEL Corp.	Phones	1	$1,000	$1,000
Qwest Communications International Inc.	Phones	1	$1,000	$1,000
National Telephone Cooperative Association	Phones	1	$1,000	$1,000
Covad Communications Co.	Phones	1	$500	$500
Time Warner	PayTV - Cable	1	$250	$250
	Total:		$140,424	

Source: Federal Election Commission contribution records from January 1998 to September 2004

Telecommunications Company Provided Trips to Committee Member's Staff

Company	Sector	#	Total $
National Cable and Telecommunications Association	PayTV - Cable	3	$4,464
SBC Communications Inc.	Phones	2	$2,793
United States Telecom Association	Phones	1	$1,351
NBC-Universal Inc (controlled by General Electric)	Broadcast	1	$810
	Total:	7	$9,418

Source: Congressional office travel records for members of the Senate Committee on Commerce, Science & Transportation and the House Committee on Energy and Commerce for the period of January 2000 to March 2004.

Trips by Committee Member's Staff Sponsored by the Telecommunications Industry

Individual	#	Total $
Zuckerman, Laura	3	$4,405
Copher, Michael	3	$4,203
Buyer, Steve	1	$810
Total:	7	$9,418

Source: Congressional office travel records for members of the Senate Committee on Commerce, Science & Transportation and the House Committee on Energy and Commerce for the period of January 2000 to March 2004.

Capps, Lois

Representative (D-CA)

House Committee on Energy and Commerce

1707 Longworth House Office Building
Washington, DC 20515
Phone: (202) 225-3601
Fax: (202) 225-5632

Web Page: http://www.house.gov/capps/
Email: http://www.house.gov/writerep/

Contribution Summary By Telecommunications Sector	
Union	$59,500
Phones	$42,705
PayTV - Cable	$33,699
Broadcast	$30,198
Other	$2,500
PayTV - Satellite	$2,000
Satellite	$500
Total:	$171,102

Source: Federal Election Commission contribution records from January 1998 to September 2004

Contributions by Telecommunications Sector Organizations				
Company	Sector	#	Total	Avg.
International Brotherhood of Electrical Workers (IBEW)	Union	13	$38,500	$2,962
Communications Workers of America	Union	7	$19,500	$2,786
National Cable and Telecommunications Association	PayTV - Cable	9	$11,549	$1,283
AT&T Wireless	Phones	16	$11,455	$716
Walt Disney Co.	Broadcast	12	$11,000	$917
MCI (formerly WorldCom Inc.)	Phones	12	$11,000	$917
General Electric Co.	Broadcast	15	$10,700	$713
Time Warner	PayTV - Cable	11	$9,000	$818
SBC Communications Inc.	Phones	12	$8,300	$692
Charter Communications Inc.	PayTV - Cable	8	$6,500	$813
National Association of Broadcasters	Broadcast	4	$4,248	$1,062
Cox Communications Inc.	PayTV - Cable	14	$4,150	$296
SAVVIS Communications Corp.	PayTV - Cable	3	$2,500	$833
Sprint Corp.	Phones	3	$2,500	$833
Verizon Communications Inc.	Phones	3	$2,200	$733
Level 3 Communications Inc.	Other	2	$2,000	$1,000
Cingular Wireless	Phones	3	$2,000	$667
Clear Channel Communications Inc.	Broadcast	2	$2,000	$1,000
Comptel/ASCENT	Phones	2	$1,500	$750
Transportation Communications International Union	Union	2	$1,500	$750
Viacom Inc.	Broadcast	3	$1,250	$417
News Corp Ltd.	Broadcast	2	$1,000	$500
Echostar Corp.	PayTV - Satellite	1	$1,000	$1,000
The DirecTV Group Inc.	PayTV - Satellite	2	$1,000	$500
AirTouch Communications Inc.	Phones	2	$1,000	$500
ALLTEL Corp.	Phones	2	$1,000	$500
AT&T Corp.	Phones	2	$750	$375
Cellular Telecommunications & Internet Association	Phones	3	$500	$167
IDT Corp.	Other	1	$500	$500
Deutsche Telekom AG (T-Mobile)	Phones	1	$500	$500
Motorola Inc.	Satellite	1	$500	$500
		Total:	$171,102	

Source: Federal Election Commission contribution records from January 1998 to September 2004

Cox, Christopher

Representative (R-CA)

House Committee on Energy and Commerce

2402 Rayburn House Office Building
Washington, DC 20515
Phone: (202) 225-5611
Fax: (202) 225-9177

Web Page: http://cox.house.gov/
Email: http://cox.house.gov/html/contact_email.cfm

Contribution Summary By Telecommunications Sector	
Phones	$65,486
PayTV - Cable	$32,998
Broadcast	$8,800
PayTV - Satellite	$3,500
Satellite	$1,000
Total:	$111,784
Source: Federal Election Commission contribution records from January 1998 to September 2004	

Contributions by Telecommunications Sector Organizations				
Company	Sector	#	Total	Avg.
National Cable and Telecommunications Association	PayTV - Cable	6	$19,998	$3,333
MCI (formerly WorldCom Inc.)	Phones	9	$16,686	$1,854
AT&T Wireless	Phones	15	$11,000	$733
Time Warner	PayTV - Cable	9	$10,000	$1,111
SBC Communications Inc.	Phones	9	$10,000	$1,111
Verizon Communications Inc.	Phones	5	$9,000	$1,800
Sprint Corp.	Phones	7	$7,000	$1,000
General Electric Co.	Broadcast	6	$5,300	$883
Echostar Corp.	PayTV - Satellite	3	$3,500	$1,167
AT&T Corp.	Phones	3	$2,300	$767
Comcast Corp.	PayTV - Cable	2	$2,000	$1,000
Deutsche Telekom AG (T-Mobile)	Phones	2	$2,000	$1,000
Cellular Telecommunications & Internet Association	Phones	2	$1,500	$750
Comptel/ASCENT	Phones	2	$1,000	$500
SAVVIS Communications Corp.	PayTV - Cable	1	$1,000	$1,000
AirTouch Communications Inc.	Phones	1	$1,000	$1,000
Association for Local Telecommunications Services	Phones	1	$1,000	$1,000
National Association of Broadcasters	Broadcast	1	$1,000	$1,000
News Corp Ltd.	Broadcast	1	$1,000	$1,000
Viacom Inc.	Broadcast	1	$1,000	$1,000
United States Telecom Association	Phones	1	$1,000	$1,000
Motorola Inc.	Satellite	1	$1,000	$1,000
XO Communications Inc.	Phones	1	$500	$500
Personal Communications Industry Association	Phones	1	$500	$500
Qwest Communications International Inc.	Phones	1	$500	$500
Walt Disney Co.	Broadcast	3	$500	$167
ICG Communications Inc.	Phones	1	$500	$500
		Total:	$111,784	
Source: Federal Election Commission contribution records from January 1998 to September 2004				

Cubin, Barbara

Representative (R-WY)

House Committee on Energy and Commerce

1114 Longworth House Office Building
Washington, DC 20515
Phone: (202) 225-2311
Fax: (202) 225-3057

Web Page: http://www.house.gov/cubin/
Email: http://www.house.gov/cubin/zip_auth.html

Contribution Summary By Telecommunications Sector	
Phones	$98,528
PayTV - Cable	$39,708
Broadcast	$33,071
PayTV - Satellite	$4,500
Other	$2,000
Satellite	$1,000
Total:	$178,807

Source: Federal Election Commission contribution records from January 1998 to September 2004

Contributions by Telecommunications Sector Organizations				
Company	Sector	#	Total	Avg.
National Cable and Telecommunications Association	PayTV - Cable	13	$34,208	$2,631
Qwest Communications International Inc.	Phones	20	$19,778	$989
National Association of Broadcasters	Broadcast	14	$18,571	$1,327
SBC Communications Inc.	Phones	19	$17,500	$921
Verizon Communications Inc.	Phones	11	$11,500	$1,045
ALLTEL Corp.	Phones	9	$11,000	$1,222
General Electric Co.	Broadcast	6	$7,500	$1,250
Cingular Wireless	Phones	5	$5,500	$1,100
Cincinnati Bell Inc.	Phones	5	$5,000	$1,000
AT&T Wireless	Phones	6	$5,000	$833
Sprint Corp.	Phones	8	$5,000	$625
Echostar Corp.	PayTV - Satellite	4	$4,500	$1,125
CenturyTel Inc.	Phones	4	$3,500	$875
Cellular Telecommunications & Internet Association	Phones	4	$3,000	$750
Time Warner	PayTV - Cable	2	$3,000	$1,500
News Corp Ltd.	Broadcast	2	$3,000	$1,500
United States Cellular Corp.	Phones	3	$3,000	$1,000
United States Telecom Association	Phones	5	$3,000	$600
Viacom Inc.	Broadcast	4	$2,000	$500
Walt Disney Co.	Broadcast	2	$2,000	$1,000
Level 3 Communications Inc.	Other	3	$2,000	$667
Comcast Corp.	PayTV - Cable	2	$1,500	$750
AirTouch Communications Inc.	Phones	2	$1,500	$750
MCI (formerly WorldCom Inc.)	Phones	2	$1,500	$750
National Telephone Cooperative Association	Phones	2	$1,500	$750
Satellite Broadcasting & Communication Association	Satellite	2	$1,000	$500
SAVVIS Communications Corp.	PayTV - Cable	1	$1,000	$1,000
Alaska Communications Systems	Phones	2	$750	$375
Comptel/ASCENT	Phones	1	$500	$500
		Total:	$178,807	

Source: Federal Election Commission contribution records from January 1998 to September 2004

Telecommunications Company Provided Trips to Committee Member's Staff			
Company	Sector	#	Total $
Independent Telephone & Telecommunications Alliance	Phones	1	$984
AT&T Corp.	Phones	1	$590
	Total:	2	$1,574

Source: Congressional office travel records for members of the Senate Committee on Commerce, Science & Transportation and the House Committee on Energy and Commerce for the period of January 2000 to March 2004.

Trips by Committee Member's Staff Sponsored by the Telecommunications Industry		
Individual	#	Total $
Thompson, Patrick	1	$984
Jacobs, Bryan	1	$590
Total:	2	$1,574

Source: Congressional office travel records for members of the Senate Committee on Commerce, Science & Transportation and the House Committee on Energy and Commerce for the period of January 2000 to March 2004.

Davis, Jim

Representative (D-FL)

House Committee on Energy and Commerce

409 Cannon House Office Building
Washington, DC 20515
Phone: (202) 225-3376
Fax: (202) 225-5652

Web Page: http://www.house.gov/jimdavis/
Email: http://www.house.gov/jimdavis/message.html

Contribution Summary By Telecommunications Sector	
Phones	$32,550
Union	$18,100
Broadcast	$15,000
PayTV - Cable	$8,915
Satellite	$1,000
PayTV - Satellite	$500
Total:	$76,065
Source: Federal Election Commission contribution records from January 1998 to September 2004	

Contributions by Telecommunications Sector Organizations				
Company	Sector	#	Total	Avg.
International Brotherhood of Electrical Workers (IBEW)	Union	13	$15,600	$1,200
Verizon Communications Inc.	Phones	9	$9,250	$1,028
MCI (formerly WorldCom Inc.)	Phones	14	$8,800	$629
General Electric Co.	Broadcast	10	$8,000	$800
Walt Disney Co.	Broadcast	7	$5,000	$714
AT&T Wireless	Phones	5	$4,500	$900
BellSouth Corp.	Phones	6	$4,500	$750
National Cable and Telecommunications Association	PayTV - Cable	1	$4,415	$4,415
Time Warner	PayTV - Cable	4	$3,500	$875
Sprint Corp.	Phones	5	$2,500	$500
Transportation Communications International Union	Union	5	$2,500	$500
Motorola Inc.	Satellite	2	$1,000	$500
Telephone Electronics Corp.	Phones	1	$1,000	$1,000
National Telephone Cooperative Association	Phones	3	$1,000	$333
Comcast Corp.	PayTV - Cable	1	$1,000	$1,000
National Association of Broadcasters	Broadcast	1	$1,000	$1,000
News Corp Ltd.	Broadcast	1	$1,000	$1,000
AT&T Corp.	Phones	2	$1,000	$500
The DirecTV Group Inc.	PayTV - Satellite	1	$500	$500
	Total:		$76,065	
Source: Federal Election Commission contribution records from January 1998 to September 2004				

Telecommunications Company Provided Trips to Committee Member's Staff			
Company	Sector	#	Total $
Time Warner	PayTV - Cable	2	$1,840
	Total:	2	$1,840
Source: Congressional office travel records for members of the Senate Committee on Commerce, Science & Transportation and the House Committee on Energy and Commerce for the period of January 2000 to March 2004.			

Trips by Committee Member's Staff Sponsored by the Telecommunications Industry		
Individual	#	Total $
Farmer, Suzanne	1	$1,139
Callender, John	1	$701
Total:	2	$1,840
Source: Congressional office travel records for members of the Senate Committee on Commerce, Science & Transportation and the House Committee on Energy and Commerce for the period of January 2000 to March 2004.		

Deal, Nathan

Representative (R-GA)

House Committee on Energy and Commerce

2437 Rayburn House Office Building
Washington, DC 20515
Phone: (202) 225-5211
Fax: (202) 225-8272

Web Page: http://www.house.gov/deal/
Email: http://www.house.gov/deal/contact/default.shtml

Contribution Summary By Telecommunications Sector	
Phones	$67,000
PayTV - Cable	$27,853
Broadcast	$13,000
PayTV - Satellite	$1,000
Total:	$108,853

Source: Federal Election Commission contribution records from January 1998 to September 2004

Contributions by Telecommunications Sector Organizations				
Company	Sector	#	Total	Avg.
National Cable and Telecommunications Association	PayTV - Cable	11	$23,353	$2,123
SBC Communications Inc.	Phones	22	$19,000	$864
Cingular Wireless	Phones	8	$10,000	$1,250
Verizon Communications Inc.	Phones	9	$9,000	$1,000
ALLTEL Corp.	Phones	7	$6,000	$857
National Telephone Cooperative Association	Phones	7	$5,500	$786
National Association of Broadcasters	Broadcast	6	$5,000	$833
General Electric Co.	Broadcast	5	$4,500	$900
BellSouth Corp.	Phones	6	$4,500	$750
Time Warner	PayTV - Cable	4	$4,000	$1,000
MCI (formerly WorldCom Inc.)	Phones	4	$3,500	$875
AT&T Wireless	Phones	4	$3,000	$750
United States Telecom Association	Phones	3	$3,000	$1,000
Clear Channel Communications Inc.	Broadcast	2	$2,000	$1,000
Cellular Telecommunications & Internet Association	Phones	3	$1,500	$500
Qwest Communications International Inc.	Phones	3	$1,500	$500
Echostar Corp.	PayTV - Satellite	1	$1,000	$1,000
Paxson Communications Corp.	Broadcast	1	$1,000	$1,000
American Cable Association	PayTV - Cable	1	$500	$500
Meredith Corp.	Broadcast	1	$500	$500
United States Cellular Corp.	Phones	1	$500	$500
		Total:	$108,853	

Source: Federal Election Commission contribution records from January 1998 to September 2004

Telecommunications Company Provided Trips to Committee Member's Staff			
Company	Sector	#	Total $
SBC Communications Inc.	Phones	2	$3,326
National Cable and Telecommunications Association	PayTV - Cable	1	$2,471
News Corp Ltd.	Broadcast	1	$2,402
United States Telecom Association	Phones	2	$2,288
	Total:	6	$10,488

Source: Congressional office travel records for members of the Senate Committee on Commerce, Science & Transportation and the House Committee on Energy and Commerce for the period of January 2000 to March 2004.

Trips by Committee Member's Staff Sponsored by the Telecommunications Industry		
Individual	#	Total $
Herndon, Heather	6	$10,488
Total:	6	$10,488

Source: Congressional office travel records for members of the Senate Committee on Commerce, Science & Transportation and the House Committee on Energy and Commerce for the period of January 2000 to March 2004.

DeGette, Diana

Representative (D-CO)

House Committee on Energy and Commerce

1530 Longworth House Office Building
Washington, DC 20515
Phone: (202) 225-4431
Fax: (202) 225-5657

Web Page: http://www.house.gov/degette/
Email: http://www.house.gov/degette/contact/comment.html

Contribution Summary By Telecommunications Sector	
Phones	$76,184
Union	$52,250
PayTV - Cable	$48,246
Other	$13,750
PayTV - Satellite	$10,000
Broadcast	$9,200
Total:	$209,630

Source: Federal Election Commission contribution records from January 1998 to September 2004

Contributions by Telecommunications Sector Organizations				
Company	Sector	#	Total	Avg.
National Cable and Telecommunications Association	PayTV - Cable	14	$32,246	$2,303
International Brotherhood of Electrical Workers (IBEW)	Union	11	$30,500	$2,773
MCI (formerly WorldCom Inc.)	Phones	21	$23,400	$1,114
Communications Workers of America	Union	9	$20,250	$2,250
Qwest Communications International Inc.	Phones	25	$20,159	$806
AT&T Wireless	Phones	18	$16,000	$889
Level 3 Communications Inc.	Other	13	$13,750	$1,058
Time Warner	PayTV - Cable	7	$9,000	$1,286
Echostar Corp.	PayTV - Satellite	9	$8,500	$944
Comcast Corp.	PayTV - Cable	8	$5,500	$688
SBC Communications Inc.	Phones	6	$4,500	$750
AT&T Corp.	Phones	5	$3,825	$765
Viacom Inc.	Broadcast	5	$3,750	$750
ICG Communications Inc.	Phones	4	$3,300	$825
Sprint Corp.	Phones	5	$3,000	$600
General Electric Co.	Broadcast	4	$2,000	$500
National Association of Broadcasters	Broadcast	3	$2,000	$667
The DirecTV Group Inc.	PayTV - Satellite	2	$1,500	$750
SAVVIS Communications Corp.	PayTV - Cable	2	$1,500	$750
Transportation Communications International Union	Union	3	$1,500	$500
Walt Disney Co.	Broadcast	1	$1,000	$1,000
Comptel/ASCENT	Phones	1	$1,000	$1,000
AirTouch Communications Inc.	Phones	1	$500	$500
XO Communications Inc.	Phones	1	$500	$500
Liberty Media Corp.	Broadcast	2	$450	$225
		Total:	$209,630	

Source: Federal Election Commission contribution records from January 1998 to September 2004

Deutsch, Peter

Representative (D-FL)

House Committee on Energy and Commerce

2303 Rayburn House Office Building
Washington, DC 20515
Phone: (202) 225-7931
Fax: (202) 225-8456

Web Page: http://www.house.gov/deutsch/
Email: http://www.house.gov/writerep/

Contribution Summary By Telecommunications Sector	
PayTV - Cable	$51,998
Phones	$33,050
Union	$26,700
Broadcast	$21,250
Satellite	$4,500
PayTV - Satellite	$1,000
Total:	$138,498
Source: Federal Election Commission contribution records from January 1998 to September 2004	

Contributions by Telecommunications Sector Organizations				
Company	Sector	#	Total	Avg.
National Cable and Telecommunications Association	PayTV - Cable	8	$29,998	$3,750
International Brotherhood of Electrical Workers (IBEW)	Union	10	$19,000	$1,900
Time Warner	PayTV - Cable	20	$12,000	$600
AT&T Wireless	Phones	12	$11,750	$979
MCI (formerly WorldCom Inc.)	Phones	9	$7,300	$811
Comcast Corp.	PayTV - Cable	7	$7,000	$1,000
General Electric Co.	Broadcast	8	$6,500	$813
National Association of Broadcasters	Broadcast	7	$6,500	$929
Communications Workers of America	Union	5	$5,700	$1,140
Viacom Inc.	Broadcast	6	$3,750	$625
Walt Disney Co.	Broadcast	4	$3,500	$875
Adelphia Communications Corp.	PayTV - Cable	3	$3,000	$1,000
Sprint Corp.	Phones	7	$3,000	$429
Motorola Inc.	Satellite	4	$2,500	$625
AT&T Corp.	Phones	2	$2,500	$1,250
Transportation Communications International Union	Union	5	$2,500	$500
XM Satellite Radio Holdings Inc.	Satellite	2	$2,000	$1,000
XO Communications Inc.	Phones	2	$2,000	$1,000
BellSouth Corp.	Phones	3	$2,000	$667
ALLTEL Corp.	Phones	2	$2,000	$1,000
SBC Communications Inc.	Phones	3	$1,500	$500
Cellular Telecommunications & Internet Association	Phones	2	$1,000	$500
The DirecTV Group Inc.	PayTV - Satellite	1	$1,000	$1,000
Paxson Communications Corp.	Broadcast	1	$1,000	$1,000
Utility Workers Union of America	Union	1	($500)	($500)
		Total:	$138,498	
Source: Federal Election Commission contribution records from January 1998 to September 2004				

Telecommunications Company Provided Trips to Committee Member's Staff			
Company	Sector	#	Total $
Comcast Corp.	PayTV - Cable	1	$1,021
	Total:	1	$1,021
Source: Congressional office travel records for members of the Senate Committee on Commerce, Science & Transportation and the House Committee on Energy and Commerce for the period of January 2000 to March 2004.			

Trips by Committee Member's Staff Sponsored by the Telecommunications Industry		
Individual	#	Total $
Assey, Elizabeth	1	$1,021
Total:	1	$1,021
Source: Congressional office travel records for members of the Senate Committee on Commerce, Science & Transportation and the House Committee on Energy and Commerce for the period of January 2000 to March 2004.		

Dingell, John D.

Representative (D-MI)

House Committee on Energy and Commerce

Ex Officio member, Subcommittee

2328 Rayburn House Office Building
Washington, DC 20515
Phone: (202) 225-4071
Fax: (202) 226-0371

Web Page: http://www.house.gov/dingell/
Email: http://www.house.gov/writerep/

Contribution Summary By Telecommunications Sector	
Phones	$302,067
Broadcast	$137,000
PayTV - Cable	$114,159
Union	$48,500
Satellite	$12,969
PayTV - Satellite	$11,500
Total:	$626,195
Source: Federal Election Commission contribution records from January 1998 to September 2004	

Contributions by Telecommunications Sector Organizations				
Company	Sector	#	Total	Avg.
BellSouth Corp.	Phones	130	$69,875	$538
SBC Communications Inc.	Phones	44	$59,324	$1,348
Verizon Communications Inc.	Phones	34	$58,750	$1,728
Comcast Corp.	PayTV - Cable	56	$55,475	$991
National Cable and Telecommunications Association	PayTV - Cable	18	$39,684	$2,205
Walt Disney Co.	Broadcast	29	$38,500	$1,328
Cingular Wireless	Phones	21	$36,750	$1,750
International Brotherhood of Electrical Workers (IBEW)	Union	10	$35,000	$3,500
Viacom Inc.	Broadcast	14	$25,500	$1,821
National Association of Broadcasters	Broadcast	13	$24,500	$1,885
Qwest Communications International Inc.	Phones	16	$22,500	$1,406
General Electric Co.	Broadcast	15	$19,000	$1,267
United States Telecom Association	Phones	10	$17,000	$1,700
Time Warner	PayTV - Cable	9	$12,000	$1,333
Communications Workers of America	Union	7	$12,000	$1,714
ALLTEL Corp.	Phones	11	$11,000	$1,000
Echostar Corp.	PayTV - Satellite	6	$9,500	$1,583
AT&T Wireless	Phones	8	$8,500	$1,063
Loral Space & Communications Ltd.	Satellite	8	$8,500	$1,063
News Corp Ltd.	Broadcast	8	$7,500	$938
Paxson Communications Corp.	Broadcast	7	$7,000	$1,000
Clear Channel Communications Inc.	Broadcast	4	$6,000	$1,500
Cellular Telecommunications & Internet Association	Phones	5	$5,118	$1,024
Cox Communications Inc.	PayTV - Cable	5	$5,000	$1,000
AT&T Corp.	Phones	3	$3,750	$1,250
Spanish Broadcasting Systems, Inc.	Broadcast	3	$3,000	$1,000
Motorola Inc.	Satellite	2	$2,469	$1,235
Satellite Broadcasting & Communication Association	Satellite	2	$2,000	$1,000
The DirecTV Group Inc.	PayTV - Satellite	2	$2,000	$1,000
AirTouch Communications Inc.	Phones	2	$2,000	$1,000
Charter Communications Inc.	PayTV - Cable	1	$2,000	$2,000
Western Wireless Corp.	Phones	2	$2,000	$1,000
National Telephone Cooperative Association	Phones	3	$1,500	$500
Hubbard Broadcasting Inc.	Broadcast	2	$1,500	$750
Tribune Co.	Broadcast	1	$1,000	$1,000
Univision Communications Inc.	Broadcast	1	$1,000	$1,000
Emmis Communications Corp.	Broadcast	1	$1,000	$1,000
Hearst Corp.	Broadcast	1	$1,000	$1,000
Teligent	Phones	1	$1,000	$1,000
United States Cellular Corp.	Phones	1	$1,000	$1,000
XO Communications Inc.	Phones	1	$1,000	$1,000
Deutsche Telekom AG (T-Mobile)	Phones	1	$1,000	$1,000

Contributions by Telecommunications Sector Organizations				
Company	Sector	#	Total	Avg.
Utility Workers Union of America	Union	1	$1,000	$1,000
Transportation Communications International Union	Union	1	$500	$500
Gannett Co. Inc.	Broadcast	1	$500	$500
		Total:	$626,195	
Source: Federal Election Commission contribution records from January 1998 to September 2004				

Telecommunications Company Provided Trips to Committee Member's Staff			
Company	Sector	#	Total $
Walt Disney Co.	Broadcast	1	$6,295
National Association of Broadcasters	Broadcast	1	$5,754
	Total:	2	$12,049
Source: Congressional office travel records for members of the Senate Committee on Commerce, Science & Transportation and the House Committee on Energy and Commerce for the period of January 2000 to March 2004.			

Trips by Committee Member's Staff Sponsored by the Telecommunications Industry		
Individual	#	Total $
Dingell, John	2	$12,049
Total:	2	$12,049
Source: Congressional office travel records for members of the Senate Committee on Commerce, Science & Transportation and the House Committee on Energy and Commerce for the period of January 2000 to March 2004.		

Doyle, Michael F.

Representative (D-PA)

House Committee on Energy and Commerce

401 Cannon House Office Building
Washington, DC 20515
Phone: (202) 225-2135
Fax: (202) 225-3084

Web Page: http://www.house.gov/doyle/
Email: rep.doyle@mail.house.gov

Contribution Summary By Telecommunications Sector	
Union	$70,000
PayTV - Cable	$36,096
Phones	$29,591
Broadcast	$15,240
PayTV - Satellite	$10,750
Total:	$161,677
Source: Federal Election Commission contribution records from January 1998 to September 2004	

Contributions by Telecommunications Sector Organizations				
Company	Sector	#	Total	Avg.
Communications Workers of America	Union	13	$36,000	$2,769
International Brotherhood of Electrical Workers (IBEW)	Union	16	$31,000	$1,938
Comcast Corp.	PayTV - Cable	20	$21,750	$1,088
Echostar Corp.	PayTV - Satellite	12	$10,750	$896
National Cable and Telecommunications Association	PayTV - Cable	3	$7,971	$2,657
National Association of Broadcasters	Broadcast	6	$7,240	$1,207
MCI (formerly WorldCom Inc.)	Phones	6	$6,000	$1,000
AT&T Wireless	Phones	6	$5,500	$917
Verizon Communications Inc.	Phones	7	$4,500	$643
Viacom Inc.	Broadcast	5	$3,500	$700
General Electric Co.	Broadcast	3	$3,500	$1,167
Cingular Wireless	Phones	4	$3,000	$750
Transportation Communications International Union	Union	6	$3,000	$500
Sprint Corp.	Phones	3	$3,000	$1,000
Adelphia Communications Corp.	PayTV - Cable	5	$2,125	$425
Time Warner	PayTV - Cable	3	$1,750	$583
American Cable Association	PayTV - Cable	2	$1,500	$750
Covad Communications Co.	Phones	3	$1,500	$500
Comptel/ASCENT	Phones	1	$1,000	$1,000
Walt Disney Co.	Broadcast	1	$1,000	$1,000
SAVVIS Communications Corp.	PayTV - Cable	1	$1,000	$1,000
XO Communications Inc.	Phones	1	$1,000	$1,000
Focal Communications Corp.	Phones	2	$1,000	$500
AT&T Corp.	Phones	2	$858	$429
Qwest Communications International Inc.	Phones	1	$500	$500
SBC Communications Inc.	Phones	1	$500	$500
Deutsche Telekom AG (T-Mobile)	Phones	1	$500	$500
Association for Local Telecommunications Services	Phones	1	$500	$500
Cellular Telecommunications & Internet Association	Phones	1	$233	$233
		Total:	$161,677	
Source: Federal Election Commission contribution records from January 1998 to September 2004				

Telecommunications Company Provided Trips to Committee Member's Staff			
Company	Sector	#	Total $
Echostar Corp.	PayTV - Satellite	1	$825
Comptel/ASCENT	Phones	1	$706
Total:		2	$1,531
Source: Congressional office travel records for members of the Senate Committee on Commerce, Science & Transportation and the House Committee on Energy and Commerce for the period of January 2000 to March 2004.			

Trips by Committee Member's Staff Sponsored by the Telecommunications Industry		
Individual	#	Total $
Grant, Sharon	1	$825
Lucas, David	1	$706
Total:	2	$1,531
Source: Congressional office travel records for members of the Senate Committee on Commerce, Science & Transportation and the House Committee on Energy and Commerce for the period of January 2000 to March 2004.		

Engel, Eliot L.

Representative (D-NY)

House Committee on Energy and Commerce

2264 Rayburn House Office Building
Washington, DC 20515
Phone: (202) 225-2464
Fax:

Web Page: http://www.house.gov/engel/
Email: http://www.house.gov/writerep/

Contribution Summary By Telecommunications Sector	
Phones	$118,713
PayTV - Cable	$48,748
Broadcast	$44,250
Union	$43,500
Other	$11,000
Satellite	$10,000
PayTV - Satellite	$500
Total:	$276,711
Source: Federal Election Commission contribution records from January 1998 to September 2004	

Contributions by Telecommunications Sector Organizations				
Company	Sector	#	Total	Avg.
Verizon Communications Inc.	Phones	48	$57,000	$1,188
International Brotherhood of Electrical Workers (IBEW)	Union	11	$21,500	$1,955
National Cable and Telecommunications Association	PayTV - Cable	9	$21,498	$2,389
Viacom Inc.	Broadcast	12	$20,500	$1,708
Communications Workers of America	Union	16	$20,000	$1,250
Cablevision Systems Corp.	PayTV - Cable	6	$17,250	$2,875
SBC Communications Inc.	Phones	18	$16,000	$889
Cingular Wireless	Phones	16	$14,000	$875
IDT Corp.	Other	11	$11,000	$1,000
Time Warner	PayTV - Cable	7	$10,000	$1,429
Loral Space & Communications Ltd.	Satellite	11	$8,500	$773
National Association of Broadcasters	Broadcast	6	$8,000	$1,333
United States Telecom Association	Phones	8	$7,500	$938
AT&T Wireless	Phones	6	$7,000	$1,167
General Electric Co.	Broadcast	11	$6,500	$591
News Corp Ltd.	Broadcast	7	$6,000	$857
Qwest Communications International Inc.	Phones	6	$5,000	$833
Cellular Telecommunications & Internet Association	Phones	7	$4,213	$602
ALLTEL Corp.	Phones	2	$2,000	$1,000
Transportation Communications International Union	Union	3	$2,000	$667
Motorola Inc.	Satellite	3	$1,500	$500
MCI (formerly WorldCom Inc.)	Phones	3	$1,500	$500
National Telephone Cooperative Association	Phones	2	$1,500	$750
Paxson Communications Corp.	Broadcast	2	$1,250	$625
Clear Channel Communications Inc.	Broadcast	1	$1,000	$1,000
Walt Disney Co.	Broadcast	2	$1,000	$500
Deutsche Telekom AG (T-Mobile)	Phones	1	$1,000	$1,000
Sprint Corp.	Phones	1	$1,000	$1,000
Teligent	Phones	2	$1,000	$500
The DirecTV Group Inc.	PayTV - Satellite	1	$500	$500
		Total:	$276,711	
Source: Federal Election Commission contribution records from January 1998 to September 2004				

Telecommunications Company Provided Trips to Committee Member's Staff			
Company	Sector	#	Total $
National Association of Broadcasters	Broadcast	3	$11,282
National Cable and Telecommunications Association	PayTV - Cable	3	$6,642
Clear Channel Communications Inc.	Broadcast	1	$1,601
Verizon Communications Inc.	Phones	1	$625
IDT Corp.	Other	1	$187
	Total:	9	$20,337
Source: Congressional office travel records for members of the Senate Committee on Commerce, Science & Transportation and the House Committee on Energy and Commerce for the period of January 2000 to March 2004.			

Trips by Committee Member's Staff Sponsored by the Telecommunications Industry		
Individual	#	Total $
Engel, Eliot	5	$14,463
Leon, Peter	3	$5,249
Illegible	1	$625
Total:	9	$20,337

Source: Congressional office travel records for members of the Senate Committee on Commerce, Science & Transportation and the House Committee on Energy and Commerce for the period of January 2000 to March 2004.

Eshoo, Anna G.

Representative (D-CA)

House Committee on Energy and Commerce

205 Cannon House Office Building
Washington, DC 20515
Phone: (202) 225-8104
Fax: (202) 225-8890

Web Page: http://www-eshoo.house.gov/
Email: http://www-eshoo.house.gov/contact.aspx

Contribution Summary By Telecommunications Sector	
Phones	$85,006
PayTV - Cable	$55,497
Broadcast	$17,250
Other	$14,266
Satellite	$11,500
Union	$8,500
PayTV - Satellite	$3,000
Total:	$195,019
Source: Federal Election Commission contribution records from January 1998 to September 2004	

Contributions by Telecommunications Sector Organizations				
Company	Sector	#	Total	Avg.
National Cable and Telecommunications Association	PayTV - Cable	12	$30,997	$2,583
AT&T Wireless	Phones	19	$16,500	$868
MCI (formerly WorldCom Inc.)	Phones	18	$15,500	$861
Time Warner	PayTV - Cable	12	$12,000	$1,000
IDT Corp.	Other	10	$10,266	$1,027
General Electric Co.	Broadcast	12	$9,500	$792
Loral Space & Communications Ltd.	Satellite	10	$8,500	$850
International Brotherhood of Electrical Workers (IBEW)	Union	6	$8,000	$1,333
Comcast Corp.	PayTV - Cable	6	$8,000	$1,333
Sprint Corp.	Phones	8	$7,000	$875
SBC Communications Inc.	Phones	7	$5,256	$751
Covad Communications Co.	Phones	7	$5,000	$714
Level 3 Communications Inc.	Other	4	$4,000	$1,000
XO Communications Inc.	Phones	5	$4,000	$800
Verizon Communications Inc.	Phones	4	$3,500	$875
Cingular Wireless	Phones	4	$3,500	$875
Comptel/ASCENT	Phones	5	$3,500	$700
AirTouch Communications Inc.	Phones	5	$3,250	$650
SAVVIS Communications Corp.	PayTV - Cable	3	$3,000	$1,000
National Association of Broadcasters	Broadcast	4	$3,000	$750
Viacom Inc.	Broadcast	3	$3,000	$1,000
Teligent	Phones	6	$3,000	$500
Motorola Inc.	Satellite	6	$3,000	$500
Cellular Telecommunications & Internet Association	Phones	5	$2,500	$500
Deutsche Telekom AG (T-Mobile)	Phones	2	$2,000	$1,000
Focal Communications Corp.	Phones	2	$2,000	$1,000
AT&T Corp.	Phones	3	$2,000	$667
Echostar Corp.	PayTV - Satellite	2	$2,000	$1,000
Association for Local Telecommunications Services	Phones	2	$1,500	$750
ALLTEL Corp.	Phones	1	$1,000	$1,000
The DirecTV Group Inc.	PayTV - Satellite	2	$1,000	$500
Walt Disney Co.	Broadcast	1	$1,000	$1,000
Cox Communications Inc.	PayTV - Cable	1	$1,000	$1,000
Qwest Communications International Inc.	Phones	1	$1,000	$1,000
Pac-West Telecomm Inc.	Phones	1	$1,000	$1,000
Telephone Electronics Corp.	Phones	1	$1,000	$1,000
United States Telecom Association	Phones	1	$500	$500
Personal Communications Industry Association	Phones	1	$500	$500
Charter Communications Inc.	PayTV - Cable	1	$500	$500
News Corp Ltd.	Broadcast	1	$500	$500
Transportation Communications International Union	Union	1	$500	$500

Contributions by Telecommunications Sector Organizations				
Company	Sector	#	Total	Avg.
Gannett Co. Inc.	Broadcast	1	$250	$250
National Telephone Cooperative Association	Phones	2	-	-
		Total:	$195,019	

Source: Federal Election Commission contribution records from January 1998 to September 2004

Telecommunications Company Provided Trips to Committee Member's Staff			
Company	Sector	#	Total $
National Cable and Telecommunications Association	PayTV - Cable	3	$5,317
News Corp Ltd.	Broadcast	1	$2,258
Misc. telecom interests	Other	2	$1,943
Cellular Telecommunications & Internet Association	Phones	1	$1,846
	Total:	7	$11,365

Source: Congressional office travel records for members of the Senate Committee on Commerce, Science & Transportation and the House Committee on Energy and Commerce for the period of January 2000 to March 2004.

Trips by Committee Member's Staff Sponsored by the Telecommunications Industry		
Individual	#	Total $
Kolovos, Nick	6	$10,346
Olson, Eric	1	$1,018
Total:	7	$11,365

Source: Congressional office travel records for members of the Senate Committee on Commerce, Science & Transportation and the House Committee on Energy and Commerce for the period of January 2000 to March 2004.

Ferguson, Mike

Representative (R-NJ)

House Committee on Energy and Commerce

214 Cannon House Office Building
Washington, DC 20515
Phone: (202) 225-5361
Fax: (202) 225-9460

Web Page: http://www.house.gov/ferguson/
Email: http://www.house.gov/ferguson/get_address2.shtml

Contribution Summary By Telecommunications Sector	
Phones	$90,599
PayTV - Cable	$14,050
Broadcast	$6,750
Other	$4,550
Union	$500
Total:	$116,449

Source: Federal Election Commission contribution records from January 1998 to September 2004

Contributions by Telecommunications Sector Organizations				
Company	Sector	#	Total	Avg.
Verizon Communications Inc.	Phones	47	$44,899	$955
SBC Communications Inc.	Phones	9	$13,000	$1,444
Cingular Wireless	Phones	9	$8,500	$944
AT&T Wireless	Phones	6	$7,500	$1,250
Comcast Corp.	PayTV - Cable	11	$5,550	$505
United States Telecom Association	Phones	7	$5,500	$786
IDT Corp.	Other	6	$4,550	$758
AT&T Corp.	Phones	4	$4,450	$1,113
General Electric Co.	Broadcast	4	$3,750	$938
Time Warner	PayTV - Cable	3	$3,500	$1,167
National Cable and Telecommunications Association	PayTV - Cable	3	$2,500	$833
Qwest Communications International Inc.	Phones	2	$2,500	$1,250
Cablevision Systems Corp.	PayTV - Cable	1	$2,000	$2,000
Cellular Telecommunications & Internet Association	Phones	1	$1,000	$1,000
Forstmann Little & Co.	Phones	1	$1,000	$1,000
Hubbard Broadcasting Inc.	Broadcast	1	$1,000	$1,000
National Association of Broadcasters	Broadcast	1	$1,000	$1,000
Univision Communications Inc.	Broadcast	2	$1,000	$500
Sprint Corp.	Phones	2	$1,000	$500
Communications Workers of America	Union	1	$500	$500
American Cable Association	PayTV - Cable	1	$500	$500
MCI (formerly WorldCom Inc.)	Phones	1	$500	$500
Comptel/ASCENT	Phones	1	$500	$500
Covad Communications Co.	Phones	1	$250	$250
	Total:		$116,449	

Source: Federal Election Commission contribution records from January 1998 to September 2004

Fossella, Vito

Representative (R-NY)

House Committee on Energy and Commerce

1239 Longworth House Office Building
Washington, DC 20515
Phone: (202) 225-3371
Fax: (202) 226-1272

Web Page: http://www.house.gov/fossella/
Email: vito.fossella@mail.house.gov

Contribution Summary By Telecommunications Sector	
Phones	$97,925
Broadcast	$40,019
PayTV - Cable	$23,500
Satellite	$2,500
Total:	$163,944

Source: Federal Election Commission contribution records from January 1998 to September 2004

Contributions by Telecommunications Sector Organizations				
Company	Sector	#	Total	Avg.
Verizon Communications Inc.	Phones	29	$29,350	$1,012
SBC Communications Inc.	Phones	23	$23,500	$1,022
National Association of Broadcasters	Broadcast	17	$14,869	$875
Cingular Wireless	Phones	14	$13,000	$929
Cablevision Systems Corp.	PayTV - Cable	5	$11,000	$2,200
Viacom Inc.	Broadcast	9	$9,500	$1,056
National Cable and Telecommunications Association	PayTV - Cable	2	$8,500	$4,250
United States Telecom Association	Phones	8	$8,328	$1,041
News Corp Ltd.	Broadcast	6	$7,000	$1,167
General Electric Co.	Broadcast	6	$6,000	$1,000
ALLTEL Corp.	Phones	5	$5,000	$1,000
AT&T Wireless	Phones	5	$4,500	$900
Cellular Telecommunications & Internet Association	Phones	6	$4,247	$708
Qwest Communications International Inc.	Phones	5	$4,000	$800
Time Warner	PayTV - Cable	4	$4,000	$1,000
Loral Space & Communications Ltd.	Satellite	2	$2,000	$1,000
Sprint Corp.	Phones	5	$2,000	$400
Clear Channel Communications Inc.	Broadcast	1	$1,500	$1,500
Deutsche Telekom AG (T-Mobile)	Phones	1	$1,000	$1,000
MCI (formerly WorldCom Inc.)	Phones	1	$1,000	$1,000
Cincinnati Bell Inc.	Phones	1	$1,000	$1,000
Hubbard Broadcasting Inc.	Broadcast	1	$650	$650
Walt Disney Co.	Broadcast	1	$500	$500
Teligent	Phones	1	$500	$500
XO Communications Inc.	Phones	1	$500	$500
Motorola Inc.	Satellite	1	$500	$500
Total:			$163,944	

Source: Federal Election Commission contribution records from January 1998 to September 2004

Telecommunications Company Provided Trips to Committee Member's Staff			
Company	Sector	#	Total $
SBC Communications Inc.	Phones	5	$4,944
National Association of Broadcasters	Broadcast	1	$4,080
Cellular Telecommunications & Internet Association	Phones	2	$2,824
National Cable and Telecommunications Association	PayTV - Cable	1	$2,457
News Corp Ltd.	Broadcast	1	$2,258
United States Telecom Association	Phones	1	$1,768
BellSouth Corp.	Phones	2	$1,151
Total:		13	$19,483

Source: Congressional office travel records for members of the Senate Committee on Commerce, Science & Transportation and the House Committee on Energy and Commerce for the period of January 2000 to March 2004.

Trips by Committee Member's Staff Sponsored by the Telecommunications Industry		
Individual	#	Total $
Weiss, Brendon	9	$10,692
Fossella, Vito	1	$4,080
Thompson, Michael	1	$1,768
Quaadman, Thomas	1	$1,575
Daly, Justin	1	$1,368
Total:	13	$19,483
Source: Congressional office travel records for members of the Senate Committee on Commerce, Science & Transportation and the House Committee on Energy and Commerce for the period of January 2000 to March 2004.		

Gillmor, Paul E.

Representative (R-OH)

House Committee on Energy and Commerce

1203 Longworth House Office Building
Washington, DC 20515
Phone: (202) 225-6405
Fax: (800) 278-8203

Web Page: http://www.house.gov/gillmor/
Email: http://www.house.gov/gillmor/mail.htm

Contribution Summary By Telecommunications Sector	
Phones	$60,300
PayTV - Cable	$33,998
Broadcast	$10,000
Satellite	$1,000
Other	$500
Total:	$105,798

Source: Federal Election Commission contribution records from January 1998 to September 2004

Contributions by Telecommunications Sector Organizations				
Company	Sector	#	Total	Avg.
National Cable and Telecommunications Association	PayTV - Cable	9	$30,998	$3,444
SBC Communications Inc.	Phones	19	$21,800	$1,147
Cingular Wireless	Phones	10	$10,500	$1,050
Verizon Communications Inc.	Phones	12	$8,000	$667
General Electric Co.	Broadcast	6	$6,500	$1,083
AT&T Wireless	Phones	3	$4,500	$1,500
Qwest Communications International Inc.	Phones	3	$3,000	$1,000
United States Telecom Association	Phones	3	$2,500	$833
National Association of Broadcasters	Broadcast	3	$2,500	$833
Time Warner	PayTV - Cable	2	$2,000	$1,000
AT&T Corp.	Phones	3	$2,000	$667
Sprint Corp.	Phones	3	$2,000	$667
National Telephone Cooperative Association	Phones	3	$1,500	$500
ALLTEL Corp.	Phones	2	$1,000	$500
AirTouch Communications Inc.	Broadcast	2	$1,000	$500
News Corp Ltd.	Phones	1	$1,000	$1,000
Cellular Telecommunications & Internet Association	Satellite	2	$1,000	$500
Motorola Inc.	Phones	1	$500	$500
Teligent	Other	1	$500	$500
IDT Corp.	PayTV - Cable	1	$500	$500
Adelphia Communications Corp.	PayTV - Cable	1	$500	$500
Comcast Corp.				
	Total:		$105,798	

Source: Federal Election Commission contribution records from January 1998 to September 2004

Telecommunications Company Provided Trips to Committee Member's Staff			
Company	Sector	#	Total $
SBC Communications Inc.	Phones	1	$1,685
	Total:	1	$1,685

Source: Congressional office travel records for members of the Senate Committee on Commerce, Science & Transportation and the House Committee on Energy and Commerce for the period of January 2000 to March 2004.

Trips by Committee Member's Staff Sponsored by the Telecommunications Industry		
Individual	#	Total $
Beck, Andrew	1	$1,685
Total:	1	$1,685

Source: Congressional office travel records for members of the Senate Committee on Commerce, Science & Transportation and the House Committee on Energy and Commerce for the period of January 2000 to March 2004.

Gonzalez, Charles A.

Representative (D-TX)

House Committee on Energy and Commerce

327 Cannon House Office Building
Washington, DC 20515
Phone: (202) 225-3236
Fax: (202) 225-1915

Web Page: http://www.house.gov/gonzalez/
Email: http://www.house.gov/writerep

Contribution Summary By Telecommunications Sector	
Phones	$55,250
Union	$43,250
Broadcast	$25,750
PayTV - Cable	$5,499
Satellite	$500
Other	$250
Total:	$130,499

Source: Federal Election Commission contribution records from January 1998 to September 2004

Contributions by Telecommunications Sector Organizations				
Company	Sector	#	Total	Avg.
SBC Communications Inc.	Phones	31	$33,250	$1,073
Communications Workers of America	Union	9	$24,000	$2,667
International Brotherhood of Electrical Workers (IBEW)	Union	8	$14,500	$1,813
Clear Channel Communications Inc.	Broadcast	7	$12,500	$1,786
Verizon Communications Inc.	Phones	16	$8,500	$531
Cingular Wireless	Phones	6	$6,000	$1,000
General Electric Co.	Broadcast	8	$5,500	$688
Qwest Communications International Inc.	Phones	3	$5,000	$1,667
National Cable and Telecommunications Association	PayTV - Cable	2	$4,999	$2,500
Transportation Communications International Union	Union	10	$4,750	$475
Pappas Telecasting Cos.	Broadcast	1	$2,500	$2,500
News Corp Ltd.	Broadcast	2	$2,000	$1,000
United States Telecom Association	Phones	1	$1,500	$1,500
Univision Communications Inc.	Broadcast	2	$1,500	$750
Hearst Corp.	Broadcast	2	$1,250	$625
Deutsche Telekom AG (T-Mobile)	Phones	1	$1,000	$1,000
Motorola Inc.	Satellite	1	$500	$500
National Association of Broadcasters	Broadcast	1	$500	$500
Time Warner	PayTV - Cable	1	$500	$500
Telecommunication Development Fund Inc.	Other	1	$250	$250
	Total:		$130,499	

Source: Federal Election Commission contribution records from January 1998 to September 2004

Gordon, Bart

Representative (D-TN)

House Committee on Energy and Commerce

2304 Rayburn House Office Building
Washington, DC 20515
Phone: (202) 225-4231
Fax: (202) 225-6887

Web Page: http://gordon.house.gov/
Email: http://www.house.gov/writerep/

Contribution Summary By Telecommunications Sector	
Phones	$95,491
Union	$43,000
PayTV - Cable	$36,246
Broadcast	$25,750
Satellite	$7,500
PayTV - Satellite	$4,500
Other	$1,500
Total:	$213,987

Source: Federal Election Commission contribution records from January 1998 to September 2004

Contributions by Telecommunications Sector Organizations				
Company	Sector	#	Total	Avg.
International Brotherhood of Electrical Workers (IBEW)	Union	8	$25,500	$3,188
National Cable and Telecommunications Association	PayTV - Cable	10	$19,496	$1,950
Cingular Wireless	Phones	10	$18,000	$1,800
BellSouth Corp.	Phones	8	$16,400	$2,050
Communications Workers of America	Union	9	$15,000	$1,667
Time Warner	PayTV - Cable	10	$13,000	$1,300
SBC Communications Inc.	Phones	12	$12,000	$1,000
MCI (formerly WorldCom Inc.)	Phones	12	$10,500	$875
General Electric Co.	Broadcast	14	$10,000	$714
AT&T Wireless	Phones	10	$8,000	$800
Loral Space & Communications Ltd.	Satellite	13	$7,500	$577
ALLTEL Corp.	Phones	8	$6,000	$750
National Association of Broadcasters	Broadcast	8	$4,750	$594
Echostar Corp.	PayTV - Satellite	7	$4,500	$643
Viacom Inc.	Broadcast	6	$4,000	$667
Walt Disney Co.	Broadcast	4	$4,000	$1,000
Verizon Communications Inc.	Phones	7	$4,000	$571
Sprint Corp.	Phones	5	$3,500	$700
United States Telecom Association	Phones	6	$3,091	$515
United States Cellular Corp.	Phones	4	$2,500	$625
Transportation Communications International Union	Union	5	$2,500	$500
Cellular Telecommunications & Internet Association	Phones	4	$2,000	$500
Charter Communications Inc.	PayTV - Cable	7	$2,000	$286
News Corp Ltd.	Broadcast	3	$2,000	$667
IDT Corp.	Other	4	$1,500	$375
National Telephone Cooperative Association	Phones	3	$1,500	$500
Qwest Communications International Inc.	Phones	2	$1,500	$750
Comptel/ASCENT	Phones	1	$1,000	$1,000
CenturyTel Inc.	Phones	2	$1,000	$500
Telephone Electronics Corp.	Phones	1	$1,000	$1,000
Meredith Corp.	Broadcast	2	$1,000	$500
AirTouch Communications Inc.	Phones	2	$1,000	$500
SAVVIS Communications Corp.	PayTV - Cable	1	$1,000	$1,000
Comcast Corp.	PayTV - Cable	2	$750	$375
Alaska Communications Systems	Phones	2	$500	$250
Teligent	Phones	2	$500	$250
XO Communications Inc.	Phones	1	$500	$500
Cincinnati Bell Inc.	Phones	1	$500	$500
ICG Communications Inc.	Phones	1	$500	$500
		Total:	$213,987	

Source: Federal Election Commission contribution records from January 1998 to September 2004

Telecommunications Company Provided Trips to Committee Member's Staff			
Company	Sector	#	Total $
United States Telecom Association	Phones	2	$2,985
Cellular Telecommunications & Internet Association	Phones	1	$1,753
National Cable and Telecommunications Association	PayTV - Cable	1	$1,572
Time Warner	PayTV - Cable	1	$1,502
Misc. telecom interests	Other	1	$545
	Total:	6	$8,356

Source: Congressional office travel records for members of the Senate Committee on Commerce, Science & Transportation and the House Committee on Energy and Commerce for the period of January 2000 to March 2004.

Trips by Committee Member's Staff Sponsored by the Telecommunications Industry		
Individual	#	Total $
Lichtenberg, Dana	5	$6,785
Lichtneberg, Dana	1	$1,572
Total:	6	$8,356

Source: Congressional office travel records for members of the Senate Committee on Commerce, Science & Transportation and the House Committee on Energy and Commerce for the period of January 2000 to March 2004.

Green, Gene

Representative (D-TX)

House Committee on Energy and Commerce

2335 Rayburn House Office Building
Washington, DC 20515
Phone: (202) 225-1688
Fax: (202) 225-9903

Web Page: http://www.house.gov/green/
Email: http://www.house.gov/green/contact/

Contribution Summary By Telecommunications Sector	
Phones	$83,750
Union	$71,000
Broadcast	$31,148
PayTV - Cable	$29,442
Total:	$215,340

Source: Federal Election Commission contribution records from January 1998 to September 2004

Contributions by Telecommunications Sector Organizations				
Company	Sector	#	Total	Avg.
Communications Workers of America	Union	10	$35,000	$3,500
SBC Communications Inc.	Phones	33	$32,500	$985
International Brotherhood of Electrical Workers (IBEW)	Union	17	$32,000	$1,882
National Cable and Telecommunications Association	PayTV - Cable	9	$28,142	$3,127
Verizon Communications Inc.	Phones	26	$24,000	$923
National Association of Broadcasters	Broadcast	11	$15,148	$1,377
Cingular Wireless	Phones	14	$13,500	$964
General Electric Co.	Broadcast	9	$6,000	$667
Transportation Communications International Union	Union	8	$4,000	$500
Viacom Inc.	Broadcast	5	$3,500	$700
Cellular Telecommunications & Internet Association	Phones	6	$3,000	$500
ALLTEL Corp.	Phones	2	$3,000	$1,500
Belo Corp.	Broadcast	3	$2,000	$667
Clear Channel Communications Inc.	Broadcast	2	$2,000	$1,000
Qwest Communications International Inc.	Phones	3	$2,000	$667
Walt Disney Co.	Broadcast	2	$1,500	$750
AT&T Wireless	Phones	6	$1,500	$250
Time Warner	PayTV - Cable	2	$1,300	$650
MCI (formerly WorldCom Inc.)	Phones	6	$1,000	$167
United States Telecom Association	Phones	1	$1,000	$1,000
VALOR Telecommunications	Phones	1	$750	$750
Western Wireless Corp.	Phones	1	$500	$500
National Telephone Cooperative Association	Phones	1	$500	$500
Teligent	Phones	1	$500	$500
News Corp Ltd.	Broadcast	1	$500	$500
Paxson Communications Corp.	Broadcast	1	$500	$500
	Total:		$215,340	

Source: Federal Election Commission contribution records from January 1998 to September 2004

Telecommunications Company Provided Trips to Committee Member's Staff			
Company	Sector	#	Total $
National Association of Broadcasters	Broadcast	3	$12,609
National Cable and Telecommunications Association	PayTV - Cable	1	$5,641
Total:		4	$18,251

Source: Congressional office travel records for members of the Senate Committee on Commerce, Science & Transportation and the House Committee on Energy and Commerce for the period of January 2000 to March 2004.

Trips by Committee Member's Staff Sponsored by the Telecommunications Industry		
Individual	#	Total $
Green, Gene	3	$16,659
Woehrle, Patrick	1	$1,591
Total:	4	$18,251

Source: Congressional office travel records for members of the Senate Committee on Commerce, Science & Transportation and the House Committee on Energy and Commerce for the period of January 2000 to March 2004.

Greenwood, James C.

House Committee on Energy and Commerce

2436 Rayburn House Office Building
Washington, DC 20515
Phone: (202) 225-4276
Fax: (202) 225-9511

Web Page: http://www.house.gov/greenwood/
Email: http://www.house.gov/greenwood/contact.shtml

Contribution Summary By Telecommunications Sector	
Phones	$11,250
PayTV - Cable	$10,800
Satellite	$4,800
Broadcast	$500
Total:	$27,350
Source: Federal Election Commission contribution records from January 1998 to September 2004	

Contributions by Telecommunications Sector Organizations				
Company	Sector	#	Total	Avg.
Verizon Communications Inc.	Phones	32	$10,750	$336
Comcast Corp.	PayTV - Cable	18	$8,000	$444
Motorola Inc.	Satellite	10	$4,800	$480
National Cable and Telecommunications Association	PayTV - Cable	2	$1,300	$650
Time Warner	PayTV - Cable	4	$1,000	$250
Viacom Inc.	Broadcast	1	$500	$500
Adelphia Communications Corp.	PayTV - Cable	1	$500	$500
MCI (formerly WorldCom Inc.)	Phones	1	$500	$500
SBC Communications Inc.	Phones	2	-	-
Cingular Wireless	Phones	2	-	-
		Total:	$27,350	
Source: Federal Election Commission contribution records from January 1998 to September 2004				

Networks of Influence **Appendix B – Page 241**

Issa, Darrell

Representative (R-CA)

House Committee on Energy and Commerce

211 Cannon House Office Building
Washington, DC 20515
Phone: (202) 225-3906
Fax: (202) 225-3303

Web Page: http://www.issa.house.gov/
Email: http://issa.house.gov/contact/dsp_contact.asp

Contribution Summary By Telecommunications Sector	
Phones	$45,268
PayTV - Cable	$15,000
Broadcast	$12,000
PayTV - Satellite	$2,000
Satellite	$1,000
Total:	$75,268

Source: Federal Election Commission contribution records from January 1998 to September 2004

Contributions by Telecommunications Sector Organizations				
Company	Sector	#	Total	Avg.
SBC Communications Inc.	Phones	15	$20,000	$1,333
National Cable and Telecommunications Association	PayTV - Cable	2	$8,500	$4,250
United States Telecom Association	Phones	4	$5,768	$1,442
Verizon Communications Inc.	Phones	4	$5,000	$1,250
Cingular Wireless	Phones	5	$5,000	$1,000
National Association of Broadcasters	Broadcast	4	$4,000	$1,000
News Corp Ltd.	Broadcast	3	$3,500	$1,167
AT&T Wireless	Phones	4	$3,500	$875
Cox Communications Inc.	PayTV - Cable	10	$2,500	$250
Qwest Communications International Inc.	Phones	3	$2,500	$833
Time Warner	PayTV - Cable	2	$2,000	$1,000
Echostar Corp.	PayTV - Satellite	2	$2,000	$1,000
General Electric Co.	Broadcast	2	$2,000	$1,000
Sprint Corp.	Phones	2	$2,000	$1,000
Motorola Inc.	Satellite	1	$1,000	$1,000
Clear Channel Communications Inc.	Broadcast	1	$1,000	$1,000
SAVVIS Communications Corp.	PayTV - Cable	2	$1,000	$500
Viacom Inc.	Broadcast	1	$1,000	$1,000
Comcast Corp.	PayTV - Cable	1	$1,000	$1,000
MCI (formerly WorldCom Inc.)	Phones	2	$1,000	$500
Covad Communications Co.	Phones	1	$500	$500
Pappas Telecasting Cos.	Broadcast	1	$500	$500
		Total:	$75,268	

Source: Federal Election Commission contribution records from January 1998 to September 2004

Telecommunications Company Provided Trips to Committee Member's Staff			
Company	Sector	#	Total $
National Cable and Telecommunications Association	PayTV - Cable	3	$5,563
United States Telecom Association	Phones	1	$2,577
SBC Communications Inc.	Phones	1	$1,266
Telecommunications Industry Association	Other	1	$539
	Total:	6	$9,945

Source: Congressional office travel records for members of the Senate Committee on Commerce, Science & Transportation and the House Committee on Energy and Commerce for the period of January 2000 to March 2004.

Trips by Committee Member's Staff Sponsored by the Telecommunications Industry		
Individual	#	Total $
Issa, Darrell	2	$5,315
Brown, Joshua	2	$1,805
Anderson, Mark	1	$1,537
Anderson, Paige	1	$1,288
Total:	6	$9,945

Source: Congressional office travel records for members of the Senate Committee on Commerce, Science & Transportation and the House Committee on Energy and Commerce for the period of January 2000 to March 2004.

John, Christopher

Representative (D-LA)

House Committee on Energy and Commerce

403 Cannon House Office Building
Washington, DC 20515
Phone: (202) 225-2031
Fax: (202) 225-5724

Web Page: http://www.house.gov/john/
Email: http://www.house.gov/writerep/

Contribution Summary By Telecommunications Sector	
Phones	$53,906
Broadcast	$32,943
PayTV - Cable	$19,278
Union	$5,000
Total:	$111,127
Source: Federal Election Commission contribution records from January 1998 to September 2004	

Contributions by Telecommunications Sector Organizations				
Company	Sector	#	Total	Avg.
General Electric Co.	Broadcast	15	$13,000	$867
Verizon Communications Inc.	Phones	13	$12,500	$962
SBC Communications Inc.	Phones	10	$12,000	$1,200
National Association of Broadcasters	Broadcast	8	$8,693	$1,087
National Cable and Telecommunications Association	PayTV - Cable	4	$8,528	$2,132
Cingular Wireless	Phones	3	$6,500	$2,167
BellSouth Corp.	Phones	6	$6,250	$1,042
Walt Disney Co.	Broadcast	7	$6,000	$857
United States Telecom Association	Phones	6	$5,906	$984
Time Warner	PayTV - Cable	6	$5,500	$917
International Brotherhood of Electrical Workers (IBEW)	Union	1	$5,000	$5,000
AT&T Wireless	Phones	5	$4,000	$800
Comcast Corp.	PayTV - Cable	4	$3,250	$813
Clear Channel Communications Inc.	Broadcast	2	$2,000	$1,000
American Cable Association	PayTV - Cable	4	$2,000	$500
Viacom Inc.	Broadcast	2	$2,000	$1,000
Qwest Communications International Inc.	Phones	2	$2,000	$1,000
Cellular Telecommunications & Internet Association	Phones	3	$1,250	$417
Liberty Corp.	Broadcast	2	$1,250	$625
ALLTEL Corp.	Phones	1	$1,000	$1,000
MCI (formerly WorldCom Inc.)	Phones	1	$1,000	$1,000
Sprint Corp.	Phones	1	$1,000	$1,000
National Telephone Cooperative Association	Phones	1	$500	$500
	Total:		$111,127	
Source: Federal Election Commission contribution records from January 1998 to September 2004				

Telecommunications Company Provided Trips to Committee Member's Staff			
Company	Sector	#	Total $
United States Telecom Association	Phones	2	$3,190
National Cable and Telecommunications Association	PayTV - Cable	2	$3,004
Misc. telecom interests	Other	2	$1,452
Cellular Telecommunications & Internet Association	Phones	1	$951
BellSouth Corp.	Phones	1	$921
	Total:	8	$9,518
Source: Congressional office travel records for members of the Senate Committee on Commerce, Science & Transportation and the House Committee on Energy and Commerce for the period of January 2000 to March 2004.			

Trips by Committee Member's Staff Sponsored by the Telecommunications Industry		
Individual	#	Total $
Taylor, Gordon	7	$8,930
Kay, David	1	$589
Total:	8	$9,518
Source: Congressional office travel records for members of the Senate Committee on Commerce, Science & Transportation and the House Committee on Energy and Commerce for the period of January 2000 to March 2004.		

Markey, Edward J.

House Committee on Energy and Commerce

2108 Rayburn House Office Building
Washington, DC 20515
Phone: (202) 225-2836
Fax: (202) 226-0092

Representative (D-MA)

Ranking Member

Web Page: http://www.house.gov/markey/
Email: http://www.house.gov/writerep/

Contribution Summary By Telecommunications Sector	
Phones	$163,650
Broadcast	$141,050
PayTV - Cable	$67,250
PayTV - Satellite	$25,500
Other	$25,000
Union	$12,000
Satellite	$5,000
Total:	$439,450

Source: Federal Election Commission contribution records from January 1998 to September 2004

Contributions by Telecommunications Sector Organizations				
Company	Sector	#	Total	Avg.
Time Warner	PayTV - Cable	30	$33,250	$1,108
Walt Disney Co.	Broadcast	28	$33,050	$1,180
Echostar Corp.	PayTV - Satellite	25	$22,500	$900
News Corp Ltd.	Broadcast	18	$22,000	$1,222
AT&T Corp.	Phones	30	$21,650	$722
Viacom Inc.	Broadcast	19	$21,000	$1,105
XO Communications Inc.	Phones	18	$19,500	$1,083
MCI (formerly WorldCom Inc.)	Phones	13	$17,750	$1,365
Sprint Corp.	Phones	10	$16,000	$1,600
Verizon Communications Inc.	Phones	14	$14,500	$1,036
General Electric Co.	Broadcast	13	$14,500	$1,115
National Cable and Telecommunications Association	PayTV - Cable	5	$14,000	$2,800
AT&T Wireless	Phones	8	$13,250	$1,656
Comptel/ASCENT	Phones	11	$13,250	$1,205
Global Crossing Ltd.	Other	12	$12,500	$1,042
Cingular Wireless	Phones	24	$11,300	$471
National Association of Broadcasters	Broadcast	5	$11,000	$2,200
Comcast Corp.	PayTV - Cable	5	$10,000	$2,000
Communications Workers of America	Union	2	$10,000	$5,000
Cellular Telecommunications & Internet Association	Phones	10	$9,250	$925
Clear Channel Communications Inc.	Broadcast	5	$9,000	$1,800
Cablevision Systems Corp.	PayTV - Cable	7	$8,000	$1,143
Tribune Co.	Broadcast	11	$7,750	$705
Pappas Telecasting Cos.	Broadcast	3	$7,000	$2,333
Teligent	Phones	6	$6,000	$1,000
Hubbard Broadcasting Inc.	Broadcast	6	$5,500	$917
IDT Corp.	Other	5	$5,000	$1,000
Loral Space & Communications Ltd.	Satellite	4	$5,000	$1,250
Deutsche Telekom AG (T-Mobile)	Phones	4	$5,000	$1,250
Misc. telecom interests	Other	6	$4,500	$750
Qwest Communications International Inc.	Phones	10	$4,000	$400
BellSouth Corp.	Phones	7	$3,200	$457
The DirecTV Group Inc.	PayTV - Satellite	3	$3,000	$1,000
Level 3 Communications Inc.	Other	2	$3,000	$1,500
Westwood One Inc.	Broadcast	2	$2,000	$1,000
Univision Communications Inc.	Broadcast	1	$2,000	$2,000
Emmis Communications Corp.	Broadcast	2	$2,000	$1,000
Transportation Communications International Union	Union	4	$2,000	$500
Hearst Corp.	Broadcast	2	$1,500	$750
Paxson Communications Corp.	Broadcast	2	$1,500	$750
Belo Corp.	Broadcast	2	$1,250	$625
American Cable Association	PayTV - Cable	1	$1,000	$1,000
SAVVIS Communications Corp.	PayTV - Cable	4	$1,000	$250

Contributions by Telecommunications Sector Organizations				
Company	Sector	#	Total	Avg.
Covad Communications Co.	Phones	1	$1,000	$1,000
Western Wireless Corp.	Phones	1	$1,000	$1,000
SBC Communications Inc.	Phones	2	$1,000	$500
Telephone Electronics Corp.	Phones	1	$1,000	$1,000
Forstmann Little & Co.	Phones	1	$1,000	$1,000
ICG Communications Inc.	Phones	1	$1,000	$1,000
National Telephone Cooperative Association	Phones	3	$1,000	$333
Nextel Communications	Phones	1	$500	$500
United States Cellular Corp.	Phones	1	$500	$500
VALOR Telecommunications	Phones	1	$500	$500
AirTouch Communications Inc.	Phones	1	$500	$500
		Total:	$439,450	

Source: Federal Election Commission contribution records from January 1998 to September 2004

Telecommunications Company Provided Trips to Committee Member's Staff			
Company	Sector	#	Total $
National Association of Broadcasters	Broadcast	1	$958
Comptel/ASCENT	Phones	1	$425
	Total:	2	$1,383

Source: Congressional office travel records for members of the Senate Committee on Commerce, Science & Transportation and the House Committee on Energy and Commerce for the period of January 2000 to March 2004.

Trips by Committee Member's Staff Sponsored by the Telecommunications Industry		
Individual	#	Total $
Crowell, Colin	2	$1,383
Total:	2	$1,383

Source: Congressional office travel records for members of the Senate Committee on Commerce, Science & Transportation and the House Committee on Energy and Commerce for the period of January 2000 to March 2004.

McCarthy, Karen

Representative (D-MO)

House Committee on Energy and Commerce

1436 Longworth House Office Building
Washington, DC 20515
Phone: (202) 225-4535
Fax: (202) 225-4403

Web Page: http://mccarthy.house.gov/
Email:
http://mccarthy.house.gov/feedback.cfm?campaign=mccarthy&type=Contact%20Karen

Contribution Summary By Telecommunications Sector	
Phones	$34,351
PayTV - Cable	$28,464
Union	$11,000
Broadcast	$7,750
Satellite	$2,000
Other	$1,500
Total:	$85,065

Source: Federal Election Commission contribution records from January 1998 to September 2004

Contributions by Telecommunications Sector Organizations				
Company	Sector	#	Total	Avg.
National Cable and Telecommunications Association	PayTV - Cable	9	$18,214	$2,024
Sprint Corp.	Phones	15	$11,851	$790
International Brotherhood of Electrical Workers (IBEW)	Union	6	$9,000	$1,500
MCI (formerly WorldCom Inc.)	Phones	10	$8,500	$850
AT&T Wireless	Phones	10	$7,000	$700
Charter Communications Inc.	PayTV - Cable	7	$4,000	$571
General Electric Co.	Broadcast	4	$3,000	$750
National Association of Broadcasters	Broadcast	3	$2,500	$833
Time Warner	PayTV - Cable	3	$2,250	$750
Cablevision Systems Corp.	PayTV - Cable	1	$2,000	$2,000
ALLTEL Corp.	Phones	3	$2,000	$667
Loral Space & Communications Ltd.	Satellite	4	$2,000	$500
Communications Workers of America	Union	2	$2,000	$1,000
Comcast Corp.	PayTV - Cable	4	$1,500	$375
Meredith Corp.	Broadcast	3	$1,500	$500
IDT Corp.	Other	1	$1,000	$1,000
Cellular Telecommunications & Internet Association	Phones	2	$1,000	$500
Cingular Wireless	Phones	1	$1,000	$1,000
Comptel/ASCENT	Phones	2	$1,000	$500
SBC Communications Inc.	Phones	2	$1,000	$500
Personal Communications Industry Association	Phones	1	$500	$500
Misc. telecom interests	Other	1	$500	$500
Viacom Inc.	Broadcast	1	$500	$500
SAVVIS Communications Corp.	PayTV - Cable	1	$500	$500
AirTouch Communications Inc.	Phones	1	$500	$500
Paxson Communications Corp.	Broadcast	1	$250	$250
Walt Disney Co.	Broadcast	2	-	-
		Total:	$85,065	

Source: Federal Election Commission contribution records from January 1998 to September 2004

Telecommunications Company Provided Trips to Committee Member's Staff			
Company	Sector	#	Total $
Clear Channel Communications Inc.	Broadcast	1	$1,344
	Total:	1	$1,344

Source: Congressional office travel records for members of the Senate Committee on Commerce, Science & Transportation and the House Committee on Energy and Commerce for the period of January 2000 to March 2004.

Trips by Committee Member's Staff Sponsored by the Telecommunications Industry		
Individual	#	Total $
Mott, David	1	$1,344
Total:	1	$1,344

Source: Congressional office travel records for members of the Senate Committee on Commerce, Science & Transportation and the House Committee on Energy and Commerce for the period of January 2000 to March 2004.

Norwood, Charlie

Representative (R-GA)

House Committee on Energy and Commerce

2452 Rayburn House Office Building
Washington, DC 20515
Phone: (202) 225-4101
Fax: (202) 226-0776

Web Page: http://www.house.gov/norwood/
Email: http://www.house.gov/writerep/

Contribution Summary By Telecommunications Sector	
Phones	$64,791
PayTV - Cable	$33,852
Broadcast	$16,418
Total:	$115,061
Source: Federal Election Commission contribution records from January 1998 to September 2004	

Contributions by Telecommunications Sector Organizations				
Company	Sector	#	Total	Avg.
National Cable and Telecommunications Association	PayTV - Cable	9	$21,552	$2,395
SBC Communications Inc.	Phones	22	$17,000	$773
Viacom Inc.	Broadcast	19	$9,750	$513
Cingular Wireless	Phones	10	$9,500	$950
BellSouth Corp.	Phones	8	$7,000	$875
ALLTEL Corp.	Phones	11	$6,700	$609
National Association of Broadcasters	Broadcast	8	$6,668	$834
Comcast Corp.	PayTV - Cable	7	$5,800	$829
United States Telecom Association	Phones	5	$5,091	$1,018
Verizon Communications Inc.	Phones	5	$5,000	$1,000
AT&T Wireless	Phones	6	$5,000	$833
Time Warner	PayTV - Cable	3	$4,000	$1,333
MCI (formerly WorldCom Inc.)	Phones	5	$4,000	$800
Cellular Telecommunications & Internet Association	Phones	3	$2,000	$667
Charter Communications Inc.	PayTV - Cable	4	$2,000	$500
Sprint Corp.	Phones	5	$1,500	$300
AirTouch Communications Inc.	Phones	2	$1,000	$500
American Cable Association	PayTV - Cable	1	$500	$500
United States Cellular Corp.	Phones	1	$500	$500
National Telephone Cooperative Association	Phones	1	$500	$500
		Total:	$115,061	
Source: Federal Election Commission contribution records from January 1998 to September 2004				

Telecommunications Company Provided Trips to Committee Member's Staff			
Company	Sector	#	Total $
National Cable and Telecommunications Association	PayTV - Cable	1	$3,750
	Total:	1	$3,750
Source: Congressional office travel records for members of the Senate Committee on Commerce, Science & Transportation and the House Committee on Energy and Commerce for the period of January 2000 to March 2004.			

Trips by Committee Member's Staff Sponsored by the Telecommunications Industry		
Individual	#	Total $
Norwood, Charlie	1	$3,750
Total:	1	$3,750
Source: Congressional office travel records for members of the Senate Committee on Commerce, Science & Transportation and the House Committee on Energy and Commerce for the period of January 2000 to March 2004.		

Otter, C.L. "Butch"

Representative (R-ID)

House Committee on Energy and Commerce

1711 Longworth House Office Building
Washington, DC 20515
Phone: (202) 225-6611
Fax: (202) 225-3029

Web Page: http://www.house.gov/otter/
Email: http://www.house.gov/otter/email.htm

Contribution Summary By Telecommunications Sector	
Phones	$44,665
Broadcast	$6,000
PayTV - Cable	$1,000
Total:	$51,665
Source: Federal Election Commission contribution records from January 1998 to September 2004	

Contributions by Telecommunications Sector Organizations				
Company	Sector	#	Total	Avg.
Qwest Communications International Inc.	Phones	23	$17,665	$768
Verizon Communications Inc.	Phones	8	$9,000	$1,125
SBC Communications Inc.	Phones	7	$8,500	$1,214
Cingular Wireless	Phones	7	$7,500	$1,071
General Electric Co.	Broadcast	5	$5,000	$1,000
National Association of Broadcasters	Broadcast	1	$1,000	$1,000
American Cable Association	PayTV - Cable	2	$1,000	$500
AT&T Wireless	Phones	2	$1,000	$500
United States Telecom Association	Phones	2	$1,000	$500
		Total:	$51,665	
Source: Federal Election Commission contribution records from January 1998 to September 2004				

Telecommunications Company Provided Trips to Committee Member's Staff			
Company	Sector	#	Total $
Clear Channel Communications Inc.	Broadcast	1	$1,296
	Total:	1	$1,296
Source: Congressional office travel records for members of the Senate Committee on Commerce, Science & Transportation and the House Committee on Energy and Commerce for the period of January 2000 to March 2004.			

Trips by Committee Member's Staff Sponsored by the Telecommunications Industry		
Individual	#	Total $
Heiner, Brandon	1	$1,296
Total:	1	$1,296
Source: Congressional office travel records for members of the Senate Committee on Commerce, Science & Transportation and the House Committee on Energy and Commerce for the period of January 2000 to March 2004.		

Pallone, Jr., Frank

Representative (D-NJ)

House Committee on Energy and Commerce

420 Cannon House Office Building
Washington, DC 20515
Phone: (202) 225-4671
Fax: (202) 225-9665

Web Page: http://www.house.gov/pallone/
Email: http://www.house.gov/writerep/

Contribution Summary By Telecommunications Sector	
PayTV - Cable	$50,893
Union	$50,000
Phones	$39,250
Broadcast	$22,240
PayTV - Satellite	$2,500
Satellite	$500
Total:	$165,383

Source: Federal Election Commission contribution records from January 1998 to September 2004

Contributions by Telecommunications Sector Organizations				
Company	Sector	#	Total	Avg.
International Brotherhood of Electrical Workers (IBEW)	Union	22	$30,000	$1,364
National Cable and Telecommunications Association	PayTV - Cable	9	$21,193	$2,355
AT&T Wireless	Phones	18	$17,500	$972
National Association of Broadcasters	Broadcast	15	$17,490	$1,166
Communications Workers of America	Union	7	$16,500	$2,357
Cablevision Systems Corp.	PayTV - Cable	13	$15,200	$1,169
Comcast Corp.	PayTV - Cable	6	$13,500	$2,250
MCI (formerly WorldCom Inc.)	Phones	13	$11,750	$904
Verizon Communications Inc.	Phones	5	$6,000	$1,200
Transportation Communications International Union	Union	7	$3,500	$500
The DirecTV Group Inc.	PayTV - Satellite	4	$2,500	$625
News Corp Ltd.	Broadcast	5	$2,500	$500
General Electric Co.	Broadcast	4	$2,000	$500
Sprint Corp.	Phones	2	$2,000	$1,000
Comptel/ASCENT	Phones	1	$1,000	$1,000
Adelphia Communications Corp.	PayTV - Cable	2	$1,000	$500
AT&T Corp.	Phones	1	$500	$500
SBC Communications Inc.	Phones	1	$500	$500
Loral Space & Communications Ltd.	Satellite	1	$500	$500
Viacom Inc.	Broadcast	1	$250	$250
		Total:	$165,383	

Source: Federal Election Commission contribution records from January 1998 to September 2004

Telecommunications Company Provided Trips to Committee Member's Staff			
Company	Sector	#	Total $
News Corp Ltd.	Broadcast	1	$2,258
National Association of Broadcasters	Broadcast	1	$1,430
United States Telecom Association	Phones	1	$1,202
	Total:	3	$4,890

Source: Congressional office travel records for members of the Senate Committee on Commerce, Science & Transportation and the House Committee on Energy and Commerce for the period of January 2000 to March 2004.

Trips by Committee Member's Staff Sponsored by the Telecommunications Industry		
Individual	#	Total $
Yehl, Tim	2	$2,632
Carroll, Jeffrey	1	$2,258
Total:	3	$4,890

Source: Congressional office travel records for members of the Senate Committee on Commerce, Science & Transportation and the House Committee on Energy and Commerce for the period of January 2000 to March 2004.

Pickering, Charles W. "Chip"

Representative (R-MS)

House Committee on Energy and Commerce

229 Cannon House Office Building
Washington, DC 20515
Phone: (202) 225-5031
Fax: (202) 225-5797

Web Page: http://www.house.gov/pickering/
Email: http://www.house.gov/pickering/Form.htm

Contribution Summary By Telecommunications Sector	
Phones	$264,031
PayTV - Cable	$82,848
Broadcast	$55,250
Other	$13,250
PayTV - Satellite	$3,500
Satellite	$2,500
Total:	$421,379

Source: Federal Election Commission contribution records from January 1998 to September 2004

Contributions by Telecommunications Sector Organizations				
Company	Sector	#	Total	Avg.
MCI (formerly WorldCom Inc.)	Phones	39	$46,550	$1,194
AT&T Wireless	Phones	28	$36,250	$1,295
XO Communications Inc.	Phones	33	$33,350	$1,011
National Cable and Telecommunications Association	PayTV - Cable	11	$31,498	$2,863
Comcast Corp.	PayTV - Cable	24	$28,850	$1,202
National Association of Broadcasters	Broadcast	11	$20,000	$1,818
Cingular Wireless	Phones	17	$16,500	$971
Sprint Corp.	Phones	13	$16,000	$1,231
Time Warner	PayTV - Cable	10	$15,500	$1,550
AT&T Corp.	Phones	22	$14,950	$680
Verizon Communications Inc.	Phones	13	$14,500	$1,115
General Electric Co.	Broadcast	14	$12,500	$893
BellSouth Corp.	Phones	14	$11,950	$854
ALLTEL Corp.	Phones	15	$10,709	$714
Viacom Inc.	Broadcast	6	$9,000	$1,500
Cellular Telecommunications & Internet Association	Phones	13	$8,564	$659
SBC Communications Inc.	Phones	9	$8,500	$944
Comptel/ASCENT	Phones	7	$7,000	$1,000
Walt Disney Co.	Broadcast	8	$6,750	$844
Teligent	Phones	10	$6,000	$600
Level 3 Communications Inc.	Other	6	$5,500	$917
Association for Local Telecommunications Services	Phones	8	$5,208	$651
Covad Communications Co.	Phones	5	$5,000	$1,000
Deutsche Telekom AG (T-Mobile)	Phones	4	$4,000	$1,000
IDT Corp.	Other	5	$4,000	$800
News Corp Ltd.	Broadcast	4	$3,000	$750
Western Wireless Corp.	Phones	5	$3,000	$600
Misc. telecom interests	Other	6	$2,500	$417
Echostar Corp.	PayTV - Satellite	3	$2,500	$833
SAVVIS Communications Corp.	PayTV - Cable	3	$2,500	$833
CenturyTel Inc.	Phones	3	$2,000	$667
Focal Communications Corp.	Phones	2	$2,000	$1,000
National Telephone Cooperative Association	Phones	4	$2,000	$500
Charter Communications Inc.	PayTV - Cable	3	$2,000	$667
Paxson Communications Corp.	Broadcast	2	$2,000	$1,000
Clear Channel Communications Inc.	Broadcast	1	$2,000	$2,000
United States Cellular Corp.	Phones	2	$2,000	$1,000
Telephone Electronics Corp.	Phones	2	$1,500	$750
Motorola Inc.	Satellite	2	$1,500	$750
Pac-West Telecomm Inc.	Phones	2	$1,500	$750
AirTouch Communications Inc.	Phones	2	$1,500	$750
Global Crossing Ltd.	Other	2	$1,250	$625
Cablevision Systems Corp.	PayTV - Cable	1	$1,000	$1,000
The DirecTV Group Inc.	PayTV - Satellite	2	$1,000	$500

Contributions by Telecommunications Sector Organizations				
Company	Sector	#	Total	Avg.
Salem Communications Corp.	PayTV - Cable	1	$1,000	$1,000
Qwest Communications International Inc.	Phones	2	$1,000	$500
Satellite Broadcasting & Communication Association	Satellite	1	$1,000	$1,000
United States Telecom Association	Phones	1	$1,000	$1,000
U.S. LEC Corp.	Phones	1	$1,000	$1,000
Cincinnati Bell Inc.	Phones	1	$500	$500
American Cable Association	PayTV - Cable	1	$500	$500
		Total:	$421,379	

Source: Federal Election Commission contribution records from January 1998 to September 2004

Telecommunications Company Provided Trips to Committee Member's Staff			
Company	Sector	#	Total $
Cellular Telecommunications & Internet Association	Phones	7	$11,125
National Cable and Telecommunications Association	PayTV - Cable	1	$1,538
United States Telecom Association	Phones	1	$1,464
Lockheed Martin	Satellite	2	$1,127
Misc. telecom interests	Other	1	$589
AT&T Corp.	Phones	2	$555
	Total:	14	$16,397

Source: Congressional office travel records for members of the Senate Committee on Commerce, Science & Transportation and the House Committee on Energy and Commerce for the period of January 2000 to March 2004.

Trips by Committee Member's Staff Sponsored by the Telecommunications Industry		
Individual	#	Total $
Pickering, Charles	3	$5,415
Chappell, Mike	2	$3,042
Pickering, Chip	4	$2,598
Chappell, Michael	3	$2,340
Butler, Susan	1	$1,538
Hurst, David Michael	1	$1,464
Total:	14	$16,397

Source: Congressional office travel records for members of the Senate Committee on Commerce, Science & Transportation and the House Committee on Energy and Commerce for the period of January 2000 to March 2004.

Pitts, Joseph R.

Representative (R-PA)

House Committee on Energy and Commerce

204 Cannon House Office Building
Washington, DC 20515
Phone: (202) 225-2411
Fax: (202) 225-2013

Web Page: http://www.house.gov/pitts/
Email: http://www.house.gov/pitts/service/correspond.htm

Contribution Summary By Telecommunications Sector	
Phones	$34,000
PayTV - Cable	$14,291
Broadcast	$9,410
Other	$1,000
PayTV - Satellite	$1,000
Total:	$59,701

Source: Federal Election Commission contribution records from January 1998 to September 2004

Contributions by Telecommunications Sector Organizations				
Company	Sector	#	Total	Avg.
AT&T Wireless	Phones	10	$12,000	$1,200
National Cable and Telecommunications Association	PayTV - Cable	2	$7,791	$3,896
Verizon Communications Inc.	Phones	9	$7,000	$778
Hearst Corp.	Broadcast	5	$5,000	$1,000
Sprint Corp.	Phones	5	$4,500	$900
MCI (formerly WorldCom Inc.)	Phones	4	$4,000	$1,000
National Association of Broadcasters	Broadcast	2	$2,910	$1,455
Qwest Communications International Inc.	Phones	2	$2,000	$1,000
Comcast Corp.	PayTV - Cable	2	$2,000	$1,000
Covad Communications Co.	Phones	2	$1,500	$750
General Electric Co.	Broadcast	2	$1,500	$750
American Cable Association	PayTV - Cable	3	$1,500	$500
SAVVIS Communications Corp.	PayTV - Cable	1	$1,500	$1,500
Time Warner	PayTV - Cable	1	$1,000	$1,000
The DirecTV Group Inc.	PayTV - Satellite	2	$1,000	$500
Misc. telecom interests	Other	1	$1,000	$1,000
Cellular Telecommunications & Internet Association	Phones	1	$1,000	$1,000
Cingular Wireless	Phones	1	$1,000	$1,000
Salem Communications Corp.	PayTV - Cable	1	$500	$500
AT&T Corp.	Phones	1	$500	$500
XO Communications Inc.	Phones	1	$500	$500
SBC Communications Inc.	Phones	2	-	-
		Total:	$59,701	

Source: Federal Election Commission contribution records from January 1998 to September 2004

Telecommunications Company Provided Trips to Committee Member's Staff			
Company	Sector	#	Total $
Misc. telecom interests	Other	2	$1,304
	Total:	2	$1,304

Source: Congressional office travel records for members of the Senate Committee on Commerce, Science & Transportation and the House Committee on Energy and Commerce for the period of January 2000 to March 2004.

Trips by Committee Member's Staff Sponsored by the Telecommunications Industry		
Individual	#	Total $
Carr, Julie	2	$1,304
Total:	2	$1,304

Source: Congressional office travel records for members of the Senate Committee on Commerce, Science & Transportation and the House Committee on Energy and Commerce for the period of January 2000 to March 2004.

Rush, Bobby L.

House Committee on Energy and Commerce

2416 Rayburn House Office Building
Washington, DC 20515
Phone: (202) 225-4372
Fax: (202) 226-0333

Web Page: http://www.house.gov/rush/
Email: http://www.house.gov/rush/zipauth.html

Contribution Summary By Telecommunications Sector	
Phones	$80,214
Union	$27,000
PayTV - Cable	$21,498
Broadcast	$12,000
Total:	$140,712

Source: Federal Election Commission contribution records from January 1998 to September 2004

Contributions by Telecommunications Sector Organizations				
Company	Sector	#	Total	Avg.
SBC Communications Inc.	Phones	38	$34,464	$907
Verizon Communications Inc.	Phones	16	$23,000	$1,438
International Brotherhood of Electrical Workers (IBEW)	Union	11	$17,500	$1,591
National Cable and Telecommunications Association	PayTV - Cable	6	$17,498	$2,916
Cingular Wireless	Phones	7	$7,250	$1,036
Communications Workers of America	Union	5	$7,000	$1,400
National Association of Broadcasters	Broadcast	4	$4,500	$1,125
Viacom Inc.	Broadcast	3	$4,000	$1,333
United States Telecom Association	Phones	4	$4,000	$1,000
Qwest Communications International Inc.	Phones	5	$4,000	$800
Comcast Corp.	PayTV - Cable	3	$3,000	$1,000
Transportation Communications International Union	Union	4	$2,500	$625
Walt Disney Co.	Broadcast	2	$2,000	$1,000
MCI (formerly WorldCom Inc.)	Phones	4	$2,000	$500
AT&T Corp.	Phones	3	$2,000	$667
AT&T Wireless	Phones	2	$1,500	$750
Covad Communications Co.	Phones	1	$1,000	$1,000
Clear Channel Communications Inc.	Broadcast	1	$1,000	$1,000
Time Warner	PayTV - Cable	1	$1,000	$1,000
ALLTEL Corp.	Phones	3	$1,000	$333
News Corp Ltd.	Broadcast	1	$500	$500
		Total:	$140,712	

Source: Federal Election Commission contribution records from January 1998 to September 2004

Telecommunications Company Provided Trips to Committee Member's Staff			
Company	Sector	#	Total $
SBC Communications Inc.	Phones	1	$2,178
	Total:	1	$2,178

Source: Congressional office travel records for members of the Senate Committee on Commerce, Science & Transportation and the House Committee on Energy and Commerce for the period of January 2000 to March 2004.

Trips by Committee Member's Staff Sponsored by the Telecommunications Industry		
Individual	#	Total $
Parker, Kimberly	1	$2,178
Total:	1	$2,178

Source: Congressional office travel records for members of the Senate Committee on Commerce, Science & Transportation and the House Committee on Energy and Commerce for the period of January 2000 to March 2004.

Schakowsky, Jan

House Committee on Energy and Commerce

515 Cannon House Office Building
Washington, DC 20515
Phone: (202) 225-2111
Fax: (202) 226-6890

Web Page: http://www.house.gov/schakowsky/
Email: http://www.house.gov/schakowsky/contact.html

Contribution Summary By Telecommunications Sector	
Union	$36,500
Phones	$11,550
Broadcast	$1,500
Total:	$49,550
Source: Federal Election Commission contribution records from January 1998 to September 2004	

Contributions by Telecommunications Sector Organizations				
Company	Sector	#	Total	Avg.
International Brotherhood of Electrical Workers (IBEW)	Union	12	$26,000	$2,167
Communications Workers of America	Union	9	$9,000	$1,000
SBC Communications Inc.	Phones	11	$5,750	$523
AT&T Wireless	Phones	3	$3,000	$1,000
MCI (formerly WorldCom Inc.)	Phones	4	$2,800	$700
Transportation Communications International Union	Union	3	$1,500	$500
General Electric Co.	Broadcast	1	$1,000	$1,000
Viacom Inc.	Broadcast	1	$500	$500
		Total:	$49,550	
Source: Federal Election Commission contribution records from January 1998 to September 2004				

Shadegg, John B.

Representative (R-AZ)

House Committee on Energy and Commerce

306 Cannon House Office Building
Washington, DC 20515
Phone: (202) 225-3361
Fax: (202) 225-3462

Web Page: http://johnshadegg.house.gov/
Email: http://www.house.gov/formshadegg/emailtemplate.htm

Contribution Summary By Telecommunications Sector	
Phones	$62,000
PayTV - Cable	$18,749
Broadcast	$10,000
Satellite	$1,500
Total:	$92,249
Source: Federal Election Commission contribution records from January 1998 to September 2004	

Contributions by Telecommunications Sector Organizations				
Company	Sector	#	Total	Avg.
AT&T Wireless	Phones	14	$20,000	$1,429
National Cable and Telecommunications Association	PayTV - Cable	4	$9,499	$2,375
MCI (formerly WorldCom Inc.)	Phones	7	$8,000	$1,143
Qwest Communications International Inc.	Phones	4	$8,000	$2,000
Time Warner	PayTV - Cable	6	$6,500	$1,083
Sprint Corp.	Phones	7	$6,000	$857
Cingular Wireless	Phones	6	$4,000	$667
ALLTEL Corp.	Phones	2	$3,000	$1,500
Viacom Inc.	Broadcast	3	$3,000	$1,000
National Association of Broadcasters	Broadcast	3	$3,000	$1,000
Covad Communications Co.	Phones	3	$2,500	$833
SBC Communications Inc.	Phones	2	$2,000	$1,000
SAVVIS Communications Corp.	PayTV - Cable	2	$2,000	$1,000
Comptel/ASCENT	Phones	3	$2,000	$667
Cellular Telecommunications & Internet Association	Phones	2	$1,500	$750
News Corp Ltd.	Broadcast	1	$1,500	$1,500
XO Communications Inc.	Phones	2	$1,500	$750
Motorola Inc.	Satellite	3	$1,500	$500
Verizon Communications Inc.	Phones	1	$1,000	$1,000
Focal Communications Corp.	Phones	1	$1,000	$1,000
Meredith Corp.	Broadcast	2	$1,000	$500
Walt Disney Co.	Broadcast	1	$1,000	$1,000
Association for Local Telecommunications Services	Phones	1	$1,000	$1,000
AirTouch Communications Inc.	Phones	1	$500	$500
Salem Communications Corp.	PayTV - Cable	1	$500	$500
General Electric Co.	Broadcast	1	$500	$500
Cox Communications Inc.	PayTV - Cable	1	$250	$250
		Total:	$92,249	
Source: Federal Election Commission contribution records from January 1998 to September 2004				

Telecommunications Company Provided Trips to Committee Member's Staff			
Company	Sector	#	Total $
National Association of Broadcasters	Broadcast	1	$265
	Total:	1	$265
Source: Congressional office travel records for members of the Senate Committee on Commerce, Science & Transportation and the House Committee on Energy and Commerce for the period of January 2000 to March 2004.			

Trips by Committee Member's Staff Sponsored by the Telecommunications Industry		
Individual	#	Total $
Noble, Sean	1	$265
Total:	1	$265
Source: Congressional office travel records for members of the Senate Committee on Commerce, Science & Transportation and the House Committee on Energy and Commerce for the period of January 2000 to March 2004.		

Shimkus, John

Representative (R-IL)

House Committee on Energy and Commerce

513 Cannon House Office Building
Washington, DC 20515
Phone: (202) 225-5271
Fax: (202) 225-5880

Web Page: http://www.house.gov/shimkus/
Email: http://www.house.gov/shimkus/emailme.htm

Contribution Summary By Telecommunications Sector	
Phones	$125,497
Broadcast	$44,198
PayTV - Cable	$42,746
Union	$13,000
Satellite	$1,650
PayTV - Satellite	$1,000
Total:	$228,091

Source: Federal Election Commission contribution records from January 1998 to September 2004

Contributions by Telecommunications Sector Organizations				
Company	Sector	#	Total	Avg.
SBC Communications Inc.	Phones	26	$39,000	$1,500
National Cable and Telecommunications Association	PayTV - Cable	12	$27,046	$2,254
Verizon Communications Inc.	Phones	21	$27,000	$1,286
National Association of Broadcasters	Broadcast	18	$22,198	$1,233
Cingular Wireless	Phones	16	$17,750	$1,109
International Brotherhood of Electrical Workers (IBEW)	Union	3	$12,500	$4,167
General Electric Co.	Broadcast	13	$9,500	$731
AT&T Wireless	Phones	13	$9,500	$731
Time Warner	PayTV - Cable	6	$8,500	$1,417
Qwest Communications International Inc.	Phones	8	$8,000	$1,000
United States Telecom Association	Phones	9	$7,609	$845
Viacom Inc.	Broadcast	6	$5,500	$917
Charter Communications Inc.	PayTV - Cable	11	$5,500	$500
Cellular Telecommunications & Internet Association	Phones	7	$4,000	$571
AT&T Corp.	Phones	1	$3,138	$3,138
Clear Channel Communications Inc.	Broadcast	2	$3,000	$1,500
National Telephone Cooperative Association	Phones	3	$2,500	$833
Sprint Corp.	Phones	3	$2,000	$667
ALLTEL Corp.	Phones	2	$2,000	$1,000
Motorola Inc.	Satellite	4	$1,650	$413
MCI (formerly WorldCom Inc.)	Phones	2	$1,500	$750
News Corp Ltd.	Broadcast	2	$1,500	$750
Emmis Communications Corp.	Broadcast	4	$1,250	$313
Walt Disney Co.	Broadcast	1	$1,000	$1,000
Echostar Corp.	PayTV - Satellite	1	$1,000	$1,000
Salem Communications Corp.	PayTV - Cable	1	$1,000	$1,000
XO Communications Inc.	Phones	1	$1,000	$1,000
Transportation Communications International Union	Union	1	$500	$500
Telephone Electronics Corp.	Phones	1	$500	$500
American Cable Association	PayTV - Cable	1	$500	$500
Tribune Co.	Broadcast	1	$250	$250
Cox Communications Inc.	PayTV - Cable	1	$200	$200
		Total:	$228,091	

Source: Federal Election Commission contribution records from January 1998 to September 2004

Telecommunications Company Provided Trips to Committee Member's Staff			
Company	Sector	#	Total $
National Cable and Telecommunications Association	PayTV - Cable	3	$4,431
SBC Communications Inc.	Phones	2	$3,667
United States Telecom Association	Phones	2	$2,396
Clear Channel Communications Inc.	Broadcast	1	$1,547
BellSouth Corp.	Phones	1	$1,215
Cellular Telecommunications & Internet Association	Phones	1	$1,094
	Total:	10	$14,349

Source: Congressional office travel records for members of the Senate Committee on Commerce, Science & Transportation and the House Committee on Energy and Commerce for the period of January 2000 to March 2004.

Trips by Committee Member's Staff Sponsored by the Telecommunications Industry		
Individual	#	Total $
Anderson, Courtney	8	$11,292
Childress, Kelly	1	$2,026
Shimkus, John	1	$1,032
Total:	10	$14,349

Source: Congressional office travel records for members of the Senate Committee on Commerce, Science & Transportation and the House Committee on Energy and Commerce for the period of January 2000 to March 2004.

Solis, Hilda L.

Representative (D-CA)

House Committee on Energy and Commerce

1725 Longworth House Office Building
Washington, DC 20515
Phone: (202) 225-5464
Fax: (202) 225-5467

Web Page: http://solis.house.gov/
Email: http://www.house.gov/writerep

Contribution Summary By Telecommunications Sector	
Union	$37,000
Broadcast	$18,686
PayTV - Cable	$9,500
Phones	$9,203
PayTV - Satellite	$1,000
Total:	$75,389

Source: Federal Election Commission contribution records from January 1998 to September 2004

Contributions by Telecommunications Sector Organizations				
Company	Sector	#	Total	Avg.
International Brotherhood of Electrical Workers (IBEW)	Union	9	$20,000	$2,222
Communications Workers of America	Union	5	$8,500	$1,700
Utility Workers Union of America	Union	6	$6,000	$1,000
Walt Disney Co.	Broadcast	8	$5,350	$669
Time Warner	PayTV - Cable	10	$5,250	$525
National Association of Broadcasters	Broadcast	3	$4,586	$1,529
AT&T Wireless	Phones	6	$4,500	$750
National Cable and Telecommunications Association	PayTV - Cable	1	$3,500	$3,500
General Electric Co.	Broadcast	4	$3,000	$750
News Corp Ltd.	Broadcast	2	$2,500	$1,250
Transportation Communications International Union	Union	5	$2,500	$500
Verizon Communications Inc.	Phones	7	$1,703	$243
SBC Communications Inc.	Phones	2	$1,500	$750
Viacom Inc.	Broadcast	2	$1,250	$625
Univision Communications Inc.	Broadcast	2	$1,000	$500
Clear Channel Communications Inc.	Broadcast	1	$1,000	$1,000
Sprint Corp.	Phones	3	$1,000	$333
Echostar Corp.	PayTV - Satellite	1	$1,000	$1,000
Charter Communications Inc.	PayTV - Cable	2	$750	$375
Qwest Communications International Inc.	Phones	1	$500	$500
Cellular Telecommunications & Internet Association	Phones	2	-	-
		Total:	$75,389	

Source: Federal Election Commission contribution records from January 1998 to September 2004

Stearns, Cliff

Representative (R-FL)

House Committee on Energy and Commerce

2370 Rayburn House Office Building
Washington, DC 20515
Phone: (202) 225-5744
Fax: (202) 225-3973

Web Page: http://www.house.gov/stearns/
Email: wyr.fl06@mail.house.gov

Contribution Summary By Telecommunications Sector	
Phones	$104,000
Broadcast	$81,810
PayTV - Cable	$22,499
Other	$2,500
PayTV - Satellite	$1,000
Satellite	$500
Total:	$212,309

Source: Federal Election Commission contribution records from January 1998 to September 2004

Contributions by Telecommunications Sector Organizations				
Company	Sector	#	Total	Avg.
Verizon Communications Inc.	Phones	12	$19,500	$1,625
SBC Communications Inc.	Phones	17	$17,500	$1,029
National Association of Broadcasters	Broadcast	13	$16,560	$1,274
Viacom Inc.	Broadcast	13	$16,000	$1,231
Walt Disney Co.	Broadcast	10	$16,000	$1,600
Cingular Wireless	Phones	14	$16,000	$1,143
General Electric Co.	Broadcast	15	$13,500	$900
AT&T Wireless	Phones	12	$10,000	$833
Time Warner	PayTV - Cable	7	$9,500	$1,357
Paxson Communications Corp.	Broadcast	9	$9,000	$1,000
BellSouth Corp.	Phones	6	$8,000	$1,333
ALLTEL Corp.	Phones	9	$8,000	$889
National Cable and Telecommunications Association	PayTV - Cable	4	$7,999	$2,000
MCI (formerly WorldCom Inc.)	Phones	5	$6,000	$1,200
News Corp Ltd.	Broadcast	6	$5,500	$917
Cellular Telecommunications & Internet Association	Phones	4	$3,000	$750
Sprint Corp.	Phones	8	$3,000	$375
United States Telecom Association	Phones	4	$3,000	$750
Clear Channel Communications Inc.	Broadcast	3	$2,750	$917
Qwest Communications International Inc.	Phones	3	$2,500	$833
Comcast Corp.	PayTV - Cable	2	$2,250	$1,125
Teligent	Phones	2	$2,000	$1,000
AT&T Corp.	Phones	2	$1,500	$750
Misc. telecom interests	Other	3	$1,500	$500
American Cable Association	PayTV - Cable	2	$1,500	$750
Meredith Corp.	Broadcast	3	$1,500	$500
Tribune Co.	Broadcast	1	$1,000	$1,000
Level 3 Communications Inc.	Other	1	$1,000	$1,000
SAVVIS Communications Corp.	PayTV - Cable	1	$1,000	$1,000
The DirecTV Group Inc.	PayTV - Satellite	1	$1,000	$1,000
AirTouch Communications Inc.	Phones	2	$1,000	$500
Association for Local Telecommunications Services	Phones	1	$1,000	$1,000
National Telephone Cooperative Association	Phones	2	$1,000	$500
XO Communications Inc.	Phones	1	$1,000	$1,000
Loral Space & Communications Ltd.	Satellite	1	$500	$500
Cox Enterprises Inc.	PayTV - Cable	1	$250	$250
	Total:		$212,309	

Source: Federal Election Commission contribution records from January 1998 to September 2004

Telecommunications Company Provided Trips to Committee Member's Staff			
Company	Sector	#	Total $
Time Warner	PayTV - Cable	3	$4,806
National Cable and Telecommunications Association	PayTV - Cable	2	$4,074
United States Telecom Association	Phones	2	$3,249
Cellular Telecommunications & Internet Association	Phones	2	$2,500
News Corp Ltd.	Broadcast	1	$2,258
SBC Communications Inc.	Phones	1	$1,771
National Association of Broadcasters	Broadcast	1	$1,461
	Total:	12	$20,119
Source: Congressional office travel records for members of the Senate Committee on Commerce, Science & Transportation and the House Committee on Energy and Commerce for the period of January 2000 to March 2004.			

Trips by Committee Member's Staff Sponsored by the Telecommunications Industry		
Individual	#	Total $
Amirhooshmand, Ali	12	$20,119
Total:	12	$20,119
Source: Congressional office travel records for members of the Senate Committee on Commerce, Science & Transportation and the House Committee on Energy and Commerce for the period of January 2000 to March 2004.		

Strickland, Ted

Representative (D-OH)

House Committee on Energy and Commerce

336 Cannon House Office Building
Washington, DC 20515
Phone: (202) 225-5705
Fax: (202) 225-5907

Web Page: http://www.house.gov/strickland/
Email: http://www.house.gov/writerep/

Contribution Summary By Telecommunications Sector	
Union	$96,500
Phones	$64,900
PayTV - Cable	$21,262
Broadcast	$8,250
Total:	$190,912

Source: Federal Election Commission contribution records from January 1998 to September 2004

Contributions by Telecommunications Sector Organizations				
Company	Sector	#	Total	Avg.
Communications Workers of America	Union	20	$55,500	$2,775
International Brotherhood of Electrical Workers (IBEW)	Union	10	$40,000	$4,000
SBC Communications Inc.	Phones	24	$26,000	$1,083
National Cable and Telecommunications Association	PayTV - Cable	6	$10,997	$1,833
Time Warner	PayTV - Cable	9	$8,265	$918
MCI (formerly WorldCom Inc.)	Phones	6	$7,500	$1,250
Verizon Communications Inc.	Phones	7	$7,000	$1,000
AT&T Wireless	Phones	6	$5,500	$917
Cincinnati Bell Inc.	Phones	6	$5,400	$900
National Association of Broadcasters	Broadcast	7	$4,500	$643
ALLTEL Corp.	Phones	4	$4,000	$1,000
Sprint Corp.	Phones	6	$4,000	$667
General Electric Co.	Broadcast	3	$2,000	$667
Cingular Wireless	Phones	2	$2,000	$1,000
American Cable Association	PayTV - Cable	2	$1,500	$750
CenturyTel Inc.	Phones	1	$1,000	$1,000
Walt Disney Co.	Broadcast	1	$1,000	$1,000
Qwest Communications International Inc.	Phones	1	$1,000	$1,000
Telephone Electronics Corp.	Phones	1	$1,000	$1,000
Transportation Communications International Union	Union	2	$1,000	$500
National Telephone Cooperative Association	Phones	1	$500	$500
Comcast Corp.	PayTV - Cable	1	$500	$500
News Corp Ltd.	Broadcast	1	$500	$500
Morris Communications Company LLC	Broadcast	1	$250	$250
		Total:	$190,912	

Source: Federal Election Commission contribution records from January 1998 to September 2004

Stupak, Bart

Representative (D-MI)

House Committee on Energy and Commerce

2352 Rayburn House Office Building
Washington, DC 20515
Phone: (202) 225-4735
Fax: (202) 225-4744

Web Page: http://www.house.gov/stupak/
Email: http://www.house.gov/writerep/

Contribution Summary By Telecommunications Sector	
Phones	$90,771
Union	$41,000
PayTV - Cable	$37,747
Broadcast	$16,284
Other	$3,500
PayTV - Satellite	$3,000
Satellite	$1,000
Total:	$193,302

Source: Federal Election Commission contribution records from January 1998 to September 2004

Contributions by Telecommunications Sector Organizations				
Company	Sector	#	Total	Avg.
International Brotherhood of Electrical Workers (IBEW)	Union	8	$28,500	$3,563
MCI (formerly WorldCom Inc.)	Phones	24	$28,488	$1,187
National Cable and Telecommunications Association	PayTV - Cable	9	$20,247	$2,250
AT&T Wireless	Phones	21	$18,500	$881
National Association of Broadcasters	Broadcast	11	$14,034	$1,276
SBC Communications Inc.	Phones	16	$12,550	$784
Sprint Corp.	Phones	10	$8,500	$850
Communications Workers of America	Union	3	$8,000	$2,667
Time Warner	PayTV - Cable	8	$8,000	$1,000
Teligent	Phones	10	$4,250	$425
ALLTEL Corp.	Phones	3	$4,000	$1,333
Qwest Communications International Inc.	Phones	4	$3,500	$875
Echostar Corp.	PayTV - Satellite	3	$3,000	$1,000
Charter Communications Inc.	PayTV - Cable	3	$3,000	$1,000
Comcast Corp.	PayTV - Cable	2	$3,000	$1,500
IDT Corp.	Other	3	$2,500	$833
National Telephone Cooperative Association	Phones	4	$2,500	$625
Utility Workers Union of America	Union	3	$2,500	$833
Transportation Communications International Union	Union	4	$2,000	$500
SAVVIS Communications Corp.	PayTV - Cable	2	$2,000	$1,000
Cellular Telecommunications & Internet Association	Phones	4	$1,733	$433
American Cable Association	PayTV - Cable	3	$1,500	$500
Verizon Communications Inc.	Phones	2	$1,250	$625
XO Communications Inc.	Phones	2	$1,000	$500
Motorola Inc.	Satellite	2	$1,000	$500
Telephone Electronics Corp.	Phones	1	$1,000	$1,000
Comptel/ASCENT	Phones	2	$1,000	$500
Covad Communications Co.	Phones	1	$1,000	$1,000
Level 3 Communications Inc.	Other	1	$1,000	$1,000
Clear Channel Communications Inc.	Broadcast	1	$1,000	$1,000
Belo Corp.	Broadcast	1	$500	$500
Paxson Communications Corp.	Broadcast	1	$500	$500
Cingular Wireless	Phones	1	$500	$500
Association for Local Telecommunications Services	Phones	1	$500	$500
Deutsche Telekom AG (T-Mobile)	Phones	1	$500	$500
Tribune Co.	Broadcast	1	$250	$250
		Total:	$193,302	

Source: Federal Election Commission contribution records from January 1998 to September 2004

Telecommunications Company Provided Trips to Committee Member's Staff			
Company	Sector	#	Total $
National Cable and Telecommunications Association	PayTV - Cable	1	$1,608
National Association of Broadcasters	Broadcast	1	$455
	Total:	2	$2,062

Source: Congressional office travel records for members of the Senate Committee on Commerce, Science & Transportation and the House Committee on Energy and Commerce for the period of January 2000 to March 2004.

Trips by Committee Member's Staff Sponsored by the Telecommunications Industry		
Individual	#	Total $
Peled, Daphna	1	$1,608
Stupak, Bart	1	$455
Total:	2	$2,062

Source: Congressional office travel records for members of the Senate Committee on Commerce, Science & Transportation and the House Committee on Energy and Commerce for the period of January 2000 to March 2004.

Sullivan, John

Representative (R-OK)

House Committee on Energy and Commerce

114 Cannon House Office Building
Washington, DC 20515
Phone: (202) 225-2211
Fax: (202) 225-9187

Web Page: http://sullivan.house.gov/
Email: http://sullivan.house.gov/contact.shtml

Contribution Summary By Telecommunications Sector	
Phones	$42,500
PayTV - Cable	$8,000
Broadcast	$4,000
Total:	$54,500

Source: Federal Election Commission contribution records from January 1998 to September 2004

Contributions by Telecommunications Sector Organizations				
Company	Sector	#	Total	Avg.
SBC Communications Inc.	Phones	11	$20,500	$1,864
National Cable and Telecommunications Association	PayTV - Cable	1	$5,000	$5,000
Cingular Wireless	Phones	5	$5,000	$1,000
Verizon Communications Inc.	Phones	3	$4,500	$1,500
VALOR Telecommunications	Phones	3	$3,500	$1,167
Qwest Communications International Inc.	Phones	2	$3,000	$1,500
Cox Communications Inc.	PayTV - Cable	2	$3,000	$1,500
United States Telecom Association	Phones	3	$2,500	$833
National Association of Broadcasters	Broadcast	1	$2,000	$2,000
News Corp Ltd.	Broadcast	1	$1,000	$1,000
General Electric Co.	Broadcast	1	$1,000	$1,000
Cellular Telecommunications & Internet Association	Phones	1	$1,000	$1,000
MCI (formerly WorldCom Inc.)	Phones	1	$1,000	$1,000
National Telephone Cooperative Association	Phones	1	$1,000	$1,000
Comptel/ASCENT	Phones	1	$250	$250
AT&T Corp.	Phones	1	$250	$250
	Total:		$54,500	

Source: Federal Election Commission contribution records from January 1998 to September 2004

Tauzin, W.J. "Billy"

House Committee on Energy and Commerce

2183 Rayburn House Office Building
Washington, DC 20515
Phone: (202) 225-4031
Fax: (202) 225-0563

Representative (R-LA)

Web Page: http://www.house.gov/tauzin/
Email: http://www.house.gov/writerep/

Contribution Summary By Telecommunications Sector	
Phones	$377,041
Broadcast	$183,777
PayTV - Cable	$93,498
PayTV - Satellite	$14,500
Other	$13,300
Satellite	$12,500
Total:	$694,616
Source: Federal Election Commission contribution records from January 1998 to September 2004	

Contributions by Telecommunications Sector Organizations				
Company	Sector	#	Total	Avg.
SBC Communications Inc.	Phones	25	$64,750	$2,590
Verizon Communications Inc.	Phones	35	$64,750	$1,850
BellSouth Corp.	Phones	94	$63,400	$674
National Association of Broadcasters	Broadcast	15	$46,500	$3,100
Cingular Wireless	Phones	16	$34,500	$2,156
United States Telecom Association	Phones	18	$31,736	$1,763
AT&T Wireless	Phones	23	$28,500	$1,239
General Electric Co.	Broadcast	23	$27,000	$1,174
National Cable and Telecommunications Association	PayTV - Cable	10	$26,998	$2,700
Time Warner	PayTV - Cable	16	$25,000	$1,563
Viacom Inc.	Broadcast	15	$24,277	$1,618
Walt Disney Co.	Broadcast	13	$23,500	$1,808
Qwest Communications International Inc.	Phones	12	$21,250	$1,771
Paxson Communications Corp.	Broadcast	14	$18,500	$1,321
Comcast Corp.	PayTV - Cable	7	$17,500	$2,500
News Corp Ltd.	Broadcast	10	$15,500	$1,550
Cellular Telecommunications & Internet Association	Phones	17	$15,405	$906
Clear Channel Communications Inc.	Broadcast	5	$14,000	$2,800
Cox Communications Inc.	PayTV - Cable	12	$10,500	$875
Cablevision Systems Corp.	PayTV - Cable	4	$10,500	$2,625
ALLTEL Corp.	Phones	10	$10,000	$1,000
Echostar Corp.	PayTV - Satellite	9	$9,500	$1,056
AirTouch Communications Inc.	Phones	6	$7,500	$1,250
Pappas Telecasting Cos.	Broadcast	3	$7,500	$2,500
Global Crossing Ltd.	Other	7	$7,000	$1,000
Sprint Corp.	Phones	5	$7,000	$1,400
Loral Space & Communications Ltd.	Satellite	6	$6,500	$1,083
Teligent	Phones	8	$5,500	$688
Tribune Co.	Broadcast	9	$5,000	$556
The DirecTV Group Inc.	PayTV - Satellite	5	$5,000	$1,000
Deutsche Telekom AG (T-Mobile)	Phones	1	$5,000	$5,000
Level 3 Communications Inc.	Other	3	$4,000	$1,333
Western Wireless Corp.	Phones	5	$4,000	$800
Satellite Broadcasting & Communication Association	Satellite	4	$4,000	$1,000
MCI (formerly WorldCom Inc.)	Phones	2	$3,000	$1,500
AT&T Corp.	Phones	4	$3,000	$750
Comptel/ASCENT	Phones	2	$2,000	$1,000
Charter Communications Inc.	PayTV - Cable	2	$2,000	$1,000
Motorola Inc.	Satellite	2	$2,000	$1,000
National Telephone Cooperative Association	Phones	2	$1,500	$750
Misc. telecom interests	Other	2	$1,300	$650
American Cable Association	PayTV - Cable	1	$1,000	$1,000
Computer & Communications Industry Association	Other	1	$1,000	$1,000
Hubbard Broadcasting Inc.	Broadcast	1	$1,000	$1,000

Contributions by Telecommunications Sector Organizations

Company	Sector	#	Total	Avg.
Meredith Corp.	Broadcast	1	$1,000	$1,000
Personal Communications Industry Association	Phones	1	$1,000	$1,000
Covad Communications Co.	Phones	1	$1,000	$1,000
CenturyTel Inc.	Phones	1	$1,000	$1,000
XO Communications Inc.	Phones	1	$1,000	$1,000
United States Cellular Corp.	Phones	1	$250	$250
		Total:	$694,616	

Source: Federal Election Commission contribution records from January 1998 to September 2004

Telecommunications Company Provided Trips to Committee Member's Staff

Company	Sector	#	Total $
National Cable and Telecommunications Association	PayTV - Cable	18	$33,492
United States Telecom Association	Phones	7	$13,955
National Association of Broadcasters	Broadcast	7	$10,913
Cellular Telecommunications & Internet Association	Phones	7	$10,907
SBC Communications Inc.	Phones	5	$7,992
Misc. telecom interests	Other	6	$7,277
Walt Disney Co.	Broadcast	5	$5,032
Viacom Inc.	Broadcast	4	$4,776
Time Warner	PayTV - Cable	3	$4,545
News Corp Ltd.	Broadcast	2	$4,285
BellSouth Corp.	Phones	1	$1,890
Verizon Communications Inc.	Phones	3	$1,825
Telecommunications Industry Association	Other	1	$536
	Total:	69	$107,424

Source: Congressional office travel records for members of the Senate Committee on Commerce, Science & Transportation and the House Committee on Energy and Commerce for the period of January 2000 to March 2004.

Trips by Committee Member's Staff Sponsored by the Telecommunications Industry

Individual	#	Total $
Tauzin, W. J. "Billy"	13	$22,195
Waltzman, Howard	13	$19,112
Wallace, Jessica	9	$15,446
Bloss-Baum, Linda	7	$11,866
Johnson, Ken	6	$7,088
Marventano, David	4	$6,567
Bonnin, Nydia	2	$4,241
Zerzan, Kelly	2	$2,723
Kidd, Hollyn	1	$2,527
Murventano, David	1	$2,173
Connaughton, Jaylyn	1	$2,018
Fried, Neil	2	$1,883
Marventano, Dave	1	$1,662
Simison, Robert	1	$1,600
Betfarhad, Ramsen	1	$1,596
Terry, Lee	1	$1,303
Berfarhad, Ramsen	1	$1,292
Azare, Monica	1	$1,065
Patterson, Byron	1	$571
Barrette, James	1	$496
Total:	69	$107,424

Source: Congressional office travel records for members of the Senate Committee on Commerce, Science & Transportation and the House Committee on Energy and Commerce for the period of January 2000 to March 2004.

Terry, Lee

Representative (R-NE)

House Committee on Energy and Commerce

1524 Longworth House Office Building
Washington, DC 20515
Phone: (202) 225-4155
Fax: (202) 226-5452

Web Page: http://leeterry.house.gov/
Email: http://leeterry.house.gov/contact.asp

Contribution Summary By Telecommunications Sector	
Phones	$108,717
Broadcast	$30,532
PayTV - Cable	$28,776
Other	$9,500
PayTV - Satellite	$6,000
Total:	$183,525

Source: Federal Election Commission contribution records from January 1998 to September 2004

Contributions by Telecommunications Sector Organizations				
Company	Sector	#	Total	Avg.
Qwest Communications International Inc.	Phones	35	$34,076	$974
Verizon Communications Inc.	Phones	18	$19,000	$1,056
National Cable and Telecommunications Association	PayTV - Cable	8	$18,026	$2,253
SBC Communications Inc.	Phones	15	$18,000	$1,200
National Association of Broadcasters	Broadcast	11	$14,032	$1,276
Cingular Wireless	Phones	10	$9,000	$900
ALLTEL Corp.	Phones	10	$8,400	$840
Level 3 Communications Inc.	Other	5	$8,000	$1,600
Echostar Corp.	PayTV - Satellite	3	$6,000	$2,000
Time Warner	PayTV - Cable	5	$5,000	$1,000
AT&T Wireless	Phones	3	$3,500	$1,167
Cellular Telecommunications & Internet Association	Phones	3	$3,500	$1,167
Sprint Corp.	Phones	4	$3,500	$875
United States Telecom Association	Phones	5	$3,500	$700
National Telephone Cooperative Association	Phones	6	$3,241	$540
General Electric Co.	Broadcast	5	$3,000	$600
Viacom Inc.	Broadcast	3	$3,000	$1,000
Walt Disney Co.	Broadcast	2	$2,500	$1,250
News Corp Ltd.	Broadcast	1	$2,500	$2,500
Western Wireless Corp.	Phones	4	$2,500	$625
Clear Channel Communications Inc.	Broadcast	2	$2,000	$1,000
Univision Communications Inc.	Broadcast	2	$2,000	$1,000
American Cable Association	PayTV - Cable	3	$2,000	$667
Comcast Corp.	PayTV - Cable	2	$2,000	$1,000
Cox Communications Inc.	PayTV - Cable	4	$1,750	$438
Telecommunications Industry Association	Other	1	$1,500	$1,500
Pappas Telecasting Cos.	Broadcast	1	$1,000	$1,000
Paxson Communications Corp.	Broadcast	1	$500	$500
VALOR Telecommunications	Phones	1	$500	$500
	Total:		$183,525	

Source: Federal Election Commission contribution records from January 1998 to September 2004

Telecommunications Company Provided Trips to Committee Member's Staff			
Company	Sector	#	Total $
National Cable and Telecommunications Association	PayTV - Cable	3	$7,966
Misc. telecom interests	Other	1	$5,515
National Association of Broadcasters	Broadcast	1	$4,329
United States Telecom Association	Phones	2	$2,647
News Corp Ltd.	Broadcast	1	$2,258
SBC Communications Inc.	Phones	1	$1,685
	Total:	9	$24,400

Source: Congressional office travel records for members of the Senate Committee on Commerce, Science & Transportation and the House Committee on Energy and Commerce for the period of January 2000 to March 2004.

Trips by Committee Member's Staff Sponsored by the Telecommunications Industry		
Individual	#	Total $
Stien, Robert	7	$14,955
Terry, Lee	2	$9,445
Total:	9	$24,400

Source: Congressional office travel records for members of the Senate Committee on Commerce, Science & Transportation and the House Committee on Energy and Commerce for the period of January 2000 to March 2004.

Towns, Edolphus

Representative (D-NY)

House Committee on Energy and Commerce

2232 Rayburn House Office Building
Washington, DC 20515
Phone: (202) 225-5936
Fax: (202) 225-1018

Web Page: http://www.house.gov/towns/
Email: http://www.house.gov/writerep/

Contribution Summary By Telecommunications Sector	
Phones	$98,364
PayTV - Cable	$58,897
Broadcast	$45,350
Union	$24,500
PayTV - Satellite	$2,000
Other	$400
Total:	$229,511

Source: Federal Election Commission contribution records from January 1998 to September 2004

Contributions by Telecommunications Sector Organizations				
Company	Sector	#	Total	Avg.
National Cable and Telecommunications Association	PayTV - Cable	9	$29,997	$3,333
Verizon Communications Inc.	Phones	23	$24,000	$1,043
SBC Communications Inc.	Phones	15	$20,500	$1,367
Cingular Wireless	Phones	14	$15,000	$1,071
Cablevision Systems Corp.	PayTV - Cable	6	$14,400	$2,400
International Brotherhood of Electrical Workers (IBEW)	Union	10	$13,500	$1,350
Time Warner	PayTV - Cable	9	$13,000	$1,444
General Electric Co.	Broadcast	15	$12,350	$823
AT&T Wireless	Phones	10	$9,000	$900
Viacom Inc.	Broadcast	10	$8,500	$850
Walt Disney Co.	Broadcast	9	$8,000	$889
Communications Workers of America	Union	5	$8,000	$1,600
National Association of Broadcasters	Broadcast	4	$6,500	$1,625
News Corp Ltd.	Broadcast	9	$6,000	$667
BellSouth Corp.	Phones	12	$4,500	$375
United States Telecom Association	Phones	5	$4,364	$873
MCI (formerly WorldCom Inc.)	Phones	5	$3,500	$700
Qwest Communications International Inc.	Phones	5	$3,500	$700
Transportation Communications International Union	Union	5	$3,000	$600
Cellular Telecommunications & Internet Association	Phones	4	$3,000	$750
Echostar Corp.	PayTV - Satellite	2	$2,000	$1,000
ALLTEL Corp.	Phones	2	$2,000	$1,000
AT&T Corp.	Phones	1	$2,000	$2,000
Radio One, Inc.	Broadcast	1	$2,000	$2,000
Deutsche Telekom AG (T-Mobile)	Phones	2	$2,000	$1,000
Focal Communications Corp.	Phones	2	$2,000	$1,000
Clear Channel Communications Inc.	Broadcast	2	$2,000	$1,000
Sprint Corp.	Phones	2	$1,500	$750
Comcast Corp.	PayTV - Cable	2	$1,500	$750
Covad Communications Co.	Phones	2	$1,500	$750
IDT Corp.	Other	1	$400	$400
	Total:		$229,511	

Source: Federal Election Commission contribution records from January 1998 to September 2004

Telecommunications Company Provided Trips to Committee Member's Staff			
Company	Sector	#	Total $
United States Telecom Association	Phones	1	$3,429
SBC Communications Inc.	Phones	1	$1,791
National Cable and Telecommunications Association	PayTV - Cable	1	$1,325
	Total:	3	$6,545

Source: Congressional office travel records for members of the Senate Committee on Commerce, Science & Transportation and the House Committee on Energy and Commerce for the period of January 2000 to March 2004.

Trips by Committee Member's Staff Sponsored by the Telecommunications Industry		
Individual	#	Total $
Davis, Jeffrey	2	$4,754
Mccollum, Jesse	1	$1,791
Total:	3	$6,545

Source: Congressional office travel records for members of the Senate Committee on Commerce, Science & Transportation and the House Committee on Energy and Commerce for the period of January 2000 to March 2004.

Upton, Fred

House Committee on Energy and Commerce

2161 Rayburn House Office Building
Washington, DC 20515
Phone: (202) 225-3761
Fax: (202) 225-4986

Representative (R-MI)

Chair, Subcommittee

Web Page: http://www.house.gov/upton/
Email: http://www.house.gov/writerep/

Contribution Summary By Telecommunications Sector	
Phones	$147,500
Broadcast	$105,339
PayTV - Cable	$66,498
PayTV - Satellite	$11,000
Satellite	$5,000
Other	$2,750
Total:	$338,087

Source: Federal Election Commission contribution records from January 1998 to September 2004

Contributions by Telecommunications Sector Organizations

Company	Sector	#	Total	Avg.
SBC Communications Inc.	Phones	15	$46,500	$3,100
National Cable and Telecommunications Association	PayTV - Cable	15	$34,998	$2,333
National Association of Broadcasters	Broadcast	23	$31,250	$1,359
Verizon Communications Inc.	Phones	19	$23,800	$1,253
Cingular Wireless	Phones	18	$17,000	$944
General Electric Co.	Broadcast	20	$16,589	$829
Comcast Corp.	PayTV - Cable	6	$16,500	$2,750
Viacom Inc.	Broadcast	12	$15,000	$1,250
Walt Disney Co.	Broadcast	7	$13,500	$1,929
Time Warner	PayTV - Cable	9	$9,500	$1,056
Echostar Corp.	PayTV - Satellite	9	$9,500	$1,056
News Corp Ltd.	Broadcast	8	$8,000	$1,000
AT&T Wireless	Phones	11	$7,600	$691
Cellular Telecommunications & Internet Association	Phones	11	$7,500	$682
Qwest Communications International Inc.	Phones	4	$7,000	$1,750
United States Telecom Association	Phones	6	$6,500	$1,083
Sprint Corp.	Phones	7	$6,000	$857
ALLTEL Corp.	Phones	5	$6,000	$1,200
Paxson Communications Corp.	Broadcast	6	$6,000	$1,000
Clear Channel Communications Inc.	Broadcast	4	$6,000	$1,500
Tribune Co.	Broadcast	5	$5,000	$1,000
AT&T Corp.	Phones	4	$4,500	$1,125
MCI (formerly WorldCom Inc.)	Phones	6	$4,500	$750
National Telephone Cooperative Association	Phones	3	$4,100	$1,367
Charter Communications Inc.	PayTV - Cable	3	$4,000	$1,333
Western Wireless Corp.	Phones	4	$3,000	$750
Loral Space & Communications Ltd.	Satellite	3	$3,000	$1,000
Motorola Inc.	Satellite	3	$2,000	$667
Deutsche Telekom AG (T-Mobile)	Phones	2	$2,000	$1,000
Cumulus Media Inc.	Broadcast	2	$2,000	$1,000
Misc. telecom interests	Other	4	$1,750	$438
American Cable Association	PayTV - Cable	2	$1,500	$750
The DirecTV Group Inc.	PayTV - Satellite	2	$1,500	$750
AirTouch Communications Inc.	Phones	2	$1,000	$500
Emmis Communications Corp.	Broadcast	1	$1,000	$1,000
Level 3 Communications Inc.	Other	1	$1,000	$1,000
Univision Communications Inc.	Broadcast	1	$1,000	$1,000
United States Cellular Corp.	Phones	1	$500	$500
	Total:		$338,087	

Source: Federal Election Commission contribution records from January 1998 to September 2004

Telecommunications Company Provided Trips to Committee Member's Staff			
Company	Sector	#	Total $
National Cable and Telecommunications Association	PayTV - Cable	5	$10,389
Cellular Telecommunications & Internet Association	Phones	2	$4,679
Tribune Co.	Broadcast	1	$3,337
SBC Communications Inc.	Phones	2	$3,141
Echostar Corp.	PayTV - Satellite	1	$2,048
National Association of Broadcasters	Broadcast	2	$1,919
United States Telecom Association	Phones	1	$1,885
	Total:	14	$27,398

Source: Congressional office travel records for members of the Senate Committee on Commerce, Science & Transportation and the House Committee on Energy and Commerce for the period of January 2000 to March 2004.

Trips by Committee Member's Staff Sponsored by the Telecommunications Industry		
Individual	#	Total $
Upton, Fred	5	$12,872
Nordwind, William	8	$12,566
Waldron, Michael	1	$1,959
Total:	14	$27,398

Source: Congressional office travel records for members of the Senate Committee on Commerce, Science & Transportation and the House Committee on Energy and Commerce for the period of January 2000 to March 2004.

Walden, Greg

Representative (R-OR)

House Committee on Energy and Commerce

1404 Longworth House Office Building
Washington, DC 20515
Phone: (202) 225-6730
Fax: (202) 225-5774

Web Page: http://walden.house.gov/
Email: http://walden.house.gov/contactgreg

Contribution Summary By Telecommunications Sector	
Phones	$63,331
Broadcast	$54,947
Union	$15,000
PayTV - Cable	$14,499
Total:	$147,777

Source: Federal Election Commission contribution records from January 1998 to September 2004

Contributions by Telecommunications Sector Organizations				
Company	Sector	#	Total	Avg.
National Association of Broadcasters	Broadcast	25	$37,747	$1,510
International Brotherhood of Electrical Workers (IBEW)	Union	4	$15,000	$3,750
SBC Communications Inc.	Phones	10	$12,500	$1,250
Verizon Communications Inc.	Phones	11	$10,000	$909
Cingular Wireless	Phones	9	$9,000	$1,000
National Cable and Telecommunications Association	PayTV - Cable	4	$8,499	$2,125
Qwest Communications International Inc.	Phones	12	$8,099	$675
Sprint Corp.	Phones	13	$7,500	$577
General Electric Co.	Broadcast	9	$6,000	$667
Walt Disney Co.	Broadcast	5	$5,000	$1,000
AT&T Wireless	Phones	5	$5,000	$1,000
National Telephone Cooperative Association	Phones	4	$4,500	$1,125
American Cable Association	PayTV - Cable	6	$3,500	$583
Viacom Inc.	Broadcast	4	$3,000	$750
United States Telecom Association	Phones	4	$2,732	$683
Western Wireless Corp.	Phones	2	$2,000	$1,000
Clear Channel Communications Inc.	Broadcast	2	$2,000	$1,000
Charter Communications Inc.	PayTV - Cable	1	$1,000	$1,000
SAVVIS Communications Corp.	PayTV - Cable	1	$1,000	$1,000
Deutsche Telekom AG (T-Mobile)	Phones	1	$1,000	$1,000
Cellular Telecommunications & Internet Association	Phones	1	$1,000	$1,000
Salem Communications Corp.	PayTV - Cable	1	$500	$500
Emmis Communications Corp.	Broadcast	1	$500	$500
Meredith Corp.	Broadcast	1	$500	$500
Entercom Communications Corp.	Broadcast	1	$200	$200
	Total:		$147,777	

Source: Federal Election Commission contribution records from January 1998 to September 2004

Telecommunications Company Provided Trips to Committee Member's Staff			
Company	Sector	#	Total $
National Association of Broadcasters	Broadcast	3	$7,327
SBC Communications Inc.	Phones	1	$1,965
	Total:	4	$9,292

Source: Congressional office travel records for members of the Senate Committee on Commerce, Science & Transportation and the House Committee on Energy and Commerce for the period of January 2000 to March 2004.

Trips by Committee Member's Staff Sponsored by the Telecommunications Industry		
Individual	#	Total $
Walden, Greg	3	$7,327
Hard, Brian	1	$1,965
Total:	4	$9,292

Source: Congressional office travel records for members of the Senate Committee on Commerce, Science & Transportation and the House Committee on Energy and Commerce for the period of January 2000 to March 2004.

Waxman, Henry A.
Representative (D-CA)

House Committee on Energy and Commerce

2204 Rayburn House Office Building
Washington, DC 20515
Phone: (202) 225-3976
Fax: (202) 225-4099

Web Page: http://www.house.gov/waxman/
Email: http://www.house.gov/waxman/contact.htm

Contribution Summary By Telecommunications Sector	
Broadcast	$71,500
PayTV - Cable	$47,500
Phones	$33,750
Union	$8,000
Other	$4,000
Total:	$164,750

Source: Federal Election Commission contribution records from January 1998 to September 2004

Contributions by Telecommunications Sector Organizations				
Company	Sector	#	Total	Avg.
Viacom Inc.	Broadcast	19	$29,500	$1,553
National Cable and Telecommunications Association	PayTV - Cable	8	$26,500	$3,313
Walt Disney Co.	Broadcast	6	$21,000	$3,500
MCI (formerly WorldCom Inc.)	Phones	8	$13,500	$1,688
General Electric Co.	Broadcast	7	$12,500	$1,786
Time Warner	PayTV - Cable	5	$10,500	$2,100
AT&T Wireless	Phones	7	$9,500	$1,357
Communications Workers of America	Union	4	$7,000	$1,750
National Association of Broadcasters	Broadcast	4	$6,500	$1,625
Sprint Corp.	Phones	5	$5,000	$1,000
Charter Communications Inc.	PayTV - Cable	4	$4,000	$1,000
Comcast Corp.	PayTV - Cable	2	$3,000	$1,500
SAVVIS Communications Corp.	PayTV - Cable	3	$2,500	$833
Global Crossing Ltd.	Other	2	$2,000	$1,000
AT&T Corp.	Phones	2	$1,250	$625
Cellular Telecommunications & Internet Association	Phones	1	$1,000	$1,000
ALLTEL Corp.	Phones	1	$1,000	$1,000
IDT Corp.	Other	1	$1,000	$1,000
Level 3 Communications Inc.	Other	1	$1,000	$1,000
Adelphia Communications Corp.	PayTV - Cable	1	$1,000	$1,000
Hearst Corp.	Broadcast	1	$1,000	$1,000
Meredith Corp.	Broadcast	1	$1,000	$1,000
Teligent	Phones	1	$1,000	$1,000
International Brotherhood of Electrical Workers (IBEW)	Union	1	$1,000	$1,000
Covad Communications Co.	Phones	3	$1,000	$333
Comptel/ASCENT	Phones	1	$500	$500
Total:			$164,750	

Source: Federal Election Commission contribution records from January 1998 to September 2004

Telecommunications Company Provided Trips to Committee Member's Staff			
Company	Sector	#	Total $
Comptel/ASCENT	Phones	2	$1,569
Telecommunications Industry Association	Other	1	$493
Total:		3	$2,062

Source: Congressional office travel records for members of the Senate Committee on Commerce, Science & Transportation and the House Committee on Energy and Commerce for the period of January 2000 to March 2004.

Trips by Committee Member's Staff Sponsored by the Telecommunications Industry		
Individual	#	Total $
Delgado, Patricia	3	$2,062
Total:	3	$2,062

Source: Congressional office travel records for members of the Senate Committee on Commerce, Science & Transportation and the House Committee on Energy and Commerce for the period of January 2000 to March 2004.

Whitfield, Ed

Representative (R-KY)

House Committee on Energy and Commerce

301 Cannon House Office Building
Washington, DC 20515
Phone: (202) 225-3115
Fax: (202) 225-3547

Web Page: http://www.house.gov/whitfield/
Email: http://www.house.gov/whitfield/whitfield/contactform/index2.shtml

Contribution Summary By Telecommunications Sector

Phones	$111,690
PayTV - Cable	$38,013
Broadcast	$19,750
Satellite	$1,000
Total:	**$170,453**

Source: Federal Election Commission contribution records from January 1998 to September 2004

Contributions by Telecommunications Sector Organizations

Company	Sector	#	Total	Avg.
SBC Communications Inc.	Phones	25	$31,000	$1,240
National Cable and Telecommunications Association	PayTV - Cable	8	$27,013	$3,377
Cingular Wireless	Phones	13	$21,000	$1,615
Verizon Communications Inc.	Phones	16	$19,500	$1,219
BellSouth Corp.	Phones	13	$12,500	$962
General Electric Co.	Broadcast	13	$10,500	$808
United States Telecom Association	Phones	8	$8,190	$1,024
Qwest Communications International Inc.	Phones	7	$7,000	$1,000
Comcast Corp.	PayTV - Cable	4	$5,000	$1,250
Clear Channel Communications Inc.	Broadcast	3	$4,000	$1,333
National Association of Broadcasters	Broadcast	4	$4,000	$1,000
ALLTEL Corp.	Phones	4	$4,000	$1,000
Time Warner	PayTV - Cable	2	$3,000	$1,500
AT&T Wireless	Phones	4	$2,000	$500
Charter Communications Inc.	PayTV - Cable	3	$2,000	$667
National Telephone Cooperative Association	Phones	3	$2,000	$667
Sprint Corp.	Phones	2	$1,500	$750
Cincinnati Bell Inc.	Phones	1	$1,000	$1,000
Motorola Inc.	Satellite	1	$1,000	$1,000
Viacom Inc.	Broadcast	1	$1,000	$1,000
Adelphia Communications Corp.	PayTV - Cable	1	$1,000	$1,000
MCI (formerly WorldCom Inc.)	Phones	1	$1,000	$1,000
Cellular Telecommunications & Internet Association	Phones	1	$500	$500
United States Cellular Corp.	Phones	1	$500	$500
Gannett Co. Inc.	Broadcast	1	$250	$250
	Total:		**$170,453**	

Source: Federal Election Commission contribution records from January 1998 to September 2004

Telecommunications Company Provided Trips to Committee Member's Staff

Company	Sector	#	Total $
SBC Communications Inc.	Phones	1	$1,575
National Cable and Telecommunications Association	PayTV - Cable	1	$1,572
	Total:	**2**	**$3,146**

Source: Congressional office travel records for members of the Senate Committee on Commerce, Science & Transportation and the House Committee on Energy and Commerce for the period of January 2000 to March 2004.

Trips by Committee Member's Staff Sponsored by the Telecommunications Industry

Individual	#	Total $
Hale, Brett	1	$1,575
Beaton, Benjamin	1	$1,572
Total:	**2**	**$3,146**

Source: Congressional office travel records for members of the Senate Committee on Commerce, Science & Transportation and the House Committee on Energy and Commerce for the period of January 2000 to March 2004.

Wilson, Heather

Representative (R-NM)

House Committee on Energy and Commerce

318 Cannon House Office Building
Washington, DC 20515
Phone: (202) 225-6316
Fax: (202) 225-4975

Web Page: http://wilson.house.gov/
Email: http://wilson.house.gov/Contact.asp

Contribution Summary By Telecommunications Sector	
Phones	$185,569
PayTV - Cable	$93,448
Broadcast	$54,300
Other	$4,000
Satellite	$1,500
PayTV - Satellite	$500
Total:	$339,317

Source: Federal Election Commission contribution records from January 1998 to September 2004

Contributions by Telecommunications Sector Organizations				
Company	Sector	#	Total	Avg.
MCI (formerly WorldCom Inc.)	Phones	26	$37,000	$1,423
AT&T Wireless	Phones	35	$36,000	$1,029
National Cable and Telecommunications Association	PayTV - Cable	10	$34,998	$3,500
Comcast Corp.	PayTV - Cable	30	$33,950	$1,132
National Association of Broadcasters	Broadcast	14	$18,500	$1,321
Time Warner	PayTV - Cable	12	$17,000	$1,417
Verizon Communications Inc.	Phones	11	$16,500	$1,500
Sprint Corp.	Phones	20	$14,000	$700
General Electric Co.	Broadcast	12	$13,000	$1,083
Qwest Communications International Inc.	Phones	17	$12,950	$762
XO Communications Inc.	Phones	13	$12,750	$981
SBC Communications Inc.	Phones	10	$8,500	$850
Hubbard Broadcasting Inc.	Broadcast	7	$7,000	$1,000
SAVVIS Communications Corp.	PayTV - Cable	7	$7,000	$1,000
Clear Channel Communications Inc.	Broadcast	6	$6,500	$1,083
Viacom Inc.	Broadcast	7	$6,000	$857
Telephone Electronics Corp.	Phones	6	$5,500	$917
Cingular Wireless	Phones	6	$5,000	$833
Covad Communications Co.	Phones	6	$5,000	$833
ALLTEL Corp.	Phones	5	$4,500	$900
Association for Local Telecommunications Services	Phones	5	$4,250	$850
Comptel/ASCENT	Phones	3	$4,000	$1,333
Cellular Telecommunications & Internet Association	Phones	6	$3,619	$603
United States Telecom Association	Phones	3	$3,000	$1,000
Level 3 Communications Inc.	Other	3	$3,000	$1,000
AT&T Corp.	Phones	5	$2,750	$550
News Corp Ltd.	Broadcast	3	$2,000	$667
AirTouch Communications Inc.	Phones	4	$2,000	$500
Focal Communications Corp.	Phones	2	$2,000	$1,000
VALOR Telecommunications	Phones	4	$1,750	$438
National Telephone Cooperative Association	Phones	3	$1,500	$500
Motorola Inc.	Satellite	3	$1,500	$500
Walt Disney Co.	Broadcast	2	$1,300	$650
IDT Corp.	Other	1	$1,000	$1,000
Pac-West Telecomm Inc.	Phones	1	$1,000	$1,000
United States Cellular Corp.	Phones	1	$1,000	$1,000
Deutsche Telekom AG (T-Mobile)	Phones	1	$500	$500
American Cable Association	PayTV - Cable	1	$500	$500
The DirecTV Group Inc.	PayTV - Satellite	1	$500	$500
Western Wireless Corp.	Phones	1	$500	$500
	Total:		$339,317	

Source: Federal Election Commission contribution records from January 1998 to September 2004

Telecommunications Company Provided Trips to Committee Member's Staff			
Company	Sector	#	Total $
Cellular Telecommunications & Internet Association	Phones	2	$1,361
Total:		2	$1,361

Source: Congressional office travel records for members of the Senate Committee on Commerce, Science & Transportation and the House Committee on Energy and Commerce for the period of January 2000 to March 2004.

Trips by Committee Member's Staff Sponsored by the Telecommunications Industry		
Individual	#	Total $
Rose, Luke	2	$1,361
Total:	2	$1,361

Source: Congressional office travel records for members of the Senate Committee on Commerce, Science & Transportation and the House Committee on Energy and Commerce for the period of January 2000 to March 2004.

Wynn, Albert Russell

Representative (D-MD)

House Committee on Energy and Commerce

434 Cannon House Office Building
Washington, DC 20515
Phone: (202) 225-8699
Fax: (202) 225-8714

Web Page: http://www.wynn.house.gov/
Email:
http://www.wynn.house.gov/feedback.cfm?campaign=wynn&type=Interactive%20Wynn

Contribution Summary By Telecommunications Sector	
Phones	$89,341
PayTV - Cable	$47,305
Union	$21,000
Broadcast	$16,300
Total:	$173,946
Source: Federal Election Commission contribution records from January 1998 to September 2004	

Contributions by Telecommunications Sector Organizations				
Company	Sector	#	Total	Avg.
Verizon Communications Inc.	Phones	37	$33,710	$911
National Cable and Telecommunications Association	PayTV - Cable	12	$26,055	$2,171
SBC Communications Inc.	Phones	18	$21,000	$1,167
Comcast Corp.	PayTV - Cable	11	$15,250	$1,386
Cingular Wireless	Phones	15	$11,500	$767
Communications Workers of America	Union	5	$8,500	$1,700
International Brotherhood of Electrical Workers (IBEW)	Union	4	$7,000	$1,750
Time Warner	PayTV - Cable	3	$6,000	$2,000
Transportation Communications International Union	Union	10	$5,500	$550
United States Telecom Association	Phones	10	$5,219	$522
ALLTEL Corp.	Phones	6	$5,000	$833
General Electric Co.	Broadcast	7	$4,300	$614
Viacom Inc.	Broadcast	5	$4,000	$800
Walt Disney Co.	Broadcast	4	$4,000	$1,000
Cellular Telecommunications & Internet Association	Phones	5	$3,912	$782
National Association of Broadcasters	Broadcast	3	$3,000	$1,000
AT&T Wireless	Phones	5	$2,000	$400
MCI (formerly WorldCom Inc.)	Phones	3	$2,000	$667
Qwest Communications International Inc.	Phones	2	$1,500	$750
Sprint Corp.	Phones	2	$1,500	$750
Deutsche Telekom AG (T-Mobile)	Phones	1	$1,000	$1,000
AirTouch Communications Inc.	Phones	1	$1,000	$1,000
Clear Channel Communications Inc.	Broadcast	1	$1,000	$1,000
Paxson Communications Corp.	Broadcast	2	-	-
		Total:	$173,946	
Source: Federal Election Commission contribution records from January 1998 to September 2004				

Telecommunications Company Provided Trips to Committee Member's Staff			
Company	Sector	#	Total $
Cellular Telecommunications & Internet Association	Phones	1	$1,486
	Total:	1	$1,486
Source: Congressional office travel records for members of the Senate Committee on Commerce, Science & Transportation and the House Committee on Energy and Commerce for the period of January 2000 to March 2004.			

Trips by Committee Member's Staff Sponsored by the Telecommunications Industry		
Individual	#	Total $
Wynn, Albert	1	$1,486
Total:	1	$1,486
Source: Congressional office travel records for members of the Senate Committee on Commerce, Science & Transportation and the House Committee on Energy and Commerce for the period of January 2000 to March 2004.		

Senate Committee on Commerce, Science & Transportation (2003-2004)

Allen, George

Senator (R-VA)

Senate Committee on Commerce, Science & Transportation

204 Russell Senate Office Bldg., Room 204
Washington, DC 20510
Phone: (202) 224-4024
Fax: (202) 224-5432

Web Page: http://allen.senate.gov/
Email: http://allen.senate.gov/?c=email

Contribution Summary By Telecommunications Sector	
Phones	$105,150
PayTV - Cable	$55,750
Broadcast	$42,200
Other	$7,500
Satellite	$7,000
PayTV - Satellite	$3,000
Total:	$220,600

Source: Federal Election Commission contribution records from January 1998 to September 2004

Contributions by Telecommunications Sector Organizations				
Company	Sector	#	Total	Avg.
Verizon Communications Inc.	Phones	23	$31,400	$1,365
Time Warner	PayTV - Cable	29	$28,250	$974
General Electric Co.	Broadcast	19	$21,500	$1,132
AT&T Wireless	Phones	7	$11,000	$1,571
MCI (formerly WorldCom Inc.)	Phones	8	$10,500	$1,313
SAVVIS Communications Corp.	PayTV - Cable	5	$8,500	$1,700
Comcast Corp.	PayTV - Cable	3	$8,500	$2,833
Cingular Wireless	Phones	7	$8,000	$1,143
Qwest Communications International Inc.	Phones	6	$8,000	$1,333
Motorola Inc.	Satellite	7	$7,000	$1,000
Viacom Inc.	Broadcast	5	$6,500	$1,300
AT&T Corp.	Phones	7	$6,250	$893
Clear Channel Communications Inc.	Broadcast	5	$5,450	$1,090
National Cable and Telecommunications Association	PayTV - Cable	2	$5,250	$2,625
Comptel/ASCENT	Phones	5	$4,750	$950
SBC Communications Inc.	Phones	2	$4,500	$2,250
Sprint Corp.	Phones	3	$4,500	$1,500
Level 3 Communications Inc.	Other	4	$4,500	$1,125
Teligent	Phones	3	$4,000	$1,333
XO Communications Inc.	Phones	4	$3,500	$875
Covad Communications Co.	Phones	3	$3,000	$1,000
Echostar Corp.	PayTV - Satellite	2	$3,000	$1,500
Walt Disney Co.	Broadcast	4	$2,750	$688
National Association of Broadcasters	Broadcast	1	$2,500	$2,500
News Corp Ltd.	Broadcast	2	$2,500	$1,250
ALLTEL Corp.	Phones	3	$2,500	$833
Cox Communications Inc.	PayTV - Cable	3	$2,250	$750
Global Crossing Ltd.	Other	2	$2,000	$1,000
Adelphia Communications Corp.	PayTV - Cable	2	$1,500	$750
Cellular Telecommunications & Internet Association	Phones	2	$1,500	$750
Western Wireless Corp.	Phones	1	$1,000	$1,000
Salem Communications Corp.	PayTV - Cable	1	$1,000	$1,000
IDT Corp.	Other	1	$1,000	$1,000
Gannett Co. Inc.	Broadcast	1	$1,000	$1,000
Americable Inc	PayTV - Cable	1	$500	$500
Leap Wireless International	Phones	1	$500	$500
BellSouth Corp.	Phones	1	$250	$250
		Total:	$220,600	

Source: Federal Election Commission contribution records from January 1998 to September 2004

Telecommunications Company Provided Trips to Committee Member's Staff			
Company	Sector	#	Total $
Time Warner	PayTV - Cable	3	$3,843
National Cable and Telecommunications Association	PayTV - Cable	1	$1,835
SBC Communications Inc.	Phones	1	$1,685
Telecommunications Industry Association	Other	1	$629
BellSouth Corp.	Phones	1	$612
	Total:	7	$8,604

Source: Congressional office travel records for members of the Senate Committee on Commerce, Science & Transportation and the House Committee on Energy and Commerce for the period of January 2000 to March 2004.

Trips by Committee Member's Staff Sponsored by the Telecommunications Industry		
Individual	#	Total $
Cavaliere, Frank	4	$4,761
Unger, Paul	2	$2,581
Timmons, Jay	1	$1,262
Total:	7	$8,604

Source: Congressional office travel records for members of the Senate Committee on Commerce, Science & Transportation and the House Committee on Energy and Commerce for the period of January 2000 to March 2004.

Boxer, Barbara

Senator (D-CA)

Senate Committee on Commerce, Science & Transportation

112 Hart Senate Office Bldg
Washington, DC 20510
Phone: (202) 224-3553
Fax:

Web Page: http://boxer.senate.gov/
Email: http://boxer.senate.gov/contact/webform.cfm

Contribution Summary By Telecommunications Sector	
Broadcast	$187,432
PayTV - Cable	$119,350
Phones	$47,600
Union	$44,200
Other	$19,675
Satellite	$6,000
PayTV - Satellite	$2,750
Total:	$427,007

Source: Federal Election Commission contribution records from January 1998 to September 2004

Contributions by Telecommunications Sector Organizations				
Company	Sector	#	Total	Avg.
Time Warner	PayTV - Cable	82	$115,350	$1,407
Viacom Inc.	Broadcast	44	$81,175	$1,845
News Corp Ltd.	Broadcast	42	$36,125	$860
Walt Disney Co.	Broadcast	32	$31,482	$984
Misc. telecom interests	Other	13	$19,675	$1,513
Communications Workers of America	Union	9	$18,000	$2,000
Westwood One Inc.	Broadcast	6	$16,500	$2,750
Transportation Communications International Union	Union	7	$16,000	$2,286
General Electric Co.	Broadcast	18	$14,150	$786
AT&T Wireless	Phones	14	$13,000	$929
International Brotherhood of Electrical Workers (IBEW)	Union	3	$10,200	$3,400
MCI (formerly WorldCom Inc.)	Phones	7	$9,500	$1,357
Loral Space & Communications Ltd.	Satellite	6	$6,000	$1,000
Cingular Wireless	Phones	4	$5,500	$1,375
Deutsche Telekom AG (T-Mobile)	Phones	4	$4,000	$1,000
Clear Channel Communications Inc.	Broadcast	3	$4,000	$1,333
Covad Communications Co.	Phones	3	$3,000	$1,000
ICG Communications Inc.	Phones	4	$2,500	$625
SBC Communications Inc.	Phones	5	$2,100	$420
Sprint Corp.	Phones	2	$2,000	$1,000
Teligent	Phones	3	$2,000	$667
Working Assets	Phones	1	$2,000	$2,000
Univision Communications Inc.	Broadcast	2	$2,000	$1,000
Echostar Corp.	PayTV - Satellite	2	$2,000	$1,000
Comcast Corp.	PayTV - Cable	2	$2,000	$1,000
AT&T Corp.	Phones	2	$1,500	$750
Charter Communications Inc.	PayTV - Cable	2	$1,250	$625
Hearst Corp.	Broadcast	1	$1,000	$1,000
Radio One, Inc.	Broadcast	1	$1,000	$1,000
National Cable and Telecommunications Association	PayTV - Cable	2	$750	$375
The DirecTV Group Inc.	PayTV - Satellite	2	$750	$375
Cellular Telecommunications & Internet Association	Phones	1	$500	$500
		Total:	$427,007	

Source: Federal Election Commission contribution records from January 1998 to September 2004

The Center for Public Integrity

Breaux, John B.

Senate Committee on Commerce, Science & Transportation

503 Hart Senate Office Bldg
Washington, DC 20510
Phone: (202) 224-4623
Fax: (202) 228-2577

Web Page: http://breaux.senate.gov/
http://breaux.senate.gov/index_contact.html
Email: http://breaux.senate.gov/index_contact.html

Contribution Summary By Telecommunications Sector	
Phones	$100,250
Broadcast	$37,050
PayTV - Cable	$11,250
Satellite	$3,000
Other	$1,000
Total:	$152,550

Source: Federal Election Commission contribution records from January 1998 to September 2004

Contributions by Telecommunications Sector Organizations				
Company	Sector	#	Total	Avg.
SBC Communications Inc.	Phones	18	$33,250	$1,847
General Electric Co.	Broadcast	19	$20,500	$1,079
Verizon Communications Inc.	Phones	9	$18,000	$2,000
Cingular Wireless	Phones	9	$10,500	$1,167
AT&T Wireless	Phones	6	$7,000	$1,167
Viacom Inc.	Broadcast	4	$7,000	$1,750
BellSouth Corp.	Phones	6	$6,500	$1,083
Qwest Communications International Inc.	Phones	7	$6,500	$929
United States Telecom Association	Phones	2	$6,000	$3,000
National Cable and Telecommunications Association	PayTV - Cable	1	$5,000	$5,000
Time Warner	PayTV - Cable	2	$4,000	$2,000
MCI (formerly WorldCom Inc.)	Phones	3	$3,000	$1,000
National Association of Broadcasters	Broadcast	3	$3,000	$1,000
News Corp Ltd.	Broadcast	1	$3,000	$3,000
Walt Disney Co.	Broadcast	1	$3,000	$3,000
CenturyTel Inc.	Phones	2	$2,000	$1,000
ALLTEL Corp.	Phones	2	$2,000	$1,000
AT&T Corp.	Phones	2	$1,500	$750
Cellular Telecommunications & Internet Association	Phones	5	$1,000	$200
Level 3 Communications Inc.	Other	1	$1,000	$1,000
Comcast Corp.	PayTV - Cable	1	$1,000	$1,000
SAVVIS Communications Corp.	PayTV - Cable	1	$1,000	$1,000
Loral Space & Communications Ltd.	Satellite	1	$1,000	$1,000
Motorola Inc.	Satellite	1	$1,000	$1,000
Satellite Broadcasting & Communication Association	Satellite	1	$1,000	$1,000
Sprint Corp.	Phones	1	$1,000	$1,000
Teligent	Phones	1	$1,000	$1,000
United States Cellular Corp.	Phones	1	$1,000	$1,000
Gannett Co. Inc.	Broadcast	2	$550	$275
Cox Communications Inc.	PayTV - Cable	1	$250	$250
	Total:		$152,550	

Source: Federal Election Commission contribution records from January 1998 to September 2004

Telecommunications Company Provided Trips to Committee Member's Staff			
Company	Sector	#	Total $
National Cable and Telecommunications Association	PayTV - Cable	6	$11,527
News Corp Ltd.	Broadcast	1	$1,897
SBC Communications Inc.	Phones	1	$1,769
United States Telecom Association	Phones	1	$1,410
Cellular Telecommunications & Internet Association	Phones	1	$425
	Total:	10	$17,028

Source: Congressional office travel records for members of the Senate Committee on Commerce, Science & Transportation and the House Committee on Energy and Commerce for the period of January 2000 to March 2004.

Trips by Committee Member's Staff Sponsored by the Telecommunications Industry		
Individual	#	Total $
Vermilye, Andrew	7	$12,922
Breaux, John	2	$2,696
Vermilye, Andy	1	$1,410
Total:	10	$17,028
Source: Congressional office travel records for members of the Senate Committee on Commerce, Science & Transportation and the House Committee on Energy and Commerce for the period of January 2000 to March 2004.		

Brownback, Sam
Senator (R-KS)

Senate Committee on Commerce, Science & Transportation

303 Hart Senate Office Bldg
Washington, DC 20510
Phone: (202) 224-6521
Fax: (202) 228-1265

Web Page: http://brownback.senate.gov/
Email: http://brownback.senate.gov/CMEmailMe.htm

Contribution Summary By Telecommunications Sector	
Phones	$173,956
Broadcast	$40,000
PayTV - Cable	$25,500
Other	$9,000
Satellite	$3,000
PayTV - Satellite	$2,000
Total:	$253,456

Source: Federal Election Commission contribution records from January 1998 to September 2004

Contributions by Telecommunications Sector Organizations				
Company	Sector	#	Total	Avg.
SBC Communications Inc.	Phones	44	$48,900	$1,111
Verizon Communications Inc.	Phones	17	$31,000	$1,824
Cingular Wireless	Phones	22	$28,000	$1,273
United States Telecom Association	Phones	19	$19,256	$1,013
Qwest Communications International Inc.	Phones	15	$14,050	$937
General Electric Co.	Broadcast	9	$12,000	$1,333
Clear Channel Communications Inc.	Broadcast	8	$10,500	$1,313
National Cable and Telecommunications Association	PayTV - Cable	2	$10,000	$5,000
Sprint Corp.	Phones	12	$10,000	$833
National Association of Broadcasters	Broadcast	9	$9,500	$1,056
AT&T Wireless	Phones	7	$8,500	$1,214
Time Warner	PayTV - Cable	5	$7,000	$1,400
Comcast Corp.	PayTV - Cable	5	$6,500	$1,300
Cellular Telecommunications & Internet Association	Phones	6	$6,000	$1,000
IDT Corp.	Other	4	$5,000	$1,250
Global Crossing Ltd.	Other	1	$4,000	$4,000
Viacom Inc.	Broadcast	2	$3,000	$1,500
ALLTEL Corp.	Phones	3	$2,500	$833
Deutsche Telekom AG (T-Mobile)	Phones	2	$2,000	$1,000
Western Wireless Corp.	Phones	2	$2,000	$1,000
Loral Space & Communications Ltd.	Satellite	2	$2,000	$1,000
Paxson Communications Corp.	Broadcast	2	$2,000	$1,000
Echostar Corp.	PayTV - Satellite	1	$2,000	$2,000
AirTouch Communications Inc.	Phones	1	$1,000	$1,000
Salem Communications Corp.	PayTV - Cable	1	$1,000	$1,000
Cox Communications Inc.	PayTV - Cable	1	$1,000	$1,000
Walt Disney Co.	Broadcast	1	$1,000	$1,000
News Corp Ltd.	Broadcast	1	$1,000	$1,000
Meredith Corp.	Broadcast	1	$1,000	$1,000
Motorola Inc.	Satellite	1	$1,000	$1,000
National Telephone Cooperative Association	Phones	1	$500	$500
AT&T Corp.	Phones	1	$250	$250
		Total:	$253,456	

Source: Federal Election Commission contribution records from January 1998 to September 2004

Burns, Conrad R.   Senator (R-MT)

Senate Committee on Commerce, Science & Transportation   Chair, Subcommittee

187 Dirksen Senate Office Bldg   Web Page: http://burns.senate.gov/
Washington, DC 20510   Email: http://burns.senate.gov/index.cfm?FuseAction=Home.Contact
Phone: (202) 224-2644
Fax: (202) 224-8594

Contribution Summary By Telecommunications Sector	
Phones	$289,632
PayTV - Cable	$152,200
Broadcast	$108,500
Other	$46,500
Satellite	$13,500
PayTV - Satellite	$3,000
Total:	$613,332

Source: Federal Election Commission contribution records from January 1998 to September 2004

Contributions by Telecommunications Sector Organizations				
Company	Sector	#	Total	Avg.
Time Warner	PayTV - Cable	38	$44,700	$1,176
Bresnan Communications	PayTV - Cable	23	$35,500	$1,543
SBC Communications Inc.	Phones	34	$34,750	$1,022
Comcast Corp.	PayTV - Cable	29	$34,500	$1,190
Qwest Communications International Inc.	Phones	74	$33,450	$452
AT&T Wireless	Phones	32	$33,000	$1,031
MCI (formerly WorldCom Inc.)	Phones	14	$25,000	$1,786
Cingular Wireless	Phones	14	$24,500	$1,750
General Electric Co.	Broadcast	23	$24,000	$1,043
Verizon Communications Inc.	Phones	26	$23,497	$904
Global Crossing Ltd.	Other	28	$22,750	$813
Walt Disney Co.	Broadcast	14	$17,500	$1,250
United States Telecom Association	Phones	12	$16,750	$1,396
IDT Corp.	Other	16	$14,750	$922
Cellular Telecommunications & Internet Association	Phones	13	$14,685	$1,130
Viacom Inc.	Broadcast	11	$12,500	$1,136
National Cable and Telecommunications Association	PayTV - Cable	5	$12,500	$2,500
AT&T Corp.	Phones	10	$12,500	$1,250
National Association of Broadcasters	Broadcast	8	$11,000	$1,375
Cincinnati Bell Inc.	Phones	5	$11,000	$2,200
Sprint Corp.	Phones	11	$10,500	$955
BellSouth Corp.	Phones	23	$10,000	$435
Salem Communications Corp.	PayTV - Cable	2	$10,000	$5,000
Level 3 Communications Inc.	Other	3	$9,000	$3,000
Paxson Communications Corp.	Broadcast	8	$8,500	$1,063
Clear Channel Communications Inc.	Broadcast	8	$8,000	$1,000
News Corp Ltd.	Broadcast	7	$7,500	$1,071
Sinclair Broadcast Group Inc.	Broadcast	5	$7,000	$1,400
ALLTEL Corp.	Phones	6	$7,000	$1,167
Deutsche Telekom AG (T-Mobile)	Phones	7	$6,500	$929
Western Wireless Corp.	Phones	5	$6,000	$1,200
Cox Communications Inc.	PayTV - Cable	5	$5,500	$1,100
Loral Space & Communications Ltd.	Satellite	5	$5,000	$1,000
XO Communications Inc.	Phones	5	$4,500	$900
Motorola Inc.	Satellite	3	$4,000	$1,333
Satellite Broadcasting & Communication Association	Satellite	4	$3,500	$875
Covad Communications Co.	Phones	3	$3,000	$1,000
Tribune Co.	Broadcast	7	$3,000	$429
Pappas Telecasting Cos.	Broadcast	4	$3,000	$750
Adelphia Communications Corp.	PayTV - Cable	3	$2,500	$833
Hubbard Broadcasting Inc.	Broadcast	5	$2,500	$500
National Telephone Cooperative Association	Phones	2	$2,500	$1,250
United States Cellular Corp.	Phones	3	$2,500	$833
Charter Communications Inc.	PayTV - Cable	2	$2,000	$1,000

Contributions by Telecommunications Sector Organizations

Company	Sector	#	Total	Avg.
The DirecTV Group Inc.	PayTV - Satellite	2	$2,000	$1,000
AirTouch Communications Inc.	Phones	2	$2,000	$1,000
SAVVIS Communications Corp.	PayTV - Cable	2	$2,000	$1,000
ICG Communications Inc.	Phones	2	$1,500	$750
Telephone Electronics Corp.	Phones	2	$1,500	$750
CenturyTel Inc.	Phones	2	$1,500	$750
Comptel/ASCENT	Phones	1	$1,000	$1,000
Sirius Satellite Radio Inc.	Satellite	1	$1,000	$1,000
Echostar Corp.	PayTV - Satellite	1	$1,000	$1,000
Washington Post Co.	Broadcast	1	$1,000	$1,000
Mediacom Communications Corp.	PayTV - Cable	1	$1,000	$1,000
Pegasus Communications Corp.	PayTV - Cable	1	$1,000	$1,000
Liberty Media Corp.	Broadcast	1	$1,000	$1,000
Univision Communications Inc.	Broadcast	1	$1,000	$1,000
American Cable Association	PayTV - Cable	1	$1,000	$1,000
Belo Corp.	Broadcast	1	$500	$500
Gannett Co. Inc.	Broadcast	1	$500	$500
Teligent	Phones	1	$500	$500
		Total:	$613,332	

Source: Federal Election Commission contribution records from January 1998 to September 2004

Telecommunications Company Provided Trips to Committee Member's Staff

Company	Sector	#	Total $
National Cable and Telecommunications Association	PayTV - Cable	8	$13,875
National Association of Broadcasters	Broadcast	6	$10,929
GCI	Phones	3	$5,969
United States Telecom Association	Phones	2	$3,133
SBC Communications Inc.	Phones	1	$1,641
Bresnan Communications	PayTV - Cable	4	$1,639
Cellular Telecommunications & Internet Association	Phones	1	$1,608
Lockheed Martin	Satellite	3	$1,464
AT&T Corp.	Phones	2	$1,180
Western Wireless Corp.	Phones	1	$92
	Total:	31	$41,529

Source: Congressional office travel records for members of the Senate Committee on Commerce, Science & Transportation and the House Committee on Energy and Commerce for the period of January 2000 to March 2004.

Trips by Committee Member's Staff Sponsored by the Telecommunications Industry

Individual	#	Total $
Burns, Conrad	10	$15,045
Rawson, Michael	6	$11,372
Brooke, Will	6	$5,578
Hellickson, Renny	3	$3,681
Rawson, Mike	2	$1,829
Thompson, Jarrod	1	$1,792
Hajela, Prabhat	1	$1,341
Pierce, Erin	1	$488
Molen, Ric	1	$404
Total:	31	$41,529

Source: Congressional office travel records for members of the Senate Committee on Commerce, Science & Transportation and the House Committee on Energy and Commerce for the period of January 2000 to March 2004.

Cantwell, Maria

Senator (D-WA)

Senate Committee on Commerce, Science & Transportation

717 Hart Senate Office Bldg
Washington, DC 20510
Phone: (202) 224-3441
Fax: (202) 228-0514

Web Page: http://cantwell.senate.gov/
Email: http://cantwell.senate.gov/contact/index.html

Contribution Summary By Telecommunications Sector	
PayTV - Cable	$45,500
Phones	$26,500
Other	$11,505
Broadcast	$8,550
Total:	$92,055

Source: Federal Election Commission contribution records from January 1998 to September 2004

Contributions by Telecommunications Sector Organizations				
Company	Sector	#	Total	Avg.
Time Warner	PayTV - Cable	30	$25,000	$833
Comcast Corp.	PayTV - Cable	16	$11,500	$719
AT&T Wireless	Phones	13	$10,250	$788
Global Crossing Ltd.	Other	10	$10,000	$1,000
Charter Communications Inc.	PayTV - Cable	10	$7,000	$700
AT&T Corp.	Phones	9	$5,750	$639
Emmis Communications Corp.	Broadcast	3	$2,500	$833
Deutsche Telekom AG (T-Mobile)	Phones	4	$2,250	$563
Qwest Communications International Inc.	Phones	5	$2,250	$450
XO Communications Inc.	Phones	3	$2,000	$667
Viacom Inc.	Broadcast	2	$2,000	$1,000
Misc. telecom interests	Other	4	$1,505	$376
Bresnan Communications	PayTV - Cable	1	$1,000	$1,000
Cablevision Systems Corp.	PayTV - Cable	1	$1,000	$1,000
Entercom Communications Corp.	Broadcast	1	$1,000	$1,000
Liberty Media Corp.	Broadcast	1	$1,000	$1,000
MCI (formerly WorldCom Inc.)	Phones	1	$1,000	$1,000
Covad Communications Co.	Phones	1	$1,000	$1,000
BellSouth Corp.	Phones	3	$750	$250
General Electric Co.	Broadcast	2	$550	$275
Walt Disney Co.	Broadcast	1	$500	$500
News Corp Ltd.	Broadcast	1	$500	$500
Cellular Telecommunications & Internet Association	Broadcast	1	$500	$500
Comptel/ASCENT	Phones	1	$500	$500
Nextel Communications	Phones	1	$500	$500
Belo Corp.	Phones	1	$250	$250
National Association of Broadcasters	Broadcast	1	$250	$250
	Broadcast	1	$250	$250
	Total:		$92,055	

Source: Federal Election Commission contribution records from January 1998 to September 2004

Telecommunications Company Provided Trips to Committee Member's Staff			
Company	Sector	#	Total $
National Cable and Telecommunications Association	PayTV - Cable	3	$6,356
	Total:	3	$6,356

Source: Congressional office travel records for members of the Senate Committee on Commerce, Science & Transportation and the House Committee on Energy and Commerce for the period of January 2000 to March 2004.

Trips by Committee Member's Staff Sponsored by the Telecommunications Industry		
Individual	#	Total $
Fredrickson, Caroline	3	$6,356
Total:	3	$6,356

Source: Congressional office travel records for members of the Senate Committee on Commerce, Science & Transportation and the House Committee on Energy and Commerce for the period of January 2000 to March 2004.

Dorgan, Byron L.   Senator (D-ND)

Senate Committee on Commerce, Science & Transportation

713 Hart Senate Office Bldg
Washington, DC 20510
Phone: (202) 224-2551
Fax: (202) 224-1193

Web Page: http://Dorgan.senate.gov/
Email: senator@dorgan.senate.gov

Contribution Summary By Telecommunications Sector	
Phones	$199,579
Union	$56,000
Broadcast	$52,940
PayTV - Cable	$40,647
Other	$35,500
PayTV - Satellite	$7,500
Satellite	$4,500
Total:	$396,666
Source: Federal Election Commission contribution records from January 1998 to September 2004	

Contributions by Telecommunications Sector Organizations				
Company	Sector	#	Total	Avg.
International Brotherhood of Electrical Workers (IBEW)	Union	9	$27,500	$3,056
Cingular Wireless	Phones	23	$26,400	$1,148
General Electric Co.	Broadcast	19	$21,000	$1,105
Level 3 Communications Inc.	Other	14	$21,000	$1,500
AT&T Wireless	Phones	20	$20,700	$1,035
Communications Workers of America	Union	5	$19,000	$3,800
Sprint Corp.	Phones	19	$18,000	$947
Western Wireless Corp.	Phones	22	$17,500	$795
National Cable and Telecommunications Association	PayTV - Cable	8	$14,997	$1,875
XO Communications Inc.	Phones	13	$12,898	$992
MCI (formerly WorldCom Inc.)	Phones	15	$12,500	$833
AT&T Corp.	Phones	18	$12,450	$692
Time Warner	PayTV - Cable	13	$10,000	$769
Transportation Communications International Union	Union	8	$9,500	$1,188
National Association of Broadcasters	Broadcast	9	$9,440	$1,049
Deutsche Telekom AG (T-Mobile)	Phones	5	$8,500	$1,700
IDT Corp.	Other	8	$8,000	$1,000
Cellular Telecommunications & Internet Association	Phones	9	$7,733	$859
Comcast Corp.	PayTV - Cable	8	$7,650	$956
Hubbard Broadcasting Inc.	Broadcast	7	$7,500	$1,071
Walt Disney Co.	Broadcast	8	$7,000	$875
Verizon Communications Inc.	Phones	5	$7,000	$1,400
Comptel/ASCENT	Phones	6	$6,500	$1,083
Qwest Communications International Inc.	Phones	10	$6,250	$625
SBC Communications Inc.	Phones	9	$6,000	$667
Cablevision Systems Corp.	PayTV - Cable	2	$6,000	$3,000
Echostar Corp.	PayTV - Satellite	7	$5,000	$714
National Telephone Cooperative Association	Phones	3	$5,000	$1,667
United States Telecom Association	Phones	4	$5,000	$1,250
BellSouth Corp.	Phones	7	$4,500	$643
ALLTEL Corp.	Phones	4	$3,500	$875
Misc. telecom interests	Other	3	$3,500	$1,167
Global Crossing Ltd.	Other	3	$3,000	$1,000
Satellite Broadcasting & Communication Association	Satellite	3	$3,000	$1,000
Viacom Inc.	Broadcast	2	$2,500	$1,250
The DirecTV Group Inc.	PayTV - Satellite	4	$2,500	$625
Covad Communications Co.	Phones	2	$2,000	$1,000
CenturyTel Inc.	Phones	2	$2,000	$1,000
Focal Communications Corp.	Phones	2	$2,000	$1,000
American Cable Association	PayTV - Cable	2	$2,000	$1,000
Telephone Electronics Corp.	Phones	2	$2,000	$1,000
U.S. LEC Corp.	Phones	2	$2,000	$1,000
United States Cellular Corp.	Phones	2	$2,000	$1,000

Company	Sector	#	Total	Avg.
Teligent	Phones	4	$1,500	$375
Clear Channel Communications Inc.	Broadcast	3	$1,500	$500
AirTouch Communications Inc.	Phones	2	$1,148	$574
Association for Local Telecommunications Services	Phones	1	$1,000	$1,000
Forstmann Little & Co.	Phones	1	$1,000	$1,000
ICG Communications Inc.	Phones	1	$1,000	$1,000
Cincinnati Bell Inc.	Phones	1	$1,000	$1,000
Hearst Corp.	Broadcast	1	$1,000	$1,000
News Corp Ltd.	Broadcast	1	$1,000	$1,000
Paxson Communications Corp.	Broadcast	1	$1,000	$1,000
Univision Communications Inc.	Broadcast	1	$1,000	$1,000
Loral Space & Communications Ltd.	Satellite	1	$1,000	$1,000
Motorola Inc.	Satellite	1	$500	$500
Pac-West Telecomm Inc.	Phones	1	$500	$500
		Total:	$396,666	

Source: Federal Election Commission contribution records from January 1998 to September 2004

Telecommunications Company Provided Trips to Committee Member's Staff			
Company	Sector	#	Total $
SBC Communications Inc.	Phones	1	$2,051
United States Telecom Association	Phones	1	$1,481
Walt Disney Co.	Broadcast	1	$571
Misc. telecom interests	Other	1	$251
	Total:	4	$4,355

Source: Congressional office travel records for members of the Senate Committee on Commerce, Science & Transportation and the House Committee on Energy and Commerce for the period of January 2000 to March 2004.

Trips by Committee Member's Staff Sponsored by the Telecommunications Industry		
Individual	#	Total $
O'Keefe, Emmett	3	$2,873
Walker, G Franklin	1	$1,481
Total:	4	$4,355

Source: Congressional office travel records for members of the Senate Committee on Commerce, Science & Transportation and the House Committee on Energy and Commerce for the period of January 2000 to March 2004.

Ensign, John

Senator (R-NV)

Senate Committee on Commerce, Science & Transportation

364 Russell Senate Building
Washington, DC 20510
Phone: (202) 224-6244
Fax: (202) 228-2193

Web Page: http://ensign.senate.gov/
Email: http://ensign.senate.gov/contact_john/contactjohn_email.html

Contribution Summary By Telecommunications Sector	
Phones	$91,083
Broadcast	$36,700
PayTV - Cable	$8,750
PayTV - Satellite	$5,000
Satellite	$2,000
Other	$1,000
Total:	$144,533

Source: Federal Election Commission contribution records from January 1998 to September 2004

Contributions by Telecommunications Sector Organizations				
Company	Sector	#	Total	Avg.
AT&T Wireless	Phones	19	$20,600	$1,084
Verizon Communications Inc.	Phones	8	$15,000	$1,875
General Electric Co.	Broadcast	12	$14,000	$1,167
SBC Communications Inc.	Phones	5	$13,250	$2,650
Sprint Corp.	Phones	12	$9,000	$750
National Association of Broadcasters	Broadcast	3	$7,000	$2,333
Clear Channel Communications Inc.	Broadcast	3	$6,000	$2,000
Cingular Wireless	Phones	4	$6,000	$1,500
MCI (formerly WorldCom Inc.)	Phones	8	$6,000	$750
National Cable and Telecommunications Association	PayTV - Cable	1	$5,000	$5,000
Echostar Corp.	PayTV - Satellite	1	$5,000	$5,000
Cellular Telecommunications & Internet Association	Phones	6	$4,233	$706
United States Telecom Association	Phones	4	$4,000	$1,000
News Corp Ltd.	Broadcast	3	$3,500	$1,167
ALLTEL Corp.	Phones	3	$3,000	$1,000
AT&T Corp.	Phones	4	$3,000	$750
Sinclair Broadcast Group Inc.	Broadcast	3	$2,200	$733
Cox Communications Inc.	PayTV - Cable	3	$1,750	$583
Deutsche Telekom AG (T-Mobile)	Phones	2	$1,500	$750
Teligent	Phones	1	$1,000	$1,000
Pac-West Telecomm Inc.	Phones	1	$1,000	$1,000
Qwest Communications International Inc.	Phones	1	$1,000	$1,000
Covad Communications Co.	Phones	1	$1,000	$1,000
Western Wireless Corp.	Phones	1	$1,000	$1,000
Motorola Inc.	Satellite	1	$1,000	$1,000
Sirius Satellite Radio Inc.	Satellite	1	$1,000	$1,000
SAVVIS Communications Corp.	PayTV - Cable	1	$1,000	$1,000
Time Warner	PayTV - Cable	1	$1,000	$1,000
Viacom Inc.	Broadcast	1	$1,000	$1,000
Walt Disney Co.	Broadcast	1	$1,000	$1,000
Level 3 Communications Inc.	Other	1	$1,000	$1,000
Paxson Communications Corp.	Broadcast	1	$1,000	$1,000
Hubbard Broadcasting Inc.	Broadcast	1	$1,000	$1,000
XO Communications Inc.	Phones	1	$500	$500
		Total:	$144,533	

Source: Federal Election Commission contribution records from January 1998 to September 2004

Telecommunications Company Provided Trips to Committee Member's Staff			
Company	Sector	#	Total $
United States Telecom Association	Phones	4	$5,981
National Cable and Telecommunications Association	PayTV - Cable	3	$5,854
News Corp Ltd.	Broadcast	1	$1,897
SBC Communications Inc.	Phones	1	$1,821
National Association of Broadcasters	Broadcast	1	$1,041
Telecommunications Industry Association	Other	1	$540
	Total:	11	$17,135

Source: Congressional office travel records for members of the Senate Committee on Commerce, Science & Transportation and the House Committee on Energy and Commerce for the period of January 2000 to March 2004.

Trips by Committee Member's Staff Sponsored by the Telecommunications Industry		
Individual	#	Total $
Cunningham, William	7	$10,106
Sullivan, Mike	2	$3,857
Lopez, John	1	$1,897
Cunningham, Wm Bryant	1	$1,275
Total:	11	$17,135

Source: Congressional office travel records for members of the Senate Committee on Commerce, Science & Transportation and the House Committee on Energy and Commerce for the period of January 2000 to March 2004.

Fitzgerald, Peter G.

Senator (R-IL)

Senate Committee on Commerce, Science & Transportation

555 Dirksen Senate Office Bldg
Washington, DC 20510
Phone: (202) 224-2854
Fax:

Web Page: http://Fitzgerald.senate.gov/
Email: http://fitzgerald.senate.gov/index.cfm?FuseAction=Offices.Contact

Contribution Summary By Telecommunications Sector	
Phones	$82,091
Broadcast	$7,850
Satellite	$6,000
PayTV - Cable	$4,000
Other	$2,000
PayTV - Satellite	$1,000
Total:	$102,941
Source: Federal Election Commission contribution records from January 1998 to September 2004	

Contributions by Telecommunications Sector Organizations				
Company	Sector	#	Total	Avg.
XO Communications Inc.	Phones	19	$20,999	$1,105
SBC Communications Inc.	Phones	13	$18,500	$1,423
MCI (formerly WorldCom Inc.)	Phones	17	$12,800	$753
Verizon Communications Inc.	Phones	6	$6,900	$1,150
Motorola Inc.	Satellite	8	$6,000	$750
Focal Communications Corp.	Phones	4	$5,500	$1,375
AT&T Wireless	Phones	5	$4,500	$900
Time Warner	PayTV - Cable	3	$3,000	$1,000
Sprint Corp.	Phones	3	$3,000	$1,000
General Electric Co.	Broadcast	3	$2,350	$783
Cingular Wireless	Phones	2	$2,000	$1,000
Walt Disney Co.	Broadcast	1	$2,000	$2,000
Covad Communications Co.	Phones	3	$1,892	$631
Viacom Inc.	Broadcast	2	$1,500	$750
United States Telecom Association	Phones	2	$1,500	$750
United States Cellular Corp.	Phones	1	$1,000	$1,000
Qwest Communications International Inc.	Phones	1	$1,000	$1,000
Comptel/ASCENT	Phones	1	$1,000	$1,000
National Association of Broadcasters	Broadcast	1	$1,000	$1,000
Tribune Co.	Broadcast	1	$1,000	$1,000
Level 3 Communications Inc.	Other	1	$1,000	$1,000
Misc. telecom interests	Other	1	$1,000	$1,000
Echostar Corp.	PayTV - Satellite	1	$1,000	$1,000
Association for Local Telecommunications Services	Phones	1	$1,000	$1,000
Charter Communications Inc.	PayTV - Cable	1	$500	$500
Cox Communications Inc.	PayTV - Cable	1	$500	$500
Forstmann Little & Co.	Phones	1	$500	$500
AT&T Corp.	Phones	2	-	-
	Total:		$102,941	
Source: Federal Election Commission contribution records from January 1998 to September 2004				

Hollings, Ernest F.

Senate Committee on Commerce, Science & Transportation

Senator (D-SC)

Ranking Democrat

125 Russell Senate Office Bldg
Washington, DC 20510
Phone: (202) 224-6121
Fax: (202) 224-4293

Web Page: http://hollings.senate.gov/
Email: http://hollings.senate.gov/contact/Webform.cfm

Contribution Summary By Telecommunications Sector	
Phones	$119,580
Broadcast	$84,782
PayTV - Cable	$70,283
Union	$24,750
Other	$18,000
Satellite	$13,500
PayTV - Satellite	$5,000
Total:	$335,895

Source: Federal Election Commission contribution records from January 1998 to September 2004

Contributions by Telecommunications Sector Organizations				
Company	Sector	#	Total	Avg.
Time Warner	PayTV - Cable	39	$30,533	$783
Comcast Corp.	PayTV - Cable	29	$25,000	$862
Viacom Inc.	Broadcast	29	$23,882	$824
Walt Disney Co.	Broadcast	20	$19,000	$950
XO Communications Inc.	Phones	13	$17,000	$1,308
AT&T Corp.	Phones	16	$13,750	$859
AT&T Wireless	Phones	27	$13,250	$491
Communications Workers of America	Union	4	$13,000	$3,250
News Corp Ltd.	Broadcast	14	$12,500	$893
Loral Space & Communications Ltd.	Satellite	12	$11,500	$958
Teligent	Phones	14	$9,250	$661
National Association of Broadcasters	Broadcast	4	$9,000	$2,250
Sprint Corp.	Phones	13	$8,250	$635
Global Crossing Ltd.	Other	8	$8,000	$1,000
Cellular Telecommunications & Internet Association	Phones	8	$8,000	$1,000
Cingular Wireless	Phones	5	$8,000	$1,600
Transportation Communications International Union	Union	8	$7,000	$875
General Electric Co.	Broadcast	10	$6,700	$670
Comptel/ASCENT	Phones	6	$5,500	$917
Charter Communications Inc.	PayTV - Cable	10	$5,250	$525
MCI (formerly WorldCom Inc.)	Phones	10	$5,250	$525
Qwest Communications International Inc.	Phones	1	$5,000	$5,000
Misc. telecom interests	Other	5	$5,000	$1,000
International Brotherhood of Electrical Workers (IBEW)	Union	3	$4,750	$1,583
Paxson Communications Corp.	Broadcast	4	$4,000	$1,000
The DirecTV Group Inc.	PayTV - Satellite	5	$4,000	$800
ALLTEL Corp.	Phones	3	$3,500	$1,167
Cox Communications Inc.	PayTV - Cable	4	$3,500	$875
IDT Corp.	Other	4	$3,500	$875
Liberty Corp.	Broadcast	2	$3,500	$1,750
ICG Communications Inc.	Phones	2	$3,500	$1,750
Clear Channel Communications Inc.	Broadcast	3	$3,000	$1,000
Adelphia Communications Corp.	PayTV - Cable	2	$3,000	$1,500
BellSouth Corp.	Phones	3	$2,830	$943
United States Cellular Corp.	Phones	1	$2,500	$2,500
Verizon Communications Inc.	Phones	2	$2,000	$1,000
Focal Communications Corp.	Phones	2	$2,000	$1,000
Association for Local Telecommunications Services	Phones	2	$2,000	$1,000
National Telephone Cooperative Association	Phones	2	$1,500	$750
Telephone Electronics Corp.	Phones	2	$1,500	$750
SBC Communications Inc.	Phones	3	$1,000	$333
Motorola Inc.	Satellite	1	$1,000	$1,000
Satellite Broadcasting & Communication Association	Satellite	1	$1,000	$1,000

Contributions by Telecommunications Sector Organizations				
Company	Sector	#	Total	Avg.
AirTouch Communications Inc.	Phones	1	$1,000	$1,000
Corvis Corporation	Phones	1	$1,000	$1,000
Covad Communications Co.	Phones	1	$1,000	$1,000
Cablevision Systems Corp.	PayTV - Cable	1	$1,000	$1,000
Echostar Corp.	PayTV - Satellite	1	$1,000	$1,000
National Cable and Telecommunications Association	PayTV - Cable	1	$1,000	$1,000
SAVVIS Communications Corp.	PayTV - Cable	1	$1,000	$1,000
Hubbard Broadcasting Inc.	Broadcast	1	$1,000	$1,000
Level 3 Communications Inc.	Other	1	$1,000	$1,000
Univision Communications Inc.	Broadcast	1	$1,000	$1,000
Telecommunications Industry Association	Other	1	$500	$500
Hearst Corp.	Broadcast	1	$500	$500
Pac-West Telecomm Inc.	Phones	1	$500	$500
Forstmann Little & Co.	Phones	1	$500	$500
Gannett Co. Inc.	Broadcast	1	$450	$450
Meredith Corp.	Broadcast	1	$250	$250
		Total:	$335,895	
Source: Federal Election Commission contribution records from January 1998 to September 2004				

Telecommunications Company Provided Trips to Committee Member's Staff			
Company	Sector	#	Total $
Cellular Telecommunications & Internet Association	Phones	1	$1,020
MCI (formerly WorldCom Inc.)	Phones	1	$865
Misc. telecom interests	Other	1	$725
	Total:	3	$2,610
Source: Congressional office travel records for members of the Senate Committee on Commerce, Science & Transportation and the House Committee on Energy and Commerce for the period of January 2000 to March 2004.			

Trips by Committee Member's Staff Sponsored by the Telecommunications Industry		
Individual	#	Total $
Cooper, Ashley	3	$2,610
Total:	3	$2,610
Source: Congressional office travel records for members of the Senate Committee on Commerce, Science & Transportation and the House Committee on Energy and Commerce for the period of January 2000 to March 2004.		

Hutchison, Kay Bailey
Senator (R-TX)

Senate Committee on Commerce, Science & Transportation

284 Russell Senate Office Bldg
Washington, DC 20510
Phone: (202) 224-5922
Fax: (202) 224-0776

Web Page: http://hutchison.senate.gov/
Email: http://hutchison.senate.gov/e-mail.htm

Contribution Summary By Telecommunications Sector	
Phones	$51,800
Broadcast	$17,000
PayTV - Cable	$7,000
Satellite	$1,000
Other	$0
Total:	$76,800
Source: Federal Election Commission contribution records from January 1998 to September 2004	

Contributions by Telecommunications Sector Organizations				
Company	Sector	#	Total	Avg.
SBC Communications Inc.	Phones	30	$21,800	$727
Verizon Communications Inc.	Phones	8	$17,500	$2,188
Clear Channel Communications Inc.	Broadcast	10	$10,000	$1,000
National Cable and Telecommunications Association	PayTV - Cable	1	$5,000	$5,000
AT&T Wireless	Phones	5	$5,000	$1,000
ALLTEL Corp.	Phones	1	$3,000	$3,000
National Association of Broadcasters	Broadcast	3	$3,000	$1,000
Time Warner	PayTV - Cable	1	$2,000	$2,000
General Electric Co.	Broadcast	2	$2,000	$1,000
AirTouch Communications Inc.	Phones	1	$1,000	$1,000
News Corp Ltd.	Broadcast	1	$1,000	$1,000
Walt Disney Co.	Broadcast	1	$1,000	$1,000
Western Wireless Corp.	Phones	1	$1,000	$1,000
Motorola Inc.	Satellite	1	$1,000	$1,000
MCI (formerly WorldCom Inc.)	Phones	1	$1,000	$1,000
Sprint Corp.	Phones	5	$1,000	$200
Pac-West Telecomm Inc.	Phones	1	$500	$500
Global Crossing Ltd.	Other	3	-	-
		Total:	$76,800	
Source: Federal Election Commission contribution records from January 1998 to September 2004				

Inouye, Daniel K.

Senator (D-HI)

Senate Committee on Commerce, Science & Transportation

722 Hart Senate Office Bldg
Washington, DC 20510
Phone: (202) 224-3934
Fax: (202) 224-6747

Web Page: http://inouye.senate.gov/
Email: http://inouye.senate.gov/abtform.html

Contribution Summary By Telecommunications Sector	
Phones	$66,352
Broadcast	$42,500
PayTV - Cable	$34,999
Union	$9,000
Satellite	$3,500
Other	$3,000
Total:	$159,351
Source: Federal Election Commission contribution records from January 1998 to September 2004	

Contributions by Telecommunications Sector Organizations				
Company	Sector	#	Total	Avg.
National Cable and Telecommunications Association	PayTV - Cable	7	$19,999	$2,857
AT&T Wireless	Phones	15	$15,000	$1,000
National Association of Broadcasters	Broadcast	3	$9,000	$3,000
Viacom Inc.	Broadcast	7	$8,500	$1,214
Walt Disney Co.	Broadcast	4	$8,000	$2,000
General Electric Co.	Broadcast	9	$8,000	$889
Verizon Communications Inc.	Phones	8	$7,500	$938
Comcast Corp.	PayTV - Cable	2	$7,000	$3,500
Time Warner	PayTV - Cable	7	$7,000	$1,000
XO Communications Inc.	Phones	5	$6,000	$1,200
MCI (formerly WorldCom Inc.)	Phones	5	$6,000	$1,200
International Brotherhood of Electrical Workers (IBEW)	Union	5	$6,000	$1,200
Cingular Wireless	Phones	4	$5,000	$1,250
Sprint Corp.	Phones	6	$4,000	$667
News Corp Ltd.	Broadcast	2	$4,000	$2,000
Clear Channel Communications Inc.	Broadcast	4	$3,000	$750
Deutsche Telekom AG (T-Mobile)	Phones	2	$3,000	$1,500
Focal Communications Corp.	Phones	3	$3,000	$1,000
Cellular Telecommunications & Internet Association	Phones	3	$2,500	$833
Misc. telecom interests	Other	2	$2,000	$1,000
United States Telecom Association	Phones	2	$2,000	$1,000
Western Wireless Corp.	Phones	2	$2,000	$1,000
Transportation Communications International Union	Union	2	$2,000	$1,000
Motorola Inc.	Satellite	1	$2,000	$2,000
Covad Communications Co.	Phones	2	$1,500	$750
Pac-West Telecomm Inc.	Phones	2	$1,500	$750
Qwest Communications International Inc.	Phones	2	$1,500	$750
AT&T Corp.	Phones	2	$1,352	$676
ALLTEL Corp.	Phones	1	$1,000	$1,000
Association for Local Telecommunications Services	Phones	1	$1,000	$1,000
SAVVIS Communications Corp.	PayTV - Cable	1	$1,000	$1,000
Level 3 Communications Inc.	Other	1	$1,000	$1,000
Emmis Communications Corp.	Broadcast	1	$1,000	$1,000
Pappas Telecasting Cos.	Broadcast	1	$1,000	$1,000
SBC Communications Inc.	Phones	1	$1,000	$1,000
United States Cellular Corp.	Phones	1	$1,000	$1,000
Communications Workers of America	Union	1	$1,000	$1,000
Loral Space & Communications Ltd.	Satellite	1	$1,000	$1,000
Intelsat Ltd.	Satellite	1	$500	$500
Comptel/ASCENT	Phones	1	$500	$500
	Total:		$159,351	
Source: Federal Election Commission contribution records from January 1998 to September 2004				

Telecommunications Company Provided Trips to Committee Member's Staff			
Company	Sector	#	Total $
National Cable and Telecommunications Association	PayTV - Cable	1	$1,572
	Total:	1	$1,572

Source: Congressional office travel records for members of the Senate Committee on Commerce, Science & Transportation and the House Committee on Energy and Commerce for the period of January 2000 to March 2004.

Trips by Committee Member's Staff Sponsored by the Telecommunications Industry		
Individual	#	Total $
Cummisky, Margaret	1	$1,572
Total:	1	$1,572

Source: Congressional office travel records for members of the Senate Committee on Commerce, Science & Transportation and the House Committee on Energy and Commerce for the period of January 2000 to March 2004.

Kerry, John F.

Senator (D-MA)

Senate Committee on Commerce, Science & Transportation

304 Russell Senate Office Bldg
Washington, DC 20510
Phone: (202) 224-2742
Fax: (202) 224-8525

Web Page: http://kerry.senate.gov
Email: http://kerry.senate.gov/bandwidth/contact/email.html

Contribution Summary By Telecommunications Sector	
Broadcast	$385,921
PayTV - Cable	$322,753
Phones	$305,794
Other	$48,500
Satellite	$24,400
Union	$7,875
PayTV - Satellite	$2,250
Total:	$1,097,493

Source: Federal Election Commission contribution records from January 1998 to September 2004

Contributions by Telecommunications Sector Organizations				
Company	Sector	#	Total	Avg.
Time Warner	PayTV - Cable	318	$241,959	$761
Viacom Inc.	Broadcast	155	$117,911	$761
Verizon Communications Inc.	Phones	184	$116,083	$631
News Corp Ltd.	Broadcast	110	$90,036	$819
Walt Disney Co.	Broadcast	80	$59,645	$746
General Electric Co.	Broadcast	88	$58,929	$670
Comcast Corp.	PayTV - Cable	41	$33,450	$816
AT&T Corp.	Phones	58	$31,496	$543
SBC Communications Inc.	Phones	59	$29,226	$495
MCI (formerly WorldCom Inc.)	Phones	32	$22,734	$710
Cablevision Systems Corp.	PayTV - Cable	26	$22,550	$867
Misc. telecom interests	Other	28	$21,500	$768
Clear Channel Communications Inc.	Broadcast	17	$15,750	$926
Global Crossing Ltd.	Other	16	$15,500	$969
Sprint Corp.	Phones	30	$14,800	$493
BellSouth Corp.	Phones	21	$13,250	$631
Qwest Communications International Inc.	Phones	25	$11,455	$458
AT&T Wireless	Phones	20	$11,250	$563
Cellular Telecommunications & Internet Association	Phones	10	$10,250	$1,025
Level 3 Communications Inc.	Other	12	$10,000	$833
Nextel Communications	Phones	16	$9,450	$591
California Microwave Inc.	Satellite	5	$9,000	$1,800
Tribune Co.	Broadcast	13	$9,000	$692
Loral Space & Communications Ltd.	Satellite	9	$8,900	$989
National Cable and Telecommunications Association	PayTV - Cable	13	$8,644	$665
Western Wireless Corp.	Phones	3	$8,000	$2,667
Cox Communications Inc.	PayTV - Cable	9	$7,650	$850
Working Assets	Phones	10	$6,950	$695
Univision Communications Inc.	Broadcast	9	$6,400	$711
Entercom Communications Corp.	Broadcast	4	$6,000	$1,500
Covad Communications Co.	Phones	9	$5,750	$639
International Brotherhood of Electrical Workers (IBEW)	Union	13	$5,375	$413
Hearst Corp.	Broadcast	10	$4,950	$495
Charter Communications Inc.	PayTV - Cable	4	$4,750	$1,188
Cingular Wireless	Phones	11	$4,700	$427
Hubbard Broadcasting Inc.	Broadcast	6	$4,500	$750
Emmis Communications Corp.	Broadcast	4	$4,000	$1,000
Westwood One Inc.	Broadcast	6	$3,900	$650
Deutsche Telekom AG (T-Mobile)	Phones	7	$3,400	$486
XO Communications Inc.	Phones	3	$3,250	$1,083
Intelsat Ltd.	Satellite	5	$3,000	$600
Sirius Satellite Radio Inc.	Satellite	2	$2,500	$1,250
Communications Workers of America	Union	15	$2,500	$167

Contributions by Telecommunications Sector Organizations

Company	Sector	#	Total	Avg.
VALOR Telecommunications	Phones	2	$2,000	$1,000
Pegasus Communications Corp.	PayTV - Cable	1	$2,000	$2,000
The DirecTV Group Inc.	PayTV - Satellite	5	$2,000	$400
Liberty Media Corp.	Broadcast	2	$2,000	$1,000
Pappas Telecasting Cos.	Broadcast	2	$1,900	$950
United States Cellular Corp.	Phones	3	$1,250	$417
XM Satellite Radio Holdings Inc.	Satellite	2	$1,000	$500
NTT America Inc.	Other	1	$1,000	$1,000
Mediacom Communications Corp.	PayTV - Cable	1	$1,000	$1,000
Adelphia Communications Corp.	PayTV - Cable	2	$750	$375
Washington Post Co.	Broadcast	2	$750	$375
IDT Corp.	Other	1	$500	$500
Cumulus Media Inc.	Broadcast	1	$250	$250
ALLTEL Corp.	Phones	1	$250	$250
Echostar Corp.	PayTV - Satellite	1	$250	$250
United States Telecom Association	Phones	1	$250	$250
		Total:	$1,097,493	

Source: Federal Election Commission contribution records from January 1998 to September 2004

Telecommunications Company Provided Trips to Committee Member's Staff

Company	Sector	#	Total $
News Corp Ltd.	Broadcast	1	$1,957
Walt Disney Co.	Broadcast	1	$1,828
United States Telecom Association	Phones	1	$1,774
Cellular Telecommunications & Internet Association	Phones	1	$1,171
General Electric Co.	Broadcast	1	$620
	Total:	5	$7,349

Source: Congressional office travel records for members of the Senate Committee on Commerce, Science & Transportation and the House Committee on Energy and Commerce for the period of January 2000 to March 2004.

Trips by Committee Member's Staff Sponsored by the Telecommunications Industry

Individual	#	Total $
Rothschild, Gregg	3	$4,772
Rosenberg, Lisa	1	$1,957
Kerry, John	1	$620
Total:	5	$7,349

Source: Congressional office travel records for members of the Senate Committee on Commerce, Science & Transportation and the House Committee on Energy and Commerce for the period of January 2000 to March 2004.

Lautenberg, Frank

Senator (D-NJ)

Senate Committee on Commerce, Science & Transportation

324 Hart Senate Office Building, Suite 324
Washington, DC 20510
Phone: (202) 224-3224
Fax: (202) 228-4054

Web Page: http://lautenberg.senate.gov/
Email: lautenberg.senate.gov/webform.html

Contribution Summary By Telecommunications Sector	
PayTV - Cable	$20,250
Union	$13,500
Phones	$6,000
Broadcast	$1,000
Other	$1,000
Satellite	-
Total:	$41,750

Source: Federal Election Commission contribution records from January 1998 to September 2004

Contributions by Telecommunications Sector Organizations				
Company	Sector	#	Total	Avg.
Comcast Corp.	PayTV - Cable	2	$6,000	$3,000
National Cable and Telecommunications Association	PayTV - Cable	1	$5,000	$5,000
Communications Workers of America	Union	1	$5,000	$5,000
International Brotherhood of Electrical Workers (IBEW)	Union	2	$5,000	$2,500
Cablevision Systems Corp.	PayTV - Cable	1	$5,000	$5,000
Time Warner	PayTV - Cable	4	$4,250	$1,063
Transportation Communications International Union	Union	4	$3,500	$875
Cingular Wireless	Phones	2	$3,000	$1,500
AT&T Wireless	Phones	3	$2,000	$667
MCI (formerly WorldCom Inc.)	Phones	1	$1,000	$1,000
Spanish Broadcasting Systems, Inc.	Broadcast	1	$1,000	$1,000
Misc. telecom interests	Other	1	$1,000	$1,000
Loral Space & Communications Ltd.	Satellite	2	-	-
	Total:		$41,750	

Source: Federal Election Commission contribution records from January 1998 to September 2004

Telecommunications Company Provided Trips to Committee Member's Staff			
Company	Sector	#	Total $
National Cable and Telecommunications Association	PayTV - Cable	1	$1,300
	Total:	1	$1,300

Source: Congressional office travel records for members of the Senate Committee on Commerce, Science & Transportation and the House Committee on Energy and Commerce for the period of January 2000 to March 2004.

Trips by Committee Member's Staff Sponsored by the Telecommunications Industry		
Individual	#	Total $
Yehl, Tim	1	$1,300
Total:	1	$1,300

Source: Congressional office travel records for members of the Senate Committee on Commerce, Science & Transportation and the House Committee on Energy and Commerce for the period of January 2000 to March 2004.

Lott, Trent

Senator (R-MS)

Senate Committee on Commerce, Science & Transportation

487 Russell Senate Office Bldg
Washington, DC 20510
Phone: (202) 224-6253
Fax: (202) 224-2262

Web Page: http://lott.senate.gov/
Email: http://lott.senate.gov/index.cfm?FuseAction=Contact.Email

Contribution Summary By Telecommunications Sector	
Phones	$231,720
Broadcast	$75,000
PayTV - Cable	$66,000
Other	$18,000
Total:	$390,720

Source: Federal Election Commission contribution records from January 1998 to September 2004

Contributions by Telecommunications Sector Organizations				
Company	Sector	#	Total	Avg.
MCI (formerly WorldCom Inc.)	Phones	12	$46,500	$3,875
Verizon Communications Inc.	Phones	13	$44,500	$3,423
Time Warner	PayTV - Cable	18	$43,000	$2,389
Cingular Wireless	Phones	11	$32,000	$2,909
AT&T Wireless	Phones	13	$31,500	$2,423
National Association of Broadcasters	Broadcast	7	$31,000	$4,429
BellSouth Corp.	Phones	13	$28,970	$2,228
SBC Communications Inc.	Phones	10	$27,500	$2,750
Global Crossing Ltd.	Other	14	$18,000	$1,286
General Electric Co.	Broadcast	8	$16,500	$2,063
Walt Disney Co.	Broadcast	7	$11,000	$1,571
Viacom Inc.	Broadcast	2	$9,000	$4,500
National Cable and Telecommunications Association	PayTV - Cable	3	$7,000	$2,333
Cellular Telecommunications & Internet Association	Phones	4	$6,750	$1,688
News Corp Ltd.	Broadcast	6	$6,500	$1,083
Comcast Corp.	PayTV - Cable	2	$6,000	$3,000
United States Telecom Association	Phones	5	$6,000	$1,200
Qwest Communications International Inc.	Phones	1	$5,000	$5,000
Cox Communications Inc.	PayTV - Cable	4	$4,000	$1,000
Cablevision Systems Corp.	PayTV - Cable	2	$3,500	$1,750
Pegasus Communications Corp.	PayTV - Cable	2	$1,500	$750
Clear Channel Communications Inc.	Broadcast	1	$1,000	$1,000
Adelphia Communications Corp.	PayTV - Cable	1	$1,000	$1,000
Comptel/ASCENT	Phones	1	$1,000	$1,000
XO Communications Inc.	Phones	1	$1,000	$1,000
National Telephone Cooperative Association	Phones	1	$500	$500
AT&T Corp.	Phones	1	$500	$500
		Total:	$390,720	

Source: Federal Election Commission contribution records from January 1998 to September 2004

Telecommunications Company Provided Trips to Committee Member's Staff			
Company	Sector	#	Total $
National Cable and Telecommunications Association	PayTV - Cable	2	$2,633
News Corp Ltd.	Broadcast	1	$1,651
United States Telecom Association	Phones	1	$1,035
Association for Local Telecommunications Services	Phones	1	$905
Sprint Corp.	Phones	1	$828
Misc. telecom interests	Other	1	$649
AT&T Corp.	Phones	1	$520
Cellular Telecommunications & Internet Association	Phones	1	$502
	Total:	9	$8,723

Source: Congressional office travel records for members of the Senate Committee on Commerce, Science & Transportation and the House Committee on Energy and Commerce for the period of January 2000 to March 2004.

Trips by Committee Member's Staff Sponsored by the Telecommunications Industry		
Individual	#	Total $
Wall, Steven	7	$6,860
Mashburn, John	1	$1,035
Bennett, Renee	1	$828
Total:	9	$8,723
Source: Congressional office travel records for members of the Senate Committee on Commerce, Science & Transportation and the House Committee on Energy and Commerce for the period of January 2000 to March 2004.		

McCain, John

Senate (R-AZ)

Senate Committee on Commerce, Science & Transportation

Chairman

241 Russell Senate Office Bldg
Washington, DC 20510
Phone: (202) 224-2235
Fax: (202) 228-2862

Web Page: http://mccain.senate.gov/
Email: http://mccain.senate.gov/index.cfm?fuseaction=Contact.Home

Contribution Summary By Telecommunications Sector

Phones	$475,142
Broadcast	$227,300
PayTV - Cable	$143,519
PayTV - Satellite	$23,100
Other	$20,000
Satellite	$16,200
Total:	**$905,261**

Source: Federal Election Commission contribution records from January 1998 to September 2004

Contributions by Telecommunications Sector Organizations

Company	Sector	#	Total	Avg.
Qwest Communications International Inc.	Phones	196	$116,700	$595
Verizon Communications Inc.	Phones	59	$77,400	$1,312
Viacom Inc.	Broadcast	74	$70,450	$952
Time Warner	PayTV - Cable	59	$61,775	$1,047
SBC Communications Inc.	Phones	48	$57,550	$1,199
BellSouth Corp.	Phones	84	$40,050	$477
AT&T Wireless	Phones	27	$37,000	$1,370
News Corp Ltd.	Broadcast	48	$29,550	$616
General Electric Co.	Broadcast	42	$29,200	$695
AT&T Corp.	Phones	45	$28,850	$641
Comcast Corp.	PayTV - Cable	27	$26,400	$978
Univision Communications Inc.	Broadcast	23	$25,000	$1,087
MCI (formerly WorldCom Inc.)	Phones	22	$21,400	$973
Cablevision Systems Corp.	PayTV - Cable	8	$21,000	$2,625
Echostar Corp.	PayTV - Satellite	44	$20,600	$468
Cingular Wireless	Phones	8	$20,000	$2,500
Sinclair Broadcast Group Inc.	Broadcast	22	$19,100	$868
National Cable and Telecommunications Association	PayTV - Cable	10	$18,644	$1,864
Paxson Communications Corp.	Broadcast	15	$16,000	$1,067
Cellular Telecommunications & Internet Association	Phones	12	$13,500	$1,125
Motorola Inc.	Satellite	18	$12,200	$678
United States Telecom Association	Phones	10	$12,192	$1,219
IDT Corp.	Other	8	$11,500	$1,438
Sprint Corp.	Phones	8	$11,000	$1,375
Cox Communications Inc.	PayTV - Cable	14	$9,400	$671
Walt Disney Co.	Broadcast	11	$9,000	$818
AirTouch Communications Inc.	Phones	10	$7,050	$705
Global Crossing Ltd.	Other	10	$6,000	$600
National Association of Broadcasters	Broadcast	4	$6,000	$1,500
Tribune Co.	Broadcast	5	$5,000	$1,000
ALLTEL Corp.	Phones	4	$4,250	$1,063
Spanish Broadcasting Systems, Inc.	Broadcast	2	$4,000	$2,000
Teligent	Phones	4	$4,000	$1,000
Nextel Communications	Phones	5	$3,500	$700
XO Communications Inc.	Phones	4	$3,500	$875
Belo Corp.	Broadcast	4	$3,500	$875
Hearst Corp.	Broadcast	3	$3,000	$1,000
Personal Communications Industry Association	Phones	3	$3,000	$1,000
Western Wireless Corp.	Phones	3	$3,000	$1,000
The DirecTV Group Inc.	PayTV - Satellite	3	$2,500	$833
Charter Communications Inc.	PayTV - Cable	3	$2,250	$750
Hubbard Broadcasting Inc.	Broadcast	3	$2,250	$750
Adelphia Communications Corp.	PayTV - Cable	4	$2,050	$513
Gannett Co. Inc.	Broadcast	4	$2,000	$500

Contributions by Telecommunications Sector Organizations				
Company	Sector	#	Total	Avg.
Loral Space & Communications Ltd.	Satellite	2	$2,000	$1,000
Satellite Broadcasting & Communication Association	Satellite	2	$2,000	$1,000
Telephone Electronics Corp.	Phones	2	$2,000	$1,000
ICG Communications Inc.	Phones	2	$2,000	$1,000
Forstmann Little & Co.	Phones	2	$1,500	$750
Misc. telecom interests	Other	2	$1,500	$750
Meredith Corp.	Broadcast	1	$1,250	$1,250
Liberty Media Corp.	Broadcast	1	$1,000	$1,000
Westwood One Inc.	Broadcast	1	$1,000	$1,000
Level 3 Communications Inc.	Other	1	$1,000	$1,000
SAVVIS Communications Corp.	PayTV - Cable	1	$1,000	$1,000
CenturyTel Inc.	Phones	1	$1,000	$1,000
Cincinnati Bell Inc.	Phones	1	$1,000	$1,000
Leap Wireless International	Phones	1	$1,000	$1,000
NextWave Telecom Inc.	Phones	1	$1,000	$1,000
United States Cellular Corp.	Phones	1	$1,000	$1,000
National Telephone Cooperative Association	Phones	2	$700	$350
Pegasus Communications Corp.	PayTV - Cable	1	$500	$500
Mediacom Communications Corp.	PayTV - Cable	1	$500	$500
		Total:	$905,261	

Source: Federal Election Commission contribution records from January 1998 to September 2004

Nelson, Bill

Senator (D-FL)

Senate Committee on Commerce, Science & Transportation

716 Hart Senate Office Bldg
Washington, DC 20510
Phone: (202) 224-5274
Fax: (202) 228-2183

Web Page: http://billnelson.senate.gov/
Email: billnelson.senate.gov/contact/index.cfm#email

Contribution Summary By Telecommunications Sector	
Broadcast	$71,500
Phones	$62,500
PayTV - Cable	$28,750
Union	$28,500
Other	$12,250
Satellite	$8,000
PayTV - Satellite	$2,000
Total:	$213,500

Source: Federal Election Commission contribution records from January 1998 to September 2004

Contributions by Telecommunications Sector Organizations				
Company	Sector	#	Total	Avg.
Walt Disney Co.	Broadcast	46	$42,500	$924
Time Warner	PayTV - Cable	10	$14,250	$1,425
International Brotherhood of Electrical Workers (IBEW)	Union	9	$13,000	$1,444
Verizon Communications Inc.	Phones	3	$12,000	$4,000
BellSouth Corp.	Phones	11	$10,250	$932
Communications Workers of America	Union	2	$10,000	$5,000
Global Crossing Ltd.	Other	9	$9,000	$1,000
Paxson Communications Corp.	Broadcast	7	$8,000	$1,143
Loral Space & Communications Ltd.	Satellite	7	$8,000	$1,143
Comcast Corp.	PayTV - Cable	4	$7,000	$1,750
Sprint Corp.	Phones	6	$6,500	$1,083
AT&T Wireless	Phones	9	$6,000	$667
Cingular Wireless	Phones	5	$6,000	$1,200
General Electric Co.	Broadcast	6	$6,000	$1,000
National Association of Broadcasters	Broadcast	2	$6,000	$3,000
Transportation Communications International Union	Union	6	$5,500	$917
Viacom Inc.	Broadcast	4	$5,250	$1,313
National Cable and Telecommunications Association	PayTV - Cable	1	$5,000	$5,000
SBC Communications Inc.	Phones	4	$5,000	$1,250
MCI (formerly WorldCom Inc.)	Phones	2	$4,000	$2,000
United States Telecom Association	Phones	4	$3,000	$750
Misc. telecom interests	Other	3	$2,250	$750
Adelphia Communications Corp.	PayTV - Cable	2	$2,000	$1,000
Covad Communications Co.	Phones	2	$2,000	$1,000
Clear Channel Communications Inc.	Broadcast	2	$2,000	$1,000
News Corp Ltd.	Broadcast	2	$1,500	$750
Level 3 Communications Inc.	Other	1	$1,000	$1,000
Echostar Corp.	PayTV - Satellite	1	$1,000	$1,000
The DirecTV Group Inc.	PayTV - Satellite	1	$1,000	$1,000
Association for Local Telecommunications Services	Phones	1	$1,000	$1,000
Focal Communications Corp.	Phones	1	$1,000	$1,000
Comptel/ASCENT	Phones	1	$1,000	$1,000
XO Communications Inc.	Phones	1	$1,000	$1,000
Pac-West Telecomm Inc.	Phones	1	$1,000	$1,000
Qwest Communications International Inc.	Phones	1	$1,000	$1,000
United States Cellular Corp.	Phones	1	$1,000	$1,000
Cellular Telecommunications & Internet Association	Phones	1	$500	$500
Charter Communications Inc.	PayTV - Cable	1	$500	$500
AT&T Corp.	Phones	1	$250	$250
Washington Post Co.	Broadcast	1	$250	$250
	Total:		$213,500	

Source: Federal Election Commission contribution records from January 1998 to September 2004

Rockefeller, John D.

Senator (D-WV)

Senate Committee on Commerce, Science & Transportation

531 Hart Senate Office Bldg
Washington, DC 20510
Phone: (202) 224-6472
Fax: (202) 224-7665

Web Page: http://rockefeller.senate.gov/
Email: senator@rockefeller.senate.gov

Contribution Summary By Telecommunications Sector

Phones	$49,550
PayTV - Cable	$21,000
Union	$20,000
Broadcast	$16,000
Other	$3,000
PayTV - Satellite	$2,000
Satellite	$2,000
Total:	**$113,550**

Source: Federal Election Commission contribution records from January 1998 to September 2004

Contributions by Telecommunications Sector Organizations

Company	Sector	#	Total	Avg.
National Cable and Telecommunications Association	PayTV - Cable	3	$11,000	$3,667
Communications Workers of America	Union	3	$10,000	$3,333
AT&T Wireless	Phones	8	$9,000	$1,125
General Electric Co.	Broadcast	8	$8,000	$1,000
Time Warner	PayTV - Cable	6	$7,000	$1,167
Cingular Wireless	Phones	3	$7,000	$2,333
Qwest Communications International Inc.	Phones	5	$7,000	$1,400
Verizon Communications Inc.	Phones	7	$5,750	$821
International Brotherhood of Electrical Workers (IBEW)	Union	3	$5,000	$1,667
Transportation Communications International Union	Union	5	$5,000	$1,000
Sprint Corp.	Phones	7	$4,000	$571
SBC Communications Inc.	Phones	3	$3,000	$1,000
ALLTEL Corp.	Phones	3	$3,000	$1,000
MCI (formerly WorldCom Inc.)	Phones	3	$2,500	$833
Cellular Telecommunications & Internet Association	Phones	2	$2,000	$1,000
Echostar Corp.	PayTV - Satellite	2	$2,000	$1,000
Misc. telecom interests	Other	2	$2,000	$1,000
Charter Communications Inc.	PayTV - Cable	2	$2,000	$1,000
National Association of Broadcasters	Broadcast	2	$2,000	$1,000
Viacom Inc.	Broadcast	2	$2,000	$1,000
Walt Disney Co.	Broadcast	2	$2,000	$1,000
California Microwave Inc.	Satellite	2	$2,000	$1,000
Clear Channel Communications Inc.	Broadcast	1	$2,000	$1,000
Western Wireless Corp.	Phones	1	$1,000	$1,000
Teligent	Phones	1	$1,000	$1,000
Level 3 Communications Inc.	Other	1	$1,000	$1,000
News Corp Ltd.	Broadcast	1	$1,000	$1,000
Comcast Corp.	PayTV - Cable	1	$1,000	$1,000
CenturyTel Inc.	Phones	1	$1,000	$1,000
National Telephone Cooperative Association	Phones	1	$1,000	$1,000
Comptel/ASCENT	Phones	1	$1,000	$1,000
Deutsche Telekom AG (T-Mobile)	Phones	1	$1,000	$1,000
AT&T Corp.	Phones	1	$300	$300
		Total:	**$113,550**	

Source: Federal Election Commission contribution records from January 1998 to September 2004

Telecommunications Company Provided Trips to Committee Member's Staff

Company	Sector	#	Total $
National Cable and Telecommunications Association	PayTV - Cable	2	$4,229
Cellular Telecommunications & Internet Association	Phones	2	$3,407
	Total:	**4**	**$7,636**

Source: Congressional office travel records for members of the Senate Committee on Commerce, Science & Transportation and the House Committee on Energy and Commerce for the period of January 2000 to March 2004.

Trips by Committee Member's Staff Sponsored by the Telecommunications Industry		
Individual	#	Total $
Nilsson, Michael	2	$4,229
Margie, Paul	2	$3,407
Total:	4	$7,636

Source: Congressional office travel records for members of the Senate Committee on Commerce, Science & Transportation and the House Committee on Energy and Commerce for the period of January 2000 to March 2004.

Smith, Gordon

Senator (R-OR)

Senate Committee on Commerce, Science & Transportation

404 Russell Senate Office Bldg
Washington, DC 20510
Phone: (202) 224-3753
Fax: (202) 228-3997

Web Page: http://gsmith.senate.gov/
Email: http://gsmith.senate.gov/webform.htm

Contribution Summary By Telecommunications Sector	
Phones	$88,910
Broadcast	$38,250
PayTV - Cable	$21,310
Other	$2,000
Total:	$150,470

Source: Federal Election Commission contribution records from January 1998 to September 2004

Contributions by Telecommunications Sector Organizations				
Company	Sector	#	Total	Avg.
AT&T Wireless	Phones	13	$13,500	$1,038
Qwest Communications International Inc.	Phones	13	$13,250	$1,019
General Electric Co.	Broadcast	14	$12,250	$875
Cingular Wireless	Phones	8	$12,000	$1,500
Walt Disney Co.	Broadcast	5	$10,000	$2,000
Time Warner	PayTV - Cable	9	$9,500	$1,056
National Cable and Telecommunications Association	PayTV - Cable	3	$9,360	$3,120
SBC Communications Inc.	Phones	7	$9,160	$1,309
Verizon Communications Inc.	Phones	11	$8,000	$727
Sprint Corp.	Phones	6	$7,000	$1,167
Viacom Inc.	Broadcast	7	$7,000	$1,000
National Association of Broadcasters	Broadcast	5	$7,000	$1,400
United States Telecom Association	Phones	3	$4,000	$1,333
Western Wireless Corp.	Phones	5	$4,000	$800
MCI (formerly WorldCom Inc.)	Phones	4	$4,000	$1,000
Deutsche Telekom AG (T-Mobile)	Phones	3	$3,000	$1,000
XO Communications Inc.	Phones	3	$2,500	$833
Covad Communications Co.	Phones	2	$2,000	$1,000
News Corp Ltd.	Broadcast	2	$2,000	$1,000
Charter Communications Inc.	PayTV - Cable	2	$2,000	$1,000
ALLTEL Corp.	Phones	2	$2,000	$1,000
Cellular Telecommunications & Internet Association	Phones	2	$1,500	$750
Association for Local Telecommunications Services	Phones	1	$1,000	$1,000
AT&T Corp.	Phones	1	$1,000	$1,000
IDT Corp.	Other	1	$1,000	$1,000
Level 3 Communications Inc.	Other	1	$1,000	$1,000
Misc. telecom interests	Other	1	$500	$500
Forstmann Little & Co.	Phones	1	$500	$500
Pac-West Telecomm Inc.	Phones	1	$500	$500
Comcast Corp.	PayTV - Cable	2	$450	$225
		Total:	$150,470	

Source: Federal Election Commission contribution records from January 1998 to September 2004

Telecommunications Company Provided Trips to Committee Member's Staff			
Company	Sector	#	Total $
United States Telecom Association	Phones	2	$2,223
National Cable and Telecommunications Association	PayTV - Cable	1	$1,791
SBC Communications Inc.	Phones	1	$1,630
Walt Disney Co.	Broadcast	1	$571
	Total:	5	$6,215

Source: Congressional office travel records for members of the Senate Committee on Commerce, Science & Transportation and the House Committee on Energy and Commerce for the period of January 2000 to March 2004.

Trips by Committee Member's Staff Sponsored by the Telecommunications Industry		
Individual	#	Total $
Hsueh, Wallace	5	$6,215
Total:	5	$6,215

Source: Congressional office travel records for members of the Senate Committee on Commerce, Science & Transportation and the House Committee on Energy and Commerce for the period of January 2000 to March 2004.

Snowe, Olympia J.

Senator (R-ME)

Senate Committee on Commerce, Science & Transportation

154 Russell Senate Office Building
Washington, DC 20510
Phone: (202) 224-5344
Fax: (202) 224-1946

Web Page: http://snowe.senate.gov
Email: http://snowe.senate.gov/Webform.htm

Contribution Summary By Telecommunications Sector	
Phones	$24,750
PayTV - Cable	$18,000
Broadcast	$15,450
PayTV - Satellite	$1,000
Satellite	$1,000
Total:	$60,200

Source: Federal Election Commission contribution records from January 1998 to September 2004

Contributions by Telecommunications Sector Organizations				
Company	Sector	#	Total	Avg.
National Cable and Telecommunications Association	PayTV - Cable	2	$10,000	$5,000
Verizon Communications Inc.	Phones	6	$8,250	$1,375
Time Warner	PayTV - Cable	5	$8,000	$1,600
AT&T Wireless	Phones	8	$6,500	$813
General Electric Co.	Broadcast	5	$5,000	$1,000
National Association of Broadcasters	Broadcast	5	$5,000	$1,000
MCI (formerly WorldCom Inc.)	Phones	3	$4,000	$1,333
SBC Communications Inc.	Phones	2	$2,000	$1,000
News Corp Ltd.	Broadcast	2	$2,000	$1,000
Viacom Inc.	Broadcast	2	$2,000	$1,000
The DirecTV Group Inc.	PayTV - Satellite	1	$1,000	$1,000
XO Communications Inc.	Phones	1	$1,000	$1,000
Motorola Inc.	Satellite	1	$1,000	$1,000
National Telephone Cooperative Association	Phones	1	$1,000	$1,000
Cellular Telecommunications & Internet Association	Phones	1	$1,000	$1,000
Cingular Wireless	Phones	1	$1,000	$1,000
Walt Disney Co.	Broadcast	3	$950	$317
Paxson Communications Corp.	Broadcast	1	$500	$500
	Total:		$60,200	

Source: Federal Election Commission contribution records from January 1998 to September 2004

Stevens, Ted

Senator (R-AK)

Senate Committee on Commerce, Science & Transportation

522 Hart Senate Office Bldg
Washington, DC 20510
Phone: (202) 224-3004
Fax: (202) 224-2354

Web Page: http://stevens.senate.gov/
Email: http://stevens.senate.gov/contact_form.htm

Contribution Summary By Telecommunications Sector	
Phones	$141,950
Broadcast	$99,511
PayTV - Cable	$34,250
Other	$13,000
PayTV - Satellite	$3,000
Satellite	$3,000
Union	$2,000
Total:	$296,711

Source: Federal Election Commission contribution records from January 1998 to September 2004

Contributions by Telecommunications Sector Organizations				
Company	Sector	#	Total	Avg.
General Electric Co.	Broadcast	26	$32,500	$1,250
AT&T Wireless	Phones	26	$32,500	$1,250
MCI (formerly WorldCom Inc.)	Phones	15	$26,500	$1,767
National Association of Broadcasters	Broadcast	10	$23,761	$2,376
Walt Disney Co.	Broadcast	8	$20,500	$2,563
Verizon Communications Inc.	Phones	7	$12,250	$1,750
Cingular Wireless	Phones	4	$12,000	$3,000
National Cable and Telecommunications Association	PayTV - Cable	4	$11,500	$2,875
Time Warner	PayTV - Cable	6	$11,500	$1,917
Viacom Inc.	Broadcast	8	$11,000	$1,375
XO Communications Inc.	Phones	9	$11,000	$1,222
Comcast Corp.	PayTV - Cable	5	$10,250	$2,050
Paxson Communications Corp.	Broadcast	8	$8,000	$1,000
IDT Corp.	Other	7	$6,500	$929
Cellular Telecommunications & Internet Association	Phones	5	$5,000	$1,000
Deutsche Telekom AG (T-Mobile)	Phones	5	$5,000	$1,000
Sprint Corp.	Phones	8	$5,000	$625
Qwest Communications International Inc.	Phones	3	$4,000	$1,333
Association for Local Telecommunications Services	Phones	4	$3,750	$938
BellSouth Corp.	Phones	7	$3,500	$500
Alaska Communications Systems	Phones	9	$3,450	$383
ALLTEL Corp.	Phones	2	$3,000	$1,500
Echostar Corp.	PayTV - Satellite	3	$3,000	$1,000
Level 3 Communications Inc.	Other	3	$3,000	$1,000
Focal Communications Corp.	Phones	3	$3,000	$1,000
Loral Space & Communications Ltd.	Satellite	3	$3,000	$1,000
Transportation Communications International Union	Union	2	$2,000	$1,000
Teligent	Phones	2	$2,000	$1,000
Comptel/ASCENT	Phones	2	$2,000	$1,000
Covad Communications Co.	Phones	2	$2,000	$1,000
Misc. telecom interests	Other	2	$2,000	$1,000
Belo Corp.	Broadcast	2	$2,000	$1,000
Global Crossing Ltd.	Other	2	$1,500	$750
National Telephone Cooperative Association	Phones	1	$1,500	$1,500
Pac-West Telecomm Inc.	Phones	1	$1,000	$1,000
U.S. LEC Corp.	Phones	1	$1,000	$1,000
United States Cellular Corp.	Phones	1	$1,000	$1,000
News Corp Ltd.	Broadcast	1	$1,000	$1,000
SAVVIS Communications Corp.	PayTV - Cable	1	$1,000	$1,000
Western Wireless Corp.	Phones	1	$1,000	$1,000
Tribune Co.	Broadcast	1	$750	$750
AT&T Corp.	Phones	2	$500	$250
		Total:	$296,711	

Source: Federal Election Commission contribution records from January 1998 to September 2004

Telecommunications Company Provided Trips to Committee Member's Staff			
Company	Sector	#	Total $
United States Telecom Association	Phones	3	$12,765
National Cable and Telecommunications Association	PayTV - Cable	2	$1,321
AT&T Corp.	Phones	2	$1,180
Walt Disney Co.	Broadcast	1	$895
Telecommunications Industry Association	Other	1	$539
	Total:	9	$16,700

Source: Congressional office travel records for members of the Senate Committee on Commerce, Science & Transportation and the House Committee on Energy and Commerce for the period of January 2000 to March 2004.

Trips by Committee Member's Staff Sponsored by the Telecommunications Industry		
Individual	#	Total $
Stevens, Ted	3	$5,479
Sutherland, Lisa	2	$4,871
Givens, Andrew	2	$4,810
Drager, Christine	2	$1,540
Total:	9	$16,700

Source: Congressional office travel records for members of the Senate Committee on Commerce, Science & Transportation and the House Committee on Energy and Commerce for the period of January 2000 to March 2004.

Sununu, John

Senator (R-NH)

Senate Committee on Commerce, Science & Transportation

111 Russell Senate Office Building
Washington, DC 20510
Phone: (202) 224-2841
Fax: (202) 228-4131

Web Page: http://sununu.senate.gov/
Email: http://www.sununu.senate.gov/webform.html

Contribution Summary By Telecommunications Sector	
Phones	$54,100
Broadcast	$32,900
PayTV - Cable	$16,000
Other	$1,000
Total:	$104,000
Source: Federal Election Commission contribution records from January 1998 to September 2004	

Contributions by Telecommunications Sector Organizations				
Company	Sector	#	Total	Avg.
Verizon Communications Inc.	Phones	19	$12,250	$645
Clear Channel Communications Inc.	Broadcast	6	$10,000	$1,667
Cingular Wireless	Phones	6	$9,500	$1,583
General Electric Co.	Broadcast	12	$9,150	$763
AT&T Wireless	Phones	4	$7,500	$1,875
National Association of Broadcasters	Broadcast	3	$6,500	$2,167
Adelphia Communications Corp.	PayTV - Cable	3	$6,000	$2,000
News Corp Ltd.	Broadcast	4	$5,250	$1,313
Time Warner	PayTV - Cable	4	$5,000	$1,250
MCI (formerly WorldCom Inc.)	Phones	4	$5,000	$1,250
AT&T Corp.	Phones	8	$4,750	$594
Comcast Corp.	PayTV - Cable	2	$4,000	$2,000
United States Cellular Corp.	Phones	2	$4,000	$2,000
Forstmann Little & Co.	Phones	7	$3,100	$443
XO Communications Inc.	Phones	1	$2,500	$2,500
SBC Communications Inc.	Phones	1	$1,000	$1,000
Sprint Corp.	Phones	1	$1,000	$1,000
Covad Communications Co.	Phones	1	$1,000	$1,000
Focal Communications Corp.	Phones	1	$1,000	$1,000
Salem Communications Corp.	PayTV - Cable	1	$1,000	$1,000
ALLTEL Corp.	Phones	1	$1,000	$1,000
Univision Communications Inc.	Broadcast	1	$1,000	$1,000
Walt Disney Co.	Broadcast	1	$1,000	$1,000
Global Crossing Ltd.	Other	1	$1,000	$1,000
BellSouth Corp.	Phones	1	$500	$500
		Total:	$104,000	
Source: Federal Election Commission contribution records from January 1998 to September 2004				

Telecommunications Company Provided Trips to Committee Member's Staff			
Company	Sector	#	Total $
Cellular Telecommunications & Internet Association	Phones	1	$1,240
Comcast Corp.	PayTV - Cable	1	$251
	Total:	2	$1,491
Source: Congressional office travel records for members of the Senate Committee on Commerce, Science & Transportation and the House Committee on Energy and Commerce for the period of January 2000 to March 2004.			

Trips by Committee Member's Staff Sponsored by the Telecommunications Industry		
Individual	#	Total $
O'Rielly, Michael	2	$1,491
Total:	2	$1,491
Source: Congressional office travel records for members of the Senate Committee on Commerce, Science & Transportation and the House Committee on Energy and Commerce for the period of January 2000 to March 2004.		